Psychodynamic Psychiatry
in Clinical Practice

Psychodynamic Psychiatry
in Clinical Practice

Glen O. Gabbard, M.D.

American Psychiatric Press, Inc.

Washington, DC
London, England

To My Teachers, My Patients, and My Students

About the Author

Glen O. Gabbard, M.D., is Director, C. F. Menninger Memorial Hospital; Training and Supervising Analyst, Topeka Institute for Psychoanalysis; and serves as a member of the faculty of the Karl Menninger School of Psychiatry and Mental Health Sciences.

CONTENTS

Foreword

The growth of biological psychiatry over the past two decades has effected an almost paradigmatic shift in the prevailing understanding of psychiatric illness, a shift back into a more "medical" illness model, more exactly akin to the natural science explanatory model of somatic medicine in general. This had been the model of the first scientific descriptive nosology of psychiatric illness devised by Kraepelin a century ago, from which the field was subsequently swung into the psychodynamically conceptualized psychological understanding of mental functioning and its disorders based on the theory of the psychoanalysis created and elaborated by Freud and his followers. This psychodynamic (and to some extent, a psycho-educational) understanding held an almost exclusive sway throughout the middle decades of this century—until the recent knowledge surge in neurobiology and the growth of modern day biological psychiatry under the attractive banner of "remedicalization."

A major reflection of this pendular to-and-fro in the conceptualization of psychiatric illness enterprise has been in the structure and the philosophic tenets of the official psychiatric nomenclature. The American Psychiatric Association's *Diagnostic and Statistical Manual of Mental Disorders* (DSM-I), which appeared in 1952, and even more so its successor, DSM-II, were both underpinned by the prevailing psychological paradigms of mental illness of the period. DSM-I contained a lingering reflection of Adolf Meyer's psychobiological view that mental disorders represented reactions of the total personality to the converging relevant psychological, social, and biological factors, and DSM-II was more unreservedly psychoanalytic in its psychological framework. It was within this predominantly psychoanalytic, called euphemistically *psychodynamic,* understanding of mental health and illness and the DSM-I and DSM-II nomenclatures that reigned for a combined quarter century, that the post–World War II generations of psychiatrists were taught the fundamentals of psychodynamic case formulation and treatment planning, and the practice of the psychoanalytically oriented expressive and supportive psychotherapies based on those case formulations and the derived psychoanalytically informed treatment plans.

The major sea change embodied in DSM-III (approved by the American Psychiatric Association in 1979) was both a major aspect and a signal reflection of the concomitant shifting conceptual emphases impelled by the rise of biological psychiatry and of modern psychopharmacology, with its proliferation of putatively specifically targeted psychoactive drugs. The dissatisfactions with DSM-II had indeed been serious. A psychoanalytically based nomenclature was imprecise with ambiguous and elastic diagnostic boundaries and contained high levels of (often unspecifiable) inferential reasoning. Case formulations were therefore notoriously unreliable, and professional disagreements seemed often to be rather arbitrarily resolved simply by the weight of authority or seniority. Questions of validity could hardly even be approached for purposes of research classification, medical record keeping, or reimbursement.

The intent of the creators of DSM-III was in the first instance to enhance diagnostic reliability and precision; the guiding framework was to be a closer modeling of the kinds of clearer delineations of medical somatic illness by symptom picture in the *International Classification of Diseases* (ICD). The path toward this was to classify only *descriptively*, rigorously eschewing the levels of inference inherent in the psychodynamic, or psychoanalytically based, viewpoint— that is, to be specifically atheoretical and theory-neutral as far as human intention could ensure. The result has been a new nomenclature, with us now for a decade, that is indeed more stable, more precise, and more reliable across individuals and across time and space. For the purposes of empirical research studies on the clinical trials model, for statistical, epidemiological, and treatment reimbursement purposes, and for purposes of clinical treatment with the ever-widening array of psychoactive drugs, the gains have indeed been impressive. The thinking of DSM-III (and its successors in the DSM-III-R and the presently in-process DSM-IV) is now the centerpiece of current academic psychiatric education and research. Within the governmental research-grant-giving structure, it is currently extremely difficult to garner funding support for clinical psychotherapeutic *or* psychopharmacological treatment research unless it is embedded within the specific nosological categories of DSM-III, the specific syndromes of Axis I, and the specific personality disorders as delineated by Axis II.

The gains that have accrued to psychiatry with the newer "atheoretical" nomenclature of DSM-III and its successors, and specifically the greatly enhanced gains to the understanding and treatment of many psychiatric illnesses that have derived from the burgeoning biological (including of course genetic) and also epidemiological understandings of these disorders have also unhappily had their price. Every swing of the pendulum in the historic unfolding of psychiatric understandings has brought important new emphases and new advances in relation to the fathoming of the ideally integrated overall "biopsychosocial" conceptual framework (to which we will all pay at least lip service). But with each swing there has been a concomitant unnecessary de-emphasis and condoned neglect of the immediately prior dominant arm of the tripartite psychiatric explanatory structure, biological, psychological, and so-

cial. We are now solidly in an era in psychiatric education of
de-emphasis of psychodynamic understanding and case formulation and treatment planning as if enhanced knowledge of the
biological dimensions of mental disorders renders psychosocial and
psychological approaches far less relevant if not completely obso-
lete.

It is the implicit challenge in this state of affairs, to accept the
current "atheoretical" diagnostic framework of the DSM-III (and
DSM-III-R and the forthcoming DSM-IV) classification of psychiatric
disorders by symptom cluster, and to demonstrate specifically, even
within that framework, the continued usefulness, or rather the
continued necessity, for the fullest psychodynamic exploration and
understanding in order to ensure the most comprehensive treatment, the continuingly relevant psychotherapeutic in proper interaction with the newly relevant psychopharmacological, for the array
of defined psychiatric disorders—it is this formidable challenge that
Glen Gabbard so successfully takes on. Briefly put, the intent of the
book is to persuade that psychoanalytically based understandings of
the disorders of the mind and the paths toward their amelioration
must not be lost today in the illusory expectation that biological
understanding and remediation is sufficient to the effective reversal
of disordered mental functioning and behavior. It would be to
everyone's loss, most directly to that of the patients, if this were
allowed to happen. It is books just like this one by Gabbard that will
therefore play a vital role in ensuring that the imbalances in our
diagnostic understandings, our conceptual frameworks, and our
therapeutic armamentaria created by our dramatic pendular paradigmatic swings are properly self-corrected, in this particular case to
maintain the full value of the psychodynamic orientation within the
current house of psychiatry. No one book can be completely successful in attaining so ambitious a goal, and each of us will find our
points of disagreement or disappointment with the author's effort.
What is more important is how much of the overall message does
get conveyed and does persuade.

Robert S. Wallerstein, M.D.

Source Acknowledgments

The author gratefully acknowledges permission to reprint portions of the following material:

Gabbard GO: A contemporary perspective on psychoanalytically informed hospital treatment. Hosp Community Psychiatry 39:1291–1295, 1988. Portions reprinted with permission.

Gabbard GO: The exit line: heightened transference-countertransference manifestations at the end of the hour. J Am Psychoanal Assoc 30:579–598, 1982. Portions reprinted with permission.

Gabbard GO: Patients who hate. Psychiatry 52:96–106, 1989. Portions reprinted with permission.

Gabbard GO: The psychology of the physician (Ch 3), in Medical Marriages. Edited by Gabbard GO, Menninger RW. Washington, DC, American Psychiatric Press, 1988, pp 23–38. Portions reprinted with permission.

Gabbard GO: The role of compulsiveness in the normal physician. JAMA 254:2926–2929. Copyright 1985, American Medical Association. Portions reprinted with permission.

Gabbard GO: Splitting in hospital treatment. Am J Psychiatry 146:444–451. Copyright 1989, American Psychiatric Association. Portions reprinted with permission.

Gabbard GO: Therapeutic approaches to erotic transference. Directions in Psychiatry 10(4), 1990. Portions reprinted with permission.

Gabbard GO: The treatment of the "special" patient in a psychoanalytic hospital. International Review of Psycho-Analysis 13:333–347, 1986. Portions reprinted with permission.

Gabbard GO: Two subtypes of narcissistic personality disorder. Bull Menninger Clin 53:527–532, 1989. Portions reprinted with permission.

Gabbard GO, Coyne L: Predictors of response of antisocial patients to hospital treatment. Hosp Community Psychiatry 38:1181–1185, 1987. Portions reprinted with permission.

Gabbard GO, Horwitz L, Frieswyk S, et al: The effect of therapist interventions on the therapeutic alliance with borderline patients. J Am Psychoanal Assoc 36:697–727, 1988. Portions reprinted with permission.

Gabbard GO, Nemiah JC: Multiple determinants of anxiety in a patient with borderline personality disorder. Bull Menninger Clinic 49:161–172, 1985. Portions reprinted with permission.

Introduction

When Carol Nadelson, editor-in-chief of American Psychiatric Press, first invited me to write a book that approached DSM-III-R from a psychodynamic perspective, I asked her why she had selected me for the task. She replied that she felt I was the logical person to do it. At that moment I was like the man who one day discovered that he had been speaking prose all his life. I realized that indeed I had been practicing psychodynamic psychiatry all my professional life. I had treated a broad array of outpatients and inpatients with individual psychotherapy, psychoanalysis, medications, family/marital therapy, and group therapy, but these therapeutic approaches had always been informed by psychodynamic understanding of the clinical situation.

After accepting the challenge, I set to work on a prospectus for the book. I originally proposed an edited volume with multiple authors. The APPI Board responded to the proposal by making a compelling case for a single-authored volume. The advantage of having one author, they argued, would be cohesive and unified application of theory to diagnostic understanding and treatment from chapter to chapter. One author could lay down the theoretical principles at the beginning of the book and then proceed to demonstrate how those principles apply to DSM-III-R disorders. An edited volume would be prone to fragmentation of theory and practice because of the multiple perspectives and approaches of diverse authors.

Having been persuaded by the argument of the APPI Board, I developed a working outline of the book. I immediately confronted the fact that no one clinician could possibly be equally knowledgeable about the treatment of every major diagnostic entity. As a result, in some chapters involving disorders with which I have limited clinical experience, I have had to rely more on the experience and writings of others who are more expert than I. When writing about other conditions, I have drawn more from my own clinical experience. I also realized that my review of the relevant literature would have to be selective rather than comprehensive if I were to complete the task during my lifetime.

While in the process of writing this volume, I had the opportunity to lecture to residents, psychiatrists in private practice, and other groups of mental health professionals throughout the country. My interactions with these clinicians convinced me that a book such as this one was sorely needed. Residents repeatedly expressed concern that their programs were not providing an adequate foundation in psychodynamic psychiatry. They could diagnose a psychiatric disorder according to symptoms, course, and history, but they could not understand the person with the disorder. Psychiatrists in practice repeatedly complained of "getting stuck" when their patients would not respond to psychopharmacologic agents. I was also struck by the unnecessary polarization between biological and psychodynamic approaches within psychiatry. It had always seemed to me that medications were part of the dynamic psychiatrist's therapeutic armamentarium and that a sophisticated knowledge of transference, countertransference, and resistance was extraordinarily helpful in the practice of pharmacotherapy. This book is written in that spirit of integration, with the hope that biological psychiatrists will find it as useful as those who are more dynamically oriented. The audiences I have targeted are psychiatric residents and psychiatrists in clinical practice. Those involved in hospital work and the treatment of severely disturbed patients may find it useful as well.

The book is organized into three sections. Section I discusses the basic theoretical principles of dynamic psychiatry and the major treatment modalities, including individual psychotherapy, group psychotherapy, family/marital therapy, dynamic pharmacotherapy, and dynamically informed hospital treatment. Section II applies the theoretical principles and therapeutic approaches described in Section I to the major Axis I disorders of DSM-III-R. Since my goal was to produce a reasonably slender one-volume text that does not require a forklift to transport it, I have not been able to include every Axis I disorder listed in the manual. Forced to be selective, I have focused on the most common Axis I disorders and those conditions for which a psychodynamic approach is most useful. To keep the scope of the book manageable for a single author, I have further limited myself to adult psychiatry.

Section III addresses Axis II disorders, with chapters subdivided according to the DSM-III-R clusters. One chapter each is devoted to Cluster A (comprising those personality disorders that appear "eccentric") and to Cluster C (subsuming personality disorders that share in common the feature of anxiety). Cluster B personality disorders—borderline, narcissistic, antisocial, and histrionic—are grouped together because of their more dramatic nature. Moreover, they are the personality disorders most commonly encountered in the practice of dynamic psychiatry and the Axis II conditions about which more is known. Accordingly, a separate chapter is devoted to each Cluster B personality disorder in order to cover the relevant literature and theoretical controversies more comprehensively.

All of us are shaped by our environments, and my 15 years of clinical work at the Menninger Clinic have profoundly influenced my perspective on psychiatric practice. To a large extent, the psychodynamic psychiatry described in this volume reflects the nature of Menninger practice. I must acknowledge a debt of gratitude to my teachers over the years who have taught me the importance of listening to and understanding patients. These mentors are too numerous to mention by name, and I would not want to run the risk of omitting someone in an attempt to list them. My psychoanalytic training at the Topeka Institute for Psychoanalysis was also of enormous value in my professional development. I am particularly grateful to my training analyst, Dr. Ramon Ganzarain, and to my teachers and supervisors: Drs. Ishak Ramzy, Irwin Rosen, Jack Ross, Jerome Katz, Stuart Averill, Alfred Namnum, and J. Cotter Hirschberg.

Patients, of course, are our most important teachers, and I wish to acknowledge their contribution to my development as a clinician. The residents and other trainees I have taught during my years as a teacher and supervisor in the Karl Menninger School of Psychiatry have also been an important source of stimulation and education for me.

Writing a book of this nature is truly a team effort. Alice Brand Bartlett and Marcy Schott of the Menninger Professional Library were most helpful in their provision of up-to-date literature searches. Mary Ann Clifft, Phil Beard, and Eleanor Bell spent many hours with early manuscript drafts meticulously copyediting and checking references. I am especially grateful to Faye Schoenfeld for patiently and enthusiastically typing many drafts of each chapter. I have also greatly appreciated the administrative support of my colleagues, Dr. Roy Menninger and Dr. Walt Menninger, without which the writing of this book would not have been possible. Other colleagues, including Drs. Donald Colson, James Eyman, Leonard Horwitz, Lisa Lewis, Donald Rinsley, and Kathryn Zerbe, graciously read portions of the manuscript and contributed constructive suggestions for revision. Several other colleagues—including Drs. Steve Katz, Joel Nance, Tom Picard, Victoria Spinazzola, Howard Rosenfield, and Mrs. Alice Brand Bartlett—provided clinical material for the book or added supplemental information to my own cases. Dr. Robert Wallerstein has been most generous in sharing a portion of his much-sought-after time to carefully read the manuscript and write a foreword.

The American Psychiatric Press staff were, as usual, a superb support system. Carol Nadelson provided encouragement and moral support from the project's inception right on through to its completion. Tim Clancy and Claire Reinburg efficiently kept the project on schedule and contained my anxieties when necessary. Karen Loper and Margaret Gore were involved in the planning of a marketing program far in advance of the book's completion. I am grateful to all of them.

Finally, I wish to thank my wife and best friend, Dr. Joyce Davidson Gabbard, who sustained me emotionally so I could face the challenge of this project with energy and enthusiasm.

Glen O. Gabbard, M.D.

SECTION I

Basic Principles and Treatment Approaches in Dynamic Psychiatry

CHAPTER 1

Basic Principles of
Dynamic Psychiatry

It would be far easier if we could avoid the patient as we explore
the realm of psychopathology; it would be far simpler if we
could limit ourselves to examining the chemistry and physiology of his brain, and to treating mental events as objects alien
to our immediate experience, or as mere variables in impersonal statistical formulae. Important as these approaches are
for the understanding of human behavior, they cannot alone
uncover or explain all the relevant facts. To see into the mind
of another, we must repeatedly immerse ourselves in the flood
of his associations and feelings; we must be ourselves the
instrument that sounds him.

— John Nemiah, 1961, p. 4

Psychodynamic psychiatry (used interchangeably with dynamic
psychiatry in this volume) is celebrating its 100th birthday.
Ellenberger (1970) has traced the first usage of the term to the
period between 1880 and 1900. Leibniz originally used *dynamic* to
emphasize the contrast with *static*. Herbart applied this distinction
to states of consciousness. Fechner appropriated the term to refer
to mental energy and probably influenced Freud in this regard.
Dynamic then came to be used by the French physiologists to connote *functional* as opposed to *organic*. Eventually, the eminent neu-
rologist Hughlings Jackson borrowed the term to mean physiological as opposed to anatomic, functional as opposed to organic, and
regressive as opposed to the status quo. In fact, Jackson's notion of
mental energy very likely caught Freud's eye.

Dynamic psychiatry owes its greatest debt to Freud. Whatever
else it may be, this approach is steeped in psychoanalytic theory and
knowledge. (While some would argue that dynamic psychiatry subsumes a broader purview than that of psychoanalytic psychiatry, the
predominant contemporary usage is to equate *psychodynamic* with
psychoanalytic.) For much of this century, modern dynamic psychiatry has been viewed as a branch of psychiatry that explains mental
phenomena as the outgrowth of *conflict*. This conflict derives from

3

powerful unconscious forces that seek expression and require constant monitoring from opposing forces to prevent their expression. These interacting forces may be conceptualized (with some overlap) as: 1) a wish and a defense against the wish; 2) different intrapsychic agencies or "parts" with different aims and priorities; or 3) an impulse in opposition to an internalized awareness of the demands of external reality.

In the last couple of decades, psychodynamic psychiatry has come to connote more than the conflict model of illness. Today's dynamic psychiatrist must also understand what is commonly referred to as the "deficit model" of illness. This model is applied to patients who, for whatever developmental reasons, suffer from weakened or absent psychic structures. This compromised state prevents them from feeling whole and secure about themselves, so they therefore require inordinate responses from persons in the environment to maintain psychological homeostasis. Also contained within the purview of psychodynamic psychiatry is the unconscious internal world of relationships. All patients carry within them a host of different mental representations of aspects of themselves and others, many of which may create characteristic patterns of interpersonal difficulties. These representations of self and others reside in the patient's unconscious, where they form the world of internal object relations.

Above all, psychodynamic psychiatry is a *way of thinking*—not only about one's patients but also about oneself in the interpersonal field between patient and treater. In fact, to characterize the essence of dynamic psychiatry, one might well use the following definition: *Psychodynamic psychiatry is an approach to diagnosis and treatment characterized by a way of thinking about both patient and clinician that includes unconscious conflict, deficits and distortions of intrapsychic structures, and internal object relations.*

Although dynamic psychotherapy is one of the foremost tools in the dynamic psychiatrist's therapeutic armamentarium, dynamic psychotherapy is not synonymous with dynamic psychiatry. The dynamic psychiatrist uses a *wide range* of treatment interventions that depend on a dynamic assessment of the patient's needs. Dynamic psychiatry simply provides a coherent conceptual framework within which all treatments are prescribed. Regardless of whether the treatment is dynamic psychotherapy or pharmacotherapy, it is *dynamically informed*. Indeed, a crucial component of the dynamic psychiatrist's expertise is knowing when to avoid exploratory psychotherapy in favor of treatments that do not threaten the patient's psychic equilibrium.

Psychiatry has grown beyond the era when typical practitioners passed their days in the privacy of their consulting rooms, seeing one neurotic patient after another in long-term, insight-oriented psychotherapy. Just as psychiatry as a field has changed, so has dynamic psychiatry. Today's dynamic psychiatrist must practice in the context of impressive advances in the neurosciences, integrating psychoanalytic insight with biologic understanding of illness. Nevertheless, the dynamic psychiatrist is still guided by a handful of time-honored principles derived from psychoanalytic theory and technique that provide psychodynamic psychiatry with its unique character.

The Unique Value of Subjective Experience

Dynamic psychiatry is further defined by contrasting it with descriptive psychiatry. Practitioners of the latter approach categorize patients according to common behavioral and phenomenological features. They develop symptom checklists that allow them to classify patients according to similar clusters of symptoms. The patient's subjective experience, except as used to report items in the checklist, is less important. Descriptive psychiatrists with a behavioral orientation would argue that the patient's subjective experience is peripheral to the essence of psychiatric diagnosis and treatment, which must be based on observable behavior. The most extreme behavioral view is that behavior and mental life are synonymous (Watson 1930). Moreover, the descriptive psychiatrist is more interested in how a patient is *similar* to rather than different from other patients with congruent features.

In contrast, dynamic psychiatrists approach their patients by trying to determine what is unique about each one—how a particular patient *differs* from other patients as a result of a life story like no other. Symptoms and behaviors are viewed only as the final common pathways of highly personalized subjective experiences, which filter the biological and environmental determinants of illness. Furthermore, dynamic psychiatrists place paramount value on the patient's internal world—fantasies, dreams, fears, hopes, impulses, wishes, self-images, perceptions of others, and psychological reactions to symptoms.

A descriptive psychiatrist approaching an occluded cave nestled in the side of a mountain might well describe in detail the characteristics of the massive rock obstructing the cave's opening, while dismissing the interior of the cave beyond the rock as inaccessible and therefore unknowable. In contrast, dynamic psychiatrists would be curious about the dark recesses of the cave beyond the boulder. Like the descriptive psychiatrists, they would note the markings of the opening, but they would regard them differently. They would want to know how the cave's exterior reflected the inner contents. They might be curious about why it was necessary to protect the interior with a boulder at the opening.

The Unconscious

Continuing with our cave metaphor, the dynamic psychiatrist would figure out a way to remove the boulder, enter the dark recesses of the cave, and, perhaps with a flashlight, illuminate the interior. Artifacts on the floor or markings on the wall would be of special interest to the explorer because they would shed light on the history of this particular cave. A steady gurgling of water coming up through the floor might suggest an underground spring applying pressure from below. The dynamic psychiatrist would be particularly interested in exploring the depths of the cave. How far into the mountainside does it extend? Is the back wall the true limit that defines the inner space, or is it a "false wall" that gives way to even greater depths?

As the cave metaphor suggests, a second defining principle of dynamic psychiatry is a conceptual model of the mind that includes the unconscious. Freud (1915) recognized two different kinds of unconscious mental content: 1) the preconscious (i.e., mental contents that can easily be brought into conscious awareness by merely shifting one's attention) and 2) the unconscious proper (i.e., mental contents that are censored because they are unacceptable and therefore are repressed and not easily brought into conscious awareness). Throughout this book, *the unconscious* will be used to refer exclusively to those mental contents in this second category. The preconscious can be illustrated by a memory of your first grade teacher—although not generally conscious of him or her, you can retrieve an image of the teacher simply by shifting your attention. A common example of unconscious thought is the murderous wish an older sibling directs at a new baby brother or sister. Because this wish is unacceptable, it is repressed and buried in the unconscious.

Together, the unconscious, the preconscious, and the conscious systems of the mind compose what Freud (1900) termed the *topographic model.* He became convinced of the unconscious because of two major pieces of clinical evidence: dreams and parapraxes. Analysis of dreams revealed that an unconscious childhood wish was usually the motivating force of dreams (1900). The dreamwork disguised the wish, so analysis of the dream was necessary to discern the true nature of the wish. Reflecting on the manifest or overt content of your own dreams should be enough to convince you that dreams provide a forum for ideas that are not acceptable during waking life.

Parapraxes consist of such phenomena as slips of the tongue, "accidental" actions, and forgetting or substituting names or words. A typist, for example, repeatedly typed "murder" when she intended to type "mother." The notion of the "Freudian slip" is now a thoroughly entrenched part of our culture that connotes the unwitting revelation of a person's unconscious wishes or feelings. Freud (1901) used these embarrassing incidents to illustrate the breakthrough of repressed wishes and to demonstrate the parallels between the mental processes of everyday life and those of neurotic symptom formation.

The dynamic psychiatrist views symptoms and behaviors as reflections of unconscious processes that defend against repressed wishes and feelings, just as the boulder protects the contents of the cave from exposure. Moreover, dreams and parapraxes are like the artwork on the walls of the cave—communications, symbolic or otherwise, in the present that deliver messages from the forgotten past. The dynamic psychiatrist must develop sufficient comfort with this dark realm to explore it without stumbling.

Psychic Determinism

To assert that symptoms and behavior are external manifestations of unconscious processes is to touch on a third principle of dynamic psychiatry—psychic determinism. The psychodynamic approach asserts that we are consciously confused and unconsciously controlled. We go through our daily lives as though we have freedom of choice, but we are actually far more restricted than we think. In actuality, we are but characters living out a script written by the unconscious. Our choices of marital partners, our vocational interests, even our leisure-time pursuits are not randomly selected; they are shaped by unconscious forces in dynamic relationship with one another.

At the risk of oversimplifying, an obstetrician who is the oldest of four children may have chosen her profession partly because she unconsciously wishes to kill off all sibling rivals and avoid repeated displacement by the birth of a new baby. She defends against this unconscious wish by devoting herself professionally to bringing new life into the world, thereby reassuring herself that she cannot possibly harbor destructive wishes toward babies. But on the conscious level, she may regard her specialty choice simply as the one she liked best during her clinical clerkship experiences in medical school.

When human behavior becomes markedly symptomatic, the limits of free will become more obvious. An obsessive-compulsive patient who must retrace the route from the subway to the office three times a day is consciously aware of being out of control, but simply does not understand the nature of the unconscious forces at work. A man who can only reach orgasm during masturbation by imagining humiliation at the hands of a muscle-bound sadist has similarly lost the freedom to choose his sexual fantasies. The dynamic psychiatrist approaches these symptoms with the understanding that they represent adaptation to the demands of an unconscious script forged by a mixture of drives, defenses, object relations, and disturbances in the self. In short, behavior has meaning.

The meaning is rarely as simple and straightforward as the foregoing example involving the obstetrician. More commonly, a single behavior or symptom serves several functions and solves many problems—a notion that Waelder (1930) referred to as the principle of multiple function. He developed the principle out of dissatisfaction with Freud's more restrictive concept of overdetermination, which implied that several intrapsychic factors must operate together to create sufficient cause for a specific effect (a behavior or symptom). As Sherwood (1969) pointed out, "Freud clearly held that the causes of behavior were *both* complex (overdetermined) and multiple (in the sense of their being alternate sets of sufficient conditions)" (p. 181). In other words, certain behaviors or symptoms are at times caused by a specific intrapsychic constellation of factors, but in other instances they are produced by a multitude of other etiological forces in the unconscious. Suffice it to say that the psychodynamic view of human behavior defines it as the end result of many different conflicting forces that serve a variety of different functions corresponding both to the demands of reality and to the needs of the unconscious.

The principle of psychic determinism, although certainly a bedrock notion, calls for two disclaimers. First, unconscious factors do not determine all behaviors or symptoms. When a patient with Alzheimer's disease forgets the name of his spouse, it probably is not a parapraxis. When a patient with partial complex seizures ritualistically buttons and unbuttons his shirt during the aura of his seizure, the symptom can likely be attributed to an irritable focus of the temporal lobe. The dynamic psychiatrist's task is to sort out which symptoms and behaviors can or cannot be explained by dynamic factors.

The second caveat derives from experience with patients who make no effort to change their behavior because they claim to be passive victims of unconscious forces. Within the concept of psychic determinism, there *is* room for choice. Although it may be more restricted than we like to think, conscious intention to change can be an influential factor in recovery from symptoms (Appelbaum 1981). The dynamic psychiatrist must be wary of the patient who justifies remaining ill by invoking psychic determinism.

Past Is Prologue

A fourth basic principle of dynamic psychiatry is that the experiences of infancy and childhood are crucial determinants of the adult personality. In the succinct words of William Wordsworth, "The child is father of the man." The dynamic psychiatrist listens intently when a patient speaks of childhood memories, knowing that these experiences may play a critical role in the current presenting problems. Indeed, etiology and pathogenesis are often linked to childhood events in the dynamic view. In some cases, overt trauma, such as incest or physical abuse, leads to disturbances in the adult personality. More often, the chronic, repetitive patterns of interaction within a family are of greater etiological significance.

The dynamic point of view also takes into consideration the fact that infants and children perceive their environment through highly subjective filters that may distort the real qualities of the figures around them. Similarly, certain children are constitutionally difficult to raise no matter how effective their parents may be. Research has revealed several discrete constitutional temperaments in newborn infants (Thomas and Chess 1984). The etiology of some psychiatric illness may be related to how good the "fit" is between the temperament of the child and the temperament of the parenting figure. The hyperirritable child who does reasonably well with a calm and low-key mother may do poorly with a high-strung mother. This model of "goodness of fit" avoids blaming either parents or children for the latter's psychiatric problems. Longitudinal studies now reveal that shyness, for example, may be an inherited variation in the threshold of arousal in selected limbic sites in the brain (Kagan et al. 1988). The same research also suggests, however, that for shy behavior to be actualized, some variety of chronic environmental stress needs to act on the basic temperamental disposition present at birth.

Theories of childhood development have always been central to dynamic psychiatry. Freud postulated that a child passes through three principal psychosexual stages on the road to maturity. Each of these—the oral, the anal, and the genital—is associated with a particular bodily zone where Freud believed that the libido, or sexual energy, of the child was concentrated. As a result of environmental trauma, constitutional factors, or both, a child may become developmentally arrested at the oral or anal phase, resulting in a fixation that is retained into adult life. Under stress, the adult may regress to this more primitive phase of development and manifest the mental organization of the instinctual gratification associated with that phase. Although Freud reconstructed childhood development retrospectively based on the reports of adult patients in psychoanalysis, subsequent psychoanalytic investigators have studied development prospectively through direct infant and child observation. These studies (Mahler et al. 1975; Stern 1985) have led to more elaborate developmental theories of normal and abnormal personality and to a greater emphasis on the nature of the child's relatedness to others as opposed to the vicissitudes of instinctual energies. These theories will be discussed in more detail in Chapter 2.

Transference

The persistence of childhood patterns of mental organization in adult life implies that the past is repeating itself in the present. Perhaps the most compelling example of this is the core psychodynamic concept of transference, in which the patient experiences the doctor as a significant figure from the patient's past. Qualities of that past figure will be attributed to the doctor, and feelings associated with that figure will be experienced in the same way with the doctor. The two outstanding characteristics of transference are that it is inappropriate to the current relationship and that it is a repetition of the past (Greenson 1967). The patient unconsciously *reenacts* the past relationship, instead of remembering it, and in so doing introduces to the treatment a wealth of information about past relationships.

Although the concept of transference is generally associated with psychoanalysis or psychotherapy, the therapeutic relationship is merely one example of a more general phenomenon. As Brenner (1982) put it: "*Every* object relation is a new addition of the first, definitive attachments of childhood. . . . Transference is ubiquitous, it develops in every psychoanalytic situation because it develops in every situation where another person is important in one's life" (pp. 194–195). To be more precise, every relationship is a mixture of a real relationship and transference phenomenon, since transference is superimposed on real characteristics.

The dynamic psychiatrist recognizes the pervasiveness of transference phenomena and realizes that the relationship problems of which the patient complains will eventually manifest themselves in the patient's relationship with the treater. What is unique, then, about the doctor-patient relationship in dynamic psychiatry is not the presence of the transference, but the fact that it is therapeutic material to be understood. Dynamic psychiatrists do not respond to transference with the same actions as everyone else. When subjected to hateful invectives from their patients, they do not angrily reject them as others would. Instead, an attempt is made to determine what past relationship is being repeated in the present. In this sense, dynamic psychiatrists are defined by what they do *not* do as much as by what they do.

Countertransference

An overarching principle embraced by those of us who practice dynamic psychiatry is that we are basically more similar to our patients than we are different from them. The psychological mechanisms in pathological states are merely extensions of principles involved in normal developmental functioning. Doctor and patient are both human beings. Just as patients have transference, treaters have countertransference. Since every current relationship is a new addition of old relationships, it follows logically that countertransference in the psychiatrist and transference in the patient are essentially identical processes—each unconsciously experiences the other as someone from the past. The difference lies in how the feelings are handled in the therapeutic encounter (Brenner 1982). While transference is discussed and analyzed as part of the therapeutic process, countertransference is monitored by the constant internal vigilance of the psychiatrist, who notes the emergence of powerful positive and negative feelings toward the patient and reflects silently on the possible origin of those feelings in the context of past relationships. This monitoring process is a deliberate attempt to remember that helps avoid repeating or reenacting the old object relationship.

The concept of countertransference has undergone considerable evolution since its inception (Hamilton 1988; Kernberg 1965). Freud's (1912) narrow definition referred to the analyst's transference to the patient or the analyst's response to the patient's transference. Implicit in this conceptualization is the emergence of unresolved conflicts from the analyst's unconscious. Winnicott (1949), however, in working with psychotic patients and those with severe personality disorders, noted a different form of countertransference. He termed the feeling *objective hate,* because it was not a reaction stemming from unresolved unconscious conflicts in the treater, but rather was a natural reaction to the patient's outrageous behavior. It is objective in the sense that virtually everyone would react similarly to the patient's provocative behavior.

As Kernberg (1965) pointed out, this broader definition of countertransference as the therapist's conscious and appropriate total emotional reaction to the patient is gaining greater acceptance, particularly because it helps characterize the work with severe personality disorders, which are an increasingly common segment of the dynamic psychiatrist's practice. This definition serves to attenuate the pejorative connotation of countertransference—unresolved problems in the treater that require more analysis—and to replace it with a conceptualization that views countertransference as a major diagnostic and therapeutic tool that tells the treater a good deal about the patient's internal world. In this volume I will attempt to clarify whether the narrower or broader sense of countertransference is being used in a given instance.

Resistance

The last major principle of dynamic psychiatry involves the patient's wish to preserve the status quo, to oppose the treater's efforts to produce insight and change. In his early papers on technique, Freud (1912) had already noted these powerful oppositional forces: "The resistance accompanies the treatment step by step. Every single association, every act of the person under treatment must reckon with the resistance and represents a compromise between the forces that are striving towards recovery and the opposing ones" (p. 103). Resistances to treatment are as ubiquitous as transference phenomena and may take many forms, including lateness to appointments, refusal to take medications, forgetting the psychiatrist's advice or interpretations, silence in therapy sessions, focusing on unimportant material during the sessions, or forgetting to pay the therapy bill, to name only a few. Resistance may be conscious, preconscious, or unconscious. All resistance has in common an attempt to avoid unpleasant feelings, whether anger, guilt, hate, love (if directed toward a forbidden object such as the therapist), envy, shame, grief, anxiety, and so on. The dynamic psychiatrist notes that treatment threatens the repression of unacceptable impulses, feelings, and thoughts, and so must expect to encounter resistance in the service of protecting repression.

Resistance defends the patient's illness. The patient's characteristic defense mechanisms designed to safeguard against unpleasant affects come to the fore during dynamic treatment. In fact, resistance may be defined as the patient's defenses as they manifest themselves in psychodynamic treatment (Greenson 1967). The difference between resistances and defense mechanisms is simply that the former can be observed while the latter must be inferred (Thomä and Kächele 1987). The strength of the defense or resistance is necessarily proportional to the strength of the underlying impulse. As Ralph Waldo Emerson once observed, "The louder he talked of his honor, the faster we counted our spoons." Similarly, those who most speak out *against* sin may be struggling with powerful urges *to* sin, a conjecture amply supported by the fates of several prominent televangelists in the past decade.

The dynamic psychiatrist expects to encounter resistance to treatment and is prepared to address this phenomenon as part and parcel of the treatment process. While other treaters may get angry at noncompliance with prescribed treatment, the dynamic psychiatrist is curious to know what this resistance is protecting and what past situation is being reenacted.

Mind and Brain in Psychiatry

One of the most unfortunate developments in contemporary psychiatry is the polarization between biologically oriented and dynamically oriented psychiatrists. At the root of this conflict lies the age-old mind-body problem. Is the etiology of mental illness in the brain or in the mind? Should the treatment of mental illness be somatic or psychotherapeutic? The main problem with the debate between these polarized factions is the questions posed. It is not a situation of "either-or," but "both-and." As Nemiah (1961) noted nearly 30 years ago, "For a practical understanding of the human being, sometimes it is the language of psychology and sometimes the language of physiology and biochemistry that is more apposite; and when we are lucky, we occasionally catch a glimpse of the complex interrelations between these modes of discourse" (p. 9). The dynamic psychiatrist who neglects the biological dimension of experience and the biologically oriented psychiatrist who neglects the psychological realm are both guilty of narrow-minded reductionism.

Putting aside the enormous philosophical literature on the mind-body problem, from the standpoint of hard science, any distinction between functional and organic psychiatric illness is somewhat artificial. In the words of Kandel (1979), "What we conceive of as our mind is an expression of the functioning of our brain" (p. 1037). In a series of highly creative experiments with the marine snail *Aplysia*, Kandel (1979, 1983) has demonstrated that experiences with the environment alter the functional effectiveness of synaptic connections by modulating calcium influx in the presynaptic terminals. In this sense, disturbances of a psychological nature are reflected in specific changes in neuronal and synaptic function. Kandel shared Freud's view that all mental disturbances must fundamentally be biological in nature. Environmental factors, like genetic/constitutional factors and infectious or toxic agents, affect the mind at the level of brain function.

Kandel (1979) extrapolated implications for psychotherapy from his molecular research. Since experience appears to modify brain function through altering synaptic strength and regulating gene expression, "it is only insofar as our words produce changes in each other's brains that psychotherapeutic intervention produces changes in patients' minds. From this perspective the biological and psychological approaches are joined" (p. 1037).

Despite this promising research, we are far from being able to make one-to-one correlations between mind and brain. As Reiser (1988) observed: "Even though the brain is the organ that subserves the function of the mind, brain and mind are not the same thing. Brain science does not yet, and probably never will, fully explain the mind or make mental functions fully understandable" (p. 149). Although we fully recognize the inseparability of mind and brain, we must also acknowledge that the two domains use different languages (Edelson 1984; Reiser 1985). The parlance of the brain and the parlance of the mind depend on different conceptual models and on different levels of abstraction as well. The language of dynamic psychiatry is the language of the mind, but we must not for a moment allow the semantic demands of communication to obscure the fundamental origin of that language in the brain.

This model of the interrelationship between mind and brain is best illustrated by a brief clinical example. In the language of the brain, the locus ceruleus is associated with anxiety and panic attacks (Charney et al. 1982). Certain drugs that stimulate the locus ceruleus produce panic in patients who suffer from panic disorder. Those drugs that have been found effective in treating panic attacks also quiet the firing of the locus ceruleus. In the language of the mind, patients who lack the ability to summon up a soothing mental image of their therapists over a long weekend will also undergo a panic reaction. However, when the locus ceruleus fires, a patient's subjective experience may be a sense of terror that the therapist has died and will never be seen again. The sound of the therapist's voice over the phone may immediately diminish that terror. Hence the locus ceruleus may be quieted with words as effectively as it is with medication.

Two levels of discourse describe the same physiological and psychological phenomenon. One involves the language of the brain, and one prefers the language of the mind. Dynamic psychiatry predominantly speaks the language of meanings, a realm of discourse foreign to the locus ceruleus. Meanings reside in the domain of the mind.

The Role of the Dynamic Psychiatrist in Contemporary Psychiatry

In an age when impressive advances in the neurosciences occur almost weekly, dynamic psychiatry has lost some of its luster. Only a generation ago, psychoanalysts and dynamic psychiatrists enjoyed unparalleled prestige. They have since been upstaged by biologically oriented researchers, whose contribution to the field is beyond question. However, above the din of optimistic proclamations about the genetic-biochemical basis of all mental illness, another cry can be heard, one that is growing in intensity. Groups of psychiatric residents in biologically oriented programs complain that they know all about neurotransmitters but do not know how to talk to their patients. Freshly trained private practitioners ask analysts for consultation and supervision when their patients fail to respond to medications. Even patients are beginning to demand that they be listened to rather than simply medicated.

Advances in any scientific field conform to a predictable pattern—an initial flurry of excitement is followed by sobering disillusionment. Our own field of psychiatry is no exception in this regard. The post–World War II enthusiasm for psychoanalysis as a panacea for a host of social problems led to a bitter disenchantment in the decade of the 1960s. American psychiatrists today are encountering the limitations inherent in the tools of biological psychiatry. The alarming prevalence of tardive dyskinesia has dampened the early enthusiasm for antipsychotics. The dexamethasone suppression test that was going to revolutionize psychiatric diagnosis only a few years ago is now mired in controversy about whether it has only limited clinical usefulness or none at all. Psychiatric clinicians are frustrated when certain patients do not respond to medications or to electroconvulsive therapy. Patients are frustrated when their hallucinations remit on medication but their lives remain miserable because of numerous interpersonal problems. The fanfare accompanying advances in neurochemistry has masked the fact that there is a formidable distance between the research laboratory and the psychiatrist's consulting room.

Training in dynamic psychiatry significantly broadens the scope of the clinician's expertise. The real advantage of the dynamic approach is its attention to the role of personality factors in illness. In fact, personality and its influence on the patient is a principal area of expertise for dynamic psychiatrists (Michels 1988). As Perry et al. (1987) persuasively argue, since every treatment involves therapeutic management and modification of the patient's personality, a psychodynamic evaluation is applicable to all patients, not simply those referred for long-term psychoanalytic psychotherapy. Characterological resistances to treatment frequently torpedo the medication program designed to maintain the patient in remission. A recent study of treatment-resistant hospitalized patients (Marcus and Bradley 1987) revealed that 71 percent of such patients had an Axis II diagnosis in addition to the more obvious Axis I diagnosis of depression, schizophrenia, or other psychosis. Symptoms are embedded in character structure, and the dynamic psychiatrist recognizes that in many cases one cannot treat the symptoms without first addressing the character structure.

A dynamic therapeutic approach is certainly not necessary for every psychiatric patient. Those who respond well to medications, electroconvulsive therapy, or behavioral desensitization do not require the services of a dynamic psychiatrist. A patient with dementia may be so cognitively impaired as to be unable to think in the language of psychodynamic treatment. As with all other schools of psychiatry, the dynamic psychotherapeutic approach cannot effectively treat all psychiatric illnesses or patients. It is particularly useful with personality disorders, the paraphilias, some anxiety disorders, most eating disorders, and with treatment-resistant Axis I patients who do not respond to conventional biological treatments. The patient with dual diagnoses on Axis I and Axis II is also in need of a dynamic approach.

A strictly dynamic therapeutic approach should probably be reserved for patients who most need it and who will not respond to any other interventions. However, a *dynamically informed* approach to most—if not all—patients will enrich the psychiatrist's practice and enhance the clinician's sense of mastery over the mysteries of the human psyche. Most importantly, it will help the dynamic psychiatrist identify and understand the daily countertransference problems that interfere with effective diagnosis and treatment. In a recent survey of private psychiatric practitioners and academic psychiatrists, Langsley and Yager (1988) found that the second most highly regarded skill was the ability to "recognize countertransference problems and personal idiosyncrasies as they influence interactions with patients and be able to deal with them constructively" (p. 471). The dynamic approach is the only one that systematically addresses the psychiatrist's conscious and unconscious contributions to the process of treatment and evaluation.

References

Appelbaum SA: Effecting Change in Psychotherapy. New York, Jason Aronson, 1981
Brenner C: The Mind in Conflict. New York, International Universities Press, 1982
Charney DS, Heninger GR, Sternberg DE: Assessment of alpha-II adrenergic autoreceptor function in humans: effects of oral yohimbine. Life Sciences 30:2033–2041, 1982
Edelson M: Hypothesis and Evidence in Psychoanalysis. Chicago, University of Chicago Press, 1984
Ellenberger HF: The Discovery of the Unconscious: The History and Evolution of Dynamic Psychiatry. New York, Basic Books, 1970
Freud S: The interpretation of dreams (1900), in The Standard Edition of the Complete Psychological Works of Sigmund Freud, Vol 4,

5. Translated and edited by Strachey J. London, Hogarth Press, 1953, pp 1–627

Freud S: The psychopathology of everyday life (1901), in The Standard Edition of the Complete Psychological Works of Sigmund Freud, Vol 6. Translated and edited by Strachey J. London, Hogarth Press, 1960, pp 1–279

Freud S: The dynamics of transference (1912), in The Standard Edition of the Complete Psychological Works of Sigmund Freud, Vol 12. Translated and edited by Strachey J. London, Hogarth Press, 1958, pp 97–108

Freud S: The unconscious (1915), in The Standard Edition of the Complete Psychological Works of Sigmund Freud, Vol 14. Translated and edited by Strachey J. London, Hogarth Press, 1963, pp 159–215

Greenson RR: The Technique and Practice of Psychoanalysis. New York, International Universities Press, 1967

Hamilton NG: Self and Others: An Introduction to Object Relations Theory in Practice. Northvale, NJ, Jason Aronson, 1988

Kagan J, Reznick JS, Snidman N: Biological bases of childhood shyness. Science 240:167–171, 1988

Kandel ER: Psychotherapy and the single synapse: the impact of psychiatric thought on neurobiologic research. N Engl J Med 301:1028–1037, 1979

Kandel ER: From metapsychology to molecular biology: explorations into the nature of anxiety. Am J Psychiatry 140:1277–1293, 1983

Kernberg O: Notes on countertransference. J Am Psychoanal Assoc 13:38–56, 1965

Langsley DG, Yager J: The definition of a psychiatrist: eight years later. Am J Psychiatry 145:469–475, 1988

Mahler MS, Pine F, Bergman A: The Psychological Birth of the Human Infant. New York, Basic Books, 1975

Marcus E, Bradley S: Concurrence of Axis I and Axis II illness in treatment-resistant hospitalized patients. Psychiatr Clin North Am 10:177–184, 1987

Michels R: The future of psychoanalysis. Psychoanal Q 57:167–185, 1988

Nemiah JC: Foundations of Psychopathology. New York, Oxford University Press, 1961

Perry S, Cooper AM, Michels R: The psychodynamic formulation: its purpose, structure, and clinical application. Am J Psychiatry 144:543–550, 1987

Reiser MF: Converging sectors of psychoanalysis and neurobiology: mutual challenge and opportunity. J Am Psychoanal Assoc 33:11–34, 1985

Reiser MF: Are psychiatric educators "losing the mind"? Am J Psychiatry 145:148–153, 1988

Sherwood M: The Logic of Explanation in Psychoanalysis. New York, Academic Press, 1969

Stern DN: The Interpersonal World of the Infant: A View from Psychoanalysis and Developmental Psychology. New York, Basic Books, 1985

Thomä H, Kächele H: Psychoanalytic Practice, Vol 1: Principles. Translated by Wilson M, Roseveare D. New York, Springer-Verlag, 1987
Thomas A, Chess S: Genesis and evolution of behavioral disorders: from infancy to early adult life. Am J Psychiatry 141:1–9, 1984
Waelder R: The principle of multiple function: observations on overdetermination, in Psychoanalysis: Observation, Theory, Application. Edited by Gutman SA. New York, International Universities Press, 1930, pp 68–83
Watson JB: Behaviorism. New York, WW Norton, 1930 (originally published in 1924)
Winnicott DW: Hate in the counter-transference. Int J Psychoanal 30:69–74, 1949

CHAPTER 2

The Theoretical Basis of Dynamic Psychiatry

Nothing is as practical as a good theory.
— Kurt Lewin

L ike a sailor without a sextant, a psychiatrist who sets out to navigate the dark waters of the unconscious without a theory will soon be lost at sea. Psychoanalytic theory is the foundation of dynamic psychiatry. It brings order to the seemingly chaotic inner world of the patient. It allows the psychiatrist to supplement and transcend the descriptive level of cataloging symptoms and applying diagnostic labels. It provides a means of entering and understanding the cavernous interior of the mind. Theory not only guides clinicians toward diagnostic understanding, it also informs the choice of treatment for each patient. Theoretical understanding helps the dynamic psychiatrist decide what to say, when to say it, how to say it, and what is better left unsaid.

Contemporary dynamic psychiatry subsumes three broad psychoanalytic theoretical frameworks: 1) ego psychology, derived from the classic psychoanalytic theory of Freud; 2) object relations theory, derived from the work of Melanie Klein and members of the "British School," including Fairbairn, Winnicott, and Balint; and 3) self psychology, derived from the Sullivanian interpersonal tradition but formulated and elaborated in contemporary terms by Heinz Kohut. Although volumes have been written on each of these schools of thought, here we will merely examine the salient features of the three theories. In subsequent chapters the theories will be "fleshed out" to illustrate their application to clinical situations.

Ego Psychology

Freud's early years as a psychoanalytic investigator were heavily influenced by his topographic model (described in Chapter 1). Hysterical symptoms were seen as the result of repressed memories of events or ideas. Freud hypothesized that psychotherapeutic intervention could lift repression, leading to the recall of memories. In turn, a detailed verbal description of the remembered pathogenic idea or event, accompanied by intense affect, would lead to the symptom's disappearance. For example, a young man's paralyzed arm might be the result of a repressed wish to hit his father. According to this model, the young man might regain the use of his arm by retrieving the wish from his unconscious, verbalizing it, and expressing the anger toward his father. This cathartic method, also known as abreaction, makes conscious the unconscious pathogenic memory.

But the topographic model soon began to fail Freud. He repeatedly encountered resistances in his patients to his therapeutic maneuvers. Some memories could not be brought back into consciousness. The defense mechanisms responsible for this resistance were themselves unconscious and therefore inaccessible. These observations led Freud to conclude that the ego has both conscious and unconscious components.

With the publication of *The Ego and the Id,* Freud (1923) introduced his tripartite structural theory of ego, id, and superego. In the structural model, which superseded the topographic model, the ego was viewed as distinct from the instinctual drives. The conscious aspect of the ego was the executive organ of the psyche, responsible for decision making and integration of perceptual data. The unconscious aspect of the ego contained defense mechanisms such as repression. These defenses were necessary to counteract the powerful instinctual drives harbored in the id—specifically, sexuality (libido) and aggression.

The id is a completely unconscious intrapsychic agency that is only interested in discharging tension. The id is controlled both by the unconscious aspects of the ego and by the third agency of the structural model—the superego. For the most part, the superego is unconscious, but aspects of it are certainly conscious. This agency incorporates the moral conscience and the ego ideal. The former *proscribes* (i.e., dictates what one should *not* do based on the internalization of parental and societal values), while the latter *prescribes* (i.e., dictates what one ought to do or be). The superego tends to be more sensitive to the strivings of the id and is therefore more immersed in the unconscious than is the ego (see Figure 2-1).

Ego psychology conceptualizes the intrapsychic world as one of interagency conflict. The superego, the ego, and the id battle among themselves as sexuality and aggression strive for expression and discharge. Conflict between the agencies produces anxiety. This signal anxiety (Freud 1926) alerts the ego that a defense mechanism is required. The mechanism of neurotic symptom formation may be understood in this manner. Conflict produces anxiety, which results in defense, which leads to a compromise between the id and the

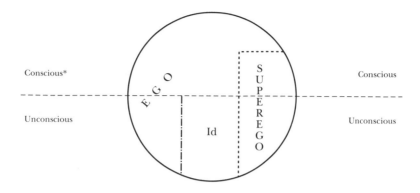

*The preconscious has been deleted for the sake of simplicity.

Figure 2-1. The structural model.

ego. A symptom, then, is a compromise formation that both defends against the wish arising from the id and gratifies the wish in disguised form.

An accountant with an obsessive-compulsive disorder was terribly concerned that he would explode in anger at his boss. He believed that he could control his anger by swallowing a hundred times in a row. This symptom defended against the eruption of anger from the id, but it also contained an attenuated form of gratification of his aggressive wish toward his boss—the process of counting and swallowing prevented him from getting his work done and therefore defied his boss and expressed his independence. Such compromise formations are a normal mental process (Brenner 1982). Neurotic symptoms represent only the pathological variety. Character traits themselves can be compromise formations and may represent adaptive and creative solutions to intrapsychic conflict.

Defense Mechanisms

Freud acknowledged the existence of other defense mechanisms, but he devoted most of his attention to repression. His daughter Anna, in her landmark work, *The Ego and the Mechanisms of Defense* (1936), expanded her father's work by describing in detail nine individual defense mechanisms: regression, reaction formation, undoing, introjection, identification, projection, turning against the self, reversal, and sublimation. Even more important, she acknowledged the implications that this increased scrutiny of the defensive operation of the ego had for treatment. No longer could the psychoanalyst simply attend to the uncovering of unacceptable wishes from the id. Equal attention would need to be paid to the vicissitudes of defensive efforts put forth by the ego, which would manifest themselves as resistances in treatment.

In shifting the emphasis of psychoanalysis from drives to ego defenses, Anna Freud anticipated the movement of psychoanalysis and dynamic psychiatry away from neurotic symptom formation and toward character pathology. We now partially define many forms of personality disorder according to their typical defensive operations. Hence the dynamic psychiatrist must be thoroughly familiar with a broad range of defense mechanisms because of their usefulness in understanding both neurotic problems and personality disorders.

All defenses have in common the protection of the ego against instinctual demands from the id (Freud 1926). Some of the principal neurotic defense mechanisms are repression, displacement, reaction formation, isolation of affect, undoing, somatization, and conversion.

1. *Repression.* Freud viewed this mechanism as the queen of all defenses. It operates unconsciously by expelling unacceptable wishes, feelings, or fantasies from conscious awareness. Although repression is used by virtually all neurotics, it is a hallmark of the hysterical neurotic and the higher-level hysterical personality (see Chapter 17).

2. *Displacement.* This defense is an unconscious process by which feelings attached to one source are redirected toward another. Transference is an obvious example of displacement, since feelings for a person in the past are transferred to a figure in the present. Phobias are the classic example of this defense, because the anxiety associated with an unconscious source is redirected to a conscious substitute, often harmless in and of itself. Displacement is also one of the chief mechanisms of disguise in dreams, where anxiety is reduced and sleep is preserved by substituting a neutral figure for a more emotionally charged one.

3. *Reaction formation.* This common defense is characterized by warding off an unacceptable wish or impulse by adopting a character trait that is diametrically opposed to it. The obstetrician in Chapter 1, who brings new babies into the world to deny her destructive childhood wishes toward her younger siblings, is using reaction formation. This defense is commonly found in obsessive-compulsive disorder and in those with obsessive-compulsive personality disorder.

4. *Isolation of affect.* This mechanism, also commonly found in obsessive-compulsive patients, divorces affect from ideation. A traumatic memory, for example, may be easily retrieved but will be stripped of any concomitant intense feelings. Isolation often operates hand in hand with intellectualization, which performs a similar function of avoiding affect.

5. *Undoing.* Sometimes referred to as doing and undoing, this mechanism is also characteristic of obsessive-compulsive patients. It involves magical thinking, with a symbolic action performed to reverse or cancel out a completed and unacceptable thought or action. One patient took literally the aphorism, "If you step on a crack, you'll break your mother's back." Whenever he inadvertently stepped on a crack in the sidewalk, he would return to retrace his steps so he could repeat them without hitting the crack.
6. *Somatization.* This defense, typical of hypochondriacal patients, involves the transfer of painful feelings to body parts. Psychotherapy with somatizing patients is often frustrating because feelings are unacceptable, and their emotional concerns can only be communicated through physical complaints.
7. *Conversion.* Most commonly, though not exclusively, associated with hysteria, this mechanism is characterized by the symbolic representation of an intrapyschic conflict in physical terms. As in the case of the young man with hysterical paralysis of his arm (referred to at the beginning of this chapter), the motor or sensory symbolization frequently involves a defense against an unacceptable wish.

Defense mechanisms have been classified according to a hierarchy from the most immature or pathological to the most mature or healthy (Vaillant 1977). The primarily neurotic defenses enumerated above are only a partial list. None of us is without defense mechanisms, once again illustrating the dynamic principle that psychological health and illness are on a continuum. In fact, a profile of your typical defense mechanisms is a good barometer of your psychological health. Vaillant (1977) emphasized four mature defenses in particular: 1) *suppression*—the *conscious* (as distinct from repression, which is unconscious) banishing of unacceptable thoughts or feelings from your mind; 2) *altruism*—the subordination of your own needs and interests to those of others; 3) *sublimation*— an unconscious process by which consciously unacceptable drives or wishes are channeled into socially acceptable alternatives (e.g., a wish to stab a sibling rival is converted into a surgical career); 4) *humor*—the ability to playfully poke fun at yourself and the situation you're in—an invaluable part of mental health. Examples of the more primitive defenses will be considered along with a discussion of object relations theory later in the chapter.

Adaptive Aspects of the Ego

The ego's importance to the psyche is not limited to its defensive operations. Heinz Hartmann established himself as one of the foremost contributors to contemporary ego psychology by focusing on the nondefensive aspects of the ego. He turned the ego away from the id and refocused it on the outside world. Hartmann (1939) insisted that there was a "conflict-free sphere of the ego" that develops independently of id forces and conflicts. Given an "average expectable environment," certain autonomous ego functions present at birth are allowed to flourish without being impeded by conflict. These include thinking, learning, perception, motor control, and language, to name a few. Hartmann's *adaptive* point of view, then, is an outgrowth of his concept of the existence of an autonomous, conflict-free area of the ego. Through neutralization of sexual and aggressive energies, Hartmann believed that even certain defenses could lose their connection with the instinctual forces of the id and become secondarily autonomous or adaptive.

David Rapaport (1951) and Edith Jacobson (1964) picked up where Hartmann left off and further refined his seminal contributions to ego psychology. It is commonplace today for clinicians to consider ego functions, ego strengths, and ego weaknesses as part of their routine psychodynamic evaluation of a patient. Bellak et al. (1973) systematized ego functions into scales used both for research and for clinical evaluation. The most important of these ego functions include reality testing, impulse control, thought processes, judgment, synthetic-integrative functioning, mastery-competence, and primary and secondary autonomy (after Hartmann).

Developmental Considerations

As with all psychoanalytic theories, ego psychology emphasizes developmental issues. The classical scheme associated with libidinal zones, that is, the oral, anal, and genital phases of Freud (see Chapter 1), has been elaborated as ego psychology has expanded. Erik Erikson (1959), following the lead of Hartmann, made an effort to weave interagency conflict into a broader fabric of ego psychology. He focused on psychosocial issues from the environment, which allowed him to evolve an epigenetic developmental scheme characterized by a psychosocial crisis at each phase. For example, during the oral phase of development, the infant must struggle with basic trust versus basic mistrust. The crisis of the anal phase involves autonomy versus shame and doubt. During the phallic-oedipal phase, the child grapples with initiative versus guilt.

The oedipal phase of development occupies a central place in the pathogenesis of neuroses (anxiety disorders), as well as in the dynamics of higher-level personality disorders (also called character neuroses), such as obsessive-compulsive personality and hysterical personality. Beginning at age three, children become more intensely focused on their genitals as a source of pleasure. Accompanying this interest is an intensified longing to be the exclusive love object of the parent of the opposite sex. However, at the same time, the child's dyadic or mother-and-child frame of reference changes to a triadic one with the child being aware of a rival for the affections of the parent of the opposite sex.

In the case of the male child, his first love object is his mother, which does not require a shift of affection. He desires to sleep with her, caress her, and be the center of her world. Since the father interferes with these plans, the child develops murderous wishes toward his rival. These wishes result in guilt, fear of retaliation by the father, and a sense of anxiety about that impending retaliation. Freud repeatedly observed that the leading source of the male child's anxiety during this phase of development is that the father's retaliation will come in the form of castration. To avoid this punishment, the boy renounces his sexual strivings for his mother and identifies with his father. This identification with the aggressor carries with it the decision to look for a woman *like* the mother so the boy can be *like* his father. As part of this oedipal resolution, the retaliatory father is internalized around the end of the fifth or sixth year, forming the superego, which Freud viewed as heir to the Oedipus complex.

Freud had more difficulty explaining the little girl's oedipal development. In a series of papers (1925, 1931, 1933), he frankly acknowledged his bewilderment at female psychology, yet struggled to chart female development. One way he dealt with this difficulty was to assume that female development was basically analogous to that of males. In Freud's view, while the Oedipus complex in boys is resolved by the castration complex, in girls it is *promulgated* by an awareness of "castration." In the preoedipal phases of development, in Freud's view, the little girl feels essentially like a little boy until she discovers the existence of the penis. At that point, she begins to feel inferior and falls victim to penis envy. She tends to blame her mother for her inferiority so she turns to her father as her love object, and the wish for a child from her father replaces her wish for a penis. Freud believed that one of three paths was available to the female child after discovery of her "genital inferiority": 1) cessation of all sexuality, that is, neurosis; 2) a defiant hypermasculinity; or 3) definitive femininity, which entailed renunciation of clitoral sexuality. In the normal oedipal resolution, loss of the mother's love, rather than fear of castration from the father, was postulated as the key factor.

More contemporary psychoanalytic authors have raised serious questions about Freud's formulations of female development. Stoller (1968) pointed out that the first phase of development in girls is clearly feminine, not masculine. Through extensive investigation of individuals with ambiguous genitalia and chromosomal anomalies, he clearly demonstrated that definitive femininity is established *before* the phallic-oedipal phase of development. Moreover, he persuasively argued that neither chromosomes nor genitalia are the primary source of femaleness—rather, it results from the parents' unswerving conviction of the child's gender. He shared the view of others, such as Lerner (1980) and Torok (1970), that penis envy is only one aspect of the development of femaleness, not the origin of it. All three authors pointed out the adverse therapeutic implications of viewing penis envy as a "bedrock" phenomenon (Freud 1937) that defies further analysis and understanding. One implication of such an approach is that it may lead therapists to help female patients accept a view of themselves as an inferior form of male. It might also strengthen a patient's defensive focus on anatomical or genital deficiency and prevent exploration of underlying wishes, conflicts, and anxieties. As Lerner (1980) pointed out, a more prominent source of concern for the little girl may be the anxiety-provoking nature of her own genitals, not the supposed superiority of the penis.

Although the Oedipus complex is central to understanding neuroses and character neurosis, regressions from the oedipal phase to anal and oral issues are also common. Finally, development does not cease with the resolution of the Oedipus complex. Defensive constellations change with each succeeding phase—latency, adolescence, young adulthood, midlife, and old age. In fact, Vaillant (1976) has documented an orderly shift during adult life from immature defenses such as hypochondriasis and acting out to more mature defenses such as altruism and sublimation, suggesting that personality is truly dynamic and malleable over the entire life cycle.

Object Relations Theory

The view of ego psychology is that drives (i.e., sexuality and aggression) are primary, while object relations are secondary. (It is a well-established, though perhaps unfortunate, tradition in psychoanalytic writing to use the term *object* to mean *person.* Despite the somewhat pejorative connotations of *object,* I will retain the usage here for the sake of consistency and clarity.) In other words, the infant's most compelling agenda is tension discharge under the pressure of drives. Object relations theory, on the other hand, holds that drives emerge in the context of a relationship (i.e., the infant-mother dyad) and therefore can never be divorced from one another. Some object relations theorists (Fairbairn 1952) would even suggest that the drives are primarily geared to object seeking rather than tension reduction.

Stated in its simplest terms, object relations theory encompasses the transformation of interpersonal relationships into internalized representations of relationships. As children develop, they do not simply internalize an object or person; rather, they internalize an entire *relationship* (Fairbairn 1940, 1944). A prototype of loving, positive experience is formed during periods when the infant is nursing (Freud 1905). This prototype includes a positive experience of the self (the nursing infant), a positive experience of the object (the attentive, caretaking mother), and a positive affective experience (pleasure, satiation). When hunger returns and the infant's mother is not immediately available, a prototype of negative experience occurs, including a negative experience of the self (the frustrated, demanding infant), an inattentive, frustrating object (the unavailable mother), and a negative affective experience of anger and perhaps terror. Ultimately, these two experiences are internalized as two opposing sets of object relationships consisting of a self-representation, an object-representation, and an affect linking the two (Ogden 1983).

The internalization of the infant's mother, usually referred to as introjection (Schafer 1968), begins with the physical sensations associated with the presence of the mother during nursing but does not become meaningful until a boundary between inner and outer has developed. Around the 16th month of life, isolated images of the mother gradually coalesce into an enduring mental representation (Sandler and Rosenblatt 1962). At the same time an enduring self-representation forms, first as a body-representation and later as a compilation of sensations and experiences perceived as belonging to the infant.

The positively colored or "good" object-representation begins as a hallucinatory wish fulfillment growing out of the hungry infant's longing for its mother (Schafer 1968) and is later transformed into an internal presence as the infant's cognitive/perceptual apparatus develops. A major motivating force in the introjection of the positive, loving aspects of the mother seems to be the infant's fear of losing the mother (Schafer 1968). The reasons for the introjection or "taking in" of the negative, "bad" aspects of the mother are more complex. Possible motivating factors include the fantasy of controlling the object by containing it within oneself (Segal 1964), gaining a sense of mastery through repeated traumatic experiences with the object (Schafer 1968), and a preference for a "bad" object over no object at all (Schafer 1968). Clinical experience suggests that intense attachment to an internalized hostile object may also be connected with the yearning for a more positive relationship with the object (Meissner 1981). Furthermore, the object that has been introjected does not necessarily correlate with the real external object. For example, a mother who is unavailable to feed her infant on demand may simply be occupied with an older sibling, but is *experienced* and *introjected* by the infant as hostile, rejecting, and unavailable. Object relations theory acknowledges that there is *not* a one-to-one correlation between the real object and the internalized object-representation.

Object relations theory also views conflict differently than it is viewed by ego psychology. Unconscious conflict is not merely the struggle between an impulse and a defense, but it is also a clash between opposing pairs of internal object relations units (Kernberg 1983; Ogden 1983; Rinsley 1977). In other words, at any one time different constellations of self-representations, object-representations, and affects vie with one another for center stage in the intrapsychic theater of internal object relations.

Internalization of object relations always involves a splitting of the ego into unconscious suborganizations (Ogden 1983). These fall into two groups:

> (1) self-suborganizations of ego, i.e., aspects of the ego in which the person more fully experiences his ideas and feelings as his own, and (2) object suborganizations of ego through which meanings are generated in a mode based upon an identification of an aspect of the ego with the object. This identification with the object is so thorough that one's original sense of self is almost entirely lost. (Ogden 1983, p. 227)

This model clearly shows the influence of Freud's notion of the superego, which is commonly experienced as though it is a "foreign body" (i.e., an object-suborganization of the ego that monitors what a self-suborganization of the ego is doing). Ogden's model also provides a pathway back from the intrapsychic to the interpersonal. In this framework, transference can be viewed as taking one of two forms—either the role of the self-subdivision of the ego or that of the object-subdivision of the ego may be externalized onto the treater, a process that will be discussed in detail later in this chapter.

A Historical Perspective

Originating in the United Kingdom, object relations theory has flourished there and in South America. Only recently has it taken hold in the United States. Melanie Klein is usually seen as the founder of the object relations movement. She emigrated from Budapest, and later from Berlin, to England in 1926, where her theory of early infantile development became highly controversial. She was influenced by Freud, but also broke new ground in her focus on internal objects. Through psychoanalytic work with children, she evolved a theory that relied heavily on unconscious intrapsychic fantasy and that compressed the developmental timetable of classical theory into the first year of life. The Oedipus complex, for example, was viewed by Klein as coinciding approximately with weaning in the latter half of the first year.

In the first few months of life, according to Klein, the infant experiences a primal terror of annihilation connected with Freud's death instinct. As a way of defending against this terror, the ego undergoes splitting, in which all "badness" or aggression deriving from the death instinct is disavowed and projected into the mother. The infant then lives in fear of the mother's persecution—which may be concretized as a fear that the mother will get inside the infant and destroy any goodness (deriving from libido) that has also been split off and is protected inside the infant. This latter fear is the primary anxiety of what Klein (1946) termed the *paranoid-schizoid position*. This early mode of organizing experience gains its name from the prominent defense mechanisms of splitting of the ego ("schizoid") and projection ("paranoid"). Indeed, projection and introjection are crucial to understanding the paranoid-schizoid position. These mechanisms are used to separate "good" and "bad" as much as possible (Segal 1964). After persecuting, or bad, objects have been projected into the mother to separate them from good, or idealized objects, they may be reintrojected (i.e., taken back inside) to gain control and mastery over them. Concomitantly, the good objects may be projected to keep them safe from the "bad," which is now inside.

These oscillating cycles of projection and introjection continue until the infant begins to realize that the "bad" mother and the "good" mother are not in fact different, but are rather the same person. As children integrate the two part-objects into one whole object, they become disturbed that their sadistic, destructive fantasies toward the mother may have destroyed her. This newfound concern for the mother as a whole object is termed *depressive anxiety* by Klein and heralds the arrival of the *depressive position*. This mode of experience involves concern that one may harm others, in contrast to the paranoid-schizoid position, where the concern is that one will be harmed by others. Guilt becomes a prominent part of the affective life of the infant, who attempts to resolve it through *reparation*. This process may involve acts toward the mother that are designed to repair the "damage" inflicted on her in actuality or in fantasy. Klein recast the Oedipus complex as an effort to resolve depressive anxieties and guilt through reparation.

Klein's formulations have been criticized for relying exclusively on fantasy and thereby minimizing the influence of real persons in the environment, for overemphasizing the death instinct—a concept that is largely discounted by contemporary psychoanalytic theorists, and for attributing sophisticated adult forms of cognition to infants in their first year of life. Nevertheless, her brilliant development of the paranoid-schizoid and depressive positions is of extraordinary clinical value, especially if we view these positions as two modes of generating experience that are lifelong and that create a dialectical interplay in the mind rather than viewing them as developmental phases that are passed through or outgrown (Ogden 1986). This conceptualization of lifelong modes of experience decreases the significance of Klein's developmental timetable.

For Klein, the drives were really complex psychological phenomena intimately tied to specific object relations. Rather than originating in the body, drives are seen as merely using the body as a vehicle for expression (Greenberg and Mitchell 1983). Similarly, the drives were not viewed as simply seeking tension reduction but as being directed toward specific objects for specific reasons. This perspective and others held by Klein led to acrimonious debate in the British Psychoanalytic Society. Anna Freud was Klein's principal nemesis, and when a schism finally ruptured the society, one segment, known as the "B" group, followed Anna Freud's leadership, while the "A" group remained loyal to Klein. A third segment, the "Independent" group, refused to take sides. These factions still exist today. The Independent group, all influenced to some degree by Klein's thinking, created the theory of object relations as we know it today (Kohon 1986). This group, often referred to collectively as constituting the "British School" of object relations (Sutherland 1980), includes such luminaries as D. W. Winnicott, Michael Balint, W. R. D. Fairbairn, Paula Heimann, Margaret Little, and Harry Guntrip. Although in fact there were significant differences in the writings of these thinkers, they are grouped together because they shared common themes. All were concerned about early development prior to the Oedipus complex, and all focused on the vicissitudes of internal object relations rather than on drive theory. Moreover, like Klein and unlike the classical analysts, they tended to treat sicker patients with psychoanalytic methods, perhaps thereby obtaining a more intimate glimpse of primitive mental states.

The British School served to counterbalance Klein's overemphasis on fantasy by stressing the influence of the infant's early environment. Winnicott (1965), for example, coined the term *the good enough mother* to characterize the minimum environmental requirements needed by the infant in order to proceed with normal development. Balint (1968) described the feeling in many patients that something was missing, which he termed *the basic fault*. He viewed this lack as caused by the mother's failure to respond to the child's basic needs. Fairbairn (1963), perhaps the most divorced from drive theory, saw the etiology of his schizoid patients' difficulties not in drive frustration but in their mothers' failure to provide experiences that reassured them they were truly loved for themselves. He believed that the instincts or drives were not pleasure seeking but rather object seeking.

These thinkers were all impressed with the fact that a theory of *deficit,* as well as a theory of conflict, was necessary for a complete psychoanalytic understanding of the human being. Analysts had another task in addition to the analysis of conflict. They also serve as a new object to be internalized by their patients so as to bolster deficient intrapsychic structures. This point is critical for a clinical theory of object relations—the patient's internal object relations are not etched in granite; they are open to modification through new experiences. This point of view is even acknowledged to some extent by proponents of classical ego psychology, such as Blum (1971), who credited Stone (1967) in noting: "Even in adult analysis the role of the analyst as a real new object rather than the object of transference must be considered along with identification with the analyst and analytic attitudes" (p. 51).

Self and Ego

While ego psychologists tend to minimize the significance of the self in their pursuit of a thoroughgoing understanding of the ego, the object relations theorists, because of their focus on the self as it relates to objects, have sought to clarify further the place of the self in the psychic apparatus. Certain American theorists, including Kernberg, Mahler, and Edith Jacobson, have worked to integrate object relations theory with ego psychology, considering the relationship of the ego and the self.

Few concepts in modern psychoanalytic discourse are more controversial than the self. The controversy has its historical roots in Freud's ambiguous usage of *Ich.* Literally translated from the German as "I," the term was used by Freud with two different connotations. At times *Ich* referred to an impersonal intrapsychic structure, while at other times it clearly connoted the individual's personal self-experience (Kernberg 1982; Meissner 1986). Strachey's subsequent translation of *Ich* as "ego" in the Standard Edition of Freud's works profoundly influenced this controversy. Ego became definitively associated with the tripartite structural theory as one of three impersonal intrapsychic agencies. Freud's other use of the term to mean self-experience became lost in the standardization of the impersonal meaning.

Hartmann (1950) further divorced the two meanings of *Ich* by differentiating ego and self according to their interactional contexts. The ego interacted with the other intrapsychic agencies, the id and superego, in this view, while the self interacted with objects.

Although critics believe that this historical development blurs the distinction between psychoanalytic and sociological concepts (Kernberg 1982), other theorists find that this clarification establishes a framework for the development of the theory of object relations. In other words, the self evolves as the result of interactions with significant objects in the environment and with corresponding internal objects (Meissner 1986).

Another major controversy surrounding the self is whether it refers to an intrapsychic representation of the individual or a source of action and agency in its own right. The tendency among ego psychological thinkers has been to view the self as representational rather than as a source of subjective autonomous activity (Meissner 1986). However, numerous authors (Guntrip 1968, 1971; Meissner 1986; Schafer 1976; Sutherland 1983) have expressed concern that the structural theory and the model of the self as an intrapsychic representation provide little basis for a concept of the self that includes subjective experience or personal agency. Structural theory, by its nature, is oriented to specific functions that are impersonal in nature. Sutherland (1983), for example, asserted that a basic feature of the self is its active initiating role with the environment—striving toward relatedness and unity.

There is room for both the self-as-representation and the self-as-agency. In fact, the self may be viewed as embedded in the ego and may be defined as the end product of the integration of the many self-representations (Kernberg 1982).

Defense Mechanisms

In the preceding section on ego psychology, we considered several neurotic defense mechanisms. In keeping with the historical trend associating object relations theory with more profoundly disturbed patients, in this section, we will discuss a number of more primitive defenses characteristic of personality disorders and psychoses: splitting, projective identification, introjection, and denial.

Splitting. This mechanism is an unconscious process that actively separates contradictory feelings, self-representations, or object-representations from one another. Although Freud (1927, 1940) made scattered references to splitting, it was Klein (1946) who exalted it to the position of the cornerstone of emotional survival during the first few months of life. Splitting allows the infant to separate good from bad, pleasure from unpleasure, love from hate so as to preserve positively colored experiences, affects, self-representations, and object-representations in safely isolated mental compartments, free from contamination by negative counterparts. Splitting may be viewed as a basic biological mode of ordering experience, by which the endangering is separated from the endangered; it is secondarily elaborated into a psychological defense (Ogden 1986). It is also a fundamental cause of ego weakness (Kernberg 1967, 1975). The integration of libidinal and aggressive drive derivatives associated with "good" and "bad" introjects serves to neutralize aggression. Splitting prevents this neutralization and thus deprives the ego of an essential source of energy for growth.

In Kernberg's view, splitting is characterized by certain clinical manifestations: 1) alternating expression of contradictory behaviors and attitudes, which the patient regards with lack of concern and bland denial; 2) selective lack of impulse control; 3) the compartmentalization of everyone in the environment into "all good" and "all bad" camps, which is often referred to as idealization and devaluation; and 4) the coexistence of contradictory self-representations that alternate with one another. Although Kernberg viewed splitting as the key defensive operation in patients with borderline personality disorder, splitting may be observed in all patients at times (Rangell 1982), and it does not clearly differentiate borderline patients from those with other personality disorders (Allen et al. 1988). Kernberg distinguished between neurotic characters and borderlines partly on the basis of the latter's preference for splitting over repression, but empirical research suggests that these two defenses operate independently and may coexist in the same individual (Perry and Cooper 1986).

Projective identification.   A second defense mechanism, projective identification, is an unconscious three-step process by which aspects of oneself are disavowed and attributed to someone else (see Figures 2-2, 2-3, and 2-4). The three steps (Ogden 1979) include: 1) The patient projects an object- or self-representation into the treater. 2) The treater unconsciously identifies with what is projected and begins to feel or behave like the projected object- or self-representation in response to interpersonal pressure exerted by the patient. This aspect of the phenomenon is sometimes referred to as projective counteridentification (Grinberg 1979). 3) The projected material is "psychologically processed" and modified by the treater, who returns it to the patient via reintrojection. The modification of the projected material, in turn, modifies the corresponding self- or object-representation and the pattern of interpersonal relatedness.

Transference and countertransference can be correlated with steps 1 and 2, respectively. As just described, projective identification has an interpersonal dimension in addition to its role as an intrapsychic defense mechanism. Splitting and projective identification, then, clearly are highly interrelated mechanisms that work together to keep "good" and "bad" separated (Grotstein 1981). The interpersonal element inherent in Ogden's definition of projective identification derives from Bion's (1962) conceptualization of the therapist

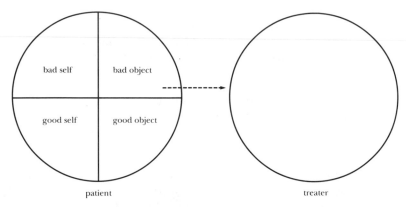

Patient disavows and projects bad internal object into treater.

Figure 2-2. Projective identification—Step 1.

as a container for the projections of the patient, much as the mother contains the projections of her infant. Other authors (Grotstein 1981; Hamilton 1988; Sandler 1987) have disagreed with broadening the definition to include a particular response of the treater to the projected aspects of the patient. They prefer a narrower view of projective identification, one that categorizes it as a purely intrapsychic defense that may or may not result in a reciprocal response from the clinician. Grotstein (1981), for example, shared Kernberg's (1987b) view that the identification occurs *within the projector* rather than within the target of the projection. By maintaining this empathic bond or identification with that which has

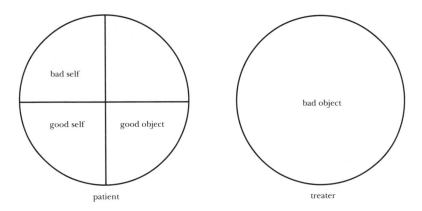

Treater unconsciously begins to feel and/or behave like the projected bad object in response to interpersonal pressure exerted by the patient. This step may be referred to as projective counteridentification.

Figure 2-3. Projective identification—Step 2.

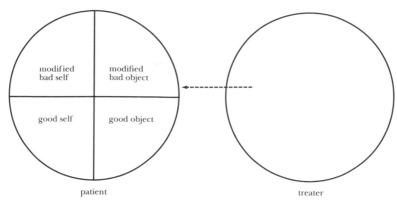

patient   treater

Treater contains and modifies the projected bad object, which is then re-introjected by the patient and assimilated (introjective identification).

Figure 2-4. Projective identification—Step 3.

been projected, the projector has the fantasy of control over the projected material. Most authors would agree that this element of control is central to the concept of projective identification. Sandler (1987) noted: "What one wants to get rid of in oneself can be disposed of by projective identification, and through controlling the object one can then gain the unconscious illusion that one is controlling the unwanted and projected aspect of the self" (p. 20). Ogden's three-step formulation is completely in keeping with this notion except that he views the identification as occurring in both the treater and the projector rather than in the projector alone.

The distinction between projection and projective identification is also somewhat controversial. Grotstein (1981) conceptualized all projection as projective identification since an empathic identification with the projected material is always retained within the projector. The projection outwards of something within the self would be meaningless unless the individual maintained some connection with that which is projected, in Grotstein's view. By Ogden's definition, however, all projection is not projective identification. A paranoid individual may project malevolent intentions into many figures in his environment with whom he never comes in contact. He simply avoids these individuals and keeps to himself. Projection becomes projective identification when the target of the projection begins to be transformed by the projection. When the paranoid individual begins to have direct contact with the object of his projections and begins to accuse that person of malevolent motives, the target of the projections is likely to identify unconsciously with the "bad object" projections and begin to become defensive and angry about the unfair accusations. A third view is suggested by

Kernberg (1987b), who disagreed with the traditional view of projection as a primitive mechanism. He sees projection as typical of
higher-level neurotic patients. He described it as involving no empathy with the material projected, no evocation in the treater of
behavior typical of the projected aspects of the patient, and no
process of reintrojection. Projective identification is a more primitive process, in Kernberg's view, because it involves more permeable
self-other boundaries in the sense that the material returns to the
patient more easily than it does in projection, where the self-other
boundary is firm.

   Introjection.   This third defense is an unconscious process by
which an external object is symbolically taken in and assimilated as
part of oneself. This mechanism may exist as a part of projective
identification, where what is taken in was originally projected, or it
may exist independently as the converse of projection. Classically,
Freud (1917) formulated depression as a result of the introjection
of an ambivalently viewed object. Anger focused on this introject
within the depressed patient resulted in self-depreciation and other
symptoms of depression.

   Denial.   The fourth defense mechanism, denial, is a direct
disavowal of traumatic sensory data. Whereas repression is generally
used as a defense against *internal* wishes or impulses, denial is
ordinarily a defense against the external world of reality when that
reality is overwhelmingly disturbing. Although associated primarily
with psychoses and severe personality disorders, this mechanism
may also be used by normal people, especially in the face of catastrophic events.

Developmental Considerations

The object relations formulations derived from clinical observations
have been bolstered and elaborated by the infant observation studies of Margaret Mahler and her colleagues (1975). Again, in keeping with the historical thrust of object relations theory, the focus of
this research has been on *preoedipal* development, specifically, from
birth to around 3 years of age. Through observation of normal and
abnormal mother-infant pairs, Mahler et al. have been able to
identify three broad phases of the development of object relations.

   In the first 2 months of life, an *autistic* phase occurs in which
the infant appears self-absorbed and concerned with survival rather
than relatedness. The period between 2 and 6 months, denoted as
symbiosis, begins with the smile response of the infant and the visual
ability to follow the mother's face. Although the infant is vaguely
aware of the mother as a separate object, the infant's primary
experience of the mother-infant dyad is of a dual unity rather than
two separate people.

The third phase, *separation-individuation,* is characterized by four subphases. Between 6 and 10 months, in the subphase of *differentiation,* the child becomes aware that the mother is a separate person. This awareness may lead to the child's need for a transitional object (Winnicott 1953), such as a blanket or pacifier, to help deal with the fact that the mother is not always available. *Practicing* is the next subphase; it occurs between 10 and 16 months. With the newfound locomotor skills of this age, toddlers love to explore the world on their own, although they frequently return to their mothers for "refueling." The third subphase, *rapprochement,* is characterized by a sharper awareness of the separateness of the mother and occurs between 16 and 24 months of age. This awareness brings with it a heightened sense of vulnerability to separations from mother. This separation anxiety punctures the narcissistic inflation of the practicing subphase and leads the child to check frequently on the mother's whereabouts during play periods.

The fourth and final subphase of separation-individuation is marked by the consolidation of individuality and the beginnings of object constancy. The achievement of this period, which roughly corresponds to the 3rd year of life, is the integration of split views of the mother into an integrated whole object that can be internalized as an emotionally soothing inner presence that sustains the child during the mother's absence. This achievement corresponds with Klein's depressive position and sets the stage for the child to enter the oedipal phase.

Mahler's empirical observations have been extraordinarily influential in our evolving understanding of the developmental pathogenesis of the borderline personality disorder (see Chapter 14). Object relations theory is particularly relevant to those disorders whose etiology appears to relate to preoedipal problems in the mother-infant dyad prior to the introduction of triangular relationships typical of the Oedipus complex. Mahler's studies also lend empirical support to the paramount importance of object-seeking in development and the impossibility of divorcing drives from object relations.

Self Psychology

While object relations theory emphasizes the *internalized* relationships between *representations* of self and object, self psychology stresses how *external* relationships help maintain self-esteem and self-cohesion. Derived from the seminal writings of Heinz Kohut (1971, 1977, 1984), this theoretical approach views the patient as in desperate need of certain responses from other persons to maintain a sense of well-being. Indeed, some observers have suggested that self psychology is fundamentally a two-person psychology (Jaenicke 1987) or a self-object psychology (Gedo 1986).

Self psychology evolved from Kohut's study of narcissistically disturbed outpatients he was treating in psychoanalysis. He noted that they seemed different from the classic neurotic patients who presented for treatment with hysterical or obsessive-compulsive symptoms. Instead, they complained of nondescript feelings of depression or dissatisfaction in relationships (Kohut 1971). They were also characterized by a vulnerable self-esteem that was highly sensitive to slights from friends, family, lovers, colleagues, and others. Kohut observed that the structural model of ego psychology did not seem adequate to explain the pathogenesis and cure of these patients' problems.

Kohut noted that these patients formed two kinds of transferences: the mirror transference and the idealizing transference. In the mirror transference the patient looks to the analyst for a confirming, validating response that Kohut linked to the "gleam in the mother's eye" in response to phase-appropriate displays of exhibitionism on the part of her small child, what Kohut called the *grandiose-exhibitionistic self.* These approving responses, according to Kohut, are essential for normal development in that they provide the child with a sense of self-worth. When a mother fails to empathize with her child's need for such a mirroring response, the latter has great difficulty in maintaining a sense of wholeness and self-regard. In response to this failure of empathy, the child's sense of self fragments, and the child desperately attempts to be perfect and to "perform" for the parent to gain the hungered-for approbation. This form of "showing off" is another manifestation of the grandiose-exhibitionistic self (Baker and Baker 1987). The same phenomena constitute the mirror transference in adults who seek treatment. The adult patient who "performs" for his or her therapist in a desperate attempt to gain approval and admiration may be developing a mirror transference.

The idealizing transference, as implied in the name, refers to a situation in which the patient perceives the therapist as an all-powerful parent whose presence soothes and heals. The wish to bask in the reflected glory of the idealized therapist is a manifestation of this transference. Just as the child may be traumatized by the empathic failures of a mother who does not provide mirroring responses to her child's grandiose-exhibitionistic self, so can that same child be traumatized by a mother who does not empathize with the child's need to idealize her or who does not provide a model worthy of idealization.

In either case, the adult patient who suffers from such early disturbances of parenting and who presents these kinds of transference dispositions is struggling with a defective or deficient self—one that is developmentally frozen at a point where it is highly prone to fragmentation. Kohut's view is that the structural model of conflict associated with ego psychology is not sufficient to explain these narcissistic needs for mirroring and idealization. Moreover, he noted a moralizing, pejorative tone in the attitudes of analysts who approached narcissism from a classical point of view. He believed that much harm was done by following Freud's (1914) model, which proposed a transition from a state of primary narcissism to object love as part of the normal maturational process. The offshoot of Freud's thinking was that one should "outgrow" narcissistic strivings and be more concerned about the needs of others.

Kohut thought that this point of view was hypocritical. He asserted that narcissistic needs persist throughout life and that they parallel development in the realm of object love. He postulated a *double axis* theory (see Figure 2-5) that allows for ongoing development in *both* narcissistic and object love realms (Ornstein 1974). As infants mature, they attempt to capture the lost perfection of the early maternal-infant bond by resorting to one of two strategies—the grandiose self, where the perfection is captured within, and the idealized parent imago, where it is assigned to the parent. These two poles constitute the *bipolar self.* In his last book (1984), Kohut expanded this conceptualization to a *tripolar* self by adding a third pole of selfobject needs, the twinship or alter ego. This aspect of the self appears in the transference as a need to be just like the therapist. It has its developmental origins in a wish for merger that is gradually transformed into imitative behavior. For example, a young boy might play at lawn mowing while his father cuts the grass. This third pole of the self has limited clinical usefulness compared to the other

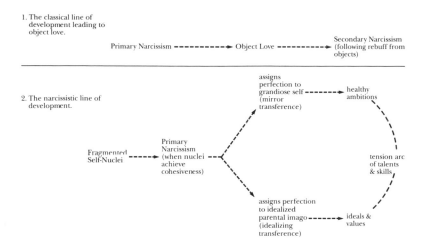

Figure 2-5. Kohut's double axis theory (1971).

two and is often excluded from discussions of selfobject transferences. If failures of empathy were typical of the parental responses
to these strategies, a developmental arrest occurs. With adequate
parenting, on the other hand, the grandiose self is transformed into
healthy ambitions, and the idealized parent imago becomes internalized as ideals and values (Kohut 1971). Hence therapists could
empathize with the narcissistic needs of their patients as developmentally normal rather than regarding them with contempt for
being self-centered and immature. Another implication of self psychology is that the goal of treatment is self-cohesion without necessarily requiring the capacity for object love (Kohut 1977).
    Kohut's first book proposed this theoretical formulation as
applicable primarily to narcissistic character pathology. By the time
his last (1984, posthumously published) book appeared, he had
greatly expanded the scope of self psychology:

> Self psychology is now attempting to demonstrate. . . that all
> forms of psychopathology are based either on defects in the
> structure of the self, on distortions of the self, or on weakness
> of the self. It is trying to show, furthermore, that all these flaws
> in the self are due to disturbances of self-selfobject relation-
> ships in childhood. (p. 53)

The term *selfobject* came to be a generic term to describe the role
that other persons perform for the self in regard to mirroring,
idealizing, and twinship needs. From the standpoint of the growth
and development of the self, others are not regarded as separate
persons but as objects to gratify these needs of the self. In a sense,
then, selfobjects may be viewed more as functions (i.e., soothing,
validating) than people. The need for selfobjects is never outgrown,
according to Kohut, but rather persists throughout life—we need
selfobjects in our environment for emotional survival much as we
need oxygen in the atmosphere for physical survival (Kohut 1984).
    One implication of Kohut's final theoretical statement is that
separation is a myth. He differs dramatically from Mahler's object
relations view, which pivots around intrapsychic separation, in that
self psychology views the separation of the self from the selfobject
as impossible. We all need affirming, empathic responses from
others throughout life to maintain our self-esteem. Maturation and
growth move away from a need for archaic selfobjects toward an
ability to use more mature and appropriate selfobjects.
    Kohut always resisted a simple definition of the self, which he
believed was such an overarching structure that it defied crisp
definition. However, by the time of his death in 1981, his view of the
self had clearly gone from that of a self-representation to that of a
"supraordinate self as the primary psychic constellation, the center
of experience and initiative and the main motivating agency" (Cur-

tis 1985, p. 343). Further implications include a pervasive de-emphasis on the ego and the vicissitudes of drives and defenses, a greater focus on conscious subjective experience, and the conceptualization of aggression as secondary to failures of selfobjects (i.e., narcissistic rage) rather than as a primary or innate drive. Defenses and resistances in this framework, or "defense-resistances," as Kohut (1984) came to refer to them, are viewed entirely differently: "My personal preference is to speak of the 'defensiveness' of patients— and to think of their defensive attitudes as adaptive and psychologically valuable—and not of their 'resistances'" (p. 114). Clearly, they are valuable and adaptive because they preserve the integrity of the self.

In contrast to the ego psychologists, Kohut viewed the Oedipus complex as of secondary importance. The oedipal conflicts involving sexuality and aggression are mere "breakdown products" of developmentally earlier failures in the self-selfobject matrix. If a mother adequately fulfills the selfobject needs of her child, the Oedipus complex can be weathered without the child becoming symptomatic. The fundamental anxiety, according to self psychology, is "disintegration anxiety," which involves the fear that one's self will fragment in response to inadequate selfobject responses, resulting in an experiencing of a nonhuman state of psychological death (Baker and Baker 1987). From the standpoint of self psychology, most forms of symptomatic behavior (e.g., drug abuse, sexual promiscuity, perversions, self-mutilation, binge eating, and purging) do *not* grow out of neurotic conflict related to castration anxiety. Rather, they reflect "an emergency attempt to maintain and/or restore internal cohesion and harmony to a vulnerable, unhealthy self" (Baker and Baker 1987, p. 51).

The emphasis of self psychology on the failures of parenting figures and the resulting deficiencies of the self resonate with the British object relations theories. Echoes of Winnicott's good enough mothering and Balint's basic fault can be heard in the themes of self psychological writings. Although Kohut does not acknowledge the contributions of these forerunners, their influence is unmistakable. However, the object relations theorists did not develop the notion of the self to the extent that Kohut did, perhaps because of their adherence to a model of maturation that retains the moralizing potential eschewed by Kohut (Bacal 1987). Kohut also has made a significant contribution in recognizing the significance of self-esteem in the pathogenesis of psychiatric disturbances.

Developmental Considerations

Kohut formulated his concept of developmental pathogenesis by reconstructing childhood experience from the analytic data he heard from adult patients. Therefore, he did not provide a specific developmental timetable in the manner of Mahler and her colleagues. However, the infant observation research of Daniel Stern (1985) has provided some support for the premises of self psychology much as Mahler's work has done for object relations theory. Stern noted that the infant's self emerges along with a growing sense of the "other" (i.e., the mother or caregiver). He delineated four different "senses of self": emergent, core, subjective, and verbal. The sense of an emergent self, predominantly a physical self, is characteristic of the first 2 months of life. From 2 to 6 months, a sense of core self with more capability for interpersonal relatedness emerges. A major step is taken in the third phase of development between 7 and 9 months. Referred to as the sense of subjective self, this stage of development is characterized by a matching of intrapsychic states between the infant and mother. The fourth and final sense of self, the verbal self, appears between 15 and 18 months of age and is a domain where symbols and verbal communication predominate.

Of paramount importance in Stern's developmental theory is the notion that the self can only emerge through connectedness with the other. Terms such as a sense of *self-with-other* and a *self-regulating other* are used to illustrate this dimension of subjective experience in the infant. He noted that throughout development, infants have an ongoing need for affirmation by the mother or caregiver. Like Kohut, Stern saw validation from external figures as crucial. Also like Kohut, he de-emphasized the role of fantasy and distortion in the internalization of relationships. Stern believed that, from the beginning of life, infants primarily experience reality rather than distortions of reality based on wishes or defenses. Kohut's emphasis on conscious subjective experience over unconscious content is in a similar vein.

The Role of Theory in Clinical Practice

Faced with a bewildering array of psychoanalytic theories, one may choose to deny the value of theory altogether. Who needs it? Why not just begin *de novo* with each patient and stick to the clinical material? To advocate this approach is simply to advocate the formation of new theories. As Kernberg (1987a) noted: "All observations of clinical phenomena depend upon theories, and when we think that we are forgetting about theory, it only means that we have a theory of which we are not aware" (pp. 181–182).

A more sensible solution is to become familiar with the phenomena described by all the major theories and to focus on each perspective as it is clinically appropriate with a given patient. Psychoanalysis and psychodynamic psychiatry are tragically beset with needless polarities—is it oedipal or preoedipal, conflict or deficit, classical theory or self psychology, tension-reduction or object-seeking? Such questions tend to be cast in terms of right or wrong. But is it possible that all models are valid in certain clinical situations? Is it not possible for both oedipal and preoedipal, conflict and deficit, to be relevant in the understanding of an individual patient? Of course it is. Wallerstein (1983) made this point eloquently in a critique of self psychology:

> For in the flow and flux of analytic clinical material we are always in the world of 'both/and.' We deal constantly, and in turn, both with the oedipal, where there is a coherent self, and the preodipal, where there may not yet be; with defensive regressions and with developmental arrests; with defensive transferences and defensive resistances and with recreations of earlier traumatic and traumatized states. (p. 31)

Wallerstein reminds us of the fundamental psychoanalytic principles of overdetermination and multiple function.

Some aspects of all three theories examined in this chapter will most likely prove useful in the treatment of the majority of patients. From a developmental perspective, certain aspects of early childhood experience are better explained by one theory than another, and with certain patients, the emphasis will be more in one direction than another, depending on the clinical data (Pine 1988). In most patients, however, we will find both deficit and conflict. As Eagle (1984) noted in his appraisal of the role of theory in psychoanalysis: "We are most conflicted in the areas in which we are deprived. . . . It is precisely the person deprived of love who is most conflicted about giving and receiving love" (p. 130). In practice, clinicians find themselves serving both as selfobjects and as real, separate objects for their patients.

Wallerstein (1988) has pointed out that it is possible for clinicians to pay attention to the *clinical phenomena* described by each theoretical perspective without embracing the entire metapsychological model. For example, one can address self- and object-representations, mirror and idealizing transferences, and impulse-defense configurations as they appear in the clinical setting without having to resort to invoking the entire theoretical edifice on which such observations are based. He believes that selfobject transferences described by self psychologists can be explained within the framework of conflict theory. Cooper (1977), on the other hand, has advocated greater theoretical flexibility. Different diagnostic categories and different patients, in his view, suggest different theoretical models. For example, to be effectively treated, certain narcissistic patients may require a self psychological approach, while individuals with neurotic conflicts may respond better to a therapeutic approach based on the principles of ego psychology.

Each of these approaches to the theoretical pluralism of modern dynamic psychiatry is workable for some clinicians. Regardless of which approach is found more suitable, all clinicians should be wary of rigidly imposing theory onto clinical material. The patient must be allowed to lead the clinician into whatever theoretical realm is the best match for the clinical material. While familiarity with all three theoretical models of dynamic psychiatry requires greater breadth of knowledge, it allows for a richer understanding of patients and their psychopathology. Finding the theoretical framework that best fits a particular patient entails a good deal of exploratory trial and error, but as we stumble through the cave, we may eventually find the path and may be far better off than other travelers with a map of an altogether different cave.

References

Allen J, Deering C, Buskirk J, et al: Assessment of therapeutic alliances in the psychiatric hospital milieu. Psychiatry 51:291–299, 1988

Bacal HA: British object-relations theorists and self psychology: some critical reflections. Int J Psychoanal 68:81–98, 1987

Baker HS, Baker MN: Heinz Kohut's self psychology: an overview. Am J Psychiatry 144:1–9, 1987

Balint M: The Basic Fault: The Therapeutic Aspects of Regression. London, Tavistock, 1968

Bellak L, Hurvich M, Gedimen HK: Ego Functions in Schizophrenics, Neurotics, and Normals: A Systematic Study of Conceptual, Diagnostic, and Therapeutic Aspects. New York, John Wiley & Sons, 1973

Bion WR: Learning from Experience. New York, Basic Books, 1962

Blum HP: On the conception and development of the transference neurosis. J Am Psychoanal Assoc 19:41–53, 1971

Brenner C: The Mind in Conflict. New York, International Universities Press, 1982

Cooper AM: Clinical psychoanalysis: one method or more—the relation of diagnosis to psychoanalytic treatment. Presented at the Fall Meeting of the American Psychoanalytic Association, December 1977

Curtis HC: Clinical perspectives on self psychology. Psychoanal Q 54:339–378, 1985

Eagle MN: Recent Developments in Psychoanalysis: A Critical Evaluation. New York, McGraw-Hill, 1984

Erikson EH: Identity and the life cycle: selected papers. Psychol Issues 1:1–171, 1959

Fairbairn WRD: Schizoid factors in the personality (1940), in Psychoanalytic Studies of the Personality. London, Routledge & Kegan Paul, 1952, pp 3–27

Fairbairn WRD: Endopsychic structure considered in terms of object-relationships (1944), in Psychoanalytic Studies of the Personality. London, Routledge & Kegan Paul, 1952, pp 82–136

Fairbairn WRD: Psychoanalytic Studies of the Personality. London, Routledge & Kegan Paul, 1952

Fairbairn WRD: Synopsis of an object-relations theory of the personality. Int J Psychoanal 44:224–225, 1963

Freud A: The Ego and the Mechanisms of Defense (1936). Translated by Baines C. New York, International Universities Press, 1946

Freud S: Three essays on the theory of sexuality (1905), in The Standard Edition of the Complete Psychological Works of Sigmund Freud, Vol 7. Translated and edited by Strachey J. London, Hogarth Press, 1953, pp 123–245

Freud S: On narcissism: an introduction (1914), in The Standard Edition of the Complete Psychological Works of Sigmund Freud, Vol 14. Translated and edited by Strachey J. London, Hogarth Press, 1963, pp 67–102

Freud S: Mourning and melancholia (1917), in The Standard Edition of the Complete Psychological Works of Sigmund Freud, Vol 14. Translated and edited by Strachey J. London, Hogarth Press, 1963, pp 237–260

Freud S: The ego and the id (1923), in The Standard Edition of the Complete Psychological Works of Sigmund Freud, Vol 19. Translated and edited by Strachey J. London, Hogarth Press, 1961, pp 1–66

Freud S: Some psychical consequences of the anatomical distinction between the sexes (1925), in The Standard Edition of the Complete Psychological Works of Sigmund Freud, Vol 19. Translated and edited by Strachey J. London, Hogarth Press, 1961, pp 241–258

Freud S: Inhibitions, symptoms and anxiety (1926), in The Standard Edition of the Complete Psychological Works of Sigmund Freud, Vol 20. Translated and edited by Strachey J. London, Hogarth Press, 1959, pp 75–175

Freud S: Fetishism (1927), in The Standard Edition of the Complete Psychological Works of Sigmund Freud, Vol 21. Translated and edited by Strachey J. London, Hogarth Press, 1961, pp 147–157

Freud S: Female sexuality (1931), in The Standard Edition of the Complete Psychological Works of Sigmund Freud, Vol 21. Translated and edited by Strachey J. London, Hogarth Press, 1961, pp 223–243

Freud S: Femininity (1933), in The Standard Edition of the Complete Psychological Works of Sigmund Freud, Vol 22. Translated and edited by Strachey J. London, Hogarth Press, 1964, pp 112–135

Freud S: Analysis terminable and interminable (1937), in The Standard Edition of the Complete Psychological Works of Sigmund Freud, Vol 23. Translated and edited by Strachey J. London, Hogarth Press, 1964, pp 209–253

Freud S: Splitting of the ego in the process of defence (1940), in The Standard Edition of the Complete Psychological Works of Sigmund Freud, Vol 23. Translated and edited by Strachey J. London, Hogarth Press, 1964, pp 271–278

Gedo JE: Conceptual Issues in Psychoanalysis: Essays in History and Method. Hillsdale, NJ, Analytic Press, 1986

Greenberg J, Mitchell SA: Object Relations in Psychoanalytic Theory. Cambridge, MA, Harvard University Press, 1983

Grinberg L: Countertransference and projective counteridentification, in Countertransference. Edited by Epstein L, Feiner A. New York, Jason Aronson, 1979, pp 169–191

Grotstein JS: Splitting and Projective Identification. New York, Jason Aronson, 1981

Guntrip H: Schizoid Phenomena, Objects-Relations, and the Self. New York, International Universities Press, 1968

Guntrip H: Psychoanalytic Theory, Therapy, and the Self. New York, Basic Books, 1971

Hamilton NG: Self and Others: Object Relations Theory in Practice. Northvale, NJ, Jason Aronson, 1988

Hartmann H: Ego Psychology and the Problem of Adaptation (1939). Translated by Rapaport D. New York, International Universities Press, 1958

Hartmann H: Comments on the psychoanalytic theory of the ego (1950), in Essays on Ego Psychology: Selected Problems in Psychoanalytic Theory. New York, International Universities Press, 1964, pp 113–141

Jacobson E: The Self and the Object World. New York, International Universities Press, 1964

Jaenicke C: Kohut's concept of cure. Psychoanal Rev 74:537–548, 1987

Kernberg OF: Borderline personality organization. J Am Psychoanal Assoc 15:641–685, 1967

Kernberg OF: Borderline Conditions and Pathological Narcissism. New York, Jason Aronson, 1975

Kernberg OF: Self, ego, affects, and drives. J Am Psychoanal Assoc 30:893-917, 1982

Kernberg OF: Object relations theory and character analysis. J Am Psychoanal Assoc [Suppl] 31:247–272, 1983

Kernberg OF: Concluding discussion, in Projection, Projective Identification. Edited by Sandler J. Madison, CT, International Universities Press, 1987a, pp 179–196

Kernberg OF: Projection and projective identification: developmental and clinical aspects, in Projection, Identification, Projective Identification. Edited by Sandler J. Madison, CT, International Universities Press, 1987b, pp 93–115

Klein M: Notes on some schizoid mechanisms (1946), in Envy and Gratitude and Other Works, 1946–1963. New York, Free Press, 1975, pp 1–24

Kohon G: The British School of Psychoanalysis: The Independent Tradition. New Haven, Yale University Press, 1986

Kohut H: The Analysis of the Self: A Systematic Approach to the Psychoanalytic Treatment of Narcissistic Personality Disorders. New York, International Universities Press, 1971

Kohut H: The Restoration of the Self. New York, International Universities Press, 1977

Kohut H: How Does Analysis Cure? Chicago, University of Chicago Press, 1984

Lerner HE: Penis envy: alternatives in conceptualization. Bull Menninger Clinic 44:39–48, 1980

Mahler MS, Pine F, Bergman A: The Psychological Birth of the Human Infant: Symbiosis and Individuation. New York, Basic Books, 1975

Meissner WW: Internalization in Psychoanalysis. New York, International Universities Press, 1981

Meissner WW: Can psychoanalysis find its self? J Am Psychoanal Assoc 34:379–400, 1986

Ogden TH: On projective identification. Int J Psychoanal 60:357–373, 1979

Ogden TH: The concept of internal object relations. Int J Psychoanal 64:227-241, 1983

Ogden TH: The Matrix of the Mind: Object Relations and the Psychoanalytic Dialogue. Northvale, NJ, Jason Aronson, 1986

Ornstein PH: On narcissism: beyond the introduction, highlights of Heinz Kohut's contributions to the psychoanalytic treatment of narcissistic personality disorders. Annual of Psychoanalysis 2:127–149, 1974

Perry JC, Cooper SII: A preliminary report on defenses and conflicts associated with borderline personality disorder. J Am Psychoanal Assoc 34:863–893, 1986

Pine F: The four psychologies of psychoanalysis and their place in clinical work. J Am Psychoanal Assoc 36:571–596, 1988

Rangell L: The self in psychoanalytic theory. J Am Psychoanal Assoc 30:863-891, 1982

Rapaport D: Organization and Pathology of Thought: Selected Sources. New York, Columbia University Press, 1951

Rinsley DB: An object relations view of borderline personality, in Borderline Personality Disorders. Edited by Hartocollis P. New York, International Universities Press, 1977, pp 47–70

Sandler J (ed): Projection, Identification, Projective Identification. Madison, CT, International Universities Press, 1987

Sandler J, Rosenblatt B: The concept of the representational world. Psychoanalytic Study of the Child 17:128–145, 1962

Schafer R: Aspects of Internalization. New York, International Universities Press, 1968

Schafer R: A New Language for Psychoanalysis. New Haven, Yale University Press, 1976

Segal H: An Introduction to the Work of Melanie Klein. New York, Basic Books, 1964

Stern DN: The Interpersonal World of the Infant: A View from Psychoanalysis and Developmental Psychology. New York, Basic Books, 1985

Stoller RJ: The sense of femaleness. Psychoanal Q 37:42–55, 1968

Stone L: The psychoanalytic situation and transference. J Am Psychoanal Assoc 15:3–58, 1967

Sutherland JD: The British Object Relations Theorists: Balint, Winnicott, Fairbairn, Guntrip. J Am Psychoanal Assoc 28:829–860, 1980

Sutherland JD: The self and object relations: a challenge to psychoanalysis. Bull Menninger Clin 47:525–541, 1983

Torok M: The significance of penis envy in women, in Female Sexuality: New Psychoanalytic Views. Edited by Chasseguet-Smirgel J. Ann Arbor, University of Michigan Press, 1970, pp 135–170

Vaillant GE: Natural history of male psychological health: V. The relation of choice of ego mechanisms of defense to adult adjustment. Arch Gen Psychiatry 33:535–545, 1976

Vaillant GE: Adaptation to Life. Boston, Little, Brown, 1977

Wallerstein RS: One psychoanalysis or many? Int J Psychoanal 69:5–21, 1988

Wallerstein RS: Self psychology and "classical" psychoanalytic psychology: the nature of their relationship (1983), in The Future of Psychoanalysis: Essays in Honor of Heinz Kohut. Edited by Goldberg A. New York, International Universities Press, 1983, pp 19–63

Winnicott DW: The Maturational Process and the Facilitating Environment: Studies in the Theory of Emotional Development. London, Hogarth Press, 1965

Winnicott DW: Transitional objects and transitional phenomena: a study of the first *not-me* possession (Int J Psychoanal 34:89–97, 1953), reprinted in Playing and Reality. New York, Basic Books, 1971, pp 1–25

CHAPTER 3

Psychodynamic Assessment of the Patient

> Whenever two people meet there are really six people present.
> There is each man as he sees himself, each man as the other
> person sees him, and each man as he really is.
>
> — William James

The psychodynamic assessment of a patient does not stand apart from the thorough evaluation of history, signs, and symptoms growing out of the medical-psychiatric tradition. Dynamic psychiatrists value such information as a crucial component of the diagnostic assessment. However, their approach to gathering that information differs from the purely descriptive approach to diagnosis. Moreover, other information is of interest to the dynamic psychiatrist, so the psychodynamic assessment may be viewed as a significant extension of the descriptive medical-psychiatric evaluation.

The Clinical Interview

Any description of the psychodynamic approach to clinical interviewing must begin with the fundamental importance of the doctor-patient relationship. When psychiatrist and patient meet for the first time, two strangers are coming into contact, each with a variety of expectations concerning the other. Establishing rapport and a shared understanding must always be the first agenda in a psychodynamic interview (MacKinnon and Michels 1971; Menninger et al. 1962; Thomä and Kächele 1987). The first task of the interviewer, then, is to convey that the patient is accepted, valued, and validated as a unique person with unique problems.

Interviewers who attempt to immerse themselves empathically in their patients' experience will promote a bond between them based on the interviewer's obvious attempt to understand the patient's point of view. Such an approach does not require reassuring comments such as, "Don't worry, everything will be all right." Rather than allaying the patient's anxiety, these hollow reassurances are usually doomed to failure because they resemble similar past comments of friends and family members. They will only lead the patient to believe that the interviewer does not appreciate true suffering. Interviewers may instead build better rapport with comments such as, "I can understand how you feel, considering what you've been through." Challenging a patient's statements early in the interview will simply confirm any preexisting fears that psychiatrists are judgmental parental figures.

Differences Between Psychodynamic and Medical Interviewing

In medical interviewing physicians pursue a direct course from the chief complaint to its etiology and pathogenesis. Patients generally cooperate with this process because they are eager to eliminate the pain or symptoms associated with their illness. Psychiatrists who attempt to steer a similarly linear course in the clinical interview will encounter potholes and detours at every turn. Moreover, psychiatrists often find that patients rarely are capable of coming quickly to the point because of their inability to pinpoint what is really bothering them (Menninger et al. 1962). They may also be highly ambivalent about giving up their symptoms because psychiatric illness is somehow always a workable adaptation. Finally, psychiatric patients are often embarrassed about their symptoms and may conceal information to make a good impression (MacKinnon and Michels 1971).

Another major difference between medical history-taking and psychodynamic interviewing is the interrelationship of diagnosis and treatment. A physician evaluating a patient for appendicitis approaches the interview with a clear mind-set—diagnosis precedes treatment. In the psychodynamic interview, however, any distinction between diagnosis and treatment would be artificial (MacKinnon and Michels 1971). The dynamic psychiatrist approaches the interview with the understanding that the manner in which the history is taken may in and of itself be therapeutic. The dynamic view, which intimately links diagnosis and treatment, is empathic in the sense that it takes into account the patient's perspective. As Menninger et al. (1962) noted: "The patient comes to be *treated* and everything that is done for him, so far as he is concerned, is treatment, whatever the doctor may call it. In a sense, therefore, treatment always *precedes* diagnosis" (p. 3).

A third distinction between medical and psychodynamic interviewing lies in the dimensions of activity and passivity. To a large extent patients are passive participants in the medical diagnostic process. The patient complies with the physician's evaluation by cooperatively answering questions. The physician, however, must fit together the pieces of the diagnostic puzzle to arrive at a definitive diagnosis. The dynamic psychiatrist tries to avoid this division of roles. Instead, the dynamic approach involves actively engaging the patient as a *collaborator* in an exploratory process (Shevrin and Shectman 1973). The patient is viewed as someone with a great deal to contribute to the ultimate diagnostic understanding. If a patient begins an interview with anxiety, the psychiatrist does not try to eliminate it to facilitate the interview. On the contrary, the psychiatrist might attempt to engage the patient in a collaborative search for the origins of the anxiety with such questions as: "What concerns about this interview might cause you to be anxious right now?"; "Does this situation remind you of any similar anxiety-provoking situations in the past?"; or "Have you heard anything about me or about psychiatrists in general that might contribute to your anxiety?"

In a productive dynamic interview, the psychiatrist will elicit information regarding symptoms and history that allow for a descriptive diagnosis. To promote more openness on the part of the patient, however, psychiatrists must guard against an overemphasis on diagnostic labeling that precludes the unfolding of the complex relationship between doctor and patient. MacKinnon and Michels (1971) warned that "the interview that is oriented only toward establishing a diagnosis gives the patient the feeling that he is a specimen of pathology being examined, and therefore actually inhibits him from revealing his problems" (pp. 6–7).

A fourth difference between the medical and the dynamic orientation in clinical interviewing revolves around the selection of relevant data. Reiser (1988) expressed alarm at the tendency of contemporary psychiatric residents to stop the data collection after eliciting a symptom inventory that satisfies a DSM-III-R (American Psychiatric Association 1987) diagnostic category and that allows for pharmacotherapeutic prescription. He warned that a DSM-III-R diagnosis is only one aspect of the diagnostic process and that the residents' lack of interest in understanding the patient as a person forms an obstacle to establishing a therapeutic relationship. For dynamic psychiatrists, the intrapsychic life of the patient is a crucial part of the data pool.

Another unique aspect of the psychodynamic interview is the emphasis on the doctor's feelings during the process. The surgeon or internist who notes feelings of anger, envy, lust, sadness, hatred, or admiration views these feelings as annoyances that interfere with evaluating the illness. The typical physician suppresses these feelings in the service of maintaining objectivity and proceeding with the examination. For the dynamic psychiatrist, such feelings constitute crucial diagnostic information. They tell the clinician something about what reactions the patient elicits in others. These considerations lead us directly to two of the most important aspects of the psychodynamic assessment—transference and countertransference.

Transference and Countertransference

Given the fact that transference is active in every significant relationship, you can be certain that transference elements exist from the first encounter between doctor and patient. Indeed, transference may even develop before the initial contact (Thomä and Kächele 1987). After making the first appointment, the soon-to-be patient may begin attributing qualities to the psychiatrist based on bits of factual information, previous experiences with psychiatrists, media portrayals of psychiatrists, positive or negative experiences with other physicians in the past, or general attitudes toward authority figures. One young man who first met his psychiatrist in the waiting room exclaimed, "Why, you're not at all like I expected you to be!" When the psychiatrist asked the patient to elaborate, the young man explained that the psychiatrist's name evoked images of a distinguished elderly man, and he was shocked at the youth of the actual psychiatrist.

Transference is a critical dimension of the evaluation because it profoundly affects the patient's cooperation with the doctor. Patients who view doctors as stern, disapproving parents, for example, will be much less forthcoming with embarrassing aspects of their history. Likewise, patients who view psychiatrists as intrusive busybodies may stubbornly withhold information and refuse to cooperate in the interview. Psychiatrists who address the transference distortions early in the interview may remove obstacles to effective history-taking.

During the first few minutes of a consultation with a psychiatrist, one patient was struggling to overcome his inhibitions about talking. The psychiatrist asked if any of his actions or comments made it difficult for the patient to talk. The patient confided that he had harbored the notion that psychiatrists were like mind readers and that he needed to be wary of what he did or said in their presence. The psychiatrist replied humorously, "I'm afraid we're not that good." Both laughed, and the patient found it much easier to open up during the rest of the interview.

By definition, transference is a repetition. The feelings associated with a figure from the past are being repeated with the psychiatrist in the present situation. This premise implies that transference patterns in a clinical interview provide glimpses of significant relationships from the patient's past. The patient's view of the examiner and the patient's feelings toward the examiner are somehow repetitions. Furthermore, these repetitions also reveal a good deal about the patient's current significant relationships. Since transference is ubiquitous, the same patterns from the past are repeated again and again in all the patient's relationships. For example, a woman patient came to a psychiatrist, complaining that men seemed uninterested in her. In response to her psychiatrist's inquiries, she was able to link this feeling of being neglected with her childhood perception that her father ignored her. When the psychiatrist looked at his clock late in the interview, she accused him of not paying attention to her—like all other men.

To keep from labeling all the patient's reactions to the doctor as transference, psychiatrists must keep in mind that the patient-doctor relationship is always a mixture of transference and a real relationship. The psychiatrist who glanced at his clock provided a kernel of reality to the patient's transference fear that yet another man was losing interest in her. Psychodynamic assessment requires continuous self-monitoring throughout the diagnostic process. The psychiatrist accused of being inattentive must question whether he really is feeling boredom (and conveying it to the patient) or whether the patient is distorting the situation. If boredom is the problem, then the psychiatrist needs to determine whether his interest is waning because of interference from his own issues, or because the patient is doing something to evoke inattentiveness, or both.

These considerations are, of course, countertransference concerns. The conceptual framework of the dynamic interview is that it involves two persons. (Dare I say two patients?) Each brings a personal past into the present and projects aspects of internal self- and object-representations into the other (Langs 1976). It is commonplace for dynamic psychiatrists to find themselves relating to a patient as though the patient were someone else. The psychiatrist might note a striking physical resemblance between a patient and someone from the past. As a result the psychiatrist then attributes qualities of the past figure to the patient.

An ongoing task for dynamic psychiatrists is to differentiate those feelings and reactions toward the patient that arise from countertransference in the narrow sense from those that arise from countertransference in the broad sense (see Chapter 1). The narrow sense involves instances where the psychiatrist's own past is being repeated in the present, while the broader definition of countertransference involves instances in which the psychiatrist's strong feelings are evoked by behavior in the patient that produces similar feelings in virtually everyone with whom the patient has contact (Hamilton 1988; Kernberg 1965). Often these two varieties of countertransference do not appear in pure form, and differentiating between the two may be a formidable task. Because the ability to make this distinction depends greatly on familiarity with one's own internal world, most dynamic psychiatrists find a personal treatment experience (either psychoanalysis or psychotherapy) of enormous value in monitoring and understanding countertransference.

The model of projective identification (see Chapter 2) is useful for understanding the broad form of countertransference (i.e., emotional reaction produced in everyone the patient encounters). Because of various provocative behaviors in the patient, the psychiatrist begins to feel like a projected object- or self-representation of the patient. One child psychiatrist, for example, observed that she could always tell when she was dealing with a victim of child abuse because she would develop an irrational feeling of anger, accompanied by an impulse to abuse the child. In other words, an internal abusing object in the child would be projected into the psychiatrist, who in turn felt like the internal object because of the child's obnoxious and provocative behavior. Indeed, psychiatrists can diagnosis a projective identification process when they detect that they are feeling or behaving in an alien or atypical manner toward their patients. Awareness of such feelings can help the psychiatrist understand the nature of the patient's internal object world and the typical problems in the patient's interpersonal relationships.

Approaches to History Taking

The history-taking aspect of the interview should involve two simultaneous goals: a descriptive diagnosis and a dynamic diagnosis. To accomplish these goals, the psychiatrist must maintain a flexible interviewing style that shifts from a structured pursuit of specific facts (e.g., about symptoms, family history, stressors, duration of illness) to an unstructured posture of listening to the natural ebb and flow of the patient's thought processes. Throughout both structured and unstructured portions of the history taking, the examiner makes a fine-tuned assessment of the patient-doctor interaction. Kernberg (1984) characterized one form of the dynamic interview—the structural interview—as a systematic movement from a symptom inventory to an active focus on defensive operations in the here-and-now relationship with the interviewer.

Initially the interviewer must simply create an atmosphere in which the patient feels free to talk. Beginning psychiatric residents commonly err in aggressively interrogating patients only to elicit history and symptoms. Another common error is the assumption of a pseudoanalytic attitude of abstinence, virtual silence, and passivity. Residents who may be warm and personable individuals suddenly become stiff, overly formal, and cold when they interview a patient. The interviewer will get much farther by becoming an active participant in the relationship—by warmly and empathically seeking to understand the patient's point of view. This posture, while dynamically informed, departs from the classical view of the analyst as a nongratifying, neutral observer (Viederman 1984). A dynamic interview is not a psychoanalytic therapy session.

The psychiatrist can learn a great deal by allowing the patient to ramble freely for a while. Initial comments should be designed to facilitate this rambling (e.g., "tell me more," "please go on," "I can understand your feeling that way," or "that must have been upsetting"). Besides eliciting essential historical and mental status data, interviewers can discern patterns of association that may reveal significant unconscious connections. The order in which events, memories, concerns, and other psychological issues are verbalized is never random. Mathematicians have long known that it is impossible for any individual to generate prolonged sequences of random numbers. Within a short time, the numbers will fall into meaningful patterns. The mind prefers order to chaos. So it is with the verbalizations of the patient. Deutsch and Murphy (1955) based their approach to interviewing—known as "associative anamnesis"—on this principle:

> The method...consists in recording not only what the patient said, but also how he gave the information. It is of consequence not only that the patient tells his complaints, but also in what phase of the interview, and in which connection he introduces his ideas, complaints and recollections of his somatic and emotional disturbances. (p. 19)

Although patients may be consciously baffled by their symptoms, the ordering of their associations may provide clues to unconscious connections. For example, a 31-year-old man who came with his parents for a psychiatric evaluation began the morning with a psychiatrist while his parents met privately with a social worker in a different building. The young man began by explaining that he had been unable to keep a job. He suddenly became overwhelmed with anxiety because he was uncertain of his parents' whereabouts. The psychiatrist clarified that they were with the social worker in the office building next door. The patient asked if he could use the psychiatrist's phone to call them. The psychiatrist silently noted that the patient's anxiety about his parents' location followed immediately on the heels of his complaint of not being able to hold a job. He asked the patient if the two concerns were connected. After a moment's reflection, the patient acknowledged that when he is away from his parents at work, he worries that something will happen to them. This interchange led to a productive discussion about the patient's concerns that growing up and becoming independent would be destructive to his parents.

Because of the central role of developmental theory in dynamic psychiatry, a developmental history must be part of a thorough dynamic assessment. Was the patient a product of an unwanted pregnancy? Did the patient's birth occur after an older sibling had died? Did the patient achieve developmental milestones such as talking, walking, and sitting up at the appropriate ages? Were there traumatic separations or losses during the formative years? Obtaining such invaluable information often necessitates interviews of parents and other family members—either by the psychiatrist or by a social worker associated with the psychiatrist. Obviously, patients will be unable to recall some significant events of childhood and will distort others.

Despite their imperfect memory for historical events, patients should nevertheless be engaged in a review of childhood and adolescent development. A fundamental principle of the dynamic interview is that the past is repeating itself in the present. To enlist the patient as a collaborator in the diagnostic process, the interviewer can encourage the patient's curiosity about links between historical events and present-day feelings. A variety of open-ended questions serve to establish this collaborative partnership: "Does the anxiety you're experiencing today remind you of feelings you've had at anytime in your past?" "Were there any events in your childhood that may have contributed to your feeling as an adult that women cannot be trusted?" "Do your current marital problems have any similarities with problems you've had in other relationships in the past?"

As the patient begins to collaborate in the search for links between past and present, the examiner should note particular historical events and periods that seem important to the patient. Similarly, conspicuous omissions from the developmental history are also noteworthy. Does the patient, for example, focus exclusively on one parent as the cause of all current problems while omitting any reference to the other parent? What about the patient's cultural and religious background? How do these factors affect family relationships and the acceptability of emotional problems?

After several minutes of open-ended questions designed to facilitate a free-flowing history of the present illness and family and developmental issues, the psychiatrist can then fill in the gaps with more specific, direct questions. These may be geared to the descriptive diagnosis (e.g., specific symptoms necessary for the DSM-III-R diagnosis, information about the duration of the illness, exclusions of other illnesses) or may be directed toward a more complete dynamic diagnosis (e.g., specific developmental traumas, relationship patterns, or recurrent fantasies and daydreams). As the patient fills in the gaps, the dynamic psychiatrist can begin to formulate hypotheses that link the patient's past relationships with current relationships and with emerging transference paradigms (Menninger 1958). In other words, how are repetitions of past relationship patterns creating problems in the present?

Axis IV of DSM-III-R mandates that stressors be considered during the diagnostic appraisal of the patient. Events that precipitate an episode of illness are vital to both the descriptive and the dynamic diagnosis. Some researchers estimate that as many as 32 percent of psychiatric illness episodes are precipitated by stressful life events (Cooke and Hole 1983). However, careful history taking is essential when evaluating Axis IV because patients may distort their memory of a stressor's timing in an effort to retrospectively explain their illness or problems as directly attributable to an external event (Andrews and Tennant 1978).

Patients can nevertheless provide important dynamic information about their perception of the connections between events and symptoms. Again the examiner should think in terms of how issues from the past are evoked by stressors in the present. One female executive developed extraordinary anxiety after receiving a promotion. She identified the promotion as the stressor, but could not determine why it provoked anxiety, because she had sought the new job for several years. In the course of the interview, she frequently referred to her younger sister, who was divorced and supporting two children through a menial job. Further exploration of intense sibling rivalry that had existed between the sisters during childhood revealed that the executive's anxiety was related to guilt feelings. She was convinced that her promotion had been destructive to her sister. These feelings resonated with her childhood wish to triumph over her sister and be the only child in the eyes of their parents.

Holmes and Rahe (1967) have developed a scale that ranks the severity of stress in a number of different life events. Although such scales can help provide consensual estimates of the effects that accompany particular life events, the dynamic psychiatrist must approach each patient as a unique individual and not assume a priori that a certain life event has only one specific meaning. For example, one young man reacted to his father's death with a liberated sense that he was finally free to pursue his career without incessant criticism. Hence the stressor resulted in improved school performance and enhanced overall functioning.

In addition, the examiner should keep in mind that some stressors may operate at an unconscious level, preventing the patient from identifying any precipitating event when asked to do so. One function of the interview may be to work together to determine whether any stressors have been overlooked. Anniversary reactions, for example, are common stressors the patient may neglect. One chronically depressed patient became acutely suicidal on the anniversary of her brother's suicide. In another instance, when a happily married physician began having marital problems for no apparent reason, he called on a psychiatric colleague for advice. During the course of their phone conversation, the doctor suddenly realized that he was calling on the 10th anniversary of his divorce from his previous wife. This insight revealed that his current anger at his present wife was actually caused by his stormy relationship with his first wife.

The Mental Status Examination

Like descriptive psychiatrists, dynamic psychiatrists are interested in mental status data, but they approach the information somewhat differently. First, to the extent that it is reasonable and possible, they prefer to weave mental status questions into the fabric of the interview rather than to add them at the end in a list of formal mental status questions (MacKinnon and Michels 1971). Although some specific mental status questions should obviously be appended to the interview if they are not elicited during it, there is an advantage in minimizing the formal mental status examination. When these questions are brought into the body of the interview, the patient views distortions of perception, thought, and affect in a meaningful context. Moreover, in determining connections between such distortions and the illness, the patient becomes more involved as a collaborator rather than as merely a passive responder to questions, like a specimen under a microscope.

   Orientation and perception.   A patient's orientation to time, place, and person is often clear in the course of history-taking. To ask specific orientation questions of someone who is obviously well oriented is likely to disturb the rapport of the doctor-patient relationship. Hyperalertness is a mental status finding that will also reveal itself without direct questioning. Significant perceptual symptoms such as auditory or visual hallucinations will often be evident at the beginning of the interview when the patient is asked to explain why psychiatric treatment is being sought. But the dynamic psychiatrist is interested in more than the presence or absence of hallucinations. If a patient hears voices, the psychiatrist wants to know what the voices say, under what circumstances they speak, whose voice it sounds like, and what the voices mean to the patient. One male paranoid schizophrenic patient always heard his father telling him that he would never amount to anything. His hallucinations correlated with his childhood experiences of never being able to do enough to please his father. Similarly, the multiply determined distortions of mind-body perception such as depersonalization may serve as windows onto intrapsychic conflicts and clashes between sets of internal object relations (Gabbard and Twemlow 1984).

Cognition. The presence of a formal thought disorder will usually be clear from the history-taking portion of the interview. As alluded to earlier, even loose associations are connected idiosyncratically in the patient's mind. The examiner's task is to understand the nature of such connections. Delusions are also more likely to be elicited by open-ended historical questions than by specific questions about "false beliefs." The presence or absence of delusions is only part of the psychodynamic assessment; their meanings and functions are equally relevant. The grandiose delusions of the paranoid patient may serve to compensate for devastating feelings of low self-esteem.

Because cognition affects language and communication, the psychiatrist must also listen for parapraxes or slips of the tongue that reveal glimpses of the unconscious at work. A pregnant woman whose obstetrician referred her for a psychiatric consultation was resentful about seeing a psychiatrist, and at one point she exclaimed, "I don't want to be a psychiatric parent—I mean patient!" The examining psychiatrist could conclude from this parapraxis that the patient was highly ambivalent about becoming a mother.

The patient's manner of answering questions may reveal a good deal about his or her unconscious character style. The obsessive-compulsive patient may respond to questions with an over-inclusive attention to detail, frequently asking the examiner to elaborate on specifically requested information. By contrast, the hysterical patient may be so completely uninterested in detail as to provide vague responses that frustrate the interviewer. The passive-aggressive patient may produce anger in the interviewer by asking for questions to be repeated and by generally thwarting attempts to elicit historical data. The paranoid patient may constantly read hidden meanings into the questions, thus placing the examiner on the defensive.

Determining the presence or absence of suicidal ideation is essential to any psychiatric evaluation. Suicidal patients should be asked outright if they have a suicide plan and if they have a support system of people they can talk to before acting impulsively. The psychodynamic assessment should discern the meaning of the contemplated suicide. Is there a reunion fantasy with a deceased loved one? Is suicide a vengeful act designed to devastate someone else just as that person once devastated the patient? Is suicide really designed to kill an internal object-representation that is hated and feared? Of the many possible solutions to a patient's problems, why is suicide so compelling?

Affect. Observations about the patient's emotional states provide a gold mine of information about defense mechanisms. After all, the management of affect is perhaps the most important function of defenses. Patients who describe extraordinarily painful events in their lives without being moved in the least may be employing intellectualization. Hypomanic patients who assert that they always are in a good mood and are unusually jocular with the examiner may be using denial to defend against feelings such as grief and anger. Borderline patients who express contempt and hostility toward the key figures in their lives may be employing splitting to ward off any integration of good and bad feelings toward others. Mood, a subcategory of affect involving a sustained, internal feeling tone, should also be assessed. Exploration of moods with a patient often reveals that they are linked with significant self- and object-representations.

Action. A wealth of information is communicated through nonverbal behavior in the clinical interview. What particularly sensitive subjects result in the patient's fidgeting? What topics evoke silence? What issues cause the patient to break off eye contact with the examiner? Despite the fact that patients attempt to conceal essential data from the examining psychiatrist, their nonverbal behaviors will consistently betray them. Freud made the following observation in 1905:

> When I set myself the task of bringing to light what human beings keep hidden within them, not by the compelling power of hypnosis, but by observing what they say and what they show, I thought the task was a harder one than it really is. He that has eyes to see and ears to hear may convince himself that no mortal can keep a secret. If his lips are silent, he chatters with his finger-tips; betrayal oozes out of him at every pore. And thus the task of making conscious the most hidden recesses of the mind is one which it is quite possible to accomplish. (pp. 77–78)

Psychological Testing

Projective psychological tests, principally the Rorschach and the Thematic Apperception Test (TAT), may be extraordinarily useful adjuncts to the psychodynamic assessment. The Rorschach consists of 10 symmetrical inkblots that present ambiguous stimuli to the patient. In the face of this ambiguity, patients will reveal a great deal about themselves through their interpretations of the amorphous shapes within the inkblots. Highly sophisticated guides to Rorschach interpretations have systematized the responses according to a psychodynamic diagnostic understanding of the patient (Kwawer et al. 1980; Rapaport et al. 1968; Schafer 1954).

The TAT operates on a similar principle. A series of drawings or woodcuts, portraying persons and situations of varying degrees of ambiguity, allow patients a good deal of latitude in interpretation. Patients are asked to invent a story to describe each picture. In making up these stories, patients project their own fantasies, wishes, and conflicts into the pictures. Projective testing is especially useful for patients who are guarded and laconic in the psychiatric interview and therefore do not share their inner life freely with the psychiatrist. Many patients, however, will reveal so much about themselves in the course of the clinical interview that psychological testing is not necessary as an adjunct.

Physical and Neurological Examination

For obvious reasons, the patient's physical and neurological status is as important to the dynamic psychiatrist as it is to the descriptive psychiatrist. "The head bone is connected to the neck bone," so whatever goes wrong in the body will affect the brain—and vice versa. If the assessment is taking place in a hospital setting, dynamic psychiatrists may or may not perform their own physical and neurological examinations. If the assessment is of an outpatient in a private office, most dynamic psychiatrists prefer that an internist do the physical. Regardless of who does it, exploring the meaning of the physical is usually beneficial—both in terms of transference issues and in terms of patients' fantasies about their body. In any case, neither a descriptive nor a dynamic assessment can be complete without this data.

The Psychodynamic Diagnosis

At the completion of the psychodynamic assessment, the clinician should arrive at a descriptive diagnosis (based on DSM-III-R criteria) and a psychodynamic diagnosis (based on one's understanding of the patient and the illness). Both diagnoses inform the treatment planning, but the descriptive diagnosis is geared to the assignment of the correct label, the latter is viewed as a summary of understanding that goes beyond the label. Menninger et al. (1963) elegantly described the dynamic approach to diagnosis:

> This means diagnosis in a new sense, not the mere application of a label. It is not a search for a proper name by which one can refer to this affliction in this and other patients. It is diagnosis in the sense of understanding just how the patient is ill and how ill the patient is, how he became ill and how his illness serves him. From this knowledge one may draw logical conclusions regarding how changes might be brought about in or around the patient which would affect his illness. (pp. 6–7)

The descriptive diagnosis may assist clinicians in planning appropriate pharmacologic interventions. The dynamic diagnosis may facilitate the clinician's understanding of what the medication prescription means to the patient and whether compliance with the medication is likely to be a problem.

In this context, I want to emphasize that the usefulness of a dynamic diagnosis is not limited to patients whose prescribed treatment is dynamic psychotherapy. The therapeutic management of the patient's personality is an integral part of all psychiatric treatment that must always be considered in treatment planning (Perry et al. 1987).

Part of the dynamic diagnosis involves understanding how the five axes of DSM-III-R interact and influence one another. Because all illness grows out of a preexisting personality, consideration must be given to how the personality diagnosis on Axis II contributes to the Axis I syndrome. Obsessive-compulsive individuals, for example, often decompensate into a major depressive episode. Clinicians might therefore evaluate how the rigid and demanding superego of the obsessive-compulsive personality structure contributed to the self-loathing characteristic of the depression. This aspect of the diagnosis would not replace the contributions of biochemical and genetic factors to the depression but rather would work synergistically to provide a more complete understanding of the patient and the illness. Similarly, an Axis III diagnosis of carcinoma of the pancreas might contribute to an Axis I major depressive episode on a biological basis, but the patient's psychological reaction to the diagnosis of a malignancy might be another determinant of the depression. The patient who is diagnosed with narcissistic personality disorder on Axis II and panic disorder on Axis I might be unwilling to take medication for the panic disorder because the notion of having a major psychiatric disorder is too narcissistically injurious to tolerate.

As previously described in this chapter, Axis IV stressors, both obvious, conscious precipitants and hidden, unconscious ones, must also be evaluated in the dynamic diagnosis. Finally, it is helpful to assess how all the findings on the other four axes affect the Axis V level of functioning. Does the Axis I diagnosis account for the severity of the patient's functional impairment, or do characterological features on Axis II contribute to a lower level of functioning than is warranted by the Axis I diagnosis? A complete psychodynamic diagnosis also involves assessing the patient from the three major theoretical perspectives discussed in Chapter 2: ego psychology, object relations theory, and self psychology.

Characteristics of the Ego

A great deal can be learned about patients' overall ego strength from their work histories and their relationship patterns. Those who have been able to hold jobs and establish committed relationships for reasonably long periods are likely to have more resilient egos than those who have not.

The assessment of certain key ego functions (Bellak et al. 1973) can help psychiatrists understand a patient's strengths and weaknesses and thus enable them to prescribe the treatment program. How is the patient's reality testing? Is there an ability to distinguish what is internal from what is external, or is there a persistent pattern of delusional misperception? Is the patient's reality testing intact in structured situations but impaired in unstructured situations? What about the patient's impulse control? Is there sufficient ego to delay the discharge of impulses, or is the patient virtually driven by impulses to the point where there is danger to others or self? Judgment is another ego function that must be assessed. Can the patient adequately anticipate the consequences of actions?

In planning for the appropriate form of psychotherapy, psychiatrists should also determine the psychological mindedness of the patient. Does the patient see problems as having an internal origin, or are all difficulties externalized and blamed on others in the environment? Can the patient synthesize and integrate various bits of data and reflect on their connections to develop meaningful explanations for symptoms and interpersonal difficulties? Does the patient think in metaphors and analogies that allow for connections between various levels of abstraction? All these considerations aid in assessing the extent of psychological mindedness.

A major portion of ego assessment focuses on the defensive functioning of the ego. In the psychoanalytic setting, Waelder (1960) developed a series of questions that addresses the defensive operations of the patient. These same questions could be adapted to the dynamic assessment: *"What are the patient's desires?* What does the patient (unconsciously) want? And *of what is he afraid? ... And when he is afraid, what does he do?"* (pp. 182–183). One can also assess the defense mechanisms on the continuum of immaturity to maturity described in Chapter 2. The patient who is able to use suppression and humor in the midst of a difficult situation is showing much greater ego strength than the patient who resorts to splitting and projective identification in the same situation.

Determining the ego's relationship to the superego is another vital part of an ego psychological assessment. Is the superego a rigid and ruthless overseer of the ego, or is there a flexibility and harmony in the relationship of superego to ego? Does the patient espouse realistic ideals, or is the patient driven by unreachable and fantastic goals? Are there antisocial tendencies in the patient characterized by an absent or underdeveloped superego? The answers to these questions also provide clues about the patient's childhood experiences with parental figures since the superego is an internalized representation of those figures.

Object Relations

As an end result of the psychodynamic assessment, the clinician has information about the patient's interpersonal relationships in three contexts: childhood relationships, the real and transferential aspects of the relationship between the patient and the examining clinician, and current relationships outside the doctor-patient relationship. The nature of these relationships provides the psychiatrist with a good deal of information about the patient's position in family and social systems. Still needed, though, is an assessment of how the patient's family relationships influence the development of the clinical picture that brings the patient to the psychiatrist. Does an adolescent patient's symptomatic picture reflect the parents' marital problems? In other words, is the patient serving as a "carrier" of illness for the entire family?

Information about the patient's interpersonal relationships also tells a great deal about the nature of the patient's internal object relations. Interviews of family members and significant others can help sort out the extent of distortion inherent in the patient's view of other relationships. Certain easily discernible patterns seem to cut across all relationships. For example, does the patient always seem to end up as a masochistic partner in a sado-masochistic bond? Is the patient always taking care of others who are less functional and more in need of caretaking?

Determining the level of maturity of object relations is an integral part of this assessment. Does the patient experience others ambivalently as whole objects having both good and bad qualities? Alternatively, does the patient view others as either idealized (all good) or devalued (all bad)? Does the patient see others as need-gratifying part-objects who serve only one function for the patient rather than as separate persons with needs and concerns of their own? Finally, what about object constancy? Can the patient tolerate being apart from significant others by summoning up a soothing internal image of the person who is missed?

The Self

A thorough dynamic assessment must evaluate several aspects of the patient's self. In the broad framework of self psychology, psychiatrists should examine the durability and cohesiveness of the self. Is it prone to fragmentation in response to the smallest slight from a friend or colleague? Does the patient need to be in the spotlight continually to receive affirming responses from selfobjects?

The maturity of the patient's selfobjects should also be assessed. Are the patient's selfobject needs satisfied by a mutually gratifying relationship in the context of a long-term commitment?

In addition to self-esteem, the psychiatrist should also assess the patient's self-continuity. Is the patient much the same over time, regardless of external circumstances, or is there a generalized identity diffusion? Evidence for the latter would indicate that different self-representations, split off from one another, are constantly jockeying for dominance over the total personality. Different self-representations would obviously arise in connection with different object-representations that are highly influenced by the interpersonal context at a given moment. The boundaries of the self are also of interest. Can the patient clearly differentiate his or her own mental contents from those of others, or is there a general blurring of self-object boundaries? A related aspect would be the patient's body perception. Are the patient's body boundaries intact, or does the patient have to engage periodically in self-mutilation to define the skin boundary? Are mind and body viewed as connected over time, or are there episodes of depersonalization or out-of-body experience where the mind seems independent of the body?

Explanatory Formulation

The different elements of the psychodynamic diagnosis enumerated above are the basis of an explanatory formulation. This tentative hypothesis or working model illustrates how the elements interact to create the clinical picture presented by the patient. This summary statement, sometimes referred to as a psychodynamic formulation (Perry et al. 1987), may also include comments on the biological aspects of the illness and on treatment implications. Although the formulation is intended to explain the patient's condition, it does not have to explain everything. It should succinctly highlight the major issues, especially their relevance to treatment planning.

With some patients, one theoretical model will appear to have more explanatory value than the other two. With other patients, however, all three theoretical perspectives may seem useful in conceptualizing various aspects of the patient's psychopathology. As suggested in Chapter 2, clinicians should be open-minded to all three theoretical frameworks and should embrace a "both/and" rather than an "either/or" attitude. The formulation should also be approached with the understanding that it undergoes continual modification as treatment proceeds. In dynamic psychiatry, diagnosis and treatment are always evolving together. A sample explanatory formulation illustrates these points:

Ms. A, a 33-year-old single woman employed as a librarian, came to the hospital in the midst of a psychotic episode with paranoid features. She had become convinced that her mother was plotting to kill her, and she had barricaded herself in the apartment she shared with her brother.

When Ms. A reorganized after a few doses of haloperidol, she presented herself as a cheerful, Pollyannaish person, commenting, "I have no anger in me." She said she felt fine and wanted to go home. Her mother was glad to see her "back to normal," but expressed concern because Ms. A's brother was still at the apartment. He had apparently exploited his sister by moving in, eating her food, and living rent-free for the past several weeks.

According to her mother, Ms. A lived an isolated existence and had few interpersonal contacts outside several superficial relationships at work. Moreover, the patient's mother revealed that Ms. A had had one previous psychotic episode 18 months earlier when her brother had moved in with her under the same exploitative circumstances. Ms. A's mother also reported a family history of bipolar affective disorder.

The following explanatory formulation was developed:

Ms. A inherited a diathesis toward bipolar affective disorder. Her cyclic psychotic episodes, which appeared schizophreniform, were possibly a variant of bipolar illness. After stabilizing the psychosis with haloperidol, the psychiatrist could taper off that medication, and consider replacing it with lithium prophylaxis.

When Ms. A is nonpsychotic, her adjustment comes at the expense of massive denial of all negative feelings, especially anger, and results in a schizoid existence. The stressor of having her brother living parasitically in her apartment provoked so much anger in Ms. A that she could not maintain her usual defensive posture. Under pressure of this intense affect, she regressed to the paranoid-schizoid position, where an unacceptable self-representation harboring angry, murderous feelings was split off and projected into her mother. After remission of Ms. A's psychosis with medication, she reintrojected the self-representation, which once again became buried under her denial.

The patient lacks the psychological mindedness to see any problems to work on in an exploratory therapy process. Casework or family therapy is therefore needed to remove the stressor (i.e., the brother) and to allow Ms. A to resume her previous adjustment with a follow-up regimen of medication and supportive psychotherapy to maintain her defenses.

While dynamic in its conceptualization, this formulation is in keeping with the biopsychosocial model of psychiatry championed by Engel (1977), Fink (1988), and others in that it takes into account genetic predisposition, social-familial influences, and intrapsychic factors.

Table 3-1. The psychodynamic assessment

Historical data
  Present illness with attention to associative linkages and
      Axis IV stressors.
  Past history with emphasis on how the past is repeating
      itself in the present.
    Developmental history.
    Family history.
    Cultural/religious background.
Mental status examination
  Orientation and perception.
  Cognition.
  Affect.
  Action.
Projective psychological testing (if necessary)
Physical and neurological examination
The psychodynamic diagnosis
  Descriptive DSM-III-R diagnosis.
  Interactions among Axes I–V.
  Characteristics of the ego.
    Strengths and weaknesses.
    Defense mechanisms and conflicts.
    Relationship to superego.
  Quality of object relations.
    Family relationships.
    Transference-countertransference patterns.
    Inferences about internal object relations.
  Characteristics of the self.
    Self-esteem and self-cohesiveness.
    Self-continuity.
    Self-boundaries.
    Mind/body relationship.
  Explanatory formulation using above data.

Conclusion

Table 3-1 summarizes the steps involved in a thorough psychodynamic assessment. In the final analysis, the purpose of the assessment is to inform and guide the overall treatment planning. The case of Ms. A illustrates how a psychodynamic diagnosis, and particularly an explanatory formulation, can be useful even when dynamic psychotherapy is contraindicated. The treatment is nevertheless dynamically informed. The dynamic assessment assists all aspects of treatment planning. An evaluation of ego functions can contribute to a decision regarding whether an individual should be an inpatient or an outpatient. For example, the extent of impulse control may be a crucial variable in deciding whether a patient should be admitted in the first place and, if so, when the patient can be discharged. A dynamic understanding of their patients can help clinicians decide whether their patients would accept a recommendation for sex therapy, behavior modification, family therapy, or group therapy. Finally, each patient's compliance with any medication regimen will be affected by that particular patient's characterological substrate. The cases discussed in subsequent chapters will illustrate how other theoretical models can be used in developing a formulation and how the dynamic assessment of the patient guides the treatment planning.

References

American Psychiatric Association: Diagnostic and Statistical Manual of Mental Disorders, 3rd Edition, Revised. Washington, DC, American Psychiatric Press, 1987

Andrews G, Tennant C: Editorial: Life event stress and illness. Psychol Med 8:545–549, 1978

Bellak L, Hurvich M, Gedimen K: Ego Functions in Schizophrenics, Neurotics, and Normals: A Systematic Study of Conceptual, Diagnostic, and Therapeutic Aspects. New York, John Wiley & Sons, 1973

Cooke DJ, Hole DJ: The aetiological importance of stressful life events. Br J Psychiatry 143:397–400, 1983

Deutsch F, Murphy WF: The Clinical Interview, Vol I: Diagnosis: A Method of Teaching Associative Exploration. New York, International Universities Press, 1955

Engel GL: The need for a new medical model: a challenge for biomedicine. Science 196:129–136, 1977

Fink PJ: Response to the presidential address: is "biopsychosocial" the psychiatric shibboleth? Am J Psychiatry 145:1061–1067, 1988

Freud S: Fragment of an analysis of a case of hysteria (1905), in The Standard Edition of the Complete Psychological Works of Sigmund Freud, Vol 7. Translated and edited by Strachey J. London, Hogarth Press, 1953, pp 1–122

Gabbard GO, Twemlow SW: With the Eyes of the Mind: An Empirical Analysis of Out-of-Body States. New York, Praeger, 1984

Hamilton NG: Self and Others: Object Relations Theory in Practice. Northvale, NJ, Jason Aronson, 1988

Holmes TH, Rahe RH: Social Readjustment Rating Scale. J Psychosomatic Research 11:213–281, 1967

Kernberg OF: Notes on countertransference. J Am Psychoanal Assoc 13:38–56, 1965

Kernberg OF: Severe Personality Disorders: Psychotherapeutic Strategies. New Haven, Yale University Press, 1984

Kwawer JS, Lerner HD, Lerner PM, et al (eds): Borderline Phenomena and the Rorschach Test. New York, International Universities Press, 1980

Langs RJ: The Bipersonal Field. New York, Jason Aronson, 1976

MacKinnon RA, Michels R: The Psychiatric Interview in Clinical Practice. Philadelphia, WB Saunders, 1971

Menninger KA: Theory of Psychoanalytic Technique. New York, Basic Books, 1958

Menninger KA, Mayman M, Pruyser PW: A Manual for Psychiatric Case Study (2nd Edition). New York, Grune & Stratton, 1962

Menninger KA, Mayman M, Pruyser PW: The Vital Balance: The Life Process in Mental Health and Illness. New York, Viking Press, 1963

Perry S, Cooper AM, Michels R: The psychodynamic formulation: its purpose, structure, and clinical application. Am J Psychiatry 144:543–550, 1987

Rapaport D, Gill MM, Schafer R: Diagnostic Psychological Testing (rev ed). Edited by Holt RR. New York, International Universities Press, 1968

Reiser MF: Are psychiatric educators "losing the mind?" Am J Psychiatry 145:148–153, 1988

Schafer R: Psychoanalytic Interpretation in Rorschach Testing: Theory and Application. New York, Grune & Stratton, 1954

Shevrin H, Shectman F: The diagnostic process in psychiatric evaluations. Bull Menninger Clin 37:451–494, 1973

Thomä H, Kächele H: Psychoanalytic Practice, Vol 1: Principles. Translated by Wilson M, Roseveare D. New York, Berlin, Heidelberg, Springer-Verlag, 1987

Viederman M: The active dynamic interview and the supportive relationship. Compr Psychiatry 25:147–157, 1984

Waelder R: Basic Theory of Psychoanalysis. New York, International Universities Press, 1960

CHAPTER 4

Treatments in Dynamic Psychiatry I: Individual Psychotherapy

Proficiency at individual psychotherapy is perhaps the hallmark of the dynamic psychiatrist. Evolving as it does from psychoanalysis, dynamic psychiatry understandably emphasizes the nuances of the healing relationship between psychotherapist and patient. Space considerations here limit us to a brief overview of the general principles derived from the vast literature on individual psychotherapy. Specific applications of those principles will be demonstrated and explicated in Sections II and III. Readers who are interested in a more comprehensive discussion of individual psychotherapy should consult any of several outstanding texts (Basch 1980; Chessick 1974; Dewald 1964; Fromm-Reichmann 1950; Luborsky 1984; Ogden 1982; Roth 1987).

The Expressive-Supportive Continuum

Psychotherapy modeled on the technical principles of formal psychoanalysis has been designated by a number of different names: expressive, dynamic, psychoanalytically oriented, insight oriented, exploratory, uncovering, and intensive, to name a few. This form of treatment, geared to analyzing defenses and uncovering the dynamically repressed material in the unconscious, has traditionally been viewed as wholly different from another entity known as supportive psychotherapy. The latter, which is more oriented to suppressing unconscious conflict and bolstering defenses, has been widely regarded as inferior to expressive therapy. This tendency is reflected in the clinical maxim that has guided psychotherapists for years: "Be as expressive as you can be, and as supportive as you have to be" (Wallerstein 1986, p. 688).

A number of authors have recently expressed concern about this traditional dichotomy (Pine 1976, 1986; Wallerstein 1986; Werman 1984). One problem with the distinction is the implication that supportive psychotherapy is not psychoanalytically oriented. In practice, supportive psychotherapy is guided by psychoanalytic understanding every step of the way. Moreover, the dichotomy portrays expressive psychotherapy and supportive psychotherapy as highly discrete entities when, in fact, they rarely occur in pure form anywhere (Wallerstein 1986; Werman 1984). Finally, the value distinction associated with the greater prestige of expressive psychotherapy or psychoanalysis has always carried with it the assumption that change achieved as a result of insight or intrapsychic conflict resolution is somehow superior to that achieved through supportive techniques. No hard data support this assumption; the changes achieved by expressive psychotherapy have not been proven in any way superior or more durable than those achieved by supportive psychotherapy (Wallerstein 1986).

At the conclusion of a monumental study of 42 patients treated in the Menninger Foundation Psychotherapy Research Project, Wallerstein (1986) determined that all forms of psychotherapy contain a mixture of expressive and supportive elements, and that changes achieved by the supportive elements are in no way inferior to those achieved by the expressive elements. Rather than regarding expressive psychotherapy and supportive psychotherapy as two distinct modalities of treatment then, we should view psychotherapy as taking place on an expressive-supportive continuum, which is in closer keeping with the reality of clinical practice and with empirical research. With certain patients, at certain points in the therapy, the therapy will be weighted more heavily toward expressive elements, while with other patients and at other times, the therapy will require more attention to supportive elements. As Wallerstein (1986) noted, "All proper therapy is always both expressive and supportive (in different ways), and the question at issue at all points in every therapy should be that of expressing *how* and *when,* and supporting *how* and *when*" (p. 689).

Individual psychotherapy geared to this continuum might best be termed *expressive-supportive* or *supportive-expressive.* Even psychoanalysis, situated at the most extreme point on the expressive end of the continuum, contains supportive elements associated with the treatment structure itself and the collaboration of analyst and patient to achieve certain goals (Luborsky 1984); meanwhile, most supportive psychotherapies at the opposite end of the continuum do provide insight and understanding from time to time. Hence the effective dynamic therapist will shift flexibly back and forth along the expressive-supportive continuum, depending on the needs of the patient at a given moment in the psychotherapy process.

The concept of the expressive-supportive continuum provides a framework for considering the goals, characteristics, and indications for individual psychotherapy. Each of these elements changes accordingly as we move back and forth along the continuum.

Goals of Expressive-Supportive Psychotherapy

The ultimate goals of psychoanalysis and those treatments weighted toward the expressive end of the continuum involve the acquisition of insight, which may be defined as the capacity to understand the unconscious meanings and origins of one's symptoms and behavior. Although Freud never used the term *insight*, he did define the goal of analysis as to make conscious what is unconscious, which is certainly a significant aspect of insight. In Freud's early clinical case reports, insight came through dramatic catharsis or abreaction, much the way it does in Hollywood portrayals of psychotherapeutic cures (Gabbard and Gabbard 1987). When Joanne Woodward in *The Three Faces of Eve,* for example, has the blinding flash of insight that her multiple personality disorder was caused by the repressed memory of having to kiss her dead grandmother, she is miraculously and dramatically cured. In real life therapy, however, insight through catharsis is rare. Ordinarily, insight is gained gradually as resistances are methodically eroded through the therapist's interventions.

Intimately related to insight is the goal of conflict resolution. A conflict is resolved when the nature of the defense and the underlying wish are understood and the wish is renounced, or at least attenuated, making the defense no longer necessary. Classically, conflict resolution refers to oedipal conflict. Another way to view this goal is greater ego mastery over the id or, as Freud (1933) put it, "where id was, there ego shall be" (p. 80).

One distinctive aspect of psychotherapies that are highly expressive is that the therapist avoids an intense investment in curing patients of their symptoms. Instead, the therapist provides insight, with the goal of giving patients greater freedom of choice. The therapist attempts to broaden the possibilities but also to maintain a profound respect for the freedom and autonomy of the patients. Warning against excessive zeal, or *furor therapeuticus,* Khan (1987) admonished "that one must not try to cure a patient beyond his need and his psychic resources to sustain and live from that cure" (p. 18).

From an object relations standpoint, an improvement in the quality of one's relationships is a goal of psychotherapy, regardless of whether it is weighted toward the supportive or the expressive end of the continuum. As internal object relations change in the course of psychotherapy, one is able to perceive and relate to external persons differently. In contemporary practice, patients are much more likely to seek therapy with complaints about the quality of their relationships rather than with discrete symptoms, as they did in Freud's day. Hence, the importance of this goal cannot be overstated. One empirical study of analysis (Kantrowitz et al. 1987) demonstrated through projective psychological testing before and after treatment that analysis produces statistically significant improvement in the level and quality of object relations.

In self psychologically oriented psychotherapy, the goals involve strengthening the cohesiveness of the self and helping the patient choose more mature selfobjects, as alluded to in Chapter 2. In Kohut's (1984) words, "The essence of the psychoanalytic cure resides in a patient's newly acquired ability to identify and seek out appropriate selfobjects...as they present themselves in his realistic surroundings and to be sustained by them" (p. 77). In other words, the goal of self psychological therapy is to help patients shift their reliance on archaic and unrealistic selfobjects to more mature and appropriate selfobjects.

The goal of psychotherapy at the supportive end of the continuum is primarily to help the patient adapt to stresses while avoiding insight into unconscious wishes and defenses (Roskin 1982). The therapist hopes to strengthen defenses to facilitate the patient's adaptive capacity to handle the stresses of daily living. This goal often involves restoring a patient to a previous level of functioning that has been compromised by a crisis. Furthermore, since supportive techniques are often used in treating patients with serious ego weaknesses, ego building is a crucial aspect of supportive psychotherapies. For example, the therapist may serve as an auxiliary ego, helping patients to test reality more accurately or to anticipate consequences of their actions and thereby improve their judgment.

Duration of Expressive-Supportive Psychotherapy

The length of expressive-supportive psychotherapy is essentially independent of the expressive-supportive continuum. Therapies that are highly supportive or highly expressive can be either brief or long. In some cases, psychoanalysis may last well over 5 years, while some supportive processes may go on even longer. On the other hand, there are instances where just one supportive or expressive therapy session (or consultation) has been highly therapeutic.

The most useful distinction is not between expressive and supportive psychotherapies but rather between open-ended psychotherapy and brief or time-limited psychotherapy. For purposes of discussion, the open-ended variety will be considered in this section and brief psychotherapy will be considered later in this chapter in recognition of its separate evolution as a special form of therapy.

Frequency of Sessions

In contrast to the duration of therapy, the frequency of sessions tends to be highly correlated with the expressive-supportive continuum. As a general rule, a greater number of weekly sessions characterizes the expressive end of the continuum. Psychoanalysis, an extremely expressive treatment, is characterized by four or five sessions a week and is usually conducted with the patient lying on a couch while the analyst sits behind the couch. Toward the center of the continuum, however, highly expressive forms of psychotherapy usually involve one to three sessions a week with the patient sitting in a chair facing the therapist. In contrast, psychotherapy with primarily supportive goals rarely takes place more than twice a week and ordinarily occurs once a week or less often. It is not uncommon for supportive processes to have a frequency of once a month.

The issue of frequency is connected with the role of transference in the psychotherapeutic process (to be discussed later in this chapter). Clinical experience has shown that transference intensifies as the frequency of sessions increases. Since the more expressive treatments focus on the transference, these therapists usually prefer to see their patients more than once a week. In contrast, supportive processes work with transference to a lesser extent and thus do not require more than one session a week. Also, while highly expressive treatments are almost invariably administered in 45- or 50-minute sessions, supportive processes tend to use time more flexibly. Certain patients who require more frequent supportive contacts with the therapist do better with two 25-minute sessions in a week than with one 50-minute session.

The reality of psychiatric practice is that practical matters may outweigh theoretical considerations in determining the frequency of sessions. Some patients may be able to afford only one session a week even though they might do better with three. Other patients, because of inconvenient work schedules or transportation problems, may be able to get to their therapist's office only once a week. Before accepting such limitations, however, the therapist should keep in mind that resistance often finds convenient hiding places. An investigation of these practical limitations may reveal that the patient has greater flexibility in regard to time and money than can be readily acknowledged.

Free Association

In the ideal psychoanalytic situation, free association is the major mode by which the patient communicates to the analyst. This requires patients to relax their usual control over their thought processes in an effort to say whatever comes to mind without censoring their words or thoughts. In actual practice, resistances inevitably intervene when patients try to free associate. It is often asserted, only half jokingly, that when a patient is able to free associate without interference from resistance, then the patient may be ready for termination. Patients may also use free association itself as a resistance (Greenson 1967) to focusing on a particular issue in their current life situation.

Free association is also useful in highly expressive therapies, although more selectively than in analysis. The therapist, for example, may ask the patient to associate to various elements of a dream to help both patient and therapist understand unconscious connections that make interpretation of the dream possible.

Free association is far less useful farther along the continuum toward the more supportively based treatments. As Greenson (1967) pointed out, the process itself requires a mature and healthy ego to maintain a split between an observing ego and an experiencing ego. Ego-deficient patients who are prone to psychosis may become increasingly regressed if allowed to free associate in a supportive process. Moreover, such patients often lack the ego capacity to reflect on their associations and to integrate them into a meaningful and coherent understanding of unconscious issues.

Neutrality

Neutrality is perhaps the most misunderstood aspect of psychotherapeutic technique. It is frequently misinterpreted to mean coldness or aloofness (Chessick 1981). Even in the most expressive treatments, emotional warmth is a necessary part of the therapeutic relationship. Similarly, concern for the patient's unique situation is essential to establish rapport. Greenson (1967) stressed that the patient in analysis deserves explanations of new or strange procedures, such as the therapist declining to answer direct questions. This humaneness and empathy are part of any effective doctor-patient relationship.

Therapists who remove themselves from the interpersonal field of the therapy by assuming an aloof, nonparticipatory attitude diminish their effectiveness by closing themselves off to the experience of the patient's internal object world (Hoffman and Gill 1988). On the other hand, therapists who allow themselves to be "roped in" to interactions with the patient allow themselves to experience the projective identification process (i.e., countertransference in the broad sense of identification with the patient's projected self- and object-representations). The ideal model would instead involve the therapist as a participant in the therapeutic process in a spontaneous, but transitory, disciplined and partial way (Hoffman and Gill 1988; Racker 1968). After the interaction, the therapist can then reflect on it and analyze it with an increased empathic appreciation of what others go through in their interactions with the patient because of having "been there." Sandler (1976) noted that the therapist may only become aware of countertransference feelings *after* responding like one of the patient's projected internal objects. This response may be an entirely silent reflection on thoughts and feelings arising within the therapist.

Neutrality, then, in no way implies detachment or emotional deadness. It is more appropriately defined as a nonjudgmental position vis-à-vis the patient's intrapsychic world (i.e., equidistant from the id, the ego, the superego, and the demands of external reality [A. Freud 1936]). In other words, the therapist does not take sides in the conflicts between the intrapsychic agencies. This position is much less applicable farther along the continuum to supportive treatments. If the superego pressure from a particular patient is so severe that it results in a suicide attempt, the therapist must take sides against the superego and restrain or hospitalize the patient. Similarly, in the supportive treatment of patients who are unable to delay the impulsive discharge of raw aggression, the therapist must side against the id.

Anonymity

Freud's (1912b) injunction that the analyst should strive for the òpacity of a mirror has led generations of analysts to scrupulously avoid any comment or action that would reveal information about themselves to their patients. In some cases, attention to anonymity has led analysts to lead a highly restricted, even cloistered, existence. The rationale has always been that divulging too much information about oneself will interfere with the development of the transference.

Nowadays analysts tend to be somewhat less rigid and restrictive because of a growing awareness that patients' reactions to information about their analysts' personal lives can usually be analyzed and understood (Katz 1978). Moreover, various kinds of personal information about therapists is available in their offices. Photographs of family, artwork, books, and so forth provide glimpses of the therapist's true nature. The therapist's various reactions to material the patient brings to therapy are also revealing.

Finally, even overt factual information is frequently distorted by the patient's transference. For example, in a group therapy process led by two cotherapists, one cotherapist fell sound asleep in the middle of one session. For a while the patients continued to talk as if nothing had happened. Finally, one patient observed that the sleeping cotherapist was pretending to be asleep as a way of testing the group's reactions.

Although knowledge about the therapist can be dealt with therapeutically, therapists in expressively oriented treatments should nevertheless refrain from volunteering personal information. Such material is unlikely to be of much value to the treatment and may inhibit the patient's freedom to speak about whatever comes to mind. However, anonymity is less crucial in the more supportive treatments. Therapists who reveal that they share the personal interests of their patients may encourage the development of trust and a common ground for collaboration in supportive psychotherapy.

Interventions

The interventions made by the therapist can be placed in seven categories along an expressive-supportive continuum: 1) interpretation, 2) confrontation, 3) clarification, 4) encouragement to elaborate, 5) empathic validation, 6) advice and praise, and 7) affirmation (Table 4-1). [This expressive-supportive continuum of interventions is derived from the work of the Menninger Clinic Treatment Interventions Project consisting of the following investigators: Jon Allen, Ph.D.; Donald Colson, Ph.D.; Lolafaye Coyne, Ph.D.; Siebolt Frieswyk, Ph.D.; Glen O. Gabbard, M.D.; Leonard Horwitz, Ph.D.; and Gavin Newsom, M.S.W.].

1. *Interpretation.* In the most expressive forms of treatment, interpretation is regarded as the therapist's ultimate decisive instrument (Greenson 1967). In its simplest form, interpretation involves making something conscious that was previously unconscious. An interpretation is an explanatory statement that links a feeling, thought, behavior, or symptom to its unconscious meaning or origin. For example, the therapist might say to a patient who is late, "Perhaps the reason you are late is that you were afraid I would react to the success you are now having the way your father reacted." Depending on the point in therapy and the patient's readiness to hear the interpretation, interpretations may focus on the transference (as in this example), on extratransference issues, the patient's past or present situation, or the patient's resistances or fantasies. As a general rule, the therapist does not address unconscious content via interpretation until the material is almost conscious and therefore relatively accessible to the patient's awareness.

Table 4-1. An expressive-supportive continuum of interventions

	Interpretation		Clarification		Encouragement to Elaborate		Empathic Validation	Advice and Praise	Affirmation	
Expressive		Confrontation								Supportive

2. *Confrontation.* The next most expressive intervention is confrontation, which addresses something the patient does not want to accept or identifies the patient's avoidance or minimization. A confrontation may be geared to clarifying how the patient's behavior affects others or to reflecting back to the patient a denied or suppressed feeling. Confrontation, which is often gentle, carries the unfortunate connotation in common parlance of being aggressive or blunt. The following example illustrates that confrontation is not necessarily forceful or hostile. In the last session of a long-term therapy process, one patient talked at great length about car problems he encountered on the way to the session. The therapist commented, "I think you'd rather talk about your car than face the sadness you're feeling about our last session."

3. *Clarification.* Farther along the continuum from expressive to supportive interventions, clarification involves a reformulation or pulling together of the patient's verbalizations to convey a more coherent view of what is being communicated. Clarification differs from confrontation because it lacks the element of denial or minimization. A clarification is aimed at helping the patient articulate something that is difficult to put into words.

4. *Encouragement to elaborate.* Closer to the center of the continuum come interventions that are neither supportive nor expressive in and of themselves. Encouragement to elaborate may be broadly defined as a request for information about a topic brought up by the patient. It may be an open-ended question such as, "What comes to mind about that?" or a more specific request as in, "Tell me more about your father." Such interventions are commonly used in both the most expressive and the most supportive treatments.

5. *Empathic validation.* This intervention is a demonstration of the therapist's empathic attunement with the patient's internal state. A typically validating comment is, "I can understand why you feel depressed about that," or "It hurts when you're treated that way." In the view of the self psychologists, empathic immersion in the patient's internal experience is essential, regardless of the location of the therapy on the expressive-supportive continuum (Kohut 1984; Ornstein 1986). When patients feel that the therapist understands their subjective experiences, they are more likely to accept interpretations.

6. *Advice and praise.* This category really includes two interventions that are linked by the fact that they both prescribe and reinforce certain activities. Advice involves direct suggestions to the patient regarding how to behave, while praise reinforces certain patient behaviors by expressing overt approval of them. An example of the former is, "I think you should stop going out with that man

immediately." An example of the latter is, "I'm very pleased that you were able to tell him that you would not see him anymore." These comments are on the opposite end of the continuum from traditional psychoanalytic interventions because they are departures from neutrality and to some extent compromise the patient's autonomy in making decisions.
7. *Affirmation.* This simple intervention involves succinct comments in support of the patient's comments or behaviors such as, "Uh-huh," or "Yes, I see what you mean."

The vast majority of psychotherapeutic processes contain all these interventions at some time during the course of treatment. However, a therapy is classified as primarily expressive or supportive based partly on which interventions predominate. These associations of interventions with the continuum are not ironclad, however. Anna Ornstein (1986) argued that empathic interpretations are the optimal therapeutic interventions for all classes of psychopathology, including the supportive psychotherapy of severely disturbed patients. Her empathic interpretations have three aspects: accepting the patient as is, understanding the patient's situation, and explaining, to give insight into the origins of the patient's difficulties. In this sense Ornstein combined a predominantly supportive intervention, empathic validation, with a highly expressive intervention (interpretation). The essence of this self psychological approach is to convey to the patient that certain emotions or attitudes with negative connotations, such as hatred, envy, or greed, originate in completely understandable early life experiences marked by parental deprivation, neglect, or failures of empathy. Pine (1986) has advocated supportive techniques to "cushion the blow" of interpretations in the supportive therapy of fragile patients. Werman (1984, p. 83) proposed making "upward interpretations" of transference behavior or feelings to relate them to current situations rather than to early experiences, thereby preventing regression in patients with serious ego weakness. These interventions are the inverse of classical interpretations in that they provide conscious, rather than unconscious, explanations of the patient's behavior or feelings.

Transference

Freud was fond of saying that what made a therapy process psychoanalytic was a focus on transference and resistance. Certainly all forms of dynamically oriented psychotherapy pay careful attention to the state of the transference. However, the specific manner in which the transference is addressed (or left unaddressed) varies considerably, depending on the expressive-supportive dimension. In formal psychoanalysis the highlighting and resolution of the transference is of paramount importance. Cooper (1987) noted: "Despite the diversity of analytic views that abound today, analysts seem to agree on the centrality of the transference and its interpretation in analytic process and cure, differing only in whether transference is everything or almost everything" (p. 78). Classically, the essence of the analytic process has been the development and resolution through interpretation of the transference neurosis, which may be defined as the reactivation in analysis of the patient's infantile oedipal situation with the analyst in the role of one or both parents.

Psychotherapy of a predominantly expressive nature also deals with strong transferences via interpretation, but in a more limited way (Roskin 1982). There is no attempt to be as pervasive or ambitious as in psychoanalysis. Those transference dispositions most closely related to the presenting problems are the focus of the interpretive effort. Also, the curative factors stem from forces other than interpretation alone (Chessick 1981). Wallerstein (1986) stressed, however, that on the basis of his research these distinctions between psychoanalysis and expressive psychotherapy are blurred in practice.

The therapist must be careful to avoid a "blaming" approach to transference interpretation. All a patient's observations about the therapist are not distortions. The patient may be responding to the therapist's real behaviors or attitudes, so the therapist must engage in ongoing self-scrutiny to sort out what is transference and what is the real contribution of the therapist to the interaction (Cooper 1987; Hoffman and Gill 1988). Attention to countertransference is the cornerstone of all treatment in dynamic psychiatry.

In therapies designed primarily to be supportive, the therapist is involved in the same process of monitoring transference developments and countertransference responses. The transference is noted inwardly but is usually not addressed or interpreted to the patient. The treatment goal in doing so is often to evoke a positive dependent transference without analyzing it (Wallerstein 1986). This transference attachment is the mechanism of the "transference cure," whereby the patient gets better to please the therapist. Although changes derived from this model have traditionally been disparaged as inferior to those stemming from conflict resolution, research (Horwitz 1974; Wallerstein 1986) suggests that they are, in fact, stable and lasting.

Resistance

As noted in Chapter 1, resistance involves the emergence of the patient's characterological defenses within the therapeutic situation. In the more expressive therapies, analyzing and understanding resistance is part of the daily bread-and-butter work of the therapist. If, for example, the patient is consistently late to sessions or consistently silent during them, therapists may regard these resistances with interest and curiosity rather than devalue them as defiant and willful behavior. Resistances are not met with proscriptions or censure. Instead, the therapist enlists the patient's help in understanding the origins of the resistance and then addresses the resistance with interpretation.

Resistance related to transference issues is referred to as transference resistance. This involves interferences with the therapeutic work deriving from transference feelings or misperceptions. For example, a patient may feel unable to talk about masturbatory fantasies because he is convinced that his therapist disapproves of masturbation. To prevent receiving a negative judgment from the therapist, the patient therefore chooses to remain silent. In the parlance of object relations theory, a transference resistance may be understood as the patient's unconscious tendency to cling tenaciously to a particular internal object relationship. This may manifest itself as a therapeutic stalemate in which the therapist is repeatedly related to as someone else.

In Chapter 2 we noted the different perspective on resistance that is held by the self psychologists. They regard resistances as healthy psychic activities that safeguard the growth of the self (Kohut 1984). Rather than interpret them, they empathize with the patient's need for them. This view is in keeping with their concern that the classical approach of pursuing the content beneath resistance has moralistic overtones. However, this empathic approach has led some analysts to regard the self psychological technique as fundamentally supportive. It should also be noted that classical analytic technique does not include insensitive "attacks" on resistance, but rather patient understanding and examination.

As implied by the previous comments about self psychology, resistance is viewed as essential and adaptive in the context of predominantly supportive psychotherapy. Resistances are often manifestations of defensive structures that need to be bolstered as part of therapy. The therapist might even encourage resistance by pointing out to the patient that certain matters are too upsetting to discuss and should be postponed until a more auspicious moment. Similarly, delay mechanisms may be reinforced in the interest of supporting a weakened ego beset by impulses. When a patient's actions usurp verbalization of painful feelings, as in acting out, the therapist may be forced to set limits on self-destructive behavior rather than to interpret the resistance to talking, as in expressive treatment. This limit-setting may involve hospitalization or insistence that the patient turn over illegal drugs to the therapist.

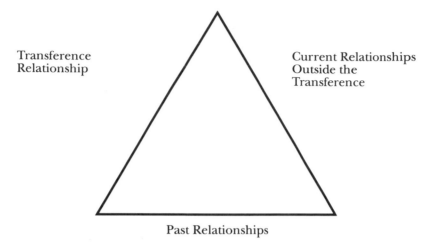

Figure 4-1.   Triangle of insight (modeled after K. Menninger, 1958).

Working Through

Interpretations delivered by the expressive therapist rarely result in "Aha!" responses and dramatic cures. Typically, they are warded off by the forces of resistance and require frequent repetition by the therapist in different contexts. This repetitive interpretation of transference and resistance until the insight has become fully integrated into the patient's conscious awareness is known as "working through." Although the therapist's efforts are necessary, the patient does part of the work of accepting and integrating the therapist's insights between the actual therapy sessions (Karasu 1977). The triangle of insight (Menninger 1958) is a useful conceptual model for the process of working through (see Figure 4-1). Over the course of therapy, the therapist notes a certain pattern 1) in the patient's outside relationships and then links it to 2) transference patterns and to 3) antecedent relationships with family members. Eventually, the patient makes these unconscious linkages conscious. This model is related to what Luborsky (1984) referred to as the core conflictual relationship theme (CCRT). This theme usually involves a wish or a need (e.g., "I want to be spontaneous with others") that is in conflict with the control function of the ego or superego (e.g., "If I try, though, I may lose control, and therefore it's better to not even try"). This theme can be tracked throughout the course of therapy as it relates to the three sides of the triangle, and it can be pointed out to the patient each time it appears. As the patient sees the pattern come up again and again in new contexts, it becomes less alien, and the patient gains greater ego mastery over it.

This same model can be restated in terms of object relations theory. A recurrent self-object-affect constellation appears in the transference, in current extratransference relationships, and in memories of past relationships. In self psychological terms, the pattern may be the expectation of mirroring or the need to idealize others. Regardless of which theoretical model is employed, however, all schools of thought view the reexperiencing of this central relationship pattern in the transference as critically important to a positive outcome. This working-through process is applied almost exclusively to treatments with a significant expressive component—it is rarely used to characterize primarily supportive processes.

Use of Dreams

In psychoanalysis and highly expressive forms of therapy, the interpretation of dreams is valued as "the royal road" to an understanding of the unconscious (Freud 1900, p. 608). The patient's associations to the dream elements are used to understand the latent or hidden content of the dream that lies behind the manifest or overt content. The symbols of the dream can then be interpreted to help the patient further understand the unconscious issues in the dream.

In psychotherapies on the supportive end of the continuum, the therapist listens carefully to the patient's dream and thinks about it in the same way as would an expressive therapist. However, the therapist limits interpretive efforts to "upward interpretations" (Werman 1978, p. 83) that help the patient associate the dream with conscious feelings and attitudes toward the therapist as a real person and to other reality situations in waking life. Free association to the dream is not encouraged because it might lead to further regression.

In between the supportive and expressive ends of the continuum, there is room for selective dream interpretation in which the therapist relates the dream to conscious or unconscious issues in a limited sector of the patient's psychological life. The focus is more on the psychological surface than on the depths of the unconscious and is geared to the specific goals of the psychotherapy (Werman 1978).

Therapeutic Alliance

As already stated, the patient's relationship to the therapist is a mixture of a transference relationship and a real relationship. This latter relationship has been termed the therapeutic alliance (Zetzel 1956) or the working alliance (Greenson 1965). Freud (1912a) originally described this aspect of the treatment as a component of transference that "is admissible to consciousness and unobjectionable...and is the vehicle of success in psychoanalysis exactly as it is in other methods of treatment" (p. 105). He was aware that patients were unlikely to be able to use interpretations unless a proper rapport had been established (Freud 1913). Greenson (1965) later noted that a number of analytic stalemates were produced by the analyst's failure to address the development of the working alliance, which he defined as "the relatively nonneurotic, rational rapport which the patient has with his analyst" (p. 202).

After intensively studying Freud's notes from his work with the "Rat Man," Lipton (1977) was impressed by the real, cordial relationship that Freud maintained with patients. This warm and genuine relationship formed an envelope outside psychoanalytic technique within which the treatment process unfolded. Lipton argued that the silent, constricted model of the analyst, which has come to be termed *classical*, is a serious distortion of the way Freud actually practiced.

Major research efforts on the therapeutic alliance have confirmed its influence on the process and outcome of psychotherapy (Frieswyk et al. 1986; Hartley and Strupp 1983; Horwitz 1974; Luborsky et al. 1980; Marziali et al. 1981). Much of this research points to the strength of the therapeutic alliance as a dominant factor in the outcome of a broad range of therapies (Bordin 1979; Hartley and Strupp 1983; Luborsky et al. 1980). These studies also suggest that the nature of the therapeutic alliance in the opening phase of psychotherapy is perhaps the best predictor of the outcome of that therapy.

One application of this extensive research is that in all psychotherapies, regardless of their point on the expressive-supportive continuum, therapists must attend early on to the establishment and maintenance of the therapeutic alliance. This focus does not require the formation of a positive transference that will not allow the expression of negative feelings. Rather, therapists must help their patients quickly identify their treatment goals and then must ally themselves with the healthy aspects of their patients' egos that are striving to reach those goals. Patients will then experience their therapists as collaborators who are working *with* them rather than *against* them. When negative transference feelings enter the process, they can be examined in the context of the therapeutic alliance rather than be allowed to disrupt treatment. When working more supportively with patients with fragile egos, therapists find that the alliance is more difficult to develop and maintain (Gabbard et al. 1988; Horwitz 1974). The borderline patient's chaotic transference reactions, for example, interfere with the formation of an alliance, and it is a major therapeutic accomplishment for the patient to eventually be able to perceive the therapist as a helpful person collaborating on common goals (Adler 1979).

Mechanisms of Change

The mechanism of change in the more expressive forms of psychotherapy is one of the most controversial issues in the field. Much of
the debate revolves around whether change results from the judicious use of explanatory interpretations or from the therapeutic
relationship itself (Hamilton 1988). The classical view is that change
depends on intrapsychic conflict resolution in response to accurate
interpretations, specifically transference interpretations (Strachey
1934). In this model, the therapist interprets the patient's id impulses and wishes toward the therapist and the defenses against
them. Ultimately, the patient realizes that these feelings are really
directed toward figures from childhood, not the analyst. Hostile
feelings toward the analyst are tamed by modification of the superego and expansion of the ego.

The last two decades have seen a gradual but profound shift
in thinking away from the classical model toward an object rela-
tions/interpersonal model emphasizing the internalization of the
relationship with the therapist (Cooper 1988). This shift was anticipated by the seminal work of Loewald (1956-57), who compared
analysis to a re-parenting process in which the child internalizes
aspects of the parent. Much of this trend is also related to the
renewed interest in the work of the British School on this side of the
Atlantic. Ogden's (1979) conceptualization of projective identification (discussed in Chapter 2) is influenced by Bion's (1962) notion
that the therapist serves as a container for the projections of the
patient in the same way as the mother serves that function for her
infant. This container model involves a "holding" function
(Winnicott 1965) for the therapist that again has a correlate in the
mother-infant relationship. By allowing the infant to be irritable,
demanding, or fussy, or by letting the infant coo, sleep, feed, and so
forth, the mother affords her child an opportunity to work through
instinctual experience and to sort out diametrically opposed feelings (Winnicott 1986). Similarly, this holding function allows the
therapist to process the projected material and return it in modified
form to the patient, who then reintrojects slightly different self- and
object-representations. Ogden (1988) has clarified that this process
actually results in a change in the interactional mode between
therapist and patient, such that patient and treater generate a new
way of experiencing old psychological contents.

Although the internalization of the therapist and the therapeutic relationship is widely recognized as a mechanism of change
in psychoanalysis and expressive forms of psychotherapy (Epstein
1979; Khan 1987; Modell 1976; Winnicott 1965), Adler (1982)
pointed out that the same process is a principal mechanism of
change in supportive psychotherapies. Pine (1976) has suggested

that the auxiliary ego function performed by the therapist is ultimately internalized and assumed by the patient. In the vast majority of therapies, as Luborsky (1984) has suggested, change occurs partly from expressive or interpretive mechanisms and partly from supportive mechanisms deriving from the relationship.

Wallerstein's (1986) research has shed a good deal of light on the underlying mechanisms of cure in noninterpretive supportive approaches. The transference cure connected with the unanalyzed positive dependent transference has already been mentioned. One variant is the "therapeutic lifer" (pp. 690–691), who loses the gains if termination is attempted but who can be sustained at a high level of functioning as long as contact with the therapist continues indefinitely. Many patients are able to reduce the contacts to once a month or less but are prone to decompensate if there is any talk of termination. Another supportive mechanism of cure is "transfer of the transference" (p. 692), in which the positive dependency in the therapeutic relationship is transferred to another person, usually a spouse. Yet another mechanism is termed "the antitransference cure" (p. 693) and involves change through defiance and acting out against the therapist. Still other patients in Wallerstein's sample changed via a narrowly defined variant of the corrective emotional experience in which the patient's transference behavior was met by the therapist with steady concern and neutrality. This mechanism, of course, is related to the re-parenting model or the internalization of the relationship model. Finally, some patients appear to benefit from a supportive treatment geared to giving direct nonjudgmental advice. Wallerstein termed this process "reality testing and re-education" (p. 694).

Indications

Before considering the indications for weighting a psychotherapy process toward the expressive or supportive end of the continuum, therapists must understand that predicting who will respond to what form of psychotherapy is an uncertain business at best. There is some indication in the literature that healthier patients tend to do better in psychotherapy than more severely ill patients (i.e., the rich get richer [Luborsky et al. 1980]). The strength of the therapeutic or helping alliance in the first session or two may be the best predictor of eventual outcome, according to empirical research on the subject (Morgan et al. 1982). However, this variable is greatly affected by the nature of the patient-therapist match, which is almost impossible to quantify. Kantrowitz (1987), in a study of 22 analytic patients, concluded that even with sophisticated psychological testing, one cannot reliably predict suitability for psychoanalysis.

Despite these caveats, it is nevertheless possible to outline patient characteristics that can help clinicians decide whether a predominantly expressive or predominantly supportive focus is indicated (see Table 4-2). Indications for a highly expressive modality, such as psychoanalysis, include: 1) a strong motivation to understand oneself, 2) suffering that interferes with life to such an extent that it becomes an incentive for the patient to endure the rigors of treatment, 3) the ability not only to regress and give up control of feelings and thoughts but also to quickly regain control and reflect on that regression (regression in the service of the ego) (Greenson 1967), 4) tolerance for frustration, 5) a capacity for insight or psychological mindedness, 6) intact reality testing, 7) meaningful and enduring object relations, 8) reasonably good impulse control, and 9) ability to sustain a job (Bachrach and Leaff 1978). The ability to think in terms of metaphor and analogy, where one set of circumstances can be grasped as parallel to another, also augurs well for expressive treatment. Finally, reflective responses to trial interpretations during the evaluation period may suggest a suitability for expressive therapy.

Two general indications for supportive psychotherapy are chronic ego weaknesses or defects and regression in a healthy person who is undergoing a severe life crisis (Wallerstein 1986; Werman 1984). The former might include problems such as im-

Table 4-2.　Indications for expressive or supportive emphasis in psychotherapy

Expressive	Supportive
Strong motivation to understand.	Significant ego defects of a chronic nature.
Significant suffering.	Severe life crisis.
Ability to regress in the service of the ego.	Low anxiety tolerance.
Tolerance for frustration.	Poor frustration tolerance.
Capacity for insight (psychological mindedness).	Lack of psychological mindedness.
Intact reality testing.	Poor reality testing.
Meaningful object relations.	Severely impaired object relations.
Good impulse control.	Poor impulse control.
Ability to sustain work.	Low intelligence.
Capacity to think in terms of analogy and metaphor.	Little capacity for self-observation.
Reflective responses to trial interpretations.	Organically based cognitive dysfunction.
	Tenuous ability to form a therapeutic alliance.

paired reality testing, poor impulse control, and poor anxiety tolerance. Organically based cognitive dysfunction and lack of psychological mindedness are other indications for weighting the psychotherapy in a supportive direction. Patients with severe personality
disorders who are prone to a great deal of acting out may also
require supportive measures (Adler 1979; Luborsky 1984). Other
patients who frequently do better with a predominantly supportive
approach are those with seriously impaired object relations and a
tenuous ability to form a therapeutic alliance (Adler 1982). Individuals who are in the midst of a serious life crisis, such as divorce or
death of a spouse or child, or who are affected by a catastrophe such
as a flood or tornado, are rarely suitable for expressive or exploratory approaches because their ego may be overwhelmed by the
recent trauma. After beginning a supportive process, however, these
patients will sometimes shift in an expressive direction.

   Although these indications are focused on the two ends of the
expressive-supportive continuum, most patients will present with a
mixture of indications, some pointing in the expressive direction
while others point toward the supportive end. The therapist must
continually assess how—and when—to be supportive or expressive
as the process proceeds.

Brief Psychotherapy

In the past 20 years there has been a burgeoning interest and
literature on forms of brief psychotherapy derived from psychoanalytic principles. A number of superb texts outline detailed guidelines for clinicians (Budman 1981; Davanloo 1980; Gustafson 1986;
Horowitz et al. 1984; Malan 1976, 1980; Mann 1973; Sifneos 1972).
Also available are several comprehensive review articles that compare and contrast the approaches and attempt to integrate them
(Gustafson 1984; MacKenzie 1988; Ursano and Hales 1986). Despite
the variations and approaches, there are striking areas of consensus
regarding the practice of brief psychotherapy. This brief discussion
will emphasize those points of agreement.

Indications and Contraindications

In many ways the indications for brief dynamic psychotherapy of an
expressive nature parallel those associated with open-ended expressive psychotherapy. Important selection criteria include: 1) the
capacity for insight or psychological mindedness, 2) high levels of
ego functioning, 3) strong motivation to understand oneself beyond
mere symptom relief, 4) the capacity to form in-depth relationships
(particularly an initial alliance with the therapist), and 5) the ability
to tolerate anxiety. An additional point, which is not applicable to

open-ended psychotherapy, is central to selecting patients for brief psychotherapy—namely, the issue of focus. By virtue of its brevity, time-limited psychotherapy must be focal in nature in contrast to the pervasive breadth of psychoanalysis and highly expressive open-ended psychotherapy. Therefore, to proceed with brief therapy, the therapist and patient must identify the dynamic focus for the problem within the first or second evaluation session. Finally, brief therapy may be particularly helpful for relatively healthy individuals going through a developmental transition, such as moving from home, changing jobs, or having a first child.

    Contraindications include the same factors that contraindicate open-ended psychotherapy of an expressive nature, but also encompass other features that might not contraindicate longer-term treatment. If a patient cannot circumscribe the problem to a focal dynamic issue, brief psychotherapy is contraindicated. Personality disorders that are amenable to longer-term expressive approaches cannot be expected to respond to short-term therapy, unless the patient presents with a situational complaint, such as grief, and unless the goals are limited to this temporary complaint (Horowitz et al. 1984). Although some authors exclude chronically phobic or obsessional patients, Davanloo (1980) views patients with such symptoms as highly amenable to his style of brief psychotherapy.

Number of Sessions

Different authors recommend different ways of handling the actual time limit of brief therapy. Mann (1973), who saw an acceptance of limits and a renunciation of magical expectations as central to the therapy process, insisted on a limit of 12 sessions. Davanloo (1980), on the other hand, averaged 15–25 sessions and does not set a specific termination at the beginning of treatment. Although Sifneos (1972) also refused to stipulate a specific number of sessions, his treatments tend to last only 12–16 sessions. As a general rule, then, brief therapy lasts as little as 2–3 months or as long as 5–6 months, and involves a range of 10–20 sessions.

Process of Therapy

Although the techniques associated with open-ended therapy are by and large applicable to brief treatments, their most striking difference is that they are markedly accelerated. Therapists must formulate their central hypothesis more quickly and must proceed to interpret resistances to insight earlier and more aggressively. Authors differ in terms of their degree of confrontation in dealing with resistances, but all acknowledge that the intensity of the process stirs up anxiety. Gustafson (1984) has stressed that confronting resistances requires an *empathic* frame of reference or else the patient will feel attacked. There is also considerable consensus among authors about the critical role played by transference interpretations in producing change. Malan (1976), appropriating Karl Menninger's triangle of insight, suggested that the therapist's primary task is to link the focused complaint to patterns in past relationships, in present relationships, and in the transference. A brief example will illustrate this process.

> Mr. B, a 35-year-old military man, came to therapy with a chief complaint of "I'm too domineering." He had been married for 8 months to his second wife, who he said was already complaining about this character trait as his first wife had. In the second session Mr. B came in and began talking about the softball game he had just left. He disagreed with the umpire's decision to call him out at home plate, but noted, "You don't argue with the umpire. What he says goes. You're asking for trouble if you do." Later in the session he spoke of his father, who was a lieutenant colonel in the army. He described his father as an arbitrary man with whom you could not negotiate. The patient had always believed that his own opinions were not valued by his father. Still later in the session, Mr. B said, "I don't think 12 sessions are enough. But I guess we have to limit it to that. You said so."
>
> At this point the therapist made an intervention that drew together the three sides of the triangle, "It sounds like your experiences with the umpire, your father, and me are all similar—you feel we make arbitrary decisions in which you have no say." The therapist was then able to formulate an interpretation regarding the way the patient treated both his first and second wife. He was turning the passively experienced trauma of being completely dominated by his father into an experience of active mastery with his wife. He dominated her the way his father had dominated him.

Brief Supportive Psychotherapy

There is much less literature on brief psychotherapies of a supportive nature. The primary indication for brief supportive psychotherapy is a relatively healthy person who is undergoing a specific life crisis. The techniques involved are similar to those of long-term supportive psychotherapy, namely, ego building, facilitating the development of a positive transference without interpreting it, and restoring previously adaptive defenses, as illustrated in this example:

> Ms. C, a 52-year-old woman, came for consultation complaining about feelings of guilt and anxiety related to her 23-year-old daughter's out-of-wedlock pregnancy. The psychiatrist listened and empathized with the patient about the difficulty parents have seeing their children turn out differently than expected. The patient ex-

plained that she was so distracted by her guilt and anxiety over the situation that she was unable to function as usual at work or at home. The consultant attempted to restore Ms. C's usual obsessive-compulsive defenses by suggesting that she establish a structured routine at home so that she could accomplish all her usual household duties. He pointed out that staying busy would help Ms. C take her mind off her daughter. Ms. C complied with this suggestion and seemed somewhat improved at the next session. During this meeting the psychiatrist pointed out that Ms. C talked as though her daughter's pregnancy was her own responsibility. The patient responded, "You mean I didn't spread her legs?" The doctor affirmed, "That's right. You didn't spread her legs." The patient experienced a flood of relief with the doctor's words and thanked him for relieving her guilt. She called the following week and said that she need not return since she felt "100 percent better."

　　In this example the psychiatrist first helped the patient restore adaptive defenses by encouraging a return to her usual schedule. He then utilized the patient's positive transference to absolve her of guilt. This absolution from an authority figure whom she regarded with respect, if not idealization, had much greater impact on her than it would have if she had merely told herself the same message.

　　Determining whether to prescribe open-ended or brief psychotherapy is a complex decision. Clearly, the presence or absence of a focal issue is of considerable relevance (Ursano and Dressler 1974). If the patient's complaint is sufficiently circumscribed, a recommendation for brief psychotherapy can put the patient to less expense and less inconvenience. However, complicated characterological problems may interfere with a patient's effective implementation of any "quick-fix" approach. Moreover, there is always a danger of therapists prescribing what they think the patient needs rather than what the patient wants. Is the patient asking for a fundamental examination and restructuring of personality, or is the request limited to assistance with one specific problem or complaint? The patient must clearly be a collaborator in determining the kind of treatment. We would be well advised to remember the dictum attributed to Freud that in some way the patient is always right.

The Application of Theory to Technique

In Chapter 3, the role of theory in the development of an explanatory formulation was discussed. As the clinician moves from a psychodynamic assessment to psychodynamic psychotherapy, the process of tentative hypothesis formation continues. The application of theory to clinical material and to technique becomes increasingly complex, however, as more and more data enter the picture.

The greatest danger is that the therapist, faced with a plethora of contradictory bits of information, will begin to organize the data by rigidly applying stereotyped theoretical formulations. All schools of thought are guilty of this tendency from time to time, as are all clinicians. To avoid this stereotyped approach, Peterfreund (1983) advocated a *heuristic* approach to the patient's verbalizations, which he defined as initiating and fostering "a process whereby patient and therapist work together to learn, discover, and understand as much as possible about the individual patient" (p. 2). The heuristic therapist does not pose as the bearer of truth who will impart it to the patient at the appropriate time. Heuristic therapists conceptualize themselves instead as barely a step ahead of the patient—a collaborator with the patient in a joint discovery of truth.

Therapists who listen carefully, without pretending to know a priori the appropriate theoretical formulation to explain the patient's psychopathology, must tolerate long periods of ambiguity wherein the etiology and pathogenesis of the patient's problems may seem puzzling. As therapists get to know their patients better, the clinical picture may or may not fit neatly into the model of self psychology, object relations theory, or ego psychology. To understand and help their patients, therapists may have to borrow bits and pieces from various theoretical models or may have to shift flexibly between models.

Wallerstein (1988) has stressed that the clinician must first and foremost address the clinical interaction with the patient in the here and now. The patient's repetition of the past in the present transference relationship does not necessarily require an extensive metapsychological model for purposes of explanation and understanding. All our theories are essentially *metaphors* that help us master the daily chaos of countertransference and ambiguity. Theory must never become our master.

Implicit in the heuristic approach to psychotherapy is acknowledgment of one's own fallibility in the therapeutic role and a special sensitivity to the patient's resistance. Whether or not we appreciate it, the patient is always "supervising" us. If a particular patient is consistently unable to make use of a particular line of interpretations, the therapist should examine the "goodness of fit" between the theoretical model and the patient's clinical picture. Rather than labeling the patient's responses to interpretations as resistance and subtly blaming the patient by repeatedly pointing out the resistance, the therapist might do far better to reconsider the theoretical model. The therapist who carefully follows the patient's lead will be able to shift approaches on a trial-and-error basis as more is learned about the patient.

Mr. D, a young professional man in expressive-supportive psychotherapy, was reacting negatively to having to change his session from

Wednesday to Thursday. He told his therapist that he felt devalued by the change in appointment times, as though he were not as important as other people on the therapist's schedule. The therapist, postulating that the patient was reexperiencing the sibling rivalry of childhood, wondered aloud if the patient might be reexperiencing a childhood feeling that his siblings got preferential treatment. The patient responded matter-of-factly that he could not relate to what the therapist had said. Mr. D reported that as a child he had been highly valued. He said that his parents had tended to treat him as if he was another parent managing the younger siblings. In fact, he often thought of himself as "the king." The therapist filed this piece of "supervision" away, until the next session, when the patient reported problems at work with his boss. This time, the therapist stayed closer to the patient's experience and offered a comment from an empathic self psychological framework, "It must hurt when your boss does not treat you like 'the king,' as your parents did." Mr. D wept in response to this comment and then opened up further about his childhood experiences, particularly the terrible burden he felt on being expected to be a parent to his siblings. He ended the session by saying that he felt understood by his therapist.

No therapy is completely free from theoretical bias. The best we can hope for is to be alert to these biases and to allow our patients to lead us into whatever theoretical domain provides the best explanation for each patient. Hypotheses are proved and disproved repeatedly as the process goes on, and the wise therapist is always eager to learn more about the human condition.

The Efficacy of Psychotherapy

The efficacy of individual psychotherapy is no longer in question. There is now overwhelming evidence that psychotherapy is an effective treatment (Luborsky et al. 1975; Smith et al. 1980). In a recent review of psychotherapy studies (Lambert et al. 1986), the authors demonstrated that the typical person seeking psychotherapy will be better off at the end of the treatment than will 80 percent of all the persons with the same problems who go untreated; this figure is in the same range as that found in comparable studies of antidepressant medications. Studies have also suggested that the changes produced by psychotherapeutic measures are lasting. Husby (1985), for example, replicated Malan's work on brief therapy and found that dynamic changes produced by treatment were still present at 5-year follow-up.

Despite this abundant evidence regarding efficacy, vexing questions remain. Studies that have compared one form of psychotherapy to another have yet to show any major advantages of one technique over another. Whether nonspecific factors involving the therapeutic relationship or the match between patient and therapist are more important than specific factors of technique is still unknown. Much of the difficulty is related to the extraordinary complexity of psychotherapy research. Between-group experimental designs analogous to those used in psychopharmacology studies run the risk of overlooking the trees because of the forest. In other words, the need for large group comparisons to gain sufficient statistical power blurs the individual factors in a given patient-therapist dyad that may be compellingly significant in determining what specific kind of patient will benefit from what specific kind of intervention (Barlow and Beck 1984).

When one adds the question of the relative benefits of pharmacotherapy versus psychotherapy, the complexity increases exponentially. Elkin et al. (1988) outlined some of the major problems in such comparisons: 1) the length of psychotherapy and drug treatment are often quite different; 2) although it is relatively simple to construct a placebo design in pharmacotherapy research, to do so in psychotherapy research presents a formidable problem; 3) relationship issues inherent in the prescribing of medication are difficult to standardize—one could argue that effective medication prescription requires supportive psychotherapeutic interventions; and 4) the patient's expectation of receiving a certain form of treatment may influence that patient's ability to benefit from treatment.

Another problem in comparing pharmacotherapy and psychotherapy is the conceptualization of them as "either-or" choices. The two forms of treatment actually complement each other by working at different levels on different aspects of the illness (Karasu 1984). This synergism will be discussed at greater length in Chapter 5.

Because the between-group comparison method of psychotherapy research is fraught with problems, there has been increasing interest in recent years in intensively studying the psychotherapy process within an individual case (Gabbard et al. 1988; Rice and Greenberg 1984). This approach emphasizes the measurable changes in the patient and their connection with the therapist's interventions. Process research begins from the premise that psychotherapy is effective. What it seeks to learn is how psychotherapy is effective within the limited framework of a single patient-therapist dyad.

References

Adler G: The myth of the alliance with borderline patients. Am J Psychiatry 47:642–645, 1979

Adler G: Supportive psychotherapy revisited. Hillside J Clin Psychiatry 4:3–3, 1982

Bachrach HM, Leaff LA: "Analyzability": a systematic review of the clinical and quantitative literature. J Am Psychoanal Assoc 26:881–920, 1978

Barlow DH, Beck JG: The psychosocial treatment of anxiety disorders: current status, future directions, in Psychotherapy Research: Where Are We and Where Should We Go? Edited by Williams JBW, Spitzer RL. New York, Guilford Press, 1984

Basch MF: Doing Psychotherapy. New York, Basic Books, 1980

Bion WR: Learning From Experience. New York, Basic Books, 1962

Bordin ES: The generalizability of the psychoanalytic concept of the working alliance. Psychotherapy: Theory, Research, and Practice 16:252–260, 1979

Budman SH (ed): Forms of Brief Therapy. New York, Guilford Press, 1981

Chessick RD: The Technique and Practice of Intensive Psychotherapy. New York, Jason Aronson, 1974

Chessick RD: What is intensive psychotherapy? Am J Psychother 35:489–501, 1981

Cooper AM: Changes in psychoanalytic ideas: transference interpretation. J Am Psychoanal Assoc 35:77–98, 1987

Cooper AM: Our changing views of the therapeutic action of psychoanalysis: comparing Strachey and Loewald. Psychoanal Q 57:15–27, 1988

Davanloo H (ed): Short-Term Dynamic Psychotherapy. New York, Jason Aronson, 1980

Dewald PA: Psychotherapy: A Dynamic Approach. New York, Basic Books, 1964

Elkin I, Pilkonis P, Docherty J, et al: Conceptual and methodological issues in comparative studies of psychotherapy and pharmacotherapy, I: active ingredients and mechanisms of change. Am J Psychiatry 145:909–917, 1988

Epstein L: Countertransference with borderline patients, in Countertransference. Edited by Epstein L, Feiner AH. New York, Jason Aronson, 1979, pp 375–405

Freud A: The Ego and the Mechanisms of Defense (1936), in The Writings of Anna Freud, Vol 2 (Revised Edition). New York, International Universities Press, 1966

Freud S: The interpretation of dreams (1900), in The Standard Edition of the Complete Psychological Works of Sigmund Freud, Vols 4, 5. Translated and edited by Strachey J. London, Hogarth Press, 1953

Freud S: The dynamics of transference (1912a), in The Standard Edition of the Complete Psychological Works of Sigmund Freud, Vol 12. Translated and edited by Strachey J. London, Hogarth Press, 1958, pp 97–108

Freud S: Recommendations to physicians practising psycho-analysis (1912b), in The Standard Edition of the Complete Psychological Works of Sigmund Freud, Vol 12. Translated and edited by Strachey J. London, Hogarth Press, 1958, pp 109–120

Freud S: On beginning the treatment (1913), in The Standard Edition of the Complete Psychological Works of Sigmund Freud, Vol 12. Translated and edited by Strachey J. London, Hogarth Press, 1958, pp 121–144

Freud S: New introductory lectures on psycho-analysis (1933), in The Standard Edition of the Complete Psychological Works of Sigmund Freud, Vol 22. Translated and edited by Strachey J. London, Hogarth Press, 1964, pp 3–182

Frieswyk SH, Allen JG, Colson DB, et al: Therapeutic alliance: its place as a process and outcome variable in dynamic psychotherapy research. J Consult Clin Psychol 54:32–38, 1986

Fromm-Reichmann F: Principles of Intensive Psychotherapy. Chicago, University of Chicago Press, 1950

Gabbard K, Gabbard GO: Psychiatry and the Cinema. Chicago, University of Chicago Press, 1987

Gabbard GO, Horwitz L, Frieswyk S, et al: The effect of therapist interventions on the therapeutic alliance with borderline patients. J Am Psychoanal Assoc 36:697–727, 1988

Greenson RR: The Technique and Practice of Psychoanalysis, Vol 1. New York, International Universities Press, 1967

Greenson RR: The working alliance and the transference neurosis (1965), in Explorations in Psychoanalysis. New York, International Universities Press, 1978, pp 119–224

Gustafson JP: An integration of brief dynamic psychotherapy. Am J Psychiatry 141:935–944, 1984

Gustafson JP: The Complex Secret of Brief Psychotherapy. New York, WW Norton, 1986

Hamilton NG: Self and Others: Object Relations Theory in Practice. Northvale, NJ, Jason Aronson, 1988

Hartley DE, Strupp HH: The therapeutic alliance: its relationship to outcome in brief psychotherapy, in Empirical Studies of Psychoanalytic Theories, Vol 1. Edited by Masling J. Hillside, NJ, Analytic Press, 1983, pp 1–37

Hoffman IZ, Gill MM: Critical reflections on a coding scheme. Int J Psychoanal 69:55–64, 1988

Horowitz M, Marmar C, Krupnick J, et al: Personality Styles and Brief Psychotherapy. New York, Basic Books, 1984

Horwitz L: Clinical Prediction in Psychotherapy. New York, Jason Aronson, 1974

Husby R: Short-term dynamic psychotherapy, IV: comparison of recorded changes in 33 neurotic patients 2 and 5 years after end of treatment. Psychother Psychosom 43:23–27, 1985

Kantrowitz JL: Suitability for psychoanalysis. Yearbook of Psychoanalysis and Psychotherapy 2:403–415, 1987

Kantrowitz JL, Katz AL, Paolitto F et al: Changes in the level and quality of object relations in psychoanalysis: followup of a longitudinal, prospective study. J Am Psychoanal Assoc 35:23–46, 1987

Karasu TB: Psychotherapies: an overview. Am J Psychiatry 134:851–863, 1977

Karasu TB: Politics, practice, and p value in psychotherapy, in Psychotherapy Research: Where Are We and Where Should We Go?

Edited by Williams JBW, Spitzer RL. New York, Guilford Press, 1984, pp 372–382

Katz JB: A psychoanalyst's anonymity: fiddler behind the couch. Bull Menninger Clin 42:520–524, 1978

Khan MMR: Introduction, in Holding and Interpretation: Fragment of an Analysis, by Winnicott DW. New York, Grove Press, 1987, pp 1–18

Kohut H: How Does Analysis Cure? Edited by Goldberg A. Chicago, University of Chicago Press, 1984

Lambert MJ, Shapiro DA, Bergin AE: The effectiveness of psychotherapy, in Handbook of Psychotherapy and Behavior Change, 3rd Edition. Edited by Garfield SL, Bergin AE. New York, Wiley, 1986, pp 157–211

Lipton SD: The advantages of Freud's technique as shown in his analysis of the Rat Man. Int J Psychoanal 58:255–273, 1977

Loewald HW: On the therapeutic action of psychoanalysis (1956-57), in Papers on Psychoanalysis. New Haven, Yale University Press, 1980, pp 221–256

Luborsky L: Principles of Psychoanalytic Psychotherapy: A Manual for Supportive-Expressive Treatment. New York, Basic Books, 1984

Luborsky L, Singer B, Luborsky L: Comparative studies of psychotherapies: is it true that "everyone has won and all must have prizes"? Arch Gen Psychiatry 32:995–1008, 1975

Luborsky L, Mintz J, Auerbach A, et al: Predicting the outcome of psychotherapy: findings of the Penn Psychotherapy Project. Arch Gen Psychiatry 37:471–481, 1980

MacKenzie KR: Recent developments in brief psychotherapy. Hosp Community Psychiatry 39:742–752, 1988

Malan DH: The Frontier of Brief Psychotherapy: An Example of the Convergence of Research and Clinical Practice. New York, Plenum, 1976

Malan DH: Toward the Validation of Dynamic Psychotherapy: A Replication. New York, Plenum, 1980

Mann J: Time-Limited Psychotherapy. Cambridge, Harvard University Press, 1973

Marziali E, Marmar C, Krupnick J: Therapeutic alliance scales: development and relationship to psychotherapy outcome. Am J Psychiatry 138:361–364, 1981

Menninger KA: Theory of Psychoanalytic Technique. New York, Basic Books, 1958

Modell AH: "The holding environment" and the therapeutic action of psychoanalysis. J Am Psychoanal Assoc 24:285–307, 1976

Morgan R, Luborsky L, Crits-Christoph P, et al: Predicting the outcomes of psychotherapy by the Penn Helping Alliance Rating Method. Arch Gen Psychiatry 39:397–402, 1982

Ogden TH: On projective identification. Int J Psychoanal 60:357–373, 1979

Ogden TH: Projective Identification and Psychotherapeutic Technique. New York, Jason Aronson, 1982

Ogden TH: On the dialectical structure of experience: some clinical and theoretical implications. Contemporary Psychoanalysis 24:17–45, 1988

Ornstein A: "Supportive" psychotherapy: a contemporary view. Clinical Social Work Journal 14:14–30, 1986

Peterfreund E: The Process of Psychoanalytic Therapy: Models and Strategies. Hillsdale, NJ, Analytic Press, 1983

Pine F: On therapeutic change: perspectives from a parent-child model. Psychoanalysis and Contemporary Science 5:537–569, 1976

Pine F: Supportive psychotherapy: a psychoanalytic perspective. Psychiatric Annals 16:526–529, 1986

Racker H: Transference and Counter-transference. New York, International Universities Press, 1968

Rice LN, Greenberg LS: Patterns of Change: Intensive Analysis of Psychotherapy Process. New York, Guilford Press, 1984

Roskin G: Changing modes of psychotherapy. Journal of Psychiatric Treatment and Evaluation 4:483–487, 1982

Roth S: Psychotherapy: The Art of Wooing Nature. Northvale, NJ, Jason Aronson, 1987

Sandler J: Countertransference and role-responsiveness. International Review Psychoanalysis 3:43–47, 1976

Sifneos PE: Short-Term Psychotherapy and Emotional Crisis. Cambridge, Harvard University Press, 1972

Smith ML, Glass GV, Miller TI: The Benefits of Psychotherapy. Baltimore, Johns Hopkins University Press, 1980

Strachey J: The nature of the therapeutic action of psycho-analysis. Int J Psychoanal 15:127–159, 1934

Ursano RJ, Dressler DM: Brief vs. long-term psychotherapy: a treatment decision. J Nerv Ment Dis 159:164–171, 1974

Ursano RJ, Hales RE: A review of brief individual psychotherapies. Am J Psychiatry 143:1507–1517, 1986

Wallerstein RS: Forty-Two Lives in Treatment: A Study of Psychoanalysis and Psychotherapy. New York, Guilford Press, 1986

Wallerstein RS: One psychoanalysis or many? Int J Psychoanal 69:5–21, 1988

Werman DS: The use of dreams in psychotherapy: practical guidelines. Canadian Psychiatric Association Journal 23:153–158, 1978

Werman DS: The Practice of Supportive Psychotherapy. New York, Brunner/Mazel, 1984

Winnicott DW: The Maturational Processes and the Facilitating Environment: Studies in the Theory of Emotional Development. London, Hogarth Press, 1965

Winnicott DW: Holding and Interpretation: Fragment of an Analysis. New York, Grove Press, 1986

Zetzel ER: Current concepts of transference. Int J Psychoanal 37:369–378, 1956

CHAPTER 5

Treatments in Dynamic Psychiatry II: Group Therapy, Family/Marital Therapy, and Pharmacotherapy

Dynamic Group Psychotherapy

We all live and work in the context of groups. Group psychotherapy provides patients an opportunity to learn how they function in groups—the roles they play, the expectations and unconscious fantasies they harbor about groups, and the obstacles they encounter in getting along with others at work and at home. Unique dimensions of group experience can only be partially explored in individual psychotherapy.

Unique Aspects of Group Experience

Much of our knowledge of the forces operating in groups is derived from the work of Wilfred Bion (1959). After World War II, Bion began conducting small group experiences at the Tavistock Clinic. His understanding of groups revolved around his observation that two groups are present in every group: 1) the "work group" and 2) the "basic assumption group." The former is involved with the actual work task of a group and is geared toward completion of the task. Few groups, however, work rationally toward attaining their goals without interference from basic assumptions (Rioch 1970).

Basic assumptions refer to the unconscious fantasies that lead groups to behave in an "as-if manner" (Rioch 1970). In other words, the group members begin to act on an assumption about the group that is different from the reality of the task at hand. Basic assumptions fall into three categories: dependency, fight/flight, and pairing. These discrete emotional states are unconscious in origin but are easily deducible from the behavior of the group. These assumptions derail the work group and prevent completion of its task. In a psychotherapy group, the task of understanding one another's problems may be steered off course by the development of basic assumptions. However, just as Freud discovered that transference in psychoanalysis is more of a therapeutic tool than an obstacle, Bion discovered that the basic assumptions themselves can be of enormous value in helping individual members of groups understand themselves in the context of the group.

Bion's initial observations of basic assumptions were at a descriptive level, but as he gained more and more experience with group dynamics, he realized that the basic assumptions were clusters of defenses against psychotic anxieties present in everyone. Groups are powerfully regressive, and they provide patients with a window into their most primitive fears. Bion realized that the mechanisms associated with the paranoid-schizoid and depressive positions identified by Melanie Klein (see Chapter 2) were also present in the basic assumptions.

The dependency basic assumption, for example, can be viewed as a cluster of defenses against depressive anxieties (Ganzarain 1980). In this basic assumption, patients behave as though they are weak, ignorant, and incapable of helping each other and as if they are totally dependent on the therapist, whom they view as godlike. The underlying fear is that their greed (i.e., their oral neediness) will engulf the therapist and result in their being abandoned. To defend against the anxiety and guilt connected with their potential destruction of the therapist (i.e., their mother at an unconscious level), the patients believe that the therapist is an inexhaustible, omniscient, and omnipotent figure who will always be there for them and who will always have the answers.

In the fight/flight basic assumption, the group has regressed to a frank paranoid-schizoid position. All "badness" is split off and projected. The wish to fight or take flight is a cluster of defenses against paranoid anxiety. To avoid an externally perceived persecutor who will destroy them, the group can either fight or run from the persecutor. The group becomes nonreflective and views action as the only solution to the perceived threat.

The pairing basic assumption is a cluster of defenses against depressive anxieties. The assumption in this instance frequently revolves around two group members who will reproduce and bring forth a messiah to rescue the group (Rioch 1970). There is a pervasive atmosphere of optimism and hopefulness, a belief that love will prevail. This Pollyannaish attitude may be viewed as a manic defense against the group's concern that destructiveness, hate, and hostility also exist within the group. Hence, in this view pairing can be viewed as a manic reparative effort (Ganzarain 1980).

Group psychotherapists must be continually vigilant for the development of basic assumptions in their groups, so that they can interpret and examine them before they become too destructive to the task of the group. Unexamined transference may lead an individual to quit psychotherapy; unexamined basic assumptions may lead to the dissolution of group therapy.

Beyond the basic assumptions, there are other unique forces operating in groups. One of the most powerful is the phenomenon of "role suction" (Redl 1963). A common observation is that an individual's behavior in a one-to-one situation may change dramatically upon entry to a group. We frequently hear, for example, about a "good boy" who "got in with the wrong crowd." Individuals who find themselves behaving differently in groups often describe themselves as being drawn or "sucked" into playing a role that seemed outside their control. An individual patient in group psychotherapy, for example, may serve as a spokesperson for the entire group, while everyone else remains silent. Another individual may serve in the role of scapegoat, behaving in such a way as to become the target for everyone's anger. Both the spokesperson and the scapegoat phenomena can be understood as group versions of projective identification (Horwitz 1983; Ogden 1982). In scapegoating, for example, the unacceptable parts of all the group members are projected into one individual who then feels coerced into responding like the projected parts of the other patients. If the therapist supports the scapegoat and interprets the group process, the projected parts may be reintrojected.

Characteristics of Psychotherapeutic Groups

Most group therapists meet with their groups once a week (Sadock 1983), although some who model group psychotherapy after classical psychoanalysis (Wolf 1983) may conduct as many as five group sessions a week. The sessions, which adhere to a strict time limit as in individual psychotherapy, usually last from one-and-a-fourth to one-and-a-half hours. Although groups vary in size, the average dynamic psychotherapy group contains 8 to 10 members (Sadock 1983). Smaller groups may be quite useful, provided that the members actively participate and are reasonably verbal.

The composition of a dynamic therapy group may vary considerably, although heterogeneous groups are thought to have advantages over homogeneous groups (Yalom 1985). The consensus of clinicians is that groups in which everyone is similar rarely get beyond superficial levels of interaction. On the other hand, if a group is too heterogeneous, it may be dysfunctional because of the lack of common ground among the patients. Moreover, certain individuals may feel isolated if they believe that they are vastly different from everyone else in the group by virtue of their age, cultural background, or socioeconomic status. Finally, if members of the group have highly variable levels of ego strength, the group may not "gel" because of the difficulty in exploring psychological issues.

The consensus of the literature is that dynamic therapy groups should be heterogeneous in terms of the conflicts of the members but homogeneous in terms of a reasonably similar level of ego strength (Whitaker and Lieberman 1964; Yalom 1985). Most of the dynamic group psychotherapy literature is weighted toward the expressive end of the expressive-supportive continuum. Groups that are more supportive in nature may be more homogeneous as well. A good example of such a group is the supportive group approach often used in the treatment of schizophrenic patients (see Chapter 7). Dynamic therapy groups are typically open-ended, and new members may be added as old members terminate. However, some homogeneous groups with a focal issue to discuss, such as victims of therapist-patient sexual abuse (Sonne 1989), may meet for a time-limited therapy process.

Dynamic group psychotherapists vary in the extent to which they use a group-centered versus an individual-centered approach. In the individual-centered form of group therapy (Wolf 1983), the process is conceptualized as similar to individual psychoanalysis in a group setting. The group process itself is relatively less important than interpretation of the individual's difficulties in dealing with the other group members and with the therapist. The more extreme advocates of the group-centered approach (Ezriel 1950) have viewed the interpretation of group forces as much more important than the interpretation of the individual's conflicts. In fact, Ezriel (1950) suggested that the therapist should refrain from interpretation until a common group tension or theme has developed. A less extreme approach was advocated by Horwitz (1977), who proposed that individual interpretations may be used in the service of building up the group's awareness of a common group issue, which is then also interpreted. There are common group experiences that everyone shares and that deserve interpretation, such as not having all one's needs met by the leader, competition for support, and anxiety about being ignored. However, if there is no focus on individual issues as well, patients may feel that their individual reasons for seeking treatment have been overlooked by the therapist. Most group therapists today ascribe to a combined model involving both individual- and group-centered interventions (Slipp 1988).

Transference, Countertransference, and Resistance

Transference, countertransference, and resistance are cornerstones of dynamic group psychotherapy, just as they are in individual work. However, the group modality itself significantly alters the transference. First, the intensity of the patients' transferences may be diluted by their redirection to fellow patients. This displacement of the transference from therapist to peer may be beneficial, however, as it allows a "practice ground" for working through a parental transference prior to its development in the relationship with the therapist (Wolf 1983). Group psychotherapy also allows for the formation of multiple transferences. The therapist then is provided with a laboratory where the patients' internal object relations are displayed for all to see through externalization in relationships with individual group members. Although different transferences develop in individual therapy as well, they tend to appear over a longer period. The group setting may allow the therapist to gain a greater familiarity with the patients' internal object relations in a much shorter time.

Although transference may be diluted in group therapy, the converse is also true. Transference may be intensified when the entire group is swept up with powerful feelings of either positive or negative valence. Therapists who serve as containers for all the bad object projections in the group members rapidly realize that countertransference may also be intensified in a group setting. The countertransferential demands on the group therapist may be formidable. Fortunately, there is built-in protection against untoward countertransference acting out because group patients will readily spot inappropriate behavior or misperceptions on the part of the therapist and insist on an explanation (Wolf 1983). To diffuse transference and countertransference, some therapists prefer to work with a co-therapist in group psychotherapy. Having a partner helps the therapist to process the intense feelings stirred up by the group.

Sibling rivalry and a transference wish to be the therapist's only or favorite child is a common development in all dynamic therapies. However, these issues may have a more compelling quality in group therapy, and the therapist must diligently avoid showing any favoritism for specific group members (Yalom 1985).

In addition to the patients' transference to the therapist and to other group members, there is a third form of transference that is truly unique to groups—transference to the group as a whole. This form of transference affords patients an opportunity to examine their expectations of other groups with which they live and work. The group as a total entity is often viewed as an idealized, completely gratifying "mother" that will satisfy the patient's yearning for a reunion with an unconditionally loving figure. In recognition of this tendency, Scheidlinger (1974) dubbed this phenomenon the "mother-group." When this form of transference is in full flower, the therapist may be viewed as a terrifying maternal figure in contrast to the all-giving benevolence of the group as a whole. Other authors

(Gibbard and Hartman 1973) have viewed the idealized transference to the group as a whole as a defensive posture that avoids seeing the group (mother) as sadistic.

The working through of transference and resistance constitutes the bulk of the dynamic therapist's task, much as it does in individual psychotherapy. Indeed, Ganzarain (1983) suggested that working through is the key characteristic that distinguishes psychoanalytic group therapy from other forms of group treatment. He particularly emphasized the working through of primitive psychotic-like anxieties and their associated defense mechanisms. The regressive forces activated by group experience bring the patient in touch with anxiety stemming from the paranoid-schizoid and depressive positions much more rapidly and more profoundly than in individual treatment. The working through of transference is also facilitated by the input of other group members. An individual patient may attempt to validate a personal impression of the therapist by "checking it out" with other group patients. When peers confront the distortions inherent in the transference perception, the patient may be much more willing to listen and accept feedback than when it is provided by the therapist.

Indications and Contraindications

A number of indications for dynamic group psychotherapy are the same as those for expressive-supportive individual therapy. These include: 1) strong motivation, 2) psychological mindedness, 3) a reasonably high level of ego strength, 4) sufficient discomfort that the patient is willing to endure the frustrations inherent in the process, and 5) problems in interpersonal relationships (Yalom 1985). However, the question that the clinician must address is: What specific criteria suggest that a patient is particularly suited for group psychotherapy rather than individual psychotherapy?

There are several kinds of problems that may be dealt with more effectively in a group setting than in individual treatment (Sadock 1983). The patient who is extraordinarily anxious around authority figures may find it easier to talk and relate in the company of peers. A patient whose primary problem seems to have originated in sibling conflicts may find that a group setting reactivates the problem in a way that makes it easier to examine and resolve. Conversely, sometimes an only child who missed out on a sibling experience and who has difficulty learning to share in adult life may find that a group is the best place to address those issues. Nonpsychotic patients who rely heavily on projection may benefit from the confrontations of other group members, who repeatedly dispute the distortions brought to the group. Borderline patients who form an intensely negative transference in individual therapy may benefit from the dilution of transference inherent in group work. However, these patients almost always require individual therapy as well (see Chapter 14).

Group therapy is generally effective for patients with higher-level personality disorders, including hysterical, obsessive-compulsive, some narcissistic, passive-aggressive, and dependent types, because a group setting may be the only place in which these patients receive feedback about how their character patterns affect others. Much of the psychopathology found in personality disordered patients involves ego-syntonic character traits (i.e., behaviors that distress others but not the patient). The feedback from peers in group therapy often helps these patients reflect about their behavior patterns so that they eventually become ego-dystonic (i.e., uncomfortable to the patients themselves), which is the first step in gaining sufficient motivation to change. The effect of group psychotherapy on particular personality disorders and the indications for combined individual and group therapy will be further addressed in Section III.

One obvious difference between individual and group psychotherapy in assessing indications is that the group therapist must constantly evaluate the fit between a prospective patient and the group as it is currently composed. One borderline patient may be quite tolerable in a group of patients with a high level of ego strength, but two may overwhelm the group with disproportionate demands for attention and disruptive acting out. Similarly, issues such as age and gender must be balanced when deciding on indications for a particular group.

Certain clinical symptomatology is consensually viewed as contraindicating dynamic group psychotherapy. These features include: 1) low motivation, 2) psychotic disorganization, 3) addiction to substances, 4) antisocial personality disorder, 5) severe somatization, 6) organically based cognitive dysfunction, and 7) serious suicide risk (Yalom 1985). Addicts and patients with antisocial features may, however, be effectively treated in homogeneous groups of a confrontational nature (see Chapters 11 and 16). As is the case with indications, some patients may be contraindicated for a particular group because of the composition of that group, but might instead be suitable for a different group.

Family and Marital Therapy

Although many family and marital therapists practicing today are not dynamically oriented, the field had its origins in the work of a number of early psychoanalytically oriented clinicians, including

Theodore Lidz, Lyman Wynne, Nathan Ackerman, Murray Bowen, and Virginia Satir. The focus of these early family therapists on the psychology of the individual was dramatically altered in the decades of the 1950s and 1960s by a group of Palo Alto researchers, including Gregory Bateson, Don Jackson, and Jay Haley (1956). Systemic family therapy grew out of the work of this group, and with it the emphasis shifted from the individual to the family system. Individual psychopathology and personal history both became secondary to the family as a whole, which was viewed as a system with a life of its own. Until recently, this systemic approach to family therapy, along with its subsequent elaborations by Minuchin (1974) and Selvini Palazzoli et al. (1978), has largely dominated the field of family therapy.

Bowen family therapy has grown increasingly popular in recent years. This approach is rooted in psychoanalytic theory, but the technique that has evolved from the ideas of Bowen (1978) is largely nondynamic. In this form of treatment, one individual family member meets with the therapist on an infrequent basis (often once a month) to carefully study the intergenerational patterns in the patient's family. The patient is helped to understand how the current patterns in family relationships are repetitions of patterns from past generations. The approach is strictly cognitive, and the patient is not encouraged to express feelings. Transference issues are not viewed as important and are not interpreted. On the contrary, once patients have gained an intellectual understanding of their family patterns, they are encouraged to address the unresolved issues directly with the appropriate family members.

In the last decade or so, object relations family therapy has also grown in popularity and now stands as the most prominent present-day example of psychodynamic family therapy. Since the discussion in this chapter is restricted to dynamic approaches, we will examine object relations family therapy in some detail while omitting consideration of the nondynamic schools of family therapy.

Theoretical Understanding

Working with married couples at the Tavistock Clinic in the 1950s and 1960s, Henry Dicks (1963) began to notice that relatively healthy couples—who appeared to have a satisfying marriage—were often working out primitive object relationships in their marriages. He observed that each spouse tended to perceive the other as though he or she were someone else. Typically, the husband would perceive the wife as though she were an internal object-representation from his own psyche, often his own mother. Similarly, the wife would relate to the husband as though he were simply a projection from her internal world. Dicks concluded that a major source of marital discord was the failure of each partner to confirm the other's true nature or identity. Instead, the partners tended to coerce each other into behaving in highly stereotyped and constricting ways. Couples tended to deteriorate into polarized units, such as sadistic-masochistic, domineering-submissive, healthy-sick, and independent-dependent. Dicks recognized that each of these polarized halves formed a whole personality in the marital dyad, but that each individual alone was incomplete. Just as his colleague Bion was noting that groups exert a regressive force on individuals, Dicks was discovering that marriage has a similar regressive effect. Even in people with considerable ego strength, marriage seemed to regress them rapidly into parent-child relationships.

What Dicks observed, of course, was a form of transference. The marital partners were reenacting a past relationship in the present. In the language of object relations theory, the spouses were using splitting and projective identification to make an *internal* conflict an *external,* or marital, conflict, with an internal object-representation, usually a parent, split off and projected into the spouse. The projector then behaved in such a way as to coerce the spouse into behaving like the projected internal object. A husband, for example, who is used to being babied by his mother, may unconsciously recreate the situation with his mother in his marriage by acting childish and evoking a motherly response from his wife. Alternatively, the marital partner may project a self-representation into the spouse and coerce the spouse into behaving like that self-representation while the projector behaves like a complementary object-representation. The case of Mr. B in Chapter 4 was such a situation. He projected a victimized, submissive self-representation onto both his first and second wife while behaving like his domineering, aggressive father.

Marital conflict may be viewed as the recreation of conflicts with one's parents, via splitting and projective identification. The selection of a mate is obviously much influenced by such processes. Dicks (1963) believed that such selections are "largely based on unconscious signals or cues by which the partners recognize in a more-or-less central ego-syntonic person the other's 'fitness' for joint working-through or repeating of still unresolved splits or conflicts inside each other's personalities, while at the same time, paradoxically, also sensing a guarantee that with that person they will not be worked-through" (p. 128). Hence couples are thrown together by conflicting desires to work through unresolved object relations, on the one hand, and simply to repeat them, on the other.

Several authors have expanded this object relations understanding of marital conflict to the entire family (Scharff and Scharff 1987; Shapiro et al. 1975; Slipp 1984, 1988; Stewart et al. 1975;

Zinner and Shapiro 1972, 1974). These authors noted that an identified patient in a family is frequently a carrier or container of the split-off unacceptable parts of other family members. In that sense the family equilibrium is maintained by this arrangement of splitting and projective identification. An adolescent boy, for example, may act on antisocial impulses that represent aspects of an unacceptable self-representation of his father that has been projectively disavowed by the father and contained by the son. A child may be idealized in the same way via projective identification of positive aspects of self- or object-representations. Object relations theory lends itself well to family therapy because its constructs (e.g., splitting and projective identification) provide a bridge from the intrapsychic to the interpersonal and from the individual to the family (Slipp 1984; Zinner 1976).

Technique

The technique of object relations therapy for couples and families grows out of the theoretical understanding. The overall goal is to help members of the family or couple reinternalize the conflicts that have been externalized via projective identification (Zinner 1976). The focus, then, must be on helping each individual to re-own projected parts (Stewart et al. 1975). To accomplish this goal, the object relations family therapist will typically meet with the family for a 50-minute session every week or every other week (Slipp 1988).

The therapy process begins with a careful diagnosis of how internal object- and self-representations have been distributed throughout the family via splitting and projective identification. When this pattern becomes apparent, the therapist attempts to explain how an unconscious collusive system is formed among family members to perpetuate pathological behavior in the identified patient. The stability of the family depends on the ability of one or more individual members to contain various projected parts of other family members. As with other forms of dynamic psychotherapy, these explanatory interpretations are usually met with resistance early on. This antitherapeutic force may take the form of attempting to get the therapist "sucked in" to the family system. In other words, family members unconsciously repeat the family's pathological patterns instead of verbalizing and exploring them. In marital therapy, for example, a husband may use projective identification with the therapist in the same way he does with his spouse.

Because of these powerful resistances, object relations family therapists must be especially attuned to their countertransference reactions in the broad or objective sense. In other words, it is critically important that the therapists allow themselves to be containers for the projected parts of the family members so that they can more adequately diagnose and interpret what happens within the family (Slipp 1988). Therapists are then in a position to point out the pathological collusive patterns in the here and now of the therapy process and to connect them with what goes on outside that process.

The most common form of resistance at the beginning of marital therapy is for both partners to expect the therapist to "fix" their spouse (Jones and Gabbard 1988). Because the externalization of the conflict into the partner is so well established, both spouses are more interested in persuading the therapist that they are "right" rather than in repairing the marriage (Berkowitz 1984). Therapists must consistently avoid taking sides in such conflicts. Instead, they must help couples expand their perspective to encompass an appreciation of their own contributions to the conflict in the marriage.

The transition from seeing the problem as a marital conflict to perceiving it as an internal conflict that is played out within the couple is a difficult task for each partner. Projective identification in the marital dyad requires a continued state of conflict—the polarization inherent in the splitting process maintains the stable balance (Zinner 1976). Any effort to destabilize this arrangement is likely to be highly threatening to both marital partners. The need for the spouse to be the "bad object" may be so compelling that all therapeutic efforts are for naught (Dicks 1963). Despite their understanding of the pathological interactions between them, some couples will choose to live in a state of turmoil rather than to face the anxiety associated with change.

In the final analysis, of course, change in marital therapy is not the therapist's responsibility—only the marital partners themselves can decide if they wish to change their marriage. As is true in all dynamic psychotherapies, the therapist must scrupulously avoid feeling driven by a need to change the couple. The therapist's task is to provide insight and understanding and to help the couple decide whether—and how—they wish to change their marriage (Jones and Gabbard 1988). When therapists find themselves highly invested in a particular outcome, they are frequently involved in a collusive interaction in which they have become identified with projected parts of the family members. Moreover, the more the therapist pushes for change, the more the couple is likely to resist. When the therapy becomes stalemated because of such resistance, it is sometimes useful for the therapist to lay out various options to the couple and to convey to them that they are free to choose how to proceed with their lives. Divorce or no change at all must be among those options and must be considered acceptable outcomes by the therapist. Only then will the couple realize that it is ultimately up to them how they choose to live their lives.

Brief Marital Therapy

Greenspan and Mannino (1974) have developed a model for brief marital therapy based on projective identification. This model is designed for couples with considerable ego strength and with no signs of any severe pathology. The goal of this form of treatment is limited: to confront each partner with those aspects of the spouse's personality that are not being perceived because of projective identification. After listening to the wife's version of the conflict, the therapist might ask the husband to repeat the essence of his wife's concern. If he omits a particular aspect of her feelings, the therapist will point out the omission.

The therapeutic process in this model of brief intervention helps both partners listen better and develop a fuller empathic appreciation for their spouse's internal experience. As marital partners come to acknowledge that they are distorting their perceptions of one another, they begin to realize that they do not know the person they married very well. When this approach is successful, it sets in motion a process of "checking out" each other's feelings rather than assuming that the partner feels a certain way.

Self Psychological Marital Therapy

In recent years the concepts of self psychology have also been applied to marital conflict. Kohut himself, in a footnote from his last book (1984), noted that "a good marriage is one in which one or the other partner rises to the challenge of providing the selfobject functions that the other's temporarily impaired self needs at a particular moment" (p. 220). He also noted that when selfobject needs are not supplied by a spouse, the result may be divorce and unending bitterness—a form of all-too-common chronic narcissistic rage.

Berkowitz (1985) has expanded Kohut's notions by examining the tendency for marital partners to develop selfobject transferences to their spouses. In this form of marital disharmony, one partner regulates self-esteem through a mirroring or idealizing relationship with the spouse. This arrangement creates problems because of the implicit demand for unconditional love and acceptance that no one can fulfill. When one spouse fails to validate or serve as an appropriate figure for idealization, the result may be self-fragmentation for the other spouse. Narcissistic rage and a wish for revenge may also appear at such times. Lansky (1982) has described such couples as having "narcissistically vulnerable" marriages, in which the dread of being shamed or humiliated is a key feature. One significant limitation to the self psychological approach to marital therapy, however,

is that Kohut's theory does not adequately account for the motivation of one spouse to assume the role of selfobject for the other
(Finkelstein 1988).

Indications and Contraindications

The "consumer" model is a commonsense approach clinicians can
use in deciding whether a patient needs individual or family/marital
therapy. What is the patient asking for? Does one "patient" come to
the office or do two? Does the discussion focus on "my problem" or
"our problem"? Is the problem viewed as having an internal origin
or an external one?

   If parents come with their adolescent child, the problem of
determining the therapy of choice may be more complex. Frequently, the adolescent is not convinced of the need for treatment
and may remain silent throughout most of the first appointment.
Meanwhile, the parents may go on and on about their son's or
daughter's problems. The evaluating clinician needs to make a
rapid determination regarding the next appointment. Will seeing
only one "patient" be a collusion with the splitting and projective
identification processes in the family (Stewart et al. 1975)? When in
doubt, of course, the clinician may simply continue an exploratory
evaluation process until the dynamics of the family are clearer. At
times when one member of a couple or certain family members
simply refuse to attend a therapy process, the therapist may be
forced to work with only one family member or to do no treatment
at all.

   Slipp (1988) stressed the identified patient's level of differentiation from the family as a good rule of thumb in determining the
therapy of choice. Individual psychotherapy is probably the treatment of choice with late adolescents or young adults who have
managed to separate, psychologically and geographically, from
their families and to live their own lives with reasonably mature
defensive operations. But family therapy or a combination of family
and individual therapy is likely to be most helpful with individuals
in the same age group who are still living at home, or who are living
separately but still find themselves emotionally involved with their
families in an intense and conflictual manner.

   A frequent problem that arises in individual psychotherapy is
the patient's request to bring the spouse to an appointment to work
on marital issues. If the individual process is well established, trying
to convert it into a marital therapy process as well is rarely successful.
The spouse who is brought in usually feels that the therapist's
primary loyalty is to the other partner and is rarely able to form an
alliance with the therapist. A better solution is to refer the couple

to a marital therapist while continuing the original individual process.

Dynamic Pharmacotherapy

Several decades ago the phrase "dynamic pharmacotherapy" would have been considered a contradiction in terms. The legacy of mind/body dualism polarized dynamic and pharmacologic approaches to psychiatric disorders for many years. Fortunately, recent integrative trends have brought contemporary psychiatry to the point where combined use of medication and psychotherapy is now almost universal practice for both nonpsychotic and psychotic conditions (Thompson and Brodie 1981). An extensive study of the combined practice of pharmacotherapy and psychotherapy by the Group for the Advancement of Psychiatry (1975) found no significant problems with combining the two approaches and suggested further efforts toward integrating the two.

Even when formal psychotherapy is not part of the treatment regimen, dynamic principles are extraordinarily useful in prescribing psychotropic agents. Indeed, the effectiveness of pharmacotherapy can be significantly enhanced by a dynamic understanding of the treatment process. In the practice of psychopharmacotherapy, noncompliance remains a serious problem. Research on noncompliance suggests that 24–63 percent of schizophrenic outpatients take less antipsychotic medication than prescribed (Van Putten 1974), while as many as 40 percent of schizophrenic patients stop medication altogether in the first year following discharge from a hospital (Hogarty et al. 1973). Among all psychiatric patients, somewhere between 18 and 50 percent will refuse medication at some point during treatment (Jamison et al. 1979; Van Putten 1975). Noncompliance can usually be understood with the aid of dynamic principles such as transference, countertransference, and resistance.

Transference

The psychiatrist prescribing medication is no less a transference figure than the psychotherapist. For patients, the decision to comply or not to comply with the doctor's recommendations activates unconscious issues of parental expectations. When patients refuse to take medication as prescribed, psychiatrists often react by becoming more authoritarian, insisting that their orders be followed without question. This approach usually backfires because it merely exacerbates the transference disposition to see the doctor as a demanding parental figure. A far more productive approach is to enlist patients' collaboration in exploring their concerns. Does the medication have a particular meaning to them? Is a situation from their past being repeated in the present? What feelings toward the doctor did the prescription evoke?

One patient experienced the prescription of an antidepressant as an empathic failure on the part of the psychiatrist. When the patient's noncompliance was explored with him, he told his doctor, "I was looking for someone to validate my feelings. Instead, you tried to medicate them away. I felt like the pill was a way of telling me to shut up." When the psychiatrist encouraged him to elaborate further, the patient was able to connect this feeling with earlier experiences with his father, whom he experienced as inattentive and uncaring about his concerns.

Other patients, especially those who have characterological tendencies to be controlling or dominating, will see medication as a threat to their counterdependent stance. Taking a pill means submitting to the domination of a powerful parental figure. These patients must be given some control over whether to take the medication (Thompson and Brodie 1981). With overly submissive patients, one often encounters the opposite situation. Pills make these patients feel "fed" and taken care of to such an extent that they may decide that they no longer need to take responsibility for any aspect of their illness.

Transference struggles may be particularly intense with whining "manipulative *help-rejecters*" (Groves 1978). These patients systematically defeat every treatment intervention, pharmacologic or otherwise. They frequently have gone through a lengthy list of psychotropic agents without feeling any benefit. Exploring the transference dynamics may lead to the uncovering of a great deal of resentment and bitterness toward parental figures who the patient believes did not give enough nurturance. By rejecting help offered to them, these patients may be unconsciously seeking revenge against their parents (Gabbard 1988). When such patients sense that they are making their doctor miserable, they often feel a secret triumph.

A unique aspect of transference in dynamic pharmacotherapy is transference to the medication itself (Gutheil 1982). Placebo responses to medications often have this same transference quality. A manic patient, for example, became markedly subdued after one 300-mg dose of lithium carbonate, a response that could not be explained pharmacologically. Placebo side effects are also common. Another manifestation of transference to medications is the response to changing the drug rituals of chronic patients (Appelbaum and Gutheil 1980). Such patients may decompensate into psychosis with the slightest alteration of their usual medication regimen.

The transference relationship to a medication may be most obvious in situations where the pill takes the place of the absent doctor. Pills may function as transitional objects for some patients, allowing them to maintain some sense of connectedness with their psychiatrists even when seeing them quite infrequently (Book 1987). Touching or looking at the pill may have a soothing effect on the patient. In training programs, where residents rotate through services on an annual basis, patients may deal with the loss of their doctor by becoming intensely attached to the medication prescribed by the departing doctor (Gutheil 1977).

Transferences of this type are powerful and may lead to another form of noncompliance—refusal to discontinue medications because of the unconscious meaning of the medication to the patient. Transference issues must always be taken into account when prescribing psychotropic agents to paranoid patients. In more subtle cases the patient may discontinue a medication for the ostensible reason of unpleasant side effects, when in actuality the patient is afraid of being poisoned. Insistence on compliance will greatly increase the paranoia, while empathic exploration of the nature of the fears may help the patient to realize that they are unfounded and to view the therapist as less threatening (Book 1987).

Countertransference

The prescribing of medication is just as likely as any other treatment intervention to be contaminated by countertransference. One common manifestation of countertransference is overprescription. It is not uncommon for a patient to arrive at a hospital or an emergency room with a brown paper bag full of psychoactive agents. One such patient was taking three antipsychotics, two antidepressants, lithium carbonate, and two benzodiazepines. After a few days in the hospital, it was apparent that this patient evoked intense feelings of impotence and anger in treaters. The excessive amounts of medication reflected the countertransference despair of the attending psychiatrist.

Narcissistic injury may also be a factor in countertransference. Some psychotherapists may fail to prescribe a much-needed medication because they believe that doing so would be tantamount to conceding that their psychotherapeutic skills were ineffective. Others may induce guilt feelings in noncompliers so that they will feel obligated to comply with the prescription out of a wish not to hurt their doctor.

Some psychiatrists become anxious about intense feelings of any kind in the transference. Medication may be viewed as a way to deal with this countertransference anxiety. The discussion of side effects may also be influenced by this anxiety. Gutheil (1982), for example, noted that psychiatrists seldom discuss the sexual side effects of phenothiazines with their patients because of their own discomfort with overt sexual discussions.

Countertransference anger, which is a common response to noncompliance in patients, may take many forms. Some psychiatrists may collude with the noncompliance to demonstrate how ill their patients will get if they do not follow the "doctor's orders" (Book 1987). Others may bully patients into taking their medications or threaten to discharge them from treatment if they do not comply. Those psychiatrists who have difficulty controlling their anger may refuse to set limits on patients who demand increasing amounts of medication. In these cases the psychiatrist hopes that gratifying the demands of the patient will keep aggression and hostility out of the therapeutic relationship. Unfortunately, the patient's demandingness and anger usually escalate.

Resistance

Resistance to treatment is as powerful a force in pharmacotherapy as it is in psychotherapy. Illness may be preferable to health for numerous reasons. It is well known, for example, that patients with bipolar affective disorder may enjoy their manic episodes so much that they will stop taking their lithium. In one study of schizophrenic patients (Van Putten et al. 1976), a similar cause of resistance was uncovered. In this investigation, side effects and secondary gain had little to do with noncompliance. An ego-syntonic grandiose psychosis was the most powerful discriminating factor that distinguished schizophrenic patients who did not comply from those who did. Clearly, the noncompliers preferred their experience of psychotic grandiosity.

Denial of illness is also a prominent cause of resistance to pharmacotherapy. For some patients any psychotropic agent carries with it the stigma of mental illness. When an acute psychotic episode goes into remission, a patient may stop the antipsychotic medication responsible for the remission because maintenance treatment connotes a chronic mental illness. Nonpsychotic patients who are quite willing to submit to psychotherapeutic treatment will balk at the suggestion of medication because they are convinced it means that they are more seriously disturbed than they like to think. Likewise, patients who have had a relative in psychopharmacologic treatment may unconsciously identify with that relative when offered the same medication (Book 1987). This identification may serve as a resistance to accepting treatment, particularly if the relative had an unfavorable outcome, such as suicide.

Finally, another form of resistance not related to compliance with the prescribed medication represents the flip side of the wish to deny illness. It is not at all uncommon for some patients who willingly take their medication to nevertheless resist the therapeutic effects of pharmacologic agents. These patients are so powerfully invested in their illness that they tenaciously cling to their symptoms even when these are challenged by potent psychotropic agents. For such patients a psychotherapeutic approach is the treatment of choice.

Therapeutic Alliance

The foregoing discussion about noncompliance should make it clear that the therapeutic alliance plays a crucial role in dynamic pharmacotherapy. Numerous authors have stressed that attending to the therapeutic alliance is part of the prescribing process (Docherty and Fiester 1985; Elkin et al. 1988; Gutheil 1982; Howard et al. 1970). Although much contemporary psychopharmacological research does not quantify the doctor-patient relationship, many investigators have noted its influence on compliance. One study (Howard et al. 1970) discovered that subtle aspects of the therapist's behavior, including vocal enthusiasm, body language, and use of the patient's name, differentiated psychiatrists with low drop-out rates from those with high attrition rates. This study also indicated that attention to the therapeutic alliance in the first session prevented noncompliance with drug treatment.

Studies of the drop-out rate in both psychotherapeutic and psychopharmacologic treatment settings have emphasized that patient expectations can influence attrition (Freedman et al. 1958; Overall and Aronson 1963). Different patients come to a psychiatrist with different expectations of the kind of treatments available. American moviegoers might well get the impression that all psychiatrists are psychotherapists, because the effective prescription of psychotropic medication is virtually absent from cinematic depictions of psychiatrists and psychiatric treatment (Gabbard and Gabbard 1987). At some point in the first interview, psychiatrists should explore their patients' expectations so that the treatment prescribed is in some way consistent with them. If the treatment of choice is counter to a patient's preconceived notions, an educational effort may be necessary to convince the patient of its usefulness.

In Chapter 4 the concept of collaboration was emphasized in the discussion of the therapeutic alliance in psychotherapy. An analogous concept of "participant prescribing" (Gutheil 1982, p. 322) is relevant for pharmacotherapy. The unconscious tendency of some psychiatrists to switch to a more authoritarian mode when prescribing medications is liable to backfire in the form of noncompliance. Even in the practice of internal medicine, sensitive internists are aware that they will evoke better compliance if they discuss with their patients the reasons for antibiotics, thus enlisting their patients' cooperation in the process of treatment. The variable of patient education positively influences the development of a therapeutic alliance in pharmacotherapy. All patients should be thoroughly informed about the therapeutic and side effects of any pharmacologic agent they receive. With acutely psychotic patients, however, this discussion sometimes must wait until the acute episode is under pharmacologic control.

Combined Treatment

Despite the history of polarization between psychotherapists and pharmacotherapists, the combination of psychotherapy and medication is a time-honored clinical practice in psychiatry. In three different analytic cases involving severe depression, Anna Freud enlisted a colleague to prescribe medication—with highly beneficial results (Lipton 1983). She was convinced that the addition of pharmacologic agents was crucial in allowing the analysis to continue. Luborsky et al. (1976) surveyed 26 research studies evaluating combined treatment and found that, in 69 percent of the comparisons, the combined approach was more effective than either psychotherapy or pharmacotherapy alone. Much of the professional resistance to developing an integrative model of combined treatment stems from the traditional view of the approaches as competitive rather than synergistic. Karasu (1984) noted, however, that:

> Psychotherapy and pharmacotherapy are not competitive or inhibitive, but [that] each has differential effects or loci of outcome (drugs have their major manifestations upon symptom formation and affective distress, where psychotherapy more directly influences interpersonal relations and social adjustment); each is activated and sustained on a different time schedule (drugs may take effect sooner and be of short-term duration, while psychotherapy results may not reveal themselves until a later point in time, but last longer); and each may best relate to different disorders or their subtypes (drugs for time-limited and autonomous "state" disorders, psychotherapy for long-lasting "trait" disorders). (p. 380)

The "state/trait" distinction of Karasu is generally valid, but there are notable exceptions. Anxiety is a "state" disorder that may respond well to either modality. The same can be said of depression. On the other hand, attention-deficit disorder is a "trait" disorder that may respond well to tricyclic antidepressants (Ostow 1983). It is certainly true that the effects of psychotherapy generally show up later than the effects of pharmacotherapy. This observation has led some to propose a "two-stage treatment strategy" (Karasu 1982; Klerman 1978). In this approach the psychopharmacologic agent is the first step, designed to relieve symptoms and set the stage for a later psychotherapy process. The goal of psychotherapy, the second step, would then be geared to interpersonal relationships, social adjustment, and improvement at work.

Despite the lack of evidence to suggest any deleterious effect of combining pharmacotherapy with psychotherapy, concern continues in some quarters about the potential for medications to obstruct or even destroy psychotherapy. Some clinicians worry, for example, that reducing anxiety will eradicate a patient's motivation for continuing the painful work of psychotherapy. Others speculate that the transference will be irreparably confounded by the introduction of medication. A comprehensive review of studies designed to investigate these concerns reveals them to be unfounded (Karasu 1982). What is required of clinicians who combine the approaches, however, is an awareness of the "bimodal relatedness" inherent in the dual role (Docherty et al. 1977). The patient must be viewed simultaneously as a disturbed person and as a diseased central nervous system. The former view requires an empathic subjective approach, while the latter demands an objective medical model approach. The clinician must be able to shift between these two modes gracefully yet also stay attuned to the impact of the shift on the patient.

Extensive case reports in the literature provide persuasive examples of the efficacy of combined treatment. Wylie and Wylie (1987) reported the case of a female analytic patient who could not work within the transference in the analysis until monoamine oxidase inhibitors were prescribed for her depression. The medication reduced her affective vulnerability sufficiently to enable her to risk dealing with transference feelings. Loeb and Loeb (1987) treated seven manic patients who were taking lithium carbonate while in either psychoanalysis or psychoanalytic psychotherapy. Through analysis or therapy, these patients became aware of a marked increase in their unconscious sexual impulses and their defenses against them. The patients were then able to learn that these impulses heralded the onset of a manic episode. By making these impulses conscious, they were able to prevent future manic episodes by increasing their lithium dosage.

The fundamental compatibility of biology and psychodynamics was emphasized in Chapter 1. One instance of this marriage is the increasing practice of combining pharmacotherapy and psychotherapy. Because conceptual bridges are still being built between the two approaches, much of the practice remains empirical at this point. As in all psychiatry, the guiding principle must be to help the patient rather than to be true to one's theoretical biases.

References

Appelbaum PS, Gutheil TG: Drug refusal: a study of psychiatric inpatients. Am J Psychiatry 137:340–346, 1980

Bateson G, Jackson DD, Haley J, et al: Toward a theory of schizophrenia. Behav Sci 1:251–264, 1956

Berkowitz DA: An overview of the psychodynamics of couples: bridging concepts, in Marriage and Divorce: A Contemporary Perspective. Edited by Nadelson CC, Polonsky DC. New York, Guilford Press, 1984, pp 117–126

Berkowitz DA: Selfobject needs and marital disharmony. Psychoanal Rev 72:229–237, 1985

Bion WR: Experiences in Groups and Other Papers. New York, Basic Books, 1961

Book HE: Some psychodynamics of non-compliance. Can J Psychiatry 32:115–117, 1987

Bowen M: Family Therapy in Clinical Practice. New York, Jason Aronson, 1978

Dicks HV: Object relations theory and marital studies. Br J Med Psychol 36:125–129, 1963

Docherty JP, Fiester SJ: The therapeutic alliance and compliance with psychopharmacology, in Psychiatry Update: American Psychiatric Association Annual Review, Vol 4. Edited by Hales RE, Frances AJ. Washington, DC, American Psychiatric Press, 1985, pp 607–632

Docherty JP, Marder SR, Van Kammen DP, et al: Psychotherapy and pharmacotherapy: conceptual issues. Am J Psychiatry 134:529–533, 1977

Elkin I, Pilkonis PA, Docherty JP, et al: Conceptual and methodological issues in comparative studies of psychotherapy and pharmacotherapy, I: active ingredients and mechanisms of change. Am J Psychiatry 145:909-917, 1988

Ezriel H: A psycho-analytic approach to group treatment. Br J Med Psychol 23:59–74, 1950

Finkelstein L: Psychoanalysis, marital therapy, and object-relations theory. J Am Psychoanal Assoc 36:905–931, 1988

Freedman N, Engelhardt DM, Hankoff LD, et al: Drop out from outpatient psychiatric treatment. Archives of Neurology and Psychiatry 80:657–666, 1958

Gabbard GO: A contemporary perspective on psychoanalytically informed hospital treatment. Hosp Community Psychiatry 39:1291–1295, 1988

Gabbard K, Gabbard GO: Psychiatry and the Cinema. Chicago, University of Chicago Press, 1987

Ganzarain R: Psychotic-like anxieties and primitive defenses in group analytic psychotherapy. Issues in Ego Psychology 3:42–48, 1980

Ganzarain R: Working through in analytic group psychotherapy. Int J Group Psychother 33:281–296, 1983

Gibbard GR, Hartman JJ: The significance of utopian fantasies in small groups. Int J Group Psychother 23:125–147, 1973

Greenspan SI, Mannino FV: A model for brief intervention with couples based on projective identification. Am J Psychiatry 131:1103–1106, 1974

Group for the Advancement of Psychiatry: Report No. 93: Pharmacotherapy and psychotherapy: paradoxes, problems, and progress. 9:261–434, 1975

Groves J: Taking care of the hateful patient. N Engl J Med 298:883–887, 1978

Gutheil TG: Psychodynamics in drug prescribing. Drug Therapy 2:35–40, 1977

Gutheil TG: The psychology of psychopharmacology. Bull Menninger Clin 46:321–330, 1982

Hogarty GE, Goldberg SC, Collaborative Study Group: Drug and sociotherapy in the aftercare of schizophrenic patients. Arch Gen Psychiatry 28:54–64, 1973

Horwitz L: A group-centered approach to group psychotherapy. Int J Group Psychother 27:423–439, 1977

Horwitz L: Projective identification in dyads and groups. Int J Group Psychother 33:259–279, 1983

Howard K, Rickels K, Mock JE, et al: Therapeutic style and attrition rate from psychiatric drug treatment. J Nerv Ment Dis 150:102–110, 1970

Jamison KR, Gerner RH, Goodwin FK: Patient and physician attitudes toward lithium. Arch Gen Psychiatry 36:866–869, 1979

Jones SA, Gabbard GO: Marital therapy of physician couples, in Medical Marriages. Edited by Gabbard GO, Menninger RW. Washington, DC, American Psychiatric Press, 1988, pp 137–151

Karasu TB: Psychotherapy and pharmacotherapy: toward an integrative model. Am J Psychiatry 139:1102–1113, 1982

Karasu TB: Politics, practice, and *p* value in psychotherapy, in Psychotherapy Research: Where Are We and Where Should We Go? Edited by Williams JBW, Spitzer RL. New York, Guilford Press, 1984, pp 372–383

Klerman GL: Combining drugs and psychotherapy in the treatment of depression, in Depression: Biology, Psychodynamics, and Treatment. Edited by Cole JO, Schatzberg AF, Frazier SH. New York, Plenum Press, 1978, pp 213–227

Kohut H: How Does Analysis Cure? Edited by Goldberg A. Chicago, University of Chicago Press, 1984

Lansky MR: Masks of the narcissistically vulnerable marriage. Int J Family Psychiatry 3:439–449, 1982

Lipton MA: A letter from Anna Freud. Am J Psychiatry 140:1583–1584, 1983

Loeb FF, Loeb LR: Psychoanalytic observations on the effect of lithium on manic attacks. J Am Psychoanal Assoc 35:877–902, 1987

Luborsky L, Singer B, Luborsky L: Comparative studies of psychotherapies: is it true that "everybody has won and all must have prizes?"

in Evaluation of Psychological Therapies: Psychotherapies, Behavior Therapies, Drug Therapies, and Their Interaction. Edited by Spitzer RL, Klein DF. Baltimore, Johns Hopkins University Press, 1976, pp 3–22

Minuchin S: Families and Family Therapy. Cambridge, MA, Harvard University Press, 1974

Ogden TH: Projective Identification and Psychotherapeutic Technique. New York, Jason Aronson, 1982

Ostow M: Interactions of psychotherapy and pharmacotherapy (letter to the editor). Am J Psychiatry 140:370–371, 1983

Overall B, Aronson H: Expectations of psychotherapy in patients of lower socioeconomic class. Am J Orthopsychiatry 33:421–430, 1963

Redl F: Psychoanalysis and group therapy: a developmental point of view. Am J Orthopsychiatry 33:135–147, 1963

Rioch MJ: The work of Wilfred Bion on groups. Psychiatry 33:56–66, 1970

Sadock BJ: Preparation, selection of patients, and organization of the group, in Comprehensive Group Psychotherapy, 2nd Edition. Edited by Kaplan HI, Sadock BJ. Baltimore, Williams & Wilkins, 1983, pp 23–32

Scharff DE, Scharff JS: Object Relations Family Therapy. Northvale, NJ, Jason Aronson, 1987

Scheidlinger S: On the concept of the "mother-group." Int J Group Psychother 24:417–428, 1974

Selvini Palazzoli M, Boscolo L, Cecchin G, et al: Paradox and Counterparadox: A New Model in the Therapy of the Family in Schizophrenic Transaction. New York, Jason Aronson, 1978

Shapiro ER, Zinner J, Shapiro RL, et al: The influence of family experience on borderline personality development. International Review of Psychoanalysis 2:399–411, 1975

Slipp S: Object Relations: A Dynamic Bridge Between Individual and Family Treatment. New York, Jason Aronson, 1984

Slipp S: The Technique and Practice of Object Relations Family Therapy. Northvale, NJ, Jason Aronson, 1988

Sonne JL: An example of group therapy for victims of therapist-client sexual intimacy, in Sexual Exploitation in Professional Relationships. Edited by Gabbard GO. Washington, DC, American Psychiatric Press, 1989, pp 101–113

Stewart RH, Peters TC, Marsh S, et al: An object-relations approach to psychotherapy with marital couples, families, and children. Fam Process 14:161–178, 1975

Thompson EM, Brodie HKH: The psychodynamics of drug therapy. Current Psychiatric Therapies 20:239–251, 1981

Van Putten T: Why do schizophrenic patients refuse to take their drugs? Arch Gen Psychiatry 31:67–72, 1974

Van Putten T: Why do patients with manic-depressive illness stop their lithium? Compr Psychiatry 16:179–183, 1975

Van Putten T, Crumpton E, Yale C: Drug refusal in schizophrenia and the wish to be crazy. Arch Gen Psychiatry 33:1443–1446, 1976

Whitaker DS, Lieberman MA: Psychotherapy Through the Group Process. New York, Atherton Press, 1964

Wolf A: Psychoanalysis in groups, in Comprehensive Group Psychotherapy, 2nd Edition. Edited by Kaplan HI, Sadock BJ. Baltimore, Williams & Wilkins, 1983, pp 113–131

Wylie HW Jr, Wylie ML: An effect of pharmacotherapy on the psychoanalytic process: case report of a modified analysis. Am J Psychiatry 144:489–492, 1987

Yalom ID: The Theory and Practice of Group Psychotherapy, 3rd Edition. New York, Basic Books, 1985

Zinner J: The implications of projective identification for marital interaction, in Contemporary Marriage: Structure, Dynamics, and Therapy. Edited by Grunebaum H, Christ J. Boston, Little, Brown, 1976, pp 293–308

Zinner J, Shapiro R: Projective identification as a mode of perception and behavior in families of adolescents. Int J Psychoanal 53:523–530, 1972

Zinner J, Shapiro R: The family as a single psychic entity: implications for acting out in adolescence. International Review of Psychoanalysis 1:179–186, 1974

CHAPTER 6

Treatments in Dynamic Psychiatry III: Dynamically Informed Hospital Treatment

B ecause psychodynamic principles evolved largely from the practice of psychoanalysis, these precepts are sometimes narrowly construed to be relevant only to outpatient treatment. One psychiatric resident asked his supervisor for help in understanding a hospitalized patient, only to be told, "Dynamics apply only to outpatients, not inpatients." Nothing could be further from the truth, of course. However, the supervisor's comment reflects an unfortunate trend in modern hospital psychiatry to use the psychiatric unit as a mere holding tank where patients wait for their medication to take effect. The treatment of many patients is greatly enhanced by approaching hospital treatment with a dynamic perspective.

A Historical Review

The practitioner can draw on a long tradition of the application of psychoanalytic principles to hospital treatment. The history of the notion of the psychoanalytic hospital began with Simmel's work at Schloss Tegel (1929), where he noted that certain patients could not be analyzed outside a hospital because of various symptomatic behaviors, such as alcoholism or phobias. He had the idea that a hospital could extend the patient's hour on the couch by training hospital staff members to conduct quasi-analytic treatment in the milieu as issues of transference and resistance arose. In his creative and brilliant *Guide to the Order Sheet,* Will Menninger (1939) de-emphasized the model of individual psychoanalysis and attempted to apply the principles of psychoanalysis directly within the hospital by manipulation of the milieu. Working from the assumption that all symptoms and disturbed behaviors derive from disturbances in the proper fusion and expression of the two major instinctual drives— libido and aggression, he evolved a system of milieu treatment based largely on sublimation and not requiring insight. Rather than frustrate or interpret unconscious wishes and conflicts, this approach focused on rechanneling energies into less harmful paths. For example, Menninger encouraged the direct expression of hostilities toward substitute objects; prescriptions for a patient might range from demolishing a building to punching a punching bag. Unfortunately, this model could not take into account those patients with ego weaknesses involving impulse control problems who required a treatment designed to help them gain more control over drive expression rather than to redirect it. Moreover, this conceptualization was limited by confining itself to the dual instinct theory of the times, which tended to neglect the object relations context in which disturbed drives occur, nor did it allow for systematic examination of transference and countertransference in the milieu.

The third model grew out of an awareness that patients were re-creating with various staff members in the hospital setting their conflicts with their own family members (Hilles 1968). Interpretation of maladaptive behavior patterns in terms of their roots in the past was common within this model, which relied less and less on providing substitute outlets for unconscious needs. The milieu was not seen as a therapeutic community in which real, constructive experiences with peers are stressed, but rather as a screen upon which archaic patterns are projected and then examined. Schlesinger and Holzman (1970), in describing the therapeutic aspects of the milieu of a psychiatric hospital, noted that the milieu could supplement the therapist-patient relationship by providing opportunities for patients to work out in a real context what had been talked about in therapy. It also served as a kind of training ground or laboratory where patients could practice trying to change in various ways as they progressed in psychotherapy. Schlesinger and Holzman asserted that prescribing milieu therapy for hospital patients was a complex process requiring a sensitivity to the multiple functions of a patient's involvement in the hospital milieu. They proposed a schema based on the five points of view of psychoanalytic metapsychology: the structural, the economic, the dynamic, the adaptive, and the genetic.

A number of authors (Gabbard 1986, 1988, 1989; Harty 1979; Stamm 1985a; Wesselius 1968; Zee 1977) have pinpointed countertransference as an integral part of the treatment process. They offer the caveat that treatment effectiveness is impaired when staff members respond in a countertransferential manner as though they are one of the patient's parents. These countertransference influences occur regularly, rather than occasionally; and the systematic examination of the countertransference should be part of the routine work of the treatment team. A recurring theme throughout the various formulations of psychoanalytically informed hospital treatment is that patients re-create in the milieu environment their own internal object relations. This point of view is reflected in Kernberg's (1973) integrative attempt to synthesize psychoanalytic object relations theory, systems theory, and the use of group process in an overall approach to hospital treatment. One basic tenet of his approach to hospital treatment is that there exists in all of us a potential for both higher-level object relationships, typical of the transference neurosis in individual psychoanalytic treatment, and more primitive levels of object relationships leading to psychotic regression in group situations. He theorized that the higher level of object relationship is activated in individual therapeutic relationships while the more primitive version is much more likely to be activated in group treatment modalities. A combination of individual and group treatment in long-term hospitalization provides for intervention at both levels. Kernberg (1973) insisted that such a two-pronged treatment approach requires a "'neutral' hospital milieu, that is, an attitude of staff basically equidistant from the different intrapsychic and external agencies involved in the patient's conflicts, and reflected in an overall friendly and generally tolerant, an interested and intellectually alert hospital atmosphere" (p. 372). In the context of this neutral atmosphere, he saw the therapeutic community and individual hospital therapy operating simultaneously to examine internal object relationships as well as to perform the ego or control function. He formulates hospital treatment "as the simultaneous diagnosis and treatment of the patient's control function and his internal world of object-relationships" (p. 379).

In summary, the application of psychoanalytic/psychodynamic principles to hospital treatment has undergone a gradual shift during the past 60 years. The notion of containment of patients undergoing psychoanalysis gradually gave way to a second model involving prescribed interactions with milieu staff. The third and current model, because it shifts the emphasis to the systematic examination of transference and countertransference, views patients as re-creating their internal object relations in the milieu.

Dynamic Principles in Contemporary Hospital Treatment

A dynamic approach provides for a diagnostic understanding that pays careful attention to patients' ego weaknesses and strengths, their intrapsychic object relations as manifested in family and social relationships, their capacity for psychological work, and the childhood origins of their current problems. A psychodynamic assessment may lead a clinician to conclude that interpretive interventions and uncovering of unconscious material are ill-advised. With patients who have significant ego weakness and/or organically based cognitive impairment, ego-supportive approaches and those geared to building self-esteem may be recommended. Because of the reality of daily hospital practice, the terms *dynamically informed* or *psychoanalytically informed* hospital treatment are preferable to *dynamic* or *psychoanalytic* hospital treatment (Gabbard 1986).

Psychoanalytic theories of development are useful in designing inpatient treatment plans. A psychoanalytically informed hospital team realizes that the majority of its patients are developmentally arrested. Knowledge of psychoanalytic theory allows the team to respond at an appropriate developmental level, accepting the notion that the patient is a child in an adult's body. This perspective helps the staff avoid the perils of depersonification (Rinsley 1982), whereby the patient is expected to behave as a mature and polite adult in spite of severe psychopathology. Such depersonification has often been the life story of the severely disturbed patient in terms of interactions with family members.

Psychoanalytic theory provides models of interventions geared to the patient's phase-appropriate developmental needs, such as empathic mirroring (Kohut 1971) and the provision of a holding environment (Stamm 1985b; Winnicott 1965). Within this context, the limits associated with hospital structure are not viewed as punishments for immature and irritating behavior but rather as external substitutes for missing intrapsychic structures. In a similar vein, staff members must perform auxiliary ego functions, such as reality testing, impulse control, anticipation of consequences (judgment), and sharpening of self-object differentiation.

These considerations lead to a consideration of two facts that are immediately apparent when applying psychodynamic principles to hospital treatment: 1) The patient population of a psychiatric hospital is generally far more disturbed than the typical outpatient in dynamic therapy, and 2) expressive interventions must be leavened with a good deal of support in light of this different patient population. For example, technique in the classical psychoanalytic situation is geared to superego modification (Strachey 1934) designed to remove neurotic inhibitions that deprive the patient of pleasure from drive expression (e.g., sexual fulfillment). The majority of psychiatric patients referred to a hospital, however, are there because of unbridled and unrestrained drive expression rather than neurotic inhibitions that restrict free drive expression. Superego lacunae are also present in many hospitalized patients, so their superego development must be fostered rather than modified. Hence, as a general rule, whereas neurotic patients in expressive therapy or analysis are approached with the aim of analyzing defensive configurations and freeing the drive derivatives inhibited by these defenses, borderline or psychotic hospitalized patients are approached with the aim of taming direct expressions of impulses and drive derivatives by strengthening the ego (or the superego) and encouraging more mature defensive configurations.

Neutrality is another principle of technique that must be modified in its application to hospital treatment. If we accept Anna Freud's (1936) definition of neutrality as the ability to remain equidistant from the id, the ego, and the superego, and from external reality factors, then we must acknowledge that in a majority of hospital cases the approach of the staff and of the hospital structure itself unquestionably sides with one intrapsychic agency or another. For example, when a hospital patient becomes violently aggressive toward a staff member or another patient, physical and structural measures such as restraints, seclusion, and antipsychotic medication are frequently used to control the direct drive expression. Likewise, a sexually promiscuous patient may be restricted to his or her room because the behavior is viewed as destructive to the patient. In both cases the hospital staff departs from neutrality to make a judgment that the patient's sexual and aggressive forces must be controlled. Alternatively, with severely depressed and self-destructive patients who are victimized by a relentlessly tormenting superego, the staff may actively side against the superego forces in the patient.

Technical neutrality also implies a certain objectivity that tempers untoward emotional involvement with the patient. This mental attitude may be achievable within the confines of a 50-minute period in the consulting room with a neurotic patient. Achieving this form of objectivity is much more difficult for the psychiatric nurse who faces an 8-hour shift of repeated encounters with the unmitigated rage of the borderline patient and the catastrophic terror of the psychotically regressed patient. Only an automaton could avoid being swept up at times by the powerful emotions engendered in such a setting, a point to which we shall return later.

Interpretation is another cornerstone of expressive technique. Interpretations *are* used and should be used in the treatment of many hospitalized patients, but usually in the context of considerable relationship building and preparatory comments, including confrontations, clarifications, ego-supportive measures, and reality-based advice and instructions regarding daily living on the unit. For an interpretation to be effective, it requires a patient whose psychological-mindedness, abstraction ability, and intelligence are sufficient to understand the interpretation and assimilate it into conscious awareness. Clearly, the expectation of understanding and assimilating an interpretation is a tall order for patients who suffer from cognitive dysfunctions of an organic nature or patients who are floridly psychotic and unable to organize their thinking. There may also be other patients in a psychiatric hospital whose egos would

be overwhelmed and fragmented by the introduction of unconscious material via an interpretation.

A Transference-Countertransference Model

The cornerstone of dynamically informed hospital treatment is, in
fact, a systematic understanding of transference and countertransference as they reflect the patient's internal object relations. Transference and countertransference in hospital treatment are best
understood as the interpersonal externalization of an internal object relationship (Ogden 1983). The drama of hospital treatment
that is played out in the milieu derives from the theater of the
patient's internal object world.

Via projective identification, the patient attributes either a self-
or object-representation to the treater through the externalization
process. When the treaters (and other patients) begin to identify
with the projected aspects of the patient, the internal world of the
patient is replicated in the interpersonal field of the milieu. The
third step of projective identification is essentially the same in
hospital treatment as it is in psychotherapy. The treaters must
process the projected material and provide an altered interpersonal
context in which the patient can reintroject the modified self- or
object-representations.

In this manner the hospital can provide a new and different
form of interpersonal relatedness that facilitates the internalization
of less pathological object relatedness. In the optimal milieu, the
goal of hospital staff members is to relate to patients so as to avoid
being provoked into responding as their internal object-representations would. By not behaving like everyone else in the patient's
world, they can offer new objects and new models of relatedness for
the patient.

Initial responses to a patient may be similar to those of others,
but as staff members familiarize themselves with the internal object
world of the patient, they strive to *contain* the projections rather than
to identify with them. In so doing, a vicious cycle is broken. The
patient is confronted with a group of persons who respond differently than everyone else. They attempt to understand the interpersonal process instead of joining the "dance."

Weiss et al. (1986), who have studied audiotaped transcripts
of analyses with neurotics, have concluded that one curative factor
of analysis is the analyst's failure to respond as the analysand expects.
According to these investigators, a patient develops pathological
beliefs based on early interactions with parental figures, and then
seeks unconsciously to disconfirm these beliefs in analysis so that
development can proceed. Their research is very much applicable

to the hospital setting, where patients continually but unconsciously test staff members to see whether they will be different from previous figures in the prehospital environment. The success of many hospital treatments depends on the ability of the hospital staff to process what is happening and to avoid identification with the projected self- and object-representations of the patient.

Within this formulation of internal object relations, the therapeutic task is to diagnose carefully the patient's self- and object-representations and to maintain a diligent vigilance regarding the nature of the projected internal selves and objects at any given time. Implied in this task is the assumption that treaters have sufficient familiarity with their own internal self- and object-configurations so that they can sort out the two varieties of countertransference.

In this transference-countertransference-based model of hospital treatment, the treatment staff must maintain an openness to the powerful feelings engendered by these patients. Examining the countertransference must be an integral part of the treatment process. The staff should freely allow themselves to serve as containers for the patient's self- and object-projections and for the affects connected with the object relations. On an individual basis, this approach means avoiding the "dedicated physician" stance described by Searles (1967), in which the treater attempts to be loving at all times as a defense against vulnerability to directing sadism and hatred toward the patient. If the treater is overcontrolled or overdefended against emotional reactions to the patient, the diagnostic process of delineating these internal object relations will be flawed. Even more importantly, the treatment process will be a charade; the patient will be unable to view the treater as a genuine person involved in a fleshed-out whole-object relationship.

Openness to countertransference reactions must similarly exist at the group level. The persons in leadership positions on the unit must foster a noncritical, accepting attitude toward the various emotional reactions of staff members to patients. If the leaders communicate that the staff is expected to keep a lid on personal feelings in the service of delivering good treatment to patients, such exhortations will resonate with the already hypertrophied superego structures of most mental health workers and further activate their internal defenses geared to repressing, suppressing, or splitting off unacceptable feelings and identifications.

Despite increasing pressure in recent years to use staff meetings for documentation of behaviorally oriented treatment plans, the staff's emotional reactions to patients must be discussed openly and with understanding. If staff meetings become merely task-oriented administrative sessions without time for processing transference/countertransference paradigms, subsequent staff dysfunction will cause the clinical work to suffer. Furthermore, the hospital will no longer be involved in dynamically informed treatment, but simply in "case management."

The attitude of the unit or team leader is crucial in setting the tone for countertransference-based discussions. The leader must model for the other staff by openly examining his or her own feelings and relating them to the internal object relations of the patient. The leader must also value and accept the expressions of feelings on the part of other staff members and avoid interpreting them as a manifestation of unresolved and unanalyzed conflicts within the individual staff member. When a staff member shares a disturbing feeling involved in treating a patient, the leader needs to ask questions such as, "Why does the patient need to evoke that reaction in you? What is he repeating? What figure in the patient's past are you identifying with? How can we use the feelings the patient evokes in you to understand how his spouse or friends must react to him?" The leader of the treatment team should also become familiar with each staff member's usual style of relating to patients. This awareness must include a knowledge of typical countertransference reactions to certain kinds of patients as well as functioning that is more adaptive and conflict-free. This familiarity will help the team leader pinpoint deviations from the characteristic patterns of relationships with patients. Obviously, in some instances the leader of a treatment team may need to approach individual staff members privately about their need for personal treatment or a change in career.

As the treatment of a patient evolves, a sense of objectivity is an important ideal toward which staff members should strive. It may be seen as an unreachable expectation early in treatment because so many patients evoke powerful feelings in treaters. As alluded to previously, such objectivity is particularly difficult for nursing staff members who must be with patients for an 8-hour shift. Although objectivity may be an ultimate ideal, members of the nursing staff as well as other members of the treatment team should be given the expectation that they will experience powerful feelings toward the patient that can be a useful diagnostic and therapeutic tool. A distinction can be made between having feelings and acting on them. Obviously, staff should be advised to note and discuss with other staff but to not act on feelings of a destructive or erotic nature. They should be encouraged to process their feelings in staff meetings and to use those feelings to diagnose and understand the internal object relations of the patient. As the treatment progresses, the staff will be armed with a greater understanding of the patient's internal object relations so that they are much less prone to countertransference identification and can instead clarify patients' distortions and the nature of their internal object worlds. Hence, if the staff members are given permission to experience powerful countertransference feelings and to discuss them early in the treatment of a given patient, they will be able to approach the patient more objectively as the treatment progresses.

If treaters are inclined to deny their countertransference hatred, anger, and contempt out of guilt, they will nevertheless communicate their intense negative feelings nonverbally (Poggi and Ganzarain 1983). Patients are extraordinarily adept at detecting these communications and may, as a result, become increasingly paranoid. As staff members acknowledge their own ambivalence and deal with it more openly, patients will be able to acknowledge their ambivalence and to be less afraid of their hatred. But as long as staff members deny their hatred, they only confirm the patient's fear that such feelings are unspeakable and must be avoided at all cost.

The model of staff-patient interaction suggested here is directly analogous to the one advocated for the psychotherapist in Chapter 4. Hospital staff members must avoid aloofness and must participate in the patient's interpersonal field in a spontaneous but controlled manner. This capacity to allow oneself to be "sucked in," but only partially, is an extraordinary asset that enables treaters to gain an empathic understanding of the patient's relationship problems (Hoffman and Gill 1988).

Splitting in Hospital Treatment

One advantage of hospital treatment over individual therapy is that the patient's self- and object-representations are externalized onto various staff members all at once rather than onto the psychotherapist alone in sequence over time. The hospital milieu, then, serves as a superb diagnostic and therapeutic tool for understanding the process of splitting (see Chapter 2).

Splitting in hospital treatment has been well described in a number of papers on the intense countertransference evoked by treatment-resistant borderline patients (Burnham 1966; Gabbard 1986; Main 1957). Empirical research suggests that splitting is not unique to borderline patients, however, but rather is characteristic of a wide variety of personality disorders (Allen et al. 1988a; Perry and Cooper 1986). Staff members find themselves assuming and defending highly polarized positions against one another with a vehemence out of proportion to the importance of the issue. The patient has presented one self-representation to one group of treaters and another self-representation to another group of treaters (Burnham 1966; Cohen 1957; Gabbard 1986; Searles 1965). Via projective identification, each self-representation evokes a corresponding reaction in the treater that can be understood as an unconscious identification with the projected internal object of the patient. The transference/countertransference paradigm produced by one self-object constellation may differ dramatically from that produced by another. This discrepancy may first manifest itself in a staff meeting where the patient is being discussed. Staff members may become puzzled by the disparate descriptions being voiced and may ask each other, "Are we talking about the same patient?"

Full-blown splitting of this variety boldly illustrates the time-honored notion that patients recapitulate their internal object world in the hospital milieu (Gabbard 1989). Various treaters become unconsciously identified with the patient's internal objects and play out roles in a script that is written by the patient's unconscious. Moreover, because of the element of control inherent in projective identification, there is often an obligatory quality to the treaters' responses. They feel compelled to behave "like someone else." If projective identification were not involved, the purely intrapsychic splitting that would result would cause little disturbance in the staff group. Nor would the staff group view the process as an instance of splitting, since they would probably not feel polarized and angry toward one another.

The splitting that occurs in hospital treatment represents a special instance where both intrapsychic and interpersonal splitting develop simultaneously (Hamilton 1988). The interpersonal aspects of splitting that occur in staff groups clearly parallel the intrapsychic splitting in the patient. Projective identification is the vehicle that converts intrapsychic splitting into interpersonal splitting.

Staff members who are singled out as recipients of projected internal objects of the patient are not randomly selected. More often than not, borderline patients have an uncanny ability to detect preexisting latent conflict among various staff members, and their projections may be guided accordingly. A vignette from an actual case (Gabbard 1989) illustrates this pattern.

Ms. E, a 26-year-old borderline patient, was admitted to the hospital in a suicidal crisis by her psychotherapist, Dr. F. Ten days after her admission, while she was still voicing suicidal ideation, Dr. F approached Mr. G, the head nurse of the unit, and said he would like to drive Ms. E to the local college campus so she could register for the semester. Mr. G replied that, according to hospital policy, patients who are on suicide precautions may not leave the unit. He suggested that Dr. F might wish to attend a unit staff meeting to further discuss the management of the patient. When Mr. G explained to Ms. E that she could not leave the unit to register, she was enraged with Mr. G and accused him of being a "tyrant" who had no regard for the individual needs of patients. She contrasted him with Dr. F, whom she idealized by saying that among all the staff members associated with her treatment, he was "the only one who understands me." At the ensuing staff meeting, a heated argument developed between Dr. F and Mr. G, who acted as a spokesperson for the unit staff. In the midst of this clash, Mr. G told Dr. F that the latter was well known for his contempt toward hospital policies and for his propensity to treat patients as "special." As a rebuttal to that accusation, Dr. F informed Mr. G that of all the nurses in the hospital, he was known as the most rigid and punitive.

This example demonstrates how splitting and projective identification do not occur in a vacuum. Ms. E clearly selected individuals who conveniently fit the internal object-relationship paradigms assigned to them. As several authors (Adler 1985; Burnham 1966; Shapiro et al. 1977) have noted, there is often a kernel of reality in the assignment of internal object projections to staff members. This vignette also reflects an observation by Burnham (1966), namely, that the cleavage is usually between those treaters who emphasize the administrative frame of reference (i.e., what is good for the group), versus those who emphasize an individualistic frame of reference based on what is good for an individual patient. Finally, while all treaters are at risk for involvement in splits, the pattern described in this vignette is perhaps most common in the treatment of borderline patients: the psychotherapist is viewed as an idealized figure, while the unit staff are devalued as insensitive and punitive. Another typical feature of this arrangement is that, in psychotherapy sessions, the patient may omit information deriving from day-to-day unit activities and instead focus exclusively on childhood memories and transference material (Adler 1985; Kernberg 1984). The psychotherapist then has no awareness of the problematic interactions on the unit and is caught by surprise when nursing staff focus attention on them.

As a result of this form of splitting, Adler (1985) noted that the hospital staff may actually exclude the psychotherapist from the process of treatment planning. In this manner the unit staff members may consolidate their alliance by projecting "badness" and incompetence outside the unit group into the psychotherapist. If this process goes on unchecked, it becomes impossible for the unit staff and the psychotherapist to reconcile their differences and meet halfway. Just like the patient's internal objects, they cannot be integrated. The regressive power of groups is well known and may result in the use of splitting and projective identification in otherwise well-integrated professionals (Bion 1961; Kernberg 1984; Oldham and Russakoff 1987).

When a staff group reaches this point of fragmentation, all too often the patient is blamed for attempting to divide and conquer (Rinsley 1980). What is often forgotten under these circumstances is that splitting is an *unconscious* process patients employ automatically to maintain their emotional survival. We do not generally blame patients for other defense mechanisms. The unique issue in splitting seems to be the treaters' perception that the patient is being consciously and maliciously destructive. An empathic frame of reference is useful for reminding staff members that splitting is the patient's attempt to *ward off* destructiveness for personal protection.

To summarize, splitting in hospital treatment involves four primary features: 1) the process occurs at an unconscious level; 2) the patient perceives individual staff members in dramatically different ways, based on projections of the patient's internal object-representations, and treats each staff member differentially according to those projections; 3) staff members react to the patient, via projective identification, as though they actually are the projected aspects of the patient; and 4) as a result, treaters assume highly polarized positions in staff discussions about the patient and defend those positions with extraordinary vehemence (Gabbard 1989).

The Management of Splitting in the Hospital

The management of splitting in a hospital setting nicely illustrates how psychodynamic principles can be practical and useful, even essential, in inpatient treatment. Any discussion of how to manage splitting in hospital treatment must begin with Burnham's (1966) caveat that the complete prevention of splitting is neither possible nor desirable. As with other defense mechanisms, splitting provides a safety valve that protects patients from what they perceive as overwhelming danger. It is a process that will develop regardless of preventive measures implemented by treaters. The essential point is that treatment staff must continuously monitor splitting to prevent it from destroying the treatment, devastating the morale of the staff, and irreparably damaging certain interstaff relationships. Instances of serious psychiatric morbidity and staff resignations have resulted from such situations (Burnham 1966; Main 1957).

Education is one important way to help staff manage splitting. All mental health professionals working with hospitalized patients should be thoroughly conversant with the concept of splitting and its variants. If unit staff members cannot recognize splitting when it develops, the management of the situation may be hopeless. In discussions of countertransference, staff members can be encouraged to work toward containing projected aspects of the patient rather than acting on them. Intense feelings toward patients should be viewed as useful material for discussion and supervision rather than as forbidden reactions that must be concealed from supervisors. By developing an understanding of the mechanism of splitting, unit staff members can learn to avoid exploiting it by refusing to accept idealization that would collude with the devaluation of other staff members (Adler 1973; Shapiro et al. 1977). Staff members must also learn to monitor their countertransference tendency to project aspects of themselves into the patient.

Education is only a beginning, however. Regular and frequent staff meetings that include the patient's psychotherapist should be part of the weekly routine of the psychiatric unit. A spirit of open communication about differences should be established and monitored by the staff. More than 30 years ago, Stanton and Schwartz (1954) persuasively demonstrated the prophylactic value of ferreting out and discussing covert staff disagreements. Psychotherapists must view themselves as part of the treatment team and ally themselves with the administrative decisions of the unit team (Adler 1985). Rigid adherence to concerns about confidentiality may feed right into the patient's splitting tendencies.

One primary goal in the treatment of patients with major character pathology is the integration of split self- and object-representations. Although interpretation of the splitting mechanism can help patients achieve more moderated and realistic views of themselves and others, it is rarely sufficient to mend the cleavage that occurs at the group level in the hospital. Interpretations to the patient are best viewed as adjuncts to other interventions at the level of staff interactions. Corresponding to the psychotherapist's approach to the internal world of the patient is the staff's goal of integrating and moderating the *external* objects.

To this end, it is often useful to have the staff member identified with the bad object and the treater identified with the good object meet jointly with the patient to frankly discuss the patient's perception of what is going on. This arrangement makes it more difficult for the patient to maintain polarized views because both treaters are acting human and reasonable. Moreover, treaters who are faced with this situation ordinarily become less polarized and move toward middle ground. The very separateness demanded by the splitting mechanism is undermined. Although this confrontation may temporarily increase the patient's anxiety, it also conveys the message that negative feelings can be contained within interpersonal relationships without disastrous consequences.

When the situation is so emotionally charged that the participants are not willing to meet, an objective consultant can be brought in to mediate the discussion (Gabbard 1986). The consultant can fulfill the role of an observing ego for the group and thereby encourage those individuals involved with the splitting to identify with that function, much as Shapiro et al. (1977) described the function of the psychotherapist when meeting with borderline adolescents and their families.

These meetings presuppose a recognition by all parties of an ongoing splitting process. Such acknowledgment constitutes a major step toward successful management of the splitting. Ordinarily, staff members will be considerably reluctant to see themselves as involved in splitting. When a special meeting is called to discuss the staff dynamics around a particular patient, there may be strong resistance on the part of treaters because such a meeting might make the patient seem too special (Burnham 1966). If the patient's psychotherapist is involved in the split, and willingly attends the staff meeting, it may be with a different agenda. Especially when idealized by the patient, the therapist is likely to assume a condescending attitude as educator so the staff will understand their countertransference reactions and the dynamics of the patient as well as the psychotherapist does. The psychotherapist's implicit message in this situation is that understanding the patient will lead the unit staff to stop blaming the patient. Rather than viewing the staff meeting as a productive way to discuss a splitting process, the psychotherapist is convinced that he or she is right while everyone else is wrong. Being idealized can be so gratifying that the therapist may not wish to examine the idealization as part of a defensive process in the patient (Finell 1985). This approach will, of course, infuriate the unit staff even further and widen the split.

When a staff meeting is called to discuss potential splitting, all parties should certainly approach one another with the assumption that they are all reasonable and competent clinicians who care about the patient's welfare. When this approach works, the group feels that each staff member has brought a piece of the puzzle so that the whole becomes more clear (Burnham 1966). However, some splits seem irreparable; and just as the internal objects of the patient cannot be integrated, neither can the external objects reconcile with one another. If the therapist is in the role of the devalued object, such stalemates occasionally end with the unit staff recommending a new therapist (Adler 1985).

The earlier that splitting is discovered, the less entrenched and the more amenable to change it will be. Certain warning signals should be continually monitored in staff meetings: 1) when a treater is uncharacteristically punitive toward a patient, 2) when a treater is unusually indulgent, 3) when one treater repeatedly defends a patient against critical comments from other staff members, and 4) when one staff member believes that no one else can understand the patient (Gabbard 1989).

When staff members can swallow their pride and accept that they may be involved in an unconscious identification with projected aspects of the patient, they can begin to empathize with their fellow staff members' feelings and perspectives. This willingness to consider someone else's point of view can lead to collaborative work on behalf of the patient that results in marked improvement in the splitting process. The patient's internal split often begins to mend at the same time the staff's external cleavage heals (Gabbard 1986).

These parallel developments may be understood as the third step of projective identification—the previously split-off and projected object-representations of the patient have been contained and modified by the treaters and have then been reintrojected (in modified form) by the patient in a meaningful interpersonal context. By approaching their own differences in good faith, staff members can provide an atmosphere in the milieu where good experiences predominate over bad ones—an essential condition for facilitating the integration of love and hate in the patient.

The Multidisciplinary Treatment Team

The typical treatment team in a psychiatric hospital is made up of representatives from several mental health disciplines—a psychiatrist, a psychologist, a social worker, an activities therapist, nurses, and mental health technicians. Latent interdisciplinary rivalries are fertile soil for the development of splits within the team. Individual team members must conceptualize their job as subsuming two different tasks: one involves the specific treatment assignment that goes with the discipline, and the other involves serving as a transference object or a container of projections (Kernberg 1984). Observations from both aspects of one's job must be continually brought into staff meetings and shared with the treatment team. All patients should understand that whatever they say will be passed on to other members of the treatment team, to gain a complete picture of the patient and to map out a more effective treatment plan. In this manner, splitting can be identified before it becomes destructive.

The social worker brings data to the treatment team from family members and other significant persons who inhabit the environment in which the patient lives. These real individuals may be compared and contrasted with the objects that inhabit the patient's internal world. As social workers perform their usual tasks of gathering data and communicating back and forth between family and patient, they soon find that they are "sucked in" to the family matrix. As they allow themselves to contain the projected aspects of the family members and significant others, they gain a greater appreciation of the forces that shape the patient's behavior. Similarly, the social worker's direct contacts with the patient can produce a greater appreciation of the patient's impact on the family. Finally, social workers may contribute a special perspective regarding the manner in which family conflicts are re-created in the milieu.

Other discipline members find that the completion of their treatment tasks is similarly affected by the patient's style of relatedness with them. The activities therapist, for example, sets out to assist the patient in completing a task. The patient's performance of that task provides a window into similar problems that the patient may encounter in vocational or educational settings. As the patient attempts to complete the task, characteristic object relations patterns are played out with the activities therapist. Nurses will encounter similar obstacles as they attempt to assist the patient with basic matters of hygiene, and psychologists will confront the same patterns as they encourage the patient to participate in psychological testing. This transference-countertransference model based on object relations theory cuts across all disciplines and forms the basis for a common language among the disciplines.

The Role of Group Treatment in the Milieu

The foregoing descriptions of the introjection and projection of self- and object-representations illustrate the need for careful monitoring of group process on every psychiatric unit. Frequent staff meetings are essential for integrating the split-off fragments circulating among staff members and patients. Similarly, regular group meetings with patients promote a careful processing of interactions between the staff and patients, and among patients themselves; they also serve to prevent acting out of conflicts that develop in these relationships. Object relations theory provides a good conceptual framework for understanding group process on the unit (Kernberg 1973, 1984; Oldham and Russakoff 1987). Stanton and Schwartz (1954) illustrated how dynamics in the patient group may directly reflect similar dynamics in the staff group. Specifically, it is commonplace for individual patients to act out covert staff conflicts. Systematic processing of interpersonal conflicts both in staff meetings and in meetings of patients and staff can be valuable in identifying parallel processes in the two groups.

   The actual focus of small patient groups in the hospital varies, depending on the ego strengths and the diagnostic categories of the patients on a particular unit. In general, however, psychotherapeutic group meetings serve as an interface between the patients' intrapsychic difficulties and their conflicts in the hospital environment. Kibel (1987) suggested that the focus of such groups should be on the interpersonal difficulties that emerge in daily life on the hospital unit. These difficulties can be linked to the patients' intrapsychic conflicts or deficiencies. He suggested de-emphasizing transference in such groups because the anxiety generated by transference work might overwhelm both the individual and collective egos of the group. Horwitz (1987), on the other hand, believed that transference focus may be of value in inpatient groups by serving to strengthen the therapeutic alliance within the group. When small group meetings are properly conducted, they may also become havens or sanctuaries in which patients can ventilate their feelings about the experience of being a psychiatric inpatient and staff members can, in turn, validate those feelings and experiences (Kibel 1987). More specific use of inpatient groups will be discussed in Sections II and III in the context of distinct diagnostic entities.

Indications

One might argue that this model of treatment based on transference and countertransference is more applicable to borderline and affectively disturbed patients than it is to schizophrenic patients. The withdrawn schizophrenic patient may not appear to form a transference relationship with treaters. In fact, the schizophrenic patient's internal object relations are re-created in the hospital milieu every bit as much as those of a borderline patient. They are simply less dramatic. Rangell (1982) noted that Freud's assertion that patients suffering from narcissistic neuroses do not form transferences is the only clinical observation he made that has not been validated by subsequent analytic experience. As Brenner (1982) pointed out, the apparent absence of transference *is* the transference. The schizophrenic patient has re-created his or her internal object world just as the borderline patient has. This relationship vis-à-vis the hospital treaters, which must be understood, clarified, and empathized with, is similar to the process of working with a nonpsychotic patient. Even schizophrenic patients have their own unique set of characterological defenses. Although many schizophrenic patients do not require the use of this model during a brief hospitalization, this form of treatment is certainly useful for those whose defenses thwart compliance (see Chapter 7).

Another potential objection is that a conceptual framework based on the modification of object relations is not applicable to short-term treatment in the same way that it is to long-term hospital treatment. The fallacy in this argument is the conceptualization of the hospital treatment as occurring in a vacuum rather than as existing as one segment of a continuous effort over many months or years. There is a cumulative effect of many different disconfirmations of the unconscious expectations of the patient over time. Only with repeated failure to provoke the same pattern of responses in treaters do patients ultimately begin to assimilate and internalize the new object relations presented to them. Long-term follow-up studies of borderline patients (McGlashan 1986; Stone et al. 1987) have indicated that maximal improvement does not occur until the second or third decade after discharge. Staff members of an inpatient unit or a partial hospitalization service, the psychotherapist, and friends and family may ultimately provide enough new experiences and responses to strengthen the patient's ego and improve his or her object relations to a level of increased functioning in society.

The indications for extended hospitalization are somewhat controversial in the current climate of cost containment. Most clinicians would agree that hospitalization should be kept as brief as possible. Ideally, psychiatric inpatient units should be used to address acute crises in the course of an illness. When the ego of the patient has been restored to its prior level of functioning, treatment can continue on an outpatient basis. This ideal model, however, addresses only a limited percentage of the psychiatric population. For the treatment-resistant patients who do not respond to somatic treatments or brief hospitalizations, who are relentlessly self-destructive or suicidal, or who lack any form of support system outside the hospital, extended hospitalization may necessarily be the treatment of choice (Allen et al. 1988b). When greater time is available to implement the transference-countertransference model described in this chapter, greater integration of split-off object relations units is possible. In view of splitting's role as a major cause of ego weakness (Kernberg 1975), the mending of splitting processes can be instrumental in the strengthening of ego functions such as impulse control, reality testing, and judgment (Gabbard 1986).

Serious treatment errors can be inflicted on the patient just as easily in a short-term setting as in a long-term setting. A sophisticated psychodynamic understanding of the patient assists the treaters in their efforts to avoid errors of technique. For example, if they understand the nature of the object relationship that is being repeated in the milieu, they may be able to resist the temptation to gratify the transference wish. Instead, they will seek to clarify and understand it. Similarly, they may avoid the pitfall of colluding with the patient's passive stance vis-à-vis treatment. A fundamental dynamic notion is that the patient is a collaborator in the treatment process. Psychodynamically informed hospital treatment encourages patients to reflect on connections between their present situation and childhood antecedents so that they can begin to understand how they are perpetuating patterns that were scripted long ago. Intimately connected with this notion is the idea that patients are capable of taking active steps to change their situation.

In Freud's (1914) original usage of the term *acting out,* he was noting the transference tendency of patients to repeat in action something from the past rather than to remember and verbalize it. The same phenomenon occurs in hospital treatment, where patients repeat their characteristic mode of engaging others in an attempt to gratify their needs and wishes. Another basic psychodynamic notion is that patients must move in the direction of reflecting and talking about their internal experience rather than allowing it to thrust them into action. This same goal is embraced by the staff members of a psychodynamically informed hospital unit. They repeatedly remind patients that they will not engage in the "dance" that is being repeated. Instead, they will ask patients to reflect and verbalize the origins of the need for the dance. Those patients who, for reasons of cognitive dysfunction, low intelligence, or psychotic withdrawal, cannot enter into a productive verbal interchange with staff members can nevertheless benefit from the nonverbal experiential aspects of new forms of object relatedness. As Ogden (1986) has stressed, a treatment does not have to be verbal to be psychoanalytic in nature.

In the contemporary psychiatric unit, psychodynamic theory and technique must take its place alongside psychopharmacologic interventions, family work, systems theory, and sociocultural considerations. Some Axis I patients and most patients with Axis II diagnoses will benefit from this model. Other Axis I patients make symptomatic improvements without the help of a psychoanalytically based understanding. In today's smorgasbord of psychiatric interventions, resistance to conventional treatment modalities may be the primary indication for psychodynamically informed hospital treatment for patients who have Axis I diagnoses. Even with nonresistant patients, however, the great advantage of the object relations approach is that it provides staff members with a sense of mastery over intense countertransference reactions. Working with difficult hospital patients is often an unrewarding line of work. The education and understanding provided for the staff by a psychodynamically informed clinician makes the job more bearable and more meaningful in the face of the continual emotional onslaught of highly disturbed patients.

References

Adler G: Hospital treatment of borderline patients. Am J Psychiatry 130:32–36, 1973

Adler G: Borderline Psychopathology and Its Treatment. New York, Jason Aronson, 1985

Allen JG, Deering CD, Buskirk JR, et al: Assessment of therapeutic alliances in the psychiatric hospital milieu. Psychiatry 51:291–299, 1988a

Allen JG, Scovern AW, Logue AM, et al: Indications for extended psychiatric hospitalization: a study of clinical opinion. Compr Psychiatry 29:604–612, 1988b

Bion WR: Experiences in Groups and Other Papers. New York, Basic Books, 1961

Brenner C: The Mind in Conflict. New York, International Universities Press, 1982

Burnham DL: The special-problem patient: victim or agent of splitting? Psychiatry 29:105–122, 1966

Cohen RA: Some relations between staff tensions and the psychotherapeutic process, in The Patient and the Mental Hospital: Contributions of Research in the Science of Social Behavior. Edited by Greenblatt M, Levinson DJ, Williams RH. Glencoe, IL, Free Press, 1957, pp 301–308

Finell JS: Narcissistic problems in analysts. Int J Psychoanal 66:433–445, 1985

Freud A: The Ego and the Mechanisms of Defense (1936), in The Writings of Anna Freud, Vol 2 (Revised Edition). New York, International Universities Press, 1966

Freud S: Remembering, repeating and working-through (further recommendations on the technique of psycho-analysis II) (1914), in The Standard Edition of the Complete Psychological Works of Sigmund Freud, Vol 12. Translated and edited by Strachey J. London, Hogarth Press, 1958, pp 145–156

Gabbard GO: The treatment of the "special" patient in a psychoanalytic hospital. International Review of Psychoanalysis 13:333–347, 1986

Gabbard GO: A contemporary perspective on psychoanalytically informed hospital treatment. Hosp Community Psychiatry 39:1291–1295, 1988

Gabbard GO: Splitting in hospital treatment. Am J Psychiatry 146:444–451, 1989

Hamilton NG: Self and Others: Object Relations Theory in Practice. Northvale, NJ, Jason Aronson, 1988

Harty MK: Countertransference patterns in the psychiatric treatment team. Bull Menninger Clin 43:105–122, 1979

Hilles L: Changing trends in the application of psychoanalytic principles to a psychiatric hospital. Bull Menninger Clin 32:203–218, 1968

Hoffman IZ, Gill MM: Critical reflections on a coding scheme. Int J Psychoanal 69:55–64, 1988

Horwitz L: Transference issues in hospital groups. Yearbook of Psychoanalysis and Psychotherapy 2:117–122, 1987

Kernberg OF: Psychoanalytic object-relations theory, group processes and administration: toward an integrative theory of hospital treatment. Annual of Psychoanalysis 1:363–388, 1973

Kernberg OF: Borderline Conditions and Pathological Narcissism. New York, Jason Aronson, 1975

Kernberg OF: Severe Personality Disorders: Psychotherapeutic Strategies. New Haven, Yale University Press, 1984

Kibel HD: Inpatient group psychotherapy—where treatment philosophies converge. Yearbook of Psychoanalysis and Psychotherapy 2:94–116, 1987

Kohut H: The Analysis of the Self: A Systematic Approach to the Psychoanalytic Treatment of Narcissistic Personality Disorders. New York, International Universities Press, 1971

Main TF: The ailment. Br J Med Psychol 30:129–145, 1957

McGlashan TH: The Chestnut Lodge follow-up study, III: long-term outcome of borderline personalities. Arch Gen Psychiatry 43:20–30, 1986

Menninger WC: Psychoanalytic principles applied to the treatment of hospitalized patients. Bull Menninger Clin 1:35–43, 1936

Menninger WC: The Menninger Hospital's Guide to the Order Sheet (1939). Bull Menninger Clin 46:1–112, 1982

Ogden TH: The concept of internal object relations. Int J Psychoanal 64:227-241, 1983

Ogden TH: The Matrix of the Mind: Object Relations and the Psychoanalytic Dialogue. Northvale, NJ, Jason Aronson, 1986

Oldham JM, Russakoff LM: Dynamic Therapy in Brief Hospitalization. Northvale, NJ, Jason Aronson, 1987

Perry JC, Cooper SH: A preliminary report on defenses and conflicts associated with borderline personality disorder. J Am Psychoanal Assoc 34:863–893, 1986

Poggi RG, Ganzarain R: Countertransference hate. Bull Menninger Clin 47:15–35, 1983

Rangell L: The self in psychoanalytic theory. J Am Psychoanal Assoc 30:863–891, 1982

Rinsley DB: Treatment of the Severely Disturbed Adolescent. New York, Jason Aronson, 1980

Rinsley DB: Borderline and Other Self Disorders: A Developmental and Object-Relations Perspective. New York, Jason Aronson, 1982

Schlesinger HJ, Holzman PS: The therapeutic aspects of the hospital milieu. Bull Menninger Clin 34:1–11, 1970

Searles HF: Collected Papers on Schizophrenia and Related Subjects. New York, International Universities Press, 1965

Searles HF: The "dedicated physician" in psychotherapy and psychoanalysis, in Crosscurrents in Psychiatry & Psychoanalysis. Edited by Gibson RW. Philadelphia, Lippincott, 1967, pp 128–143

Shapiro ER, Shapiro RL, Zinner J, et al: The borderline ego and the working alliance: indications for family and individual treatment in adolescence. Int J Psychoanal 58:77–87, 1977

Simmel E: Psycho-analytic treatment in a sanatorium. Int J Psychoanal 10:70-89, 1929

Stamm I: The hospital as a "holding environment." International Journal of Therapeutic Communities 6:219–229, 1985a

Stamm I: Countertransference in hospital treatment: basic concepts and paradigms. Bull Menninger Clin 49:432–450, 1985b

Stanton AH, Schwartz MS: The Mental Hospital: A Study of Institutional Participation in Psychiatric Illness and Treatment. New York, Basic Books, 1954

Strachey J: The nature of the therapeutic action of psycho-analysis. Int J Psychoanal 15:127–159, 1934

Stone MH, Stone DK, Hurt SW: Natural history of borderline patients treated by intensive hospitalization. Psychiatr Clin North Am 10:185–206, 1987

Weiss J, Sampson H, the Mount Zion Psychotherapy Research Group: The Psychoanalytic Process: Theory, Clinical Observations, and Empirical Research. New York, Guilford Press, 1986

Wesselius LF: Countertransference in milieu treatment. Arch Gen Psychiatry 18:47–52, 1968

Winnicott DW: The Maturational Processes in the Facilitating Environment: Studies in the Theory of Emotional Development. London, Hogarth Press, 1965

Zee HJ: Purpose and structure of a psychoanalytic hospital. Journal of the National Association of Private Psychiatric Hospitals 84:20–26, 1977

SECTION II

Dynamic Approaches to Axis I Disorders

CHAPTER 7

Schizophrenia

There is no developmental period when the human exists
outside of the realm of interpersonal relatedness.

— Harry Stack Sullivan (1947)

Genetic studies have amply demonstrated that schizophrenia is
a disease with a biological substrate (Kendler 1987; Schulsinger
et al. 1988). Research efforts in the neurosciences have resulted in
a quantum leap in our understanding of the etiology and pathogenesis of schizophrenia. The introduction of neuroleptic medication
revolutionized the treatment of chronic patients who might otherwise have been consigned to a lifetime of institutionalization. The
unfortunate downside of this progress in some quarters has been a
biological reductionism in the clinical management of schizophrenic patients. If we accept the fact that monozygotic twins have a
concordance rate of approximately 50 percent for schizophrenia
(Gottesman and Shields 1972), then we cannot escape the conclusion that environmental and psychological factors are equally important in the development of schizophrenia. A variety of individual
environmental stressors that interact with genetic vulnerability to
schizophrenia have been identified and studied in monozygotic
twins discordant for schizophrenia (Pollin and Stabeneau 1968).

None of the findings of biological research attenuates the
impact of one irreducible fact—schizophrenia is an illness that
happens to a person with a unique psychological makeup. Even if
genetic factors accounted for 100 percent of the etiology of schizophrenia, clinicians would still be faced with a dynamically complex
individual reacting to a profoundly disturbing illness. Sophisticated
psychodynamic approaches to the management of the schizophrenic patient will always be a vital component of the clinician's treatment armamentarium. Probably no more than 10 percent of schizophrenic patients are able to function successfully with a treatment
approach consisting only of antipsychotic medication and brief
hospitalization (McGlashan and Keats 1989). The remaining 90
percent require dynamically informed treatment approaches, including dynamic pharmacotherapy, individual therapy, group ther-

apy, family approaches, and dynamically informed hospital treatment, as the crucial ingredients in the successful management of their schizophrenia.

There is no such thing as *the* treatment of schizophrenia. All therapeutic interventions must be tailored to the unique needs of the individual patient. Schizophrenia is a heterogeneous illness with protean clinical manifestations. One helpful organization of the descriptive symptomatology of the disorder is a division into three clusters: 1) positive symptoms, 2) negative symptoms, and 3) disordered personal relationships (Andreasen et al. 1982; Keith and Matthews 1984; Munich et al. 1985; Strauss et al. 1974). First proposed by Strauss et al. (1974), this model distinguishes three discrete psychopathological processes found in schizophrenic patients. Positive symptoms include disturbances of thought content (such as delusions), disturbances of perception (such as hallucinations), and behavioral manifestations (such as catatonia and agitation) that develop over a short time and often accompany an acute psychotic episode.

While the florid positive symptoms constitute an undeniable "presence," the negative symptoms of schizophrenia are better categorized as an "absence" of function. These negative symptoms include restricted affect, poverty of thought, apathy, and anhedonia. Patients in which a negative symptom picture predominates tend to have poor premorbid adjustment, less education, poorer overall functioning, a greater prevalence of left-handedness, more difficulty holding jobs, and a higher ventricle/brain ratio on CT scans (Andreasen et al. 1982). These findings suggest that negative symptomatology may be more closely linked to a genetic-biological substrate. This hypothesis has been substantiated by a review of twin studies (Dworkin et al. 1988). When twins from pairs who were concordant for schizophrenia were compared with those who were discordant, the concordant pairs had poorer premorbid adjustment, more negative symptoms, earlier age of onset, and fewer paranoid symptoms than the discordant pairs, suggesting that both poor premorbid social adjustment and negative symptomatology are linked with either familial or genetic vulnerability to schizophrenia. An adoption study (Kendler et al. 1982) found that this vulnerability is most likely related to genetic influences rather than environmental familial factors.

In summary, then, considerable evidence points to a stronger genetic basis for negative symptoms, with a correspondingly weaker genetic link to paranoid and other positive symptoms. Carpenter et al. (1988) suggested a further distinction among negative symptoms. They pointed out that certain forms of social withdrawal, blunted affect, and apparent impoverishment of thought may actually be secondary to anxiety, depression, environmental deprivation, or drug effects. These manifestations should therefore not be labeled negative symptoms because they are short-lived and secondary. Carpenter et al. proposed the term deficit syndrome to refer to clearly primary negative symptoms that endure over time.

Like negative symptoms, disordered personal relationships tend to develop over a long time. These problems grow out of a characterological substrate, and include a myriad of interpersonal problems as varied as the range of human personality. Prominent manifestations of disordered interpersonal relationships include withdrawal, inappropriate expressions of aggression and sexuality, lack of awareness of the needs of others, excessive demandingness, and inability to make meaningful contact with other people. This third category is less rigorously defined than the other two because essentially every schizophrenic patient struggles with problems in interpersonal relationships. Indeed, all three categories overlap extensively, and one schizophrenic patient may move from one group to another during the course of the illness. The most useful aspect of these three models is that they facilitate categorizing the predominant manifestations of the illness at any one time so treatment can be adjusted accordingly. These distinctions are of heuristic and practical value not only at the level of descriptive symptoms but also in weighing dynamic considerations.

Psychodynamic Understanding of Schizophrenia

Many psychodynamic models have been proposed to assist clinicians in understanding the schizophrenic process. The conflict versus deficit controversy (described in Chapter 2) is a prominent feature in discussions of theories of schizophrenia. Freud himself vacillated between a conflict model and a deficit model of schizophrenia as his own conceptualization evolved (Arlow and Brenner 1969; Grotstein 1977a, 1977b; London 1973a, 1973b; Pao 1973). Much of Freud's conceptualization (1911, 1914, 1915, 1924a, 1924b) developed out of his notion of *cathexis,* by which he referred to the quantity of energy attached to any intrapsychic structure or object-representation. He was convinced that schizophrenia was characterized by a decathexis of objects. At times he used this concept of decathexis to describe a detachment of emotional or libidinal investment from intrapsychic object-representations, while at other times he used the term to describe social withdrawal from real persons in the environment (London 1973a). Freud defined schizophrenia as a regression in response to intense frustration and conflict with others. This regression from object-relatedness to an auto-erotic stage of development was accompanied by a withdrawal of emotional investment from object-representations and from ex-

ternal figures, which explained the appearance of autistic withdrawal in schizophrenic patients. Freud then postulated that the
patient's cathexis was reinvested in the self or ego (1914).

Some authors (London 1973a, 1973b; Wexler 1971) have
viewed Freud's decathexis theory as an acknowledgment of a deficit
model of schizophrenia, although Freud clearly attempted to take
conflict into account as well. After developing the structural model,
he revised his view of psychosis accordingly (1924a, 1924b). While
he viewed neurosis as a conflict between the ego and the id, he
regarded psychosis as a conflict between the ego and the external
world. Psychosis involved a disavowal and subsequent remodeling
of reality. Despite this revision, Freud continued to speak of the
withdrawal of cathexis and its reinvestment in the ego. He used the
withdrawal of object cathexis to explain his observation that, in
comparison to neurotic patients, schizophrenic patients were incapable of forming transferences.

Freud's notion that schizophrenic patients do not form transference attachments was undoubtedly related to the fact that he did
not attempt intensive therapeutic efforts with such patients. Harry
Stack Sullivan, on the other hand, devoted his life to the treatment
of schizophrenia and arrived at very different conclusions. He
believed that the etiology of the disorder resulted from early interpersonal difficulties (particularly in the child-parent relationship),
and he conceptualized the treatment as a long-term interpersonal
process that attempted to address those early problems. Faulty
mothering, according to Sullivan (1962), produced an anxiety-
laden self in the infant and prevented the child from having its needs
satisfied. This aspect of the self-experience was then dissociated, but
the damage to self-esteem was profound. The onset of the schizophrenic illness, in Sullivan's view, was a resurgence of the dissociated
self that led to a panic state and then psychotic disorganization.
Sullivan always considered the capacity for interpersonal relatedness to be present in even the most withdrawn schizophrenic. His
pioneering work with schizophrenic patients was carried on by his
disciple, Frieda Fromm-Reichmann (1950), who stressed that schizophrenic persons are not happy with their withdrawn state. They are
fundamentally lonely people who cannot overcome their fear and
distrust of others because of adverse experiences early in life.

While Sullivan and his followers were developing their interpersonal theories, early ego psychologists were observing that a
faulty ego boundary is one of the chief deficits in schizophrenic
patients. Federn (1952) did not agree with Freud's assertion that
object cathexis was withdrawn in schizophrenia. Instead, Federn
emphasized the withdrawal of ego boundary cathexis. He noted that
schizophrenic patients characteristically have no barrier between
what is inside and what is outside, because their ego boundary is no

longer psychologically invested (as it is in neurotic patients). Mahler (1952) believed that the ego boundary developed out of rhythmic cuddling, fondling, and other forms of bodily contact between infant and mother. She also believed that the absence of this normal stimulation in the mother-infant dyad led to the schizophrenic patient's difficulty with differentiating self from other. Moreover, the tendency of adult schizophrenic patients to merge or fuse psychologically with those around them can be understood as an attempt to reestablish the symbiotic bliss of early infancy. Unfortunately, this merger also creates catastrophic fears of annihilation, leading the schizophrenic patient to feel trapped between a wish for merger and a dread of disintegration. More recent authors (Blatt and Wild 1976; Grand 1982) have supported Mahler's earlier formulations by noting that the schizophrenic patients whose disturbances in body boundaries are the most severe also appear to be those with the most extensive chaos in their earliest relationships.

One question raised by the deficit versus conflict controversy is whether one theory can explain both neuroses and schizophrenia, or whether a separate, specific theory is needed to explain schizophrenia, which is fundamentally different from the neuroses. Arlow and Brenner (1969), for example, argued that the model of conflict, defense, and compromise formation applicable to neuroses requires no revision when applied to psychosis. The two conditions are *quantitatively* distinct but *qualitatively* similar. Psychosis, like neurosis, is a compromise formation, but it differs from neurosis in three ways: 1) regression is more severe, 2) conflicts related to aggression are more intense, and 3) disturbances of ego and superego functioning are more severe. What Freud described as decathexis, Arlow and Brenner viewed as a defensive retreat from conflict. They supported their theoretical framework with the observation that, contrary to Freud's assertion, schizophrenic patients do indeed form intense transferences. Some of these transference manifestations may be diametrically opposed to withdrawal, in that they involve a clinging, demanding wish to be taken care of. As noted in Chapter 6, even the apparent absence of transference *is* the transference of some schizophrenic patients (Brenner 1982). In other words, the schizophrenic patient's withdrawal from the clinician is a repetition of a past relationship. In this model, delusions and hallucinations can be understood as symptomatic compromise formations analogous to neurotic symptoms.

Deficiency models draw some support from biological research on schizophrenia. Grotstein (1977a, 1977b), for example, in his psychoanalytic formulation of schizophrenia, viewed a constitutionally based hypersensitivity to perceptual stimuli as its central defect. This notion is supported by psychopharmacological research identifying information processing and attention dysfunction as prime target areas of antipsychotic medication (Spohn et al. 1977). The inability to screen out various stimuli and to focus on one piece of data at a time is a central difficulty for most schizophrenic patients. Grotstein (1977a, 1977b) postulated that, as a result of this defective stimulus barrier, the unmodulated release of primitive destructive impulses resulted in a state of psychological emergency. To deal with these impulses, a schizophrenic person resorts early in life to massive defensive operations, such as splitting and projective identification, in a desperate effort to evacuate them into the mothering figure. Grotstein thus accommodated both the conflict model, which involves impulses and defenses against those impulses, and the deficit model, which stems from fundamental neurophysiological problems related to genetic-constitutional factors.

Ogden (1980, 1982) proposed a conflict model that differs sharply from the impulse-defense model of conflict used to explain neurosis. He believed that the key conflict in schizophrenia is "between wishes to maintain a psychological state in which meaning can exist, and wishes to destroy meaning and thought and the capacity to create experience and to think" (p. 531, 1980). In this conceptualization, schizophrenic patients unconsciously attack their own mental contents, including their perceptions, feelings, and thoughts, because they threaten the patient with overwhelming pain and unmanageable conflict. These patients can thus prevent themselves from paying attention to sources of internal misery, resulting in an extreme state of "shutdown" or psychological limitation that approximates nonexperience. The schizophrenic patient experiences persistent conflict over maintaining this state versus allowing some absorption of thoughts, feelings, and perceptions of the outside world that might lead to psychological growth. The autistic inaccessibility of the schizophrenic patient may be understood from this perspective. As this core schizophrenic conflict is resolved, the patient progresses, in three broad phases, out of this severe prohibition against experience: 1) ejecting thoughts into others through projective identification, 2) fragmenting and distorting thought content (manifested as a formal thought disorder), and 3) divesting all symbolic thought of its meaning (manifested by concreteness of thought).

The psychodynamic notion of conflict versus deficit can be integrated with the descriptive categorization of schizophrenia in terms of the three symptom clusters (London 1973a; Munich et al. 1985). Negative symptoms, which are closely linked to genetic factors and characterized by the absence of function, can clearly be viewed as deficits. Positive symptoms, however, are often associated with acute onset in response to precipitating events and are closely allied with conflict. The disorders of interpersonal relationships may arise from intrapsychic conflicts, but may also be related to basic ego defects.

Regardless of whether a conflict, deficit, or combined conflict-deficit model is invoked to explain schizophrenia, certain common threads run through all these frameworks. First, psychotic symptoms have meaning. Grandiose delusions or hallucinations, for example, often immediately follow an insult to a schizophrenic patient's self-esteem (Garfield 1985; Garfield et al. 1987). The grandiose content of the thought or perception is the patient's effort to offset the narcissistic injury. Second, human relatedness is fraught with terror for these patients. In the vast literature on the psychotherapy of schizophrenia, there is a clear consensus that an early disturbance between the infant and the mothering figure is an almost universal finding in schizophrenic patients (McGlashan 1983). In some cases, as Sullivan observed, the mothers of schizophrenic individuals are disturbed themselves and are incapable of providing a dependable, secure, holding environment for their infant. Clinicians nowadays, however, are less inclined to blame mothers for causing schizophrenia. Rather, a more balanced perspective is that it results from an interaction between an infant with an impaired stimulus barrier, based on genetic-constitutional factors, and a mother who may not be emotionally equipped to handle an unusual child. The notion of mother-infant "fit" described in Chapter 1 is certainly relevant to the etiology and pathogenesis of schizophrenia. For whatever reason, mothers are unable to serve as containers for the projective identifications of their infants, so the infants are deprived of the experience of projecting and then reinternalizing their feelings in modified form after they have been processed by their mothers (Bion 1959; Ogden 1982). Finally, although few authors speak of cure, virtually all would agree that dynamically informed therapeutic relationships with sensitive clinicians can fundamentally improve the quality of life for schizophrenic patients.

Treatment Approaches

Pharmacotherapy

Well-designed controlled studies abundantly demonstrate that antipsychotic medication is highly efficacious in managing the positive symptoms of schizophrenia. The schizophrenic patient's accessibility to all other forms of therapeutic intervention is greatly enhanced by the judicious use of neuroleptics. Keith and Matthews (1984) even asserted that "freedom from positive symptoms approaches a *sine qua non* status for psychosocial treatments" (p. 71). Negative symptoms and disordered interpersonal relationships, however, are much less affected by medication and thus require psychosocial approaches.

Because numerous outstanding psychopharmacology texts are available, we will focus on dynamic approaches to treatment. As discussed in Chapter 5, noncompliance with prescribed medication is an ongoing problem in the treatment of many schizophrenic patients. Dynamic psychiatrists involved in the long-term management of patients suffering from schizophrenia must view medication compliance as a treatment concern. Each patient must be educated about the likelihood of relapse if medication is stopped, about signs of tardive dyskinesia, and about management of the more benign side effects. In addition, the meaning of the medication to the patient must be explored from time to time, particularly at the first sign of noncompliance. As emphasized in Chapter 5, the prescribing of antipsychotic medication must occur in the context of a therapeutic alliance that is carefully fostered through sensitivity to the patient's internal experience of all treatments.

Individual Psychotherapy

For the patient whose positive symptoms remit as a result of antipsychotic medication, treatment has just begun. Even when the hallucinations are gone, the challenge of life can be overwhelming. Relationships appear fraught with peril. Each day may bring a new wave of unspeakable terror and multiple uncertainties. The demands of a job seem out of the question. The expectations of the patient's family may appear as harsh and unrealistic. To navigate these perilous waters, such patients need a consistent, reliable, supportive human relationship.

Despite a rich clinical tradition of individual psychoanalytically oriented psychotherapy of schizophrenia, research studies have been hard pressed to demonstrate that the average schizophrenic patient is likely to reap significant benefit from such efforts (Gomez-Schwartz 1984). The Camarillo State Hospital Study (May 1968) is often cited because it was the first large-scale study that compared outcomes of schizophrenic patients according to whether they were treated with psychotherapy or neuroleptic medication. The patient groups who received medication showed significantly greater improvement than those who did not receive it and those who received psychotherapy alone. Moreover, no interaction effect was noted between psychotherapy and antipsychotic medication. This study has been criticized, however, because it relied on inexperienced therapists who had no particular commitment to the type of psychotherapy they were instructed to practice with their research subjects. Also, the outcome measures were not sensitive enough to pick up changes in interpersonal and general psychological functioning that might specifically respond to psychotherapy (Conte and Plutchik 1986). Two other studies that were also fraught with methodological problems (Grinspoon et al. 1972; Rogers et al. 1967) found questionable benefit from psychotherapy. Karon and VandenBos (1981) demonstrated more improvement in schizophrenic patients treated by experienced therapists, as compared with a control group of patients who received routine treatment with phenothiazines and supportive therapy, but this study has also been criticized for such methodological problems as a lack of random assignment and early transfer of patients in the drug treatment group to a chronic unit (Keith and Matthews 1984; Klein 1980).

By far the most elegantly designed study on the effects of psychotherapy with schizophrenic patients is the Boston study reported by Stanton, Gunderson, and colleagues (Gunderson et al. 1984; Stanton et al. 1984). A principal failure in previous studies had been the lack of definition in the form of psychotherapy being administered by project therapists. In the Boston study, nonchronic schizophrenic patients from diverse institutional and outpatient settings were assigned either to reality-adaptive, supportive psychotherapy (RAS) or to exploratory, insight-oriented psychotherapy (EIO). Those included in the analysis (95 of the original 164 patients) remained in their assigned treatment situation for at least 6 months. At 2-year follow-up, the investigators obtained complete data on 47 of the original sample. At this point in the data analysis, patients receiving RAS showed less recidivism and better role performance. On the other hand, patients who received EIO had greater improvements in cognition and ego functioning. The investigators concluded that overall differences between the two groups were relatively minor.

Unfortunately, despite the sophisticated methodology and design of the Boston study, generalizability of the results must be limited for several reasons. First, only 47 patients completed the 2-year course of the project; thus many of the definitive comparisons were based on approximately 20 subjects in each treatment group (Carpenter 1984). Second, the data collection stopped after 2 years. Many experienced therapists of schizophrenic patients would consider 2 years as merely the beginning of the middle phase of therapy. Schizophrenic patients are notoriously difficult to engage in a psychotherapeutic process. It is common for such patients to take a whole year just to be able to "say hello" to their doctor. Moreover, expecting a therapist to adhere to either a more-or-less expressive or more-or-less supportive model in the treatment of a schizophrenic patient introduces an artificiality into the treatment being evaluated. Nowhere is flexibility more important than in the psychotherapy of schizophrenia. As stressed in Chapter 4, in a naturalistic setting, the psychotherapist will shift back and forth from expressive to supportive interventions, depending on the needs of the patient at a given moment.

The investigators themselves (Glass et al. 1989) subsequently blindly rated the actual process of therapy from audiotaped transcripts and concluded that the earlier finding of little overall differences between the two groups "concealed discrete processes within the therapies that have important and specific effects" (p. 607). Therapists who were rated as skilled in dynamic exploration produced greater improvements in global psychopathology, denial of illness, and retardation-apathy.

Finally, one other irreducible difference between the needs of research and the ambience of clinical practice should be taken into account in interpreting the data from the Boston study. The motivations, both conscious and unconscious, that lead a psychotherapist to enter into what could become a lifelong commitment to treating a schizophrenic patient are both mysterious and highly personal. Whatever forces lead a therapist and patient to "choose" each other are ignored by large group designs that require, with scientific rigor, random assignment of patient to therapist (Müller 1984). Only intensive study of individual cases can shed light on this significant contributor to psychotherapeutic success.

In a subsequent report, Gunderson (1987) acknowledged the difficulty of engaging schizophrenic patients in a long-term psychotherapy process. He noted that his study and others suggested that about two-thirds of schizophrenic patients will drop out of psychotherapy when assigned nonspecifically as part of a research study. Gunderson carefully examined the data from the Boston study to determine the typical characteristics of those who continued in psychotherapy. His surprising finding was that they were characterized by social isolation, emotional flatness, and internal disorganization. However, they tended to have more consistent role performance than the dropout group. He also determined that dropout rate is affected by cultural norms within the hospital milieu. For example, patients from the Veterans Administration hospital used in the study were much more likely to drop out than those hospitalized at McLean Hospital, where psychotherapy is a standard part of treatment. Gunderson also concluded that longer-term hospitalization may be helpful in engaging patients. When he divided the patients according to whether they received RAS or EIO therapy, he determined that emotionally distant, thought-disordered patients with an optimistic view of their illness were most likely to continue with the former modality, while patients who were more likely to continue with the latter treatment had fairly intact reality testing, reasonably good interpersonal relatedness, and a view of their psychotic episode as an unfortunate event.

Gunderson's findings resonate with those of McGlashan's (1984, 1987) long-term follow-up study of patients treated at Chestnut Lodge. In this study, 163 schizophrenic patients previously hospitalized at Chestnut Lodge while receiving intensive psychoanalytically oriented psychotherapy were followed up an average of 15 years after discharge. About one-third of these patients had moderate to good outcomes (McGlashan 1984). Of the two identifiable groups whose psychosis remitted, one group attempted to integrate the psychotic experience into their life. They believed that they had gained important information from the psychotic episode, and they were curious about the meaning of their symptoms. The second group showed another pathway to stable recovery, namely, by sealing over the illness. These patients tended to have a fixed negative view of their illness and no interest in understanding their psychotic symptoms. Although both groups had achieved reasonably stable adjustments, those who integrated the experience appear to have had somewhat superior outcomes.

These findings suggest that patients who can integrate a psychotic experience into their life may benefit from exploratory work in the context of psychotherapy, while those who seal over a psychotic episode will probably not benefit or will perhaps be harmed by persistent exploratory attempts. Even psychotherapies that involve some insight will require significant support by the therapist. The expressive-supportive distinction is certainly less rigid in the psychotherapy of schizophrenia than in the treatment of higher-functioning patients. Regardless of whether exploratory work accompanies the supportive efforts of the therapist, certain principles of technique (Table 7-1) can guide the psychotherapy of any schizophrenic patient.

Table 7-1. Principles of technique in the psychotherapy of schizophrenia

1. The main focus should be on building a relationship.
2. The therapist must maintain a flexible stance regarding the mode and content of therapy.
3. For psychotherapy to proceed, therapists and patients must find and maintain an optimal distance.
4. The therapist must create a holding environment.
5. The therapist must serve as a "container" for the patient.
6. The therapist must serve as an auxiliary ego for the patient.
7. The therapist must be genuine and open with the patient.
8. The therapist should postpone interpretation until the therapeutic alliance is solid.
9. The therapist must maintain respect for the patient's need to be ill.

1. *The main focus should be on building a relationship.* Most schizophrenic patients will experience human relationships as risky
undertakings. No significant therapeutic work is likely without a
solid therapeutic alliance. Schizophrenic patients often must
struggle to trust a therapist enough to form a therapeutic alliance.
Hence much of the early work must be directive and designed to
repair the patient's deficits that impede development of a therapeutic alliance (Selzer 1983). Therapists must help their patients
test reality, strengthen their ego boundaries (by pointing out
what belongs to the patient and what belongs to others), and
assist them in fostering an observing ego so that these patients
can maintain some objectivity about their experiences and can
therefore reflect on them. Following supportive work with these
deficits, patients may be able to engage in a therapeutic alliance
that can lead to some exploratory work (Selzer 1983). This initial
process can take as long as a year or more.
2. *The therapist must maintain a flexible stance regarding the mode and
content of therapy.* Some patients may simply feel that sitting and
talking in an office is not a viable situation. With such patients,
the therapist may have to conduct the therapy while taking a walk
or while sitting at a table over a cup of coffee. Some patients may
communicate much better through an artistic medium, such as
drawing or painting, and the therapist should be prepared to
engage patients wherever they feel most comfortable. Playing
cards or table tennis enables some patients to talk who would
otherwise pass each session in anxious silence. In some ways, the
model of play therapy used by child therapists is applicable to
psychotherapy of schizophrenia, in that it implies an absence of
rigidity in relating to the patient.
3. *For psychotherapy to proceed, therapists and patients must find and
maintain an optimal distance.* Interpersonal boundaries are subject to highly idiosyncratic perceptions and distortions by the
schizophrenic patient. Therapists must allow their patients to
adopt a spatial and temporal distance that frees therapy from
excessive anxiety. For example, patients should be informed that
they can move their chair to any part of the office where they feel
comfortable. Similarly, the frequency of appointments should be
decided collaboratively with the patient. One hospitalized patient
told her doctor, who had been seeing her four times a week, that
she felt pressured by such frequent visits and simply could not
talk because of that pressure. She promised that if he would come
only twice a week, she would have a great deal to say. The quality
of their sessions improved markedly after the therapist acceded
to her request. In addition, the therapist should not be rigidly
locked into 50-minute appointments. Many patients feel much
more comfortable with frequent 25- or 30-minute appointments

rather than less frequent 50-minute sessions. The establishment of optimal distance also allows for silence. Some patients maintain a comfortable distance by periodically "shutting down," and the therapist must be able to accept this withdrawal as a necessary break from the intensity of their relationship.

4. *The therapist must create a holding environment.* McGlashan and Keats (1989) emphasized that, above all, psychotherapy should offer *asylum.* Patients must experience each psychotherapeutic session as "a safe place" where they are encircled by the caring and concern of the therapist. Feelings and thoughts that others do not understand are accepted by the psychotherapist. Similarly, withdrawal or bizarre behavior is accepted and understood without any demand that the patient must change to be acceptable. Much of this aspect of technique consists of "being-with" (McGlashan and Keats 1989, p. 159), a willingness to consistently put oneself in the company of another human being without making inordinate demands.

5. *The therapist must serve as a "container" for the patient.* Powerful feelings are stirred up in the psychotherapeutic relationship, and the patient may need to project these disturbing affects into the therapist to gain distance from them. Therapists must be able to process and detoxify these affects without acting on them (Grotstein 1976; Ogden 1980). The therapist thus contains both transference and countertransference feelings and provides a new model of relatedness to be reinternalized by the patient.

6. *The therapist must serve as an auxiliary ego for the patient.* The profound ego weaknesses found in the schizophrenic patient may be bolstered by the therapist's activity. If the patient's judgment is impaired, the therapist may have to help the patient think through consequences of actions. If the patient's reality testing is faulty, the therapist may have to point out the difference between internal and external stimuli. This auxiliary ego function may be particularly helpful in the here-and-now situation of the therapeutic relationship. One patient, for example, said to his therapist, "You're feeling hungry, aren't you?" The therapist responded by saying, "I just had lunch before we met, so I bet that you're probably feeling hungry and figured that I shared your feeling."

7. *The therapist must be genuine and open with the patient.* The opacity and anonymity characteristic of the classical analytic position are not appropriate for the treatment of patients with schizophrenia who are in desperate need of a genuine relationship. If all negative feelings are denied and split off in the therapeutic relationship, the patient will experience the therapist as unreal. Moreover, the therapist's apparent ability to transcend all feelings of anger, boredom, hatred, and frustration simply increases

the patient's envy of the therapist (Searles 1967). This posture does not imply that the therapist should engage in extensive self-disclosure or reveal insensitive expressions of negative affects toward the patient. Therapists may, however, share items of personal interest with the patient and may wish to validate the patient's perception of feelings such as irritation, sadness, and other unpleasant sensations.

8. *The therapist should postpone interpretation until the therapeutic alliance is solid.* McGlashan and Nayfack (1988) studied the detailed records of three different psychotherapy processes with one patient hospitalized at Chestnut Lodge. The first therapist, working from a defense-conflict model, made frequent interpretations of unconscious content, while the latter two employed a predominantly supportive strategy. The authors noted that the patient benefited far more from the latter two therapists' efforts to establish a positive, trusting relationship than from the first therapist's efforts to analyze unconscious meaning. They noted that intense demands for relatedness and in-depth exploration are likely to promote relapse in schizophrenic patients. Instead, resistance must be respected and gently eroded over a long time through gentle but persistent curiosity. Just as a surgeon must use anesthesia to operate, the therapist must carefully create an ambience of trusting relatedness to pave the way for an interpretation.

9. *The therapist must maintain respect for the patient's need to be ill.* No matter how pathological, the illness of schizophrenia is some form of intrapsychic solution for the patient. The omnipotent fantasy of rescuing the patient from schizophrenia is doomed to failure; it is the worst possible psychological attitude for a therapist (McGlashan 1983). Therapists must be comfortable with the possibility that patients will choose the "devil they know" rather than face the uncertainties of change and improvement. Effective psychotherapy requires an attitude in the therapist that allows the patient's wish to remain ill as an acceptable alternative to psychotherapeutic change (Searles 1979).

Why, then, should clinicians undertake psychotherapy with schizophrenic patients, given the lack of sterling research data to demonstrate its efficacy, and knowing the painstaking slowness and psychological tribulations of the process itself? Group research designs mask the shining success stories with individual patients. More significantly, small improvements in disorders of interpersonal relatedness and negative symptoms, following remission of positive symptoms through antipsychotic medication, may significantly enhance the schizophrenic person's quality of life. In the recent professional literature, schizophrenic patients have spoken eloquently about the benefits of individual psychotherapy (Anonymous 1986; Ruocchio 1989). These patients comment on the importance of having one consistent figure in their lives who is there through any adversity over many years. These patients convey how their subjective experience of themselves and their lives was significantly altered by a long-term psychotherapeutic relationship, even though outcome measures may not be sensitive enough to record such alterations. In the words of one patient (Anonymous 1986), "A fragile ego left alone remains fragile. . . . Medication or superficial support alone is not a substitute for the feeling that one is understood by another human being" (p. 70).

Group Psychotherapy

Studies of group psychotherapy with schizophrenic patients suggest that this modality may be useful, but emphasize the timing of its implementation. The optimal time appears to be after positive symptoms are stabilized through pharmacologic intervention (Kanas et al. 1980; Keith and Matthews 1984). The acutely disorganized patient is unable to screen out environmental stimuli, and the multiple inputs from a group setting may overwhelm the patient's beleaguered ego just when it is attempting to reestablish itself. One review of controlled studies of group therapy for schizophrenia (Kanas 1986) found considerable evidence for the efficacy of inpatient group psychotherapy but a clear trend for greater success on long-term chronic units than on acute wards. After positive symptomatology is controlled, inpatient groups can be highly supportive for schizophrenic patients as they are reorganizing and as they see others preparing for discharge. Efficacy studies suggest that, as an outpatient modality, group therapy may be as effective as individual therapy (O'Brien 1983). For the patient who is stabilized on medication, weekly sessions of 60–90 minutes can serve to build trust and can provide a support group where patients can freely discuss concerns such as how to manage auditory hallucinations and how to deal with the stigma of mental illness.

Family Intervention

In the empirical research literature on the efficacy of psychosocial interventions with schizophrenia, no modality has been substantiated more than family interventions. Numerous studies (Falloon et al. 1982; Goldstein et al. 1978; Hogarty 1984; Leff et al. 1982) have demonstrated that family treatment plus antipsychotic medication is three times as effective as medication alone in preventing relapse.

These investigations used a factor known as expressed emotion (EE), first identified by Brown et al. (1972). This term was coined to describe a style of interaction between family members and the patient that is characterized by intense overinvolvement and excessive criticism. Although this concept does not blame parents for causing schizophrenia in their children, it does acknowledge that families are affected by schizophrenia and that they may become secondary contributors to relapse through an intensification of their interactions with the schizophrenic patient. In brief, high EE families produce a greater frequency of relapse in a schizophrenic member than low EE families.

The extensive research on expressed emotion has led to a sophisticated psychoeducational approach with families of schizophrenic persons. The families are trained to recognize prodromal signs and symptoms that presage relapse, are taught to reduce criticism and overinvolvement, and are helped to see that a consistent medication program can preserve optimal functioning. Other areas of education include instruction about the side effects of medications and their management, the long-term course and prognosis of schizophrenia, and the genetic and biological basis of schizophrenia. Clinicians using this approach can effectively enlist the family's help as collaborators in the prevention of relapse.

The impressive results obtained with this conceptual model of family intervention have recently been challenged, however. Some investigators have questioned whether controlling expressed emotion is the exclusive factor involved in relapse prevention. One study (MacMillan et al. 1986) found that the regular ingestion of neuroleptic medication and preadmission duration of illness were factors that, when taken into account, canceled out the effect of expressed emotion in predicting relapse. A more recent study (Parker et al. 1988) examined 57 schizophrenic patients from the standpoint of the expressed emotion level of the household. Relapse was predicted by a one-parent household and by a poor course of prior illness, but the level of expressed emotion was not predictive. The investigators speculated that those patients with a poor course may evoke responses in relatives that are high in expressed emotion, particularly if the patient lives in a one-parent household.

As new research continues to refine our understanding of the factors involved in relapse, a sophisticated psychoeducational approach with families of schizophrenic patients makes sound clinical sense. Overinvolvement challenges the tenuously maintained ego boundary of the schizophrenic patient, while barrages of criticism erode the already beleaguered self-esteem of the patient who is struggling to reorganize after a psychotic episode. Finally, family members who can establish greater distance in their relationship with a schizophrenic relative will decrease the amount of stimuli with which the patient must contend. If optimal distance makes good sense in psychotherapy, it makes equally good sense in the home environment.

Hospital Treatment

Short-term hospitalization. For the schizophrenic patient who has an acute psychotic break, brief hospitalization provides "time out," a chance to regroup and gain new direction for the future. Antipsychotic medication provides relief from most positive symptoms. The structure of the hospital unit provides a safe haven to prevent patients from hurting themselves or others. Nursing staff members in the milieu perform auxiliary ego functions for the patient. The treatment team can also diagnose stressors on Axis IV of DSM-III-R (American Psychiatric Association 1987) that might contribute to a psychotic episode at this particular time in the patient's life. A psychoeducational effort can begin with the patient and family to establish an optimal posthospital environment. They should be prepared for the fact that they are dealing with a lifelong disease, and that the goal is to minimize disability, not effect a lasting cure. The importance of staying on medication is emphasized, and the concept of expressed emotion may be explained as well. At the same time, the treatment team needs to convey a sense of hope. It is often useful to point out that although the disease is chronic, considerable research suggests that aging schizophrenic patients become more and more functional (Harding et al. 1987).

The thrust of brief hospitalization is counterregressive. Defenses are restored, and the patient should be returned to functioning as expeditiously as possible. If the patient is not established in psychotherapy, the hospital may be used as a preparatory phase to get the patient ready for an outpatient psychotherapy process (Selzer 1983). The patient's omnipotence is challenged by the necessity of accommodating to the needs of others. By enforcing a routine schedule in patients' lives, some frustration of their needs and wishes is unavoidable. This optimal level of frustration helps patients improve reality testing and other ego functions (Selzer 1983). If psychotherapy can be started during the hospitalization, the patient can then maintain a sense of continuity by continuing the therapeutic relationship outside the hospital. After the patient's positive symptomatology is relieved to some extent, group treatment may be instituted and may also be continued on an outpatient basis, depending on the patient's amenability to the group format. For some isolated outpatients, group meetings may be their only significant social contact.

Extended hospitalization. Although brief hospitalization with rapid restoration of function and return to posthospital life is the optimal scenario, a significant percentage of schizophrenic patients are simply too impaired to work within this model. This subgroup requires extended hospitalization. These patients include those who adamantly refuse medication, do not respond to medication, are relentlessly self-destructive or suicidal, are aggressive toward others, and have no family or other support system to help them manage the vicissitudes of daily existence. These patients require a sophisticated milieu approach that combines dynamically informed hospital treatment, psychotherapy, and repair of vocational, social, and cognitive deficits (Munich et al. 1985).

For those patients with predominantly negative symptoms, diagnosis and medication can be reassessed. Are there secondary reasons, such as depression, anxiety, and medication side effects, that might account for the negative symptoms? Similarly, the psychotherapy process, if ongoing, can be reevaluated with the collaboration of the therapist to determine whether to make a shift in strategy. Family work can proceed in a psychoeducational fashion, and family members can be enlisted in the search for ongoing stressors that prevent the patient from responding to conventional treatment. Most of all, the negative symptom group requires social and vocational rehabilitation. Social skills groups that focus on behavioral improvement in such simple daily behaviors as eating, conversation, walking, and manners can be extraordinarily valuable for the negative symptom group. Similarly, a careful vocational evaluation in a supervised situation in which concrete job skills are taught and developed is an essential component of extended hospitalization. As Munich et al. (1985) noted, "extended treatment designed to bring about symptom reduction and 'insight' into intrapsychic conflict alone is insufficient to return chronically schizophrenic patients to the community and sustain them there" (p. 161).

Research on posthospital adjustment and rehospitalization rates demonstrates that patients are more likely to stay out of the hospital when they have been taught adaptive behaviors and skills and have learned to control symptomatic and maladaptive behaviors during their inpatient stay (Mosher and Keith 1979). Although the behavioral focus of such milieu programs may seem antithetical to dynamic psychiatrists, this focus actually may work synergistically with dynamic approaches. Patients who improve their interpersonal relations as a result of behaviorally oriented social skills training will begin to experience changes in their object relations, which then stir up material for discussion in psychotherapy.

Schizophrenic patients who are treatment resistant and therefore require extended hospitalization may also display a predominant picture of disordered interpersonal relatedness. These patients frequently have serious characterological difficulties that coexist with schizophrenia. Clinicians are sometimes prone to forget that every schizophrenic patient also has a personality. These characterological problems may therefore result in noncompliance with medication, alienation of family members and other supportive persons in the environment, denial of illness, and inability to function in a vocational setting. Extended hospitalization may be the ideal setting in which to address the characterological dimension accompanying the schizophrenia and to examine the underpinnings of the patient's noncompliance.

To a large extent, the hospital treatment of such patients follows the model outlined in Chapter 6. Via projective identification, patients attempt to reestablish their internal object world in the hospital. Hospital staff members contain those projections and provide new models of relatedness for reinternalization. In addition, patients are informed about maladaptive interactional patterns as they occur in the here-and-now of the hospital setting.

Many of the treatment principles described in this chapter can be illustrated in a detailed case example.

Mr. H, a 22-year-old single man from the southeastern United States, had a three-year history of schizophrenia that had not responded either to outpatient treatment with medication or to brief hospitalization. Referred for extended psychiatric hospitalization, he came for admission accompanied by his parents. When asked to describe his problems, he recited a litany of physical complaints involving virtually every anatomical area of his body, but steadfastly denied any psychiatric problems. When he learned that he was being admitted to a psychiatric facility, he was reluctant to sign himself into the hospital. Only with repeated reassurances that a complete physical and neurological workup was part of the psychiatric evaluation would he consent to hospitalization.

The patient's somatic preoccupations precluded any history-taking of his psychiatric disorder. Fortunately, his parents were able to fill in the gaps. Mr. H was the third of three children born to highly successful parents. The patient's father was a respected business executive, while his mother had a prominent administrative position in the school system. His older brother was a graduate of a prestigious medical school, and his older sister was an honors student in her MBA program. The patient himself had briefly attended college, but was forced to drop out after the onset of his illness. He complained of hypersensitivity to noise in his dormitory, and he expressed concern that others were talking about him. He finally demanded to be taken home so that he would not be humiliated by other boys in the dormitory, who he claimed were calling him "loser," "fag," and "crazy" in the middle of the night.

After leaving college, Mr. H returned to live with his parents, where he became increasingly demanding of their time. When his father attempted to leave for work in the morning, the patient would run out the door after him and sometimes jump on the hood of his car to prevent him from leaving. He would also wake his father in the middle of the night to demand that he listen to a recital of his physical complaints. He repeatedly accused his father of neglect by saying, "What are you going to do about my pain?" Mr. H had been seen by numerous specialists, and often several specialists in one field, without any diagnosis of physical disease. He insisted that he needed continual "monitoring" from his parents so that they would be aware of the waxing and waning of his physical symptoms. Mr. H was blessed with loving and concerned parents, who attempted to accommodate his pleas for attention by spending long periods with him. On one occasion, the patient's father sat and listened to the patient's somatic preoccupations for 10 hours without a break.

Mr. H also continued to hear voices condemning him, and in one instance he assaulted a stranger on the street because he was convinced that the stranger was saying unpleasant things about him. Mr. H had been hospitalized for a few weeks on two different occasions and had been prescribed four different antipsychotic medications at various times. Each time the patient discontinued the medication because of his denial that he had a psychiatric condition that warranted psychotropic medication and because of anticholinergic side effects that bothered him.

Shortly after admission, a mental status examination revealed that the patient continued to suffer from auditory hallucinations, although he did not complain of "hearing voices." Rather, he was convinced that people were actually talking about him. On several occasions during the first few days of his hospitalization, he angrily confronted other patients because he thought that they were ridiculing him. All the patients vehemently denied talking about him. In addition, Mr. H found it difficult to complete a thought because of a formal thought disorder that consisted of blocking and derailment. He would stop in midsentence, change the subject, then begin another sentence.

Mr. H displayed much anxiety in the hospital because none of the staff members would "monitor" his physical symptoms as his parents did. As expected, the patient attempted to recreate his family situation in the milieu. He developed intense transference attachments to his doctor and his primary nurse, whom he expected to be with him at all times. When his doctor left the unit after a meeting with him, Mr. H attempted to run out the door after him just as he had tried to stop his father from going to work.

Physical and neurological examinations revealed no significant findings. After a careful psychiatric evaluation, the treatment team developed an explanatory formulation. The patient's paranoid concerns and somatic preoccupations masked an extraordinarily low sense of self-esteem. Mr. H had grown up feeling like the "black sheep" of the family, because his limitations had precluded competition with the high achievers surrounding him. To preserve some semblance of self-esteem, he formed an identity as a "victim" of disabling physical problems that kept him from performing at an acceptable level. Mr. H was then able to attribute his failures in school and in various jobs to physical illnesses.

The somatic concerns also provided an organizing focus for the patient's thoughts, thereby preventing a more profound state of psychotic fragmentation or self-dissolution. This severe somatic preoccupation was linked to his paranoid perception of ridicule from others through the mechanisms of introjection and projection. Early in life, Mr. H had internalized (as persecuting objects) the expectations and demands of his parents. Thus, strangers on the street or in the hallway who were perceived as talking about him had become these persecuting objects that he had projected into the environment. When the persecutors were reintrojected, they became internal persecutors in the form of various aches and pains requiring immediate attention. Hence the patient felt constantly under siege by a host of tormentors both in his environment and within his body.

On a neurophysiological level, Mr. H's inability to screen out various stimuli may have compounded his feeling of numerous sources of pain and torment. Finally, the somatizing performed yet another function: it was the only way the patient knew to maintain object relatedness and therefore defend against severe separation anxiety. This patient clearly had little interest in any diagnostic evaluations or treatment suggestions from consultants. Such findings and recommendations were far less significant to him than his concern that he needed to be continuously "monitored." The patient's litany of physical complaints was not truly designed to elicit an ameliorating response from those around him. Rather, its purpose was to maintain a continual external presence so that he would not have to face his anxieties about abandonment. Paradoxically, his barrage of complaints tended to evoke the opposite response, namely, to alienate and drive away others. Initially, the treatment team attempted to control Mr. H's positive symptoms through medication. However, the patient adamantly refused the medication because he associated it with previous doctors who had told him that his pain was "all in your head."

Respecting Mr. H's need to preserve self-esteem and organize his thinking through intense investment in physical symptoms, his hospital doctor assured him that no one was questioning the severity of Mr. H's pain. The doctor explained that the patient's illness had both psychological and physical aspects. The doctor further explained that one physical manifestation of the illness was difficulty filtering out various stimuli in the environment and within the body. Through this educational approach, Mr. H's doctor thus convinced the patient that the antipsychotic medication might be worth a trial because it often had a beneficial effect on the "filtering" system. After the patient agreed to take the medication, his thought disorder greatly improved, allowing him to talk more coherently with staff members and other patients. His auditory hallucinations continued despite the medication, but abated somewhat in frequency and severity.

The treatment team then attempted to repair some of the patient's ego deficits by functioning as auxiliary egos. On one occasion, for example, a nurse was meeting with Mr. H in a closed room on the hospital unit when he began to claim that people were talking about him outside in the hallway. To demonstrate that no one was there, the nurse opened the door and walked with Mr. H into the hallway. She then explained to the patient that his illness involved voices that originated on the inside, which were then perceived as though coming from outside sources. This approach was reinforced by feedback from fellow patients in group meetings.

This patient had initially been held out of group meetings on the unit because of the overstimulating nature of that treatment modality. After being stabilized on medication, however, Mr. H began to attend the groups and frequently brought up his concern that others were talking about him. The other patients steadfastly denied these accusations, and they all encouraged him to "check it out" whenever he heard the voice. The patient's hostile accusations toward other patients and toward staff members gradually shifted to gentle inquiries as he realized that the voices did indeed emanate from within.

As Mr. H gained greater control over his positive symptoms, the treatment focus shifted to his disordered interpersonal relatedness. Via projective identification, the patient attempted to establish the same relationship with his hospital doctor that he had with his father. The hospital doctor found himself spending more time in interaction with Mr. H than with any of his other patients. The urgency with which Mr. H presented his complaints of diarrhea, stomachaches, joint pain, and so on, made his hospital doctor reluctant to disengage from Mr. H and leave the unit. One day when Mr. H frantically followed him out of the unit and continued to walk down the sidewalk with him, the doctor realized the extent to which the patient had replicated his family situation in the hospital. Mr. H felt as though he deserved the complete attention of his doctor and was oblivious to the needs of other patients who shared the same physician. The doctor then told Mr. H that he should lower his expectations of how much time the doctor would spend with him. The doctor explained to Mr. H that he would set up specific 30-minute appointments with him and would not meet with him at other times. This limit-setting approach addressed the patient's sense of entitlement.

This approach also presented a new form of object relatedness for the patient to internalize. The object-relationship paradigm of a complaining, demanding self linked to an indulgent object was modified by Mr. H's experience of a new object that was caring but also limit setting. The experience with this new object correspondingly brought about changes in the patient's self-representation. Although initially frustrated, the patient became more tolerant of the doctor's absences and more accepting of limitations on his expectations of others. Moreover, the limitations Mr. H encountered in this relationship led him to discuss his separation anxiety with his doctor. Mr. H began to express concern that in the absence of a caretaking figure, his basic needs would go unmet.

When the patient was able to address these and other psychological concerns, he was referred to an individual psychotherapist not connected with the unit. The early phase of this psychotherapy was characterized by the patient's extensive reports about his physical symptoms. The patient's therapist listened to these reports with interest and concern, empathizing with his need to focus on the somatic rather than the psychological. Periodically, however, the therapist would comment that he was really unable to help the patient with any physical ailments because he had nothing to add to the extensive work of the treatment team and the consultants. As trust developed, the patient began to discuss his profound feelings of inferiority within his family context. Although his brother and sister had distinguished themselves academically, his only distinction was that he suffered from a variety of bizarre ailments that prevented him from similar success. The patient's denial of psychiatric illness, his lack of psychological-mindedness, and his lack of curiosity about his symptoms all led the therapist to take a predominantly supportive approach. Within that context, then, the patient was finally able to explore a surprisingly broad range of feelings about himself and his place in his family.

As part of the overall treatment plan, the patient became involved in a social skills group with a small number of his peers. In this setting, he received gentle confrontation about his hygiene problems, his failure to answer conversational questions, his self-absorption, and his obliviousness to the needs of others. He began to improve in all these areas in addition to generally improving his interpersonal functioning. For example, he began to say "good morning" to others who spoke to him, and he would even inquire as to their well-being. The patient also entered a vocational assessment and training program where he had to perform simple tasks under supervision. The activities therapist in charge of the program was careful to gear the level of complexity of the tasks to the patient's ability so that his self-esteem was not seriously damaged. Finally, a psychoeducational approach was employed with the patient's parents to help them accept their son's limitations. They were told that overinvolvement and excessive expectations would be counterproductive because the patient would experience them as pressure to succeed beyond his capacities.

This fragment of dynamically informed treatment illustrates how all three theoretical frameworks discussed in Chapter 2 may be useful in the treatment of one patient. Self psychological principles led the treatment team to an empathic awareness of this patient's need to maintain self-esteem, and his treaters therefore chose not to challenge his somatization. An object relations theoretical framework facilitated the doctor's understanding of this patient's problematic relationship with the doctor. Finally, the ego-psychological perspective was helpful in two ways: 1) An ego-deficit model was applied in the milieu in the form of the nursing staff's ego-building techniques, and 2) a conflict model was used to understand the auditory hallucinations. The persecutory voices this patient heard calling him a "loser" or "crazy" grew out of a painful conflict between the internalized expectations of his parents (in the form of his ego ideal and superego) and the reality of his limitations (realistic ego functioning). These voices always seemed more evident after the patient experienced any failure in his vocational program.

In summary, patients with schizophrenia need therapeutic figures in their lives. They need help navigating through the complicated realities of the mental health system. They also need someone to facilitate their understanding of the fears and fantasies that prevent them from complying with the various components of their overall treatment plan. Indeed, a central role of the psychotherapist is to explore compliance problems that arise in other areas of treatment. In contemporary practice, this role is often assigned to a clinical case manager, usually because the patient is not interested in therapy or because community resources cannot provide psychotherapy. Case managers serve as patient advocates, guides to mental health resources, and coordinators of the total treatment plan. Even though case management is oriented to reality and to adaptation, transference and countertransference issues arise; case managers must thus be capable of providing effective psychotherapeutic interventions (Kanter 1989). What schizophrenic patients most need, whether they are called case managers or psychotherapists, are concerned individuals who can offer compassionate human relationships for sanctuary from a confusing and threatening world.

References

American Psychiatric Association: Diagnostic and Statistical Manual of Mental Disorders, 3rd Edition, Revised. Washington, DC, American Psychiatric Association, 1987

Andreasen NC, Olsen SA, Dennert JW, et al: Ventricular enlargement in schizophrenia: relationship to positive and negative symptoms. Am J Psychiatry 139:297–302, 1982

Anonymous: Can we talk? The schizophrenic patient in psychotherapy. Am J Psychiatry 143:68–70, 1986

Arlow JA, Brenner C: The psychopathology of the psychoses: a proposed revision. Int J Psychoanal 50:5–14, 1969

Bion WR: Attacks on linking (1959), in Second Thoughts: Selected Papers on Psycho-Analysis. New York, Jason Aronson, 1967, pp 93–109

Blatt SJ, Wild CM: Schizophrenia: A Developmental Analysis. New York, Academic Press, 1976

Brenner C: The Mind in Conflict. New York, International Universities Press, 1982

Brown GW, Birley JLT, Wing JK: Influence of family life on the course of schizophrenic disorders: a replication. Br J Psychiatry 121:241–258, 1972

Carpenter WT Jr: A perspective on the psychotherapy of schizophrenia project. Schizophr Bull 10:599–602, 1984

Carpenter WT Jr, Henrichs DW, Wagman AMI: Deficit and nondeficit forms of schizophrenia: the concept. Am J Psychiatry 145:578–583, 1988

Conte HR, Plutchik R: Controlled research and supportive psychotherapy. Psychiatric Annals 16:530–533, 1986

Dworkin RH, Lenzenweger MF, Moldin SO, et al: A multidimensional approach to the genetics of schizophrenia. Am J Psychiatry 145:1077–1083, 1988

Falloon IRH, Boyd JL, McGill CW, et al: Family management in the prevention of exacerbations of schizophrenia: a controlled study. N Engl J Med 306:1437–1440, 1982

Federn P: Ego Psychology and the Psychoses. New York, Basic Books, 1952

Freud S: Psycho-analytic notes on an autobiographical account of a case of paranoia (dementia paranoides) (1911), in The Standard Edition of the Complete Psychological Works of Sigmund Freud, Vol 12. Translated and edited by Strachey J. London, Hogarth Press, 1958, pp 1–82

Freud S: On narcissism: an introduction (1914), in The Standard Edition of the Complete Psychological Works of Sigmund Freud, Vol 14. Translated and edited by Strachey J. London, Hogarth Press, 1963, pp 67–102

Freud S: The unconscious (1915), in The Standard Edition of the Complete Psychological Works of Sigmund Freud, Vol 14. Translated and edited by Strachey J. London, Hogarth Press, 1963, pp 159–215

Freud S: Neurosis and psychosis (1924a), in The Standard Edition of the Complete Psychological Works of Sigmund Freud, Vol 19. Translated and edited by Strachey J. London, Hogarth Press, 1961, pp 147–153

Freud S: The loss of reality in neurosis and psychosis (1924b), in The Standard Edition of the Complete Psychological Works of Sigmund Freud, Vol 19. Translated and edited by Strachey J. London, Hogarth Press, 1961, pp 181–187

Fromm-Reichmann F: Principles of Intensive Psychotherapy. Chicago, University of Chicago Press, 1950

Garfield D: Self-criticism in psychosis: enabling statements in psychotherapy. Dynamic Psychotherapy 3:129–137, 1985

Garfield D, Rogoff M, Steinberg S: Affect-recognition and self-esteem in schizophrenia. Psychopathology 20:225–233, 1987

Glass LL, Katz IIM, Schnitzer RD, et al: Psychotherapy of schizophrenia: an empirical investigation of the relationship of process to outcome. Am J Psychiatry 146:603–608, 1989

Goldstein MJ, Rodnick EH, Evans JR, et al: Drug and family in the aftercare of acute schizophrenics. Arch Gen Psychiatry 35:1169–1177, 1978

Gomez-Schwartz B: Individual psychotherapy of schizophrenia, in Schizophrenia: Treatment, Management, and Rehabilitation. Edited by Bellack AS. Orlando, FL, Grune & Stratton, 1984, pp 307–335

Gottesman II, Shields J: Schizophrenia and Genetics: A Twin Study Vantage Point. New York, Academic Press, 1972

Grand S: The body and its boundaries: a psychoanalytic view of cognitive process disturbances in schizophrenia. International Review of Psychoanalysis 9:327–342, 1982

Grinspoon L, Ewalt JR, Shader RI: Schizophrenia: Pharmacotherapy and Psychotherapy. Baltimore, Williams & Wilkins, 1972

Grotstein JS: Psychoanalytic therapy of schizophrenia, in Treatment of Schizophrenia: Progress and Prospects. Edited by West LJ, Flinn DE. New York, Grune & Stratton, 1976, pp 131–145

Grotstein J: The psychoanalytic concept of schizophrenia, I: the dilemma. Int J Psychoanal 58:403–425, 1977a

Grotstein J: The psychoanalytic concept of schizophrenia, II: reconciliation. Int J Psychoanal 58:427–452, 1977b

Gunderson JG: Engagement of schizophrenic patients in psychotherapy, in Attachment and the Therapeutic Process: Essays in Honor of Otto Allen Will, Jr. Edited by Sacksteder JL, Schwartz DP, Akabane Y. Madison, CT, International Universities Press, 1987, pp 139–153

Gunderson JG, Frank AF, Katz HM, et al: Effects of psychotherapy in schizophrenia, II: comparative outcome of two forms of treatment. Schizophr Bull 10:564–598, 1984

Harding CM, Zubin J, Strauss JS: Chronicity in schizophrenia: fact, partial fact, or artifact? Hosp Community Psychiatry 38:477–486, 1987

Hogarty GE: Depot neuroleptics: the relevance of psychosocial factors—a United States perspective. J Clin Psychiatry 45(5,2):36–42, 1984

Kanas N: Group therapy with schizophrenics: a review of controlled studies. Int J Group Psychother 36:339–351, 1986

Kanas N, Rogers M, Kreth E, et al: The effectiveness of group psychotherapy during the first three weeks of hospitalization: a controlled study. J Nerv Ment Dis 168:487–492, 1980

Kanter J: Clinical case management: definition, principles, components. Hosp Community Psychiatry 40:361–368, 1989

Karon BP, VandenBos G: Psychotherapy of Schizophrenia. New York, Jason Aronson, 1981

Keith SJ, Matthews SM: Schizophrenia: a review of psychosocial treatment strategies, in Psychotherapy Research: Where Are We and Where Should We Go? Edited by Williams JBW, Spitzer RL. New York, Guilford Press, 1984, pp 70–88

Kendler KS: The genetics of schizophrenia: a current perspective, in Psychopharmacology: The Third Generation of Progress. Edited by Meltzer HY. New York, Raven Press, 1987, pp 705–713

Kendler KS, Gruenberg AM, Strauss JS: An independent analysis of the Copenhagen sample of the Danish adoption study of schizophrenia, V: the relationship between childhood social withdrawal and adult schizophrenia. Arch Gen Psychiatry 39:1257–1261, 1982

Klein DF: Psychosocial treatment of schizophrenia, or psychosocial help for people with schizophrenia? Schizophr Bull 6:122–130, 1980

Leff J, Kuipers L, Berkowitz R, et al: A controlled trial of social intervention in the families of schizophrenic patients. Br J Psychiatry 141:121–134, 1982

London NJ: An essay on psychoanalytic theory: two theories of schizophrenia, part I: review and critical assessment of the development of the two theories. Int J Psychoanal 54:169–178, 1973a

London NJ: An essay on psychoanalytic theory: two theories of schizophrenia, part II: discussion and restatement of the specific theory of schizophrenia. Int J Psychoanal 54:179–193, 1973b

MacMillan JF, Gold A, Crow TJ, et al: IV. Expressed emotion and relapse. Br J Psychiatry 148:133–143, 1986

Mahler M: On child psychosis and schizophrenia: autistic and symbiotic infantile psychoses. Psychoanal Study Child 7:286–305, 1952

May PRA: Treatment of Schizophrenia: A Comparative Study of Five Treatment Methods. New York, Science House, 1968

McGlashan TH: Intensive individual psychotherapy of schizophrenia: a review of techniques. Arch Gen Psychiatry 40:909–920, 1983

McGlashan TH: The Chestnut Lodge follow-up study, II: long-term outcome of schizophrenia and the affective disorders. Arch Gen Psychiatry 41:586–601, 1984

McGlashan TH: Recovery style from mental illness and long-term outcome. J Nerv Ment Dis 175:681–685, 1987

McGlashan TH, Keats CJ: Schizophrenia: Treatment Process and Outcome. Washington, DC, American Psychiatric Press, 1989

McGlashan TH, Nayfack B: Psychotherapeutic models and the treatment of schizophrenia: the records of three successive psychotherapists with one patient at Chestnut Lodge for 18 years. Psychiatry 51:340–362, 1988

Mosher LR, Keith SJ: Research on the psychosocial treatment of schizophrenia: a summary report. Am J Psychiatry 136:623–631, 1979

Müller C: Psychotherapy and schizophrenia: the end of the pioneers' period. Schizophr Bull 10:618–620, 1984

Munich RL, Carsky M, Appelbaum A: The role and structure of long-term hospitalization: chronic schizophrenia. Psychiatric Hospital 16:161–169, 1985

O'Brien C: Group psychotherapy with schizophrenia and affective disorders, in Comprehensive Group Psychotherapy, 2nd Edition. Edited by Kaplan HI, Sadock BJ. Baltimore, Williams & Wilkins, 1983, pp 242–249

Ogden TH: On the nature of schizophrenic conflict. Int J Psychoanal 61:513-533, 1980

Ogden TH: The schizophrenic state of nonexperience, in Technical Factors in the Treatment of the Severely Disturbed Patient. Edited by Giovacchini PL, Boyer LB. New York, Jason Aronson, 1982, pp 217–260

Pao P-N: Notes on Freud's theory of schizophrenia. Int J Psychoanal 54:469–476, 1973

Parker G, Johnston P, Hayward L: Parental "expressed emotion" as a predictor of schizophrenic relapse. Arch Gen Psychiatry 45:806–813, 1988

Pollin W, Stabeneau JR: Biological, psychological and historical differ-
    ences in a series of monozygotic twins discordant for schizophre-
    nia, in The Transmission of Schizophrenia. Edited by Rosenthal
    D, Kety SS. New York, Pergamon Press, 1968, pp 317–332.
Rogers CR, Gendlin ET, Kiesler DJ et al (eds): The Therapeutic
    Relationship and Its Impact: A Study of Psychotherapy with Schiz-
    ophrenics. Madison, WI, University of Wisconsin Press, 1967
Ruocchio PJ: How psychotherapy can help the schizophrenic patient.
    Hosp Community Psychiatry 40:188–190, 1989
Schulsinger F, Parnas J, Schulsinger H, et al: Recent trends from
    nature-nurture research in schizophrenia, in Schizophrenia: Re-
    cent Biosocial Developments. Edited by Stefanis CN, Rabavilas
    AD. New York, Human Sciences Press, 1988, pp 39–53
Searles HF: The "dedicated physician" in psychotherapy and psycho-
    analysis, in Crosscurrents in Psychiatry & Psychoanalysis. Edited
    by Gibson RW. Philadelphia, Lippincott, 1967, pp 128–143
Searles HF: Psychoanalytic therapy with schizophrenic patients in a
    private-practice context, in Countertransference and Related
    Subjects: Selected Papers. New York, International Universities
    Press, 1979, pp 582–602
Selzer MA: Preparing the chronic schizophrenic for exploratory psycho-
    therapy: the role of hospitalization. Psychiatry 46:303–311, 1983
Spohn HE, Lacoursiere RB, Thompson K, et al: Phenothiazine effects
    on psychological and psychophysiological dysfunction in chronic
    schizophrenics. Arch Gen Psychiatry 34:633–644, 1977
Stanton AH, Gunderson JG, Knapp PH, et al: Effects of psychotherapy
    on schizophrenic patients, I: design and implementation of a
    controlled study. Schizophr Bull 10:520–563, 1984
Strauss JS, Carpenter WT, Bartko JJ: The diagnosis and understanding
    of schizophrenia, part III: speculations on the process that under-
    lie schizophrenic symptoms and signs. Schizophr Bull 11:61–69,
    1974
Sullivan HS: Schizophrenia as a Human Process. New York, WW Nor-
    ton, 1962
Wexler M: Schizophrenia: conflict and deficiency. Psychoanal Q 40:83–
    99, 1971

CHAPTER 8

Affective Disorders

Affective disorders, like schizophrenia, are illnesses with a strong biological component. Familial transmission of mania and depression clearly suggests that genetic factors may be crucial to their etiology. Disturbances of neurochemistry are also present. Bipolar illnesses may be effectively controlled with lithium carbonate and carbamazepine, while unipolar depression often lifts when treated with tricyclic antidepressants, monoamine oxidase inhibitors, or electroconvulsive therapy. The impressive research efforts of neuroscientists in the area of affective disorders raise the question of whether there is indeed a role for the dynamic psychiatrist in these conditions.

The answer is an unqualified "yes." This affirmative response is supported by the results of the NIMH Treatment of Depression Collaborative Research Program (Elkin et al. 1989). This project examined the impact of four different treatment conditions on 239 nonbipolar, nonpsychotically depressed outpatients. One group of patients received a 16-week course of cognitive behavior therapy (CBT), and a second group received 16 weeks of interpersonal psychotherapy (IPT), while a third group was placed on imipramine plus clinical management, and a fourth received a placebo plus clinical management, both administered in double-blind fashion. Sixty-eight percent of the patients completed at least 15 weeks and 12 sessions of treatment.

When the investigators examined overall functioning and reduction of depressive symptoms at 16 weeks, none of the three active treatments demonstrated any specific effectiveness over the placebo and clinical management in the mildly depressed subgroup (Elkin et al. 1989). However, when the more severely depressed and functionally impaired patients were studied, there were clear differences in outcome among the various treatment groups. The imipramine and clinical management condition produced the best outcomes, while the two psychotherapies also produced significant improvement, with IPT doing better than CPT. Those patients in the placebo with clinical management condition did poorly. Examination of recovery data indicated that both IPT and imipramine with clinical management were far superior to placebo with clinical management.

177

These findings reflect the fundamental interconnectedness of mind and brain, as described in Chapter 1. A condition involving aberrant neurochemical functioning in the brain can apparently be altered by psychotherapeutic intervention. Conversely, psychological dimensions of the same condition apparently respond to psychopharmacologic measures. One might argue that the prescription of medication is a simpler and more cost-effective treatment, so psychotherapy is unnecessary. Certain patients may do well with nothing more than a pill. However, such a reductionistic approach to treatment does not address a large percentage of patients with affective disturbances. Included in this problematic group are those patients who cannot take antidepressant medications because of a preexisting medical condition, those who cannot tolerate the side effects, those who refuse medications for psychological reasons, those who respond only slightly to the medication, those who are refractory to any biological treatment, and those who view their depression as emanating from a psychological matrix they wish to understand and master. Moreover, at least one study (DiMascio et al. 1979) suggested patients who receive a combination of a tricyclic antidepressant and psychotherapy gain more symptom reduction than those who receive either treatment alone. Finally, depression may be far more pervasive than a discrete episode precipitated only by presumably biochemical factors.

The clinician commonly encounters patients with depressive conditions that are complicated by long-standing characterological features. Among these patients, only 40–45 percent respond to tricyclic antidepressants (Akiskal et al. 1980; Kocsis et al. 1988). Many of these patients also suffer from "double-depression" (Keller and Shapiro 1982; Kocsis et al. 1988), whereby major depressive episodes are superimposed on a chronic characterological depression. Even when episodically depressed patients respond to medication, up to half may show considerable personality disturbance (Pilkonis and Frank 1988). One study (Zimmermann et al. 1988) suggested that a higher incidence of personality disorder might be found by interviewing relatives of depressed patients rather than relying only on the self-reports of patients. Chronically depressed patients or acutely depressed patients who are refractory to conventional treatments may have strong characterological features that defeat all treatment efforts. With this subgroup of patients, Hendin's (1982) observation may well be applicable: "Life is not, as it seems, or as the individual often says, unbearable with depression, but it may sometimes be inconceivable without it" (p. 164). For these patients, an intensive psychodynamic approach may be the only viable treatment intervention.

For all the foregoing reasons, psychodynamic understanding and treatment still play a major role in the treatment of mood disorders, despite impressive advances in the biological understanding of mania and depression. The psychiatrist who combines psychodynamic approaches with psychopharmacologic measures will be better equipped to treat the broad range of affectively disturbed patients seen in clinical practice.

Psychodynamic Understanding of Depression and Mania

In Freud's classic 1917 paper, "Mourning and Melancholia," he differentiated between grief and melancholic depression. In the former, the precipitating event is the real loss of a significant figure. In melancholia, by contrast, the lost object is *emotional* rather than real. Moreover, the melancholic patient feels a profound loss of self-esteem, accompanied by self-reproach and guilt, while the mourner maintains a reasonably stable sense of self-esteem. Freud explained the marked self-depreciation common in depressed patients as the result of anger turned inward. More specifically, the rage is directed internally because the self of the patient has identified with the lost object. In 1923, Freud noted that such introjection may be the only way for the ego to give up an object. That same year, in "The Ego and the Id," he postulated that melancholic patients have a severe superego, which he related to their guilt over having shown aggression toward loved ones.

Melanie Klein (1940) linked depression to the depressive position (see Chapter 2). She understood manic-depressive states as a reflection of childhood failure to establish good internal objects. Depressed people, in other words, have never overcome the depressive position common to childhood. She contrasted this state with normal mourning, in which the depressive position is reactivated as a result of losing a loved one, but is then overcome and worked through by reestablishing the lost figure as an internal object, as well as by reinstating the good parents in the process. In Klein's view, then, depressed patients are desperately concerned that they have destroyed the loved good objects within themselves as a result of their own greed and destructiveness. As a consequence of that destruction, they feel persecuted by hated bad objects that remain. This feeling of being persecuted by bad objects while "pining" for the lost good objects is what constitutes the essence of the depressive position, which is reactivated in melancholic states. In other words, patients may feel worthless because they sense that they have changed their good internal parents into persecutors as a result of their own destructive impulses and fantasies.

Klein noted that manic defenses, such as omnipotence, denial, contempt, and idealization, develop in response to the painful affects produced by "pining" for the lost love objects. These defenses are used in the service of 1) rescuing and restoring the lost love objects, 2) disavowing the bad internal objects, and 3) denying slavish dependency on love objects. Clinically, patients may express these manic operations through a denial of any aggression or destructiveness toward others, a euphoric disposition that is contrary to their actual life situation, an idealization of others, or a scornful, contemptuous attitude toward other people that serves to disavow the need for relationships. An integral aspect of the manic defensive posture is often a wish to triumph over parents and thus reverse the child-parent relationship. This desire for triumph may in turn give rise to guilt and depression. In Klein's view, this mechanism is partly responsible for the depression that frequently develops after success or promotion.

Klein's formulation is useful because it helps clinicians to understand how the psychological function of a manic episode can coexist with any biological determinants. The defensive function of mania is most clearly evident in dysphoric manic patients (Post et al. 1989), whose anxiety and depression "break through" a manic episode, necessitating a resurgence of manic denial. Moreover, in a much more attenuated form, hypomanic defenses are typically enlisted to defend against the threat of depressive affects or grief. One patient, for example, described feeling "high" after learning of his mother's death. He felt powerful, expansive, and liberated from dependency. Despite these feelings, he was able to note how odd it was that he was not grief stricken.

Although both Freud and Klein saw aggression as pivotal to the understanding of depression, Bibring (1953) believed that depression was a primary affective state unrelated to aggression turned inward. He viewed depression as arising from the tension between ideals and reality. Three highly invested narcissistic aspirations—to be worthy and loved, to be strong or superior, and to be good and loving—are held up as standards of conduct. However, the ego's awareness of its actual or imagined inability to measure up to these standards produces depression. As a result, the depressed person feels helpless and powerless. Bibring thought that, in certain cases, the ego's awareness of its helplessness may lead to aggression turned inward, but only as a secondary phenomenon. He believed that any narcissistic frustration or injury that lowers self-esteem might precipitate a clinical depression. Alone among all authors writing on the psychodynamics of depression, Bibring (1953) did not postulate that the superego played a key role. Rather, he postulated that tension arises within the ego itself, not between the ego and another intrapsychic agency. He succinctly described this depression as "a partial or complete collapse of the self-esteem of the ego, since it feels unable to live up to its aspirations (ego ideal, superego) while they are strongly maintained" (p. 26). He understood manic elation either as a compensating secondary reaction to depression or as an expression of the fantasy fulfillment of the individual's narcissistic aspirations.

Revising Freud's formulation, Jacobson (1971a) suggested that melancholic patients actually act as if they were the worthless, lost love object, even though they do not assume all the characteristics of that object. The self then is experienced as the bad object, and eventually, this bad internal object or the lost external love object is transformed into the sadistic superego. The ego then becomes "a victim of the superego, as helpless and powerless as a small child who is tortured by his cruel, powerful mother" (p. 252).

> Ms. I was a 49-year-old housewife who became psychotically depressed. She became convinced that she was thoroughly worthless, and she was preoccupied with how her father had beaten her as a child because she was such a "bad little girl." At times the bad introject of the abusive, hated father was absorbed into the patient's self-view, and she would cut herself both as self-punishment and as a way of attacking the internal object. At other times, the father would be experienced as a separate internal object, or a harsh superego, who would rebuke her for being bad. In these instances, Ms. I would hear a hallucinated voice, saying, "You are bad" and "You deserve to die."

The internal object world of Ms. I indicates how, in psychotic depression, there may be a fusion of the self with the object, on the one hand, or a reactivation of an internal object relationship in which a tormenting bad object, or primitive superego, persecutes a bad self, on the other. Jacobson believed that mania could be understood as a magical reunion of the self with the harsh superego figure, thus changing that figure from a punitive tormenter into a loving, all-good, forgiving figure. This idealized object may then be projected into the external world to establish highly idealized relationships with others whereby all aggression and destructiveness are denied.

Based on extensive experience in the psychotherapy of severely depressed patients, Arieti (1977) postulated a preexisting ideology in persons who become severely depressed—namely, living not for oneself, but for another person—what Arieti termed the *dominant other*. Most commonly, the spouse is the dominant other, but an organization or an ideal may also serve that function. When a transcendent purpose or aim occupies this place in the individual's psychological world, it is referred to as the dominant goal or dominant ideology. Arieti's concept is somewhat reminiscent of Bibring's, because of its emphasis on the patient's helplessness upon realizing that the goal is unattainable. These patients generally cannot imagine or accept any alternate frameworks that might allow them to give up the dominant goal. They realize that living for someone or something else is not working out for them, but they feel unable to change. They believe that life is worthless if they cannot elicit the response they wish from the dominant other or if they cannot achieve their impossible goal. They adhere rigidly to an unrealistic life plan that they cannot give up.

We can summarize the various theoretical formulations of depression by concluding that whatever biochemical contributions there may be, patients experience depression psychologically as a disturbance of self-esteem in the context of failed interpersonal relationships. These childhood relationships are internalized and then are reactivated in adulthood with the onset of major affective disorders. The tormenting internal world of object relationships is then also externalized into current relationships in the patient's world. Depression illustrates the close relationship between an individual's intimate interpersonal interactions and the maintenance of self-esteem (Strupp et al. 1982). In self psychological terms, depression may be viewed as the despair resulting from the failure of selfobjects to gratify the self's needs for mirroring, twinship, or idealization.

Psychodynamics of Suicide

Many different psychiatric disorders can culminate in the tragic outcome of suicide. Suicide is most prominently associated with major affective disorders, however, so it is therefore considered in detail in the context of this chapter. Before examining the psychodynamic perspective on suicide, a caveat is in order. Determinants of suicidal behavior may be biological as well as psychological. The psychodynamics revealed by psychotherapeutic work with suicidal patients may in some respects be *secondary* to neurochemical changes, so all available somatic treatment modalities must be used aggressively along with the psychotherapeutic approach. In many cases, psychotherapy alone is insufficient with seriously suicidal patients. In one comparison study (Lesse 1978), only 16 percent of the severely depressed psychotherapy patients had a positive outcome, while 83 percent of the patients who received both psychotherapy and pharmacotherapy and 86 percent of those who received electroconvulsive therapy had good results. Saving the patient's life is far more important than theoretical purity.

Suicidal behavior and ideation, like all other acts and thoughts, are the end products of the principles of overdetermination and multiple function (see Chapter 1). Motivations for suicide are highly varied and often obscure (Meissner 1986). The clinician must therefore listen carefully to each patient, noting the particular transference-countertransference developments before reaching any closure on the dynamic underpinnings of suicide.

In keeping with his understanding of the dynamics of depression, Freud (1917) assumed that the ego could only kill itself by treating itself as an object, so he postulated that suicide results from displaced murderous impulses—destructive wishes toward an internalized object are directed instead against the self. After the development of the structural model (1923), Freud redefined suicide as the victimization of the ego by a sadistic superego. Karl Menninger's (1933) view of suicide was a bit more complex. He believed that at least three wishes might contribute to a suicidal act—the wish to kill, the wish to be killed, and the wish to die. The wish to kill someone else may be directed not only toward an *internal* object. Clinical experience confirms again and again that suicide is often designed to destroy the lives of the survivors. Depressed patients often feel, for example, that suicide is the only satisfactory revenge against their parents. The patient's spouse may similarly be the "target" of a suicide.

A recurring theme in the object relations of suicidal patients is the drama between a sadistic tormentor and a tormented victim. As in the case of Ms. I, there is often a persecuting internal object that makes the patient miserable. Alternatively, the patient who identifies with the persecutor may torment everyone in the environment. In some cases, the patient may believe that the only possible outcome of the drama is to submit to the tormentor through suicide (Meissner 1986). This internal persecuting figure has been referred to as the "hidden executioner" (Asch 1980).

In other cases, aggression plays a far less prominent role in the motivation for suicide. Fenichel (1945) noted that suicide may be the fulfillment of a reunion wish, that is, a joyous and magical rejoining with a lost loved one, or a narcissistic union with a loving superego figure. Object loss frequently lies behind suicidal behavior, and many suicidal patients reveal strong dependency yearnings toward a lost object (Dorpat 1973). In this regard, suicide may be a regressive wish for reunion with a lost maternal figure. The last words of the Reverend Jim Jones in the 1978 mass homicide and suicide in Guyana were "Mother. . .Mother," spoken just before he shot himself in the head. A pathological grief process is often involved in suicides, particularly those that occur on the anniversary of the death of a loved one. Research has demonstrated, for example, that there is a statistically significant correlation between suicide and the anniversary of a parent's death (Bunch and Barraclough 1971). When an individual's self-esteem and self-integrity depend on attachment to a lost object, suicide may seem to be the only way to restore self-cohesion.

Ms. J was a 24-year-old psychotically depressed woman who, 2 years earlier, had lost her twin brother to suicide. Following his death, she had withdrawn from life, intent on killing herself. Moreover, she had become psychotically identified with her brother to the point that she identified herself as male and as having his first name. She had been refractory to antidepressant medication, lithium carbonate, and electroconvulsive therapy. She felt that she could not continue living in the absence of her brother. She ultimately committed suicide on the anniversary of her brother's death.

Hopelessness appears to be a better predictor of suicide risk than depression per se (Fawcett et al. 1987). Patients who kill themselves often are so cognitively constricted that they simply can see no other alternative (Beck 1963; Shneidman 1976). They cannot imagine themselves existing in the future, and as Arieti (1977) has noted, they cannot shift their dominant ideology or their expectations of the dominant other.

To put suicide in a psychodynamic context, clinicians must understand the nature of the precipitating event, the conscious and unconscious motivations, and the preexisting psychological variables that increase the likelihood of acting on suicidal thoughts. Through the use of projective psychological testing, researchers (Smith 1983; Smith and Eyman 1988) have studied and identified four patterns of ego functioning and internal object-relations paradigms that differentiate individuals who made serious attempts from those who merely made gestures to control significant others. The serious attempters exhibited: 1) an inability to give up infantile wishes for nurturance associated with conflict about being openly dependent; 2) a sober but ambivalent view toward death; 3) excessively high self-expectations; and 4) overcontrol of affect, particularly aggression. Although this pattern applies more to men than to women (Smith and Eyman 1988), an inhibitory attitude toward aggression distinguishes serious female attempters from those who make mild gestures. These test findings imply that the preexisting psychological structures that favor suicide are more consistent across individual patients than are the various motivations behind a particular suicidal act.

Treatment Considerations

Research Findings

Highly expressive psychotherapy specifically aimed at relieving depression has not been rigorously tested. After reviewing the literature on short-term dynamic psychotherapy of depression, Strupp et al. (1982) concluded that although some reports indicated improvement of depressive symptomatology, "no definitive statement can be made regarding the unique effectiveness of short-term dynamic treatment approaches for the amelioration of depression" (p. 238). They further concluded that because the patients had not been selected on the basis of depression and because most of the studies had not isolated changes in depression, the research simply had not specifically addressed the issue. Moreover, the tradition in psychoanalytic psychotherapy is not to develop specific technical approaches for specific diagnostic entities, but rather to strengthen the patient's adaptive capacities by improving self-esteem, by modifying the superego, by strengthening and expanding the ego, and by altering the patient's internal object relations. Finally, studies of brief dynamic psychotherapy are more concerned with the strengths and weaknesses of the patient's personality than with a specific intervention or a specific symptom.

Although more expressive forms of psychotherapy have not been rigorously tested, a modified version of dynamic psychotherapy—interpersonal therapy (IPT)—has been. The NIMH Collaborative Study clearly demonstrated that 16 weeks of this treatment was much more effective than placebo in alleviating depression, particularly the more severe forms of depressions. Moreover, IPT has shown considerable value in preventing recurrent episodes in patients with unipolar depression (Frank et al. 1989). In a study of 74 patients with recurrent unipolar depression, those who received once-monthly sessions of IPT were significantly less likely to experience a subsequent episode of depression when compared at the end of an 18-month follow-up to those who received imipramine. Although this treatment is not always identified as dynamically informed supportive psychotherapy, IPT can be regarded as such. It was developed with the assumption that depression occurs in an interpersonal context and will improve as relationships improve (Elkin et al. 1985). It derives explicitly from a psychodynamic model, even though the focus is interpersonal rather than intrapsychic. Interventions, which tend to be noninterpretive, are focused more on the here-and-now than on childhood experiences.

Four basic problem areas are identified in the course of IPT: 1) role transitions, 2) interpersonal deficits, 3) role disputes, and 4) pathological grief (Rounsaville et al. 1984). The therapist actively helps the patient develop strategies to manage problems in each area, providing reassurance and some education about problem-solving skills as well. From a relatively neutral position, the therapist allows the patient to identify the topic to discuss in each session and then offers advice rather sparingly. The therapist is more active and practical than in expressive psychotherapy, and the major technical approach is not guided by any attempt to bring about major personality change through the achievement of insight into underlying conflicts. Instead, change is sought through education, combating demoralization, social manipulation, or problem solving, and the IPT therapist addresses underlying psychological conflict if work at these levels stalls or if the patient shows strong resistance to the treatment (Rounsaville et al. 1984).

Treatment Principles

Even though the research literature on specific treatment techniques for depression is limited, there is certainly compelling evidence that psychodynamically derived psychotherapy is effective. The abundant clinical literature on the treatment of affective disorders fleshes out the research data with rich descriptions of case material that capture a feeling of "being there" with the patient. Because the general principles to be gleaned from this literature apply equally to hospital treatment and to psychotherapy, the two forms of treatment will be considered together in this discussion.

Mania. The treatment of the bipolar patient is somewhat more straightforward than that of the unipolar patient. By and large, manic patients will not benefit from psychotherapeutic interventions until they are first pharmacologically controlled. The very nature of the manic defensive position mandates denial of all psychological problems. It is rarely possible to penetrate this denial when the patient is in a full-blown manic episode. After pharmacological stabilization, psychotherapy of an expressive-supportive nature may play a key role in several different respects. First, problems with medication compliance may require psychotherapeutic exploration before they can be resolved. In addition, psychotherapeutic or psychoanalytic work while patients are in the euthymic phase of the illness may help prevent manic or depressive episodes. A 10-year follow-up study (Feinstein and Wolpert 1973; Wolpert 1983) identified two types of therapeutic failure. One, a pharmacotherapeutic failure, involved a reluctance to increase the lithium dose when the patient became more physiologically activated just prior to a manic episode. The other, a psychotherapeutic failure, stemmed from lack of attention to psychological issues that precipitated episodes. These two types of failures are similar to the two precipitants of manic or depressive episodes, biological factors in some cases, and in others, psychological factors.

As briefly noted in Chapter 5, Loeb and Loeb (1987) found the combination of lithium carbonate and psychoanalysis or psychoanalytically oriented psychotherapy useful with a series of bipolar patients, because the psychoanalytic techniques allowed the patients to become consciously aware of a resurgence of sexual fantasies and wishes prior to the onset of a manic episode. These previously unconscious thoughts served as a signal to these patients that they needed to increase their lithium dose. Pollock (1977) advocated the psychoanalysis of manic-depressive patients medicated on lithium during the euthymic phase because of the frequent presence of obsessive-compulsive character pathology. Finally, patients settling down after a manic episode in which they were floridly out of control must frequently deal with feelings of intense guilt and shame about their behavior during the episode. Psychotherapeutic assistance may help these patients come to terms with such feelings.

From a Kleinian perspective, the fundamental psychotherapeutic task with the bipolar patient is to facilitate the work of mourning, that is, to work through the depressive position more successfully. The threat of aggressive, persecutory feelings leads to the need for manic defenses to deny them. Following a manic episode, patients may be acutely aware of their own destructiveness and may feel remorseful about the harm they have caused others during the manic phase. The psychotherapist may be presented, then, with an optimal moment to help the patient integrate the loving and aggressive sides of the internal self- and object-representations. If the therapist can maintain a supportive, holding environment while exploring the patient's concerns about aggression, the patient will become more capable of internalizing a relationship in which good predominates over bad and love predominates over hate. Klein (1940) noted that as feelings of persecution and aggression decrease, manic defenses become less necessary to the patient. Finally, the internalization of the therapist reinstates the lost "good objects" from childhood.

Depression. Contrary to conventional wisdom, the usefulness of psychodynamic approaches to depression are not limited to the milder, more neurotic forms of the condition. Psychotherapeutic intervention may, in fact, be essential to the treatment of more severe, psychotic forms of depression, especially in those cases where somatic treatments have been ineffective or refused by the patient. Arieti (1977) reported on the intensive psychotherapy of 12 severely depressed patients for whom he had follow-up data for 3 years or more. Seven had shown full recovery and an additional 4 were markedly improved. Regardless of the severity of the depression, however, certain fundamental technical principles should guide the clinician.

The first step in treatment, regardless of whether the patient is in a hospital or is an outpatient, is the establishment of a therapeutic alliance. To build the necessary rapport, the clinician must simply listen and empathize with the patient's point of view. Perhaps the most common error both of family members and of beginning mental health professionals is to try to cheer up the patient by focusing on the positive. Comments such as, "You have no reason to be depressed—you have so many good qualities," or "Why should you be suicidal? There's so much to live for," are likely to backfire. These "cheerleading" comments are experienced by depressed patients as profound failures of empathy, which may lead patients to feel more misunderstood and alone and therefore more suicidal.

On the contrary, clinicians who work with these patients must convey their understanding that there is indeed a reason to be depressed. They can empathize with the painfulness of the depression, while also enlisting the patient's help in a collaborative search for its underlying causes. The initial approach must be supportive but firm (Arieti 1977; Lesse 1978). Premature interpretations, such as, "You're not really depressed—you're angry," will also be experienced as unempathic and as off the mark. The clinician will be most helpful simply by listening and attempting to comprehend the patient's understanding of the illness.

During the early phases of information-gathering, the clinician develops an explanatory formulation of the patient's depression. What events apparently precipitated the depression? What narcissistically valued aspiration has the patient failed to achieve? What is the patient's dominant ideology? Who is the dominant other for whom the patient is living and from whom the patient is not receiving the desired responses? Is there guilt connected with aggression or anger, and if so, toward whom is the patient angry? Is there frustration of the self's strivings for selfobject responses?

While the clinician listens to the patient's story and develops hypotheses about the psychodynamic basis of the depression, the patient will form a transference attachment to the therapist. In Arieti's (1977) terms, the therapist becomes a "dominant third," in addition to the dominant other in the patient's life. Many of the same concerns that are problematic in the patient's primary relationships will also surface in the transference. Arieti pointed out that building a therapeutic alliance may require therapists to conform to certain of the patient's expectations during the initial stages of psychotherapy, thus facilitating the repetition of the patient's pathology in the therapeutic relationship. When enough information has been gathered, the therapist may have to shift to a more expressive approach and interpret to the patient the dominant-other pattern that has caused so much difficulty. Arieti (1977) observed that "the patient must come to the conscious realization that he did not know how to live for himself. He never listened to himself; in situations of great affective significance he was never able to assert himself. He cared only about obtaining the approval, affection, love, admiration, or care of the dominant other" (p. 866). After this realization, a good deal of anger toward the dominant other may surface.

After the dominant ideology has been laid bare, the therapist's task is then to help the patient conceive of new ways of living. In

Bibring's (1953) terms, either the idealized aspirations must be modified sufficiently to be realized, or they must be relinquished and replaced with other goals and objectives. At the prospect of developing new life patterns and purposes, these patients may depend on their therapist for answers. If therapists collude by telling their patients what to do, it will simply reinforce any feelings of low self-esteem and ineffectiveness (Betcher 1983; Maxmen 1978). Pleas from patients to solve their dilemmas can simply be turned back to them with the explanation that they are in the best position to make alternative life plans.

Central to the psychodynamic approach to depressed patients is the establishment of the interpersonal meaning and context of their depression. Unfortunately, patients often tenaciously resist these interpersonal implications (Betcher 1983). They often prefer to view their depression and their suicidal wishes as occurring in a vacuum, fervently insisting that no one is to blame but themselves. Careful attention to transference-countertransference developments may lead to breakthroughs with this form of resistance. In both psychotherapy and hospital treatment, patients recapitulate their internal object relationships as well as their patterns of relatedness with external figures. Depressed patients in particular engender strong feelings. In the course of such treatment, the therapist may experience despair, anger, wishes to be rid of the patient, powerful rescue fantasies, and a myriad of other feelings. All these emotional responses may reflect how others in the patient's life feel as well. These interpersonal dimensions of the depression may be involved in causing or perpetuating the condition. To examine the impact of the patient's condition on others, the therapist must enlist the patient's collaboration by using these feelings constructively in the therapeutic relationship. Many refractory cases of depression have become deadlocked in the repetition of a characteristic pattern of object relatedness that has strong characterological underpinnings and is therefore difficult to alter.

Mr. K was a respected chemist who required hospitalization when he became suicidally depressed at the age of 41. While Mr. K had been an outpatient, every known antidepressant medication had been tried in therapeutic doses with monitored serum levels, and then electroconvulsive therapy had been used during the first weeks of his hospital stay. None of these somatic interventions had alleviated his depression in the least. Nevertheless, the patient continued to maintain that he was a victim of a "chemical imbalance" which was the doctor's responsibility to restore. Mr. K complained of self-doubt, feelings of worthlessness, inability to sleep, inability to work or concentrate, and hopelessness about the future. He felt that all his accomplishments were meaningless, and that he had driven his wife to distraction by his repeated demands to comfort him. Mrs. K despaired because everything she offered her husband seemed to be of no help whatsoever. Whenever she attempted to point out positive aspects of her husband's life, he would respond with a "yes, but" comeback, dismissing her points as irrelevant.

The resident in charge of Mr. K's treatment and the other unit staff members on the treatment team shared Mrs. K's frustration. Mr. K demanded that they attend to his needs, but then dismissed all their suggestions and insights as useless. The entire treatment staff felt deskilled, impotent, and exhausted in the face of Mr. K's depression. Whenever the various residents on call during the evening hours made rounds on the hospital unit, Mr. K engaged them in long discussions about his depression. He would list the medications that had been tried and would expound on the role of neurotransmitters in depression. He would then ask for advice on his condition. Inevitably, the resident making rounds would be drawn into this discussion in an attempt to alleviate the suffering of this obviously intelligent and well-informed individual. Every suggestion made by any resident, however, would be discounted by Mr. K as "not helpful." By the end of these discussions, the on-call residents would feel that all the time spent with Mr. K was for naught, and they would leave feeling drained and devalued.

The resident in charge of Mr. K's treatment and the staff of the hospital team presented their dilemma with Mr. K to the resident's supervisor, who pointed out how the patient's internal world was being re-created in the milieu. By assuming the role of the "help-rejecting complainer," Mr. K was reestablishing an internal object relationship characterized by a long-suffering and victimized self-representation connected to an impotent and useless object-representation. Mr. K used the reactivation of this internal object relationship to torment everyone around him. He was thus able to discharge an enormous reservoir of rage stemming from his childhood interactions with his mother, whom he felt had failed to provide for his needs.

As a result of this consultation, a dramatic shift took place in the treatment approach. The resident and the nursing staff primarily involved with Mr. K were able to disengage from their heroic therapeutic efforts and began to enlist the patient's collaboration in figuring out what was happening. No longer a passive recipient of "medical" treatment, the patient was now involved as an active collaborator in a psychological process of reflection and understanding.

The object relations paradigm that was being acted out in the milieu was clarified and described for the patient. At the same time, the case social worker explained the psychoanalytically based understanding to Mrs. K to facilitate alleviation of her extraordinary guilt and to help her understand that the present situation was a recapitulation of an unresolved childhood experience. When the treatment team stopped responding like Mr. K's internal object-representation, Mr. K began presenting himself differently. He was initially enraged at their suggestion that he should accept any responsibility for his condition. The resident explained to him, however, that everything possible in terms of pharmacologic interventions had been tried and that now Mr. K would have to consider his own contributions to the feeling that he was "stuck" in the depths of despair. This change in approach presented Mr. K with a new object relationship to contend with. After his initial stubbornness, he did a good deal of psychological work. He got in touch with his rage at his mother for not giving him the validation and love that he felt he required, as well as his delight in tormenting his wife to get back at his mother.

The case of Mr. K illustrates how a severe depression that is refractory to conventional somatic treatments may be related to formidable characterological resistances that cause the patient to become "stuck" in an unresolved self-object relationship. As described in Chapter 6 on hospital treatment, a breakthrough in such treatment can occur when the treatment staff begins to disconfirm the patient's expectation that they will respond like the projected object-representation; instead, the staff members provided a new model of understanding as well as a new series of objects and interactions for internalization by the patient.

Another aspect of the breakthrough with Mr. K was that staff members realized that he was not only a victim of an illness but was also a victimizer of those around him. In discussing the secondary gain frequently associated with depression, Bibring (1953) noted that some depressed patients exploit their illness to justify their veiled expression of destructive and sadistic impulses toward others. Mr. K had forced his wife into a maternal role with him, only to deem her maternal treatment of him worthless. In commenting on the hidden sadism frequently found in the depressed patient, Jacobson (1971b) noted, "The depressive never fails to make his partner, often his whole environment, and especially his children feel terribly guilty, pulling them down into a more and more depressed state as well" (p. 295). Indeed, the entire treatment staff had begun to feel like Mrs. K. They felt increasingly guilty because they could not find any way to intervene therapeutically with Mr. K, and they became more depressed and drained as a result of each successive failure. Jacobson also pointed out that some depressed patients (such as Mr. K) may establish a vicious cycle that drives their partners away just when their love is most needed. Spouses of such patients rapidly get fed up and may begin to act cruelly or neglectfully as a result of their feelings of inadequacy, thus hurting these patients when they are most needy and vulnerable. Treaters may fall into a similar pattern by becoming sarcastic or cold because their patients repeatedly reject their help.

Treatment of the Suicidal Patient

Few events in a psychiatrist's professional life are more disturbing than the suicide of a patient. In one study (Chemtob et al. 1988), approximately half of those psychiatrists who had lost a patient to suicide experienced stress levels comparable to persons recovering from the death of a parent. A completed suicide is a reminder of the limitations inherent in our craft. The natural tendency, whether in hospital practice or in psychotherapy, is for clinicians to go to great lengths to prevent suicide. To implement reasonable measures to prevent patients from taking their life is certainly good judgment from a clinical standpoint, responsible behavior from an ethical standpoint, and sound defensive medicine from a medicolegal standpoint. However, when the role of savior becomes all-consuming, the results may be countertherapeutic.

First, clinicians must always keep in mind one unassailable fact—patients who are truly intent on killing themselves will ultimately do so. No amount of physical restraint, careful observation, and clinical skill can stop the truly determined suicidal patient. One such patient was placed in a seclusion room with nothing but a mattress. All his clothing and possessions were taken away, and he was checked at regular 15-minute intervals around the clock. Between the 15-minute rounds, the patient began jumping on the mattress so hard that he was able to repeatedly bang his head against the ceiling until he finally broke his neck. Such incidents illustrate that hospital staff members must acknowledge to themselves that they cannot prevent all suicides from occurring on an inpatient unit. Olin (1976) has even suggested that if suicides never occur in a particular hospital, the staff members in the milieu may be taking too much responsibility for the behavior of the patients. Instead, clinicians should repeatedly stress that it is ultimately each patient's responsibility to learn to verbalize suicidal impulses rather than act on them.

Psychodynamic clinicians tend to agree that treaters who fall prey to the illusion that they can save their patients from suicide are actually decreasing their chances of doing so (Hendin 1982; Meissner 1986; Richman and Eyman, in press; Searles 1967; Zee 1972). One salient psychological concern in the seriously suicidal patient is the desire to be taken care of by an unconditionally loving mother (Richman and Eyman, in press; Smith and Eyman 1988). Some therapists err in attempting to gratify this fantasy by meeting the patient's every need. They may accept phone calls from the patient any time of the day or night and throughout their vacations. They may see the patient seven days a week in their office. Some have even become sexually involved with their patients in a desperate effort to gratify the unending demands associated with the depression (Twemlow and Gabbard 1989). This kind of behavior exacerbates what Hendin (1982) has described as one of the most lethal features of suicidal patients—namely, their tendency to assign others the responsibility for their staying alive. By attempting to gratify these ever-escalating demands, the therapist colludes with the patient's fantasy that there really is an unconditionally loving mother out there somewhere who is different from everyone else. Therapists cannot possibly sustain that illusion indefinitely; those who attempt to do so are setting up the patient for a crushing disappointment that may increase the risk of suicide.

Clinicians who are drawn into the role of savior with suicidal patients often operate on the conscious or unconscious assumption that they can provide the love and concern that others have not, thus magically transforming the patient's wish to die into a desire to live. This fantasy is a trap, however, because, as Hendin (1982) has noted, "The patient's hidden agenda is an attempt to prove that nothing the therapist can do will be enough. The therapist's wish to see himself as the suicidal patient's savior may blind the therapist to the fact that the patient has cast him in the role of executioner" (pp. 171–172). Therapists are more useful to suicidal patients when they diligently try to understand and analyze the origin of the suicidal wishes instead of placing themselves in bondage to the patient.

It is useful to distinguish between *treatment* and *management* of the suicidal patient. The latter includes measures such as continuous observation, physical restraints, and removal of sharp objects from the environment. Although these interventions are useful in preventing the patient from acting on suicidal urges, management techniques do not necessarily decrease a patient's future vulnerability to resort to suicidal behavior. *Treatment* of suicidal patients—consisting of a psychotherapeutic approach to understanding the internal factors and external stressors that make the patient suicidal—is needed to alter the fundamental wish to die.

The countertransference elicited by the suicidal patient presents a formidable obstacle to treatment. Some clinicians simply avoid any responsibility for seriously depressed patients who are at risk for killing themselves. Those who do attempt to treat such patients often believe that their *raison d'être* is negated by the patient's wish to die. Suicide is also the ultimate narcissistic injury for the treater. Clinicians' anxiety about the suicide of the patient may stem more from the fear that others will blame them for the death than from concern for the individual patient's welfare (Hendin 1982). It is commonplace for therapists to set one standard for others and another for themselves—therapists who assure others that they are not responsible for their patient's suicide may feel an exaggerated sense of responsibility for keeping their own patients alive, often with the assumption that others will be critical if the patient dies.

Therapists who treat seriously suicidal patients will eventually begin to feel tormented by the repeated negation of their efforts. Countertransference hate is likely to develop at such times, and

treaters will often harbor an unconscious wish for the patient to die
so that the torment will end. Maltsberger and Buie (1974) have
noted that feelings of malice and aversion are among the most
common countertransference reactions connected with the treatment of severely suicidal patients. The inability to tolerate one's own
sadistic wishes toward the patient may lead a treater to act out
countertransference feelings. The authors caution that while malice
may be more unacceptable and uncomfortable, aversion is potentially more lethal because it can lead clinicians to neglect the patient
and provide an opportunity for a suicide attempt. On an inpatient
unit, this form of countertransference may be manifested by simply
"forgetting" to check on the patient as dictated by the suicidal
observation ordered.

    Countertransference hatred must be accepted as part of the
experience of treating suicidal patients. It often arises in direct
response to the patient's aggression. Suicide threats may be held
over the therapist's head like the mythical sword of Damocles,
tormenting and controlling the therapist night and day. Similarly,
the family members of patients may be plagued with the concerns
that if they make one false move or one unempathic comment, they
will be responsible for a suicide. If countertransference hate is split
off and disavowed by the therapist, it may be projected into the
patient, who then must deal with the therapist's murderous wishes
in addition to the preexisting suicidal impulses. Clinicians may also
deal with their feelings of aggression by reaction formation, which
may lead to rescue fantasies and exaggerated efforts to prevent
suicide. Searles (1967) has warned therapists of the perils of this
defensive style:

> And the suicidal patient, who finds us so unable to be aware of the
> murderous feelings he fosters in us through his guilt- and anxiety-
> producing threats of suicide, feels increasingly constricted, perhaps
> indeed to the point of suicide, by the therapist who, in reaction
> formation against his intensifying, unconscious wishes to kill the
> patient, hovers increasingly "protectively" about the latter, for whom
> he feels an omnipotence-based physicianly concern. Hence it is,
> paradoxically, the very physician most anxiously concerned *to keep the
> patient alive* who tends most vigorously, at an unconscious level, to
> drive him to what has come to seem the only autonomous act left to
> him—namely, suicide. (p. 74)

    Psychotherapists who treat suicidal patients must help them
come to terms with their dominant ideology (Arieti 1977) and their
rigidly held life fantasies (Richman and Eyman, in press; Smith and
Eyman 1988). When there is a disparity between reality and the
patient's constricted view of what life should be like, the therapist
can help the patient mourn the loss of the life fantasy. This tech-

nique may paradoxically require the therapist to acknowledge the patient's hopelessness so that the lost dreams can be mourned and replaced by new ones that are more realistic. For example, one 23-year-old man became suicidal when he realized that he would never be accepted to Harvard, a dream he had cherished since early childhood. The therapist acknowledged that admission to Harvard was highly unlikely and then helped the patient accept the loss of that dream. At the same time, he helped the patient consider alternative pathways to an education that would build the patient's self-esteem. Thus the therapist helped the patient see how much misery is caused by unrealistically high expectations (Richman and Eyman, in press).

To treat suicidal patients effectively, clinicians must distinguish the patient's responsibility from the treater's responsibility. Physicians in general and psychiatrists in particular are characterologically prone to an exaggerated sense of responsibility (Gabbard 1985). We tend to blame ourselves for adverse outcomes beyond our control. Ultimately, we must reconcile ourselves to the fact that there are terminal psychiatric illnesses. Patients must bear the responsibility for deciding whether they will commit suicide or work collaboratively with their therapist to understand the wish to die. Fortunately, the vast majority of patients contemplate suicide with some ambivalence. The part of the suicidal individual that questions the suicidal solution may lead these patients to choose life over death.

References

Akiskal HS, Rosenthal TL, Haykal RF, et al: Characterological depressions: clinical and sleep EEG findings separating "subaffective dysthymias" from "character spectrum disorders." Arch Gen Psychiatry 37:777–783, 1980

Arieti S: Psychotherapy of severe depression. Am J Psychiatry 134:864–868, 1977

Asch SS: Suicide and the hidden executioner. International Review of Psychoanalysis 7:51–60, 1980

Beck AT: Thinking and depression, I: idiosyncratic content and cognitive distortions. Arch Gen Psychiatry 9:324–333, 1963

Betcher RW: The treatment of depression in brief inpatient group psychotherapy. Int J Group Psychother 33:365–385, 1983

Bibring E: The mechanism of depression, in Affective Disorders: Psychoanalytic Contributions to Their Study. Edited by Greenacre P. New York, International Universities Press, 1953, pp 13–48

Bunch J, Barraclough B: The influence of parental death and anniversaries upon suicide dates. Br J Psychiatry 118:621–626, 1971

Chemtob CM, Hamada RS, Bauer G, et al: Patients' suicides: frequency and impact on psychiatrists. Am J Psychiatry 145:224–228, 1988

DiMascio A, Weissman MA, Prusoff BA, et al: Differential symptom reduction by drugs and psychotherapy in acute depression. Arch Gen Psychiatry 36:1450–1456, 1979

Dorpat TL: Suicide, loss, and mourning. Suicide Life Threat Behav 3:213–224, 1973

Elkin I, Parloff MB, Hadley SW, et al: NIMH Treatment of Depression Collaborative Research Program. Arch Gen Psychiatry 42:305–316, 1985

Elkin I, Shea T, Watkins J, et al: NIMH Treatment of Depression Collaborative Research Program: general effectiveness of treatments. Arch Gen Psychiatry 46:971–982, 1989

Fawcett J, Scheftner W, Clark D, et al: Clinical predictors of suicide in patients with major affective disorders: a controlled prospective study. Am J Psychiatry 144:35–40, 1987

Feinstein SC, Wolpert EA: Juvenile manic-depressive illness: clinical and therapeutic considerations. J Am Acad Child Psychiatry 12:123–136, 1973

Fenichel O: The Psychoanalytic Theory of Neurosis. New York, WW Norton, 1945

Frank E, Kupfer DJ, Perel JM: Early recurrence in unipolar depression. Arch Gen Psychiatry 46:397–400, 1989

Freud S: The ego and the id (1923), in The Standard Edition of the Complete Psychological Works of Sigmund Freud, Vol 19. Translated and edited by Strachey J. London, Hogarth Press, 1961, pp 3–69

Freud S: Mourning and melancholia (1917), in The Standard Edition of the Complete Psychological Works of Sigmund Freud, Vol 14. Translated and edited by Strachey J. London, Hogarth Press, 1963, pp 237–260

Gabbard GO: The role of compulsiveness in the normal physician. JAMA 254:2926–2929, 1985

Hendin H: Psychotherapy and suicide, in Suicide in America. New York, WW Norton, 1982, pp 160–174

Jacobson E (ed): Psychotic identifications, in Depression: Comparative Studies of Normal, Neurotic, and Psychotic Conditions. New York, International Universities Press, 1971a, pp 242–263

Jacobson E (ed): Transference problems in depressives, in Depression: Comparative Studies of Normal, Neurotic, and Psychotic Conditions. New York, International Universities Press, 1971b, pp 284–301

Keller MB, Shapiro RW: "Double-depression": superimposition of acute depressive episodes on chronic depressive disorders. Am J Psychiatry 139:438–442, 1982

Klein M: Mourning and its relation to manic-depressive states (1940), in Love, Guilt and Reparation and Other Works 1921–1945. New York, Free Press, 1975, pp 344–369

Kocsis JH, Frances AJ, Voss C, et al: Imipramine treatment for chronic depression. Arch Gen Psychiatry 45:253–257, 1988

Lesse S: Psychotherapy in combination with antidepressant drugs in severely depressed outpatients—20-year evaluation. Am J Psychother 32:48–73, 1978

Loeb FF, Loeb LR: Psychoanalytic observations on the effect of lithium on manic attacks. J Am Psychoanal Assoc 35:877–902, 1987

Maltsberger JT, Buie DH: Countertransference hate in the treatment of suicidal patients. Arch Gen Psychiatry 30:625–633, 1974

Maxmen JS: An educative model for inpatient group therapy. Int J Group Psychother 28:321–338, 1978

Meissner WW: Psychotherapy and the Paranoid Process. Northvale, NJ, Jason Aronson, 1986

Menninger KA: Psychoanalytic aspects of suicide. Int J Psychoanal 14:376–390, 1933

Olin HS: Psychotherapy of the chronically suicidal patient. Am J Psychother 30:570–575, 1976

Pilkonis PA, Frank E: Personality pathology in recurrent depression: nature, prevalence, and relationship to treatment response. Am J Psychiatry 145:435–441, 1988

Pollock GH: Foreword, in Manic-Depressive Illness: History of a Syndrome. Edited by Wolpert EA. New York, International Universities Press, 1977, pp 1–2

Post RM, Rubinow ER, Uhde TW, et al: Dysphoric mania: clinical and biological correlates. Arch Gen Psychiatry 46:353–358, 1989

Richman J, Eyman JR: Psychotherapy of suicide: individual, group, and family approaches, in Understanding Suicide: The State of the Art. Edited by Lester D. Philadelphia, Charles C Thomas (in press)

Rounsaville BJ, Chevron ES, Weissman MM: Specification of techniques in interpersonal psychotherapy, in Psychotherapy Research: Where Are We and Where Should We Go? Edited by Williams JBW, Spitzer RL. New York, Guilford Press, 1984, pp 160–172

Shneidman ES (ed): Suicidology: Contemporary Developments. New York, Grune & Stratton, 1976

Searles HF: The "dedicated physician" in the field of psychotherapy and psychoanalysis (1967), in Countertransference and Related Subjects. Madison, CT, International Universities Press, 1979, pp 71–88

Smith K: Using a battery of tests to predict suicide in a long term hospital: a clinical analysis. Omega 13:261–275, 1983

Smith K, Eyman J: Ego structure and object differentiation in suicidal patients, in Primitive Mental States of the Rorschach. Edited by Lerner HD, Lerner PM. Madison, CT, International Universities Press, 1988, pp 175–202

Strupp HH, Sandell JA, Waterhouse GJ, et al: Psychodynamic therapy: theory and research, in Short-Term Psychotherapies for Depression. Edited by Rush AJ. New York, Guilford Press, 1982, pp 215–250

Twemlow SW, Gabbard GO: The lovesick therapist, in Sexual Exploitation in Professional Relationships. Edited by Gabbard GO. Washington, DC, American Psychiatric Press, 1989, pp 71–87

Wolpert EA: On the nature of manic-depressive illness, in The Course of Life: Psychoanalytic Contributions Toward Understanding Personality Development, Vol III: Adulthood and the Aging Process. Edited by Greenspan SI, Pollock GH. Adelphi, MD, National

Institute of Mental Health (DHHS Pub No [ADM] 81-1000), 1981, pp 443–452

Zee HJ: Blindspots in recognizing serious suicidal intentions. Bull Menninger Clin 36:551–555, 1972

Zimmermann M, Pfohl B, Coryell W: Diagnosing personality disorder in depressed patients: a comparison of patient and informant interviews. Arch Gen Psychiatry 45:733–737, 1988

CHAPTER 9

Anxiety Disorders

As a rule, what is out of sight disturbs men's minds more
seriously than what they see.

—Julius Caesar

Anxiety is an affect that was instrumental to the birth of psychoanalysis and psychodynamic psychiatry. Nearly 100 years ago
Freud (1895) coined the term *anxiety neurosis* and identified two
forms of anxiety. One form was the diffuse sense of worry or dread
that originated in a repressed thought or wish and was curable
through psychotherapeutic intervention. The second form of anxiety was characterized by an overwhelming sense of panic, accompanied by manifestations of autonomic discharge, including profuse
sweating, increased respiratory and heart rates, diarrhea, and a
subjective sense of terror. This latter form, in Freud's view, did not
result from psychological factors. Rather, it was conceptualized as
the result of the physiological build-up of libido related to a lack of
sexual activity. He referred to this form as *actual neurosis.*

By 1926 Freud had further refined his understanding of anxiety as a result of his recent creation, the structural model. Anxiety
was now viewed as the result of psychic conflict between unconscious
sexual or aggressive wishes stemming from the id and corresponding threats of punishment from the superego. Anxiety was understood as a *signal* of the presence of danger in the unconscious. In
response to this signal, the ego mobilized defense mechanisms to
prevent unacceptable thoughts and feelings from emerging into
conscious awareness. If signal anxiety failed to adequately activate
the ego's defensive resources, then intense, more persistent anxiety
or other neurotic symptoms would result. In this sense, anxiety was
conceptualized by Freud as both a symptomatic manifestation of
neurotic conflict as well as an adaptive signal to ward off awareness
of neurotic conflict.

In Freud's model, anxiety is an ego affect. The ego controls
access to consciousness and, through repression, divorces itself from
any association with instinctual impulses from the id. It censors both
the impulse itself and the corresponding intrapsychic representa-

tion. A repressed instinctual wish or impulse may still find expression as a symptom, although it is likely to be displaced and disguised by the time it reaches symptomatic expression. Depending on the defensive operations and symptomatic manifestations, the resulting neurosis might take the form of an obsessional thought, a compulsive ritual, a hysterical paralysis, or a phobia.

One unfortunate consequence of the deliberate effort to be atheoretical in the development of the DSM-III-R (American Psychiatric Association 1987) nosology is the resulting sacrifice of classical neurotic entities and the psychodynamic model of symptom formation associated with them. They have been replaced by three separate categories: anxiety disorders, somatoform disorders, and dissociative disorders. The first of these categories, anxiety disorders, has been further subdivided into panic disorder, phobias, obsessive-compulsive disorder, posttraumatic stress disorder, and generalized anxiety disorder. Although this classification accommodates the recent biological research delineating different kinds of anxiety, it also encourages clinicians to think about anxiety as an *illness* rather than as an overdetermined *symptom* of unconscious conflict. In many cases, patients presenting with anxiety have no idea what they are anxious about.

In other cases, the anxiety may be attached to a conscious, acceptable fear that masks a deeper, less acceptable concern. The task of the psychodynamic clinician is to understand the unconscious origins of such anxiety. Freud originated the idea that each successive developmental period in a child's life produces a characteristic fear associated with that phase. Based on Freud's discoveries and those of subsequent psychoanalytic investigators, a developmental hierarchy of anxiety (see Table 9-1) can be constructed to assist the psychodynamic clinician in determining the unconscious sources of a patient's symptomatic anxiety.

At the most mature level, anxiety originating in the superego can be understood as guilt feelings or pangs of conscience about not living up to an internal standard of moral behavior. During the oedipal phase, anxiety focuses on potential damage to or loss of the genitals at the hands of a retaliatory parental figure. This fear may be expressed metaphorically as loss of another body part or any

Table 9-1.　A developmental hierarchy of anxiety

Superego anxiety
Castration anxiety
Fear of loss of love
Fear of loss of the object (separation anxiety)
Persecutory anxiety
Disintegration anxiety

other form of physical injury. Moving back in the developmental hierarchy to a somewhat earlier anxiety, we find the fear of losing the love or approval of a significant other (originally a parent). A developmentally more primitive source of anxiety is the possibility of losing not just the object's love, but also the object itself—what is usually referred to as separation anxiety. The most primitive forms of anxiety are persecutory anxiety and disintegration anxiety. The former derives from the Kleinian paranoid-schizoid position, in which the primary anxiety is that persecuting objects from outside will invade and annihilate the patient from within. Disintegration anxiety may derive either from the fear of losing one's sense of self or boundedness through merger with an object, or from concern that one's self will fragment and lose its integrity in the absence of mirroring or idealizing responses from others in the environment.

Whenever anxiety forms part of the clinical picture, the psychodynamic psychiatrist must enlist the patient's collaboration in identifying the developmental origins of the anxiety. This information may be ascertained within a 1-hour interview, or it may take an extensive evaluation. Anxiety, like most symptoms, is often multiply determined by issues deriving from a variety of developmental levels, as illustrated in the following case example. (An earlier version of this case was published in the Bulletin of the Menninger Clinic [Gabbard and Nemiah 1985]):

> Mr. L was a never-married, unemployed, 20-year-old who was hospitalized with free-floating anxiety and hypochondriacal concerns. Although he had experienced these difficulties for several years, they had been exacerbated several months before admission when his parents separated and indicated that they were intent on divorce. His anxiety and hypochondria became so overwhelming that he was unable to function in school or to hold a job. He deteriorated until he began to spend most of each day in bed, arising in the late afternoon to go to a local video arcade for the evening with younger adolescents. Several times a week his absorption in the video games was interrupted by an anxious conviction that he was suffering from a serious illness and might die at any moment. Seeking reassurance, he would abruptly rush to the office of his family internist or to the local hospital's emergency room. This behavior pattern resulted in several thousand dollars of medical bills that were charged to the patient's father.
>
> Mr. L indicated that his problems had begun in the 10th grade, when he felt as if his life was falling apart. He had found the sexual awakening that accompanied puberty highly disturbing, and he still longed to return to an earlier time when gender distinction seemed irrelevant. In describing his developmental years, the patient portrayed both his father and his mother as intrusive and voyeuristic parents who violated generational boundaries and failed to respect his privacy. Mr. L recalled that when he was 7, his father had once forced him to pose nude in the backyard of his grandmother's house

for a photograph. He also reported that his father had often watched him dress for hockey practice and had even suggested that underpants were not necessary. As he reached puberty, he began to leave his shirttails untucked to avoid his father's "ogling." Mr. L said that his mother would sometimes playfully try to remove his towel when he left the shower. His mother also complained to him about his father's sexual inadequacy, even speculating that her husband might be worried about the patient growing up and taking his place. Thus, Mr. L thought that both his parents viewed him as a "sex object."

Physical and neurological examinations were entirely normal. Routine laboratory examinations were also within normal limits. The only significant medical history was that the patient had had a congenital residual appendage of the left testicle surgically removed when he was 10.

Mr. L described himself as "asexual" but reported homosexual fantasies regarding young men in their late adolescence, whom he admired and idolized from a distance. He had, however, refused sexual interaction with those young men who had offered it. He reported limited experience with heterosexual necking and petting that had always stopped short of genital involvement. Voyeuristic tendencies were reflected in his view of himself as a person content with watching others. He indicated that he enjoyed seeing healthy, virile young men and happy young women together. The role of sex partner was clearly too anxiety-provoking for him.

Mr. L had considerable difficulty with self-other differentiation. Whenever he interacted with other patients on the unit, he began to assume their characteristics. For example, when a young female patient became psychotic, Mr. L was convinced that he, too, was disorganizing. When another patient needed bladder surgery, Mr. L reported urinary symptoms to his doctor and suggested that he might need such surgery as well. This tendency to overidentify with his peers and to take on their attributes led him to distance himself from other patients. Similarly, he would not work closely with staff members. However, this self-imposed distance made him feel anxious about being alone. As a compromise between too much distance or too much closeness, he would provoke staff members and other patients into negative interactions with him. He repeatedly broke the structure established for him in order to evoke persecutory attacks from staff members or peers. He would then feel victimized and would lash out with contempt and outrage at those he perceived as persecuting him. This pattern of interactions seemed repetitive of behavior that had occurred with his father. At times during the patient's hospitalization, his father would scream at him over the phone about his lack of motivation and his irresponsibility, occasionally reducing him to tears. As a result, Mr. L often complained about his father's tyrannical tendencies: "I'm angry at him. I feel smothered and exploited by my father. He controls my life, but if he doesn't, my life falls apart."

This patient met the criteria for the Axis I diagnoses of generalized anxiety disorder and hypochondriasis. He also met the Axis II criteria for borderline personality disorder because of his multiple "neurotic" symptoms, including free-floating anxiety and hypochondriacal concerns; his profound identity disturbance; his inappropriate and intense anger; his pattern of unstable and intense interpersonal relationships; his affective instability; and his intense separation anxiety.

As a result of a thorough evaluation of the patient's anxiety, an explanatory formulation was derived that illustrated the multiple determinants of that symptom. At the phallic-oedipal level, his anxiety was related to castration concerns. His perception of his mother as seductive and exhibitionistic led him to flee her house and live with his father after his parents had separated. Projective psychological testing with the Thematic Apperception Test was highly revealing, as in the following story the patient told:

> This woman is the mother of a male child who is masturbating. She opens the door, and with a look of disgust, yet happiness, she sees her young son masturbating. He is confused and doesn't understand what he is doing. It was just instinctual. She gets a vicarious thrill over seeing her child do this, but they also both feel guilty—a perverse pleasure. She takes an intense interest in her son's sex life.

In addition to illustrating the threat of a possible incestuous relationship, this story also reflects the presence of inadequately repressed polymorphous perverse sexual impulses, particularly along the exhibitionistic-scopophilic axis. This perceived availability of his mother made Mr. L particularly fearful of retaliation by his father. In the patient's own words, "Virility is linked to an explosive instinct. It must be controlled." His homosexual preoccupations may also have been an effort to defend against his castration anxiety by avoiding the competitive heterosexual arena with its risks of retaliation. The castration threat may similarly come from the opposite sex, as revealed in his comment, "I'm afraid of intercourse. I'm afraid my penis will be slashed if I were to have intercourse." The surgery on Mr. L's testicular appendage at age 10 may have further reinforced his castration anxiety.

Mr. L's anxiety, however, cannot be explained by relying solely on phallic-oedipal determinants. The origins of his problems with self-other differentiation may have been partially linked with the history of sexual intrusiveness of both parents and their failure to establish firm generational boundaries between the patient and themselves. During a visit from Mr. L's father, the patient and his father spent almost 2 hours in the patient's room, lying opposite each other (on the couch and on the bed), simply staring at one another, and talking only briefly. Nursing staff who observed them noted that they seemed like mirror images of one another.

Another determinant of Mr. L's anxiety was his sense that others could violate his boundaries to take him over from within. He felt as if this takeover happened whenever he became close to other patients on the unit because he began to assume their symptoms. He experienced this invasion as a threat to the integrity of his tenuously organized sense of self, and he was terrified of disintegrating and disappearing as he was engulfed by the object with which he fused. Thus his reaction to this combination of persecutory anxiety and disintegration anxiety led him to maintain more distance from others to avoid fusing with them. However, this defensive maneuver in turn created intense separation anxiety. Of note is that Mr. L linked his first attack of anxiety to leaving home for college. To deal with his separation concerns, the patient provoked others into relating to him as though they were persecutors. Via projective identification, the patient would externalize an internal object relationship of persecutor-victim and attempt to enact it with staff members. In an effort to obtain reassurance that he was loved, he pressured staff members to act like his angry and controlling father. He could gain this form of reassurance only through a struggle or argument, since a loving and more positive interaction threatened him with fusion. He would frequently leave a particular hospital activity because of unbearable anxiety. When questioned about this pattern, he confided that he was attracted to another young man who also participated in that activity and often had homosexual fantasies about him. Whenever he felt threatened by becoming physically close to the other man, Mr. L would return to the unit. However, upon arriving there, he would then become anxious about being separated from this fantasy object, and to feel less alone and abandoned, he would provoke struggles with the staff members.

Mr. L's dilemma of needing to attach and merge himself with someone else in order to survive, yet fearing engulfment and loss of identity, was a prominent resistance to treatment. He saw any movement from the primitive persecutor-victim stance to a more mature object relationship as abandonment of the only familiar form of relatedness. He repeatedly expressed a wish to leave the hospital but indicated that his father would fall apart if he improved—a projective description of what he perceived would happen to *him* upon improvement. The primitive nature of Mr. L's anxiety was vividly evident in a parapraxis he had made once while complaining about his psychotherapy and expressing a wish to leave the hospital. Changing the subject to a physical complaint about some insect bites on his legs, he complained, "I am being completely eaten up by all these insights—I mean, insects."

The principle of multiple function is particularly well illustrated by exploring the patient's hypochondriacal anxiety about becoming seriously or fatally ill. Like Mr. H in Chapter 7, Mr. L had anxiety that can be viewed as an introjection of the persecutory object. In other words, Mr. L's anxiety that an outside persecutor would invade him and take over was transformed into a fear that he was being destroyed from within by an *internal* persecutor in the form of an illness. His constant attention to his body was an extraordinary effort to shore up his weakly cathected body boundaries and to distinguish the external from the internal.

The case of Mr. L illustrates how anxiety may serve as a window onto the relevant developmental issues with which the patient struggles. Analogous to a stream of light passing through a prism, his anxiety breaks into at least four components: castration anxiety, separation anxiety, persecutory anxiety, and disintegration anxiety.

Biological Dimensions of Anxiety

Recent neurobiological research has confirmed Freud's original observation that there are essentially two forms of anxiety: one largely determined by psychological issues, and another driven by autonomous biological factors outside the realm of psychological content. It is now well established that panic attacks respond to imipramine and monoamine oxidase inhibitors, while anticipatory anxiety does not (Cooper 1985; Kandel 1983; Nemiah 1981). Panic attacks may also be experimentally induced by an infusion of lactate. In a significant number of patients with panic disorder, psychological concerns do not appear etiologically significant, so psychotherapeutic exploration may be of limited value (Cooper 1985).

As noted in Chapter 1, research on the locus ceruleus has been productive in defining the biological dimensions of anxiety. As the source of nearly three-quarters of the brain's norepinephrine supply, the locus ceruleus is the largest noradrenergic nucleus in the brain (Redmond 1987). While Freud viewed the ego as the *psychological* seat of anxiety, modern neurobiological researchers have identified the locus ceruleus as the *biological* seat of anxiety. Neural pathways enter this nucleus from every level of the central nervous system, and efferent pathways lead to all the major physiological systems involved in panic attacks. The locus ceruleus appears to regulate the anxiety level of the organism through the activation or deactivation of inhibitory neurons, which are activated by gamma-aminobutyric acid (GABA). Benzodiazepines appear to work similarly by activating the inhibitory neurons in the locus ceruleus. Conversely, a feeling of panic can be created in human subjects by deactivating the GABA-controlled neurons with piperoxane and yohimbine (Redmond 1987). Hence, dysregulation of the GABA system in the locus ceruleus may serve as a biologically based etiology of panic disorder, irrespective of psychological concerns (Cooper 1985).

Cooper (1985) has noted that certain patients may have a heightened sensitivity to separation anxiety, leading to panic attacks unrelated to psychological conflict or disturbances of internal object relations. He has cautioned that these patients should not be held psychologically responsible for their symptoms because psychological mastery of reasons for the anxiety might not eliminate it. On the other hand, it would be naive to assume that all panic attacks are unrelated to psychological concerns. Some panic attacks are clearly precipitated by specific environmental or psychological triggers, and apparently "contentless" anxiety may simply indicate the presence of unconscious factors. These patients may have a biological vulnerability that requires a psychological stimulus to produce a full-blown panic attack.

Although Freud appeared to grow more interested in the notion of signal anxiety later in his career, he always maintained that physiological anxiety was instrumental to the development of panic states. More recently, Nemiah (1981) has linked Freud's early formulations with the biological differences between panic attacks and anticipatory anxiety. To produce classical panic disorder, an underlying neural structure must be triggered by psychological or physiological factors. Without this neural structure, the end result will be a milder form of anticipatory anxiety. Nemiah (1981) noted that "in patients with a diathesis for panic attacks resulting from specific, predisposing neural structures, the anxiety aroused by the psychological conflicts, when these are present, will take the form of panic; whereas in individuals without this neural predisposition, it will appear in the less intense form of anticipatory, signal anxiety" (p. 119). The existence of a neural mechanism for anxiety does not, however, preclude the usefulness of psychotherapeutic technique. Effective psychotherapy most likely results in long-term structural and functional changes in the brain that are related to changes in the expression of specific genes (Kandel 1983). Moreover, as noted in Chapter 1, with certain patients who have intense separation anxiety, just hearing the therapist's voice over the telephone can quiet a panic attack as rapidly as the most potent pharmacologic agent.

Panic Disorder

Panic attacks generally last only a matter of minutes but produce considerable distress within the patient. In addition to alarming physiological symptoms, such as choking, dizziness, sweating, shaking, and tachycardia, patients with panic disorder often sense imminent doom. Most patients with panic disorder also have agoraphobia (i.e., a fear of being trapped in a location or situation where escape will be difficult or extremely embarrassing). Because panic attacks are recurrent, patients often develop a secondary form of anticipatory anxiety, worrying constantly about when and where the next attack will occur. Panic-disordered patients with agoraphobia often restrict their travel to try to control the dreaded situation of having a panic attack in a place they cannot leave easily.

Panic disorder, as discussed in the previous section, may appear psychologically contentless. The attacks may come "out of the blue," without apparent environmental or intrapsychic precipitants. As a result, the psychodynamic psychiatrist's role is often—and unfortunately—deemed as irrelevant in treating these patients. A significant percentage of panic-disordered patients have such attacks because of psychodynamic factors and thus may respond to psychological interventions (Nemiah 1981, 1984). Psychodynamic clinicians should thoroughly investigate the circumstances of the attacks and the history of each panic-disordered patient to determine whether psychological factors are relevant.

Several lines of evidence support the view that panic attacks have psychological meaning. First, there is a close link between separation anxiety and panic disorder. One study found that 50 percent of 32 agoraphobic patients had a history of separation anxiety and that their panic attacks often followed the loss of a significant person (Klein 1964). Also, compared to controls, patients with panic disorder have a documented higher incidence of stressful life events, particularly loss, in the months preceding the onset of panic disorder (Faravelli and Pallanti 1989). In another investigation of patients with panic attacks and agoraphobia, 1 in 4 improved dramatically with placebo (Coryell and Noyes 1988). When these placebo responders were studied in more detail, they tested normally for dexamethasone suppression and exhibited somewhat lower anxiety than nonresponders. In another study (Ballenger et al. 1988), 43 percent of the patients with panic disorder and agoraphobia showed at least "moderate improvement" by the fourth week of placebo administration. Placebo response suggests that psychological factors, such as the interaction with a concerned physician and the belief that symptoms can be reduced through pharmacologic intervention, result in significant amelioration of panic disorder.

These research findings are borne out by clinical experience with patients who suffer from poorly developed object constancy (see Chapter 14). Such patients cannot summon an internal image of their therapist in times of distress to soothe their anxiety. Over long weekends or during their therapist's vacations, these patients may develop full-blown panic attacks triggered by the thought of losing their therapist. They may fear that their therapist has died or is on the verge of rejecting or abandoning them. In such circumstances, just hearing their therapist's voice over the telephone can completely eliminate the panic within a few seconds. One psychiatrist in private practice characteristically left a message on his answering machine over the weekend so that his patients would know where to reach him. Upon hiring a secretary, he relegated to her the task of recording the answering machine message. On the first Monday morning after the secretary recorded the message, three angry patients called him to complain. One patient angrily stated, "I need to hear *your* voice, not hers! It's either your voice or a Xanax!"

As poignantly illustrated by this comment, the *sound* of the therapist's voice was enough to reassure this patient that he was truly still available. Indeed, in this case the therapist's voice had a therapeutic effect as potent as a pharmacologic agent. Patients suffering from a lack of object constancy often are able to ultimately develop an internalized image of their therapist over the course of long-term, expressive-supportive psychotherapy. As a result of this internalization process, both the separation anxiety and the panic attacks may improve considerably.

Panic-disordered patients frequently require a combination of drug therapy and psychotherapy (Nemiah 1984). Even when patients with panic attacks and agoraphobia have their symptoms pharmacologically controlled, they are often reluctant to venture out into the world again and may require psychotherapeutic interventions to help overcome this fear (Cooper 1985; Zitrin et al. 1978). Some patients will adamantly refuse any medication because they believe that it stigmatizes them as being mentally ill, so psychotherapeutic intervention is required to help them understand and eliminate their resistance to pharmacotherapy. The presence of personality disorders, particularly those in Cluster B (e.g., antisocial, borderline, narcissistic, histrionic), has been shown to adversely affect the treatment outcome of patients with panic disorder (Reich 1988). For a comprehensive and effective treatment plan, these patients require psychotherapeutic approaches in addition to appropriate medications. In all patients with symptoms of panic disorder or agoraphobia, a careful psychodynamic evaluation will help weigh the contributions of biological and dynamic factors.

Mr. M, a 27-year-old office worker, came to an outpatient clinic with a complaint of panic attacks that occurred whenever he attempted to leave town. He was initially unable to link the panic to any psychological content, but further exploration by the evaluating psychiatrist revealed a number of contributing factors. Mr. M had just purchased a new house, and his wife was pregnant with their first child. When the psychiatrist commented on the increased responsibility associated with these events, the patient replied that he felt more like 7 than 27. He went on to say that he was not sure that he was prepared to shoulder the responsibilities of a husband and father accountable for the mortgage on a house. The psychiatrist asked Mr. M to describe in more detail the circumstances of the panic attacks. Mr. M again explained that he had them whenever he started to leave town. The psychiatrist asked about the purpose of these trips, which Mr. M explained was to go hunting with his father. The psychiatrist asked if anything unpleasant had ever happened on these trips. After a few moments' reflection, Mr. M replied that he had accidentally shot his father in two different hunting accidents, although fortunately his father had sustained only minor wounds on each occasion.

The psychiatrist then developed a tentative explanatory formulation based on his evaluation that Mr. M's panic disorder was related to psychological conflict. Recent events in his life had placed him more squarely in competition with his father as a husband, father, and breadwinner. These events activated long-standing aggressive wishes toward the father that were based on repressed and unconscious oedipal rivalry. The impulse to destroy his father had emerged in the form of accidents on two previous hunting trips. Now whenever Mr. M planned to leave town with his father to go hunting, the threatened emergence of the aggressive impulses created signal anxiety that was transformed into a full-blown panic attack because this particular patient had the underlying neural substrate necessary to transform anxiety into panic. The result was an avoidance of situations in which the destructive wishes and the imagined retaliation (castration) would be activated.

To understand the dynamic factors involved in triggering the panic, the patient began expressive-supportive psychotherapy with an expressive emphasis. As the process proceeded, Mr. M began to talk more and more about his attachment to his mother. It soon emerged that his mother had also been terrified of separations herself. As a child, each time Mr. M went outside, his mother would warn him about the many dangers he might encounter. Through the psychotherapy process, Mr. M eventually realized that he shared his mother's anxiety about separations. He noted that whenever his wife was away on business, he worried the entire time because he feared that she might die and thus abandon him. The patient's oedipal anxieties were clearly compounded by more primitive anxieties about object loss, originally of his mother but now his wife.

After approximately 2 years of psychotherapy, Mr. M was free from panic attacks and from anticipatory anxiety as well. He had received a promotion at work that he was able to handle without anxiety. His new job necessitated driving out of town almost every workday, and he was able to do so without experiencing any panic.

Several years later, Mr. M returned for further treatment when two life events reactivated the underlying neural structure that mediated his panic attacks. A private business he had started had become enormously successful, resulting in a much more affluent life-style. Moreover, his father had been diagnosed as having incurable cancer. This time a combination of medication (alprazolam) and psychotherapy was required to reduce Mr. M's panic attacks to manageable proportions.

Phobias

Anxiety disorders as a group are the most prevalent of all major groups of mental disorders (Regier et al. 1988), and among anxiety disorders, phobias are by far the most common. Phobias are divided into three categories in DSM-III-R: 1) agoraphobia (without panic disorder), 2) social phobia, and 3) simple phobia. Social phobia involves a variety of fears whereby patients imagine that they will be exposed to the criticism or disapproval of others, which will be embarrassing or even humiliating. These fears include stage fright or performance anxiety, fear of speaking in public in front of other people, and anxiety about interacting with others at parties. To avoid the intense anxiety associated with the feared situation, persons with this diagnosis usually restrict their lives to avoid the situation in which they are phobic. In simple phobia, the fear is more circumscribed and may involve such items as heights, airplanes, dogs, and snakes. Anticipatory anxiety is triggered when these patients must face the feared stimulus, so they also construct their lives to avoid it.

The psychodynamic understanding of phobias illustrates the neurotic mechanism of symptom formation described previously. When forbidden sexual or aggressive thoughts that might lead to retaliatory punishment threaten to emerge from the unconscious, signal anxiety is activated, which leads to the deployment of three defense mechanisms—displacement, projection, and avoidance (Nemiah 1981). These defenses eliminate the anxiety by once again repressing the forbidden wish, but the anxiety is controlled at the cost of creating a phobic neurosis. A clinical example will illustrate the phobic symptom formation more concretely:

> Mr. N was a 25-year-old junior executive who had just completed an MBA and taken his first position with a corporation. He had developed a social phobia that involved an intense fear of meeting new people at work or in social situations. He also developed intense anxiety whenever he had to speak in front of a group of people at work. When forced to confront the feared situations, he would become short of breath and stumble over his words to such an extent that he could not complete sentences.
>
> Brief dynamic therapy was recommended for Mr. N because of his notable ego strengths, the focal nature of his symptom, his good overall functioning, a high level of motivation, and considerable psychological-mindedness. In the third session, Mr. N clarified for the therapist that the worst part of meeting new people was having to introduce himself. The following exchange took place:
>
> Therapist: What's difficult about saying your name?
> Patient: I have no idea.
> Therapist: If you reflect about your name for a minute, what comes to mind?
> Patient: (after a pause) Well, it's also my father's name.
> Therapist: How does that make you feel?
> Patient: A bit uncomfortable, I guess.
> Therapist: Why is that?
> Patient: Well, I haven't had a great relationship with him. Ever since he left my mom when I was 4 years old, I've seen very little of him.

Therapist:	So you had to live alone with your mother after he left?
Patient:	That's right. My mom never remarried, so I had to be the man of the house from an early age, and I didn't feel ready to take on so much responsibility. I've always resented that. When I was a kid, everybody always said that I acted like such an adult. That used to bother me because I felt like I was just pretending to be an adult when I was really a child inside. I felt like I was fooling everybody, and if they found out, they would be mad at me.
Therapist:	I wonder if that's how you feel now when you introduce yourself.
Patient:	I think that's exactly how I feel. To say my name is to say I'm trying to be my father.

The therapist's interpretation helped Mr. N realize that his anxiety was related to guilt and shame about prematurely filling his father's shoes. He imagined that others would see through this charade, or deceit, and disapprove of him. After 10 sessions of brief dynamic therapy, the patient overcame his social phobia and was able to function well at work and in social settings.

At the height of Mr. N's oedipal phase of development, his father left him alone with his mother. In that original anxiety-generating situation, he had feared castration or retaliatory punishment (from his father) for taking his father's place with his mother. As an adult, Mr. N dealt with anxiety by displacing the original feared situation onto an insignificant and seemingly trivial derivative of that situation, namely, saying his name during introductions. Symbolically, this simple social grace had taken on the meaning of replacing his father. The patient's second defensive maneuver was to project the feared situation outward into the environment so that the threatened punishment or disapproval came from external rather than internal sources (i.e., the superego). The patient's third and final defense mechanism was avoidance. By avoiding all situations in which he had to introduce himself or speak in front of others, Mr. N could maintain control over his anxiety, but at the cost of restricting his social life and jeopardizing his performance at work.

Mr. N's anxiety about speaking in front of others is widely shared. In one metropolitan survey (Pollard and Henderson 1988), one-fifth of the individuals contacted in the city of St. Louis had a social phobia about public speaking or performing. When the investigators modified that figure by including the "significant distress" criteria of DSM-III (American Psychiatric Association 1980), the prevalence rate fell to 2 percent. Exact figures on social phobia are difficult to ascertain, however, because the diagnosis is often applied to general interpersonal patterns of shyness and avoidance of the opposite sex for fear of rejection. The continuum ranges from social phobia at one end to a generalized characterological style of relating, known as avoidant personality disorder (see Chapter 18), at the other. Thus differentiating between discrete phobias and personality styles is not an easy task.

Because of considerable success in treating phobias with behavioral desensitization and, to a lesser extent, tricyclic antidepressants such as imipramine, psychodynamic approaches have fallen out of favor to some degree in the treatment of phobias. In patients with characteristics similar to Mr. N, expressive psychotherapy is often effective. Other patients may benefit from a more supportive approach with or without medication. A controlled study of 111 patients with simple phobia, agoraphobia, or mixed phobia confirmed the effectiveness of supportive psychotherapy plus medication (Zitrin et al. 1978). One group of patients received behavioral therapy plus a placebo, a second group received behavioral therapy plus imipramine, and a third group received supportive therapy plus imipramine. No differences were found between the supportive therapy group and behavioral therapy groups that received imipramine; both improved considerably in 70–86 percent of the cases. At 1-year follow-up, 83 percent of the patients in all three groups who had shown improvement had not relapsed. The investigators concluded that psychotherapy's greatest influence was in those patients whose core phobic disorder had been brought under pharmacological control with imipramine.

The interpersonal ramifications of phobias often benefit from a dynamic approach as well. By virtue of being housebound, severely agoraphobic individuals often require caretaking from another significant person, such as a spouse or parent. It is common, for example, for an agoraphobic woman and her husband to have accommodated to her condition over a period of many years. The husband may actually feel more secure knowing that his wife is always in the house. If the agoraphobia is treated, the couple's equilibrium may destabilize. The husband may become more anxious because of a fear that his wife will begin to seek out other men now that she is leaving the house. Adequate assessment and treatment of phobias must include a careful assessment of how the phobia fits into the patient's network of relationships. A psychodynamic understanding of the interpersonal context of a phobia may thus be crucial to dealing with resistances to conventional treatments such as behavioral desensitization and medication.

Obsessive-Compulsive Disorder

Obsessions are defined as recurrent ego-dystonic thoughts, while compulsions are ritualized actions that *must* be performed to relieve anxiety. The complaints of these patients fit into five primary categories: 1) rituals involving checking, 2) rituals involving cleaning, 3) obsessive thoughts unaccompanied by compulsions, 4) obsessional slowness, and 5) mixed rituals (Baer and Jenike 1986). Those patients who are involved in cleaning rituals or obsessive thoughts about germs and contamination bear considerable resemblance to phobic patients. Recent research has suggested that obsessive-compulsive disorder (OCD) is much more common than had been previously thought (Karno et al. 1988). Even with strict DSM-III exclusion criteria, the lifetime prevalence is between 1.2 and 2.4 percent, a figure many times greater than all previous estimates. Obsessive-compulsive disorder is often complicated by depression and by serious impairment in occupational and social functioning so that family members and coworkers of OCD patients may be significantly affected by the illness as well.

Despite the long-established tradition of the diagnosis of obsessive-compulsive neurosis, DSM-III reclassified OCD as an anxiety disorder because the primary function of an obsession or ritual seems to be regulation of anxiety. The classical formulation of the defensive regression inherent in obsessive-compulsive neurosis has been succinctly summarized by Nemiah (1988):

> In the face of stimuli that arouse anxiety-provoking oedipal libido, instead of repressing the drive and converting the energy into somatic symptoms as in hysteria or displacing and projecting it as in the phobic neurosis, the patient with an obsessive-compulsive neurosis retreats from the oedipal position and regresses along the path of psychosexual development to the anal phase, a regression often aided by the presence of anal fixations resulting from disturbances in the patient's initial passage through that developmental stage during early childhood. (p. 243)

Another product of the regression is the unraveling of the smooth fusion between aggressive and sexual drives that is characteristic of the oedipal phase. Feelings of love and hatred are no longer fused, so the obsessive-compulsive neurotic is typically plagued with intense ambivalence. The simultaneous presence of loving and hateful feelings leaves the patient consumed with doubt about the appropriate course of action and, like Hamlet, paralyzed with indecision. As noted in Chapter 2, the obsessive-compulsive neurotic characteristically uses the defenses of isolation, reaction formation, intellectualization, and undoing to cope with the primitive sexual and aggressive drives that must be contained and controlled.

The psychodynamic explanation of OCD has been challenged by recent biological research. A number of investigators have suggested that there is a biological basis for the disorder because of several observations, including a higher rate of concordance for

OCD in monozygotic than dizygotic twins, an increased prevalence in patients with Tourette's syndrome and in their families, and a dramatic response in some patients to psychosurgery (Elkins et al. 1980; Lieberman 1984; Turner et al. 1985). Moreover, a recent quantitative study using computerized tomography revealed that the caudate nucleus volume in OCD patients is significantly less than in healthy controls (Luxenberg et al. 1988). The consensus of current thinking is that OCD involves a biological predisposition that interacts with psychological and environmental factors (Rachman and Hodgson 1980).

The literature on treatment outcome has also suggested a biological component. Medications such as clomipramine and fluvoxamine have been found to be effective with some OCD patients (Jenike et al. 1986; Perse 1988; White and Cole 1988). Also, the symptoms of OCD patients are notoriously refractory to psychoanalysis and insight-oriented psychotherapy (Jenike et al. 1986; Nemiah 1988; Perse 1988; Zetzel 1970). (Obsessive-compulsive personality disorder responds well to these treatments, as discussed in Chapter 18.) The best response rates reported in the literature have been to behavioral techniques involving in vivo exposure combined with response prevention (Barlow and Beck 1984). However, pharmacologic and behavioral treatments have had only limited success. Although the symptoms may be controlled initially by behavioral modification, there is a high relapse rate (Barlow and Beck 1984), and Marks (1981) has pointed out that such treatment requires extensive cooperation from the patient, which may not be forthcoming in most OCD patients. Even without treatment, an estimated 40 percent of OCD patients will have their symptoms go into remission or at least experience considerable improvement (Baer and Jenike 1986). Although medications can be helpful, symptoms are reduced on most rating scales an average of 30–60 percent at best (White and Cole 1988), with the patients relapsing when the drug is discontinued unless they have received some form of psychotherapeutic treatment in addition to pharmacotherapy.

Many OCD patients seem to hang onto their symptoms, tenaciously resisting treatment efforts. The symptoms themselves may fend off psychotic disintegration in some patients, therefore performing a highly useful function in terms of psychological homeostasis. The symptoms of OCD may accompany any level of underlying personality or ego organization (Cornfield and Malen 1978), so a careful psychodynamic evaluation should also focus on the function of the symptoms in the patient's overall intrapsychic structure. Despite the refractory nature of many obsessive-compulsive symptoms, psychodynamic therapy may considerably improve the interpersonal functioning of OCD patients. Frequently, the symptoms have led to extraordinary relationship problems for these patients,

and dynamic therapy may be the only helpful modality for addressing these problems. Dynamic group psychotherapy, in particular,
may be useful in this realm, as illustrated in the following clinical
example:

> Mr. O was a 33-year-old law clerk who had suffered from OCD since
> childhood. He had been in individual psychotherapy for 1 year with
> no improvement, so his individual therapist, thinking that group
> psychotherapy might more adequately address his interpersonal
> problems, referred him to an expressive therapy group with a male
> and female cotherapist. During the first few months of his participa-
> tion in the group, Mr. O tended to monopolize the discussion with
> long, rambling, self-absorbed discourses that effectively shut out
> other group members. When they attempted to comment or react to
> what he was saying, he would raise his voice and speak more rapidly
> to drown them out. Much of what he said was designed to convince
> the group that he harbored no sexual or aggressive feelings. Para-
> doxically, Mr. O's manner seemed quite aggressive to the other group
> members. They gradually but forcefully began to confront him about
> his monopolistic tendencies. As is frequently the case with OCD
> patients, Mr. O was able to hear and accept confrontation from other
> patients in the group much better than from the two cotherapists.
>
> Over several years, gradual changes emerged in Mr. O. He began
> to listen to others in response to being confronted so many times.
> For the first time, he became aware that his obsessionalism had an
> impact on others. As he listened more, he also became more em-
> pathic and sensitive to other people's concerns. As he developed
> more trust in the group, he was able to confide in them about his
> compulsive rituals. When a group session went badly, he would drive
> from the therapist's office back to his office along the same route he
> followed to come to therapy. Sometimes he would even drive back
> and forth several times before going home, having fantasies that he
> could erase whatever had happened in the therapy session (an
> example of the defense mechanism of undoing). To his surprise, the
> other patients in the group were able to accept that he had symptoms
> without condemning him for them.
>
> Similarly, Mr. O was gradually able to share his sexual conflicts
> with the group. He had originally stated that he never looked at a
> woman "below the neck," as a way of reassuring the group that his
> sexual feelings were under control. As he felt more comfortable,
> however, he was able to say that he struggled daily with erotic feelings
> toward a variety of people in his life. He was even able to express
> erotic transference feelings toward the female cotherapist. To his
> amazement, no retaliation or censure was forthcoming from either
> the male cotherapist or from the other patients. With the help of
> such benign and accepting responses from the group, Mr. O began
> to learn that his expectation of criticism from others was a projection
> of his own harsh superego. After many years of group therapy, he was
> finally able to experience greatly improved interpersonal function-
> ing, which paid off both in his personal life and in his work relation-
> ships. Moreover, with the superego modification achieved through

group therapy, Mr. O's anxiety had decreased considerably. As his anxiety level fell, his need for compulsive rituals and obsessional thoughts also decreased accordingly.

The case of Mr. O demonstrates how interpersonal relatedness can be intimately linked to the need for obsessive-compulsive symptoms. Throughout the course of his group psychotherapy, he was able to repeatedly express his forbidden thoughts, feelings, and fantasies, with no disastrous consequences from either the cotherapists or his peers in the group. From an object-relations standpoint, Mr. O internalized new forms of object relatedness that led to decreased anxiety and therefore to less of a need for the symptoms.

Like agoraphobic patients, those with OCD may derive considerable secondary gain from their symptoms. For whatever reasons the symptoms initially appear, their role in family relationships may perpetuate and solidify them. Just as Mr. O controlled the group with his obsessional rambling, other patients with OCD may control their entire family, so effective treatment must often include attention to the family dynamics.

Ms. P was a 45-year-old married mother of two children who was consumed with obsessive-compulsive cleaning rituals in her household. She was convinced that germs and vomit had contaminated various items in her household, and as a result, she spent most of each day scrubbing things and washing her family's clothing. Whenever her husband and two children returned from work or school, she insisted that they immediately shower and hand over all the clothes they had worn that day so that she could place them in the washing machine. Ms. P would also go through her daughter's purse, compulsively cleaning every item that might be contaminated and checking for new contents brought in from outside the home. Her husband and children felt so controlled that they felt guilty about leaving the house. Finally their exasperation led them to take her to a psychiatrist, seeking hospitalization. Immediately after she was admitted, her cleaning rituals completely disappeared. Because her symptoms were no longer useful in controlling the family, Ms. P lost psychological investment in them. After discharge, however, her symptoms returned as soon as she arrived at her house again.

Posttraumatic Stress Disorder

Until recently, posttraumatic stress disorder (PTSD) went largely unrecognized by the majority of American psychiatrists. Because of its long-time exclusion from the official diagnostic nomenclature, many clinicians did not include it in their differential diagnosis of syndromes associated with anxiety. Years of diligent lobbying by veterans' groups spurred the American Psychiatric Association to officially recognize PTSD as a diagnostic entity worthy of inclusion in the 1980 version of DSM-III. Even today, some psychiatrists do not believe that PTSD is truly a discrete diagnostic category, but rather that it is a mixture of depression and anxiety. The delay in recognizing PTSD is ironic in light of the extensive reports of "shell shock" from World War I, "traumatic war neuroses" from World War II, and other long-term psychological reactions of holocaust survivors and survivors of various civilian disasters.

The long overdue realization of the high prevalence of stress-related disorders resulted from a confluence of several factors. First of all, the severe and disabling effects of the trauma of the Vietnam War simply would not go away. We now know, as a result of a painstaking survey by the Centers for Disease Control in Atlanta (1988), that 15 percent of all Vietnam veterans have suffered PTSD at some time since their service discharge. Second, the devastating effects of incest, sexual abuse, and rape have finally been fully recognized by the psychiatric profession. Some clinicians have noted a prevalence rate in clinical populations approaching 30–33 percent (Rosenfeld 1979; Spencer 1978). Finally, in 1976 Horowitz published his landmark work on the impact of trauma on personality. He observed that trauma victims alternate between denying the event and compulsively repeating it through flashbacks or nightmares. Thus the mind attempts to process and organize overwhelming stimuli. He identified eight common psychological themes that follow severe trauma. These include grief or sadness, guilt about one's angry or destructive impulses, fear that one will become destructive, guilt about surviving, fear that one will identify with the victims, shame over feeling helpless and empty, fear that one will repeat the trauma, and intense anger directed toward the source of the trauma.

The inclusion of PTSD in the DSM-III category of anxiety disorders has been somewhat controversial, because anxiety is merely one of a whole constellation of symptoms. To qualify for the diagnosis, a person must have experienced an extraordinarily distressing traumatic event that is well outside the normal range of human experience. Also required are three sets of symptom clusters: 1) reexperiencing the trauma through dreams or intrusive thoughts, 2) avoidance or numbing of responsiveness, and 3) symptoms of increased arousal, such as difficulty sleeping or an exaggerated startle response. The symptoms must be present for at least 1 month; for delayed onset, they must not appear until 6 months after the trauma. The diagnosis frequently is complicated by the presence of associated psychiatric disorders, such as alcohol or drug abuse, social phobia, depression, psychosomatic disorders, assorted personality disorders, and violent behavior (Rundell et al. 1989). The presence of these other disorders may interfere with a clinical determination of cause and effect.

Another complicating factor in detecting the syndrome of PTSD is the nature of the trauma itself. Individuals will differ greatly in how they react to the same stressor. Seemingly minor stressors may trigger severe symptomatology in certain vulnerable individuals. There is a documented positive correlation between the severity of the stressor and the severity of the resulting PTSD syndrome (Rundell et al. 1989). Psychodynamic assessment must therefore take into account the individual patient's particular psychological vulnerability and the meanings of various environmental triggers (Ursano 1987; West and Coburn 1984). For example, if many months or years pass before the appearance of PTSD, other intervening factors might have precipitated the onset at this particular time.

The modern psychodynamic view of PTSD has been greatly influenced by the work of Krystal (1968, 1984, 1988). Through extensive investigations of survivors of Nazi persecution, Krystal has connected impairment in the expression and tolerance of affects to psychic trauma. He noted a high prevalence of psychosomatic diseases both in concentration camp survivors and in veterans of war. Like most psychosomatic patients, these individuals also suffer from alexithymia—the inability to identify or verbalize feeling states. In Krystal's view, psychic trauma in childhood results in an *arrest* of affective development, while trauma in adulthood leads to a *regression* in affective development. The end result in both cases is that the survivors of trauma cannot use affects as signals. Any powerful emotion is viewed as a threat that the original trauma will return, so these patients somatize affects or medicate them by abusing medications. Krystal also observed that in posttraumatic states, these individuals may suffer impairment in their ability to perform self-caring and self-soothing functions. They can no longer relax and calm themselves sufficiently to fall asleep naturally.

The treatment of choice is still unclear at this point. One implication of Krystal's observations about PTSD is that exploratory psychotherapy designed to help "reenact" the trauma may be harmful to these patients. Those with alexithymia will experience only the physiological correlates of the emotional states without registering feelings in the psychological realm, resulting in further deterioration in their psychosomatic condition (Sifneos 1973). Even getting patients to talk about the trauma may be a formidable task. Krystal has pointed out that in situations of incest or child abuse, the victimized children have usually been threatened with disaster if they break their silence. He also has observed characteristic countertransference reactions to victims of disasters. Psychiatrists and other mental health professionals may avoid such patients or regard them with scorn, resulting in less than adequate treatment. This countertransference may be exacerbated by a certain subgroup of trauma survivors who feign the syndrome of PTSD or who fiercely hold on to their symptoms with no wish to change. For those patients with preexisting personality disorders, a stressor may be a convenient nidus for externalization of their problems and disavowal of any responsibility for their situation. If PTSD is associated with reimbursement or restitution by the government or other agency, the resistance may intensify. The devastating effects of psychic trauma may well be so unpleasant to confront that treaters will conveniently lump together genuine victims and assorted malingerers.

No treatment is wholly satisfactory for PTSD. There are no double-blind controlled studies of pharmacotherapeutic interventions (Lydiard et al. 1988). Propranolol has been somewhat successful in reducing autonomic activation (Van der Kolk 1983). Benzodiazepines should generally be avoided since this group of patients has a high potential for substance abuse. Behavioral techniques such as relaxation and biofeedback may be difficult for these patients to utilize because of their impairment in self-soothing ability (Krystal 1984). Reconstructions of traumatic experiences with accompanying emotional catharsis may be helpful (West and Coburn 1984), but a careful assessment of the patient's ego capacities must precede such therapeutic work. Certain patients will be overwhelmed by such reconstruction and will react with clinical deterioration. Individual psychotherapy must be applied cautiously, and the integration of split-off traumatic experiences must be titrated in keeping with the particular patient's capacity for such integration. The therapist may have to contain projected aspects of the traumatized self until the patient is ready for reintegration (Peebles 1989). Goals of psychotherapy with these patients should be modest—cure or complete removal of symptoms is probably too ambitious. A more reasonable ambition is to halt any further decline, support areas of adequate functioning, and reestablish the patient's personal integrity (Lindy et al. 1984).

Generalized Anxiety Disorder

In the DSM-III-R classification, generalized anxiety disorder is a "wastebasket" diagnosis designed to accommodate all other worriers who do not fit into the categories of panic disorder, phobia, OCD, or PTSD. The quality of life for these patients is materially affected by their continual apprehension about their future, their current life circumstances, their financial situation, the possibility of harm coming to their family members, and assorted other aspects of life.

They may experience physical tension and mild symptoms of sympathetic discharge, but nothing approaching the level of panic disorder.

When psychodynamic clinicians evaluate patients whose chief complaint is anxiety, they must make a critical decision about which treatment to prescribe—a decision that is likely to be influenced by theoretical bias, by political forces in contemporary psychiatry, and by concerns about cost-effectiveness. Shectman et al. (1989) have nicely captured the nature of this dilemma:

> Are we growth facilitators, or are we removers and suppressors of circumscribed psychological distress? Just what is the object of our efforts? In its most extreme form, do we address the problem (i.e., the symptom) in a patient or deal with a patient who has a problem? And who is to make the determination about such matters: the patient? us? both of us together? But what if there is a difference of opinion about what ought or should be done? (p. 494)

Turning to the literature can, of course, provide essential information to help with such decisions. Numerous studies demonstrate the efficacy of behavioral techniques, pharmacotherapeutic techniques—and even brief dynamic psychotherapy—in treating patients with anxiety. However, large-scale group designs tell clinicians nothing about how to determine which individual is likely to benefit from which treatment (Barlow and Beck 1984).

Antianxiety agents may decrease or remove anxiety, but they may ultimately prove to be a dead-end solution. The most obvious problem is that medication is likely to be effective only as long as the patient continues to take it. The frequency of relapse after patients stop taking benzodiazepines, for example, is estimated at 63–81 percent (Rickels et al. 1980, 1986). Pharmacotherapeutic measures do not address the underlying factors that create the anxiety either. Another compelling reason to question the regular use of benzodiazepines for generalized anxiety disorder is that they produce dependence and withdrawal syndromes in nearly half the patients who use them for more than 1 year (Noyes et al. 1988). Even when used in low doses for short-term treatment, benzodiazepines can cause significant withdrawal symptoms in patients with generalized anxiety disorders (Fontaine et al. 1984; Lapierre et al. 1982; Pecknold et al. 1982; Preskorn and Denner 1977). Alprazolam, a benzodiazepine that has enjoyed considerable popularity in recent years, has come to be recognized as causing a particularly thorny set of problems. Besides creating dependence and withdrawal symptoms, this drug's period of effectiveness becomes shorter and shorter over time. Patients find themselves anxiously watching the clock as they await their next dose, and they often report early morning "rebound," when they wake up filled with anxiety because the medication's calming effect has worn off (Herman et al. 1987). Although clonazepam seems to alleviate some of these problems, patients may still encounter dependence and withdrawal symptoms (Lydiard et al. 1988).

To deal with these difficulties, alternative nonbenzodiazepine antianxiety agents have been developed, but results with them have been less than satisfactory as well. Beta blockers, such as propranolol, are no more effective in generalized anxiety disorder than placebo (Noyes 1985). Although buspirone eliminates the danger of dependence, it has rather limited efficacy in patients with chronic anxiety. In one study (Rickels et al. 1988), nearly half the subjects discontinued treatment during the first month, while another 26 percent stopped taking the medication during the next 5 months. The main complaint of these subjects was that their anxiety was not relieved. Moreover, patients who have already tried benzodiazepines derive even less anxiolytic effect from buspirone (Schweizer et al. 1986).

Medication may at times be a crucial short-term adjunct to psychotherapeutic interventions for generalized anxiety disorder. However, they must not be oversold to patients as definitive treatments for anxiety. Patients need to learn to tolerate anxiety as a meaningful signal in the course of psychotherapy. Those with reasonably good ego strength come to view anxiety as a window into the unconscious.

The treatment of anxiety must begin with a thoughtful and thorough psychodynamic evaluation, with anxiety conceptualized as a multidetermined "tip of the iceberg." The clinician must diagnose the nature of the patient's underlying fear (see Table 9-1). In addition, the role of anxiety in the patient's personality organization must be assessed. What is the ego's capacity to tolerate anxiety and to endure an exploration of its origins? Do particular constellations of internal object relations seem to evoke anxiety? Is the anxiety connected with concerns about dissolution of the self?

Prescribing the appropriate psychodynamic intervention depends partly on the patient's clinical situation and interests. Some patients may quickly respond well to brief educational and clarifying comments and then require no further treatment. Others, such as Mr. N, who have highly focal symptoms and certain notable ego strengths, may have their anxiety ameliorated with brief dynamic therapy. Neurotic patients with fewer focal complaints and a more thoroughgoing interest in fundamental personality change may require psychoanalysis. Finally, patients with serious character pathology who complain of anxiety, such as Mr. L, will need long-term expressive-supportive psychotherapy before they are likely to experience symptom relief.

References

American Psychiatric Association: Diagnostic and Statistical Manual of Mental Disorders, 3rd Edition. Washington, DC, American Psychiatric Association, 1980

American Psychiatric Association: Diagnostic and Statistical Manual of Mental Disorders, 3rd Edition, Revised. Washington, DC, American Psychiatric Association, 1987

Baer L, Jenike MA: Introduction, in Obsessive-Compulsive Disorders: Theory and Management. Edited by Jenike MA, Baer L, Minichiello WE. Littleton, MA, PSG Publishing Co, 1986, pp 1–9

Ballenger JC, Burrows GD, DuPont RL Jr, et al: Alprazolam in panic disorder and agoraphobia: results from a multicenter trial, I: efficacy in short-term treatment. Arch Gen Psychiatry 45:413–422, 1988

Barlow DH, Beck JG: The psychosocial treatment of anxiety disorders: current status, future directions, in Psychotherapy Research: Where Are We and Where Should We Go? Edited by Williams JBW, Spitzer RL. New York, Guilford Press, 1984, pp 29–69

Centers for Disease Control Vietnam Experience Study: Health status of Vietnam veterans, I: psychosocial characteristics. JAMA 259:2701–2707, 1988

Cooper AM: Will neurobiology influence psychoanalysis? Am J Psychiatry 142:1395–1402, 1985

Cornfield RB, Malen RL: A multidimensional view of the obsessive character. Compr Psychiatry 19:73–78, 1978

Coryell W, Noyes R: Placebo response of panic disorder. Am J Psychiatry 145:1138–1140, 1988

Elkins R, Rapoport JL, Lipsky A: Obsessive-compulsive disorder of childhood and adolescence: a neurobiological viewpoint. J Am Acad Child Psychiatry 19:511–524, 1980

Faravelli C, Pallanti S: Recent life events and panic disorder. Am J Psychiatry 146:622–626, 1989

Fontaine R, Chouinard G, Annable L: Rebound anxiety in anxious patients after abrupt withdrawal of benzodiazepine treatment. Am J Psychiatry 141:848–852, 1984

Freud S: On the grounds for detaching a particular syndrome from neurasthenia under the description "anxiety neurosis" (1895), in The Standard Edition of the Complete Psychological Works of Sigmund Freud, Vol 3. Translated and edited by Strachey J. London, Hogarth Press, 1962, pp 85–117

Freud S: Inhibitions, symptoms and anxiety (1926), in The Standard Edition of the Complete Psychological Works of Sigmund Freud, Vol 20. Translated and edited by Strachey J. London, Hogarth Press, 1959, pp 75–175

Gabbard GO, Nemiah JC: Multiple determinants of anxiety in a patient with borderline personality disorder. Bull Menninger Clin 49:161–172, 1985

Herman JB, Rosenbaum JF, Brotman AW: The alprazolam to clonazepam switch for the treatment of panic disorder. J Clin Psychopharmacol 7:175–178, 1987

Horowitz MJ: Stress Response Syndromes. New York, Jason Aronson, 1976

Jenike MA, Baer L, Minichiello WE (eds): Obsessive-Compulsive Disorders: Theory and Management. Littleton, MA, PSG Publishing Co, 1986

Kandel ER: From metapsychology to molecular biology: explorations into the nature of anxiety. Am J Psychiatry 140:1277–1293, 1983

Karno M, Golding JM, Sorenson SB: The epidemiology of obsessive-compulsive disorder in five US communities. Arch Gen Psychiatry 45:1094–1099, 1988

Klein DF: Delineation of two drug-responsive anxiety syndromes. Psychopharmacologia 5:397–408, 1964

Krystal H (ed): Massive Psychic Trauma. New York, International Universities Press, 1968

Krystal H: Psychoanalytic views on human emotional damages, in Post-Traumatic Stress Disorder: Psychological and Biological Sequelae. Edited by Van der Kolk BA, Washington, DC, American Psychiatric Press, 1984, pp 1–28

Krystal H: Integration and Self-Healing: Affect, Trauma, Alexithymia. Hillsdale, NJ, Analytic Press, 1988

Lapierre YD, Tremblay A, Gagnon A, et al: A therapeutic and discontinuation study of clobazam and diazepam in anxiety neurosis. J Clin Psychiatry 43:372–374, 1982

Lieberman J: Evidence for a biological hypothesis of obsessive-compulsive disorder. Neuropsychobiology 11:14–21, 1984

Lindy JD, Grace MC, Green BL: Building a conceptual bridge between civilian trauma and war trauma: preliminary psychological findings from a clinical sample of Vietnam veterans, in Post-Traumatic Stress Disorder: Psychological and Biological Sequelae. Edited by Van der Kolk BA, Washington, DC, American Psychiatric Press, 1984, pp 43–57

Luxenberg JS, Swedo SE, Flament MF, et al: Neuroanatomical abnormalities in obsessive-compulsive disorder detected with quantitative X-ray computed tomography. Am J Psychiatry 145:1089–1093, 1988

Lydiard RB, Roy-Byrne PP, Ballenger JC: Recent advances in the psychopharmacological treatment of anxiety disorders. Hosp Community Psychiatry 39:1157–1165, 1988

Marks IM: Review of behavioral psychotherapy, I: obsessive-compulsive disorders. Am J Psychiatry 138:584–592, 1981

Nemiah JC: A psychoanalytic view of phobias. Am J Psychoanal 41:115–120, 1981

Nemiah JC: The psychodynamic view of anxiety, in Diagnosis and Treatment of Anxiety Disorders. Edited by Pasnau RO. Washington, DC, American Psychiatric Press, 1984, pp 115–137

Nemiah JC: Psychoneurotic disorders, in The New Harvard Guide to Psychiatry. Edited by Nicholi AM Jr. Cambridge, MA, Belknap Press of Harvard University Press, 1988, pp 234–258

Noyes R Jr: Beta-adrenergic blocking drugs in anxiety and stress. Psychiatr Clin North Am 8:119–132, 1985

Noyes R Jr, Garvey MJ, Cook BL, et al: Benzodiazepine withdrawal: a review of the evidence. J Clin Psychiatry 49:382–389, 1988

Pecknold JC, McClure DJ, Fleuri D, et al: Benzodiazepine withdrawal effects. Prog Neuropsychopharmacol Biol Psychiatry 6:517–522, 1982

Peebles MJ: Posttraumatic stress disorder: a historical perspective on diagnosis and treatment. Bull Menninger Clin 53:274–286, 1989

Perse T: Obsessive-compulsive disorder: a treatment review. J Clin Psychiatry 49:48–55, 1988

Pollard CA, Henderson JG: Four types of social phobia in a community sample. J Nerv Ment Dis 176:440–445, 1988

Preskorn SH, Denner LJ: Benzodiazepines and withdrawal psychosis: report of three cases. JAMA 237:36–38, 1977

Rachman S, Hodgson R: Obsessions and Compulsions. Englewood Cliffs, NJ, Prentice-Hall, 1980

Redmond DE Jr: Studies of the nucleus locus coeruleus in monkeys and hypotheses for neuropsychopharmacology, in Psychopharmacology: The Third Generation of Progress. Edited by Meltzer HY. New York, Raven Press, 1987, pp 967–983

Regier DA, Boyd JH, Burke JD, et al: One-month prevalence of mental disorders in the United States. Arch Gen Psychiatry 45:977–986, 1988

Reich JH: DSM-III personality disorders and the outcome of treated panic disorder. Am J Psychiatry 145:1149–1152, 1988

Rickels K, Case WG, Diamond L: Relapse after short-term drug therapy in neurotic outpatients. International Pharmacopsychiatry 15:186–192, 1980

Rickels K, Case WG, Downing RW, et al: One-year follow-up of anxious patients treated with diazepam. J Clin Psychopharmacol 6:32–36, 1986

Rickels K, Schweizer E, Csanalosi I, et al: Long-term treatment of anxiety and risk of withdrawal: prospective comparison of clorazepate and buspirone. Arch Gen Psychiatry 45:444–450, 1988

Rosenfeld AA: Incidence of a history of incest among 18 female psychiatric patients. Am J Psychiatry 136:791–795, 1979

Rundell JR, Ursano RJ, Holloway HC, et al: Psychiatric responses to trauma. Hosp Community Psychiatry 40:68–74, 1989

Schweizer E, Rickels K, Lucki I: Resistance to anti-anxiety effect of buspirone in patients with a history of benzodiazepine use (letter to the editor). N Engl J Med 314:719–720, 1986

Shectman F, Ross JL, Simpson W: Controversial issues in psychodynamic and symptom-focused treatment. Bull Menninger Clin 53:493–500, 1989

Sifneos PE: The prevalence of "alexithymic" characteristics in psychosomatic patients. Psychother Psychosom 22:257–262, 1973

Spencer J: Father-daughter incest: a clinical view from the corrections field. Child Welfare 57:581–590, 1978

Turner SM, Beidel DC, Nathan RS: Biological factors in obsessive-compulsive disorders. Psychol Bull 97:430–450, 1985

Ursano RJ: Posttraumatic stress disorder: the stressor criterion (commentary). J Nerv Ment Dis 175:273–275, 1987

Van der Kolk BA: Psychopharmacological issues in posttraumatic stress disorder. Hosp Community Psychiatry 34:683–684, 691, 1983

West LJ, Coburn K: Posttraumatic anxiety, in Diagnosis and Treatment of Anxiety Disorders. Edited by Pasnau RO. Washington, DC, American Psychiatric Press, 1984, pp 79–133

White K, Cole JO: Is there a drug treatment for obsessive-compulsive disorder? (forum) Harvard Medical School Mental Health Letter 5(3):8, September 1988

Zetzel ER: The Capacity for Emotional Growth. New York, International Universities Press, 1970

Zitrin CM, Klein DF, Woerner MG: Behavior therapy, supportive psychotherapy, imipramine, and phobias. Arch Gen Psychiatry 35:307–316, 1978

CHAPTER 10

Paraphilias and Sexual Dysfunctions

Paraphilias

Few psychiatric disorders are fraught with as many moralistic over-tones as the paraphilias. To determine that an individual is deviant in the area of sexuality implies the establishment of a clear norm for sexual behavior. Who will establish such norms? Shall psychiatry be the moral guardian of sexual behavior? Can we use terms such as *sexual deviation, perversion,* or even *paraphilia* without sounding pejorative?

The evolution of the definition of perverse activity reveals the extent to which psychiatric nosology mirrors the society from which it emanates. In the context of a culture that viewed normal sexuality in relatively narrow terms, Freud (1905) defined sexual activity as perverse according to several criteria: 1) it focused on nongenital regions of the body; 2) rather than coexisting with the standard practice of genital intercourse with an opposite-sex partner, it su-perseded and replaced such practice; and 3) it tended to be the exclusive sexual practice of the individual. Freud noted that traces of perversion could be found in virtually anyone whose unconscious was subject to psychoanalytic exploration.

Since Freud's early paper, cultural attitudes about sexuality have undergone dramatic changes. As sexuality became a legitimate area for scientific study, it became apparent that "normal" couples engage in a variety of sexual behaviors. Oral-genital relations, for example, became widely accepted as healthy sexual behavior. Ho-mosexuality and anal intercourse similarly were removed from the list of perverse activities. Most recently, concern about AIDS has increased the public's awareness of the relatively high prevalence of anal sexual relations among heterosexual couples.

Psychoanalytic writers have repeatedly confirmed Freud's ob-servation that there is a latent perverse core in all of us (Chasseguet-Smirgel 1983; McDougall 1980, 1986; Stoller 1975, 1985). Thus a more accepting attitude about perverse sexuality has accompanied psychoanalytic advances. McDougall (1986) pointed out that per-verse fantasies are regularly found in all adult sexual behavior, but tend to cause few problems because they are not experienced as compulsive. She has suggested using the term *neosexuality,* to reflect the innovative nature of the practice and the individual's intense investment in its pursuit. She has stressed that clinicians must be empathic with their patients, who experience these sexual demands as necessary for emotional survival.

Stoller (1975, 1985) has advocated a narrowed definition of perverse activity. Referring to perversion as "the erotic form of hatred" (1975, p. 4), he asserted that cruelty and the wish to humiliate and degrade the sexual partner, as well as oneself, is the crucial determinant of whether a behavior is perverse. From this perspective, the individual's intent is a critical variable in defining perversion. As his view evolved (1985), Stoller added another dimension to this definition. Recognizing that in *normal* sexual arousal there is a touch of hostility and a desire to humiliate, he concluded that intimacy was a critical differentiating factor. An individual is perverse only when the erotic act is used to avoid a long-term, emotionally intimate relationship with another person. Conversely, sexual behavior is not perverse when it is in the service of establishing a stable intimate relationship.

The DSM-III-R (American Psychiatric Association 1987) definition of paraphilias, in an effort to be nonjudgmental, has suggested restricting the term to situations where nonhuman objects are used, or where actual humiliation or pain is inflicted on oneself or one's partner, and where children or nonconsenting adults are involved. To deal with a continuum between fantasy and action, DSM-III-R has developed a spectrum of severity. In "mild" forms, patients are quite distressed about their paraphilic sexual urges but do not act on them. In "moderate" degrees of severity, patients translate the urge into action, but only occasionally. In "severe" cases, patients repeatedly act on their paraphilic urges. Finally, in an effort to be more scientific and less pejorative, DSM-III-R uses *paraphilia* rather than *perversion* or *deviation.*

Although the intent of DSM-III-R is admirable, Stoller (1985) has taken the authors to task for attempting to sanitize perversions by changing the official term to *paraphilias.* Perversion, in his view, is useful precisely because it has nasty and sinful connotations:

> *Perversion* is so pejorative. It wreaks of sin, accusation, vindictiveness, and righteousness. It has its absoluteness. In it thunder God and his agents on earth. (p. 4)

Stoller has argued for retaining the term *perversion* because a sense of sinning is a prerequisite for a perverse activity to create erotic excitement. Since both points of view have merit, the two terms will be used interchangeably in this chapter.

Psychodynamic Understanding of Paraphilias

To a large extent the etiology of paraphilias remains shrouded in mystery. Although certain studies have suggested that biological factors contribute to the pathogenesis of perversions (Berlin and Meinecke 1981), the data are far from definitive. Even if biological factors are present, psychological issues obviously play a crucial role in determining the choice of paraphilia and the underlying meaning of the sexual acts. Psychoanalytic understanding has greatly illuminated the dark recesses of the perverse psyche. However, we must appropriately and modestly note that psychodynamic models can shed light on the meaning of a perversion without necessarily establishing a definitive etiology (Person 1986).

The classical view of perversions is deeply embedded in drive theory. Freud (1905) believed that these disorders illustrated how instinct and object are divorced from one another: "It seems probable that the sexual instinct is in the first instance independent of its object" (p. 148). Moreover, he defined perversions in part by contrasting them with neuroses. In the latter condition, neurotic symptoms represent a transformation of repressed perverse fantasies. In perversions, however, the fantasies become conscious and are directly expressed as ego-syntonic pleasurable activities. Hence, Freud described neuroses as the negative of perversions; neurotic symptoms were desexualized perverse fantasies. In the classical view, perversions may be fixations or regressions to infantile forms of sexuality persisting into adult life (Fenichel 1945; Sachs 1986). Some remnant of infantile experience is preserved in consciousness and is the carrier of all infantile sexuality through the process of displacement. A perverse act becomes a fixated and ritualized procedure that is the only route to genital orgasm. In the classical formulation (Fenichel 1945), the decisive factor that prevents orgasm through conventional genital intercourse is castration anxiety. Perversions thus serve the function of denying castration. (Because the overwhelming majority of patients suffering from paraphilias are male, the formulations presented here will presume male gender.)

Freud (1905) appreciated the complexity of perversions, which are multilayered. He noted, for example, the myriad unconscious determinants of voyeurism and exhibitionism, which are opposite sides of the same coin. In his clinical work, he observed that any "active" perversion was always accompanied by a "passive" counterpart. In this formulation, the sadist would have a masochistic core, while the voyeur would suffer from unconscious exhibitionistic desires.

More recent psychoanalytic investigators have concluded that drive theory alone is insufficient to explain much of the perverse fantasy and behavior seen clinically and that the relational aspects of perversions are crucial for a comprehensive understanding (Mc-Dougall 1980, 1986; Mitchell 1988). According to Stoller (1975, 1985), the essence of perversion is a conversion of "childhood trauma to adult triumph" (1975, p. 4). Patients are driven by their fantasies of avenging humiliating childhood traumas caused by their parents. Their method of revenge is to dehumanize and humiliate their partner during the perverse act or fantasy.

Perverse sexual activity may also be a flight from object relatedness (Mitchell 1988). Many persons suffering from paraphilias have incompletely separated and individuated from their intrapsychic representations of their mother. As a result, they feel that their identity as a separate person is constantly being threatened by fusion or engulfment from internal or external objects. Sexual expression may be the one domain where they can assert their independence. Whereas Stoller (1975, 1985) viewed perversions as expressions of the desire to humiliate, Mitchell (1988) understood them as a defiance of the overbearing influence of the internal mothering figure. One aspect of the relief experienced by paraphilic patients after they have acted on their sexual desires is their feeling of triumph over the controlling mother within.

McDougall (1986) has noted other object-relational meanings of the *neosexualities.* She has suggested that sexual behavior evolves from a complicated matrix of identifications and counter-identifications with our parents. Each child is involved in an unconscious psychological drama that stems from the parents' unconscious erotic desires and conflicts. Hence, the obligatory nature of any neosexuality is programmed by parental scripts internalized by the child. In McDougall's view, deviant sexual behavior may function partly to protect the introjected objects from the patient's aggression by acting out the unconscious drama "written" by the parents.

Kohut (1971, 1977) has offered a self psychological perspective on the function of perversions. In his view, perverse activity involves a desperate attempt to restore the integrity and cohesiveness of the self in the absence of empathic selfobject responses from others. The sexual activity or fantasy may help the patient feel alive and intact when threatened by abandonment or separation. Perverse behavior in the course of psychotherapy or analysis may thus be a reaction to failures in empathy by the therapist, leading to a temporary disruption of the self-selfobject matrix established between patient and therapist (Miller 1985). In Kohut's (1977) view, the behavioral manifestations of perversions are secondary phenomena: "After the breakup of the primary psychological unit (assertively demanded empathy-merger with the self-object), the drive appears as a disintegration product; the drive is then enlisted in the attempt to bring about the lost merger (and thus the repair of the self) by pathological means, i.e., as enacted in the fantasies and actions of the pervert" (p. 128).

Although not a self psychologist, McDougall (1986) has also noted a profound fear of loss of identity or sense of self at the core of much perverse activity. Certain sexual practices or sexual objects become like a drug that the patient uses to "medicate" a sense of inner deadness and a fear of self-disintegration. In these patients, McDougall has observed a faulty internalization process that impeded their use of transitional objects in childhood during their efforts to separate from maternal figures.

Before considering the dynamics of each individual paraphilia, we should note that the reasons remain obscure for individual preference of one perverse fantasy or act over another. Also, different paraphilias often coexist in the same individual. Finally, a wide range of psychiatric diagnoses and levels of personality organization may be present in someone with a paraphilia. Perversions have been observed, for example, in psychotic patients, in those with personality disorders, and in relatively intact or neurotic patients. Polymorphous perverse sexuality is commonly found in patients with borderline personality organization (Kernberg 1975). Paraphilias that involve overt cruelty to others are often present in patients with antisocial personality disorder. Thus a psychodynamic understanding of any individual patient involved in perverse sexual activity implies a thoroughgoing understanding of how the perversion interacts with the patient's underlying character structure. For example, patients with neurotic organization may use a paraphilic activity to facilitate genital potency, while patients near the psychotic border may use the same activity to fend off a sense of dissolution of the self (Person 1986).

Exhibitionism and Voyeurism

By publicly exposing his genitals to strange women or girls, the exhibitionist reassures himself that he is not castrated (Fenichel 1945; Freud 1905). The reaction of shock that his actions produce helps him deal with castration anxiety and gives him a feeling of power over the opposite sex. Stoller (1985) has pointed out that exhibitionistic acts typically follow a situation in which the offender felt humiliated, often at the hands of a woman. In turn, the exhibitionist avenges this humiliation by shocking strange women. Moreover, displaying his genitals enables the man to regain some sense of worth and positive masculine identity. Frequently these men reveal a profound insecurity about their sense of maleness. Stoller (1985) noted that castration anxiety does not completely capture the motivation for the exhibitionistic act. In his view, the threat "is best put in identity terms; for humiliation is about 'existence anxiety,' threat to core gender identity" (p. 20). Exhibitionists often feel that they made no impact on anyone in their family, and thus they have had to resort to extraordinary measures to be noticed (Mitchell 1988). Each exhibitionistic act may therefore be an attempt to reverse a childhood traumatic situation.

The flip side of exhibitionism—voyeurism—also involves a violation of a strange woman's privacy, an aggressive but secretive triumph over the female sex. Fenichel (1945) linked voyeuristic tendencies to a fixation on the primal scene of childhood, in which the child either witnesses or overhears parental intercourse. This early traumatic experience could arouse the child's castration anxiety and then lead him to reenact the scene again and again as an adult in an attempt to actively master a passively experienced trauma. Fenichel also identified an aggressive component in looking, conceptualizing it as a guilt-avoiding displacement of the wish to be directly destructive to women. Even patients who are not prone to overtly voyeuristic activities may exhibit common derivatives such as curiosity and anxiety about looking. Some patients are even reluctant to glance around their therapist's office for fear that their curiosity will be construed as destructive or that they will see something forbidden. Mitchell (1988) has observed that exhibitionism and voyeurism capture an essential quality typical of all perversions: "a dialectic between surface and depth, between the visible and the secret, between the available and the withheld" (p. 111).

Sadism and Masochism

Persons who require sadistic fantasies or actions to achieve sexual gratification are often unconsciously attempting to reverse childhood scenarios in which they were the victim of physical or sexual abuse. By inflicting on others what happened to them as children, they gain revenge and a sense of mastery over the childhood trauma at the same time. Masochistic patients who require humiliation and even pain to achieve sexual pleasure may also be repeating childhood experiences of abuse. Fenichel (1945) believed that masochistic patients are making a sacrifice—accepting a "lesser evil" in place of castration. They may also be firmly convinced that they deserve punishment for their conflictual sadistic wishes. In some cases, these patients defend against separation anxiety by submitting to abuse. They are frequently convinced that a sado-masochistic relationship is the only available form of object relatedness; an abusive relationship is better than no relationship.

Sadism and masochism are unique in that they are the only paraphilias occurring regularly in both sexes (Person 1986). Although masochism has been stereotypically linked to women, muted forms of sadistic and masochistic fantasies are regularly found in almost everyone. The practices of male homosexuals and the reports of female prostitutes even suggest that masochistic sexual activities may be more common in men. Sacher-Masoch, the 19th century Austrian writer from whom the term derives, was, in fact, a poet of male masochism. All sexual arousal may indeed be linked to aggressive wishes (Stoller 1985). Patients who come to psychotherapy or psychoanalysis with sexual inhibitions often reveal highly sadistic fantasies that prevent them from becoming sexually involved with other people.

In relational terms, sadism often develops from a particular internal object relationship in which the withholding and distant object requires a forceful effort to overcome its resistance to the corresponding self-representation (Mitchell 1988). Similarly, masochistic surrender may be an enactment of an internal object relationship in which the object will respond to the self only when humiliated.

From a self psychological perspective, masochistic behavior is a frantic effort to restore a sense of aliveness or self-cohesion. Although apparently self-destructive, masochism may be experienced by the patient as self-restorative. Stolorow et al. (1988) reported the treatment of a highly disturbed 19-year-old patient who repeatedly asked the therapist to hit her. In response to the therapist's persistent inquiries about why she would want him to strike her, she wrote, "Physical pain is better than spiritual death" (p. 506). In the absence of physical pain and abuse at the hands of others, this patient felt that she did not exist and was not connected with anyone else. These authors noted that masochistic patients often organize their entire lives to meet their parents' needs. As a result, their own internal affective experience becomes remote and unavailable because it has been sacrificed in the service of their parents.

Fetishism

To achieve sexual arousal, fetishists require the use of an inanimate object, often an article of women's underwear, or a shoe, or a nongenital body part. Freud originally explained fetishism as stemming from castration anxiety. The object chosen as a fetish symbolically represented the "female penis," a displacement that helped the fetishist overcome castration anxiety. Following the premise that male awareness of the female genitals increased the man's fear of losing his own genitals and becoming like a woman, Freud thought that this unconscious symbolization explained the relatively common occurrence of fetishism. He also used this formulation to develop his concept of the splitting of the ego (1940)—coexisting in the fetishist's mind are two contradictory ideas: denial of castration and affirmation of castration. The fetish represents both.

Although Greenacre (1970, 1979) also viewed castration anxiety as central to the understanding of fetishism, she noted that it has its origins in earlier pregenital disturbances. Chronic traumatic interactions in the first few months of life may thus be instrumental in producing fetishism. Because of severe problems in the mother-infant relationship, the infant is unable to be soothed by the mother or by transitional objects. To experience body integrity, the child thus requires a fetish, something "reassuringly hard, unyielding, unchanging in shape, and reliably durable" (1979, p. 102). These early pregenital disturbances are reactivated later when the male child or adult is concerned about genital integrity. In essence, Greenacre saw the fetish as functioning like a transitional object.

Kohut (1977) held a somewhat similar view about fetishism, although couched in self psychological terms. He described a male patient whose childhood was characterized by the traumatic unavailability of his mother. The patient made a fetish of underpants, which served as a substitute for the unavailable selfobject. In contrast to this patient's feelings of helplessness about his mother, he could maintain total control over this nonhuman version of a selfobject. Thus what appears to be an intense sexual need for a fetishistic object may actually reflect severe anxiety about the loss of one's sense of self (Mitchell 1988).

Pedophilia

Of all the perversions, pedophilia is the most likely to create feelings of disgust and contempt in treaters. In fulfilling his sexual desires, the pedophile may irreparably damage innocent children. Some conceptual framework or psychodynamic formulation can enable clinicians to maintain a semblance of empathy and understanding when attempting to treat these patients. According to the classical view (Fenichel 1945; Freud 1905), pedophilia represents a narcissistic object choice, that is, the pedophile sees a child as a mirror image of himself as a child. Pedophiles were also regarded as impotent and weak individuals who sought children as sexual objects because they would offer less resistance or create less anxiety than adult partners, thus enabling pedophiles to avoid castration anxiety.

In clinical practice, many pedophiles are found to suffer from narcissistic character pathology, including psychopathic variants of narcissistic personality disorder (see Chapter 16 for a detailed discussion of the interface between narcissistic and antisocial personality disorders). Sexual activity with prepubescent children may shore up the pedophile's fragile self-esteem. Similarly, many individuals with this perversion choose professions in which they can interact with children because the idealizing responses of children help them maintain their positive self-regard. In turn, the pedophile often idealizes these children; thus sexual activity with them involves the unconscious fantasy of fusion with an ideal object or restoration of a youthful, idealized self. Anxiety about aging and death may be warded off through sexual activity with children. Socarides (1988) described a pedophilic patient who fended off engulfment from his mother through his pedophilic activities. This patient sought to escape his unconscious feminine identification by incorporating masculinity from a prepubescent male child. Sexual relations with a boy made this patient feel as if he were part of the boy. At a deeper level, merger with the boy represented a wish to incorporate the breast of the mother and thus compensate for an absence of effective mothering early in life.

When pedophilic activity occurs in conjunction with a narcissistic personality disorder with severe antisocial features, or as part of an outright psychopathic character structure (see Chapter 16), the unconscious determinants of the behavior may be closely linked to the dynamics of sadism. Sexual conquest of the child is the tool of vengeance. Pedophiles are frequently victims of childhood sexual abuse themselves, and a sense of triumph and power may accompany their transformation of a passive trauma into an actively perpetrated victimization.

Power and aggression are also prominent concerns of pedophiles whose sexual activity is limited to incestuous relationships with their children or stepchildren. These men often feel unloved by their wives, and they elicit caretaking responses from their children by portraying themselves as victims (Ganzarain and Buchele, in press). The flip side of their martyred self-presentation, however, is a sense of control and power over their sexual partners. These incestuous fathers harbor extraordinary hostility toward women, and they often think of the penis as a weapon to be used in acts of vengeance against women. Some have even acknowledged that feelings of intense anger produce erections (Ganzarain and Buchele, in press).

Transvestism

In this common paraphilia, the male patient dresses as a woman to create sexual arousal in himself that leads to heterosexual intercourse or masturbation. The patient may behave in a traditionally masculine manner while dressed as a man but then become effem-

inate when dressed as a woman. The classic psychoanalytic understanding of cross-dressing involves the notion of the phallic mother.
By imagining that his mother possesses a penis, even if it is not clearly
visible, the male child overcomes his castration anxiety. The act of
cross-dressing may thus be an identification with the phallic mother
(Fenichel 1945).

At a more primitive level, the little boy may identify with his
mother to avoid anxiety about separation. His awareness of genital
differences between him and his mother may activate anxiety that
he will lose her because they are separate individuals. Clinical work
with transvestites reveals that when they cross-dress, they commonly
experience some degree of fusion with an intrapsychic maternal
object. This reassures them that they are not in danger of losing the
soothing maternal presence within. These men are always heterosexual, but their sexuality is often inhibited (Person 1986).

Treatment Approaches

Patients with paraphilias are notoriously difficult to treat. Over many
years, they have developed a carefully crafted erotic solution to their
problems, and they are rarely interested in giving it up (McDougall
1986). Why would someone wish to halt a practice that produces
great pleasure? Most perversions are ego-syntonic; only exceptional
patients who are distressed by their symptoms willingly seek treatment. Persons with fetishes generally view their fetishism as nothing
more than a personal idiosyncrasy, not a psychiatric symptom
(Greenacre 1979). They typically seek treatment for other reasons,
and the fetishism emerges in the course of therapy or analysis.

The vast majority of paraphilic patients come to treatment
under pressure. A marital crisis may bring a transvestite to clinical
attention under threat of divorce. In instances of voyeurism, exhibitionism, and particularly pedophilia, legal pressures often man-
date treatment as a condition of probation or as an alternative to
incarceration. A court date may be pending, so the patient will go
through the motions of treatment to "look good" in court and to
influence the judge to drop any charges. In every case of paraphilia,
the first order of business is to clarify the legal situation. The
clinician may decide to defer a decision on long-term treatment
until after the disposition of the case in court. Those patients who
continue to seek treatment after all legalities have been resolved may
have a better prognosis (Reid 1989).

Another major impediment to the treatment of patients with
perversions is the countertransference responses they evoke. If
indeed we all struggle with unconscious perverse wishes, as Freud
and countless others since his time have repeatedly suggested, then

it is reasonable to assume that we may react to the perverse patient as we would to our own perverse impulses. We are filled with disgust, anxiety, and contempt. Our natural impulse is to respond puni- tively—to moralize, to chide, to lecture, and to do what we can to "stamp out" this perversity. We also recoil in horror at the prospect of anyone allowing full rein to such impulses when we ourselves carefully control them. Finally, another countertransference ten- dency is to collude with the patient's avoidance of the perversion by talking about other aspects of his life. Clinicians can avoid their own feelings of disgust and contempt by avoiding the whole area of sexual pathology. With some patients—pedophiles, in particular— some therapists may feel that they simply cannot be effective because of their intense countertransference hatred. In these instances, it is best to refer the patient elsewhere.

One final reason for treatment difficulty with persons suffer- ing from perversions is the associated psychopathology. Perverse fantasy and behavior are difficult enough to alter, but when the patient's condition is complicated by borderline, narcissistic, or antisocial character pathology, the prognosis becomes even more guarded.

In spite of, or perhaps because of, all these difficulties in the treatment of paraphilias, psychodynamic approaches are generally the preferred form of treatment (McDougall 1980, 1986; Person 1986; Rosen 1964, 1979; Stoller 1985). Although outcome studies are lacking, and results are modest, treatment of any kind has limited effectiveness with this group of patients. While behavioral techniques have had some success on a short-term basis, long-term results are disappointing (Person 1986). Antiandrogen medica- tions, such as cyproterone acetate (CPA) and medroxyprogesterone acetate (MPA, Depo-Provera), are sometimes useful but their effi- cacy is limited. First, they have serious side effects, including pulmo- nary embolism and thrombophlebitis. Second, the problem of non- compliance must be dealt with; one study (Berlin and Meinecke 1981) had a dropout rate of greater than 50 percent. That same study also revealed that 15 percent of the subjects had recurrent perverse behavior even while taking the medication. A final disad- vantage of antiandrogen agents is that they lower the sexual drive by reducing plasma testosterone levels, but do nothing to alter the deviation itself. If the medication is discontinued, within a week or so the patient's deviant behavior recurs (Travin et al. 1985). Dynam- ically oriented psychotherapy in combination with antiandrogen medications might increase compliance and lower the dropout rate (Reid 1989).

Psychotherapeutic treatments. Individual expressive-sup- portive psychotherapy with an expressive emphasis is often the preferred method of treatment, but a therapist's expectations must nevertheless be modest. Although many patients will make considerable gains in object relatedness and ego functioning, their underlying perverse tendencies may be modified to a lesser degree. In general, those patients with higher-level character organizations have a better outcome than those with borderline levels of organization (Person 1986). More specifically, when the perversion primarily functions to increase and facilitate sexual potency secondary to phallic-oedipal conflict, psychotherapeutic intervention is likely to be more effective than in those cases where the paraphilia functions to prevent disintegration of the self.

Similarly, those patients who are psychologically minded, who possess some degree of motivation, who have some distress about their symptoms, and who are curious about the origins of their symptom are likely to do better than those who lack such qualities. Socarides (1988) has reported that pedophiles fixated at a phallic-oedipal level with considerable ego strength may do quite well in psychoanalysis. Other clinicians have also reported positive results with highly expressive therapy and psychoanalysis (McDougall 1980; Rosen 1964, 1979).

Certain typical problems arise when paraphilic persons are treated with dynamic psychotherapy. These patients rarely wish to focus on the perversion itself and often actively assert that it is no longer a problem for them. Although psychotherapists must treat disorders associated with the paraphilia, they must also vigorously confront such denial from the beginning. As Kohut (1971) has pointed out, the perverse activity and fantasy often exist in a split-off and compartmentalized area of the personality. One therapeutic task is to integrate the perverse behavior with the central sector of the patient's personality functioning so that it can be addressed along with the rest of the patient's life.

Another frequently encountered dilemma in psychotherapy is the avoidance of a punitive stance vis-à-vis the patient's perverse activity. Some states have reporting laws that require a therapist to break confidentiality if pedophilic activity is uncovered during psychiatric treatment. Even apart from the legal and ethical considerations, perverse behavior is likely to evoke highly disapproving responses in therapists. Sensitive patients often detect the therapist's struggle to refrain from being punitive. Clever patients may exploit this countertransference struggle by accusing their therapist of being harsh and cruel because of the therapy's focus on the perverse symptom. Patients may also avoid discussing the symptom by instead professing their feelings of shame, embarrassment, and humiliation.

If the patient can overcome his initial resistance to forming a therapeutic alliance in the service of understanding the perverse symptom, then both patient and therapist can begin to search for unconscious meanings of the symptom and its function within the patient's personality. Most paraphilias operate in an object relations context outside the patient's awareness. Many patients with paraphilias experience their fantasies and behavior as essentially non-psychological, and they are unaware of any connections between their symptom and feeling states, or between their symptom and life events, that may increase their need for the symptom. Much of the therapist's effort must therefore go into explaining these connections. The therapist can also point out the relational aspect of the perverse fantasy or behavior.

> Mr. Q, a 22-year-old college student, was hospitalized following an arrest for exposing himself to female students on the campus. He would sit in his car in the parking lot of the women's dormitory with his genitals exposed. As female students walked by, some would look in the car and react with shock, which substantially excited him. During his brief hospitalization, Mr. Q agreed to start psychotherapy, but he was basically a reluctant participant. He told his therapist that his embarrassment and depression upon being arrested and hospitalized would prevent him from ever resorting to exhibitionism again. He preferred to use the therapy to talk about other problems, such as his difficulties with self-esteem and with applying himself to his studies at college.
>
> The therapist confronted this denial and suggested that the problem of exhibitionism had not disappeared simply because Mr. Q had been hospitalized. Following discharge from the hospital, Mr. Q continued to struggle with exhibitionistic impulses, occasionally giving in to them. Each time that he reported such impulses in therapy, his therapist would invite reflection on possible precipitants of the impulses or actions. Mr. Q seemed genuinely perplexed as he searched his memory for antecedent events or feelings. The wish to expose himself was so integral to his identity that he did not think of it as developing out of any affective or relational context.
>
> On one occasion after Mr. Q exposed himself, his therapist pointed out that the episode of exposure had occurred immediately after a young woman in one of his classes had turned him down when he asked her out for a date. Mr. Q acknowledged that he had felt rebuffed and humiliated and that he could understand the possibility that exposing himself was an expression of his anger and revenge when women failed to respond to him. He began to notice a pattern of increasing exhibitionistic impulses whenever he experienced a rebuff or rejection from any woman he pursued romantically. With help from the therapist, Mr. Q was able to link his anger at women with his deep resentment of his mother for returning to full-time work outside the home when Mr. Q was 2 years old.
>
> When the therapy began to address these sensitive aspects of Mr. Q's relationships with women, he abruptly terminated treatment. Several years later, however, he wrote his therapist, indicating that he had found the key to overcoming his urge to expose himself. Although his exhibitionistic tendency still haunted him once in a

while, he had managed to control it by teaching himself "to learn to love women." He had discovered, through a positive relationship with a young woman, that some women actually did care about him. He thanked the therapist for helping him see that he had been distorting the feelings women had toward him. When he realized that women did not automatically resent him because he was a man, he felt less fearful around them and less compelled to take revenge against them through exhibitionistic activity.

Marital therapy may be critical to the successful treatment of paraphilias. A marital crisis may precipitate the patient's seeking of treatment in the first place. Marital therapy can often help delineate how the perverse activity reflects sexual and emotional difficulties in the marital dyad. It may also alleviate the wife's unwarranted feelings of guilt and responsibility for behavior and can instead facilitate a sense that she is part of its solution rather than part of its cause (Kentsmith and Eaton 1978). An exploration of marital discord may also reveal that the paraphilia is a container or "scapegoat" that deflects the focus from other more problematic areas in the marriage (Reid 1989). Clinicians must therefore be innovative in using the patient's spouse as an adjunctive therapist in refractory cases of paraphilia. For example, one man who was unresponsive to a number of treatments for his exhibitionism was able to control the symptom only when his wife agreed to drive him everywhere he went.

In cases of pedophilia that occur in the context of incest, family therapy is ordinarily an integral part of the overall treatment plan. Mothers typically collude in these incestuous arrangements by scotomizing the abundant evidence of father-daughter (or occasionally father-son) sexual relations. These mothers frequently grew up as parentified children who never received the nurturance they needed in childhood because they were too busy taking care of their own parents and siblings (Gelinas 1986). They tend to marry highly needy, dependent men as a continuation of their propensity for caretaking. Because of chronic feelings of neglect, the mother in such families is likely to be highly ambivalent about raising children, and when they arrive, she may feel overwhelmed and neglect her husband as a result. As mother and father become more estranged, the father turns to one of the children—usually the eldest daughter—for nurturance, leading to a second generation of the parentified-child pattern. This child is likely to feel responsible for filling the mother's shoes, and when part of that responsibility entails sexually satisfying her own father, she may subordinate her own needs and rights to his. She exists to satisfy the needs of others. Indeed, family therapy in cases of incest often reveals that the victim protects the offender and maintains loyalty toward him. Effective family therapy requires careful attention to these dynamics. The victim's loyalty to the offender must be acknowledged and respected. It is also helpful to focus on the father's wish for relatedness and emotional connectedness rather than on sexuality or perversion (Gelinas 1986). Incest victims often report that the only warmth they ever received in their family of origin was from the father. The depletion of the mother's emotional resources must also be addressed empathically, and the therapist must bolster her ego capacities. The therapist who approaches the family by identifying and seeking to punish villains will be met with massive resistance—the family members will "circle the wagons" to exclude an outside attacker who does not appreciate the homeostatic balance within the family system.

Dynamic group psychotherapy is another modality that has been used effectively with patients suffering from perversions. Voyeurs and exhibitionists may respond well to group modalities. In one study (Rosen 1964), 21 of 24 patients were recovered or improved at follow-up 6–36 months later. Legally enforced group therapy with sex offenders, such as pedophiles, has also obtained satisfactory results, even on an outpatient basis (Ganzarain and Buchele, in press; Rappeport 1974). These groups provide a mixture of support and confrontation from other offenders who are intimately familiar with the patient's problem, just as homogeneous groups of drug addicts and alcoholics bring group pressure to bear to change destructive behavior. Ganzarain and Buchele (in press) have found that excluding severely disturbed pedophiles—those with organic brain syndrome, psychosis, substance abuse, pure sociopathy, and exclusive perversions—can facilitate identification of a subgroup of pedophiles who will respond well to expressive group psychotherapy. Although patients in their group of offenders frequently denied responsibility and externalized blame, many suffered from unconscious guilt feelings and a profound sense of shame and humiliation about having been discovered. Typically, however, these feelings were fended off by considerable resistance to psychotherapeutic exploration. Because the treatment was legally mandated, many of the offenders viewed the group therapists as agents of the court and therefore assumed the posture of "doing time." Those patients with lower degrees of sociopathy and greater unconscious guilt feelings ultimately were able to use the group therapy process to understand that their hatred of women grew out of their wish to be loved. This understanding led to greater control of sexual impulses and general improvement in their capacity for object relations.

Hospital treatment. Those paraphilic patients most likely to be hospitalized are pedophiles, and to a lesser extent, exhibitionists, who are simply unable to control their behavior on an outpatient basis. Many of the same countertransference problems previously described also arise in hospital treatment. The patient's denial of his perversion may lead staff members to collude with him by focusing on other problems. One exhibitionist would regularly sit in the lounge of the hospital unit with an erection visible underneath his sweatpants. However, no one on the nursing staff reported noticing this behavior until the doctor pointed out that one manifestation of countertransference with this patient was a fear of looking. This same patient would also often stand nude in his room until a female nurse made rounds; he would then act surprised and indignant when she saw him. When the patient's doctor brought up this behavior in a group meeting on the unit, the patient tried to marshal support from his fellow patients by accusing the doctor of being insensitive and cruel by embarrassing him in front of his peers.

In general, patients with paraphilias will object to discussing their problems in group meetings or community meetings on an inpatient unit. However, when staff members comply with requests to avoid sexual issues in treatment meetings, they are colluding with the patient's tendency to go through an entire hospitalization without dealing with the perversity that necessitated hospitalization. Patients must be told initially that all treatment issues will be discussed in group meetings. Many pedophiles are extraordinarily smooth individuals who will charm other patients into avoiding confrontations. Thus, patients with paraphilias may never benefit from feedback from other patients about the paraphilia's impact on them.

> Mr. R, a 41-year-old teacher, had been extensively involved in pedophilic sexual activities for many years. When the hospital staff insisted that he mention his child-molesting in the community meeting on the unit, Mr. R complied, but in such a manner that he received no feedback from any other patient. He began by saying that he loved children and was concerned about the future of America. He talked at great length about his love for his own two daughters and his concern about how his hospitalization might affect them. He admitted to sexual behavior with children, but made it sound benign. He explained that he had never forced any sexual activity on any child and he claimed that, in fact, all his victims had enjoyed their physical contact with him. He spoke of it in terms of "hugging" and "stroking," and he maintained that it had always occurred in the context of a loving friendship. By the time he finished his narrative account, the other patients were quite sympathetic. The psychiatrist in charge of the meeting asked if anyone were shocked or repulsed by Mr. R's behavior. Everyone denied any such reaction.

Pedophiles on a hospital unit may virtually paralyze the patient group from giving them the effective feedback it gives other patients. In addition, those with striking antisocial personality features may simply lie so that their perverse behavior is never dealt with during their hospitalization. One such patient maintained for all 6 weeks of his hospitalization that he had been falsely accused. On the day of his discharge, he acknowledged to his doctor with a chuckle that he actually had molested a child but had not wanted to admit it. As this patient packed his bags to leave the unit, his doctor was left feeling frustrated and impotent to do anything to improve the patient's condition.

Other pedophiles may convince staff members that they are complying with treatment by going through the motions required by it. They appear to use the insights gained in psychotherapy about the origin of their impulses and desires but secretly have no interest in changing themselves. They "play the game" of hospital treatment because it is far preferable to prison, where pedophiles are often subject to gang rape. One pedophile who was a model patient during his hospitalization reported that his pedophilic impulses were thoroughly under control at discharge. He even said that he was no longer turned on by children. Upon transfer to a halfway house after discharge, he continued to report that he was no longer troubled by his pedophilic desires. This illusion was shattered when the police issued a warrant for his arrest stemming from two instances of child molestation. This pattern of deceiving staff members while going through the motions of treatment is all too common among this patient population. Some pedophiles may therefore do far better in correctional facilities with specialized programs for sex offenders that involve group confrontational approaches.

Sexual Dysfunctions

The increased popularity of behavioral techniques in the treatment of sexual dysfunctions (Masters and Johnson 1970) may have led some clinicians to view psychodynamic approaches as less relevant to the treatment of these disorders. Over the past two decades, however, sex therapists have encountered numerous individuals and couples who, for a variety of reasons, are unsuited for brief behavioral sex therapy. As a result, the prescription of specific treatments for specific sexual dysfunctions has become increasingly sophisticated. Moreover, these disorders have served as models for the development of combined therapeutic techniques that include mixtures of behavioral and dynamic interventions (Kaplan 1974, 1979, 1986).

There is little question that certain patients can benefit from the techniques of Masters and Johnson. They originally reported an 80 percent success rate with their 2-week intensive sex therapy program in St. Louis (1970). Data on the efficacy of psychodynamic psychotherapy in the treatment of sexual dysfunctions, however, are less available. One study that appeared shortly after the original

Masters and Johnson report suggested less impressive results (O'Connor and Stern 1972). Ninety-six patients who were treated 2–4 times a week for at least 2 years with psychoanalysis or psycho-analytically oriented psychotherapy for functional disorders had a success rate of 25 percent for the female subgroup and 57 percent for the males. Kaplan (1986) has pointed out that comparisons such as these are inappropriate since the patients in the O'Connor and Stern study probably had a much greater degree of associated psychopathology. Much of the effectiveness of the Masters and Johnson approach can be attributed to the select group of patients who sought their treatment. By and large, they were highly moti-vated, financially secure professional couples who could take 2 weeks out of their lives to devote themselves intensively to a sex therapy program. Kaplan also noted that specific diagnoses greatly influenced the success of sex therapy. Problems intrinsic to the desire phase are often resistant to sex therapy, and most results for this disorder would be comparable to the O'Connor and Stern (1972) data. Discrepancy of sexual desire between partners is the most commonly treated sexual dysfunction, and one survey of sex therapists revealed that only half such couples were cured with sex therapy (Kilmann et al. 1986).

The fact that the most common sexual dysfunction is effec-tively treated by sex therapy only half the time reflects the need for dynamic approaches in addition to behavioral treatments. Clini-cians have long known that when a sexual problem is the chief complaint in an initial interview, it is often only the tip of the iceberg. In some cases, the sexual problem may be a "red herring" to distract the clinician from far more serious and urgent problems. In other cases, it may serve to "contain" a variety of intimately related intra-psychic, marital, and family problems. Patients most likely to re-spond to brief sex therapy are usually suffering from mild perfor-mance anxiety in the context of a reasonably healthy personality structure and a reasonably gratifying marital relationship. Patients whose sexual problems are associated with severe character pathol-ogy (e.g., borderline and narcissistic personality disorders) or seri-ous Axis I syndromes (e.g., panic disorder, schizophrenia, and major affective disorder) will not benefit from brief behavioral sex therapy so they should not be assigned that form of treatment (Kaplan 1986). Similarly, couples with entrenched patterns of pathological relatedness and chronic feelings of resentment and bitterness are not suitable candidates for brief sex therapy. Typically, these couples will not practice the assigned sex therapy exercises but will instead become more openly conflictual (Lansky and Davenport 1975). Even couples with greater psychological health may resist practicing the sensate focus exercises that are often part of behavioral sex therapy treatment because the exercises activate unconscious anxiety (Kaplan 1986). The treatment of sexual symptoms must therefore be highly individualized and must be based on a careful psychiatric and psychodynamic evaluation. Organic causes, especially for erectile disorders, must be ruled out, thereby facilitating an accurate psychiatric diagnosis.

Psychodynamic Understanding of Sexual Dysfunctions

Most sexual dysfunctions catalogued in DSM-III-R may be categorized as disorders of desire, arousal, or orgasm. Problems related to orgasm are generally improved with brief behaviorally oriented sex therapy, which illustrates that symptoms produced by unconscious determinants can be alleviated by behavioral techniques without recourse to dynamic understanding. Indeed, brief sex therapy may be the most cost-effective treatment for individuals and couples who have difficulty attaining orgasm but who have no serious associated psychopathology. Disorders associated with desire and arousal tend to be more refractory to brief sex therapy because they are anchored in more deep-seated psychopathological factors (Kaplan 1986; Reid 1989). This discussion will focus on problems in these areas.

The psychodynamic understanding of the male or female patient who has no desire for sex, or of the male patient who has desire but is unable to achieve an erection, begins with a careful understanding of the symptom's situational context. If the patient is involved in an intimate relationship, the clinician must determine whether the problem of desire or arousal is specific to the partner or is generalized to all potential sexual partners. Sexual difficulties that are specific to the couple must be understood in the context of the interpersonal dynamics of the dyad, while other, primarily intrapsychic difficulties occur with any partner. Clinicians must remember, though, that desire problems, like all other psychological symptoms, are multiply determined.

Levine (1988) has delineated three discrete elements of sexual desire that must function in synchrony for adequate desire and arousal: drive, wish, and motive. Drive is rooted in biology and may be affected by physical factors, such as hormonal levels, medical illnesses, and medications. The wish element is more intimately connected to conscious cognitive or ideational factors. For example, in the presence of a normal drive component, an individual may wish to not have sex because of religious prohibitions or because of a fear of contracting AIDS. The third element, motive, is intimately related to unconscious object relational needs and is the component most likely to be the focus of therapeutic intervention.

The clinician must assess all three elements, according to Levine, and they must attempt to understand why they are not integrated into a functional whole. Numerous factors may interfere with an individual's motivation. One partner in the marriage may be having an extramarital affair and may simply have no interest in the spouse. Or one spouse may feel so chronically resentful and angry toward the other that sexual relations are out of the question. Problems in the couple's nonsexual relationship probably account for most instances of inhibited sexual desire (ISD). A sexual partner's distortions can also play a key role in disturbing motivation. In many couples who enter sex or marital therapy, the spouses are unconsciously relating to one another as if to the opposite-sex parent. When this occurs, sexual relations may unconsciously be experienced as incestuous, so the partners manage the anxiety associated with this taboo by avoiding sex altogether. Simpson (1985) has reported a case of sex therapy in which the wife was highly resistant to carrying out the prescribed exercises. When this resistance was explored dynamically, the wife was able to acknowledge to the therapist that part of her wanted her husband to fail in sex therapy. She revealed her fear that her husband would become a "womanizer" like her father if he regained adequate sexual functioning. This transference distortion of her husband threatened to undermine the success of the sex therapy. Even single individuals in therapy or analysis may experience transference-like attachments to a potential sex partner that result in disorders of motivation.

> Mr. S was a 25-year-old, single professional man who entered psychoanalysis because of various problems in his capacity to work and love. The drive component of Mr. S's sexual desire was entirely adequate— he masturbated several times a day to relieve intense sexual tension. The wish component of desire was also intact. He aspired to sexual relations with an appropriate female and fantasized about doing so. However, the motivational element seemed lacking, as evidenced by his characteristic behavior pattern each time he became attracted to a woman. As he talked about the woman in analysis, he would become tearfully convinced that he would ultimately lose the current object of his longings. His anticipation of the loss aroused such intense feelings of grief and so overwhelmed him that he would decide not to pursue a relationship at all but instead to simply retreat into solitary masturbation.
>
> Each time Mr. S experienced these feelings of anticipatory loss, his analyst would try to elicit any associations to previous events or life experiences that might bring up analogous feelings. After a considerable period of analytic work, the patient finally began to make sense of his feelings. When the patient was 5 years old, his father had been away at war for a year. During this time, Mr. S had been "the man of the house," occupying a special position with his mother in the absence of his chief rival for her affections. At times he had even slept in bed with her. When Mr. S's father returned, however, the patient suffered a devastating loss of this special, intimate relationship with his mother.

The patient's memory of this period in his life helped him understand his motives not to pursue sexual relations. As soon as he became infatuated with a woman, he began to form a maternal transference attachment. Reexperiencing her (at an unconscious level) as his mother, he became convinced that she, too, would "dump" him for another man, just as his mother had turned him aside for his father. Mr. S feared confronting that grief again, which led him to avoid sexual relations. This insight also put Mr. S in touch with considerable castration anxiety. He realized that he was deeply worried that his penis might be injured during sex, a concern that he eventually associated with his fear of retaliation for having taken his father's place in mother's bed.

Our capacity for sexual arousal and desire is clearly connected intimately with our internal object relations. Scharff (1988) has developed an object relations model of inhibited sexual desire based on Fairbairn's (1952) theories of development (see Chapter 2). Fairbairn postulated two "bad object" systems, the libidinal ego and object, in which the ego longs for a tantalizing object, and the antilibidinal ego and object, in which the ego feels hatred and anger toward an attacking, abandoning, and negligent object. The rejecting or antilibidinal object attempts to eliminate the exciting or libidinal object. In Scharff's model, then, this antilibidinal system interferes with sexual excitement, which derives from the libidinal system.

These metapsychological abstractions can be more easily understood by examining the development of a typical relationship. Individuals are attracted to one another as a result of activation of the libidinal or need-exciting object system. Via mutual projective identification, each regards the other as the exciting object. To maintain the idealized "in love" state, each must repress the antilibidinal or rejecting object. However, as the luster and freshness of the relationship wear off, the repressed object relations unit begins to surface, particularly when needs are inevitably frustrated. At this point, the rejecting object of the antilibidinal system is projected into the partner, and sexual excitement is contaminated by the perception of the partner as persecuting or abandoning.

In Scharff's model, clinicians must evaluate disturbances of desire according to three different areas of internal and external object relations: 1) the external realities of the couple's current marital relationship; 2) the internal object world of each individual and how it affects the capacity for sexual intimacy; and 3) the current family constellation (including children, elderly parents, and other factors) and how it affects sexual desire. Scharff has noted that sexual desire is greatly affected by the developmental stage of the marriage itself.

A psychodynamic assessment of inhibited sexual desire must acknowledge the possibility that the "designated patient" may not be the one who needs the treatment. Kaplan (1988) has studied couples in which one partner is so exquisitely sensitive to rejection that the other partner will lose interest in having sexual relations. In many of these cases, the female partner suffers from panic disorder in which the man's absorption in pleasure is perceived as an abandonment of her. No amount of reassurance from the male partner will convince the woman of his commitment to her. Kaplan recommended that the apparently "asymptomatic" partner may need to realize that her efforts at control instead lead her partner to withdraw from sexual intimacy.

Primitively disturbed patients, especially those with schizophrenia and severe borderline features, may find the prospect of genital fusion overwhelming to their fragile ego. Motivational factors in these patients that lead to ISD are related to the primitive anxiety states described in Chapter 9, including disintegration anxiety, persecutory anxiety, and a fear of fusing with one's partner. Abstaining from sexual relations may thus appear to safeguard the integrity of the self.

Treatment Considerations

The clinician who assesses functional sexual disorders must decide whether to prescribe brief behavioral sex therapy, couples therapy, psychoanalysis or expressive-supportive psychotherapy, pharmacotherapy, or any combination of these. Lief (1981) estimated that 30–40 percent of all sexual dysfunctions will improve symptomatically with brief behavioral techniques. Of those who do not benefit from behavioral therapy, 20 percent will require marital therapy, 10 percent will need long-term individual expressive-supportive psychotherapy, and about 30 percent will need some combination of marital and sex therapy. Kaplan's (1986) estimates are similar, but she has also advocated pharmacotherapy. Approximately one-fourth of the patients at her sex clinic whose problems involved sexual aversion or phobic sex avoidance also met the diagnostic criteria for panic disorder. Prescribing sensate focus techniques for these patients only increases their anxiety, and will defeat the treatment. Antipanic medication, such as desipramine, imipramine, monoamine oxidase inhibitors, and clonazepam, all may be helpful for these patients. But Kaplan (1988) has also found that these medications do not cure the patient, and that attention to dynamic issues should accompany pharmacotherapeutic intervention.

Indications for the various modalities may not always be clear during the initial evaluation. Brief behavioral sex therapy is likely to be successful if a couple is highly motivated, if neither partner suffers from serious psychopathology, if each partner is reasonably satisfied with their relationship, and if the dysfunction is based on performance anxiety and related to the orgasm phase. Couples who have ISD and are generally disillusioned with the relationship may require marital therapy for a period of time to address basic problems in their relationship. If the couple decides to stay together after marital therapy, then sex therapy techniques can be more appropriately recommended.

Couples who seem appropriate candidates for brief sex therapy techniques but who undermine the process by not practicing the exercises may require a hybrid treatment that Kaplan (1979) has labeled *psychosexual therapy*. In this treatment, the therapist prescribes behavioral exercises and then addresses any resistance to practicing the exercises with dynamic psychotherapy. Kaplan has found this combination of techniques to be critical to successful treatment with certain patients. The dynamic portion of the treatment allows exploration of themes such as the patient's intense guilt feelings about sexual pleasure. Parental transferences to the partner can also be uncovered and explored. In addition, many patients have unconscious conflicts about being successful in any endeavor, including sexual performance, which may have to be examined. Kaplan (1986) has also found that some patients unconsciously act out the role of "loser" or "failure" that they have been assigned in their family of origin.

A strong consensus in the literature indicates that patients suffering from severe character pathology or deeply ingrained neurotic conflicts about sexuality should be treated in psychoanalysis or expressive-supportive psychotherapy (Kaplan 1986; Levine 1988; Reid 1989; Scharff 1988). Sometimes these problems surface only during an extended evaluation with sex therapy (Scharff 1988). Certain patients may remain unconvinced of the need for long-term intensive individual psychotherapy until they have tried brief methods and found them ineffective. Extended sex therapy also allows the therapist to gain a greater grasp of the internal object relations of each member of the couple. As described in the section on object relations family and marital therapy in Chapter 5, the therapist "contains" the various projective identifications from both spouses. Therapists who are open to this process can diagnose problematic patterns of object relatedness in the couple through "firsthand experience." When there is deep-seated neurotic conflict about sexuality or when there is severe character pathology, however, sex therapy will often exacerbate these problems (Lansky and Davenport 1975). The prescribed sensate focus exercises will force the couple to confront issues that are habitually avoided because of the way their relationship has been organized.

Mrs. T was a 46-year-old housewife who entered sex therapy with her husband because of her total lack of interest in sexual relations. After several unproductive sessions, the sex therapist referred Mrs. T for individual expressive-supportive psychotherapy. She felt relieved when she first saw her individual psychotherapist because she realized that she would not be "forced into sexual relations" with her husband.

She described her marital relationship as involving a caretaking role for herself that produced no gratitude from her husband. He had retired 4 years earlier and now spent his days lying around the house watching television. She was not happy with their relationship, but she seemed to have little interest in changing it. She repeatedly berated herself, saying that she did not deserve a better life than what she had. When this pattern of being unable to enjoy success was pointed out to her by the therapist, Mrs. T confided that every time she had felt good in her life, she had been "zapped." She then recounted numerous examples, including the death of one of her children, to illustrate how she had always been punished for any positive feelings she had about events in her life.

Although Mrs. T talked about a wide range of topics in her psychotherapy, she steadfastly refused to mention anything about her sexuality or the sexual problems that brought her to treatment in the first place. Her therapist began to feel as though he were coercing her into dealing with her sexual problems. When he gently asked her about them, she responded as though to a rapist, feeling violated and withdrawing into silence. The therapist used his countertransference feelings to diagnose an internal object relation that had been externalized in the psychotherapy. He said to Mrs. T, "You seem to react as though I am traumatizing you with my questions about sexuality. Is this repeating any sexually related trauma from your past?" Mrs. T broke down and tearfully acknowledged a history of early sexual trauma at the hands of an uncle. She also opened up further about her first marriage, explaining that she had had a number of extramarital affairs that led to two illegal abortions. She had always been a "daddy's girl," and she wondered if she had been looking for her father in all those affairs. This insight was coupled with an awareness that she had stopped having affairs when her father died about 18 years earlier. Her father had been involved in some of her marital problems that had resulted from her promiscuity, and he had seemed highly distressed by her unfaithfulness to her husband. She even speculated that her promiscuous behavior in her first marriage might have caused her father's death. With interpretations from the therapist, Mrs. T began to understand that her self-sacrifice and selfless devotion to caring for her husband was a form of psychological reparation for the damage she believed she had inflicted on her father. She also began to understand that she denied herself sexual pleasure to punish herself for her promiscuity and the two abortions.

The case of Mrs. T illustrates how deeply ingrained sexual problems may be ego-syntonic because they fulfill certain psychological needs. Many patients with sexual dysfunctions are actually convinced that they should not experience sexual pleasure so they are therefore invested in maintaining their symptomatology. The treatment of sexual dysfunctions is a highly value-laden area of psychiatry. Clinicians must temper their countertransference need to cure with a respect for the patient's right to choose a particular pattern of sexual adjustment. Kaplan (1986) has noted that some women who fail to reach orgasm nevertheless report satisfying sexual relations; such women usually do not seek treatment for sexual dysfunction. In addition, many voluntary celibates in religious orders lead happy and productive lives. Finally, clinicians must keep in mind that, for some patients, a sexual symptom is nothing more than an admission ticket to psychotherapy. Once inside the door, these patients become more interested in other areas of their life and the sexual symptoms lose significance.

References

American Psychiatric Association: Diagnostic and Statistical Manual of Mental Disorders, 3rd Edition, Revised. Washington, DC, American Psychiatric Association, 1987

Berlin FS, Meinecke CF: Treatment of sex offenders with antiandrogenic medication: conceptualization, review of treatment modalities, and preliminary findings. Am J Psychiatry 138:601–607, 1981

Chasseguet-Smirgel J: Perversion and the universal law. International Review of Psychoanalysis 10:293–301, 1983

Fairbairn WRD: Psychoanalytic Studies of the Personality. London, Routledge & Kegan Paul, 1952

Fenichel O: The Psychoanalytic Theory of Neurosis. New York, WW Norton, 1945

Freud S: Three essays on the theory of sexuality (1905), in The Standard Edition of the Complete Psychological Works of Sigmund Freud, Vol 7. Translated and edited by Strachey J. London, Hogarth Press, 1953, pp 123–245

Freud S: Splitting of the ego in the process of defence (1940), in The Standard Edition of the Complete Psychological Works of Sigmund Freud, Vol 23. Translated and edited by Strachey J. London, Hogarth Press, 1964, pp 271–278

Ganzarain R, Buchele BJ: Psychodynamics of incest perpetrators. Bull Menninger Clin (in press)

Gelinas DJ: Unexpected resources in treating incest families, in Family Resources: The Hidden Partner in Family Therapy. Edited by Karpel MA. New York, Guilford Press, 1986, pp 327–358

Greenacre P: The transitional object and the fetish: with special reference to the role of illusion. Int J Psychoanal 51:447–456, 1970

Greenacre P: Fetishism, in Sexual Deviation, 2nd Edition. Edited by Rosen I. Oxford, Oxford University Press, 1979, pp 79–108

Kaplan HS: The New Sex Therapy: Active Treatment of Sexual Dysfunctions. New York, Brunner/Mazel, 1974

Kaplan HS: Disorders of Sexual Desire and Other New Concepts and Techniques in Sex Therapy. New York, Simon & Schuster, 1979

Kaplan HS: The psychosexual dysfunctions (Ch 36), in Psychiatry, Revised Edition. Edited by Cavenar JO Jr. Vol 1: The Personality Disorders and Neuroses. Edited by Cooper AM, Frances AJ, Sacks MH. Philadelphia, JB Lippincott, 1986, pp 467–479

Kaplan HS: Intimacy disorders and sexual panic states. J Sex Marital Ther 14:3–12, 1988

Kentsmith DK, Eaton MT: Treating Sexual Problems in Medical Practice. New York, Arco, 1978

Kernberg OF: Borderline Conditions and Pathological Narcissism. New York, Jason Aronson, 1975

Kilmann PR, Boland JP, Norton SP, et al: Perspectives of sex therapy outcome: a survey of AASECT providers. J Sex Marital Ther 12:116–138, 1986

Kohut H: The Analysis of the Self: A Systematic Approach to the Treatment of Narcissistic Personality Disorders. New York, International Universities Press, 1971

Kohut H: The Restoration of the Self. New York, International Universities Press, 1977

Lansky MR, Davenport AE: Difficulties of brief conjoint treatment of sexual dysfunction. Am J Psychiatry 132:177–179, 1975

Levine SB: Intrapsychic and individual aspects of sexual desire, in Sexual Desire Disorders. Edited by Leiblum SR, Rosen R. New York, Guilford Press, 1988, pp 21–44

Lief HI (ed): Sexual Problems in Medical Practice. Monroe, WI, American Medical Association, 1981

Masters WH, Johnson V: Human Sexual Inadequacy. Boston, Little, Brown, 1970

McDougall J: Plea for a Measure of Abnormality. New York, International Universities Press, 1980

McDougall J: Identifications, neoneeds and neosexualities. Int J Psychoanal 67:19–31, 1986

Miller JP: How Kohut actually worked. Progress in Self-Psychology 1:13–30, 1985

Mitchell SA: Relational Concepts in Psychoanalysis: An Integration. Cambridge, MA, Harvard University Press, 1988

O'Connor JF, Stern LO: Results of treatment in functional sexual disorders. NY State J Med 72:1927–1934, 1972

Person ES: Paraphilias and gender identity disorders (Ch 35), in Psychiatry, Revised Edition. Edited by Cavenar JO Jr. Vol 1: The Personality Disorders and Neuroses. Edited by Cooper AM, Frances AJ, Sacks MH. Philadelphia, JB Lippincott, 1986, pp 447–465

Rappeport JR: Enforced treatment—is it treatment? Bull Am Acad Psychiatry Law 2:148–158, 1974

Reid WH: The treatment of psychiatric disorders: revised for the DSM-III-R. New York, Brunner/Mazel, 1989

Rosen I (ed): Pathology and Treatment of Sexual Deviation: A Methodological Approach. London, Oxford University Press, 1964

Rosen I (ed): Sexual Deviation, 2nd Edition. London, Oxford University Press, 1979

Sachs H: On the genesis of perversions. Translated by Goldberg RB. Psychoanal Q 55:477–488, 1986

Scharff DE: An object relations approach to inhibited sexual desire, in Sexual Desire Disorders. Edited by Leiblum SR, Rosen R. New York, Guilford Press, 1988, pp 45–74

Simpson WS: Psychoanalysis and sex therapy: a case report. Bull Menninger Clin 49:565–582, 1985

Socarides CW: The Preoedipal Origin and Psychoanalytic Therapy of Sexual Perversions. Madison, CT, International Universities Press, 1988

Stoller RJ: Perversion: The Erotic Form of Hatred. New York, Pantheon, 1975

Stoller RJ: Observing the Erotic Imagination. New Haven, Yale University Press, 1985

Stolorow RD, Atwood GE, Brandchaft B: Masochism and its treatment. Bull Menninger Clin 52:504–509, 1988

Travin S, Bluestone H, Coleman E, et al: Pedophilia: an update on theory and practice. Psychiatr Q 57:89–103, 1985

CHAPTER 11

Psychoactive Substance Use Disorders and Eating Disorders

In this chapter we consider two diagnostic categories that involve discrete self-destructive symptoms. Psychoactive substance abuse is defined by the ingestion of chemicals that may lead to addiction, life-threatening physical problems, and a host of emotional problems. Eating disorders are defined by overeating, voluntary purging, and starvation. Both groups of disorders present a complex problem for psychodynamic clinicians: What is the role of dynamic approaches in disorders that require symptom control as a major thrust of the therapeutic effort? In some quarters, psychodynamic understanding is considered irrelevant to the management of addiction and eating disorders. However, a considerable body of clinical and research literature suggests otherwise.

Psychoactive Substance Use Disorders

Because psychodynamic psychiatrists often become frustrated in their efforts to treat alcoholics, they may abandon or avoid such efforts. Relapse is common, and interpretations of unconscious motivations often seem to have little impact on the drinking behavior itself. Psychodynamic models of alcoholism are regarded with skepticism both by mental health professionals and by society at large.

Two other models—the moral model and the disease model—receive much greater support (Cooper 1987). The moral model views alcoholics as bearing complete responsibility for their alcoholism. From this point of view, alcoholics are hedonistic individuals interested only in their own pursuit of pleasure, with no regard for the feelings of others. This model has its roots in the fundamentalist religious belief that alcoholism is a sign of moral turpitude. Failings of willpower are closely linked to notions of sin, and punishment through the legal system is often regarded as the appropriate way to deal with alcoholics. Eliminating drinking behavior is a matter of overcoming weak willpower to pull oneself up by the "bootstraps."

The phenomenal success of Alcoholics Anonymous (AA) has led to increasing popularity of the disease model of alcoholism. In contrast to the moral model, this paradigm relieves the alcoholic of responsibility for illness. Just as the diabetic is not held responsible for diabetes, the alcoholic is not held responsible for alcoholism. Alcoholics are viewed as having an inherent predisposition to addiction to exogenous substances; psychological factors are irrelevant. Although this model originated as a backlash to moralizing reactions to—and inhumane treatment of—alcoholics, it has recently gained support from genetic studies of the offspring of alcoholics. Even when raised apart from the alcoholic parents, these children have an increased risk of becoming alcoholics as adults (Goodwin 1979; Schuckit 1985).

Further support for the disease model has come from Vaillant's (1983) prospective study of male alcoholics throughout the course of their adult life cycle. He found that the eventual development of alcoholism could not be predicted from adverse childhood experiences or even from psychological profiles of these subjects as young adults. The only reliable predictor of adult alcoholism was antisocial behavior. Vaillant concluded that depression, anxiety, and other psychological characteristics often associated with alcoholics were *consequences,* rather than *causes,* of the disorder. Furthermore, psychotherapy and psychological conceptualizations of alcoholism play a minor role in clinical understanding and treatment planning. Vaillant thus decided that enforced abstinence through AA has the greatest likelihood of success.

A shift in focus from alcoholic patients to those who abuse drugs reveals wide usage of the same two models. The moral model is more widely applied to drug abusers than to alcoholics, however, largely because of the extensive overlap between crime and drug abuse. Much of the controversy over the appropriate response to the national drug problem involves whether addicts are more effectively handled through legalistically oriented punitive approaches or medically oriented therapeutic approaches. Drug abusers have sought to replicate the success of AA by developing organizations such as Narcotics Anonymous (NA). But the disease model and its associated self-help groups have been less successful with drug abusers, as Vaillant himself (1988) has pointed out, because of apparent fundamental differences between alcoholics and polydrug abusers that require differential approaches. In view of these essential differences, the ensuing section will examine the psychodynamic understanding of alcoholics and drug abusers one at a time.

Psychodynamic Approaches to Alcoholism

The AA approach to the problem of alcoholism has been highly effective in the treatment of many individuals. Although the AA organization itself promotes the disease model, its methods address psychological needs and facilitate lasting structural personality change (Mack 1981). Abstinence is achieved in an interpersonal context where alcoholics can experience a caring and concerned community of fellow sufferers. These caring figures can be internalized in the same manner that a psychotherapist is internalized, and they can assist the alcoholic with affect management, impulse control, and other ego functions, also as a psychotherapist would. Hence the psychodynamic model can facilitate an understanding of some of the changes rendered by the AA approach (Mack 1981).

For many alcoholics, the psychological changes encouraged by AA and the abstinence associated with commitment to its ideals and regular attendance at the meetings are sufficient treatment. The psychodynamically sensitive clinician, understanding the value of this approach, must have the good judgment to leave well enough alone. Clinical experience has repeatedly demonstrated, however, that AA is not suitable for all patients who suffer from alcoholism. It apparently works best for those who can accept the idea that they have no control over their drinking and thus need to surrender to a "higher power," and for those who are essentially free of other psychiatric disorders.

Most alcoholism experts would agree that alcoholism is a heterogeneous disorder with a multifactorial etiology (Donovan 1986). What works for one patient may not work for another, and all the treatments are surrounded with controversy. Clinicians should keep in mind that a myriad of evaluation studies on the effectiveness of various treatments for alcoholism suggests that only 26 percent of treated alcoholics are still abstinent 1 year later (Parloff et al. 1986), in contrast to the "spontaneous remission" rate of 19 percent. Clearly, no treatment is definitive, and clinicians must consider each patient individually, making a careful psychiatric evaluation before developing an individually tailored treatment plan.

Unfortunately, the disease model has promulgated the "depsychologizing" of alcoholism. The conclusions drawn by Vaillant (1983) are in conflict with those based on other longitudinal studies, which suggest that personality factors may be important to an understanding of vulnerability to alcoholism (Sutker and Allain 1988). Moreover, Vaillant's conclusions are only as valid as his instruments of measurement. Dodes (1988) has observed that Vaillant's methods are not capable of identifying a critical feature in alcoholic patients, namely, their disturbance in self-esteem as revealed by an inability to care for themselves. Also, those people predisposed to alcoholism may be vulnerable to regression, despite the presence of overtly positive childhood relationships (Mack 1981).

Perhaps the major difficulty with the treatment approach suggested by Vaillant and other strict adherents to the disease model is that it ignores the heterogeneity of the disorder. Alcoholism is not a monolithic entity. In fact, one might more accurately refer to the "alcoholisms" (Donovan 1986). Numerous studies attest that there is no single "alcoholic personality" that predisposes to alcoholism (Donovan 1986; Nathan 1988; Sutker and Allain 1988). Nonetheless, personality variables and psychological issues are highly relevant in the treatment of many alcoholics. A narrow interpretation of the disease model might lead clinicians to ignore how these factors contribute to relapse in the course of the illness.

Although no specific personality traits are connected with alcoholism, psychoanalytic observers have repeatedly noted structural defects, such as ego weakness and difficulty in maintaining self-esteem (Donovan 1986). Both Kohut (1971) and Balint (1968) noted that alcohol serves the function of replacing missing psychological structures and thereby restores some sense of self-regard and inner harmony. Unfortunately, these effects last only as long as the intoxication. Khantzian (1982) also observed that alcoholic patients had problems with self-esteem, the modulation of affect, and the capacity for self-care. Investigators of borderline personality disorder have consistently noted parallels between alcoholism and the intrapsychic structure of patients with borderline personality disorder (Hartocollis 1982; Kernberg 1975; Knight 1953; Rinsley 1988); in particular, they share such traits as poor anxiety tolerance, poor affective control, and the use of splitting as a predominant defense (see Chapter 14). This linkage of alcoholism to borderline personality disorder has been further substantiated by empirical studies (Nace et al. 1983; Vaglum and Vaglum 1985) that suggest that 30–39 percent of alcoholics have coexisting borderline pathology. Other common diagnoses accompanying alcoholism are depression (Weissman and Myers 1980) and sociopathy (Schuckit et al. 1970).

These studies are not cited to convince readers that all alcoholics suffer from coexisting psychiatric disorders or preexisting intrapsychic deficits. Rather, they highlight the obvious fact that addiction to alcohol occurs in a *person*. An individual may develop alcoholism as the final common pathway of a complex interaction between structural deficits, genetic predisposition, familial influences, cultural contributions, and other assorted environmental variables. A thorough psychodynamic evaluation of the patient will consider the alcoholism and all its contributing factors in the context of the total person. Whether depression, for example, is a cause or consequence of alcoholism, or a completely separate disease state, is of more interest to researchers than to clinicians. When alcoholics sober up and look back at the wreckage caused by their alcoholic existence, they are commonly faced with a good deal of depression. Although antidepressant medication may alleviate such depression, psychotherapy is often helpful in dealing with the grief associated with working through the pain connected to the recognition of having hurt others.

Another implication of the observation that alcoholism occurs in an individual is that each person will prefer and accept different treatment options. Dodes (1988) has noted: "Some patients are able to use only psychotherapy, others can use only AA, and there are those who will best be treated with a combination of the two. Accurate prescription of treatment requires individual clinical judgment" (pp. 283–284). Many alcoholics find AA unworkable either because of their embarrassment at having to speak in front of a group or because of their philosophical opposition to the notion of a "higher power." Although Vaillant (1981) has declared psychotherapy to be wasteful in the treatment of alcoholism, some patients are able to maintain sobriety with psychotherapy alone (Dodes 1984; Khantzian 1985a). An unfortunate "straw man" stereotype often applied to the dynamic psychotherapy of alcoholics is that the therapist uncovers unconscious motivations for drinking while ignoring the patient's actual drinking behavior. The fact that psychotherapy can be misused by some patients and by some therapists does not mean, however, that the treatment should be written off (Dodes 1988).

Patients involved in AA are often in psychotherapy as well. In one study, more than 90 percent of the abstinent alcoholic patients in AA who sought psychotherapy found it helpful (Brown 1985). Psychotherapy and AA often work synergistically. Dodes (1988) has observed that alcoholic patients may develop, in self-psychological terms, an idealizing or mirror transference to the AA organization. They view it as a caring, idealized figure in their life that sustains and supports them. This transference may be split off from the psychotherapeutic transference, and the psychotherapist is wise to delay analyzing it. Eventually, the selfobject functions of AA can be internalized enough to improve self-care and heightened self-esteem. After some degree of internalization, psychotherapists can shift the therapy from a supportive to a more expressive emphasis.

Rosen (1981), who has identified separation-individuation problems in alcoholics, believed that psychotherapy is helpful in weaning patients from a symbiotic attachment to AA, but only after they have established sobriety through the help of the organization. Other researchers have argued that abstinence is not an absolute requirement for effective psychotherapy (Dodes 1984; Pattison 1976). If a therapist demands abstinence, some patients will refuse treatment altogether. In fact, it is naive to expect total abstinence in the course of long-term psychotherapy. Very few alcoholics are unambivalent about giving up their symptomatic drinking; any lack of motivation should be viewed as a symptom rather than as a contraindication for psychotherapy (Cooper 1987). However, if patients continue to drink heavily, with no capacity for or interest in exploring their reasons for drinking, they may be unable to use the psychotherapy process and may instead require hospitalization to be effectively treated. In any case, abstinence should not be an absolute requirement for establishing the psychotherapy process.

Group psychotherapy is also commonly used in both inpatient and outpatient treatment of alcoholism. As with all other treatment modalities, this modality is rarely used in isolation, so it is difficult to determine its effectiveness. More commonly, it is part of a comprehensive treatment plan that also involves many other interventions. A recent review of studies involving group psychotherapy of alcoholics suggested the empirical validity of using group psychotherapy as an adjunctive treatment (Brandsma and Pattison 1985). Group psychotherapeutic approaches often involve intense confrontation of the self-destructive nature of the addiction as a way to cut through the denial so prominent in alcoholics (Bratter 1981).

Other therapists (e.g., Khantzian 1986) have cautioned against a confrontational approach. Because of the difficulty that many alcoholics have in regulating affects such as anxiety, depression, and anger, confrontation in a group setting can be counterproductive or even harmful. Cooper (1987) shared Khantzian's view that confrontation should be used judiciously. He believed that the therapist should empathize with the alcoholic's defensive need to avoid painful affect. He has advocated inpatient groups that focus on the here-and-now but are less confrontational. He reported a 55 percent abstinence rate with patients in such groups, compared to 16 percent for patients in an inpatient group program without group psychotherapy. Those patients who remained in group therapy for at least 25 hours also demonstrated greater compliance with other aspects of the program.

Psychodynamic Approaches to Drug Abusers

Although the disease model is popular in many drug rehabilitation programs, psychodynamic approaches to drug abusers are more widely accepted and valued than they are in the treatment of alcoholics. Vaillant (1988), for example, noted that polydrug abusers, in contrast to alcoholics, are more likely to have had unstable childhoods, more likely to use substances as "self-medication" for psychiatric symptoms, and more likely to benefit from psychotherapeutic efforts to address their underlying symptomatology and character pathology.

A considerable body of research literature supports the association of personality disorder and depression with the development of drug addiction (Blatt et al. 1984a; Kandel et al. 1978; Paton et al. 1977; Treece 1984; Treece and Khantzian 1986). These studies suggested that while initiation to marijuana use may be related to peer pressure in adolescence, use of and eventual addiction to hard drugs are not. One study found impaired relationships with parents and depression to be highly significant predictors of eventual abuse of illicit drugs, while sociodemographic variables were not (Kandel et al. 1978). Another study of high school students who became involved in heavy drug use identified depression as the most potent predictor of all personality variables (Paton et al. 1977). Treece (1984) concluded that the key factor differentiating the chronic drug addict from the controlled or casual abuser is the presence in the former of severe personality disorder. Compared with alcoholics, drug abusers are much more likely to have significant coexisting psychiatric disorders. One survey of narcotics addicts determined that up to 93 percent of opiate abusers also met criteria for other psychiatric diagnoses (Khantzian and Treece 1985). Another study of opioid addicts found that more than 80 percent had a psychiatric history, with affective disorder and antisocial personality disorder the most common diagnostic entities (Rounsaville et al. 1982).

These research findings have played a key role in the development of sophisticated psychodynamic formulations of substance abuse problems. The early psychoanalytic interpretation of all substance abuse as a regression to the oral stage of psychosexual development has been replaced by an understanding of most drug abuse as *defensive* and *adaptive* rather than regressive (Khantzian 1985b, 1986; Wurmser 1974). Drug use may actually reverse regressive states by reinforcing defective ego defenses against powerful affects such as rage, shame, and depression. The early psychoanalytic formulations often depicted drug addicts as pleasure-seeking hedonists bent on self-destruction. Contemporary psychoanalytic investigators understand addictive behavior more as a reflection of a deficit in self-care rather than as a self-destructive impulse (Khantzian 1986). This impairment in self-care results from early developmental disturbances that lead to an inadequate internalization of parental figures, leaving the addict without the capacity for self-protection. Hence the majority of chronic drug addicts exhibit a fundamental impairment of judgment about the dangers of drug abuse.

Equally important in the pathogenesis of drug addiction is the impaired regulatory function in affect and impulse control and in maintenance of self-esteem (Treece and Khantzian 1986). These deficits create corresponding problems in object relations. Heavy polydrug use has been related directly to the addict's incapacity for tolerating and regulating interpersonal closeness (Nicholson and

Treece 1981; Treece 1984). Contributing to these relationship problems are the narcissistic vulnerability inherent in interpersonal risks
and the inability to modulate the affects associated with closeness.
The ingestion of a drug can thus be viewed as a desperate attempt
to compensate for deficits in ego functioning, self-esteem, and
related interpersonal problems. Treece and Khantzian (1986) succinctly noted that, "The critical factor in both severe and mild
disturbances is that a given substance or substances be experienced
as meeting a peremptory adaptive need, thus providing not only
relief, but the experience, at least temporarily, of increased capacity
to cope and to function" (p. 405). In this sense, most drug use that
is severe enough to lead to dependency may be a form of self-medication (Khantzian 1985b).

The notion that drug addicts are medicating themselves to
obtain relief from painful affect states leads directly to another
observation of contemporary psychodynamic investigators—
namely, that specific substances are chosen for specific psychological and pharmacologic effects according to each abuser's needs.
The most painful affect is likely to be what determines the choice of
drug. Khantzian (1985a) has noted that cocaine appears to relieve
distress associated with depression, hyperactivity, and hypomania,
while narcotics apparently tone down feelings of rage in opiate
addicts.

An in-depth study of narcotics addicts led Blatt et al. (1984a,
1984b) to conclude that heroin addiction is multiply determined by
1) the need to contain aggression, 2) a yearning for gratification of
longings for a symbiotic relationship with a maternal figure, and 3)
a desire to alleviate depressive affects. Although the research data
indicate that a small subgroup of narcotics addicts also suffer from
antisocial personality disorder (Rounsaville et al. 1982), Blatt et al.
have identified a larger group of severely neurotic opiate addicts,
which may represent the majority. These individuals struggle with
feelings of worthlessness, guilt, self-criticism, and shame. Their
depression appears to intensify when they attempt to become close
to others, so they withdraw into isolated "bliss" brought on by heroin
or other narcotics, which has both regressive and defensive dimensions. The depressive core of the opiate addict was further substantiated by a comparison study (Blatt et al. 1984a, 1984b), which found
opiate addicts to be significantly more depressed than polydrug
abusers. This study also identified self-criticism as a main component of their depression.

The finding of Blatt and his colleagues of a high correlation
between superego-ridden, self-critical, depression-prone personality features and opiate addiction has received support from
Wurmser's (1974, 1987a, 1987b) psychoanalytic work with addicts.
He has argued that those addicts amenable to psychoanalytic ther-

apy do not suffer from underdeveloped superegos, like the antisocial addict, but rather from an excessively harsh conscience. The intoxicating substance is sought as an escape from a tormenting superego. Many drug abusers employ the defense of splitting to disavow a drug-abusing self-representation that alternates with a non-drug-abusing self-representation. These individuals often feel as if someone else has taken over for a brief period. Wurmser has identified success as a prominent trigger for an episode of drug abuse. Positive feelings associated with successful achievement seem to produce an altered state of consciousness characterized by feelings of guilt and shame. Impulsive drug use is seen as the solution to these painful affects. These recurring crises are characterized by an overbearing conscience that becomes so unbearable that temporary defiance seems the only means of relief.

Although early studies with narcotics addicts suggested that psychotherapy materially contributes to the recovery of addicts, much of this research was discounted because of methodological problems. More recently, a number of reports from the Veterans Administration–Penn Study (Woody et al. 1983, 1984, 1985, 1986, 1987) have persuasively demonstrated with rigorous methodology that adding psychotherapy to the overall treatment plan of opiate addicts produces clear benefits. Narcotics addicts in a methadone maintenance program were randomly assigned to one of three treatment conditions: 1) drug counseling alone with paraprofessionals, 2) expressive-supportive psychotherapy plus drug counseling, or 3) cognitive-behavioral psychotherapy plus counseling. Of 110 patients who completed the full treatment program, those receiving psychotherapy improved considerably more than those who received counseling alone. Expressive-supportive psychotherapy based on dynamic principles resulted in greater improvement in psychiatric symptoms and employment than did cognitive-behavioral psychotherapy (Woody et al. 1983). Those patients who were depressed showed the most improvement, followed by patients who had opiate dependency alone but no other psychiatric disorder. Those with antisocial personality disorder alone did not benefit from psychotherapy (Woody et al. 1985). Antisocial patients only improved when depression was also a symptom.

When the researchers divided the 110 psychotherapy patients into groups according to the severity of their psychiatric symptoms, they noted that patients in the low-severity group made equal progress either with counseling or with psychotherapy, while patients with a medium degree of severity had better outcomes with both (although some improved just with counseling). However, the group with extremely severe psychiatric symptoms achieved little progress with counseling alone, but made considerable progress when psychotherapy was added; in this group those patients who received psychotherapy used both illicit and prescribed drugs far less often than did those who did not receive psychotherapy. The changes measured at 7-month follow-up were sustained at 12-month follow-up (Woody et al. 1987), even though the subjects were no longer in psychotherapy (the duration of psychotherapeutic treatment was 6 months).

The investigators (Woody et al. 1986) drew several conclusions about the psychotherapy of opiate addicts: 1) Both expressive-supportive and cognitive-behavioral psychotherapy can help those narcotic addicts who can become engaged in and will regularly attend such a treatment process. 2) Patients with significant psychiatric disturbances are the best candidates for psychotherapy and will benefit from it the most. 3) The psychotherapist must be integrated into the overall treatment program and must collaborate with other staff members in the treatment. The researchers believed that there were clear benefits to locating the psychotherapy in the same facility as the rest of the methadone maintenance program. Psychotherapy that is fragmented from the rest of the treatment is unlikely to succeed.

Psychotherapy with drug abusers is a treatment approach that indirectly addresses the addiction by focusing on the associated psychopathology. Most clinicians believe that abstinence from the abused substance is a prerequisite to adequate treatment through psychotherapeutic technique of the underlying disturbances—anxiety, depression, personality disorder, self-esteem problems, or ego deficits. The exception would be a drug substitution program such as methadone maintenance. Once abstinence is achieved, the addict often feels despair at having given up something more than a drug—a valued part of the self (Treece and Khantzian 1986). Both therapist and patient realize that abstinence alone does not automatically lead to changes in other areas of life. As abstinent addicts struggle with their longing for the drug and their grief over its loss, the therapist must address their tenaciously defended belief that drug use is an adaptive solution to life's problems. The therapist must identify the underlying problems of modulating affects, of regulating self-esteem, and of relating to others, so as to help the addict discover alternative answers to those problems.

One difficulty that psychotherapists will most likely encounter is the alexithymia common in many addicts (Krystal 1982-83). In other words, most of these patients are unable to recognize and identify their internal feeling states. A good deal of education may have to occur during the early phases of therapy, with the therapist explaining how the experience of unpleasant feelings initially leads to drug abuse. These patients must be helped to contain and tolerate their affects so that they can substitute words describing their inner states for actions such as the ingestion of a drug. The therapist can assist patients in this regard by identifying feelings that occur during the therapy hour.

An individual psychotherapy process is much more likely to be successful in the context of a comprehensive program. Khantzian (1986) suggested the concept of the primary care therapist—an individual who facilitates the addict's involvement with all treatment modalities. The therapist analyzes the addict's resistance to accepting other forms of treatment, such as NA or group therapy, but also provides a holding environment to deal with the strong affects mobilized in the treatment process. The primary care therapist must also participate in treatment decisions involving other modalities. In this model, the emphasis is more supportive than expressive at the beginning of treatment, and the therapist's role is similar to that of the hospital doctor working with an inpatient.

Treece and Khantzian (1986) have identified four essential components of a treatment program for mastery of drug dependence: 1) a substitute for the dependency on chemicals (e.g., NA, an alternative system of beliefs, or a benign dependency on a person or religious institution); 2) adequate treatment for other psychiatric disorders, including appropriate psychotropic medication and psychotherapy; 3) enforced abstinence (e.g., drug antagonists, urine surveillance, probation, drug substitutes such as methadone, external support systems) during a psychological maturational process; and 4) promotion of growth and structural personality change through psychotherapy.

Wurmser (1987b) also advocated a multi-pronged approach, but with more expressive psychotherapy. Since he conceptualized an overbearing superego as central to the pathogenesis of compulsive drug use, he cautioned therapists to avoid being punitive or critical. He suggested that therapists must not punish or warn their patients about drug use. A more appropriate role, in Wurmser's view, is to understand the superego pressures on the patient, much as in work with a severely neurotic patient. He also believed that therapists should have the luxury of looking at underlying issues rather than of just focusing on the drug abuse, which can be taken up by other members of the treatment team.

Although no major controlled studies of dynamic group psychotherapy with addicts share the methodological sophistication of the Veterans Administration–Penn Study on individual psychotherapy, group psychotherapy has become a component of many programs because of the clinical impression that it is helpful to many patients. Since group psychotherapy is rarely the only treatment modality, it is difficult to determine whether any specific therapeutic aspects of group therapy are not also present in other modalities. However, practically speaking, many addicts feel support by talking with others who have had the same problem. Also, since denial is a prominent defense in all substance abusers, a group setting of peers facilitates a powerful confrontation of the denial, and it gets addicts to accept the seriousness of their substance abuse. The same caveats about the negative effects of overly aggressive confrontation that were mentioned in the section on group psychotherapy of alcoholics also apply to group psychotherapy of addicts. Effective groups provide as much support as they do confrontation. Inpatient programs often rely more on groups for the practical reason that enforcing attendance is easier with inpatients than with outpatients (Woody et al. 1986). A commonly encountered resistance to groups in both inpatient and outpatient facilities is that many members may have committed crimes and are therefore reluctant to open up in groups for fear that confidentiality will be breached.

In summary, the indications for expressive-supportive psychotherapy can be conceptualized as the following: 1) serious psychopathology other than drug abuse; 2) engagement in an overall treatment program that includes NA or another support group, enforced abstinence, possibly a drug substitute such as methadone, and appropriate psychotropic medication; 3) no diagnosis of antisocial personality disorder (unless depression is also present) (treatment considerations with antisocial personality disorder are discussed in detail in Chapter 16); and 4) sufficient motivation to attend appointments and become engaged in the process. The indications for an expressive or supportive emphasis after the process is well launched are largely determined by the same factors that determine the emphasis in any other psychotherapeutic process (Table 4-2 in Chapter 4).

Eating Disorders

Anorexia nervosa and bulimia nervosa appear to be disorders of our time. The electronic media bombard the public with images of slender women who "have it all." In many areas of Western culture, food is in abundance, a precondition for binge eating behavior. Individuals affected by these disorders tend to be Caucasian, educated, female, economically advantaged, and ensconced in Western cultures (Johnson et al. 1989). Anorexia nervosa is virtually unknown in countries where thinness is not considered a virtue (Powers 1984). Media images of females, moreover, suggest that external appearance is far more important than internal identity. Although intrapsychic and biological factors should not be minimized in the etiology and pathogenesis of eating disorders, those factors clearly interface with a particular sociocultural period in Western civilization to produce a syndrome that reflects the culture. Anorexia nervosa has more than doubled in incidence since the 1960s, while the prevalence of bulimia nervosa has been found to be 1–5 percent among high school and college females (Mitchell and Eckert 1987). These disturbing figures indicate that the disorder may be an increasingly common solution to a variety of intrapsychic, familial, and environmental stressors.

Anorexia Nervosa

The label *anorexia nervosa* can be misleading, since the first word of the phrase implies that loss of appetite is the central problem. The diagnostic hallmark of anorexia nervosa is actually a fanatical pursuit of thinness related to overwhelming fear of becoming fat. An arbitrary cutoff of less than 85 percent of minimal normal body weight for age and height is often used to make the diagnosis. Amenorrhea is a prominent feature of anorexia nervosa in females. Although 5-10 percent of cases are male, their clinical features and psychodynamics are remarkably similar to those of females.

Psychodynamic understanding. For the last two decades, the seminal contributions of Hilde Bruch (1973, 1978, 1982, 1987) have served as a beacon in the darkness for clinicians treating anorexic patients. She observed that the preoccupation with food and weight is a relatively late occurrence emblematic of a more fundamental disturbance in self-concept. Most patients with anorexia nervosa have a thoroughgoing conviction that they are utterly powerless and ineffective. The illness often occurs in "good girls" who have spent their life trying to please their parents, only to suddenly become stubborn and negativistic in adolescence. The body is often experienced as separate from the self, as though it belongs to the parents. These patients lack any sense of autonomy to the point that they do not even feel in control of their bodily functions. The premorbid defensive posture of being a perfect little girl ordinarily defends against a profound underlying feeling of worthlessness. Anorexia nervosa develops, in Bruch's (1987) own words, as "an attempt at self-cure, to develop through discipline over the body a sense of selfhood and interpersonal effectiveness. Anorexics transform their anxiety and psychological problems through manipulation of food intake and size" (p. 211).

Bruch traced the developmental origins of anorexia nervosa back to a disturbed relationship between the infant and its mother. Specifically, the mother appears to parent the child according to her own needs rather than those of the child. When the child-initiated cues do not receive confirming and validating responses, the child cannot develop a healthy sense of self. Instead, the child experiences herself simply as an extension of her mother, not as a center of autonomy in her own right. This understanding is in

keeping with early psychoanalytic formulations about the pathogenesis of psychosomatic disorders in children in which an "appersonation" of the child was noted (Sperling 1944). The child is not
perceived as a separate individual, but rather as the "right arm" of
the mother.

Bruch, then, understood the behavior of the anorexic patient
as a frantic effort to gain admiration and validation as a unique and
special person with extraordinary attributes. More recently, Bruch
(1987) has suggested that the clinical picture may be changing
somewhat because it is more and more difficult for the anorexic
patient to feel unique, given the increasing prevalence of the disorder and the media attention on eating disorders of all kinds. The
illness has now become imbued with a sense of competition to be
the thinnest or the most unique.

Masterson (1972, 1977) has noted a similarity between the
dynamics of certain anorexic patients and those of patients with
borderline personality disorders (see Chapter 14). Lacking any
sense of identity, the child develops a false self to please the mother.
The little girl tries to be the perfect child as a way to reassure herself
that her mother will not abandon her. This forced role causes
resentment to build up over the years, however, and the anorexic
syndrome develops as a full-scale rebellion in which the patient
attempts to assert her true self which has long lain dormant and
undeveloped.

Family therapists, such as Selvini Palazzoli (1978) and
Minuchin (Minuchin et al. 1978), have confirmed and elaborated
some of the dynamic concepts of Bruch and Masterson. Minuchin
and his colleagues have described a pattern of enmeshment in the
families of anorexic patients, where there is a general absence of
generational and personal boundaries. Each family member is overinvolved in the life of every other family member to the extent that
no one feels a sense of separate identity apart from the family matrix.
Selvini Palazzoli (1978) has also noted that patients with anorexia
nervosa have been unable to psychologically separate from their
mother, which results in a failure to achieve any stable sense of their
own body. The body is thus often perceived as if it is inhabited by a
bad maternal introject, and starvation may be an attempt to stop the
growth of this hostile, intrusive internal object.

The extreme defensive posture of anorexia nervosa suggests
that a powerful underlying impulse warrants such a strategy. Indeed,
Boris (1984a) has noted that intense greed forms the core of
anorexia nervosa. Oral desires are so unacceptable, however, that
they must be dealt with projectively. Through projective identification, the greedy, demanding self-representation is transferred to the
parents. In response to the patient's refusal to eat, the parents
become obsessed with whether or not the patient is eating; they

become the ones who have desires. In a formulation influenced by Kleinian thinking, Boris conceptualized anorexia nervosa as an inability to receive good things from others because of an inordinate desire to possess. Any act of receiving food or love confronts these patients squarely with the fact that they cannot possess what they desire. Their solution is to not receive anything from anyone. Envy and greed are often closely linked in the unconscious. The patient envies the mother's good possessions—love, compassion, nurturance—but to receive them simply increases the envy. Renouncing them supports the unconscious fantasy of spoiling what is envied, not unlike the fox in Aesop's fable about the "sour grapes." The patient conveys the following message: "There is nothing good available for me to possess, so I will simply renounce all my desires." Such renunciation makes the anorexic patient the object of the desire of others and, in her fantasy, the object of their envy and admiration, because they are "impressed" by her self-control. Food symbolizes their positive qualities that she desires in herself; being enslaved by hunger is preferable to desiring to possess the maternal figure.

Most developmental formulations of the origins of anorexia nervosa focus on the mother-daughter dyad. Bemporad and Ratey (1985), however, have observed a characteristic pattern of paternal involvement with anorexic daughters. The typical father was superficially caring and supportive but emotionally abandoning of his daughter whenever she truly needed him. In addition, many fathers of anorexic patients seek emotional nurturance from—rather than give it to—their daughters. Both parents often are experiencing serious disappointment in their marriage, leading each parent to seek emotional sustenance from their daughter. In self psychological terms, the daughter may be treated as a selfobject that provides mirroring and validating functions for each parent but denies her own sense of self.

To summarize our psychodynamic understanding of anorexia nervosa, the overt behavior of self-starvation is a multiply determined symptom. It is 1) a desperate attempt to be special and unique, 2) an attack on the false sense of self fostered by parental expectations, 3) an assertion of a nascent true self, 4) an attack on a hostile maternal introject viewed as equivalent to the body, 5) a defense against greed and desire, and 6) an effort to make others rather than the patient feel greedy and helpless.

These psychodynamic factors are also accompanied by certain characteristic cognitive features. These features include misperception of one's own body image, all-or-none thinking, magical thinking, and obsessive-compulsive thoughts and rituals. The presence of obsessive-compulsive symptoms has led some researchers to wonder whether obsessive-compulsive personality disorder coexists with anorexia nervosa. This assumption is confounded by the notorious unreliability of personality disorder diagnoses in the presence of starvation (Kaplan and Woodside 1987; Powers 1984). Many symptoms, including obsessive-compulsive behavior, appear secondary to starvation. Also, premorbid personality characteristics are accentuated in states of nutritional deficiency. The fear of being fat itself has been shown to moderate when the patient begins to eat and gain weight (Garfinkel and Garner 1982).

Treatment approaches.   Clinicians who treat patients who have anorexia nervosa are in consensus that the treatment goals must not be focused narrowly on weight gain (Boris 1984a, 1984b; Bruch 1973, 1978, 1982, 1987; Chessick 1985; Hsu 1986; Powers 1984). A "two-track" approach, advocated by Garner et al. (1986), includes a first step of restoration of eating for weight gain. Once this step is accomplished, the second step of psychotherapeutic intervention can begin. Anorexic patients will show much greater improvement when provided with a mixture of family therapy and dynamic individual therapy than when they are simply managed with educational measures designed to control weight (Hall and Crisp 1983). Long-term, individual, expressive-supportive psychotherapy is the cornerstone of the treatment. Unless the patient's underlying disturbance of the self and the associated distortions of internal object relations are addressed, the patient will follow a course of repeated relapse and revolving-door hospital admissions (Bruch 1982). For those patients living at home, family therapy may be a valuable adjunct to individual therapy. Although some patients appear to benefit from group psychotherapy (Lieb and Thompson 1984; Polivy 1981) the limited data suggest that those who benefit most do not have associated personality disorders (Maher 1984).

Hospitalization may also be a beneficial adjunct to individual psychotherapy. Although no indications for inpatient treatment are universally agreed on, a weight loss of 30 percent of normal body weight is a good rule of thumb to use to determine whether inpatient treatment is necessary (Garfinkel and Garner 1982). Approximately 80 percent of all anorexic patients will gain weight with hospital treatment (Hsu 1986) provided that the hospital staff can create a specific milieu. As described in Chapter 6, the hospital staff members must be wary of the patient's unconscious efforts to reenact the family struggle in the hospital milieu. They must convey an interest in helping the patient restore weight without becoming excessively concerned about it and without making demands similar to those the patient's parents would make. The patient can be helped to cope with the fear of losing control by arranging frequent but small meals with a member of the nursing staff available to discuss the patient's anxiety about eating. Weight gains should be reported to the patient with concomitant positive reinforcements. Any surreptitious vomiting or purging should be confronted and controlled with structural measures such as locking the bathroom door. Members of the treatment staff may need to reassure the patient that they will not allow too much weight gain, thus helping the patient develop a sense of trust in them.

If individual and family therapy were being conducted prior to admission, they should continue during hospitalization. If the patient's hospitalization is her first treatment contact, however, these adjunctive therapies should be implemented as part of the hospital treatment. Antidepressant medication is helpful with patients who meet the criteria for major depression. (Milder forms of depression improve with weight gain.) Brief hospitalizations are rarely curative, as are treatment programs that demand a normal average weight and then ignore the intense anxiety aroused by such a demand (Bruch 1982). At least 50 percent of the patients who successfully control their anorexia nervosa with inpatient treatment will relapse within a year (Hsu 1980). For the 20 percent who do not respond to brief hospitalization, long-term hospitalization is indicated.

Individual expressive-supportive psychotherapy often takes several years of painstaking work because of the formidable resistance posed by the anorexic patient. Four guiding principles of technique are useful (see Table 11-1).

1. *Avoid excessive investment in trying to change the eating behavior.* As Boris (1984a) observed, "What we call their symptoms they call their salvation" (p. 315). The patient views anorexia nervosa as the solution to an internal problem. Psychotherapists who immediately define it as a problem that must be changed reduce their chances of forming a viable therapeutic alliance. The behavior associated with anorexia nervosa elicits demands and expectations for change from the patient's parents. Through projective identification, the therapist is likely to experience powerful pressure to identify with the patient's projected internal objects that are associated with the parents. Instead of acting on that pressure and becoming a parental figure, the therapist must try to understand the patient's internal world. One form of this reenactment is the equation of eating and talking. Just as the patient provokes

Table 11-1.   Technical principles in the psychotherapy of anorexic patients

1. Avoid excessive investment in trying to change the eating behavior.
2. Avoid interpretations early in the therapy.
3. Carefully monitor countertransference.
4. Examine cognitive distortions.

her parents by refusing to eat, she will attempt to provoke the therapist by refusing to talk (Mintz 1988). At the beginning of the therapy, it may thus be helpful to clarify that the primary goal of the treatment is to understand the patient's underlying emotional disturbance rather than the problem of not eating (Bruch 1982; Chessick 1985). Although Boris (1984b) advocated complete avoidance of psychotherapeutic focus on eating, Bruch (1982) suggested that psychotherapy is not feasible unless the patient weighs in the neighborhood of 95 pounds. She explains to her patients that their capacity for thinking and communicating will improve if they can get their weight at least to that level.

2. *Avoid interpretations early in the therapy.* Interpretations of unconscious wishes or fears will be experienced by the anorexic patient as a repetition of her life story. *Someone else* is telling her what she really feels, while her conscious experience is minimized and invalidated. On the contrary, the therapist's task should be to validate and empathize with the patient's internal experience (Bruch 1987; Chessick 1985). The therapist should take an active interest in what the patient thinks and feels, conveying the message that the patient is an autonomous person entitled to her own ideas about her illness. Of major importance is helping the patient define her own feeling states. The actions and decisions stemming from these feelings must be legitimized and respected. The therapist can help the patient explore various options but should refrain from telling her what to do (Chessick 1985). This empathic, ego-building, supportive approach in the early phases of therapy will facilitate introjection of the therapist as a benign object. Bruch (1987) suggested emphasizing the positive and conceptualizing the therapy as an experience in which patients will discover their positive qualities. She acknowledged that her approach has many similarities to Kohut's (1984) self psychological approach. Chessick (1985) shared this view that insight into unconscious conflict is unlikely to be curative with these patients. Although slightly more optimistic about the use of interpretations, Boris (1984b) recommended withholding interpretations until the patient finds herself. Even then, he advocated talking "to the air" instead of directly to the patient, thus providing some distance in the relationship and respecting her boundaries. Such interpretations should be delivered as hypotheses, as though talking to an imaginary colleague rather than as making a definitive pronouncement directly to the patient.

3. *Carefully monitor countertransference.* Anorexic patients commonly believe that their parents want them to gain weight so that other people won't view the parents as failures (Powers 1984). The therapist is likely to become anxious about similar matters. Therapists who work within the framework of a comprehensive treat-

ment team, in particular, may begin to feel that others are negatively judging their work if their patient fails to gain weight. This countertransference concern may lead the therapist to fall into the trap of identifying with the patient's parents. The ideal situation for individual psychotherapy is for another treater to monitor weight gain, leaving the therapist free to explore the patient's underlying psychological issues. When hospitalization is required for weight control, the admitting psychiatrist can manage food intake while the psychotherapist continues the psychotherapeutic work in the hospital. In this setting the psychotherapist can work productively with the team.

4. *Examine cognitive distortions.* Misperceptions of the patient's body and illogical cognitive beliefs should be explored with the patient nonjudgmentally (Powers 1984). The therapist thus serves as an auxiliary ego to help the patient sharpen her powers of observation and her critical thinking (Chessick 1985). Clearly, the psychotherapist must assume an educative role with these patients, helping them understand the effects of starvation on cognition. However, the therapist must seek to educate while making no demand for change. Alternatively, the therapist can simply explore the consequences of the patient's choices.

These technical guidelines, while useful, are not to be taken as a "cookbook" formula for the psychotherapy of anorexic patients. Therapists must be flexible, persistent, and durable in the face of the patient's tendency to "wait out" the therapy process until she can once again be left alone. Body image distortions, which often approach delusional proportions, may be particularly refractory to educational and therapeutic efforts. Therapists must be wary of countertransference despair and frustration that lead them to force the patient to "see things as they really are."

Bulimia Nervosa

Patients with bulimia nervosa are generally distinguished from those with anorexia nervosa on the basis of relatively normal weight and the presence of binge eating and purging. Emaciated patients who are also binge eating and purging are often classified as anorexics, bulimic subgroup (Hsu 1986). This diagnostic classification reflects how the concept of anorexia nervosa has become blurred by the cultural fascination with bulimia (Bruch 1987). In Bruch's view, the two syndromes have little in common—the rigid self-discipline and harsh conscience of the anorexic patient contrast sharply with the impulse-ridden, irresponsible, and undisciplined behavior of the bulimic. The condensed term *bulimarexia* is thus a "semantic atrocity" (Bruch 1987, p. 216), in that it mistakenly implies similarity.

Bruch's view, however, is not supported by accumulating data that suggest considerable linkage between the two disorders (Garner et al. 1986). At least 40–50 percent of all anorexic patients also have bulimia (Garfinkel et al. 1980; Hall et al. 1984; Hsu et al. 1979). Long-term follow-up research indicates that eating-disordered patients commonly move between the two syndromes during the course of their lives (Vandereycken and Pierloot 1983). Finally, the clinical features and psychometric profiles of both groups have many similarities (Garner et al. 1985).

Part of the reason for the blurring of diagnostic boundaries between anorexic and bulimic behavior is that the clinical picture can be so varied. Concurrent psychiatric disorders are common (Yager 1984), and over half of all bulimic patients may suffer from associated personality disorders (Johnson et al. 1989). Yager (1984) has eloquently stated this observation:

> Bulimia is not a disease. Nor is it a simple habit. Bulimia is heterogeneous and, like pneumonia, it may result from a variety of causes. I have found it useful to conceptualize bulimia as a habit or behavioral pattern embedded in a personality, in turn embedded in a biology, and all this embedded in a culture in which bulimia seems to be developing at an increasing rate. (p. 63)

Psychodynamic understanding. When considering the psychodynamics of bulimia, therapists must keep in mind this heterogeneity. The various contributors to our dynamic understanding of bulimia are likely to be analogous to the proverbial blind men reporting their perceptions of an elephant based on their particular vantage point. As always, dynamic understanding must be individualized. A clinical picture of bulimia may be observed in patients with vastly different character structures, ranging from psychotic through borderline to neurotic (Wilson 1983). The two disorders are essentially opposite sides of the same coin (Mintz 1988). While the anorexic patient is characterized by both greater ego strength and greater superego control, the bulimic patient may suffer from a generalized inability to delay impulse discharge, based on a weakened ego and a lax superego. Binge eating and purging are not usually isolated impulse problems. They typically coexist with impulsive, self-destructive sexual relationships and with polydrug abuse.

Mintz (1988) has observed that patients may shift from anorexia to bulimia when powerful urges to binge finally overcome and erode defense mechanisms such as repression and denial. The object relations of the bulimic patient can be the flip side of those of the anorexic patient as well. Bulimic patients typically use interpersonal relationships as a way to receive damage or punishment from external sources, while anorexic patients tend to withdraw from interpersonal relationships. Mintz explained the source of the bulimic patient's need for punishment as an enormous reservoir of unconscious aggression directed toward parental figures. This rage is displaced onto food, which is then cannibalistically destroyed. Neither anorexic patients nor bulimic patients can regulate their relationships satisfactorily, so they also displace conflicts in relationships onto food. The anorexic patient maintains control over her aggressive feelings toward people by refusing to eat, while the bulimic patient symbolically destroys and incorporates people by gorging.

Those authors who have studied the developmental origins of bulimia have identified extensive difficulty with separation both in the parents and in the individual patient. A common theme in the developmental history of bulimic patients is the absence of a transitional object, such as a pacifier or blanket, to help the child separate psychologically from her mother (Goodsitt 1983). This developmental struggle to separate may be played out instead by using the body itself as a transitional object (Sugarman and Kurash 1982), with the ingestion of food representing a wish for symbiotic merger with the mother and the expulsion of food an effort at separation from her. Like the mothers of anorexic patients, the parents of children who grow up to be bulimic often relate to their children as extensions of themselves (Humphrey and Stern 1988; Strober and Humphrey 1987). These children are used as selfobjects to validate the self of the parent. Each member of the family depends on all the other members to maintain a sense of cohesion. Although this pattern characterizes the families of anorexic patients, a particular mode of managing unacceptable "bad" qualities is predominant in bulimic families. The bulimic family system apparently has a strong need for everyone to see themselves as "all good." Unacceptable qualities in the parents are often projected into the bulimic child, who becomes the repository of all "badness." By unconsciously identifying with these projections, she becomes the carrier of all the family's greed and impulsivity. The resulting homeostatic balance keeps the focus on the "sick" child rather than on conflicts in or between the parents.

In many instances, then, bulimic patients concretize the object-relations mechanisms of introjection and projection. Ingestion and expulsion of food may directly reflect the introjection and projection of aggressive, or "bad," introjects. In many cases, this splitting process is further concretized by the patient. She may regard protein as "good" food, which is therefore retained rather than purged, and carbohydrates or junk food as "bad" food, which is consumed in huge quantities, only to be regurgitated. On the surface, this strategy of managing aggression may be compelling—

the expulsion of badness in the form of vomit leaves the patient feeling good. However, the residual feeling of "goodness" is unstable because it is based on splitting, denial, and projection of aggression rather than integration of the bad with the good.

Treatment considerations. The most important single principle in the treatment of bulimia is individualization of the treatment plan. Concurrent psychiatric disorders, such as depression, personality disorders, and drug abuse, should be addressed as part of comprehensive treatment planning. "Assembly line treatment programs" (Yager 1984, p. 64) that treat all bulimic patients alike will only help a fraction of them because of a failure to recognize and appreciate the inherent heterogeneity of the bulimic population. About one-third of all bulimic patients represent a relatively healthy subgroup who will respond well to a time-limited approach involving brief cognitive-behavioral therapy and a psychoeducational program (Johnson and Connors 1987; Johnson et al 1989). Support groups, such as Overeaters Anonymous (OA), may also sustain this subgroup of patients without further treatment.

Although dynamic approaches may not be indicated or necessary for this subgroup, they still may benefit the majority of bulimic patients. Among these nonresponders, as many as two-thirds may have borderline personality disorder (Johnson et al. 1989), while others may have other personality disorders or significant depression. These patients usually require long-term, expressive-supportive psychotherapy and often require psychopharmacologic intervention as well. Many patients also frankly resent a behavioral approach to their bulimic symptoms (Yager 1984). Focusing on the patient's overt behavior, while neglecting her internal world, may recapitulate the patient's experience of growing up with parents who are more concerned about surface than substance. Yager (1984) has suggested that as many as 50 percent of all bulimic patients are dissatisfied with behavior modification techniques. Some patients will even experience the task of writing a daily diary about their eating habits as demeaning, because they may view their eating problems as symptomatic of more fundamental disturbances. Treatment that does not match the patient's interests and belief system is doomed to failure (Yager 1984).

Moreover, effective behavioral approaches, whether with sexual disorders or eating disorders, require a solid therapeutic alliance. Johnson et al. (1987) found that symptomatic management of bulimia from a cognitive-behavioral perspective depends on a strong therapeutic alliance and that the analysis of transference facilitates the development and maintenance of that alliance. In their model, one therapist performs both tasks (i.e., reinforcement of symptom control and analysis of transference that interferes with the follow-through of behavioral techniques).

Bulimia nervosa can be life-threatening. Patients have been known to alter their electrolyte balance sufficiently to precipitate cardiac arrest. Blood chemistry monitoring should therefore be part of the outpatient management of these patients, with hospitalization as a backup strategy. Since many bulimic patients also suffer from borderline personality and major affective disorders, hospitalization may be required in the face of a suicide attempt or severe self-mutilation. The hospital treatment must follow an individualized comprehensive treatment plan, in addition to the task of gaining symptom control through locking bathrooms, implementing a normal meal schedule, providing psychoeducational assistance from a dietitian, and encouraging the keeping of a diary. Hospitalization often provides the therapist with an opportunity to better understand the patient's internal object relations; thus, it facilitates more sophisticated diagnostic understanding and more precise treatment planning:

Ms. U was a 19-year-old college student with a mixture of bulimic and anorexic symptoms. She was hospitalized after "firing" her psychotherapist and completely losing control of her binge eating and purging. Her parents, who were quite exasperated with her behavior, brought her to the hospital because they felt hopeless about ever getting her to eat properly. During the first week of hospitalization, Ms. U informed her hospital doctor that she planned to remain aloof and distant because she did not want to get attached to a doctor again only to be disappointed. Regular meals and group meetings were immediately implemented, but the patient refused to go to meals or to attend the group. She insisted that she was capable of dieting by only eating when and what she wanted. She pointed out to her doctor that her weight was remaining constant, so there was no need for concern.

The nursing staff became increasingly irritated with Ms. U for her utter lack of cooperation. The more stubborn and resistant the patient became, the more the staff insisted that she follow the structure of the hospital program. In one staff meeting, the hospital doctor observed that the patient had succeeded in recapitulating her family situation. By asserting that she should have control over her diet, she provoked others into attempting to take control of her eating. She could then feel victimized by the controlling forces around her, just as she felt victimized by her parents.

Ms. U's doctor met with her and pointed out to Ms. U that she was attempting to provoke the staff into a reenactment of her family situation. She asked the patient to reflect on what she might gain from this reenactment. Ms. U responded by indicating to her doctor that she was not interested in talking. Three days later, she told her doctor that she had been hoarding medications and sharp objects in a locked drawer in her hospital room so that she might attempt suicide. She said that she had decided to tell her doctor because she really did not want to die. She also indicated that it was terribly difficult for her to communicate feelings to her doctor because she believed that she would become uncontrollably dependent and would lose any sense of her own self. She was certain that dependency on her doctor would lead to her being exploited and mistreated according to the doctor's needs rather than her own treatment needs.

This information helped the hospital staff understand Ms. U's resistance to the treatment structure. By refusing to cooperate, this patient was attempting to establish a sense of self independent of the demands and expectations of others. Cooperation with the staff and collaboration with her hospital doctor carried the risk that she would become a mere extension of others, as she had in her family. Once this underlying anxiety surfaced, the staff members allowed Ms. U to have more say in her eating program. With a member of the nursing staff, she was able to collaborate on and then follow a program that was acceptable to both of them.

Just when Ms. U seemed to be improving, however, her hospital doctor received a call at home on Christmas morning as her family was opening presents. A hospital nurse was calling to inform her that Ms. U had smuggled in and then taken a large number of laxatives and had been having diarrhea all morning. The nurse was worried that Ms. U might require emergency medical treatment, so Ms. U's doctor felt compelled to go to the hospital to see the patient. Two days later, when Ms. U was medically stable, her doctor confronted her about the transference hostility involved in her purging, then suggested that perhaps Ms. U had wished to spoil her doctor's Christmas morning. Although the patient blandly denied any such possibility, her doctor had to suppress intense anger at Ms. U for the timing of her acting out. It gradually dawned on the doctor that the act of purging had enabled the patient to expel her own aggression. As a result, she could not relate to the doctor's interpretation of her act as hostile. The doctor's anger suggested projective identification, however, with the doctor unconsciously serving as a container of the patient's projected anger.

Although this case illustrates a more refractory patient with borderline personality disorder as part of the clinical picture, the transference/countertransference struggles are not atypical of what individual therapists commonly encounter with these patients. Therapists may find themselves repeatedly provoked into accepting the "badness" the patient is attempting to expel. They may also feel "vomited on" when the patient repeatedly spits back at them all their therapeutic efforts. The recapitulation of the family pattern in hospital treatment or in individual psychotherapy helps the clinician understand the patient's role within the family system. Because bulimia is so often part of a homeostatic balance in the family, family therapy or family intervention in association with individual therapy is frequently needed. By ignoring the family system, the therapist runs the risk that the patient's improvement will be terribly threatening to other family members. Defensive reactions to this threat may include an insidious undermining of the bulimic patient's treatment or the development of serious dysfunction in another family member. The family's need for the bulimic patient's illness must be respected, and the parents must feel "held" and validated so that they will not sabotage the treatment (Humphrey and Stern 1988).

Dynamic group psychotherapy may also be a useful adjunctive treatment. In a review of 18 different reports of this modality with bulimic patients in an outpatient setting, Oesterheld et al. (1987) found reason for guarded optimism. The consensus was that group psychotherapy effectively reduced bulimic symptoms by an average of 70 percent. However, the figures appear inflated because most studies excluded dropouts from their calculations. Dropout rates tended to be high even though most groups had excluded patients with borderline personality disorder and other severe character pathology. Long-term follow-up data were also lacking. The group therapists appeared to agree, much as did the individual therapists, that a stable remission requires both insight and symptom control.

In summary, the indication for a dynamic approach to bulimia nervosa is a lack of response to time-limited psychoeducational and cognitive-behavioral methods. As with anorexia nervosa, individual psychotherapy of an expressive-supportive nature is the cornerstone of treatment. Family interventions in the form of support, education, and possibly family therapy are also generally necessary to validate the individual therapy. Some form of symptom control is required in conjunction with the other approaches. Brief hospitalization, support groups such as OA, and group psychotherapy can all assist the patient with symptom control. Some individual psychotherapists also consider symptom control as part of the treatment process. A substantial subset of bulimic patients with associated severe character pathology, suicidal tendencies, and propensities toward life-threatening electrolyte disturbances will require psychotherapy in the context of long-term hospitalization. These patients defy the most diligent efforts of treaters to structure their lives. They seem bent on a self-destructive course that may indeed be fatal without extended hospital treatment.

References

Balint M: The Basic Fault: Therapeutic Aspects of Regression. London, Tavistock Publications, 1968

Bemporad JR, Ratey J: Intensive psychotherapy of former anorexic individuals. Am J Psychother 39:454–466, 1985

Blatt SJ, McDonald C, Sugarman A, et al: Psychodynamic theories of opiate addiction: new directions for research. Clinical Psychology Review 4:159–189, 1984a

Blatt SJ, Rounsaville B, Eyre SL, et al: The psychodynamics of opiate addiction. J Nerv Ment Dis 172:342–352, 1984b

Boris HN: The problem of anorexia nervosa. Int J Psychoanal 65:315–322, 1984a

Boris HN: On the treatment of anorexia nervosa. Int J Psychoanal 65:435–442, 1984b

Brandsma JM, Pattison EM: The outcome of group psychotherapy [with] alcoholics: an empirical review. Am J Drug Alcohol Abuse 11:151–162, 1985

Bratter TE: Some pre-treatment group psychotherapy considerations with alcoholic and drug-addicted individuals. Psychotherapy: Theory, Research and Practice 18:508–515, 1981

Brown S: Treating the Alcoholic: A Developmental Model of Recovery. New York, John Wiley, 1985

Bruch H: Eating Disorders: Obesity, Anorexia Nervosa, and the Person Within. New York, Basic Books, 1973

Bruch H: The Golden Cage: The Enigma of Anorexia Nervosa. Cambridge, MA, Harvard University Press, 1978

Bruch H: Psychotherapy in anorexia nervosa. International Journal of Eating Disorders 1(4):3–14, 1982

Bruch H: The changing picture of an illness: anorexia nervosa, in Attachment and the Therapeutic Process. Edited by Sacksteder JL, Schwartz DP, Akabane Y. Madison, CT, International Universities Press, 1987, pp 205–222

Chessick RD: Clinical notes toward the understanding and intensive psychotherapy of adult eating disorders. Annual of Psychoanalysis 22/23:301–322, 1985

Cooper DE: The role of group psychotherapy in the treatment of substance abusers. Am J Psychother 41:55–67, 1987

Dodes LM: Abstinence from alcohol in long-term individual psychotherapy with alcoholics. Am J Psychother 38:248–256, 1984

Dodes LM: The psychology of combining dynamic psychotherapy and Alcoholics Anonymous. Bull Menninger Clin 52:283–293, 1988

Donovan JM: An etiologic model of alcoholism. Am J Psychiatry 143:1–11, 1986

Garfinkel PE, Garner DM: Anorexia Nervosa: A Multidimensional Perspective. New York, Brunner/Mazel, 1982

Garfinkel PE, Moldofsky H, Garner DM: The heterogeneity of anorexia nervosa: bulimia as a distinct subgroup. Arch Gen Psychiatry 37:1036–1040, 1980

Garner DM, Garfinkel PE, O'Shaughnessy M: The validity of the distinction between bulimia with and without anorexia nervosa. Am J Psychiatry 142:518–587, 1985

Garner DM, Garfinkel PE, Irvine MJ: Integration and sequencing of treatment approaches for eating disorders. Psychother Psychosom 46:67–75, 1986

Goodsitt A: Self-regulatory disturbances in eating disorders. International Journal of Eating Disorders 2(3):51–60, 1983

Goodwin DW: Alcoholism and heredity. Arch Gen Psychiatry 36:57–61, 1979

Hall A, Crisp AH: Brief psychotherapy in the treatment of anorexia nervosa: preliminary findings, in Anorexia Nervosa: Recent Developments in Research. Edited by Darby PL, Garfinkel PE, Garner DM, et al. New York, Alan R Liss, 1983, pp 427–439

Hall A, Slim E, Hawker F, et al: Anorexia nervosa: long-term outcome in 50 female patients. Br J Psychiatry 145:407–413, 1984

Hartocollis P: Borderline syndrome and alcoholism, in Encyclopedic Handbook of Alcoholism. Edited by Pattison EM, Kaufman E. New York, Gardner Press, 1982, pp 628–635

Hsu LKG: Outcome of anorexia nervosa: a review of the literature (1954 to 1978). Arch Gen Psychiatry 37:1041–1046, 1980

Hsu LKG: The treatment of anorexia nervosa. Am J Psychiatry 143:573–581, 1986

Hsu LKG, Crisp AH, Harding B: Outcome of anorexia nervosa. Lancet 1:61–65, 1979

Humphrey LL, Stern S: Object relations and the family system in bulimia: a theoretical integration. Journal of Marital and Family Therapy 14:337–350, 1988

Johnson C, Connors ME: The Etiology and Treatment of Bulimia Nervosa: A Biopsychosocial Perspective. New York, Basic Books, 1987

Johnson C, Connors ME, Tobin D: Symptom management of bulimia. J Consult Clin Psychol 55:668–676, 1987

Johnson C, Tobin DL, Enright A: Prevalence and clinical characteristics of borderline patients in an eating-disordered population. J Clin Psychiatry 50:9–15, 1989

Kandel DB, Kessler RC, Margulies RZ: Antecedents of adolescent initiation into stages of drug use: a developmental analysis, in Longitudinal Research on Drug Use. Edited by Kandel DB. New York, Hemisphere, 1978, pp 73–78

Kaplan AS, Woodside DB: Biological aspects of anorexia nervosa and bulimia nervosa. J Consult Clin Psychol 55:645–653, 1987

Kernberg OF: Borderline Conditions and Pathological Narcissism. New York, Jason Aronson, 1975

Khantzian EJ: Psychopathology, psychodynamics, and alcoholism, in Encyclopedic Handbook of Alcoholism. Edited by Pattison EM, Kaufman E. New York, Gardner Press, 1982, pp 581–597

Khantzian EJ: Psychotherapeutic interventions with substance abusers—the clinical context. J Subst Abuse Treat 2:83–88, 1985a

Khantzian EJ: The self-medication hypothesis of addictive disorders: focus on heroin and cocaine dependence. Am J Psychiatry 142:1259–1264, 1985b

Khantzian EJ: A contemporary psychodynamic approach to drug abuse treatment. Am J Drug Alcohol Abuse 12:213–222, 1986

Khantzian EJ, Treece C: DSM-III psychiatric diagnosis of narcotic addicts: recent findings. Arch Gen Psychiatry 42:1067–1071, 1985

Knight RF: Borderline states. Bull Menninger Clin 17:1–12, 1953

Kohut H: The Analysis of the Self: A Systematic Approach to the Psychoanalytic Treatment of Narcissistic Personality Disorder. New York, International Universities Press, 1971

Kohut H: How Does Analysis Cure? Edited by Goldberg A. Chicago, University of Chicago Press, 1984

Krystal H: Alexithymia and the effectiveness of psychoanalytic treatment. International Journal of Psychoanalytic Psychotherapy 9:353–378, 1982-83

Lieb RC, Thompson TL II: Group psychotherapy of four anorexia nervosa inpatients. Int J Group Psychother 34:639–642, 1984

Mack JE: Alcoholism, AA, and the governance of the self, in Dynamic Approaches to the Understanding and Treatment of Alcoholism. Edited by Bean MH, Zinberg NE. New York, Free Press, 1981, pp 128–162

Maher MS: Group therapy for anorexia nervosa, in Current Treatment of Anorexia Nervosa and Bulimia. Edited by Powers PS, Fernandez RC. Basel, Switzerland, Karger, 1984, pp 265–276

Masterson JF: Treatment of the Borderline Adolescent: A Developmental Approach. New York, John Wiley, 1972

Masterson JF: Primary anorexia nervosa in the borderline adolescent: an object-relations view, in Borderline Personality Disorders: The Concept, the Syndrome, the Patient. Edited by Hartocollis P. New York, International Universities Press, 1977, pp 475–494

Mintz IL: Self-destructive behavior in anorexia nervosa and bulimia, in Bulimia: Psychoanalytic Treatment and Theory. Edited by Schwartz HJ. Madison, CT, International Universities Press, 1988, pp 127–171

Minuchin S, Rosman BL, Baker L: Psychosomatic Families: Anorexia Nervosa in Context. Cambridge, MA, Harvard University Press, 1978

Mitchell JE, Eckert ED: Scope and significance of eating disorders. J Consult Clin Psychol 55:628–634, 1987

Nace EP, Saxon JJ Jr, Shore N: A comparison of borderline and non-borderline alcoholic patients. Arch Gen Psychiatry 40:54–56, 1983

Nathan PE: The addictive personality is the behavior of the addict. J Consult Clin Psychol 56:183–188, 1988

Nicholson B, Treece C: Object relations and differential treatment response to methadone maintenance. J Nerv Ment Dis 169:424–429, 1981

Oesterheld JR, McKenna MS, Gould NB: Group psychotherapy of bulimia: a critical review. Int J Group Psychother 37:163–184, 1987

Parloff MB, London P, Wolfe B: Individual psychotherapy and behavior change. Annu Rev Psychol 37:321–349, 1986

Paton S, Kessler R, Kandel D: Depressive mood and adolescent illicit drug use: a longitudinal analysis. J Genet Psychol 131:267–289, 1977

Pattison EM: Nonabstinent drinking goals in the treatment of alcoholism: a clinical typology. Arch Gen Psychiatry 33:923–930, 1976

Polivy J: Group psychotherapy as an adjunctive treatment for anorexia nervosa. Journal of Psychiatric Treatment and Evaluation 3:279–283, 1981

Powers PS: Psychotherapy of anorexia nervosa, in Current Treatment of Anorexia Nervosa and Bulimia. Edited by Powers PS, Fernandez RC. Basel, Switzerland, Karger, 1984, pp 18–47

Rinsley DB: The Dipsas revisited: comments on addiction and personality. J Subst Abuse Treat 5:1–7, 1988

Rosen A: Psychotherapy and Alcoholics Anonymous: can they be coordinated? Bull Menninger Clin 45:229–246, 1981

Rounsaville BJ, Weissman MM, Kleber H, et al: Heterogeneity of psychiatric diagnosis in treated opiate addicts. Arch Gen Psychiatry 39:161–166, 1982

Schuckit MA: Genetics and the risk for alcoholism. JAMA 254:2614–2617, 1985

Schuckit MA, Rimmer J, Reich T, et al: Alcoholism: antisocial traits in male alcoholics (abstract). Br J Psychiatry 117:575–576, 1970

Selvini Palazzoli M: Self-Starvation: From Individual to Family Therapy in the Treatment of Anorexia Nervosa. Translated by Pomerans A. New York, Jason Aronson, 1978

Sperling O: On appersonation. Int J Psychoanal 25:128–132, 1944

Strober M, Humphrey LL: Familial contributions to the etiology and course of anorexia nervosa and bulimia. J Consult Clin Psychol 55:654–659, 1987

Sugarman A, Kurash C: The body as a transitional object in bulimia. International Journal of Eating Disorders 1(4):57–67, 1982

Sutker PB, Allain AN: Issues in personality conceptualizations of addictive behaviors. J Consult Clin Psychol 56:172–182, 1988

Treece C: Assessment of ego functioning in studies of narcotic addiction, in The Broad Scope of Ego Function Assessment. Edited by Bellak L, Goldsmith LA. New York, John Wiley, 1984, pp 268–290

Treece C, Khantzian EJ: Psychodynamic factors in the development of drug dependence. Psychiatr Clin North Am 9:399–412, 1986

Vaglum S, Vaglum P: Borderline and other mental disorders in alcoholic female psychiatric patients: a case control study. Psychopathology 18:50–60, 1985

Vaillant GE: Dangers of psychotherapy in the treatment of alcoholism, in Dynamic Approaches to the Understanding and Treatment of Alcoholism. Edited by Bean MH, Zinberg NE. New York, Free Press, 1981, pp 36–54

Vaillant GE: The Natural History of Alcoholism. Cambridge, MA, Harvard University Press, 1983

Vaillant GE: The alcohol-dependent and drug-dependent person, in The New Harvard Guide to Psychiatry. Edited by Nicholi AM Jr. Cambridge, MA, Belknap Press of Harvard University Press, 1988, pp 700–713

Vandereycken W, Pierloot R: Long-term outcome research in anorexia nervosa: the problem of patient selection and follow-up duration. International Journal of Eating Disorders 2(4):237–242, 1983

Weissman MM, Myers JK: Clinical depression in alcoholism. Am J Psychiatry 137:372–373, 1980

Wilson CP (ed): Fear of Being Fat: The Treatment of Anorexia Nervosa and Bulimia. New York, Jason Aronson, 1983

Woody GE, Luborsky L, McLellan AT, et al: Psychotherapy for opiate addicts: does it help? Arch Gen Psychiatry 40:639–645, 1983

Woody GE, McLellan AT, Luborsky L, et al: Severity of psychiatric symptoms as a predictor of benefits from psychotherapy: the Veterans Administration–Penn Study. Am J Psychiatry 141:1172–1177, 1984

Woody GE, McLellan AT, Luborsky L, et al: Sociopathy and psychotherapy outcome. Arch Gen Psychiatry 42:1081–1086, 1985

Woody GE, McLellan AT, Luborsky L, et al: Psychotherapy for substance abuse. Psychiatr Clin North Am 9:547–562, 1986

Woody GE, McLellan AT, Luborsky L, et al: Twelve-month follow-up of psychotherapy for opiate dependents. Am J Psychiatry 144:590–596, 1987

Wurmser L: Psychoanalytic considerations of the etiology of compulsive drug use. J Am Psychoanal Assoc 22:820–843, 1974

Wurmser L: Flight from conscience: experience with the psychoanalytic treatment of compulsive drug abusers, part I: dynamic sequences, compulsive drug use. J Subst Abuse Treat 4:157–168, 1987a

Wurmser L: Flight from conscience: experience with the psychoanalytic treatment of compulsive drug abusers, part II: dynamic and therapeutic conclusions from the experiences with psychoanalysis of drug users. J Subst Abuse Treat 4:169–179, 1987b

Yager J: The treatment of bulimia: an overview, in Current Treatment of Anorexia Nervosa and Bulimia. Edited by Powers PS, Fernandez RC. Basel, Switzerland, Karger, 1984, pp 63–91

CHAPTER 12

Organic Mental Syndromes

It is faulty in principle to try to make a distinction between
so-called organic and functional diseases, as far as symptomatology and therapy are concerned. In both conditions, one is
dealing with abnormal functioning of the same psychophysical
apparatus and with the attempts of the organism to come to
terms with that. If the disturbances—whether they are due to
damage to the brain or to psychological conflicts—do not
disappear spontaneously or cannot be eliminated by therapy,
the organism has to make a new adjustment to life in spite of
them. Our task is to help the patients in this adjustment by
physical and psychological means; the procedure and goal of
the therapy in both conditions is, in principle, the same.
—Kurt Goldstein (1952, p. 245)

In this classic cautionary statement against mind-brain dualism,
Goldstein reminds us of the fundamental interdependence of
psychology and biology. The traditional distinction between organic
and functional syndromes implies that psychology is irrelevant to
the former and biology irrelevant to the latter. Because the term
organic generally denotes the presence of actual anatomical damage
to neuronal and glial structures, some psychiatrists view such disorders as outside their purview and therefore refer patients with them
to neurologists. Dynamic psychiatrists in particular may view patients with structural brain damage as so lacking in the capacity for
abstraction that they are inaccessible to psychotherapeutic intervention. This abdication is unfortunate because dynamic clinicians have
much to contribute to the organically impaired patient.

Psychodynamic understanding of organic mental syndromes
dates back to the seminal work of Hollós and Ferenczi on general
paresis in 1925. They noted that damage to brain tissue sets off a
process of psychological regression designed to maintain self-esteem. The organic patient regresses, in their view, to an earlier
developmental stage in which the damaged ego functions are not
yet fully evolved. In this regressed state, the patient can deny the
significance of the impairments since they are not necessary for
intact functioning at that developmental level.

As Hollós and Ferenczi were aware, conditions that affect the brain also affect the mind. The personality is the end result of a series of complex functions occurring in cortical (and subcortical) structures. Psychodynamic factors in disorders involving brain damage can most productively be discussed by dividing the conditions into those present from birth and those involving insult to brain tissue later in the life cycle (Lewis 1986). In those conditions present from birth, the psychological issues of each developmental phase throughout the life cycle are shaped by the patient's neuroanatomical deficits. In those conditions occurring later, development has been unencumbered by neural dysfunction, so the major issue is adjustment to the loss of a previous level of functioning. The discussion in this chapter will focus on those organic mental syndromes for which dynamic approaches are particularly useful. Adult minimal brain dysfunction (developmental learning disabilities and residual attention-deficit disorder) and organic personality syndrome are two disturbances present from birth in which the dynamic psychiatrist may play a key role. (Although organic personality syndrome can also arise from injuries to the brain later in life, in this section the discussion will be confined to those instances that are part of a life-long pattern of developmental deficits secondary to brain damage present from early in life.) Brain injury and dementia are conditions of later onset that will also be discussed.

Conditions Present From Birth: Adult Minimal Brain Dysfunction and Organic Personality Syndrome

Genetic-constitutional and perinatal sources of brain damage play a key role in each subsequent developmental phase throughout the life cycle. Although at one time children were believed to "outgrow" the syndrome of minimal brain dysfunction or attention deficit disorder, it is now clear that residual problems, although somewhat masked, may persist into adult life (Bellak 1977; Hartocollis 1968). Clinicians should therefore have a high index of suspicion when a patient presents with a history of poor response to conventional psychiatric or psychological treatments, a chronic inability to perform at the level expected by teachers and parents, a history of repeated life frustrations, problems with spatial orientation (such as getting lost or experiencing difficulty distinguishing between left and right), emotional outbursts, restlessness, a spotty job history, memory impairment, and marked discrepancies between performance and verbal IQ scores.

Patients who grow up with minimal brain dysfunction frequently have a host of subtle deficits that can be categorized according to specific ego functions (Bellak 1977). Primary autonomous functions (such as perception, memory, and motoric abilities) are the most commonly affected ego capacities. Next are impairments in the ability to regulate and control impulses and affects, which will be manifested as frequent temper outbursts, assaults, and poor tolerance for frustration. The ego function involved with providing a barrier to internal and external stimuli is also easily overloaded. Although the thought processes of such patients may be formally intact, their abstract thinking ability is typically compromised. The ego function known as sense of reality will often show several characteristic deficits, including spatial disorientation, unclear body boundaries, and difficulty discriminating between right and left. Finally, because these patients suffer a fundamental impairment in synthetic-integrative functioning, they may struggle to bring contradictory ideas or feelings together into a unified whole.

Psychodynamic Understanding

To understand adult patients with congenital forms of brain impairment, clinicians must consider the impact of a compromised neural substrate on the achievement of normal developmental tasks. The growing infant struggles daily with an underlying tension between the pressure of drives and affects, on the one hand, and cortical control, on the other. Drive pressures resist mastery when the infant lacks the usual endowment of functioning cortex (Weil 1978). Similarly, the conflict-free or autonomous spheres of ego functioning (such as intellect, thinking, perception, motility, and language) are dependent on constitutional endowment (Hartmann 1939).

Numerous authors have commented on the effects of organically based cognitive deficits on the development of the self and on the internalization of object relations (Allen et al. 1988; Buchholz 1987; Kafka 1984; Lewis 1986; Palombo 1979; Pickar 1986; D. Stern 1985; Weil 1978). As Daniel Stern (1985) noted, the development of the self depends on mutual cuing between mother and infant that derives from an empathic bond formed by their sensitive attunement to the emotional reactions of one another. Infants with organically based cognitive dysfunction will be unable to perceive accurately or to integrate effectively the affective signals from the mother. When the child fails to respond to the mother as she expects, the mother may become anxious, thus inserting tension and discord into the infant-mother interactions. Parents may experience an infant or child who responds abnormally and who is otherwise defective as a profound narcissistic injury (Buchholz 1987). The parents may recoil from the child and convey their sense of disappointment and anxiety in all their subsequent interactions, leading to a disturbance of the child's feelings of self-esteem (Abrams and Kaslow 1976). Alternatively, the parents may become overinvolved and overprotective. As these children grow and develop, they continue to fall short of parental expectations, resulting in further feelings of failure and humiliation. Such children have poorer cortical control of impulses, leading to more parental reprimands, to more interactions in which others are angry and punitive, and to experiences with parents who convey, through their excessive anxiety, that separation from a parental figure is dangerous (Pickar 1986; Weil 1978). Because these children are often unable to effectively appreciate cause-effect sequences, they do not link the rejection responses of others to their own behavior, resulting in feelings of victimization and helplessness (Bryan 1977).

Defects in an individual's primary autonomous ego functions of visual and auditory perception and memory will adversely affect that person's ability to achieve object constancy. Children with learning disabilities and minimal brain dysfunction often suffer from an incapacity to soothe themselves because they have never been able to internalize and maintain comforting maternal figures as affectively meaningful images. As a result, they may struggle to maintain a stable sense of self. Their inability to accurately perceive social signals from others contributes to their frequently observable ineptitude in relating to others in a socially appropriate manner (Bryan et al. 1980).

To compensate for their profound feelings of inadequacy and incompetence, individuals with minimal brain dysfunction may develop a defensive grandiosity. Kafka (1984) reported on one such patient who came to analysis. Having grown up with a host of learning disabilities and other cognitive deficits, the patient had felt like a "faker" all his life. To deal with his sense that something fundamental was missing, he assumed a defensive posture of independence and grandiosity. He was embarrassed and humiliated about his dependency on others for help with his spatial disorientation. Because he associated these disabilities with a lack of masculinity, he felt deeply ashamed.

Some individuals can compensate for their neuropsychological deficits by overdeveloping other areas of ego functioning. The inventor Thomas Edison, who suffered from learning disabilities, is one famous example. However, when compensatory efforts fail, the young person may avoid dealing with the enormous frustration of repeated failure by turning to juvenile delinquency (Pickar 1986). Instead of dealing with the shame and humiliation associated with trying but failing to meet the academic and social expectations of others, the adolescent may adopt a posture of contempt toward the values of parents, teachers, and society in general. Membership in a gang of peers may also promote the adolescent's feelings of power and acceptance.

Treatment Considerations

Therapeutic nihilism with brain-damaged patients is unwarranted. As Lewis (1986) noted: "The unqualified belief that brain damage renders a person inaccessible to meaningful psychological change through psychotherapy is erroneous and derives from the misconception that brain damage is a monolithic entity" (p. 78). The therapist cannot expect the tendency toward concrete thinking to completely disappear, but many patients achieve substantial gains in their ability to think symbolically or abstractly (Buchholz 1987). Even in a highly expressive treatment like psychoanalysis, Kafka (1984) found that no significant modifications of technique were necessary for such a patient. He did note that his patient responded with narcissistic mortification to minor slips of the tongue because such incidents seemed to expose his defects. In addition, Kafka often had to repeat interpretations patiently and tactfully in various contexts using different examples.

Adapting the treatment approach to patients who suffer from more severe cognitive deficits requires a precise understanding of how those deficits affect their ability to use psychotherapy. For example, Lewis (1986) described a patient who had suffered since early childhood from memory disturbances that impaired her ability to evoke a soothing mental image of her therapist. She was unable to maintain continuity between her twice-weekly hour-long sessions because she couldn't recall the therapist's words or appearance. Simply changing the appointment time to one-half hour each weekday allowed the patient to internalize the therapeutic process more effectively because she could now remember how the therapist looked and sounded.

Repeated failures of empathy characterize the life stories of such patients. Beginning with parents, other people do not understand the nature or extent of these cognitive limitations and repeatedly expect more than these patients can deliver. Because of this life pattern, some clinicians (Buchholz 1987; Palombo 1979) have suggested using a self psychological approach. The repeated experiences of self-fragmentation and deflation connected with the lack of mirroring responses from others can be addressed as they develop in the transference. The therapist can empathically reflect the patient's strivings for admiration and approbation and can give meaning to how the cognitive impairments have interfered with those strivings. Thus the therapist serves as a selfobject who helps the patient grieve, assists the patient in building a more cohesive self, and encourages self-forgiveness as well.

When behavioral dyscontrol is a major feature of the patient's clinical picture, hospitalization may be required. Conventional psychiatric treatments usually have proved ineffective for these patients. Frequently, diagnosticians have missed the organic dimension because of its subtlety and because of more florid symptoms of personality disorder. Many patients who suffer from severe forms of adult attention-deficit disorder or minimal brain dysfunction fall into the category of organic personality syndrome. The clinician must realize that the DSM-III-R (American Psychiatric Association 1987) criteria for this disorder—affective instability, recurrent outbursts of aggression or rage, markedly impaired social judgment, marked apathy and indifference, and suspiciousness or paranoid ideation—overlap significantly with the criteria for borderline personality disorder. In the absence of information about the extent of the neurological deficit, treaters tend to have excessively high expectations of these patients. Clinicians who assume that all the symptomatology is related to character pathology may develop considerable countertransference frustration when patients react to interventions with wandering attention, poor memory, and failure to reflect on meanings. As the treater's irritation grows, the patient feels increasingly like a failure for not responding properly to treatment, thus recapitulating past experiences with parents, teachers, and employers.

One study of treatment-refractory inpatients drew a psychological profile of patients who suffered from severe psychiatric disorders complicated by organic features (Allen et al. 1988; Colson and Allen 1986); most of these patients would meet the criteria for organic personality syndrome. Problems with self-esteem and affect modulation are two commonalities in this group of patients. Rarely do they have clear-cut neurological disorders, and they are therefore difficult to diagnose. The cumulative diagnostic picture of neurological soft signs, borderline abnormalities on EEG, and spotty deficits on neuropsychological testing implicates CNS dysfunction. Subcortical involvement, manifested by episodes of behavioral dyscontrol and affective storms, appears of greater relevance than cortical impairment. These patients feel powerless in the face of overwhelming eruptions of affect. In a desperate attempt to gain some sense of mastery and control, they pretend that their episodes are volitional acts designed to intimidate others—a response similar to a grandiose delusion. Their explosions lead to increased isolation from others, great embarrassment, and decreased self-esteem. They live in fear of further loss of control. To deal with this threat, they develop extreme defensive postures against any affect whatsoever by becoming constricted and superficial, much like alexithymics. To ward off feelings, they commonly employ the defenses of denial and externalization.

The high expectations of treaters and parents contribute to a vicious cycle with these patients. Because they are unable to live up to such high expectations, their self-esteem plummets and their frustration grows, leading to further vulnerability to affective explosions. These episodes of dyscontrol elicit more negative feedback from parents and treaters and further erode their self-esteem. The diagnosis of the organic contribution often is therapeutic in and of itself, and these patients generally respond with relief to it. The diagnosis also leads to lowered expectations from both parents and clinicians. As a result, the vicious cycle is interrupted, and the patients develop better self-esteem and an increased sense of mastery as their episodes of dyscontrol decrease and their sense of chronic failure diminishes.

> Mr. V, a 20-year-old single male, was hospitalized after repeated episodes of temper outbursts leading to physical altercations with fellow employees. The patient's father, a prosperous factory owner, had given Mr. V a job because all previous attempts at gainful employment had failed. At work, Mr. V was viewed as "the boss's son." Minor allusions to preferential treatment of Mr. V by his father provoked outbursts of aggression by Mr. V. At admission, Mr. V's father clearly indicated that he was fed up with his son. He cataloged a long list of life failures, including school performance, athletic failures, and "laziness" manifested by an inability to keep a job. Mr. V hung his head in shame as this list was rattled off, and he seemed particularly wounded when his father compared him to an older brother who had recently attained a graduate professional degree.
>
> On the hospital unit, Mr. V related to others with a formal, constricted manner that made his occasional outbursts seem to come from out of the blue. In one typical instance, he was returning to the unit after an activities therapy session when he suddenly started shoving another male patient walking beside him. With a look of rage, he pinned the patient to the ground, snatched his wallet from his pants pocket, and threw it onto the roof of the hospital. Mr. V was returned to the unit and confined to his room. In a subsequent group meeting, the other patient and the staff member who had accompanied them described the incident in detail, particularly noting its inexplicability because there was no apparent trigger. With much bravado, Mr. V claimed that the other patient had provoked him by making fun of him. He maintained that the attack was justified. As a result of this and other incidents, the other patients on Mr. V's team (and several staff members) began to feel intimidated and frightened by Mr. V.
>
> Of course, Mr. V's violent outbursts led to further isolation from the patient community. He was confined to his room for much of the time to decrease stimulation and to protect the other patients. In a one-to-one session with his psychiatrist, he allowed his defensive

facade to yield to other feelings. He confided that after each episode of dyscontrol, he felt "like an idiot." He said that he had no idea why he had attacked his male peer on the way back to the hospital unit. His psychiatrist asked Mr. V what had happened in the activity period preceding the assault. He replied that he had been asked to make a wooden bowl in the wood shop. Asked how his bowl had turned out, Mr. V responded, "As usual, I screwed up." His psychiatrist then asked if it was possible that attacking the other patient was his way of dealing with his frustration. Mr. V acknowledged that it probably was, and then added that he would do anything to prevent future outbursts but that he was pessimistic about any treatment being helpful. He had dealt with such outbursts all his life and doubted that anything could control them.

A detailed neuropsychiatric evaluation revealed the following findings, which suggested an organic component to Mr. V's problems: 1) a history of learning disabilities from early grade school through high school, 2) difficulties with right-left discrimination, 3) a childhood history of hyperactivity and other symptoms of attention deficit disorder, and 4) moderate perceptual deficits on neuropsychological testing. A 24-hour sleep-deprivation EEG with nasopharyngeal leads was entirely normal, and even an ambulatory EEG monitor failed to reveal any abnormalities in the temporal lobes. Results of a CT scan were also within normal limits.

Carbamazepine was tried on an empirical basis and seemed to reduce the frequency and intensity of Mr. V's behavioral dyscontrol episodes. The main thrust of the treatment, however, was a careful explanation to Mr. V and his family about the implications of these findings. Initially, Mr. V's parents were quite resistant to the idea that their son had a subtle form of brain damage from early in life. Eventually, though, they were persuaded when the neuropsychologist discussed the testing in detail with them and explained the nature of the physical impairment. The parents' anger and frustration with their son gradually diminished as they began to understand the extent of his limitations. This diagnosis helped put the patient's history in perspective, and it led Mr. V's parents to rethink their expectations for his vocational future. After the psychiatrist explained that Mr. V's lowered stimulus barrier led to his overstimulation when he was around other people, the father arranged for a job for Mr. V at a satellite facility where he could do repetitive menial tasks in isolation from other workers. This arrangement not only lowered the expectations of high job performance but also removed interpersonal triggers of the dyscontrol episodes.

Mr. V responded favorably to the reports of the diagnostic evaluation and particularly to the lowered expectations of his parents. He said he felt like "the pressure was off." The new job arrangement worked satisfactorily for him. Although he remained socially isolated, his self-esteem increased considerably because of his improved mastery of the episodes of dyscontrol and because of his ability to perform adequately at his new job.

Conditions of Later Onset:
Brain Injury and Dementia

The human brain that receives an insult later in the developmental life cycle involves a different set of therapeutic issues. In these instances, the patient has deteriorated from a previous level of functioning, and both the patient and the family must adjust to the change. These conditions fall into two broad categories: 1) acute brain injuries with a sudden alteration of functioning, and 2) progressive degenerative diseases with a gradual decline. Both forms of insult will be considered in the ensuing discussion. Excluded from consideration are delirium, states of drug intoxication or withdrawal, and other acute insults that rapidly clear when the medical condition or toxic agent has been dealt with, because psychodynamic issues are less relevant to such conditions.

Psychodynamic Understanding

The self, at the most fundamental level, is a product of brain functioning. Damage to brain tissue may produce significant alterations in an individual's sense of identity, thus causing family and loved ones to feel that the patient is no longer the same person. Brain trauma typically affects the frontal and temporal lobes, dramatically influencing the patient's ability to interpret the meaning of stimuli and to connect them with relevant feelings (Prigatano 1989). Such alterations strike at the very heart of the personality.

The awareness of the self is difficult to localize to one area of the brain. Studies of patients whose cerebral hemispheres have been surgically disconnected (Sperry et al. 1979) have suggested that the sense of self is present in both halves of the brain. It appears to be a complex schema to which different brain regions make different contributions.

Patients react to their loss of identity in certain characteristic ways. Goldstein (1952), one of the first investigators of the psychological effects of brain damage, described an anxiety state that he termed the *catastrophic condition* or *reaction*. When brain-injured patients were asked to perform a simple task that had been no problem for them prior to the trauma, they became angry, agitated, and extremely anxious. Goldstein observed that they perceived their failure to complete the task as a danger to their very existence. As a reaction to this threat, patients characteristically restrict their lives so that they are not exposed to unfamiliar situations or impossible tasks. Thus they defend against catastrophic anxiety by avoiding awareness of their defects. These patients commonly become excessively orderly to the point of being obsessive compulsive. Keeping everything in place gives them the illusion of control over their environment. It also transforms passivity into activity and provides a concrete solution to a complex abstract problem.

When brain-injured patients can restrict their lives sufficiently, they may appear remarkably free of anxiety and oblivious to their organic deficits. They may show evidence of memory problems, childish behavior, and a short temper, but they often deny any limitations. In fact, one study (Oddy et al. 1985) found that 40 percent of the patients studied 7 years after an insult to the brain disavowed any disability whatsoever. Clinicians may struggle to differentiate between neurogenic and psychogenic denial in such patients. Lewis (in press) has pointed out that, in contrast to psychological forms of denial, neurogenic denial remits within hours or days of the injury, appears as a pattern of overall deficits rather than as an isolated symptom, and does not produce anxiety or agitation in patients who are confronted with it.

The gradual loss of functioning typical of dementia syndromes generally presents a somewhat different picture. People with dementia preserve a sense of who they are until relatively late in the course of the illness. They may be able to perform their usual work and conduct their usual social routines reasonably well. As McHugh and Folstein (1986) have noted, "It is the retention of the habitual, the concrete, and the basics of a self in the face of a progressive and severe deterioration in the skills of analysis, abstraction, comprehension, and memory that gives the demented patient his particular appearance" (p. 335). The patient may initially note some problem with recent memory. The most common alteration of personality in the early stage is a progressive indifference or apathy (Cummings 1987). As the illness progresses, the patient is likely to experience increasing difficulty with calculation, performance of complex tasks, and fluency of language. At this point in the illness, when patients realize that they cannot perform the tasks they were once able to, catastrophic reactions may emerge that are similar to those in brain-injured patients. Similarly, eruptions of anger and even combativeness may develop as the disease progresses.

In many aging patients with dementia of the Alzheimer's type, the tragedy of the illness is that self-awareness may remain intact as a number of the mental faculties deteriorate. Because recent memory tends to be sacrificed before remote memory, many patients can clearly recollect how they used to be, which makes their current dysfunctional state all the more disturbing to them. To a large extent, the continuity of the self over time depends on the capacity of memory. When remote memories begin to fade as the illness progresses, then the patient's identity begins to disappear along with the memories. Ultimately, the patient cannot recognize loved ones and family members and can no longer remember significant life events.

Treatment Considerations

Treatment planning depends on a careful assessment of several factors (Lewis 1986; Prigatano and Klonoff 1988): 1) the exact manner in which the brain insult has affected the sensory, motor, and cognitive spheres; 2) the patient's psychological reaction to the organic deficits; 3) the impact of both the brain insult and the patient's reaction on the patient's psychological and social adjustment; 4) the contribution of the patient's premorbid personality structure to the clinical picture; and 5) differentiation of those symptoms that are direct sequelae of the brain damage from those that are associated with previously defended conflicts or ego deficits, now released as a result of the trauma. This type of assessment requires a detailed history from a family member or a significant other in the patient's life.

Part of the assessment of such patients should include an evaluation of their suitability for expressive-supportive psychotherapy. Lewis and Rosenberg (1990) have delineated five useful indicators for selecting which neurologically impaired patients can benefit from dynamic therapy: 1) personal motivation, both to begin and to remain in a psychotherapeutic process; 2) a history of at least one meaningful interpersonal relationship; 3) a degree of success and active mastery in some area of life; 4) absence of serious language problems of either an expressive or receptive type; and 5) absence of frontal lobe symptoms, such as anosognosia, severe apathy, or marked impulsiveness that would make psychotherapy impossible. Another factor that may be critical in determining suitability for psychotherapy is the patient's financial situation as a result of the brain injury. When workers' compensation substantially reimburses patients for their injuries, psychotherapy may be ineffective. If patients are rewarded financially for remaining disabled, their conditions frequently deteriorate and their motivation to change through psychotherapy may be severely compromised (Prigatano and Klonoff 1988).

A growing literature documents the value of dynamic psychotherapy for brain-injured patients (Ball 1988; Lewis 1986; Lewis and Rosenberg 1990; Morris and Bleiberg 1986; Prigatano and Klonoff 1988; J. Stern 1985). A major goal of any psychotherapeutic process with these patients is to help them accept the extent of their deficits and their limitations in terms of returning to work. To accomplish this goal, the therapist must be sensitive to the narcissistic injury inherent in accepting the irreparable damage to one's skills, intellectual capabilities, talents, and even the very essence of one's personality. It is essential for the therapist to respect and empathize with the patient's need to use denial (Lewis, in press). Blunt confrontations of denial are likely to accomplish nothing and may even destroy any hope of developing a therapeutic alliance. Promoting self-acceptance of these cognitive limitations requires therapists to gradually expose their patients to the reality of the deficits in a way that allows the patients to briefly mourn week by week, over an extended period. A psychoeducational model in which the nature of the deficits and their implications are explained in small units of information that the patient is capable of assimilating may be useful at the beginning of therapy (Prigatano and Klonoff 1988). Drawings or diagrams may help patients with these limitations to visualize what the therapist is describing. As patients mourn the loss of their previous identity and their previous level of functioning, anger at themselves and others connected with the accident is likely to surface. Therapists can then help patients forgive themselves and others so that they can get on with their life.

Both individual dynamic psychotherapy and family or marital therapy may be necessary to help patients adjust to changes in intimate relationships. Spouses may be upset or bewildered by the new behaviors of their brain-damaged partner, such as childishness, concretistic thinking, paranoid accusations, and uninhibited passion (Prigatano and Klonoff 1988). Psychoeducational approaches may help family members to understand the organic contribution to these behaviors. However, explorations of themes such as guilt and anger at the patient for having the accident must also be addressed. Frequently, families will completely rearrange their lifestyle to provide round-the-clock companionship and assistance to the brain-injured patient (Ball 1988). If this unnecessarily smothering behavior goes unchecked, it will lead to increasing resentment. Interpretations of reaction formation that defend against anger may help family members return to a closer approximation of their normal lives before the accident. Family members may also find it helpful to explore guilt feelings related to fantasies of causing the accident by what they did or did not say. Reasonable expectations of the spouse and other family members should be discussed individually with the patient during the psychotherapeutic process.

The dynamic therapist of a brain-injured patient must also be cognizant of the time course of the recovery and its effect on the therapeutic process. Three general phases can be identified (J. Stern 1985). In the first phase, the patient is unable to process what has happened. The usual ego defenses are overwhelmed, and the therapist must serve the function of a consistent, supportive, auxiliary ego that provides missing functions to the patient and explains what the patient is going through. In the second phase, patients start to understand what has happened to them and are prone to feel that they have been victimized by a menacing and malevolent world. All "badness" is split off and projected into others, including the therapist. In this phase, therapists must contain the destructive impulses and the malevolent self- and object-representations projected into them and yet continue to be an observing ego for the patient. Developing trust in others is a major task in the recovery of brain-injured patients, and a trusting alliance with a therapist can be a first step in this direction. Therapists can promote trust by explaining the meaning of the patient's experience and by sharpening the differentiation between what is happening inside the patient and what is actually going on in external reality. As cognitive functioning improves, patients enter the third phase, in which intrapsychic conflicts become more prominent. The therapist's task in this phase is to help patients form a new identity by connecting past experiences and self-representations with current experiences of themselves. The patient's idealization of the past may be questioned by the therapist to facilitate integration of the past with the present. Grief and loss are central themes during this phase.

Several authors (Lewis 1986; Lewis and Rosenberg 1990; Prigatano et al. 1984; Prigatano and Klonoff 1988) have emphasized the necessity for psychotherapy to address characterological issues that predate the injury. These premorbid personality dispositions may profoundly affect the patient's rehabilitation process. For example, Morris and Bleiberg (1986) described a patient who became oppositional to a rehabilitation therapist whom he experienced as a controlling mother. This patient's characterological tendency to see others as controlling was diagnosed through the transferential relationship to the therapist. A dynamically informed decision was then made to allow the patient more control over rehabilitation and treatment planning.

Problems with self-esteem and affect modulation almost invariably surface in the psychotherapy and rehabilitation of patients suffering from brain trauma. However, these two areas are also problematic for many persons suffering from personality disorders. Psychotherapists must avoid being seduced into thinking that all psychological symptoms are directly related to the brain injury. It is common for narcissistic, antisocial, and borderline patients to place themselves in situations that involve risk of injury, and these characterological dimensions that contributed to the accident may have to be addressed during psychotherapy. Also, characterological tendencies are often exacerbated by brain damage so that patients become "more like they already are." To deal with the loss of control arising from the destruction of brain tissue, an obsessive-compulsive patient may become more obsessive compulsive. Hysterical or histrionic patients may become more cognitively diffuse and affectively labile in response to brain injury. Psychotherapists must not abandon their technique with personality disorders simply because of a patient's brain injury.

Many clinicians are guardedly optimistic about the treatment of brain-injured patients. Progressive dementia, on the other hand, often elicits profound pessimism in treaters. When treatable causes of dementia (e.g., depression, hypothyroidism, vitamin deficiencies, porphyria, neoplasm, and encephalitides) are ruled out, some clinicians reluctantly diagnose Alzheimer's disease and withdraw from a therapeutic role. This unfortunate withdrawal is associated with the view that Alzheimer's, which accounts for more than half of all dementias, is untreatable. From a psychodynamic perspective, however, there is no such thing as an untreatable dementia. Approximately one-third of these patients will require treatment for associated symptoms of depression and psychosis (Wragg and Jeste 1989). Even in the absence of such symptoms, however, much can be done to assist both the patients and their families in dealing with Alzheimer's on a daily basis. The following case example illustrates certain principles of management:

Mr. W was a 59-year-old Protestant minister with a 4-year history of deterioration in his mental functioning. Members of his congregation had noticed a sense of apathy about him and a sloppiness in his administrative functioning. Church bulletins were poorly organized, and he seemed to be less conscientious about carrying out his commitments to various parishioners. Mr. W's wife noticed that he often failed to fulfill simple requests. She would become angry at him for "selective hearing" when he indicated to her that he had forgotten what she said.

Mrs. W brought her husband for psychiatric evaluation, complaining that he was "just not the same." Mr. W acknowledged that he felt as if something was happening to him, but he was unable to be more specific than to say that he could not remember as well as he used to. Mrs. W complained that their marital relationship was deteriorating because her husband did not attend to her needs as he had in the past. Mr. W expressed hurt at the feedback from members of his congregation, and he noted that he was starting to feel like a failure.

Mental status examination revealed problems with short-term memory and calculation and minor difficulties with orientation to time. He also showed signs of mental inertia, as he was unable to move from one subject to another or from one task to another unless given considerable time. Extensive diagnostic studies ruled out causes of dementia stemming from trauma, infection, neoplasm, and normal pressure hydrocephalus, or from autoimmune, metabolic, hematologic, vascular, and toxic factors. These results were negative, as were findings from a CT scan, skull X-rays, and electroencephalography. Neuropsychological testing was more productive, with the following results noted: 1) mild-to-moderate deficits in manual dexterity, 2) mild-to-moderate deficits in perceptual functioning, 3) mild-to-moderate deficits in recent memory, 4) diffuse organic dysfunction typical of progressive neurological disease, and 5) a decrease in attention span.

After the diagnosis of dementia of unknown origin was determined (Alzheimer's in a 59-year-old man is unusual but not unheard of), the diagnostic findings were explained to the patient and his wife. When Mrs. W could accept her husband's structural brain damage, she was able to lower her expectations for his responses to her. Instead of assuming that he would always react to her verbal comments as he had in the past, she tried new ways of relating to him. At the psychiatrist's suggestion, she slowed her rate of speech and repeated comments that did not seem to register. She also tried rewording comments that Mr. W did not seem to understand. Above all, she no longer was so easily irritated with him, leading to more positive interactions between the two of them and a corresponding increase in Mr. W's self-esteem.

Mr. W had always been an orderly, fastidious person with prominent obsessive-compulsive character traits. To deal with his sense that his intellectual and administrative capacities were deteriorating, he had begun to read the Bible 2 or 3 hours a day, both to encourage divine intervention and to attempt to gain mastery over the information he hoped to impart to his congregation. The evaluating psychiatrist helped Mr. W marshal his obsessive-compulsive character traits more effectively. As a result, Mr. W began to sit down with his wife each morning to write out a daily schedule of what he had to do between breakfast and bedtime. Moreover, he began to carry a notebook at all times so he could write down what other people told him and thereby remember what he had to do.

Mr. W's self-esteem had depended on his role as minister, and his inability to continue in that capacity inflicted a deep narcissistic wound. Initially, he protested when the psychiatrist advised him to reduce his responsibilities. However, with Mr. W's permission, his associate minister was enlisted as an ally in devising ways for Mr. W to continue to serve the church without being placed in situations where he was faced with impossible tasks. For example, the associate minister began to prepare and type the weekly bulletin, but Mr. W continued to operate the printer to produce the required number for the Sunday service. Thus Mr. W continued to feel productive, which preserved some semblance of his self-esteem. By avoiding tasks that were beyond his capabilities, he also avoided repeated narcissistic injuries.

The case of Mr. W illustrates several useful principles in the dynamically informed management of dementia: 1) attend to self-esteem issues; 2) assess characteristic defense mechanisms and help the patient use them constructively; 3) find ways to replace defective ego functions and cognitive limitations, such as keeping calendars for orientation problems, taking notes for memory problems, and making schedules for problems of secondary autonomous functioning; and 4) assist family members in developing new ways of relatedness that shore up the patient's self-esteem by decreasing negative interactions.

Patients in the early stages of Alzheimer's dementia may use denial to prevent the full impact of the illness from entering conscious awareness. Clinicians treating such patients must respect the need for denial, but also help them to tie up loose ends with business and family before it is too late (Martin 1989). Those who treat Alzheimer's patients are apt to face countertransference struggles that interfere with such planning. They must be alert to feelings of helplessness, guilt, failure, wishes to abandon the patient, and hopelessness.

Although these measures do not prevent the ultimate deterioration associated with dementia of the Alzheimer's type, they do result in an increased quality of life during the gradual but inevitable downhill course of the disease. Ultimately, the patient's family members are the main focus of intervention, as they struggle with anger, guilt, grief, and exhaustion in the face of the patient's inexorable decline. In fact, family therapy is probably the dynamic treatment of choice in Alzheimer's dementia (Lansky 1984). Blaming of self and others is a frequent development in family members. Also, the readjustment of family roles may require intervention. The final task, of course, involves the acceptance of death. Clinicians who struggle along with these families in such situations will often find the treatment process a trying one, but they can pride themselves on having made a significant impact on the lives of all involved.

References

Abrams JC, Kaslow FW: Learning disability and family dynamics: a mutual interaction. Journal of Clinical Child Psychology 5:35–40, 1976

Allen JG, Colson DB, Coyne L: Organic brain dysfunction and behavioral dyscontrol in difficult-to-treat psychiatric hospital patients. Integrative Psychiatry 6:120–130, 1988

American Psychiatric Association: Diagnostic and Statistical Manual of Mental Disorders, 3rd Edition, Revised. Washington, DC, American Psychiatric Association, 1987

Ball JD: Psychotherapy with head-injured patients. Medical Psychotherapy 1:15–22, 1988

Bellak L: Psychiatric states in adults with minimal brain dysfunction. Psychiatric Annals 7:575–589, 1977

Bryan JH, Sherman RE, Fisher A: Learning disabled boys' nonverbal behaviors within a dyadic interview. Learning Disability Quarterly 3:65–72, 1980

Bryan T: Learning disabled children's comprehension of nonverbal communication. Journal of Learning Disabilities 10:501–506, 1977

Buchholz ES: The legacy from childhood: considerations for treatment of the adult with learning disabilities. Psychoanalytic Inquiry 7:431–452, 1987

Colson DB, Allen JG: Organic brain dysfunction in difficult-to-treat psychiatric hospital patients. Bull Menninger Clin 50:88–98, 1986

Cummings JL: Dementia syndromes: neurobehavioral and neuropsychiatric features. J Clin Psychiatry 48(suppl):3–8, 1987

Goldstein K: The effect of brain damage on the personality. Psychiatry 15:245–260, 1952

Hartmann H: Ego Psychology and the Problem of Adaptation (1939). Translated by Rapaport D. New York, International Universities Press, 1958

Hartocollis P: The syndrome of minimal brain dysfunction in young adult patients. Bull Menninger Clin 32:102–114, 1968

Hollós S, Ferenczi S: Psychoanalysis and the Psychic Disorder of General Paresis. Translated by Barnes GM, Keil G. New York, Normal and Mental Disease Publishing, 1925

Kafka E: Cognitive difficulties in psychoanalysis. Psychoanal Q 53:533–550, 1984

Lansky MR: Family psychotherapy of the patient with chronic organic brain syndrome. Psychiatric Annals 14:121–129, 1984

Lewis L: Individual psychotherapy with patients having combined psychological and neurological disorders. Bull Menninger Clin 50:75–87, 1986

Lewis L: The role of psychological factors in disordered awareness, in Denial of Deficit Following Brain Injury. Edited by Prigatano GP, Schacter DI. Oxford University Press (in press)

Lewis L, Rosenberg SJ: Psychoanalytic psychotherapy with brain-injured adult psychiatric patients. J Nerv Ment Dis 17:69–77, 1990

Martin RL: Update on dementia of the Alzheimer type. Hosp Community Psychiatry 40:593–604, 1989

McHugh PR, Folstein MF: Organic mental disorders (Ch 73), in Psychiatry, Revised Edition. Edited by Michels R, Cavenar JO Jr. Vol 2: Schizophrenia, Affective Disorders, and Dementias. Edited by Guze SB, Helzer JE. Philadelphia, JB Lippincott, 1986, pp 333–353

Morris J, Bleiberg J: Neuropsychological rehabilitation and traditional psychotherapy. International Journal Clinical Neuropsychology 8:133–135, 1986

Oddy M, Coughlan T, Tyreman A: Social adjustment after closed head injury: a further follow-up seven years after injury. J Neurol Neurosurg Psychiatry 48:564–568, 1985

Palombo J: Perceptual deficits and self-esteem in adolescence. Clinical Social Work Journal 7:34–61, 1979

Pickar DB: Psychosocial aspects of learning disabilities: a review of research. Bull Menninger Clin 50:22–32, 1986

Prigatano GP: Work, love, and play after brain injury. Bull Menninger Clin 53:414–431, 1989

Prigatano GP, Klonoff PS: Psychotherapy and neuropsychological assessment after brain injury. Journal of Head Trauma Rehabilitation 3:45–56, 1988

Prigatano GP, Fordyce DJ, Zeiner HK, et al: Neuropsychological rehabilitation after closed head injury in young adults. J Neurol
   Neurosurg Psychiatry 47:505–513, 1984
Sperry RW, Zaidel E, Zaidel D: Self-recognition and social awareness in
   the deconnected minor hemispheres. Neuropsychologia 17:153–
   166, 1979
Stern DN: The Interpersonal World of the Infant: A View from Psycho-
   analysis and Developmental Psychology. New York, Basic Books,
   1985
Stern JM: The psychotherapeutic process with brain-injured patients: a
   dynamic approach. Isr J Psychiatry Relat Sci 22:83–87, 1985
Weil AP: Maturational variations and genetic-dynamic issues. J Am
   Psychoanal Assoc 26:461–491, 1978
Wragg RE, Jeste DV: Overview of depression and psychosis in
   Alzheimer's disease. Am J Psychiatry 146:577–587, 1989

SECTION III

Dynamic Approaches to Axis II Disorders

CHAPTER 13

Cluster A Personality Disorders: Paranoid, Schizoid, and Schizotypal

Paranoid Personality Disorder

Paranoid thinking is not in and of itself pathological. As described in Chapter 2, the paranoid-schizoid position is a basic mode of organizing experience that persists in the human psyche throughout the life cycle. In this mode, dangerous or unpleasant thoughts and feelings are split off, projected outward, and attributed to others. This mode is readily accessible in all kinds of group experiences, such as political conventions, sporting events, and institutional dynamics. At certain historical junctures, entire cultures have been pervaded by paranoid thinking, such as in the "witch hunts" of the McCarthy era in this country.

The paranoid personality disorder, however, is a distinct pathological entity that is independent of cultural factors and is not a transient state growing out of the nexus of group dynamics. It involves a pervasive style of thinking, feeling, and relating to others that is extraordinarily rigid and unvarying. These individuals live within the paranoid-schizoid position. Seven common features comprise the diagnostic criteria; at least four must be present to make the diagnosis (see Table 13-1). Moreover, the patient's suspicious beliefs must stop short of being delusional and must occur independently of an Axis I psychotic diagnosis such as schizophrenia or delusional disorder.

As with most personality disorders, the key features of the paranoid personality disorder are ego-syntonic. Paranoid patients are often brought to treatment by family members or coworkers who are fed up with the patient's constant allegations and accusations. A boss, for example, may insist that an employee seek treatment—or look elsewhere for a job. A spouse who is tired of accusations of infidelity may use the threat of divorce to force the paranoid individual into treatment. Even when paranoid patients enter treatment willingly, they usually remain unconvinced that they are psychiatrically disturbed. Their presenting problems revolve around how others have mistreated them and betrayed them.

305

Table 13-1. DSM-III-R diagnostic criteria for paranoid
personality disorder

A. A pervasive and unwarranted tendency, beginning by early
adulthood and present in a variety of contexts, to interpret the
actions of people as deliberately demeaning or threatening, as
indicated by at least *four* of the following:
  (1) expects, without sufficient basis, to be exploited or harmed
by others
  (2) questions, without justification, the loyalty or trustworthiness of
friends or associates
  (3) reads hidden demeaning or threatening meanings into benign
remarks or events, e.g., suspects that a neighbor put out trash
early to annoy him
  (4) bears grudges or is unforgiving of insults or slights
  (5) is reluctant to confide in others because of unwarranted fear
that the information will be used against him or her
  (6) is easily slighted and quick to react with anger or to counterattack
  (7) questions, without justification, fidelity of spouse or sexual
partner
B. Occurrence not exclusively during the course of schizophrenia or
a delusional disorder.

Note. Reprinted from DSM-III-R, p. 339, with permission from the American Psychiatric Association.

The diagnostic criteria reflect a way of thinking that can be
conceptualized as a distinctly paranoid cognitive style (Shapiro
1965). This style of thinking is characterized by an unrelenting
search for hidden meanings, for clues to uncover the "truth" behind
a situation's face value. The obvious, the superficial, and the apparent merely mask the reality. This endless search involves an intense
hyperalertness of attention, evidenced by a guardedness related to
this continuous attentional monitoring. A paranoid individual constantly scans the environment for anything out of the ordinary—a
style of thinking that takes a considerable toll in physical and
emotional tension. The paranoid patient is simply unable to relax.
  Paranoid thinking is also characterized by a lack of flexibility.
The most persuasive argument will generally have no impact on the
rigid and unswerving beliefs of the paranoid person. In fact, those
persons who attempt to argue with a person who has a paranoid
personality will simply find themselves becoming the target of suspiciousness. The paranoid person's thinking differs from that of the
paranoid schizophrenic in that it is not delusional. In fact, patients
with paranoid personality disorder tend to have remarkably accurate perceptions of their environment. However, their judgments
about those perceptions are generally impaired. Reality itself is not

distorted; rather, the significance of apparent reality is (Shapiro 1965). This characteristic cognitive style may be difficult to diagnose because the paranoid individual is often closemouthed and guarded. In fact, even projective testing may only identify the paranoid individual as a more-or-less normal person who is simply inhibited.

Psychodynamics of the Paranoid Personality Disorder

An understanding of the characteristics of the paranoid-schizoid position is essential to an understanding of the paranoid patient. As noted in Chapter 2, splitting is a central defense mechanism in this mode of organizing experience. Feelings of love and hate toward the same object must be separated from one another. Any movement toward integration creates intolerable anxiety that stems from the fear that the hatred will overpower and destroy the love. From the standpoint of the paranoid patient, emotional survival requires the patient to split off all "badness" and project it into outside figures. One manifestation of this defensive maneuver is that the normal internal world of aggressor and victim is transformed into a life experience where the paranoid individual is constantly in the role of victim vis-à-vis external aggressors or persecutors. The view that paranoid patients have of the world thus relieves their internal tension between introjects. If a paranoid individual is forced to reinternalize what has been projected, the increased internal tension will result in increased rigidity and defensiveness (Shapiro 1965).

Another characteristic of the paranoid-schizoid position is that the patient's experience of others is discontinuous; no relationship is perceived as enduring over time. Rather, the patient has only the perception of the moment. Patients with paranoid personality disorder approach every relationship with the belief that the other person will eventually "slip up" and confirm their suspicions. In the paranoid-schizoid mode of existence, the patient lives in a state of unremitting anxiety that is related to a conviction that the world is peopled with untrustworthy and unpredictable strangers (Ogden 1986). Even when a stable, helpful therapist has worked with a paranoid patient over a long period, one minor disappointment can lead the patient to completely disregard the therapist's previous behavior and to feel—with unswerving conviction—that the therapist is untrustworthy. The therapist has been "unmasked." Thus good experiences with a person in the past can be totally erased by the present situation.

The self in the paranoid-schizoid mode of experience is incompletely developed. Self-experience is also equated with the current experience. There is no interpreting subject to mediate between symbol and symbolized (i.e., between perceptions and thoughts and feelings about those perceptions) (Ogden 1986). Experience is literally taken at face value. Patients with paranoid personality disorder are unable to think, "It is *as if* this other person is trying to hurt me." Instead, they *know* that the other person harbors malevolent intentions. Similarly, in the transference relationship with the therapist, the paranoid patient is unable to say, "I feel that I am reacting to you *as if* you are as sadistic as my father was." The patient simply experiences the therapist as sadistic. Feelings are not personal creations of the patient but, rather, things-in-themselves. When patients develop a mediating self that is able to interpret accurately and to think symbolically in "as if" terms, then they have achieved the depressive position (Ogden 1986).

Projection and projective identification are two key defense mechanisms of the paranoid personality disorder. Projection substitutes an external threat for an internal one; projective identification goes a step further. In addition to externalizing threats, it "controls" persons in the environment by binding them to the paranoid person in highly pathological ways. The need to control others reflects the terribly low self-esteem at the core of paranoia (Meissner 1986). Deep down, the paranoid patient feels inferior, weak, and ineffectual. Thus, the grandiosity or sense of "specialness" often seen in these patients can be understood as a compensatory defense that makes up for feelings of inferiority.

The low self-esteem at the heart of the paranoid personality disorder leads these individuals to develop a keen sense of attunement to issues of rank and power. They are terribly concerned that persons in authority will humiliate them or expect them to be submissive (Shapiro 1965). They perceive threats to their autonomy as omnipresent. A recurring fear about their interpersonal relationships is that they will result in subjection to external control; they fear that anyone who tries to be close to them is secretly trying to take over. This concern may surface as a dread of passive homosexual impulses, originally described by Freud (1911) in the case of the psychotically disturbed Judge Schreber. However, all paranoid individuals are not necessarily concerned about passive homosexual impulses. Overt homosexuality and paranoid personality disorder can and do exist in the same person. The main point is rather that the patient is concerned about *all* passive surrender to *all* impulses and to all persons (Shapiro 1965).

Successful treatment can provide a glimpse of what lies beneath the projective system: a good deal of depressive content (Meissner 1976) and diametrically opposing self-representations. Coexisting with the special, entitled, grandiose version of the self is a weak, worthless, inferior polar opposite. Therapists who are aware of this other dimension of the paranoid personality can more easily empathize with these difficult patients.

Treatment Approaches

Because of their suspiciousness, paranoid patients usually do poorly in group psychotherapy. Most treatment efforts must therefore be mounted in the context of individual therapy, despite the formidable challenge to the individual psychotherapist. As noted earlier, these patients often enter treatment under some external pressure, and they have the utmost difficulty trusting anyone. In light of these obstacles, the first step in psychotherapy should be to build a therapeutic alliance. This process is made more difficult by the tendency of paranoid patients to evoke defensive responses. The therapist is no exception, as the following vignette illustrates:

Patient:	I'm really angry with you because I've been sitting in the waiting room for half an hour. You told me to be here at 9:30 today.
Therapist:	No, that's not true. I said 10 A.M.
Patient:	You said 9:30.
Therapist:	(a little louder and more forcefully) I *said* 10 o'clock. I wrote it down in my book.
Patient:	You're trying to trick me! You won't admit you're wrong, so you try to make me think that I'm the one who's wrong.
Therapist:	(louder still) If I were wrong, I would admit it. On the contrary, I think you are the one who won't admit to being wrong, and you attribute that to me!
Patient:	I'm not going to take this harassment. I'll find another therapist!

This slightly caricatured interaction illustrates the projective identification cycle that is extraordinarily common in paranoid patients. The patient treats the therapist as a persecuting bad object. The therapist feels coerced into being defensive and ends up giving an interpretation that attempts to force the projection back into the patient. The patient responds by feeling attacked, misunderstood, and deceived. To avoid this escalating cycle, the therapist must empathize with the patient's need to project as a means of emotional survival. The therapist must be willing to serve as a container for feelings of hatred, badness, impotence, and despair (Epstein 1979). Attempting to return such feelings prematurely will simply lead the patient to feel an increased internal tension and to become more rigid. The therapist must be able to accept blame, even to the point of acknowledging a lack of ability to help the patient (Epstein 1984). Most therapists have strong countertransference resistances to accepting responsibility for a failing treatment; they just naturally become defensive when their patients accuse them of incompetence. However, by acknowledging the low self-esteem that creates the need to see fault in others, therapists can empathize with their patient's point of view and genuinely seek suggestions for how to make the treatment more productive. Becoming defensive is also a natural reaction to being accused of dishonesty. Defensiveness, however, may be misinterpreted as confirmation that the therapist has something to hide. Openness is by far the best policy with paranoid patients. If they act suspicious about the therapist's records or process notes, then the therapist would do well to share those notes with the patients and to thereby use them as a therapeutic intervention. Refusal to share notes will simply incite further paranoia.

Throughout the psychotherapy, particularly during the early phases of building an alliance, the therapist must avoid responding defensively—like everyone else in the patient's environment. The therapist should not challenge the patient's construction of events or the patient's perception of the therapist, no matter how negative. The therapist should merely ask for more detail and should empathize with the patient's feelings and perceptions. Above all, the therapist must resist the frequent countertransference tendency to be rid of undesirable projections by forcing them back into the patient via premature interpretation (Epstein 1979). As in the previous example, interpretations of this kind will simply confirm the perception that the therapist is highly invested in attacking the patient. The same situation might be handled quite differently using these principles of technique:

> Patient: I'm really angry with you because I've been sitting in
>   the waiting room for half an hour. You told me to be
>   here at 9:30 today.
> Therapist: Let me see if I understand you correctly. Your
>   understanding was that you were to see me today at
>   9:30 instead of 10 o'clock?
> Patient: You said 9:30.
> Therapist: I can certainly see why you might be angry at me then.
>   Having to wait for someone for 30 minutes would
>   make most people angry.
> Patient: You admit that you told me to come at 9:30?
> Therapist: Frankly, I don't remember saying that, but I'd like to
>   hear more about your recall of that conversation so I
>   can find out what I said to give you that impression.

In this scenario, the therapist accepts blame nondefensively without admitting to any fault. The therapist contains the patient's projection and seeks to find out more information about how it arose. By being willing to entertain the possibility of having indeed misled the patient, the therapist validates the patient's perception as legitimate and worthy of further discussion. Finally, the therapist does not attempt to return what has been projected in the form of an interpretation.

Therapists also need to empathize with the patient's tendency to be guarded. There is a certain adaptive quality in guardedness; paranoid patients who talk extensively about their perceptions are likely to alienate others. Therapists who allow for periods of silence and constriction instead of intrusively asking questions may help the patient to open up a bit more. Another technique for building an alliance is to focus on the patient's state of tension secondary to the extraordinary vigilance necessary to maintain the paranoid cognitive style. Comments such as, "Your nerves must be shot," or "You must be exhausted after all of this," may help the patient feel understood. When the patient is willing to talk, the therapist should encourage elaboration, which may reveal historical antecedents to the current situation of stress (Meissner 1976).

The overall goal of psychotherapeutic work with paranoid patients is to help them shift their perceptions of the origin of their problems from an external locus to an internal one. This shift can only follow an unhurried timetable that is unique to each patient. The therapist must withstand repeated barrages of accusations and suspicions without becoming exasperated or despairing. As the patient opens up more, the therapist can begin to label the patient's feelings and thereby help the patient distinguish between emotions and reality (Meissner 1976). Therapists can also help their patients define gaps in their knowledge. For example, a therapist might ask, "Did your boss *say* that he hates you?" When the patient responds negatively to the question, the therapist can comment matter-of-factly about the patient's limited knowledge of the boss's feelings. Such questions must be worded tactfully and neutrally so as not to inordinately challenge the patient's view of the world. The therapist need not take a pro or con position in the matter—but should only indicate that more information is necessary (Meissner 1976).

Throughout the entire psychotherapy process, the therapist must contain feelings rather than act on them. This containment will provide the patient with a new object relationship different from all others encountered. The different experience is eventually internalized over a long time. This relationship model of change is complemented by gradual changes in thinking. The key is for such patients to entertain a "creative doubt" (Meissner 1986) about their perceptions of the world. As patients move from the paranoid-schizoid position to encounter the depressive elements within, they begin to experience a sense of self that can mediate and interpret experience. Things may become "as if" they are a certain way rather than as *really* a certain way. Patients may also allow longer glimpses of their feelings of worthlessness and inferiority so that depressive elements can be worked through in the transference. In the most optimal circumstances, these patients can reveal a yearning for acceptance, love, and closeness that is associated with their frustration with early figures in their lives (Meissner 1976). As a result, they can begin the process of mourning those attachments.

Case Example

A brief report of the early stages of psychotherapy with a patient suffering from paranoid personality disorder will illustrate some of the technical principles described in the foregoing paragraphs. The bracketed comments below indicate how theory and technique relate in this case.

> Mr. X was a 42-year-old accountant who had been on disability for a year because of his continual complaints of allergies to substances in the work environment. After receiving a promotion, he had moved into a new office where he had experienced a sudden onset of several troublesome physical symptoms, including headaches, sluggish thinking, tightening in the chest, blurred vision, generalized aching, weakness, easy fatigability, and lack of motivation. The patient associated these symptoms to the new paneling and carpeting in the office and to vibrations in the floor from the blower system. The ill effects began to dissipate whenever he left the office and were often gone by the time the patient visited a doctor. He had had numerous diagnostic evaluations by various specialists, of whom only one had thought that there was any physical basis for the complaints. Mr. X used this isolated opinion to vindicate his own view. He was pressured into psychotherapy by the management of his firm, who were concerned that his disability was becoming permanent. In the initial stages of therapy, Mr. X denied any emotional problems other than marital tension, for which he blamed his wife. He spoke at length about his physical symptoms and maintained that he was convinced of their physical origin regardless of the negative findings from most of the specialists. [The patient reveals himself to be totally impervious to rational arguments from experts. He also displays grandiosity by believing that he knows more than the doctors.]
>
> When asked about his interpersonal relationships, the patient said that he and his father were not on speaking terms because his father had deceived him in business deals. Moreover, he complained that his father was always harder on him than on all his brothers. He summarized his description of his father by saying that he was an unfair and untrustworthy man. Mr. X went on to describe his wife as deceitful. She had "tricked" him into having a child by failing to use birth control and becoming pregnant. He said that he had never forgiven his wife for her trickery—8 years previously—and he said that their marriage had been a disaster ever since. He said that the

only way this situation could change would be for her to become more trustworthy. [The patient has projected malevolent persecuting objects onto close figures in his family and sees them as the source of all his problems. The patient himself acknowledges no contributions to these difficulties in family relationships and suggests that the only possible solutions involve change in others instead of in him.]

Throughout the first psychotherapy session, this patient listened intently to the therapist, often asking for further clarifications of comments. Mr. X seemed to be listening for hidden messages in the most benign communications. He was also hyperalert to any slight body movements of the therapist, often misinterpreting them as indications of boredom or disinterest. After listening for some time, the therapist commented empathically, "You must feel awful right now. Your boss is on your back to get therapy, you feel physically miserable, and your wife and you are not speaking to each other." The patient responded to this empathic comment by opening up a little more, admitting that he had always been "thin-skinned." He acknowledged that he was often considerably disturbed by minor things that did not bother other people. [The therapist's empathic validation of Mr. X's beleaguered self-esteem allowed him to feel understood. This beginning alliance allowed the patient to acknowledge a problem in himself for the first time, namely, that he was "thin-skinned."]

Mr. X described his relationship with his son in cold, calculating terms by saying, "We're together more than average for the population at large." [This description reveals the inability of the paranoid personality to feel emotional warmth and tenderness in relationships because it would produce vulnerability to rejection or attack.] Mr. X changed the subject to his concerns about the doctors who had examined him. He expressed a strong belief that all doctors are basically incompetent, and he seemed convinced that one doctor had almost caused him to have a cerebral hemorrhage with a certain medication. He described three psychiatrists who had previously examined him as all incompetent. He then asked the therapist if he knew of a particular nonpsychiatric medication. When the therapist admitted to being unfamiliar with the drug, Mr. X quickly responded that the therapist was probably as much of a "quack" as the other doctors. [The paranoid person's fear of being controlled, allied with feelings of inferiority in "one-down" relationships, often lead to a devaluation and demeaning of other people. By devaluing the therapist, Mr. X reassures himself that he has nothing to envy and no reason to feel inferior.]

When Mr. X continued to disparage the opinions of the many specialists he had seen, the therapist noted, "This must be very demoralizing for you." Mr. X responded sharply, "You're trying to lead me on!" [Here the therapist's attempt to empathize by introducing a new feeling exceeded the patient's ability to admit to that feeling. The patient's reaction might have been more positive if the therapist had stayed closer to the words and feeling states that the patient himself had described.]

As Mr. X continued to talk about his current state of affairs, he was able to acknowledge that he had found it difficult to adjust to disability and unemployment after being in an executive position. Sensing an opening regarding the self-esteem issue, the therapist noted that being unable to work must have been quite a blow. Mr. X responded by asking the therapist, "Do you think I am weak?" [Again the therapist's ability to empathize with the patient's low self-esteem rather than to become defensive allowed Mr. X to reveal concern about his underlying weakness and inferiority.]

Prevention of Violence

Although patients who suffer from any of a broad variety of psychiatric disorders may become violent, paranoid patients pose a particular threat to psychiatrists. An understanding of the dynamics of paranoia may help avert assault. To prevent the escalation of aggression, psychiatrists should keep in mind several principles of management:

1. *Do everything possible to help the patient save face.* The core of paranoia is low self-esteem, so psychiatrists should empathize with the patient's experience and not challenge the truth of what the patient says. In a busy outpatient clinic, a resident who saw a paranoid patient for the first time suspected that he was not telling the truth about his current living situation. He told the patient that he was going to check up on his statement by calling the halfway house where the patient said he lived. As the resident reached in his desk drawer for the telephone book, the patient struck him in the face with his fist. This unfortunate incident leads directly into another major principle of violence prevention.
2. *Avoid arousing further suspicion.* Because of the basic distrust of these patients, all interventions must be geared to avoiding any increase in their paranoia. Each movement should be explained slowly and carefully. The movements themselves should be performed slowly and in clear view. You might say, for example, "Now I'm going to reach in my desk and get an appointment slip so that you'll know when our next meeting is." You should also avoid being overly friendly to these patients, since such behavior is in stark contrast to their usual experience and will simply further arouse their suspicions.
3. *Help the patient maintain a sense of control.* Control is of extraordinary importance to paranoid patients, who are likely to fear loss of control as much as the therapist fears it. The therapist must avoid panic at all costs. A therapist who displays fear that the patient will lose control will only heighten the patient's own fears

of loss of control. Much of the anxiety among paranoid individuals stems from a fear that others will try to be in control, so anything the therapist can do to indicate respect for their autonomy will help reduce anxiety about passive surrender. Interventions should acknowledge their right to view the situation as they see it. For example, you might tell such a patient, "I think your feelings are legitimate about the situation, given what you've been through, and I respect your right to feel that way."

4. *Always encourage these patients to verbalize rather than to violently act out anger.* Get them to discuss their anger in as much detail as possible. Encourage a consideration of the logical consequences of becoming violent. If possible, provide constructive alternatives to violence so that these patients can begin to see that there are other options. Supporting the anger as a legitimate reaction does not mean endorsing aggressive action. The therapist who feels immediately threatened may attempt to translate this threat into words. When one psychiatric resident sensed that a new patient was about to erupt in violence, he said, "I wonder if you're feeling like you want to hit me right now." The patient nodded in assent. The resident then replied, "Maybe if we go take a walk and you tell me about the feelings you're having, you'll be able to avoid acting on those feelings." This calm, matter-of-fact approach taken helped the patient feel more in control, and the patient actually thanked the resident for his help.

5. *Always give paranoid individuals plenty of breathing room.* Their fear of passive surrender to others is heightened by physical proximity. Avoid a seating arrangement where they feel trapped in the office. Violent individuals have been shown to need greater distance from others to feel secure (Kinzel 1971). Avoid sitting too close, as well as touching them, even in the most benign manner. One paranoid woman began carrying a gun to her therapy sessions after her therapist persisted in hugging her at the end of each session.

6. *Finally, be attuned to your own countertransference in dealing with potentially violent patients* (Felthous 1984). Countertransference denial is common both in hospital staff members and in therapists who work with paranoid individuals. They may fail to ask important historical questions for fear of confirming their worst fears about their patients' potential for violence. Treaters must acknowledge their own fears and then must avoid situations of jeopardy with patients who have been assaultive in the past. Therapists may also use countertransference projection to disavow their own aggression and externalize it onto their patients. Projective identification may provoke patients to violence when therapists see destructiveness and aggression only in their patients and not in themselves.

Schizoid and Schizotypal Personality Disorders

In addition to paranoid personality disorder, Cluster A in Axis II of
DSM-III-R (American Psychiatric Association 1987) subsumes schizoid and schizotypal personality disorders. Although they are distinct
entities, they will be considered together here because both the
dynamic understanding of and the therapeutic approaches to these
disorders have much in common. Prior to DSM-III (American
Psychiatric Association 1980), a distinction was not made between
these two personality disorders. The creators of DSM-III considered
the schizoid personality disorder of DSM-II (American Psychiatric
Association 1968) too broad, however, so they divided that category
into three subtypes—schizoid, avoidant, and schizotypal—with the
publication of DSM-III in 1980. The inclusion of the avoidant
personality disorder was disturbing to many clinicians because it was
a little-used diagnosis with no clinical tradition. The decision to
distinguish between schizoid and avoidant was based on the classification system of Millon (1969, 1981), who apparently influenced
final decisions concerning diagnostic categories in Axis II (Akhtar
1987; Gunderson 1983). Millon justified the distinction because of
the different ways that persons in the two categories approached
interpersonal relationships. The schizoid individual was viewed as
incapable of and uninterested in forming relationships with others,
while the avoidant person was alleged to be both interested and
capable but afraid of humiliation and disapproval in the context of
relationships.

Criticism of this distinction has come from many quarters
(Akhtar 1987; Gunderson 1983; Kernberg 1984). Critics have
pointed out that the withdrawal of interest in others that is characteristic of schizoid individuals is only an apparent retreat. These
patients may secretly yearn for closeness but because of their fears
instead assume a defensive posture of detachment (Kernberg 1984).
Moreover, the assumption is that the schizoid personality is more
closely linked to a deficit model of psychopathology, while the
avoidant personality is a disorder of conflict, a distinction that
implies a better prognosis for the latter without any data to support
such a position (Akhtar 1987; Gunderson 1983). Empirical studies
(Morey 1985; Reich and Noyes 1986) have found the distinction
highly questionable as well. Finally, psychoanalysts and dynamically
oriented psychiatrists were concerned that the DSM-III-R version of
schizoid personality disorder deviated from the extensive psychoanalytic literature on schizoid phenomena by taking overt behavior at
face value (Akhtar 1987). (For a superb overview of the psychoanalytic and descriptive literature, see Akhtar 1987.) The DSM-III-R
version of schizoid and avoidant personality disorders improved to
some extent in response to these criticisms (see the updated diag-

nostic criteria for schizoid personality disorder contained in Table 13-2).

Although these criteria still fail to address the schizoid individual's secret longing for relationships, they do acknowledge that behind the outward appearance of detachment, the patient may experience strong emotions and may even have sexual feelings despite no such outward interest. The DSM-III-R criteria of avoidant personality also changed to more closely resemble a "phobic character."

The decision to separate schizoid and schizotypal seems to have been largely related to genetic studies (Kendler et al. 1981; Kety et al. 1971; Rosenthal et al. 1971) that suggested a muted version of schizophrenia characterized by more or less intact reality testing, disturbances of relationships, and mild thinking disturbances. The link between schizotypal personality and schizophrenia was further bolstered by McGlashan's (1983) long-term follow-up study, which demonstrated that schizotypal and schizophrenic patients had similar outcomes. The outcomes of borderline patients, on the other hand, were more typical of those associated with affective disorders. The designation of certain close relatives of schizophrenic individuals as schizotypal replaced the more problematic term *borderline schizophrenia,* which was easily confused with borderline personality disorder. Some critics (Siever and Gunder-

Table 13-2.   DSM-III-R criteria for schizoid personality disorder

A. A pervasive pattern of indifference to social relationships and a restricted range of emotional experience and expression, beginning by early adulthood and present in a variety of contexts, as indicated by at least *four* of the following:
   (1)   neither desires nor enjoys close relationships, including being part of the family
   (2)   almost always chooses solitary activities
   (3)   rarely, if ever, claims or appears to experience strong emotions, such as anger and joy
   (4)   indicates little if any desire to have sexual experiences with another person (age being taken into account)
   (5)   is indifferent to the praise and criticism of others
   (6)   has no close friends or confidants (or only one) other than first-degree relatives
   (7)   displays constricted affect, e.g., is aloof, cold, rarely reciprocates gestures or facial expressions, such as smiles or nods
B. Occurrence not exclusively during the course of schizophrenia or a delusional disorder.

Note.   Reprinted from DSM-III-R, p. 340, with permission from the American Psychiatric Association.

son 1979) have questioned the appropriateness of classifying a variant of a psychotic condition as a personality disorder. In their view the diagnosis depends to a large extent on symptoms resembling schizophrenia rather than on sustained patterns of relating to others, which are used to define the other personality disorders. Five of the nine current DSM-III-R criteria are essential to a diagnosis of schizotypal personality disorder (see Table 13-3).

As Gunderson (1983) pointed out, persons with schizotypal personality disorder are much the same as schizoid individuals except that the definition of this disorder includes a few symptoms suggestive of an attenuated form of schizophrenia. In actuality, schizoid and schizotypal patients form a continuum, so it is somewhat arbitrary to draw a dividing line between the two entities. Schizotypal patients themselves form a continuum from those on one end who are much like schizoid patients (except for a few more

Table 13-3. DSM-III-R criteria for schizotypal personality disorder

A. A pervasive pattern of deficits in interpersonal relatedness and peculiarities of ideation, appearance, and behavior, beginning by early adulthood and present in a variety of contexts, as indicated by at least *five* of the following:
  (1) ideas of reference (excluding delusions of reference)
  (2) excessive social anxiety, e.g., extreme discomfort in social situations involving unfamiliar people
  (3) odd beliefs or magical thinking, influencing behavior and inconsistent with subcultural norms, e.g., superstitiousness, belief in clairvoyance, telepathy, or "sixth sense," "others can feel my feelings" (in children and adolescents, bizarre fantasies or preoccupations)
  (4) unusual perceptual experiences, e.g., illusions, sensing the presence of a force or person not actually present (e.g., "I felt as if my dead mother were in the room with me")
  (5) odd or eccentric behavior or appearance, e.g., unkempt, unusual mannerisms, talks to self
  (6) no close friends or confidants (or only one) other than first-degree relatives
  (7) odd speech (without loosening of associations or incoherence), e.g., speech that is impoverished, digressive, vague, or inappropriately abstract
  (8) inappropriate or constricted affect, e.g., silly, aloof, rarely reciprocates gestures or facial expressions, such as smiles or nods
  (9) suspiciousness or paranoid ideation
B. Occurrence not exclusively during the course of schizophrenia or a pervasive developmental disorder

Note. Reprinted from DSM-III-R, pp. 340–341, with permission from the American Psychiatric Association.

oddities of behavior and communication), to those closer to schizophrenia who are prone to brief psychotic episodes. The ensuing discussion of the psychoanalytic understanding of these conditions assumes that they are inherently similar.

Psychodynamic Understanding

Schizoid and schizotypal patients often live on the fringes of society. They may be ridiculed as "weirdos," "oddballs," or "misfits," or they may merely be left alone to pursue a solitary and idiosyncratic existence. Their isolation and anhedonia may lead others to feel sorry for them and reach out to them. More often than not, however, the individuals who make such gestures give up after being repeatedly rebuffed. Family members may become so exasperated that they force their schizoid relative into a treatment situation. Parents of adolescents or young adults may bring their son or daughter to a psychiatrist out of concern that their child is not getting enough out of life (Stone 1985). Other schizoid and schizotypal patients come to psychiatric treatment voluntarily because of painful loneliness.

The inner world of the schizoid patient may differ considerably from the individual's outward appearance. Indeed, these people are often a bundle of contradictions. Akhtar (1987) has grouped these contradictions into overt and covert manifestations: "The schizoid individual is 'overtly' detached, self-sufficient, absent-minded, uninteresting, asexual, and idiosyncratically moral while 'covertly' being exquisitely sensitive, emotionally needy, acutely vigilant, creative, often perverse, and vulnerable to corruption" (p. 510). These polarities do not reflect conscious and unconscious personality traits. Rather, they represent a splitting or fragmentation of the self into different self-representations that remain unintegrated. From a psychodynamic perspective, the "schizoid" designation reflects this fundamental splitting of the self. The result is a diffuse identity—schizoid patients are not sure who they are, and they feel buffeted by highly conflictual thoughts, feelings, wishes, and urges. This identity diffusion makes relating to others problematic. Indeed, perhaps the most striking feature of schizoid and schizotypal patients is their apparent nonrelatedness to others. Psychoanalytic work with these patients suggests that they definitely have feelings and strivings for others, but that the patients themselves are frozen developmentally at an early stage of relatedness (Lawner 1985). These patients seem to base their decision to be isolated on a conviction that their failure to receive what they needed from their mothers means that they can make no further attempt to receive anything else from subsequent significant figures (Nachmani 1984).

Much of our understanding of the inner world of the schizoid patient derives from the work of the British object relations theorists. Balint (1968) viewed these patients as having a fundamental deficit in their ability to relate—a "basic fault" caused by significant inadequacies in the mothering they received as an infant. He believed that the schizoid patient's difficulty in relating to others stems from this basic incapacity rather than from conflict (as in neurotic patients). Fairbairn (1954), perhaps the foremost contributor to our understanding of schizoid patients, viewed the schizoid retreat as a defense against a conflict between a wish to relate to others and a fear that one's neediness would harm others. The infant who initially perceives its mother as rejecting may withdraw from the world. However, the infant's neediness grows until it is experienced as insatiable. The infant then fears that the greed will devour the mother and leave the infant alone again. Hence the very object that the infant most needs may be destroyed by its own incorporative strivings. Fairbairn termed this concern the "Little Red Riding Hood Fantasy," based on the fairy tale in which the little girl finds, to her horror, that her grandmother has disappeared, leaving her alone with her own projected oral greed—in the form of a devouring wolf.

Just as Little Red Riding Hood may project her greed into the wolf, infants may project their own greed into their mothers, whom they then view as devouring and dangerous. This infantile dilemma is frozen in time for schizoid patients, who first fear that they will devour others with their neediness, and then fear being devoured by others. This fundamental dilemma of schizoid patients mandates that they will vacillate between a fear of driving others away by their neediness, on the one hand, and fear, on the other hand, that others will smother or consume them. As a result, all relationships are experienced as dangerous and to be avoided. Because the decision to be nonrelated leaves the schizoid individual alone and empty, there is often a "schizoid compromise" (Guntrip 1968), in which the patient simultaneously clings to and rejects others.

Schizoid patients live under the constant threat of abandonment, persecution, and disintegration (Appel 1974). To take anything in from someone else risks the triggering of intense longings for dependency and merger. Love is equated with fusing with someone else, losing one's identity, and destroying the other person. Although the writing of the British School has focused on schizoid patients, the descriptions provided by Balint, Guntrip, and others refer to schizotypal patients as well (Stone 1985).

The schizoid patient's characteristic retreat from interpersonal relations may serve an important developmental function. Winnicott (1963) believed that the isolation of the schizoid patient preserves an important authenticity that is absolutely sacred to the evolving self of the patient: "There is an intermediate stage in healthy development in which the patient's most important experience in relation to the good or potentially satisfying object is the refusal of it" (p. 182). The schizoid withdrawal is a way to communicate with the "true self" within instead of sacrificing that authenticity to artificial interactions with others that would lead to a "false self." Winnicott suggested that we all have this noncommunicating core, and that we must respect the schizoid individual's right—and need—to be noncommunicative. Periods of extreme abstinence and isolation may help schizoid individuals get in touch with this sequestered self so that it can be integrated with other self-representations (Eigen 1973).

Schizoid patients who allow their therapist to have access to their inner worlds will often reveal omnipotent fantasies. These usually accompany the reclusive aspects of the self to which the patient retreats. Like other aspects of the hidden self, they serve as a "sanctuary from exposure" (Grotstein 1977) to shore up fragile self-esteem and to allay anxiety about self-disintegration. Like paranoid patients, schizoid patients have omnipotent fantasies that increase in frequency in inverse proportion to their level of self-esteem (Nachmani 1984). Lacking good internal self- and object-representations to help accomplish essential work toward success in relationships or careers, schizoid patients employ fantasies of omnipotence to bypass such work and directly achieve their grandiose fantasies. Schizoid patients often feel a great deal of shame about their fantasies, and are reluctant to share them with their therapists until they feel secure in the relationship.

Individual Psychotherapy

Schizoid and schizotypal patients may be helped with individual expressive-supportive therapy, dynamic group psychotherapy, or a combination of the two. Since the thought of the interactional demands of a group setting usually produces a good deal of anxiety, most of these patients will feel more comfortable beginning with an individual process. Much of the modern literature on the psychotherapy of schizoid and schizotypal personality disorders suggests that the mechanism of therapeutic action is likely to occur through internalization of a therapeutic relationship rather than through interpretation of conflict (Appel 1974; Gabbard 1989; Khan 1983; Nachmani 1984; Stone 1983, 1985; Winnicott 1963).

The task of the therapist is to "thaw" the patient's frozen internal object relations by providing a new experience of relatedness. The schizoid style of relatedness emerges from inadequacies in the patient's earliest relationships with parental figures—what Epstein (1979) referred to as primary maturational failure.

Throughout life, the patient has evoked similar reactions from those in the environment, producing secondary maturational failures. In other words, the schizoid patient may go through life distancing everyone. Therapists must figure out how to relate to the patient in a maturationally corrective way. Therapists must not allow themselves to be driven away or alienated like everyone else in the patient's life.

To say that the goal of therapy is to provide a new relationship for internalization is deceptively straightforward and simple. Yet this strategy presents formidable obstacles. First, the patient's basic mode of existence is nonrelatedness. The therapist is asking a nonrelating person to move in the direction of greater relatedness. As expected, the therapist's strategy will be met with emotional distance and a good deal of silence.

Therapists who attempt to treat withdrawn schizoid patients must have extraordinary patience because of the slow, painstaking internalization process. They must also adopt a permissive, accepting attitude about silence. Specifically, silence must be viewed as more than simply resistance. In addition, it is a specific form of nonverbal communication that may provide essential information about the patient.

During long periods of silence, the therapist must recognize that a relationship is still transpiring between two people. Through projective identification, the patient's behavior will evoke certain responses in the therapist that contain valuable diagnostic information about the patient's internal world (Gabbard, 1989). One patient who, throughout childhood, had been given "the silent treatment" by his father, stopped talking in his therapy; his unconscious intent was to induce the therapist to feel what the patient had experienced as a child when his father "shut down." Thus, like a mother who holds and processes the projected elements coming into her from her infant, the therapist must contain and modify the patient's projections before the patient reintrojects them.

With this model, the therapist's emotional reactions to the patient, however subtle, are the primary source of information about the patient. When the silence is prolonged, therapists must be wary of turning the tables and projecting their own self- and object-representations into the patient. This state of affairs is beautifully depicted in Ingmar Bergman's moving film, *Persona,* where a mute patient is treated by a nurse. After many unsuccessful attempts to get the patient to speak, the nurse becomes frustrated and begins to project aspects of herself into the patient. Driven crazy, the nurse begins to treat the patient as an embodiment of her own internal world (Gabbard 1989).

This model of therapy requires therapists to receive their patient's projections and to monitor their own without getting swept up into countertransference acting out. When therapists feel like quitting or giving up on a patient, they must view that feeling like any other in the process and attempt to understand it. As mentioned in Chapter 4 in the discussion of psychotherapy, the projective identifications might only be diagnosed and understood after the therapist has been "coerced" into playing a specific role vis-à-vis the patient. Therapists must silently note the interactions taking place between them and their patients and then use that information to inform subsequent interactions. Ogden (1982) summarized the therapist's task in such situations:

> The perspective of projective identification neither requires nor excludes the use of verbal interpretation; the therapist attempts to find a way of talking with and being with the patient that will constitute a medium through which the therapist may accept unintegrable aspects of the patient's internal object world and return them to the patient in a form that the patient can accept and learn from. (p. 42)

Indeed, a decision not to interpret may be the most therapeutically potent strategy with schizoid and schizotypal patients. If silence is interpreted as resistance, these patients may feel responsible and humiliated for a basic incapacity to communicate (Khan 1983; Nachmani 1984). On the other hand, by refraining from interpretation and accepting the silence, the therapist may legitimize the private, noncommunicative core of the self referred to by Winnicott (1963). With certain patients, the therapist must respect their silent self. It may be the only viable technical approach to building a therapeutic alliance (Gabbard 1989).

Therapists greatly value interpersonal relatedness. We want to mean something to our patients. Accepting silent nonrelatedness runs counter to our training and psychological predisposition. Our natural tendency is to burden our patients with the expectations that they should be different than they are. Specifically, we want our patients to talk to us and to relate to us. However, that expectation means that we must ask patients to confront the very pain they avoid by schizoid withdrawal. Greater expectations will paradoxically lead the patient to further detachment, as Searles (1986) observed:

> Winnicott's (1941) concept of the...good-enough holding environment implies that the analyst be not merely relatively stably there, for the patient, but also relatively destructible (psychologically) by the patient, time and again, as the patient's persistent needs for autistic (omnipotent) functioning still require. Hence the analyst needs intuitively to provide his own absence, perhaps as often as his own presence, to the patient at timely moments. (p. 351)

Certain patients will respond to this tolerant, empathic acceptance with greater openness in the therapeutic relationship. These patients may begin to speak about hidden aspects of the self, eventually integrating these into a more cohesive sense of self. At the beginning of a psychotherapy process, it is difficult to know which patients are likely to benefit from it. Stone (1983), writing about schizotypal (borderline schizophrenic) patients, suggested that those who do a bit better in psychotherapy have some depressive symptoms or some capacity for emotional warmth and empathy. He warned therapists to be wary of excessive countertransference expectations, because only limited progress can be expected. In Stone's view, therapists must be able to tolerate the disappointment that their patients may progress only in areas other than relatedness. In general, those patients with better ego functioning (i.e., more intact reality testing, better judgment, smaller amounts of cognitive slippage) will do better in treatment than those patients with more profoundly disturbed ego functioning. With those in the latter group, therapists may need to function as an auxiliary ego, helping patients supportively with various tasks such as reality testing, judgment, and self-object differentiation. Stone (1985) also pointed out that, like schizophrenic patients (see Chapter 7), schizoid patients need more than expressive-supportive psychotherapy. Lower-functioning schizotypal patients also need social skills training, reeducation, and various social supports. Medication is rarely useful unless the patient has a psychotic episode or affective symptoms from a concomitant Axis I disorder.

Dynamic Group Psychotherapy

In general, schizoid patients are prime candidates for dynamic group psychotherapy (Appel 1974; Azima 1983). Group therapy is oriented to helping patients with socialization, which is exactly where schizoid patients suffer most. It is also a setting in which a good deal of new parenting can take place. For many schizoid patients, their peers in a group process can function as a reconstructed family, eventually being internalized by these patients to counterbalance their more negative and frightening internal objects (Appel 1974).

Such patients can benefit considerably simply by having regular exposure to others. Some schizoid patients literally have no social outlet beyond their group therapy sessions. As they begin to feel accepted and to find that their fears are not realized, they gradually become more comfortable with people. In a manner similar to the individual therapy process described earlier, the reactions of other group members may provide a corrective experience that runs counter to all previous relationship experiences. Some difficulties that arise in the group psychotherapy of schizoid patients include resentment from other patients who have to "spill their guts" while the schizoid patient remains silent. These feelings may lead to a kind of "ganging up" to force the schizoid patient to talk. At such moments the therapist must support the schizoid member of the group and help the other patients accept that patient's need to be silent (Azima 1983). The other patients may also simply ignore a withdrawn schizoid patient and proceed as if that patient was not there. In these instances, the therapist's task is to bring the patient into the group by pointing out how a pattern that takes place outside the group is repeating itself inside the group. Schizotypal patients tend to benefit from group therapy much as schizoid patients do, but those whose behavior is bizarre or whose thinking is psychotic may become scapegoats because they are simply too different from other members of the group. With such patients, individual therapy alone may be the preferred modality.

A combination of group and individual psychotherapy is ideal for many schizoid patients because the social field they encounter in the group can be discussed and processed with their individual psychotherapist. A significant number of schizoid patients will feel, however, that a recommendation for group therapy is like "being thrown to the lions." They may even feel betrayed when their therapist makes the suggestion. A preliminary step to group referral is often the working through of their fantasies about what will happen in group psychotherapy.

Case Example

Mr. Y was a 23-year-old, single man with schizoid personality disorder. He worked as a nurse's aide on the night shift in a nursing home and took daytime classes at a local university. He liked working at night because very few interpersonal demands were made on him. His supervisor frequently slept, so he was free to read novels. When he was not sleeping, Mr. Y would spend many hours in vigorous body-building exercises. He would then pose nude in front of the mirror and flex his muscles and admire himself. Much of the posing and flexing was accompanied by omnipotent fantasies of becoming an Olympic decathlon winner. He also imagined that if he achieved a certain level of bodily perfection, he would then be attractive to a college girl in one of his classes that he could never bring himself to speak to.

Mr. Y was deeply concerned about the fact that he had been adopted. He spoke about it with great shame, as though convinced that it reflected some inherent flaw. In his view the early rejection by his biological mother was a sign that he was so inherently undesirable that others would certainly reject him if given the chance.

Like many schizoid patients, Mr. Y had a perverse streak that took the form of exhibitionism. He would place himself in situations where women would come upon him in the nude. He would then act surprised and immediately leave the scene so as to avoid prosecution. However, the sexual pleasure he derived from this activity led him into more and more risky adventures. He once switched the men's and women's labels on the locker room doors in a gymnasium so that women would enter the men's locker room and find him standing there nude, drying himself after showering.

Mr. Y eventually came to an outpatient clinic where he sought group psychotherapy. He was concerned that his exhibitionism was getting out of hand and might lead to legal consequences, and he was genuinely disturbed by the loneliness of his existence. He sought group psychotherapy because he had previously tried individual psychotherapy for 2 years. He reported that he had remained silent throughout practically the entire therapy. Finally, he and the therapist had mutually decided that there was no point in continuing. Mr. Y also reported that he had a strong desire to overcome his fear of other people, and he believed that group therapy might be a good way to deal with that fear.

Mr. Y began a dynamic group psychotherapy process with a reasonably high-functioning group of other patients with assorted personality disorders. He attended regularly but sat silently through much of the group's discussion. Little by little, he was able to reveal more and more about himself. Something of a breakthrough occurred when he mustered enough courage to talk about the female classmate who was the object of his fantasies. One female patient in the group responded by saying, "Why don't you ask her out? You're an attractive man." Moved by this comment, Mr. Y replied that no one had ever told him that before.

The support and positive feedback this patient received from other group members bolstered his self-esteem and allowed him to speak more frequently and more openly. When he finally was able to discuss his exhibitionism, he experienced considerable relief that no one recoiled in horror at his revelation.

After several years of group therapy, Mr. Y's anxieties about relationships and his self-regard had improved to the point that he was able to begin dating and to form some appropriate peer relationships with males. The episodes of exhibitionism gradually decreased, although they tended to recur whenever the group took a vacation and Mr. Y felt abandoned by the therapist and his fellow patients.

The case of Mr. Y illustrates how the overt absence of object relations in the schizoid personality disorder may be accompanied by intense fantasies of relatedness and by covert sexual activities of a perverse nature. Long periods of exercise are also fairly common in schizoid and schizotypal individuals. Physical activity of this nature may serve to "burn off" sexual energy, or as in the case of Mr. Y, it may also be a way to build self-esteem by fantasizing that others will find the individual more attractive as a result of such efforts.

Although a number of perversions are commonly found in schizoid individuals, exhibitionism seems to hold a particular significance for these patients. Fairbairn (1954) observed that schizoid individuals frequently overvalue their mental contents, perceiving them as extraordinarily precious. They fear giving anything of themselves because in so doing they would deplete their narcissistically prized contents. Fairbairn noted that schizoid patients commonly use exhibitionism as a defense against the fear of giving. To be more exact, "showing" becomes a substitute for "giving," since the latter carries the fear of losing something precious while the former does not. Although the exhibitionism was overt in the case of Mr. Y, it frequently appears in sublimated forms, such as involvement in the performing arts.

Group psychotherapy provided Mr. Y with a new series of relationships to internalize. The relatedness with his fellow patients (and with the therapist) disconfirmed his expectations of how others would respond to him. Instead of being alienated by him, the group members accepted him as he was and confirmed his desirability as a person. Thus the validation of other patients in group therapy may have a more powerful impact on a schizoid patient than similar validation by an individual therapist. The schizoid patient may write off the positive regard of the therapist as an attitude contrived for therapeutic effect; the therapist is "just doing his job."

Many schizoid and schizotypal patients are much more refractory to treatment than Mr. Y. As Stone (1985) suggested, therapists must genuinely respect their patient's need to be different and must not feel compelled to transform a patient into someone else. In treating schizoid and schizotypal patients, we would all be well advised to remember the wisdom of Thoreau: "If a man does not keep pace with his companions, perhaps it is because he hears a different drummer. Let him step to the music which he hears, however measured or far away."

References

Akhtar S: Schizoid personality disorder: a synthesis of developmental, dynamic, and descriptive features. Am J Psychother 61:499–518, 1987

American Psychiatric Association: Diagnostic and Statistical Manual of Mental Disorders, 2nd Edition. Washington, DC, American Psychiatric Association, 1968

American Psychiatric Association: Diagnostic and Statistical Manual of Mental Disorders, 3rd Edition. Washington, DC, American Psychiatric Association, 1980

American Psychiatric Association: Diagnostic and Statistical Manual of Mental Disorders, 3rd Edition, Revised. Washington, DC, American Psychiatric Association, 1987

Appel G: An approach to the treatment of schizoid phenomena. Psychoanal Rev 61:99–113, 1974

Azima FJC: Group psychotherapy with personality disorders, in Comprehensive Group Psychotherapy, 2nd Edition. Edited by Kaplan HI, Sadock BJ. Baltimore, Williams & Wilkins, 1983, pp 262–268

Balint M: The Basic Fault: Therapeutic Aspects of Regression. New York, Brunner/Mazel, 1968

Eigen M: Abstinence and the schizoid ego. Int J Psychoanal 54:493–498, 1973

Epstein L: Countertransference with borderline patients, in Countertransference. Edited by Epstein L, Feiner AH. New York, Jason Aronson, 1979, pp 375–405

Epstein L: An interpersonal-object relations perspective on working with destructive aggression. Contemp Psychoanal 20:651–662, 1984

Fairbairn WRD: An Object-Relations Theory of the Personality. New York, Basic Books, 1954

Felthous AR: Preventing assaults on a psychiatric inpatient ward. Hosp Community Psychiatry 35:1223–1226, 1984

Freud S: Psycho-analytic notes on an autobiographical account of a case of paranoia (dementia paranoides) (1911), in The Standard Edition of the Complete Psychological Works of Sigmund Freud, Vol 12. Translated and edited by Strachey J. London, Hogarth Press, 1958, pp 1–82

Gabbard GO: On "doing nothing" in the psychoanalytic treatment of the refractory borderline patient. Int J Psychoanal 70:527–534, 1989

Grotstein JS: The psychoanalytic concept of schizophrenia, I: the dilemma. Int J Psychoanal 58:403–425, 1977

Gunderson JG: DSM-III diagnoses of personality disorders, in Current Perspectives on Personality Disorders. Edited by Frosch JP. Washington, DC, American Psychiatric Press, 1983, pp 20–39

Guntrip HJS: Schizoid Phenomena, Object-Relations, and the Self. New York, International Universities Press, 1968

Kendler KS, Gruenberg AM, Strauss JS: An independent analysis of the Copenhagen sample of the Danish adoption study of schizophrenia, II: the relationship between schizotypal personality disorder and schizophrenia. Arch Gen Psychiatry 38:982–984, 1981

Kernberg OF: Severe Personality Disorders: Psychotherapeutic Strategies. New Haven, CT, Yale University Press, 1984

Kety SS, Rosenthal D, Wender PH, et al: Mental illness in the biological and adoptive families of adopted schizophrenics. Am J Psychiatry 128:302–306, 1971

Khan MR: Hidden Selves: Between Theory and Practice in Psychoanalysis. New York, International Universities Press, 1983

Kinzel AF: Violent behavior in prisons, in Dynamics of Violence. Edited by Fawcett J. Chicago, American Medical Association, 1971

Lawner P: Character rigidity and resistance to awareness of the transference. Issues in Ego Psychology 8:36–41, 1985

McGlashan T: The borderline syndrome, II: is it a variant of schizophrenia or affective disorder? Arch Gen Psychiatry 40:1319–1323, 1983

Meissner WW: Psychotherapeutic schema based on the paranoid process. Int J Psychoanal Psychother 5:87–114, 1976

Meissner WW: Psychotherapy and the Paranoid Process. Northvale, NJ, Jason Aronson, 1986

Millon T: Modern Psychopathology: A Biosocial Approach to Maladaptive Learning and Functioning. Philadelphia, WB Saunders, 1969

Millon T: Disorders of Personality: DSM-III, Axis-II. New York, John Wiley, 1981

Morey LC: An empirical comparison of interpersonal and DSM-III approaches to classification of personality disorders. Psychiatry 48:358–364, 1985

Nachmani G: Hesitation, perplexity, and annoyance at opportunity. Contemporary Psychoanalysis 20:448–457, 1984

Ogden TH: Projective Identification and Psychotherapeutic Technique. New York, Jason Aronson, 1982

Ogden TH: The Matrix of the Mind: Object Relations and the Psychoanalytic Dialogue. Northvale, NJ, Jason Aronson, 1986

Reich J, Noyes R Jr: Differentiating schizoid and avoidant personality disorders (letter to editor). Am J Psychiatry 143:1062, 1986

Rosenthal D, Wender PH, Kety SS, et al: The adopted-away offspring of schizophrenics. Am J Psychiatry 128:307–311, 1971

Searles HF: My Work With Borderline Patients. Northvale, NJ, Jason Aronson, 1986

Shapiro D: Neurotic Styles. New York, Basic Books, 1965

Siever LJ, Gunderson JG: Genetic determinants of borderline conditions. Schizophr Bull 5:59–86, 1979

Stone MH: Psychotherapy with schizotypal borderline patients. J Am Acad Psychoanal 11:87–111, 1983

Stone MH: Schizotypal personality: psychotherapeutic aspects. Schizophr Bull 11:576–589, 1985

Winnicott DW: Communicating and not communicating leading to a study of certain opposites (1963), in The Maturational Processes and the Facilitating Environment. New York, International Universities Press, 1965, pp 179–192

CHAPTER 14

The Borderline Patient

Our consideration of Cluster B personality disorders begins with the borderline patient, because borderline personality disorder serves as a reference point for the entire cluster. Narcissistic, antisocial, and histrionic personality disorders are often defined by how they differ from borderline personality disorder. Moreover, when *borderline* is used in the broad sense of a spectrum (Meissner 1988) or a personality organization (Kernberg 1967), all the personality disorders in Cluster B, along with those in Cluster A as well, may be subsumed under the general category of borderline conditions. Unfortunately, the increasing popularity of the borderline diagnosis in the last two decades has made it something of a psychiatric "wastebasket"—both overused and misused. Patients who are diagnostically confusing may receive the label *borderline* by default. A brief historical survey of the term *borderline* in American psychiatry may shed light on the place of borderline personality disorder in the current nomenclature.

Evolution of the Term

In the late 1930s and throughout the 1940s, clinicians began to describe certain patients who were not sick enough to be labeled schizophrenic but who were far too disturbed for classical psychoanalytic treatment. In an effort to capture the "in between" state typical of these patients, Hoch and Polatin (1949) referred to this group as having pseudoneurotic schizophrenia characterized by a symptomatic pattern of "panneurosis," "pananxiety," and "pansexuality." Robert Knight (1954) further characterized this ill-defined group by focusing on several impairments in ego functioning, including the inability to plan realistically, the incapacity to defend against primitive impulses, and the predominance of primary process thinking over secondary process thinking.

These early contributors were observing a "messy" syndrome that did not fit well into preexisting diagnostic rubrics. Grinker et al. (1968) brought some diagnostic rigor to the syndrome in the early 1960s with their statistical analysis of approximately 60 such patients who were hospitalized in Chicago. A cluster analysis of data

331

on these patients suggested that there were four subgroups of borderline patients (see Table 14-1). These patients appeared to occupy a continuum from the "psychotic border" (Type I) all the way to the "neurotic border" (Type IV). In between the two extremes could be found a group with predominantly negative affects and difficulty maintaining stable interpersonal relationships (Type II), and another group (Type III) characterized by a generalized lack of identity, resulting in a need to borrow identity from others.

Grinker and his associates (1968) also attempted to identify common denominators in the borderline syndrome that were present regardless of the subtype. They came up with the following four key features: 1) anger as the main or only affect, 2) defects in interpersonal relationships, 3) absence of consistent self-identity, and 4) pervasive depression. One of the most significant contributions of this empirical study was the finding that the borderline syndrome was clearly distinct from schizophrenia. Grinker et al. found that these patients do not deteriorate into frank schizophrenia over time. Rather, they are stably unstable (Schmideberg 1959) throughout the course of their illness. This discovery helped refute the belief some skeptics held that borderline patients were actually schizophrenic.

Gunderson and Singer (1975) reviewed the descriptive literature and delineated six features as the basis for a rational diagnosis of borderline patients: 1) an intense affect of a predominantly depressed or angry nature, 2) impulsivity, 3) a superficial adaptation

Table 14-1. Grinker's four subtypes of borderline patients

Type I: The Psychotic Border:
  A. Inappropriate nonadaptive behavior
  B. Problems with reality testing and sense of identity
  C. Negative behavior and openly expressed anger
Type II: Core Borderline Syndrome:
  A. Pervasive negative affect
  B. Vacillating involvement with others
  C. Anger acted out
  D. Inconsistent self-identity
Type III: As-If Group:
  A. Tendency to copy identity of others
  B. Affectless
  C. Behavior more adaptive
  D. Relationships lacking in genuineness and spontaneity
Type IV: Neurotic Border:
  A. Anaclitic depression
  B. Anxiety
  C. Neurotic and narcissistic features

Table 14-2. Discriminating characteristics of borderline
personality disorder ranked in order of importance

1. Intense and unstable interpersonal relationships
2. Chronic self-destructive behavior
3. Chronic abandonment fears
4. Chronic dysphoric affects
5. Cognitive distortions
6. Impulsivity
7. Poor social adaptation

Note. Based on Gunderson and Zanarini 1987, pp. 5–6.

to social situations (which helped differentiate these patients from schizophrenics), 4) transient psychotic episodes, 5) a proneness to loose thinking on projective testing or other unstructured situations, and 6) a vacillating pattern of relationships that shifts from extreme dependency to transient superficiality. Gunderson (1984) continued his study of the borderline diagnosis with the intent of identifying clearly discriminating criteria that would distinguish the borderline personality from other psychiatric diagnoses. By 1987, Gunderson and Zanarini were able to rank order, according to importance, discriminating features based on research focused on descriptive characteristics (see Table 14-2).

Many of these criteria are interrelated. The borderline patient is consumed with establishing exclusive one-to-one relationships with no risk whatsoever of abandonment. Since persons with borderline personality disorder find it difficult to trust others, they experience anxiety verging on panic related to the conviction that they are about to be rejected at any moment. To prevent being alone, they may resort to wrist-cutting or other self-destructive behavior to elicit rescue by the person to whom they are attached. Overdosing and bulimic behavior are other common self-destructive behaviors of those with borderline personality disorder. Dysphoric affects, such as rage and depression, result from their perception that others do not take care of their needs. Impulsive behaviors, such as ill-advised sexual encounters and substance abuse, may also relate to their desperate attempts to avoid being alone. This pattern of interpersonal relatedness obviously results in poor social adaptation, although these individuals may superficially appear to interact on an acceptable basis. Much of their cognitive distortion or strains of reality testing occur in the context of interpersonal relationships as well. In the absence of the reassuring presence of their loved ones, they may become frankly paranoid as they imagine that they are about to be abandoned.

While Gunderson and Grinker et al. focused primarily on descriptive diagnostic criteria, Otto Kernberg (1967, 1975) sought to characterize borderline patients from a psychoanalytic perspective. Using a combined ego psychological–object relations approach, he coined the term *borderline personality organization* to encompass a group of patients who showed characteristic patterns of ego weakness, primitive defensive operations, and problematic object relations. He observed a variety of symptoms in these patients, including free-floating anxiety, obsessive-compulsive symptoms, multiple phobias, dissociative reactions, hypochondriacal preoccupation, conversion symptoms, paranoid trends, polymorphous-perverse sexuality, and substance abuse. He cautioned, however, that descriptive symptoms were not sufficient for a definitive diagnosis. He believed instead that the diagnosis rested on a sophisticated structural analysis that revealed four key features (Table 14-3).

1. *Nonspecific manifestations of ego weakness.* One aspect of ego functioning is the capacity to delay the discharge of impulses and to modulate affects such as anxiety. Borderline patients, in Kernberg's view, are unable to marshal ego forces to perform those functions because of inherent nonspecific weaknesses. Similarly, they have a difficult time sublimating powerful drives and utilizing their conscience to guide behavior.
2. *Shift toward primary-process thinking.* Like Robert Knight, Kernberg noted that these patients tend to regress into psychotic-like thinking in the absence of structure or under the pressure of strong affects. However, these shifts primarily occur in the context of generally intact reality testing.

Table 14-3. Kernberg's criteria for borderline personality organization (1975)

I. Nonspecific manifestations of ego weakness
    A. Lack of anxiety tolerance
    B. Lack of impulse control
    C. Lack of developed subliminatory channels
II. Shift toward primary-process thinking
III. Specific defensive operations characteristic of borderline personality organization
    A. Splitting
    B. Primitive idealization
    C. Early forms of projection, especially projective identification
    D. Denial
    E. Omnipotence and devaluation
IV. Pathological internalized object relations

3. *Specific defensive operations.* Foremost among these defenses was splitting, which Kernberg viewed as an active process of separating contradictory introjects and affects from one another (see Chapter 2). Splitting operations in the person with borderline personality disorder manifest themselves clinically as follows: a) there is an alternating expression of contradictory behaviors and attitudes, which the patient regards with a lack of concern and bland denial; b) there is a compartmentalization of all persons in the patient's environment into "all good" and "all bad" camps, with frequent oscillations between camps for a given individual; and c) there are coexisting contradictory views and images of oneself (self-representations) that alternate in their dominance from day to day and from hour to hour.

> A 41-year-old Catholic priest was admitted to a psychiatric hospital upon discovery that he had engaged in extensive sexual behavior with children of both sexes. Shortly after admission, his routine laboratory studies revealed a positive test for syphilis. When confronted with the lab result, the priest responded, "I don't know how that's possible. I'm a celibate priest." The resident treating the priest simply pointed out that the patient had been admitted to the hospital because of his extensive sexual activity with minors. The priest blandly responded to this confrontation by saying, "What do you expect? I'm only human."

This clinical vignette illustrates how contradictory self-representations coexist in the borderline patient—a "celibate priest" coexisted with a promiscuous, bisexual pedophile. Moreover, the priest's matter-of-fact response was typical of the bland denial that many borderline patients display when confronted with the splitting maneuvers they employ. Other defenses, such as primitive idealization, omnipotence, and devaluation, similarly reflect splitting tendencies (i.e., others are seen in wholly positive or wholly negative terms). Projective identification, in which self-representations or object-representations are split off and projected into others in an effort to control them, is another prominent defense in borderline personality organization, according to Kernberg.

4. *Pathological internalized object relations.* As a result of splitting, the person with borderline personality organization does not view other people as having a mixture of positive and negative qualities. Instead, they are divided into polar extremes and are regarded, in the words of one patient, as "either gods or devils." These individuals cannot integrate libidinal and aggressive aspects of others, which inhibits their ability to truly appreciate the internal experiences of other people. Their perceptions of others

may alternate daily between idealization and devaluation, which can be highly disturbing for anyone in a relationship with such a person. Similarly, their inability to integrate positive and negative representations of the self results in profound identity diffusion, as illustrated by the previous example of the priest.

Kernberg's concept of borderline personality organization is distinct from the actual phenomenological characteristics that identify a specific personality disorder. In other words, his term encompasses many different personality disorders. In his view, patients with narcissistic, antisocial, schizoid, paranoid, infantile, and cyclothymic personality disorders, for example, are all characterized by an underlying borderline personality organization.

Because of the burgeoning literature on borderline conditions during the decades of the 1960s and 1970s, borderline personality disorder was added to DSM-III (American Psychiatric Association 1980). [There is no precise equivalent category in DSM-II. Prior to the publication of DSM-III, borderline patients were usually diagnosed with the DSM-II category of schizophrenia, latent type (American Psychiatric Association 1968).] In developing diagnostic criteria for borderline personality disorder, an effort was made both to include the descriptive features identified by Gunderson and to reflect the structural analysis of Kernberg. The revisions of the criteria in DSM-III-R (American Psychiatric Association 1987) are fairly minimal (Table 14-4).

The DSM-III criterion, "intolerance of being alone" (p. 323), was dropped from the revised criteria because of an overlap with dependent personality disorder and because it was found to have little diagnostic usefulness (Widiger et al. 1988). A new item, "frantic efforts to avoid real or imagined abandonment" (p. 347), was added to DSM-III-R to reflect the severe separation anxiety so prominent in borderline patients (Masterson and Rinsley 1975).

The DSM-III-R criteria still do not include the empirically and clinically observed brief psychotic episodes, which are identified as central features of the diagnostic entity. However, both DSM-III and DSM-III-R point out that patients with borderline personality disorder are considered particularly vulnerable to the development of brief reactive psychosis. There is an inherent ambiguity with the term *borderline* as a description of a personality disorder. Although such a designation implies that patients with this disorder are on the border of psychosis, a psychosis is a "state" disorder, while a personality diagnosis is a "trait" disorder. This mixing of distinct categorical frameworks continues to be problematic in the usage of the term *borderline personality disorder*.

There is also considerable controversy over whether the term *borderline* should be applied to a specific personality disorder or should be used broadly, as Kernberg used it, to describe a dimension

Table 14-4. DSM-III-R diagnostic criteria for borderline personality disorder

A pervasive pattern of instability of mood, interpersonal relationships, and self-image, beginning by early adulthood and present in a variety of contexts, as indicated by at least *five* of the following:

(1) a pattern of unstable and intense interpersonal relationships characterized by alternating between extremes of overidealization and devaluation

(2) impulsiveness in at least two areas that are potentially self-damaging, e.g., spending, sex, substance use, shoplifting, reckless driving, binge eating. (Do not include suicidal or self-mutilating behavior covered in [5].)

(3) affective instability: marked shifts from baseline mood to depression, irritability, or anxiety, usually lasting a few hours and only rarely more than a few days

(4) inappropriate, intense anger or lack of control of anger, e.g., frequent displays of temper, constant anger, recurrent physical fights

(5) recurrent suicidal threats, gestures, or behavior, or self-mutilating behavior

(6) marked and persistent identity disturbance manifested by uncertainty about at least two of the following: self-image, sexual orientation, long-term goals or career choice, type of friends desired, preferred values

(7) chronic feelings of emptiness or boredom

(8) frantic efforts to avoid real or imagined abandonment (Do not include suicidal or self-mutilating behavior covered in [5].)

Note. Reprinted from DSM-III-R, p. 347, with permission from American Psychiatric Association.

of personality (Gunderson and Zanarini 1987). Grinker and his associates (1968) clearly believed that there were several subcategories of the borderline syndrome, constituting a spectrum. Meissner (1984, 1988) categorized borderline conditions differently than Grinker et al., but he, too, believed that limiting the usage of the term *borderline* to a specific personality disorder is misleading. He noted that there are clear descriptive groupings within the spectrum, specifically, a hysterical continuum and a schizoid continuum. Adler (1981) and Rinsley (1985) also regarded borderline conditions as comprising a continuum in which the core borderline patient described by DSM-III-R represents the *lower end* of the continuum, while narcissistic personality disorder is located on the upper end of the continuum. In a retrospective study of 180 inpatients who had been diagnosed with borderline personality disorder by DSM-III criteria, Fyer et al. (1988) found that 91 percent had another diagnosis as well, while 42 percent had two or more additional diagnoses. They speculated that the diagnosis of borderline personality is often applied to a heterogeneous group of patients whose symptoms overlap extensively with those of other diagnoses. To avoid conceptual confusion (and because related personality disorders, such as paranoid, schizoid, narcissistic, antisocial, and histrionic are discussed at length in other chapters of this volume), the discussion in this chapter will be confined to those patients with the borderline features described by DSM-III-R. The only exception will be the inclusion of brief psychotic episodes, because they present formidable management problems for the clinicians.

Demographic Features and Course of Illness

At least two-thirds of the patients who are diagnosed with borderline personality disorder are female (Gunderson 1984). This finding may be due largely to cultural biases stemming from sex-role stereotypes, because male patients who have the features of borderline personality disorder are often diagnosed as having narcissistic or antisocial personality disorders. Borderline personality disorder is by far the most commonly used Axis II diagnosis, with a prevalence somewhere between 15 and 25 percent in clinical populations (Gunderson and Zanarini 1987). Its prevalence in the general population probably ranges between 2 and 4 percent (Baron et al. 1985; Gunderson and Zanarini 1987; Loranger et al. 1982). The legitimacy of the diagnostic category of borderline personality disorder has been substantiated by long-term follow-up studies demonstrating that, over time, borderline patients continue to manifest consistent clinical symptomatology; in the vast majority of cases, they do not shift into other major psychiatric disorders (Gunderson and Zanarini 1987).

Since all the major long-term follow-up studies (McGlashan 1986; Plakun et al. 1985; Stone et al. 1987; Werble 1970) have focused on subjects who have had rather extensive treatment experiences, the untreated course of borderline personality disorder remains something of a mystery. In fact, the key follow-up studies have been undertaken with patients who have had long-term (1–2 years), psychoanalytically oriented hospital treatment. These studies suggest that borderline personality disorder usually becomes apparent in late adolescence or young adulthood and that it runs a rocky course during the first decade, leading many clinicians to become discouraged with the patient's lack of progress. However, after approximately 5 or 6 years of treatment, borderline patients often begin to show substantial improvement that peaks in the second decade after their first hospitalization. In the sample of 251 borderline patients studied by Stone and his colleagues (1987), three-fourths were "recovered" or doing reasonably well, although many of these patients continued to have outpatient treatment. In McGlashan's (1986) follow-up study of 81 patients originally hospitalized at Chestnut Lodge, most of the patients were able to live independently and to adjust satisfactorily to work. However, the sample revealed a bimodal distribution when it came to functioning in intimate relationships: while one group managed to maintain meaningful intimate relationships over time, the other group adjusted to life by avoiding close interpersonal contact.

Stone's sample had a suicide rate of approximately 7.6 percent. Although certainly significant, this rate was lower than that for patients with schizophrenia (14.6 percent) or schizoaffective disorder (23.6 percent). Moreover, most of the borderline suicides occurred during the first decade of illness, followed by a dramatic drop-off after age 30.

Relationship With Affective Disorders

When the term *borderline* first appeared in the psychiatric literature in the 1950s and 1960s, it clearly denoted a clinical entity that was "on the border" of psychosis or, more specifically, schizophrenia. As time has passed and long-term follow-up data have accumulated on the course of borderline personality disorder, this disorder has been more closely linked to affective disorders than to schizophrenia (McGlashan 1983; Rinsley 1981b; Stone 1980; Stone et al. 1987). Whereas the course of schizotypal personality disorder is closely related to schizophrenia, that of the borderline personality disorder is distinctly different from schizophrenia but quite similar to affective disorder (McGlashan 1983).

The clinical observation that many patients with borderline personality disorder also have an Axis I diagnosis of major depression has been increasingly substantiated by research. Gunderson and Elliott (1985) concluded that the research data suggest an overlap of 40–60 percent between borderline personality disorder and major affective disorder. An even greater prevalence was found in the long-term follow-up study by Stone et al. (1987); there was a 69 percent overlap between major affective disorder and borderline personality disorder.

Further evidence for a linkage between affective disorder and borderline personality disorder comes from family studies. Stone (1980) found a high risk of affective disorder in the first-degree relatives of patients with borderline personality disorder. Other studies (Akiskal 1981; Soloff and Millward 1983) have confirmed this finding, but Pope et al. (1983) found that this higher prevalence of the disorder among first-degree relatives only applied if the index borderline patients also had an Axis I diagnosis of major affective disorder. Hence the increased risk of affective disorder in families with a relative with borderline personality disorder may be due either to 1) comorbidity with affective disorders or 2) borderline personality disorder per se. Moreover, a more recent study (Fyer et al. 1988) suggested no greater linkage between affective disorder and borderline personality disorder than between affective disorder and any other personality disorder.

All these data taken as a whole suggest that major affective disorder and borderline personality disorder are not entirely independent. Gunderson and Elliott (1985) concluded:

> For either disorder, individuals may start with a biophysiological vulnerability that increases their risk of being psychologically impaired in early development. . . . Early traumas may create vulnerability to either or both disorders, but the actual presentation varies as a function of later physiological and psychological reactions to environment and temperament. The key to the overlap and [to the] dissimilarities between these two disorders, then, may be a constellation of innate and external factors that are inconsequential individually but combine to shape depression, chronic dysphoria, or borderline behavior—alone or in any possible combination. (p. 286)

A common problem confronting the clinician is the differentiation of the characterological depression typical of borderline personality from the major affective disorder that may coexist with borderline personality disorder. A knowledge of the specific characteristics of each type of depression can assist clinicians in making this determination (Table 14-5). Borderline patients may use the term *depression* to describe chronic feelings of boredom, emptiness, and loneliness, but diagnostically may lack the vegetative signs of Axis I major depression (Gunderson and Zanarini 1987). Moreover, conscious feelings of rage are often intermingled with the characterological depression of the borderline patient, in contrast to the patient with a more autonomous and endogenous type of depression (Gunderson and Elliott 1985). Clinicians must keep in mind, however, that while these distinctions are helpful, both forms of depression may coexist in the same patient and may require pharmacologic intervention.

When psychopharmacologic agents are necessary to address the Axis I component of the depression in borderline patients, monoamine oxidase inhibitors, such as tranylcypromine, have been shown to be therapeutically effective (Cowdry and Gardner 1988). Whether tricyclic antidepressants are as useful is more controversial (Gunderson and Zanarini 1987; Soloff et al. 1986). In general, psychopharmacologic approaches to borderline personality should

Table 14-5. Differential diagnosis of major depressive episode
and characterological depression typical of
borderline personality disorder

Borderline Characterological Depression	Major Depressive Illness
1. Loneliness	1. Sleep disturbance
2. Emptiness	2. Loss of interest in pursuits that formerly produced pleasure
3. Boredom	3. Guilt
4. Inner sense of badness	4. Lack of energy
5. Conscious rage	5. Self-depreciation
	6. Loss of appetite
	7. Loss of sex drive
	8. Psychomotor retardation

be geared to target symptoms, such as the use of antidepressant medication for symptoms of depression. For behavioral dyscontrol, carbamazepine has been effective, while for psychotic or paranoid distortions of thinking, trifluoperazine has been helpful (Cowdry and Gardner 1988). Because borderline patients frequently complain of anxiety, clinicians may be tempted to prescribe antianxiety agents such as benzodiazepines. However, these agents, particularly alprazolam, may cause disinhibition, resulting in increased problems with impulse control (Cowdry and Garner 1988; Gardner and Cowdry 1985). Since drug abuse is common in borderline patients, the potential for dependency on benzodiazepines is another reason to avoid their usage.

While pharmacotherapy is an important adjunct in the treatment of borderline personality disorder, medications must be prescribed judiciously. These patients commonly accumulate large numbers of prescriptions from a variety of doctors, all of whom share feelings of frustration in their attempts to satisfy the unending demands for attention. Borderline patients may repeatedly test their treating clinicians to see if they "really care." Limiting prescription medication is only one way for the psychiatrist to use firm limits with the borderline patient. When an agent is used for a target symptom, clinicians must be careful to convey that the agent is not a panacea and that the main thrust of treatment must be a slow and painful examination of relationship patterns both in the transference and in the patient's life outside the therapeutic relationship.

In one survey of dynamic psychotherapists who were highly experienced in the treatment of borderline patients (Waldinger and Frank 1989), 90 percent of the respondents acknowledged that they prescribed medication for the borderline patients they were seeing in therapy. They were more likely to prescribe when they were feeling pessimistic about a particular patient's ability to work psychotherapeutically. These therapists also reported that nearly half the patients misused prescribed medication. This abuse was intimately connected to transference themes, and the investigators suggested that therapists should actively explore the patient's fantasies about the medication to prevent misuse.

Psychodynamic Understanding

Kernberg

Kernberg (1975) has linked the etiology and pathogenesis of borderline personality disorder to the developmental scheme of Margaret Mahler (Mahler et al. 1975). Readers may wish to review this scheme, outlined in Chapter 2, before continuing with this discussion. Specifically, Kernberg viewed borderline patients as having successfully traversed Mahler's symbiotic phase so that self and object can be clearly distinguished, but also as having become fixated during the separation-individuation phase. Kernberg targeted the rapprochement subphase, between approximately 16 and 30 months, as the chronological site of this developmental crisis. At this stage, the child becomes alarmed about the potential for its mother to disappear, and at times displays a frantic concern about her location. From this developmental standpoint, borderline patients can be viewed as repeatedly reliving an early infantile crisis in which they feared that attempts to separate from their mother would result in her disappearance and abandonment of them. In the adult form of this childhood crisis, individuals are unable to tolerate periods of being alone and fear abandonment from significant others. Patients with borderline personality disorder also may be overwhelmed with anxiety in the face of major separations from their parents or other nurturing figures. The reasons for the fixation at the rapprochement subphase are related, in Kernberg's view, to a disturbance of the mother's emotional availability during this critical period, due either to a constitutional excess of aggression in the child or to maternal problems with parenting, or even a combination of both.

An important component of this fixation is the lack of object constancy typical of the borderline patient. Like other children, throughout the period of separation-individuation, these children are unable to integrate the good and bad aspects of themselves and their mothers. These contradictory images are kept separate via splitting, so that both the mother and the self are seen as alternating between being thoroughly bad and thoroughly good. But whereas most children of nearly 3 years of age will have object constancy solidified sufficiently so that they can embrace a whole object view of the mother and the self, such is not true of borderline-prone individuals. At that point, children can generally tolerate separation somewhat better because they have internalized a whole, soothing, internal image of their mother that sustains them in times of her physical absence. Since borderline persons lack this internal image, they have little or no object constancy, which contributes significantly to their intolerance for separation and aloneness.

The end result of this developmental fixation is a condition that Kernberg characterized by its predominance of negative introjects (1966). Although he allowed for environmental sources for these negative internalized object- and self-representations, Kernberg's theory emphasized the significance of a constitutional excess of oral aggression in borderline patients. This factor reduces the ability borderline patients have for integrating good and bad images of self and other; they are convinced that the overwhelming "badness" will destroy any "goodness" in themselves or in others. When the bad introjects are projected outward, these patients feel at the mercy of malevolent persecutors. When reintrojected, the bad introjects make them feel unworthy and despicable, occasionally leading to suicidal thoughts. This innate aggression also impedes the borderline patient's passage through the oedipal phase. Thus, oedipal conflicts in borderline patients often appear more raw and primitive, compared with those in neurotic patients.

Masterson and Rinsley

The formulation of Masterson and Rinsley (1975) also focused on the rapprochement subphase of separation-individuation. However, they stressed the behavior of the mother rather than the innate aggression of the child. They found that the mothers of borderline patients, whom Masterson and Rinsley viewed as typically borderline themselves, were highly conflicted about their children growing up. As a result, the child receives a message from the mother that growing up and becoming one's own person will result in the loss of maternal love and support. A key corollary of this message is that remaining dependent constitutes the only available means of maintaining the maternal bond. This powerful maternal communication provokes "abandonment depression" any time the prospect of separation or autonomy presents itself to the child.

According to Masterson and Rinsley, this rapprochement subphase crisis between child and mother becomes rarefied as two separate split object relations units (see Table 14-6). These units are

Table 14-6. Role of the mother in the borderline syndrome
(Masterson and Rinsley 1975)

Mother-Infant Interaction in Rapprochement Subphase:
  ** Reward for regression, clinging
  ** Withdrawal for separation-individuation

Split Object Relations Units:
  ** Withdrawing (aggressive) part-unit

Maternal Part-Object	+	Affect	+	Part-Self-Representation
attacking, critical,		anger,		inadequate, bad,
hostile, withdrawing		frustration,		helpless, guilty,
approval		feeling		ugly, empty
		thwarted		

  ** Rewarding (libidinally gratifying) part-unit

Maternal Part-Object	+	Affect	+	Part-Self-Representation
approval, support, and		feeling good		good, passive,
reward for regressive,		being fed,		compliant
clinging behavior		gratification		
		of wish for		
		reunion		

constituted by a part-self-representation, a part-object-representation, and an affect that connects the two. The rewarding object relations unit (RORU) is associated with feelings of being loved and gratified. It includes a maternal part object that is affirming, loving, and supportive. In association with this positively regarded maternal introject, there is a part-self-representation of a "good child" who is obedient and passive. The withdrawing object relations unit (WORU) is associated with feelings of rage, abandonment depression, and helplessness. The maternal part object is malevolent and critical, while the part-self-representation is a "bad child" who is guilty and undesirable.

The fixation at this fragmented level leaves the borderline patient feeling that there are only two choices—you can feel abandoned and bad, or like Peter Pan, you can feel good only by denying reality and never growing up. Rinsley (1988) subsequently found this formulation of split object relations unit to be somewhat oversimplified and limiting in its therapeutic implications. He went on to apply the constructs of Fairbairn (1954) to the borderline personality (Rinsley 1987) and to focus on the developmental differences between borderline and narcissistic personality disorders (Rinsley 1984, 1985, 1989). By so doing, Rinsley has moved away from his earlier emphasis, with Masterson, on the conflict-related origin of borderline personality disorder and toward a deficit or "insufficiency" model.

In his later formulations, Rinsley (1981a, 1984, 1985, 1986, 1988, 1989), like Adler (1985), emphasized the significance of absent or seriously deficient evocative memory (object impermanency) in the pathogenesis of borderline personality disorder. He conceptualized the developmental failure of borderline individuals in terms of Mahler's interrelated processes of separation and individuation, with severe impairment of *both* separation and individuation in the borderline personality. In contrast, in the case of the "higher-level" narcissistic personality, a failure of the separation process has occurred with apparent relative intactness of the individuation process (see Chapter 15).

Adler

Whereas the psychodynamic models of Kernberg and of Masterson and Rinsley are derived essentially from conflict models of psychopathology, Adler's (1985) understanding of the borderline personality disorder is based on a deficit or "insufficiency" model. Inconsistent or unreliable mothering, in Adler's view, causes the borderline patient's failure to develop a "holding-soothing" internal object. Adler, who was heavily influenced by the self psychological theories of Kohut (see Chapter 2), understood the borderline patient as being in search of selfobject functions from *external* figures because of the absence of nurturing introjects.

Adler emphasized the developmental framework of Selma Fraiberg (1969) in contrast to that of Mahler. He noted that at approximately 18 months of age, according to Fraiberg, the normal child is ordinarily able to summon up an internal image of a maternal figure even in the physical absence of that figure. This capacity for "evocative memory," as Fraiberg termed this cognitive achievement, is only tenuously established in the borderline patient, according to Adler. In situations of stress, or in the throes of an intense transference, borderline patients tend to regress until they can no longer recall important figures in their environment who are not physically present unless an object such as a picture is available as a reminder. Adler conceptualized this observation as a regression to a developmental age between 8 and 18 months, before evocative memory has been achieved.

The borderline patient's lack of a holding-soothing internal object accounts for several aspects of borderline psychopathology. This lack creates feelings of emptiness and depressive tendencies. It is also responsible for the clinging dependency so commonly seen in borderline patients. In the absence of selfobject responses from significant others, borderline individuals have inadequate internal

resources to sustain them and are prone to fragmentations of the
self. This dissolution of the self is accompanied by a profound
emptiness described as "annihilation panic" by Adler. Finally, the
absence of the holding-soothing introject leads to a chronic oral
rage in borderline patients related to their feeling that mothering
figures were not emotionally available during childhood.

Critiques of Psychodynamic Models

Although the discussion of the three psychodynamic models presented here in no way represents a comprehensive overview of the
psychoanalytic discourse regarding borderline disorders, it does
acquaint readers with three points of view that lie at the heart of
much of the controversy centering on this diagnostic category. More
to the point, each model has specific treatment implications that are
themselves perhaps even more controversial than the diagnostic
understanding. Much of the literature involves critiques of the
positions set forth by these theorists. Those who localize the developmental disturbance to the rapprochement subphase have been
taken to task by no less a critic than Margaret Mahler herself (Mahler
and Kaplan 1977), who has pointed out that focusing on one
subphase of separation-individuation is somewhat reductionistic
rather than appreciative of the influence of other subphases, as well
as oedipal influences, in the pathogenesis of borderline personality
disorder. She doubted that there is a discrete linear relationship
between disturbances in one subphase of separation-individuation
and later adult manifestations of psychopathology. Gunderson
(1984) also has pointed out that empirical studies of parents of
borderline patients suggest that inadequate parenting is not confined to particular developmental subphases, but rather is pervasive
throughout all phases of childhood. Moreover, neglect appears
more common than overinvolvement. These studies also indicate
that both parents, rather than only the mother, are typically neglectful of their parental responsibilities. Masterson and Rinsley have
been criticized by Esman (1980) for unfairly blaming mothers in
their formulation while not sufficiently taking into account constitutional factors such as organically based cognitive dysfunction that
may contribute to problems in the separation-individuation phase.

In response to some of these criticisms, Rinsley (1988) has
acknowledged that clinicians working with adult patients may not
always be able to determine whether the patient's account of parenting is an accurate reconstruction of reality or a distortion based
on fantasy. Rinsley has also accepted the view that the father may be
as influential as the mother. Nevertheless, he reaffirms the crucial
role of the mother in reenacting her own difficulties with separation
in the parenting of her own children.

While Masterson and Rinsley have been accused of blaming mothers, Kernberg has been criticized for attributing constitutionally based oral rage to borderline patients. Atwood and Stolorow (1984), for example, have suggested that Kernberg's observations of excessive aggression in borderline patients may be viewed as an iatrogenic artifact stemming from Kernberg's early confrontation and interpretation of negative transference. Kernberg's model has also been criticized by the Kris Study Group (Abend et al. 1983) and by Meissner (1988) for underemphasizing the developmental problems of borderline patients at the genital-oedipal phase and for focusing more on the fixation at a preoedipal level rather than as a possible regression from oedipal issues to earlier conflicts. Meissner (1988) has argued that some developmental defects can be found at the lower end of the borderline spectrum, even before the separation-individuation phase, while at the opposite end of the spectrum, oedipal and postoedipal disturbances contribute to the adult clinical manifestations of borderline pathology. Stone (1987) has argued that events later in life, such as father-daughter incest, may profoundly affect children who are subsequently diagnosed as borderline. In one study (Herman et al. 1989) of borderline patients, 68 percent had a childhood history of sexual abuse, a figure significantly greater than the incidence in a control group of patients without the borderline diagnosis.

Adler has similarly been criticized for his developmental weighting toward oral issues and his relative neglect of oedipal conflicts in his understanding of the borderline patient (Finell 1988; Meissner 1988). Adler has also been taken to task for emphasizing cognitive deficits (i.e., problems with evocative memory) as a pivotal feature in psychodynamic understanding, given the fact that such defects are primarily found in borderline patients close to the psychotic border (Meissner 1988) but may be completely absent in higher-level borderline patients. Finally, Kernberg (1988) has pointed out that Adler's emphasis on the absence of "good introjects" neglects the influence of hostile introjects in borderline pathology.

All the psychodynamic models may be criticized for understating the role played by genetic-constitutional defects in the central nervous system. Stone (1980) has stressed that borderline patients tend to be extremely irritable in temperament, and that there may even be a genetic component in the etiology. Grotstein (1987) has conceptualized the essence of borderline psychopathology as impaired self-regulation related, at least in part, to neurocognitive defects. Andrulonis et al. (1981) found significant neuropsychological abnormalities in 38 percent of a sample of patients with borderline personality disorder. Other studies (Cornelius et al. 1989), however, have failed to replicate this finding.

Individual Psychotherapy

The goals involved in the individual psychotherapy of patients with borderline personality disorder are ambitious. They include strengthening the ego so that patients can better tolerate anxiety and can gain greater control over impulses, integration of split self- and object-representations so that patients have a coherent, sustained, and fully rounded view of themselves and others, and the firm establishment of a soothing-holding introject so that separations from significant figures can be tolerated. There is no shortcut to the accomplishment of these goals, which require intensive work with a therapist over a long time. Until the internal object world of these patients changes, they will have little relief from the unrelenting misery of their existence.

Expressive Versus Supportive Approaches

Although clinicians often disagree about whether psychotherapy should be weighted predominantly toward the expressive or supportive end of the expressive-supportive continuum, they concur on the extraordinary difficulty in undertaking individual psychotherapy of borderline patients. These patients are likely to quit psychotherapy, to act out self-destructively, to make inordinate demands for special treatment from their therapist, to provoke therapists into ill-advised professional boundary crossing, and to torment therapists with unrelenting phone calls at all times of the day and night. A major problem in successful psychotherapy with borderline individuals is the tenuous nature of the therapeutic alliance (Adler 1979; Gabbard et al. 1988; Gorney 1979; Kernberg 1976; Masterson 1976; Modell 1976; Zetzel 1971). These patients have great difficulty viewing their therapist as a helpful figure who is working collaboratively with them toward mutually perceived goals. Much of the controversy in the literature about the relative value of expressive versus supportive interventions revolves around which approach is more likely to foster the development and maintenance of the therapeutic alliance.

Without some semblance of a therapeutic alliance, the therapist may not have a patient. The borderline patient may rapidly develop intense negative transference, which mobilizes primitive character defenses that interfere with the establishment of an alliance (Kernberg 1976). Some clinicians (Boyer 1977; Kernberg 1975) believe that these transference distortions should be addressed early through transference interpretations. These interpretations pave the way for the patient to view the therapist more accurately and to form a therapeutic alliance with fewer psychological obstacles. Interpretation of primitive defensive operations in the here and now of the transference relationship serves to help patients integrate their "good" and "bad" views of the therapist into a more realistic "whole object" perception.

Masterson (1976) and Modell (1976) proposed quite a different technical approach. They suggested that interpretation must be delayed until the patient has developed sufficient trust in the therapist's intentions and reliability. Modell emphasized that a "holding" environment must be established as a prerequisite to interpretive interventions. This point of view is in keeping with Adler's conceptualization of the primary goal of psychotherapy as the establishment of a soothing-holding introject to sustain the patient in times of separation and aloneness. Adler (1979) saw the therapeutic alliance as something of a "myth" in the psychotherapy of borderline patients. These patients are unable to experience psychotherapy as a working collaboration, at least in the early phases. Because these patients are initially incapable of appreciating the real qualities of their therapist, they are maintained in psychotherapy by the soothing, supportive experience of a stable selfobject transference. As patients increasingly internalize the relationship, Adler believed, they are ultimately capable of allying themselves with the therapist in the service of pursuing common therapeutic goals. Adler viewed as a major therapeutic accomplishment the patient's perception of the therapist as a real and separate person who is invested in helping the patient. Zetzel (1971) was perhaps the strongest advocate of a supportive approach. She believed that interpretive psychotherapy is too disruptive of the therapeutic alliance and that low frequency supportive psychotherapy (once a week or less) is the only effective way to maintain an alliance with borderline patients.

This controversy over the relative merits of expressive and supportive interventions is reflected in the contradictory findings of the Menninger Foundation's Psychotherapy Research Project. The project's quantitative study (Kernberg et al. 1972) revealed that borderline patients treated by skilled therapists who focused intently on the transference showed a significantly better outcome than did those treated by skilled therapists who focused less on the transference. In contrast, the prediction study of the project (Horwitz 1974), using both quantitative and qualitative assessments of the treatment process, suggested that a series of patients, some of whom were borderline and were treated by predominantly supportive methods, showed greater gains in supportive treatment than anticipated. Finally, as reported in Chapter 4, Wallerstein's (1986) most recent examination of the data from this project suggested that all treatments were characterized by a mixture of expressive and supportive interventions. These apparently contradictory findings with regard

to transference focus remain unresolved, in part because the original design of the study had several shortcomings relevant to this
issue: 1) the specific diagnostic category of borderline personality
disorder was not used; 2) a detailed process study was not undertaken, so that essential treatment developments could only be
roughly approximated at the termination of treatment; and 3) the
therapeutic alliance was not one of the project's variables. Retrospectively, however, the prediction study found the therapeutic
alliance useful in conceptualizing results (Horwitz 1974).

Much of the current controversy surrounding the psychotherapy of borderline patients can be understood as another unfortunate example of the "either/or" approach to the application of
theory to clinical practice discussed at some length in Chapter 2.
Both approaches are useful for *some* patients at *some* points in the
treatment. We are dealing with a spectrum of highly heterogeneous
patients who require individually tailored psychotherapeutic approaches (Meissner 1988). To a large extent, the same indications
for expressive or supportive emphasis (see Table 4-2 in Chapter 4)
that guide the clinician's work with other diagnostic entities apply
to psychotherapy with borderline patients. Stone's (1987) follow-up
study of borderline patients who were sufficiently disturbed to
require long-term hospitalization revealed that only about one-third
of those patients who originally appeared amenable to expressive
psychotherapy were truly suited for that approach. However, large
aggregate studies of this nature, while useful, do not address the
nuances of the therapeutic process at a more microcosmic level.
Process research of individual sessions has demonstrated that, at
least with some patients, transference interpretation may serve to
improve the therapeutic alliance (Gabbard et al. 1988).

As a general rule, higher-level borderline patients with greater
ego strengths and greater psychological-mindedness will be more
able to utilize expressively oriented psychotherapy than those closer
to the psychotic border, who will need a supportive emphasis. Most
will require a flexible stance by the therapist with shifts between
interpretive and noninterpretive interventions geared to the state
of the patient's relatedness to the therapist at a given moment
(Gunderson 1984). In a study of borderline patients who discontinued psychotherapy, Gunderson et al. (1989) found that more
than half the dropouts departed in anger following early confrontation by their therapists. These findings led Gunderson and his
colleagues to advocate more supportive techniques early in therapy,
as described by Masterson (1976) and Adler (1985).

Even shifting between the conceptual frameworks of Kernberg
and Adler is both possible and reasonable with many patients,
because the common ground in these approaches serves as a basis
for integration (Goldstein, 1989). The result of the integration of

split self- and object-representations, a goal advocated by Kernberg (1975), is the development of object constancy, which is closely related to Adler's "evocative memory," in that the patient can tolerate being alone without disorganizing into a state of panic. Moreover, the patient's subjective experience of the absence of "good" soothing introjects (Adler's position) is not essentially different from the patient's experience of a predominance of "bad" hostile introjects (Kernberg's position). Adler and Rhine (1988) have demonstrated with case material how containing projections from the patient may constitute a selfobject function for the therapist, thus integrating Kernberg's object relations concept of projective identification with Adler's self psychological concept of selfobject. Finally, no single theory is likely to insulate the therapist from the tumultuous emotional upheaval experienced by both partners of the therapeutic dyad. Most therapists find themselves using a trial-and-error approach until they can clearly determine which interventions are most effective with a given patient.

Kernberg himself seems to have developed a greater regard for the effects of supportive psychotherapy as his own technique has evolved. In his 1984 examination of the psychotherapy of borderline patients, he discussed exploring transference fantasies without necessarily interpreting them as one would in highly expressive treatment: "This exploration is not connected interpretively with the patient's unconscious relation to the therapist or with his unconscious past. It is, instead, used for confronting the patient with the reality of the treatment situation and with parallel distortions in his external life" (p. 163). This modification still places Kernberg's approach at a far more expressive point on the continuum than Adler's, but more clearly emphasizes the value of noninterpretive interventions.

In a review of the literature on intensive psychotherapy with borderline patients, Waldinger (1987) has distilled the diverse technical approaches of a variety of clinicians into eight basic tenets that are consensually valued in the psychotherapy of borderline patients. These eight technical principles are also useful in organizing a discussion of interventions.

A stable treatment framework. Because of the chaotic nature of the borderline patient's life, stability must be imposed from external sources. Although a hospital milieu would be the most extreme way to provide external structure, the psychotherapist can also inject some semblance of stability in the patient's life by setting consistent appointment times, ending sessions on time even though the patient may insist on staying longer, establishing clear expectations about fee payment, and developing an explicit policy about the consequences of missed appointments.

Avoidance of a passive therapeutic stance.   The silent, reflective stance of the psychoanalyst working with a neurotic patient is usually not suitable for effective psychotherapy with borderline patients. These patients will often misinterpret silence as a lack of caring or even as a malevolent withholding of support. The alliance is facilitated instead by greater verbalizations by the therapist, even simple affirming comments such as, "I see," or open-ended questions such as, "Do you have any other thoughts about that?" When the patient is silent, the therapist would do better to inquire about the silence rather than to let it continue for a prolonged period. The only exception to this rule of thumb is a small subset of extraordinarily oppositional patients, who may take an oath of silence as a way of defeating the therapist (Gabbard 1989a). These patients are probably treatable only in an inpatient setting.

Containment of the patient's anger.   Virtually all clinicians who write about the treatment of borderline patients acknowledge the extraordinary challenge of maintaining a therapeutic posture in the face of their verbal barrages of contempt and hatred. The therapist will often feel provoked into becoming defensive or retaliating with hostile or sarcastic interpretations. Alternatively, the therapist may subtly withdraw from an emotional investment in the patient, consciously or unconsciously hoping that the patient will quit therapy and find someone else to torment. The optimal approach to containing the patient's projected hateful parts has already been described in Chapter 13 in a discussion of the psychotherapy of the paranoid patient. Indeed, anger is often part of a paranoid transference development that is a typical feature of the psychotherapy of borderline patients. The therapist should empathize with the patient's need to split good and bad self- and object-representations and to project the bad outside the self as a way to control it and keep it from destroying the good representations. The therapist who returns the "badness" prematurely will simply increase the patient's feeling of being attacked. As Grotstein (1982) has pointed out, the therapist functions essentially as a container, not an interpreter, until the patient is once again able to own these projected aspects. Until that time, transference interpretations are unlikely to be understood or processed.

Containing the patient's anger often requires the therapist to tolerate periods of psychotic transference. It is not uncommon for disturbances of reality testing to surface only in the context of the therapy session. After leaving the session, the patient may rapidly reorganize and return to normal functioning. One patient, for example, assumed a prone position on the analytic couch during each therapy session because she was convinced that her therapist would rape her. But after the hour, she would return to work with no apparent difficulty. Supportive inquiries and empathic understanding are much more useful in such situations than interpretations, which the borderline patient will only experience as an attack.

Confrontation of self-destructive behaviors. Borderline patients frequently display magical thinking about their self-destructive behavior. They may be completely oblivious to the actual consequences of their actions because they fantasize that their behavior will have different results. Waldinger (1987) stressed that therapists should make their patients look at these consequences. One patient who had been hospitalized several times because she inflicted cigarette burns on her forearms insisted that this behavior relieved her internal tension. She believed that mental health workers unnecessarily made a "big deal" out of her behavior. Whenever she was hospitalized, she complained that the nursing staff did not understand how much relief the self-burning gave her. The therapist pointed out that the actual consequence of this repeated burning was that the patient had created a "revolving-door situation" at the hospital that prevented her from maintaining stable employment or meaningful relationships.

Promiscuous sexual behavior may be similarly confronted. For example, a male homosexual patient told his therapist that he felt a strong need for homosexual encounters because the swallowing of semen from a virile, masculine male made him feel more masculine. His therapist pointed out that despite this fantasy, the *real* consequence of swallowing other men's semen would be the risk of contracting AIDS.

Establishment of the connection between feelings and actions. Action is often the language of the borderline patient. These patients feel so controlled by powerful affect states that action may seem the only viable way to achieve relief. However, much of this pattern is ego-syntonic so that patients are often unaware that their actions are motivated by feelings. Their conscious experience may be that impulses simply come "out of the blue." The therapists of borderline patients thus must look repeatedly for precipitating feeling states whenever they are confronted with acting-out behavior. One patient went out and bought eight candy bars, eating them all in the space of 10 minutes after a man had called her for a date. Although this patient saw no connection between the two events, the therapist helped her understand that the prospect of going out on a date filled her with anxiety, which she in turn tried to relieve through binge eating.

Limit setting. This form of intervention is often implemented as part of a contractual agreement at the beginning of psychotherapy (Kernberg 1984). Therapists may wish to establish a number of "ground rules," including no phone calls between sessions, the verbalization of suicidal feelings to the therapist before acting on them, and a willingness to accept hospitalization when suicidal impulses are out of control. Some therapists are flexible on these matters; others prefer more structure. Adler (1985), for example, believed that in the early phases of treatment, the therapist's availability by phone is instrumental to the establishment of a stable, holding selfobject transference. Likewise, Adler and Buie (1979) have recommended interventions such as sending a postcard during vacation to reassure the patient of the therapist's existence, providing occasional extra sessions in a crisis, and allowing the patient to know the whereabouts of the therapist during vacations. Giovacchini (1986) has noted that many patients experience some rudimentary object constancy just by knowing their therapist's phone number and whereabouts during a vacation. Even those therapists who allow for this flexibility, however, realize the importance of setting limits when such flexibility is exploited by the patient. Therapists must develop a sense of their own limits. Specifically, they should decide how much outside contact they can tolerate and still treat the patient.

Borderline patients are notorious for seducing therapists into crossing the usual professional boundaries (Gutheil 1989). One male therapist, for example, began seeing a female patient twice a week for psychotherapy but within a year, was seeing the patient seven times a week. On Sundays, he would make a special trip to his office just to see this patient. When a consultant questioned this behavior, the therapist defended it as necessary to prevent the patient from committing suicide. He also acknowledged that he allowed the patient to sit on his lap during their sessions, justifying this behavior as a way to provide the patient with the mothering that she had not received as a child. Many cases of therapist-patient sex involve borderline patients (Gabbard 1989c). One female patient insisted that nothing short of an orgasm induced by her male therapist would result in her improvement. She threatened to kill herself if her therapist would not comply. After two different therapists obliged her demands, she eventually killed herself when she still felt basically dissatisfied. The dynamics of erotic and erotized transference are discussed more fully in Chapter 17, but the tragic end of this particular patient underscores the futility of trying to gratify the patient's demands. The more gratification that borderline patients receive, the more insatiable they become.

In a succinct summary of the group of behaviors that require limit setting, Waldinger (1987) identified those that threaten the safety of the therapist or the patient, and those that jeopardize the psychotherapy itself. Suicide is an ever-present risk with borderline patients, and therapists must be ready to hospitalize their patients when these impulses become overwhelming. Therapists often find themselves in the untenable position of heroically attempting to treat lethal patients by having continuous contact with them. One therapist ended up talking on the phone to a borderline patient for an hour every night to prevent her from killing herself.

Maintaining the focus of interventions on the here and now. In the psychotherapy of borderline patients, the action is in the transference. The view of the therapist will shift kaleidoscopically from day to day or even within a single session. When the patient attempts to integrate bad and good representations of the therapist, the depressive anxieties created by that attempt at synthesis may produce intense concern about harming the therapist. If the therapist is perceived as insufficiently empathic or understanding, that concern can shift in the twinkling of an eye to anxiety more typical of the paranoid-schizoid position, namely, a perception of the therapist as a malevolent figure intent on sadistic torment. These shifts must be addressed as they occur rather than allowing the patient to take flight from transference into emotionally distant reconstructions of childhood experiences.

Ms. Z was a 24-year-old woman who came to psychotherapy after repeated failures with other therapists. She was unable to live outside her parents' home, despite the fact that she was intelligent and personally engaging. She had held countless jobs, none for more than 3 months. She was able to impress employers in an initial interview enough to convince them to hire her, but as soon as she started succeeding at the job, she would become extraordinarily anxious and would act up in a way that caused her to be fired.

As soon as she came to therapy, Ms. Z developed an immediate wish for the therapist to take care of her. She wanted to be his only patient and to be seen five times a week instead of twice a week. She told the therapist that he was "warm and wonderful," unlike the other therapists she had seen. She felt that she would greatly improve if she could just be in his presence every day of the week. This idealizing transference rapidly turned to a devaluing one when the therapist offered his opinion that twice-weekly therapy would be preferable since one of Ms. Z's difficulties was in dealing with frustration. At this point, Ms. Z exploded; she accused her therapist of being cruel and unempathic because he was simply basing the treatment on what he thought was best rather than responding to her needs. She stormed out of his office and said she was not coming back. Ten minutes later, she called her therapist from a pay phone, told him he was "a son of a bitch" and hung up. Ten minutes after that, she called again, this time to apologize and to say that she would return for her next session. The therapist simply responded that that would be fine with him.

At the next psychotherapy session, Ms. Z did not refer to the upheaval that had occurred in the previous session. She chatted amicably with the therapist as though no rift had ever occurred between them. The therapist offered an empathic interpretation: "It seems like you need to keep the hateful feelings that occurred last time out of the session today so that they won't destroy the positive feelings you're having in here today." That intervention allowed the patient to talk about how frustrating it was for her when other people would not respond to her dependency needs as she wanted them to.

This brief vignette illustrates a useful principle enunciated by Pine (1986): "Strike while the iron is cold" (p. 528). If the therapist had delivered any interpretive intervention when this patient was full of rage, she would simply have felt attacked. By waiting until Ms. Z had calmed down, however, the therapist was better able to get her to reflect on the interpretation itself. Moreover, the therapist made no effort to elaborate the interpretation by bringing in child-hood antecedents. Staying in the here and now kept this patient from taking flight from the transference situation.

Monitoring of countertransference feelings. Implicit in this entire discussion of psychotherapy has been the centrality of attend-ing to countertransference. Containing the projected parts of the patient and reflecting on the nature of these projections will help the therapist to diagnose the patient's internal world. Moreover, ongoing attention to one's own feelings prevents countertransfer-ence acting out. Each therapist has personal limits regarding how much hatred or anger is tolerable. If the therapist closely monitors countertransference feelings, this limit can be handled construc-tively rather than destructively. For example, a therapist might use countertransference feelings therapeutically by saying to the pa-tient, "I'm getting the feeling that you are trying to make me angry at you instead of letting me help you. Let's see if we can understand what's happening here." Alternatively, the therapist may have to set limits on the patient's verbal barrages based on countertransference reactions, as follows: "I really don't feel I can work with you effec-tively if you continue to shout at me. I think it's important for you to work on controlling your anger so you can express it to me without screaming." Therapists must be real and genuine with borderline patients, or they will only increase the patient's envy of them as saintly figures that are basically nonhuman (Searles 1986).

The outcome of psychotherapy with borderline patients is always uncertain. A study of completed cases by Waldinger and Gunderson (1987) indicated that even with experienced therapists and analysts, the dropout rate is high. Approximately one-third of their sample actually completed treatment. However, this research also suggested that those patients who stay in treatment derive substantial improvement from it.

Hospital Treatment

The principles of psychoanalytically informed hospital treatment are outlined in Chapter 6. In addition, the management of splitting in hospital treatment, an essential ingredient in work with border-line patients, is also discussed in that chapter. Readers are therefore referred back to Chapter 6 for the basic principles of the hospital treatment of borderline patients. Several other points specific to patients with borderline personality will be covered here.

There are essentially two models used in the treatment of borderline patients: 1) brief hospitalization for crisis intervention in the context of outpatient psychotherapy, and 2) long-term, psychodynamically informed hospital treatment with the goals of ego-building and modification of the patient's internal object world. The indications for the second model, in the simplest possible terms, involve an inability to use the first model. In actual practice, this category would include several groups of patients (with some patients overlapping different categories): 1) relentlessly self-destructive or suicidal patients who are too lethal to be treated outside an inpatient setting; 2) "special" patients, who create intense countertransference problems related to splitting and projective identification (Burnham 1966; Gabbard 1986; Main 1957); 3) extraordinarily hateful patients who venomously attack those who help them (Gabbard 1989b); and 4) passively oppositional patients who refuse to talk or participate in any aspect of the treatment plan (Gabbard 1989a). All four of these groups are occasionally characterized as negative therapeutic reactions, although some may ultimately be treatable, given the intensive approaches available in long-term hospitalization.

Short-Term Hospital Treatment

The patient who requires brief hospitalization in the course of psychotherapy is likely to be in a crisis involving a psychotic regression, self-destructive behavior, or a suicidal gesture. There may also be varying degrees of turmoil in the psychotherapy process as well. Since the goal of short-term hospitalization is rapid restoration of the patient's defenses and adaptive functioning, the inpatient staff must convey a counterregressive expectation. Treaters in the milieu must communicate to such patients that they *can* control impulses despite their disclaimers. Although external controls, such as cold, wet sheet packs, restraints, and antipsychotic medication may be necessary at times, the emphasis is on helping these patients take responsibility for self-control. The weakened ego of the patient can be supplemented with a firm, consistent structure involving a regular schedule, clear consequences for impulsive acting out, and a predictable pattern of group and individual meetings with staff members and other patients.

The usual tendency of the newly admitted borderline patient is to expect, on demand, lengthy individual sessions with members of the nursing staff. When nurses are actually "roped in" to attempting to gratify these demands, the patient typically deteriorates in direct proportion to the amount of time spent in these one-to-one "therapy" sessions. Borderline patients do much better when the nursing staff can build into the regular structure brief 5–10 minute meetings.

Staff members in the milieu and the unit structure itself function as auxiliary egos for borderline patients. Rather than attempting exploratory or interpretive work, the unit staff can help patients identify precipitants of their crisis, delay impulse discharge by seeking alternatives, anticipate consequences of their actions, and clarify their internal object relations (as described in Chapter 6). Another function of brief hospitalization is that it allows for a more exact diagnosis of the patient's internal world. Finally, the milieu staff can often assist the psychotherapist in understanding the nature of the patient's crisis or impasse that occurred during psychotherapy. In addition to addressing any splitting processes (as described in Chapter 6), the milieu staff can help the therapist by validating the therapist's competence and worth as a clinician (Adler 1984). From the self psychological perspective of Adler, the unit nurses and other personnel can perform selfobject functions for both the patient and the therapist (Adler 1987).

Long-Term Hospitalization

Long-term, psychoanalytically informed hospital treatment of borderline patients essentially follows the model outlined in Chapter 6. Much of the treatment involves ego-building, because those patients who require long-term hospital treatment have more profound ego weaknesses than patients who do not require lengthy hospitalization. The hospital's emphasis must be on the patient's substitution of words for actions, despite the patient's protestations that such a shift is impossible.

There must also be a unit norm that discourages keeping secrets. Anything the patient says to one staff member must be shared with other staff members in meetings. The staff of the unit must be able to repeatedly say "no" to the patient in a matter-of-fact, caring way that conveys no malice. Otherwise, the patient may not be able to integrate the fact that "good" caring figures are the same persons who implement restrictive measures (i.e., "bad" interventions). This integration of internal self- and object-representations is another primary goal of long-term inpatient treatment.

Limits must always be applied to the patient based on an empathic understanding of that patient's need for limits rather than on any sadistic attempt at control, which is how the patient usually views such restrictions.

Ms. AA became extremely angry and tearful when her mother left after a family visit during her long-term hospitalization. She screamed at the social worker and threw a book at him as she accused him of taking her mother away. The nursing staff asked Ms. AA to control herself and go to her room, but were forced to put her in four-point leather restraints when she continued to be assaultive toward other staff members. Throughout the process of implementing these restrictions, the nursing staff repeatedly told Ms. AA that they understood how upset she was because she missed her mother terribly and felt that she could not survive without her. Since the patient lacked a soothing maternal introject to comfort her, the nursing staff was performing that function by attempting to soothe her and reassure her as they put her into restraints. Moreover, Ms. AA's psychiatrist suggested that a photograph of her mother should be placed where the patient could see it, thereby helping Ms. AA deal with her problems with evocative memory and object constancy. The patient seemed relieved upon seeing the picture and commented that without it she could not even remember what her mother looked like. With these measures, the patient calmed down within 30 minutes, and the restraints were removed.

Suicidal and self-mutilative behavior is often a significant problem in long-term hospitalization because borderline patients attempt to control the entire treatment staff just as they have controlled their family and loved ones outside the hospital with such behavior. The staff members must stress that each patient is ultimately responsible for controlling such behavior and that realistically no one can prevent a patient from committing suicide. Borderline patients often make superficial cuts on themselves with paperclips, beverage cans, light bulbs, and other objects that are generally available even in hospitals. The actual damage from such superficial scratching may be minimal, but the behavior is used to manipulate the entire staff into giving the patient constant attention. When the mutilation is consistently mild, staff members may deal with it by establishing a weekly appointment for the patient with a nonpsychiatric physician, such as an internist, who works closely with the hospital unit (Gabbard 1986). In this manner the mutilative behavior loses its control function and allows the staff and the patient to work on other more central issues. If any serious consequences occur from the mutilation, the internist can treat them appropriately.

The chronically suicidal borderline patient may engender intense countertransference feelings in staff members, who perceive the attempts and gestures as manipulative and therefore begin to react to the patient's suicidal threats with a lack of concern. The inpatient staff must keep in mind that suicide attempters are 140 times more likely to commit suicide than nonattempters (Tuckman and Youngman 1963), and that roughly 10–20 percent of all suicide attempters eventually kill themselves (Dorpat and Ripley 1967).

Family Therapy

Therapeutic modification of the borderline patient's internal object world generally requires an intensive individual psychotherapy process. Work with the family, however, is often an essential adjunct to the overall treatment plan. The use of formal family therapy is far less common than one or more family interventions in the course of treatment (Brown 1987). Inpatient treatment, for example, provides clinicians with the opportunity to meet with the patient's family and to understand those interactions as compared and contrasted with a recapitulation of the patient's internal object world in the milieu via splitting and projective identification (see Chapter 6). In outpatient psychotherapy, the individual process may be undermined by the countertherapeutic efforts of family members who feel threatened by any change in the designated patient. Family interventions or, in severe cases, family therapy, may therefore be required for a successful individual treatment.

The first step of family intervention is to identify the role family interactions play in the pathogenesis and maintenance of the borderline patient's symptomatology. As described in Chapter 5, splitting and projective identification are extremely common mechanisms that serve to maintain a pathological homeostasis in the family system. For example, a parent may ward off bad internal self- or object-representations and project them into an adolescent or young adult offspring, who subsequently identifies with these projections and becomes the symptomatic member of the family.

In diagnosing the family patterns, therapists should avoid imposing their own theoretical constructs on the family. For example, although certain psychodynamic models (Masterson and Rinsley 1975) might presuppose overinvolvement on the part of the mother, empirical research (Gunderson and Englund 1981; Gunderson et al. 1980) has suggested that overinvolved parents are less common than neglectful ones. Neglectful parents of borderline patients tend to be needy themselves and therefore often fail to provide their children with guidance in the form of rules or "structure." This finding in Gunderson's research underscores the necessity to "reparent" the borderline patient in long-term hospital treatment by establishing firm structure and clear consequences for structure breaks in the treatment milieu. When working during inpatient treatment with a family characterized by this pattern of neglect and neediness, a social worker or other mental health professional may have to "parent the parents" of the borderline patient. Moreover, in discharge planning, the parents may need help in learning how to serve as a constructive support system for their borderline child, which may include getting help for themselves on an ongoing basis.

In families where overinvolvement is a pervasive pattern, family intervention must respect the needs of each family member for the other members. The parents may suffer from borderline psychopathology themselves and may be terribly threatened by the prospect of "losing" their borderline offspring through treatment. Clinicians must take seriously the possibility that a significant improvement in the designated patient may result in a severe decompensation in a parent, who will be thrown into a panic because of the perceived separation (Brown 1987). In these instances, a family therapist should help the family deal with the dilemmas created by change in the patient as well as in the family system as a whole. The therapist must conscientiously avoid any attempt to "pry apart" the borderline patient and the family. Such efforts will be viewed by both the family and the patient as a highly threatening attack that will simply cause them to "circle the wagons" and increase their enmeshment. Family therapists produce better results when they assume a nonjudgmental, neutral position regarding change, empathizing with the family's need to remain together because of the stability inherent in the overinvolvement (Jones 1987). Any change in the system must come from within, not from mental health professionals who place a high value on separation and autonomy.

Group Psychotherapy

Group psychotherapy may also be a beneficial adjunct to individual psychotherapy of borderline patients. As Ganzarain (1980) and Horwitz (1977) have noted, all groups are prone to employ the borderline defenses of splitting and projective identification. Group psychotherapy affords the borderline individual an opportunity to understand these defenses as they occur in a group context. Most contributors to the literature on group psychotherapy of the borderline patient, however, suggest that the borderline patient is most effectively treated in groups of patients who suffer from neuroses or higher-level personality disorders (Day and Semrad 1971; Horwitz 1977; Hulse 1958; Slavson 1964).

Likewise, the consensus of the literature is that borderline patients in group psychotherapy need concomitant individual psychotherapy (Day and Semrad 1971; Horwitz 1977; Hulse 1958; Slavson 1964; Spotnitz 1957). The dilution of transference in group psychotherapy significantly benefits both the borderline patient and the therapist. The intense rage that is ordinarily mobilized in borderline patients when they are frustrated in treatment may thus be diluted and directed toward other figures besides the individual therapist. Similarly, the strong countertransference reactions to borderline patients may be diluted by the presence of other people.

Horwitz (1977) has pointed out that the individual psychotherapist may serve a crucial supportive function when the borderline patient's anxiety escalates in response to confrontation in the group setting. The individual therapist ideally should be someone other than the group therapist, because "it is antitherapeutic for the group therapist to see some patients individually while not seeing others privately as well" (p. 415). Horwitz also identified abrasive characterological traits as an indication for group psychotherapy in addition to individual psychotherapy. He has observed that borderline patients seem more willing to accept confrontation and interpretation about such traits from their peers in group psychotherapy than from a therapist. They also may more easily accept their therapist's interpretations as part of a group-centered theme than when the interpretations single them out as individuals.

Despite the advantages of working in a group context, therapists will find certain inherent difficulties in the group psychotherapy of borderline patients. Such patients may easily become scapegoated because of their more primitive psychopathology and their greater tendency to express affect in a direct manner. The therapist may be required to support the borderline patient when scapegoating emerges as a group theme. Moreover, borderline patients may also experience an increase in their feelings of deprivation because of competition with the group for the nurturance of the therapist. Finally, borderline patients tend to maintain a certain distance in group psychotherapy because of their primary attachment to the individual therapist.

References

Abend SM, Porder MS, Willick MS: Borderline Patients: Psychoanalytic Perspectives. New York, International Universities Press, 1983

Adler G: The myth of the alliance with borderline patients. Am J Psychiatry 47:642–645, 1979

Adler G: The borderline-narcissistic personality disorder continuum. Am J Psychiatry 138:46–50, 1981

Adler G: Issues in the treatment of the borderline patient, in Kohut's Legacy: Contributions to Self Psychology. Edited by Stepansky PE, Goldberg A. Hillsdale, NJ, Analytic Press, 1984, pp 117–134

Adler G: Borderline Psychopathology and Its Treatment. New York, Jason Aronson, 1985

Adler G: Discussion: milieu treatment in the psychotherapy of the borderline patient: abandonment and containment. Yearbook of Psychoanalysis and Psychotherapy 2:145–157, 1987

Adler G, Buie DH Jr: Aloneness and borderline psychopathology: the possible relevance of child development issues. Int J Psychoanal 60:83–96, 1979

Adler G, Rhine MW: The selfobject function of projective identification: curative factors in psychotherapy. Bull Menninger Clin 52:473–491, 1988

Akiskal HS: Subaffective disorders: dysthymic, cyclothymic and bipolar II disorders in the "borderline" realm. Psychiatr Clin North Am 4:25–46, 1981

American Psychiatric Association: Diagnostic and Statistical Manual of Mental Disorders, 2nd Edition. Washington, DC, American Psychiatric Association, 1968

American Psychiatric Association: Diagnostic and Statistical Manual of Mental Disorders, 3rd Edition. Washington, DC, American Psychiatric Association, 1980

American Psychiatric Association: Diagnostic and Statistical Manual of Mental Disorders, 3rd Edition, Revised. Washington, DC, American Psychiatric Association, 1987

Andrulonis PA, Glueck BC, Stroebel CF, et al: Organic brain dysfunction and the borderline syndrome. Psychiatr Clin North Am 4:47–66, 1981

Atwood GE, Stolorow RD: Structures of Subjectivity: Explorations in Psychoanalytic Phenomenology. Hillsdale, NJ, Analytic Press, 1984

Baron M, Gruen R, Asnis L, et al: Familial transmission of schizotypal and borderline personality disorders. Am J Psychiatry 142:927–934, 1985

Boyer LB: Working with a borderline patient. Psychoanal Q 46:386–424, 1977

Brown SL: Family therapy and the borderline patient, in The Borderline Patient: Emerging Concepts in Diagnosis, Psychodynamics, and Treatment, Vol 2. Edited by Grotstein JS, Solomon MF, Lang JA. Hillsdale, NJ, Analytic Press, 1987, pp 206–209

Burnham DL: The special problem patient: victim or agent of splitting? Psychiatry 29:105–122, 1966

Cornelius JR, Soloff PH, George AWA, et al: An evaluation of the significance of selected neuropsychiatric abnormalities in the etiology of borderline personality disorder. Journal of Personality Disorders 3:19–25, 1989

Cowdry RW, Gardner DL: Pharmacotherapy of borderline personality disorder: alprazolam, carbamazepine, trifluoperazine, and tranylcypromine. Arch Gen Psychiatry 45:111–119, 1988

Day M, Semrad E: Group therapy with neurotics and psychotics, in Comprehensive Group Psychotherapy. Edited by Kaplan HI, Sadock BJ. Baltimore, Williams & Wilkins, 1971, pp 566–580

Dorpat TL, Ripley HS: The relationship between attempted suicide and committed suicide. Compr Psychiatry 8:74–79, 1967

Esman AH: Adolescent psychopathology and the rapprochement process, in Rapprochement: The Critical Subphase of Separation-Individuation. Edited by Lax RF, Bach S, Burland JA. New York, Jason Aronson, 1980, pp 295–297

Fairbairn WRD: An Object-Relations Theory of the Personality. New York, Basic Books, 1954

Finell JS: Book review of Borderline Psychopathology and Its Treatment (by Gerald Adler). Psychoanal Rev 75:491–493, 1988

Fraiberg S: Libidinal object constancy and mental representation. Psychoanal Study Child 24:9–47, 1969

Fyer MR, Frances AJ, Sullivan T, et al: Comorbidity of borderline personality disorder. Arch Gen Psychiatry 45:348–352, 1988

Gabbard GO: The treatment of the "special" patient in a psychoanalytic hospital. International Review of Psychoanalysis 13:333–347, 1986

Gabbard GO: On "doing nothing" in the psychoanalytic treatment of the refractory borderline patient. Int J Psychoanal 70:527–534, 1989a

Gabbard GO: Patients who hate. Psychiatry 52:96–106, 1989b

Gabbard GO (ed): Sexual Exploitation in Professional Relationships. Washington, DC, American Psychiatric Press, 1989c

Gabbard GO, Horwitz L, Frieswyk S, et al: The effect of therapist interventions on the therapeutic alliance with borderline patients. J Am Psychoanal Assoc 36:697–727, 1988

Ganzarain R: Psychotic-like anxieties and primitive defenses in group analytic psychotherapy. Issues in Ego Psychology 3:42–48, 1980

Gardner DL, Cowdry RW: Alprazolam-induced dyscontrol in borderline personality disorder. Am J Psychiatry 142:98–100, 1985

Giovacchini PL: Psychic integration and object constancy, in Self and Object Constancy: Clinical and Theoretical Perspectives. Edited by Lax RF, Bach S, Burland JA. New York, Guilford Press, 1986, pp 208–233

Goldstein WN: An integration of the views of Kernberg and Adler on borderline pathology. Bull Menninger Clin 53:300–309, 1989

Gorney JE: The negative therapeutic interaction. Contemp Psychoanal 15:288–337, 1979

Grinker Jr RR, Werble B, Drye RC: The Borderline Syndrome: A Behavioral Study of Ego-Functions. New York, Basic Books, 1968

Grotstein JS: The analysis of a borderline patient, in Technical Factors in the Treatment of the Severely Disturbed Patient. Edited by Giovacchini PL, Boyer LB. New York, Jason Aronson, 1982, pp 261–288

Grotstein JS: The borderline as a disorder of self-regulation, in The Borderline Patient: Emerging Concepts in Diagnosis, Psychodynamics, and Treatment, Vol 1. Edited by Grotstein JS, Solomon MF, Lang JA. Hillsdale, NJ, Analytic Press, 1987, pp 347–383

Gunderson JG: Borderline Personality Disorder. Washington, DC, American Psychiatric Press, 1984

Gunderson JG, Elliott GR: The interface between borderline personality disorder and affective disorder. Am J Psychiatry 142:277–288, 1985

Gunderson JG, Englund DW: Characterizing the families of border-
    lines: a review of the literature. Psychiatr Clin North Am 4:159–
    168, 1981
Gunderson JG, Frank AF, Ronningstam EF, et al: Early discontinuance
    of borderline patients from psychotherapy. J Nerv Ment Dis
    177:38–42, 1989
Gunderson JG, Kerr J, Englund DW: The families of borderlines: a
    comparative study. Arch Gen Psychiatry 37:27–33, 1980
Gunderson JG, Singer MT: Defining borderline patients: an overview.
    Am J Psychiatry 132:1–10, 1975
Gunderson JG, Zanarini MC: Current overview of the borderline diag-
    nosis. J Clin Psychiatry 48 (8, suppl):5–14, 1987
Gutheil T: Borderline personality disorder, boundary violations, and
    patient-therapist sex: medicolegal pitfalls. Am J Psychiatry
    146:597–602, 1989
Herman JL, Perry JC, van der Kolk BA: Childhood trauma in borderline
    personality disorder. Am J Psychiatry 146:490–495, 1989
Hoch P, Polatin P: Pseudoneurotic forms of schizophrenia. Psychiatr Q
    23:248–276, 1949
Horwitz L: Clinical Prediction in Psychotherapy. New York, Jason Aron-
    son, 1974
Horwitz L: Group psychothcrapy of thc bordcrlinc patient, in Border-
    line Personality Disorders: The Concept, the Syndrome, the Pa-
    tient. Edited by Hartocollis PL. New York, International
    Universities Press, 1977, pp 399–422
Hulse WC: Psychotherapy with ambulatory schizophrenic patients in
    mixed analytic groups. Arch Neurol Psychiatry 79:681–687,
    1958
Jones SA: Family therapy with borderline and narcissistic patients. Bull
    Menninger Clin 51:285–295, 1987
Kernberg OF: Structural derivatives of object relationships. Int J Psy-
    choanal 47:236–253, 1966
Kernberg OF: Borderline personality organization. J Am Psychoanal
    Assoc 15:641–685, 1967
Kernberg OF: Borderline Conditions and Pathological Narcissism. New
    York, Jason Aronson, 1975
Kernberg OF: Technical considerations in the treatment of borderline
    personality organization. J Am Psychoanal Assoc 24:795–829,
    1976
Kernberg OF: Severe Personality Disorders: Psychothcrapcutic Stratc-
    gies. New Haven, CT, Yale University Press, 1984
Kernberg OF: Book review of Borderline Psychopathology and Its
    Treatment (by Gerald Adler). Am J Psychiatry 145:264–265, 1988
Kernberg OF, Burstein ED, Coyne L, et al: Psychotherapy and psycho-
    analysis: final report of the Menninger Foundation's Psychother-
    apy Research Project. Bull Menninger Clin 36:3–275, 1972
Knight RP: Borderline states, in Psychoanalytic Psychiatry and Psychol-
    ogy: Clinical and Theoretical Papers (1953). Edited by Knight RP,
    Friedman CR. New York, International Universities Press, 1954,
    pp 97–109

Loranger AW, Oldham JM, Tulis EH: Familial transmission of DSM-III borderline personality disorder. Arch Gen Psychiatry 39:795–799, 1982

Mahler MS, Kaplan LJ: Developmental aspects in the assessment of narcissistic and so-called borderline personalities, in Borderline Personality Disorders: The Concept, the Syndrome, the Patient. Edited by Hartocollis PL. New York, International Universities Press, 1977, pp 71–85

Mahler MS, Pine F, Bergman A: The Psychological Birth of the Human Infant: Symbiosis and Individuation. New York, Basic Books, 1975

Main TF: The ailment. Br J Med Psychol 30:129–145, 1957

Masterson J: Psychotherapy of the Borderline Adult: A Developmental Approach. New York, Brunner/Mazel, 1976

Masterson JF, Rinsley DB: The borderline syndrome: the role of the mother in the genesis and psychic structure of the borderline personality. Int J Psychoanal 56:163–177, 1975

McGlashan TH: The borderline syndrome, II: is it a variant of schizophrenia or affective disorder? Arch Gen Psychiatry 40:1319–1323, 1983

McGlashan TH: The Chestnut Lodge follow-up study, III: long-term outcome of borderline personalities. Arch Gen Psychiatry 43:20–30, 1986

Meissner WW: The Borderline Spectrum: Differential Diagnosis and Developmental Issues. New York, Jason Aronson, 1984

Meissner WW: Treatment of Patients in the Borderline Spectrum. Northvale, NJ, Jason Aronson, 1988

Modell AH: "The holding environment" and the therapeutic action of psychoanalysis. J Am Psychoanal Assoc 24:285–307, 1976

Pine F: Supportive psychotherapy: a psychoanalytic perspective. Psychiatric Annals 16:526–529, 1986

Plakun EM, Burkhardt PE, Muller JP: 14-year follow-up of borderline and schizotypal personality disorders. Compr Psychiatry 26:448–455, 1985

Pope Jr HG, Jonas JM, Hudson JI, et al: The validity of DSM-III borderline personality disorder: a phenomenologic, family history, treatment response, and long-term follow-up study. Arch Gen Psychiatry 40:23–30, 1983

Rinsley DB: Borderline psychopathology: the concepts of Masterson and Rinsley and beyond. Adolesc Psychiatry 9:259–274, 1981a

Rinsley DB: Dynamic and developmental issues in borderline and related "spectrum" disorders. Psychiatr Clin North Am 4:117–132, 1981b

Rinsley DB: A comparison of borderline and narcissistic personality disorders. Bull Menninger Clin 48:1–9, 1984

Rinsley DB: Notes on the pathogenesis and nosology of borderline and narcissistic personality disorders. J Am Acad Psychoanal 13:317–328, 1985

Rinsley DB: Object constancy, object permanency, and personality disorders, in Self and Object Constancy: Clinical and Theoretical Perspectives. Edited by Lax RF, Bach S, Burland JA. New York, Guilford Press, 1986, pp 193–207

Rinsley DB: A reconsideration of Fairbairn's "original object" and "original ego" in relation to borderline and other self disorders, in The Borderline Patient: Emerging Concepts in Diagnosis, Psychodynamics, and Treatment, Vol 1. Edited by Grotstein JF, Solomon MF, Lang JA. Hillsdale, NJ, Analytic Press, 1987, pp 291–231

Rinsley DB: A review of the pathogenesis of borderline and narcissistic personality disorders. Adolesc Psychiatry 15:387–406, 1988

Rinsley DB: Developmental Psychodynamics of Borderline and Narcissistic Personalities. Northvale, NJ, Jason Aronson, 1989

Schmideberg M: The borderline patient, in American Handbook of Psychiatry, Vol 1. Edited by Arieti S. New York, Basic Books, 1959, pp 398–416

Searles HF: My Work With Borderline Patients. Northvale, NJ, Jason Aronson, 1986

Slavson SR: A Textbook in Analytic Group Psychotherapy. New York, International Universities Press, 1964

Soloff PH, Millward JW: Psychiatric disorders in the families of borderline patients. Arch Gen Psychiatry 40:37–44, 1983

Soloff PH, George A, Nathan RS, et al: Progress in pharmacotherapy of borderline disorders: a double-blind study of amitriptyline, haloperidol, and placebo. Arch Gen Psychiatry 43:691–697, 1986

Spotnitz H: The borderline schizophrenic in group psychotherapy: the importance of individualization. Int J Group Psychother 7:155–174, 1957

Stone MH: The Borderline Syndromes: Constitution, Personality, and Adaptation. New York, McGraw-Hill, 1980

Stone MH: Psychotherapy of borderline patients in light of long-term follow-up. Bull Menninger Clin 51:231–247, 1987

Stone MH, Stone DK, Hurt SW: Natural history of borderline patients treated by intensive hospitalization. Psychiatr Clin North Am 10:185–206, 1987

Tuckman J, Youngman WF: Suicide risk among persons attempting suicide. Public Health Rep 78:585–587, 1963

Waldinger RJ: Intensive psychodynamic therapy with borderline patients: an overview. Am J Psychiatry 144:267–274, 1987

Waldinger RJ, Frank AF: Clinicians' experiences in combining medication and psychotherapy in the treatment of borderline patients. Hosp Community Psychiatry 40:712–718, 1989

Waldinger RJ, Gunderson JG: Effective Psychotherapy With Borderline Patients: Case Studies. New York, Macmillan, 1987

Wallerstein RS: Forty-two Lives in Treatment: A Study of Psychoanalysis and Psychotherapy. New York, Guilford Press, 1986

Werble B: Second follow-up study of borderline patients. Arch Gen Psychiatry 23:3–7, 1970

Widiger TA, Frances A, Spitzer RL, et al: The DSM-III-R personality disorders: an overview. Am J Psychiatry 145:786–795, 1988

Zetzel ER: A developmental approach to the borderline patient. Am J Psychiatry 127:867–871, 1971

CHAPTER 15

The Narcissistic Patient

O, you are sick of self-love,
Malvolio, and taste with a
distempered appetite. To be generous,
guiltless, and of free disposition, is to
take those things for birdbolts* that
you deem cannon bullets.
— Olivia in Act I, Scene v,
of Shakespeare's *Twelfth Night*

blunt-head arrows for shooting birds.

Healthy Versus Pathological Narcissism

In Shakespeare's comedy, it is clear to both Olivia and the audience that Malvolio's love of himself and his tendency to experience mild slights as devastating attacks are indications that he is "sick." In contemporary psychiatric practice, however, the distinction between healthy and pathological degrees of narcissism is fraught with difficulty. A certain measure of self-love is not only normal but also desirable. Yet the point on the continuum of self-regard where healthy narcissism turns into pathological narcissism is not easy to identify.

Another confounding factor is that certain behaviors may be pathologically narcissistic in one individual while simply a manifestation of healthy self-regard in another. Let us imagine, for example, a 15-year-old boy who stands in front of the mirror blow-drying his hair for 45 minutes in order to get every hair perfectly in place. Most of us would chuckle to ourselves at this image and realize that vanity of this sort is entirely normal for a pubescent youngster. Now let us shift to an image of a 30-year-old man who spends the same amount of time every morning in front of the mirror with a blow dryer. This visual picture is a bit more disconcerting, because such excessive self-absorption is far from the norm for a man of this age. If we now imagine a 45-year-old man engaged in the same activity, we again become a bit more charitable in our attitude because, as was the case with the adolescent boy, we understand such behavior as part of a developmental phase in the life cycle that we often refer to as midlife crisis. Before making a definitive determination about the relative health or pathology in this individual, however, we would want to know more about his other activities.

The above examples illustrate how narcissism is judged differently depending on the phase of the life cycle through which one is passing. Even though we are aware of these developmental distinctions, the term *narcissistic* is rarely used as a compliment to refer to someone with healthy self-esteem. On the contrary, the term is much more commonly used pejoratively as a synonym for "son of a bitch," especially when referring to colleagues and acquaintances whom we find unpleasant. Also, the term is often invoked to refer to someone whose success and confidence we envy. Since we all struggle with narcissistic issues, we must always be wary of the potential for hypocrisy in labeling others as narcissistic. Some (Lasch 1979) would argue that the history of humankind suggests that we have always been selfish and that nothing is gained by applying a psychiatric label to such qualities.

To complicate things further, we live in a narcissistic culture (Lasch 1979; Rinsley 1986). We are slavishly devoted to electronic media that thrive on superficial images and ignore substance and depth. We view consumption of material goods as the road to happiness. Our fear of aging and death keeps plastic surgeons in business. We are consumed with the glamour of celebrity. Books with titles like *Looking Out for No. 1* make the best-seller list. Competitive sports, the great American pastime, teach us that being number one is the most important goal of all.

One of the key diagnostic criteria of narcissistic personality disorder, interpersonal exploitiveness, is highly adaptive in our society. Indeed, the very fabric of our economic system is based on rewarding those who are able to talk others into buying a product (Maccoby 1976; Person 1986). In the corporate world, "making it" has become more important than values of commitment, loyalty, integrity, and interpersonal warmth. College athletic coaches can get away with outrageous treatment of their athletes as long as they continue to bring home conference titles. Winning forgives everything.

Given this cultural ambience, it is often problematic to determine which traits indicate a narcissistic personality disorder and which are simply adaptive cultural traits. Moreover, the difference between healthy self-esteem and an artificially inflated self-esteem is often ambiguous. Let us visualize, for example, a mental health professional presenting a scientific paper to an audience of peers. The presenter notices that about half the audience is falling asleep during his presentation, while others are getting up and leaving. At the end of the presentation during the discussion period, the presenter is severely criticized for "muddy thinking," "insufficient familiarity with the literature," and "presenting nothing new." This same mental health professional responds to these criticisms by saying to himself, "No matter what they think, I know I'm competent anyway." How do we evaluate this response? Based on the information in this example, we could reach one of two conclusions: 1) this person has a healthy self-regard that does not collapse merely because of one untoward experience; or 2) the presenter's response is reflective of pathological narcissism in that it is a grandiose defensive reaction to compensate for a devastating injury to his self-esteem.

Given this bewildering array of varied usage, developmental differences, and cultural influences, what definitive criteria can be used to differentiate healthy from pathological narcissism? The time-honored criteria of psychological health—to love and to work—are only partly useful in answering this question. An individual's work history may provide little help in making the distinction. Highly disturbed narcissistic individuals may find extraordinary success in certain professions, such as big business, the arts, politics, the entertainment industry, athletics, and the televangelism field (Gabbard 1983; Rinsley 1985, 1989). In some cases, however, narcissistic pathology may be reflected in a superficial quality to one's professional interests (Kernberg 1970), as though achievement and acclaim are more important than mastery of the field itself.

Pathological forms of narcissism are more easily identified by the quality of the individual's relationships. One tragedy affecting these people is their inability to love. Healthy interpersonal relationships can be recognized by qualities such as empathy and concern for the feelings of others, a genuine interest in the ideas of others, the ability to tolerate ambivalence in long-term relationships without giving up, and a capacity to acknowledge one's own contribution to interpersonal conflicts. People whose relationships are characterized by these qualities may at times use others to gratify their own needs, but this tendency occurs in the broader context of sensitive interpersonal relatedness rather than as a pervasive style of dealing with other people. On the other hand, the person with a narcissistic personality disorder approaches people as objects to be used up and discarded according to the narcissist's needs, without regard for their feelings. People are not viewed as having a separate existence or as having needs of their own. The individual with a narcissistic personality disorder frequently ends a relationship after a short time, usually when the other person begins to make demands stemming from his or her own needs. Most importantly, such relationships clearly do not "work" in terms of the narcissist's ability to maintain his own sense of self-esteem (Stolorow 1975).

Phenomenology of Narcissistic Personality Disorder

The psychodynamic literature on narcissistic personality disorder is somewhat confusing because the label seems to apply to patients with quite different clinical pictures. DSM-III-R (American Psychiatric Association 1987) lists nine criteria for narcissistic personality disorder (Table 15-1).

These criteria identify a certain kind of narcissistic patient, specifically, the arrogant, boastful, "noisy" individual who demands to be in the spotlight. However, they fail to characterize the shy, quietly grandiose, narcissistic individual whose extreme sensitivity to slights leads to an assiduous avoidance of the spotlight (Cooper and Michels 1988).

The literature identifies something of a continuum of narcissistic personality disorder. Kernberg (1970, 1974a, 1974b) identified

Table 15-1. DSM-III-R criteria for narcissistic personality disorder

A pervasive pattern of grandiosity (in fantasy or behavior), lack of empathy, and hypersensitivity to the evaluation of others, beginning by early adulthood and present in a variety of contexts, as indicated by at least *five* of the following:

    (1) reacts to criticism with feelings of rage, shame, or humiliation (even if not expressed)

    (2) interpersonally exploitative: takes advantage of others to achieve his or her own end

    (3) has a grandiose sense of self-importance, e.g., exaggerates achievements and talents, expects to be noticed as "special" without appropriate achievement

    (4) believes that his or her problems are unique and can be understood only by other special people

    (5) preoccupied with fantasies of unlimited success, power, brilliance, beauty, or ideal love

    (6) has a sense of entitlement: unreasonable expectation of especially favorable treatment, e.g., assumes that he or she does not have to wait in line when others must do so

    (7) requires constant attention and admiration, e.g., keeps fishing for compliments

    (8) lack of empathy: inability to recognize and experience how others feel, e.g., annoyance and surprise when a friend who is seriously ill cancels a date

    (9) is preoccupied with feelings of envy

Note. Reprinted from DSM-III-R, pp. 250–251, with permission from the American Psychiatric Association.

Table 15-2. Two types of narcissistic personality disorder

The Oblivious Narcissist	The Hypervigilant Narcissist
1. Has no awareness of reactions of others	1. Is highly sensitive to reactions of others
2. Is arrogant and aggressive	2. Is inhibited, shy, or even self-effacing
3. Is self-absorbed	3. Directs attention more toward others than toward self
4. Needs to be the center of attention	4. Shuns being the center of attention
5. Has a "sender but no receiver"	5. Listens to others carefully for evidence of slights or criticisms
6. Is apparently impervious to having feelings hurt by others	6. Has easily hurt feelings; is prone to feeling ashamed or humiliated

an envious, greedy type who demands the attention and acclaim of others, while Kohut (1971, 1977, 1984) described a narcissistically vulnerable type prone to self-fragmentation. Bursten (1973) divided narcissistic patients into four groups—the craving, the paranoid, the manipulative, and the phallic-narcissistic. The various descriptions of narcissistic patients described by the authors may be conceptualized as falling between two poles on a continuum based on the typical style of interpersonal relatedness. From a descriptive standpoint, the two opposite extremes on this continuum may be labeled the oblivious narcissist and the hypervigilant narcissist (Gabbard 1989) (see Table 15-2). These terms specifically refer to the person's predominant style of interacting, both in transference relationships with a therapist and in social relationships in general.

Oblivious types appear to have no awareness whatsoever of their impact on others. They can often be observed in action at cocktail parties or in other social situations. They talk as though addressing a large audience, rarely establishing eye contact and generally looking over the heads of those around them. They talk "at" others, not "to" them. They are oblivious to the fact that they are boring and that some people will therefore leave the conversation and seek companionship elsewhere. Their talk is replete with references to their own accomplishments, and they clearly need to be the center of attention. They are insensitive to the needs of others, even to the point that they do not allow others to contribute to the conversation. They are often perceived as "having a sender but no receiver." The oblivious type is closely related to the DSM-III-R criteria, but is much more impervious to criticism than those criteria imply.

The narcissistic issues of the hypervigilant type, on the other hand, are manifested in starkly different ways. These people are exquisitely sensitive to how others react to them. In fact, their attention is continually directed toward others, in contrast to the self-absorption of the oblivious narcissist. Like the paranoid patient, they listen to others carefully for evidence of any critical reaction, and they tend to feel slighted at every turn. One narcissistic patient was so attuned to his therapist's reactions that every time the therapist shifted position in his chair or cleared his throat, the patient viewed it as a sign of boredom. When this therapist removed a dead leaf from an office plant on his desk, the patient felt humiliated and demanded a new therapist. These patients are shy and inhibited to the point of being self-effacing. They shun the limelight because they are convinced that they will be rejected and humiliated. At the core of their inner world is a deep sense of shame related to their secret wish to exhibit themselves in a grandiose manner.

Although both types struggle with maintaining their self-esteem, they deal with that issue in extremely different ways. Oblivious narcissists attempt to impress others with their accomplishments while insulating themselves from narcissistic injury by screening out the response of others. Hypervigilant narcissists attempt to maintain their self-esteem by avoiding vulnerable situations and by intensely studying others to "figure out" how to behave. They projectively attribute their own disapproval of their grandiose fantasies onto others (Gabbard 1983). This typology is closely related to Rosenfeld's (1987) distinction between "thick-skinned" and "thin-skinned" narcissistic patients and to Broucek's (1982) categories of egotistical and dissociative. However, while the oblivious narcissist is virtually identical with the egotistical type, the hypervigilant patient does not project the grandiosity onto an idealized other, as is the case with Broucek's dissociative type, but instead retains it within and regards the other as a persecutor.

These two types may occur in pure form, but many patients present with a mixture of phenomenological features from both types. Between these two endpoints on the continuum will be many narcissistic individuals who are much smoother socially and who possess a great deal of interpersonal charm.

Psychodynamic Understanding

For the last two decades the principal controversy surrounding the theoretical understanding of narcissistic personality disorder has revolved around the models of Kohut and Kernberg (Adler 1986; Glassman 1988; Kernberg 1974a, 1974b; Ornstein 1974a). The self psychology theory of Kohut was covered in some detail in Chapter 2, so it will only be schematically reviewed here.

Kohut (1971, 1977, 1984) believed that narcissistically disturbed individuals are developmentally arrested at a stage where they require specific responses from persons in their environment to maintain cohesive selves. When such responses are not forthcoming, these individuals are prone to fragmentations of the self. Kohut understood this state of affairs as the result of the parents' empathic failures. Specifically, the parents did not respond to the child's phase-appropriate displays of exhibitionism with validation and admiration, did not offer twinship experiences, and did not provide the child with a model worthy of idealization. These failures manifest themselves in the patient's tendency to form a mirror, twinship, or idealizing transference.

Kohut postulated a double axis theory (see Table 2-1 in Chapter 2) to explain how both narcissistic needs and object-related needs can coexist in the same individual. Throughout our lives, Kohut argued, we are in need of selfobject responses from the people around us. In other words, at some level we all regard others not as separate persons but as sources of gratification for the self. A need for the soothing, validating functions of selfobjects is never outgrown. The goal of treatment is to move away from a need for archaic selfobjects toward an ability to use more mature and appropriate selfobjects.

A case example may help illustrate how the theory of self psychology manifests itself in a clinical situation.

Ms. BB was a 26-year-old, single woman who came to treatment after her 4-year relationship with her boyfriend ended. She indicated that his rejection of her had been "devastating." While she specifically denied any suicidal thoughts, she did say that she felt she was no longer alive without him. Although it had been a year since the breakup, she was unable to get her life back on track. She sat around feeling empty and lonely. She continued to go to work, but then would return home each evening and just sit in her apartment staring blankly or watching television. Throughout her day at work she felt detached from any activities she pursued, as if she was on "automatic pilot." She repeatedly spoke of needing to be "plugged in" to her boyfriend to feel alive. She desperately missed having him stroke her hair to calm her down when she came home anxious from work. She poignantly stated, "Without him, I am nothing. I can't soothe myself." She lacked the symptoms necessary for a diagnosis of Axis I major depressive episode, but she described herself as depressed and empty.

She met with her therapist for several weeks and reported that she began to "feel alive again." Ms. BB then stated that she felt "plugged in" to her therapist. She tended to misinterpret her therapist's comments to mean that he was about to reject her at any

moment. She asked if her therapist would increase the number of
sessions from two to five a week so she could see him every weekday.
The therapist, on the other hand, believed that all he was doing was
listening. He noted to his supervisor, "I don't think she is really
interested in anything I say. She's perfectly content if I simply give
her my undivided attention."

Kernberg's theoretical formulations (1970, 1974a, 1974b,
1984) differ sharply from those of Kohut (Table 15-3). The major
theoretical differences in their conceptualizations of narcissistic
personality disorder may well relate to the different populations of
patients that they studied. Kohut's sample was based on relatively
well-functioning outpatients who could afford psychoanalysis. Typically, they were professional people who described vague feelings
of emptiness and depression and particular problems in their relationships. They struggled to maintain their professional self-esteem,
and they tended to feel slighted by others (Kohut, 1971). Kernberg,
on the other hand, has always worked in hospitals, and based his
conceptual framework on a mixture of inpatients and outpatients.
His clinical descriptions depict patients who are more primitive,
more arrogant, more aggressive (often with antisocial features), and
overtly grandiose (although the grandiosity may alternate with
shyness).

Kohut (1971) differentiated narcissistic personality disorders
from borderline conditions. He saw the borderline patient as not
having achieved sufficient cohesiveness of the self to be analyzed.
His diagnosis of narcissistic personality is based on the development
of either the mirror or idealizing transference in the context of a
trial analysis. In contrast, Kernberg (1970) saw the defensive
organization of narcissistic personality as strikingly *similar* to borderline personality disorder. In fact, he viewed it as one of several
personality types that operate at a borderline level of personality
organization (see Chapter 14). He differentiated narcissistic personality disorder from borderline personality on the basis of the narcissist's integrated but pathological grandiose self. This structure is
a fusion of the ideal self, the ideal object, and the real self. This
fusion results in the destructive devaluation of object-images. These
patients identify themselves with their idealized self-images in order
to deny their dependency on external objects (other people) as well
as on the inner images of those objects. At the same time, they deny
the unacceptable features of their own self-images by projecting
them into others.

The pathological grandiose self explains the paradox of relatively good ego-functioning in the presence of the primitive defenses
(splitting, projective identification, omnipotence, devaluation, idealization, and denial) typical of the borderline patient. In other
words, whereas borderline patients tend to have alternating self-rep-

Table 15-3. Dynamic understanding of narcissistic personality
disorder

Kohut	Kernberg
1. Based theory on relatively well-functioning people whose self-esteem is vulnerable to slights— all outpatients.	1. Based theory on a mixture of inpatients and outpatients, most of whom are primitive, aggressive, and arrogant, with haughty grandiosity coexisting with shyness.
2. Differentiates narcissistic personality from borderline states.	2. Defines narcissistic personality as a strikingly similar subcategory of borderline personality. While most have better ego functioning than borderline patients, some function on an overt border-line level.
3. Does not define inner world of narcissistic personality because emphasis is on internalization of missing functions.	3. Delineates primitive defenses and object relations typical of borderline personality disorder.
4. Defines archaic "normal" self as one that is develop-mentally arrested.	4. Defines self as a highly pathological structure composed of the fusion of the ideal self, ideal object, and real self.
5. Views self as nondefensive.	5. Views grandiose self as being *defensive* against investment or dependency on others.
6. Focuses mainly on libidinal/ idealizing aspects with aggression conceptualized as *secondary* to narcissistic injury.	6. Emphasizes envy and aggression.
7. Accepts idealization at face value as a normal develop-mental phase making up for missing psychic structure.	7. Views idealization as defensive against rage, envy, contempt, and devaluation.

resentations that make them look very different from day to day, narcissistic patients have a smoother, more consistent level of functioning based on an integrated pathological self. Also, the borderline personality is much more likely to have problems related to ego weaknesses, such as poor impulse control and poor anxiety tolerance. These ego weaknesses are much less common in narcissistic personalities due to the smooth functioning self-structure. However, Kernberg also added that some narcissistic patients function at an overt borderline level. These patients have the grandiosity and haughtiness of the narcissistic personality with the poor impulse control and the kaleidoscopic object relations of borderline patients. It is this subgroup that occasionally requires hospitalization. (The hospital treatment of these patients is similar to that for borderline patients discussed in Chapter 14. Inpatient treatment of narcissistic patients with serious antisocial features is described in Chapter 16.)

The detailed description of the narcissistic patient's defensive constellation and internal object relations provided by Kernberg is in contrast to Kohut's tendency to leave undefined the inner world of the narcissistic patient. He emphasized the internalization of missing functions from people in the environment, so he was less concerned about the patient's intrapsychic structure. Kohut conceptualized the self, however, as an archaic "normal" self that is simply frozen developmentally. He viewed the patient as a child in an adult's body, in other words. Unlike Kohut, Kernberg (1974a, 1974b) viewed the self as a highly pathological structure that in no way resembles the normal developing self of children. He pointed out that the exhibitionistic self-display of children is charming and endearing in contrast to the greed and demandingness of the narcissist's pathological self.

Another difference in their view of the self relates to the self's defensive functioning. Kohut saw the self as essentially nondefensive (i.e., a normally developing self that simply became stuck). Kernberg saw the pathologically grandiose self as defensive against investment in others, and specifically against dependency on others. This characteristic may manifest itself as a pseudo-self-sufficiency whereby the patient denies any need for nurturance while at the same time attempting to impress others and gain approval. Narcissistic patients frequently insist, for example, that they have no reaction to their therapists' vacations.

Kohut's view of the narcissistic personality is perhaps more charitable than Kernberg's. He focused mainly on the childhood longing for certain parental responses. Aggression is viewed as a *secondary* phenomenon (i.e., narcissistic rage in reaction to not having one's needs for mirroring and idealizing gratified). In that sense, Kohut viewed aggression as an entirely understandable response to parental failures. Kernberg saw aggression as a more primary factor. Inordinately high levels of aggression cause the narcissistic patient to be destructive toward others. In Kernberg's (1970) view, the etiology of this aggression can either be constitutional or environmental. It was seen, however, as arising from within rather than as simply an understandable reaction to the external failures of others. One manifestation of the narcissistic patient's aggression is chronic intense envy (1974b), which causes the patient to want to spoil and destroy the good things of others. Although Kohut did not view envy as having a central role, Kernberg described these patients as constantly comparing themselves to others, only to find themselves tormented with feelings of inferiority and intense yearning to possess what others have.

Idealization was viewed quite differently by Kohut and Kernberg. Kohut viewed idealization in the transference as the recapitulation of a normal developmental phase. Rather than labeling it as a defensive posture, he saw it as a way to make up for missing psychic structure. Fundamental to Kohut's understanding is the notion that the narcissistic individual is incomplete without a selfobject. Kernberg viewed idealization as a defense against a variety of negative feelings, including rage, envy, contempt, and devaluation.

In light of these point-by-point differences between Kohut and Kernberg, it should be clear that Kernberg was describing patients who more closely approximate the oblivious type, while Kohut seemed to be writing about patients who are closer to the hypervigilant type. The narcissistic patients described by Kernberg frequently appear to have nothing but the most superficial forms of object relatedness. If the patient is male, he may have a "Don Juan" syndrome in which he systematically seduces women and discards them when his idealization of them turns to devaluation. Viewing them only as "conquests," he has no capacity to empathize with their internal experience. Such a patient seems to have little interest in what others say unless the content is flattering. Although these patients are most commonly male, females may suffer from similar narcissistic pathology.

> Ms. CC came to psychotherapy because of a vague sense of unhappiness and an inability to find satisfaction in any of her relationships. She was 28 years old, attractive and intelligent, but had never found a man who had particularly interested her. She described "numbness" and boredom in relationships. She said that when other people were talking to her, she simply waited impatiently for them to finish so that she could have the floor. Several months prior to her beginning therapy, Ms. CC had been sexually assaulted in a parking lot by a man who forced her to perform fellatio on him. Attempting to empathize with the patient, the therapist said, "It must have been an awful experience for you." Ms. CC responded, "No, I actually kind of

enjoyed it. For once I actually felt something. I wasn't numb. I felt
anger, humiliation, rage—and I actually cried!"

Ms. CC had so numbed herself to experience that only an
incident as shocking as the sexual assault could make her feel alive
and related to others. The numbing state in which Ms. CC lived her
life is a reminder that the term *narcissism* is etymologically related
to the Greek word *narké,* which means numbness. Indeed, part of
the tragedy of this disorder is that these people seem to have never
awakened to the possibilities of life.

The Kohut-Kernberg controversy continues to smoulder, with
proponents on each side claiming that clinical experience validates
their own favorite theoretical perspective. In practice, some narcissistic patients seem to fit one framework better than the other. The
broad range of patients encompassed by the term *narcissistic personality disorder* may demand more than one theoretical perspective for
explanatory purposes. One research effort to validate the two constructs found data consistent with both theories but suggested that
the most parsimonious explanation was to view Kohut's model as a
special case of Kernberg's more general ego psychological–object
relations theory (Glassman 1988).

The theoretical debate between Kohut and Kernberg often
obscures other creative contributions to the understanding of the
narcissistic personality disorder. In a series of papers, Rinsley (1980,
1984, 1985, 1989) has linked the origin of narcissistic personality
disorder to Mahler's (1975) developmental framework. He postu-
lates that while the borderline patient suffers from a developmental
arrest of both separation and individuation subprocesses that
reaches a peak during the rapprochement subphase (see Chapters
2 and 14), the narcissistic patient can be characterized as having a
developmental *dissociation* of the two subprocesses—individuation
was allowed to proceed while separation was arrested. This picture
leads to a "pseudo-mature" child, who gets the message that he is
allowed to separate psychologically from his mother as long as every
achievement is ultimately in relation to her. This explanation reso-
nates with Kernberg's observation that in certain areas the narcissistic patient may function smoothly and may even be able to achieve
impressive gains at work, while still suffering from highly problematic object relations.

Rothstein (1984) has attempted to understand the narcissistic
personality disorder within the framework of the structural model
(see Chapter 2). He defines narcissism as "a felt quality of perfection" that is a universal aspect of the human psyche. This perfect
state can be integrated with either a healthy ego or a pathological
ego, but the nature of the ego determines whether the narcissism is
pathological or healthy.

Modell (1976) used the metaphor of a cocoon to describe the narcissistic individual's sense of nonrelatedness to the environment. This cocoon is like an illusion of omnipotent self-sufficiency, reinforced by grandiose fantasies, which may be initiated by a mother who has an exaggerated grandiose view of her child's capabilities. Modell believed that the noncommunicative and nonrelated facade reflects a fear of merger which the patient must defend against. The therapist's task must be to create a holding environment (Winnicott 1965) to allow development to proceed, much as in the treatment of schizoid personality disorders (described in Chapter 13).

Individual Psychotherapy and Psychoanalysis

Both Kernberg and Kohut believed that psychoanalysis is the treatment of choice for most patients with narcissistic personality disorder. Because of practical limitations of time and money, many patients are also seen in expressive-supportive psychotherapy with a predominance of expressive techniques in once- or twice-weekly sessions. The specific technical suggestions of Kohut and Kernberg reflect their differences in theoretical conceptualizations.

For Kohut, empathy was the cornerstone of the technique (Ornstein 1974b). Treaters must empathize with the patient for attempting to reactivate a failed parental relationship by coercing the therapist into meeting the patient's need for affirmation (the mirror transference), for idealization (the idealizing transference), or for being like the therapist (the twinship transference). The emergence of these selfobject transferences should not be prematurely interpreted. Kohut's emphasis on empathizing with the patient as a victim of the empathic failures of others does not imply a predominantly supportive technique. He has stressed that the analyst or therapist should not actively soothe but should rather interpret the patient's yearning to be soothed (Kohut 1984). A typical intervention might sound like this: "It hurts when you are not treated the way you feel you deserve to be treated."

Despite his insistence that his technical approach did not depart radically from classical psychoanalytic technique, his suggestions as described by supervisees (Miller 1985) revealed fundamental differences from that technique. He advised analysts to always take analytic material in a "straight" manner, just as the patient experiences it. The therapist can thus avoid repeating the empathic failures of the parents, who often try to convince the child that his or her actual feelings are *different* than what the child describes. Kohut indicated that, if the face-value approach does not bear fruit, one could always invert material or look for hidden meanings beneath the "experience-near" feelings. This approach is intimately related to Kohut's view of "resistance" as a psychic activity that safeguards the cohesiveness of the self (see Chapter 2).

Kohut was acutely sensitive to evidence of a patient's self-fragmentation in the actual analytic or therapeutic session. When these fragmentations occur, the therapist must focus on the precipitating event rather than on the content of the fragmentation itself (Miller 1985; Ornstein 1974a). For example, after one of Kohut's supervisees sneezed in an analytic session and the patient found it difficult to continue, Kohut advised the analyst to focus on the naturalness of the patient's response to such an unexpected stimulus rather than on the patient's special sensitivity to the stimulus (Miller 1985). This focus is in keeping with a general premise of self psychology that therapists must be continually attuned to how they recapitulate infantile traumas with their patients. Kohut believed that the patient is always right; if the patient feels deflated or hurt, it is reasonable to assume that the analyst or therapist has made an error. He noted that patients frequently feel exposed and ashamed when the analyst calls attention to slips of the tongue, so he did not stress the interpretation of parapraxes. Kohut was always sensitive to the proneness of narcissistic patients to feel shame. The therapist must avoid bypassing the patient's conscious subjective experience to address unconscious material outside the patient's awareness. Interpretations of unconscious motives will only make the patient feel "caught," misunderstood, and ashamed.

Kohut stressed the importance of looking at the *positive* side of the patient's experience, and he scrupulously avoided comments that might be viewed as harshly critical. He called attention to the patient's progress and shunned the asking of questions. He believed that it was the therapist's job to understand, not the patient's (Miller 1985).

Kohut asserted that the goal of psychoanalytic and psychotherapeutic treatment of the narcissistic personality disorder is to help the patient identify and seek out appropriate selfobjects. Kohut believed that mental health professionals tend to overvalue separation and autonomy. He was concerned that they might use a moralistic tone to convey to patients the expectation that they *should* become more independent.

Kohut's technical approach has been criticized on many counts. His refusal to integrate self psychology with more classical approaches has led to charges of isolationism (Wallerstein 1985). Similarly, his tendency to separate the development of the self from classical structural theory and from the vicissitudes of object relations has been criticized as artificial and needlessly polarizing (Kernberg 1974a, 1974b; Meissner 1986; Rangell 1982). His reduction of all psychopathology to empathic failures on the part of parents has been criticized as oversimplified "parent blaming" and as being out of keeping with the core psychoanalytic principle of overdetermination (Curtis 1985; Stein 1979). His emphasis on staying "experience near" in the therapeutic technique has also been challenged as having the potential to overlook important unconscious issues that should be addressed during treatment (Curtis 1985).

Kernberg (1974a, 1974b) observed some of the same transference phenomena as Kohut, but he believed that different technical approaches are indicated. For example, he conceptualizes the mirror and idealizing transference in a more parsimonious manner (see Table 15-4). Kernberg saw the patient's grandiose self as being

Table 15-4. Psychotherapeutic technique—Kohut vs. Kernberg

Kohut	Kernberg
1. Views mirror and idealizing transferences as two different poles of bipolar (Kohut 1977) or tripolar (Kohut 1984) self.	1. Views mirror and idealizing as aspects of transference related to projection and reintrojection of patient's grandiose self.
2. Accepts idealization of patient as normal developmental need.	2. Interprets idealization as a defense.
3. Empathizes with patient's feelings as an understandable reaction to failures of parents and others.	3. Helps patient see his or her own contribution to problems in relationships.
4. Accepts patient's comments at face value, viewing resistances as healthy psychic activities that safeguard the self.	4. Confronts and interprets resistances as defensive maneuvers.
5. Looks at the positive side of patient's experience.	5. Examines both positive and negative aspects of patient's experience—if only positive experiences are emphasized, the patient may develop an increased fear of internal envy and rage.
6. Calls attention to patient's progress.	6. Focuses on envy and how it prevents patient from acknowledging and receiving help.
7. Has treatment goal of helping patient acquire ability to identify and seek out appropriate selfobjects.	7. Has treatment goal of helping patient to develop guilt and concern, and to integrate idealization and trust with rage and contempt.

alternately projected and reintrojected so that one idealized figure is always in the room while the other figure is devalued and in the shadow of the idealized person. He also viewed idealization as a frequent defensive operation that involves splitting. In other words, idealization of the therapist may be a way to defend against split-off feelings of contempt, envy, and rage, so the therapist should interpret idealization as a defense rather than simply accepting it as a normal developmental need, as Kohut advocated.

Kernberg's approach in general is much more confrontative than Kohut's. Convinced that the greed and demandingness typical of the narcissistic personality disorder are not simply aspects of normal development, Kernberg believed that these traits must be confronted and examined from the standpoint of their impact on others. Whereas Kohut has emphasized the positive side of the patient's experience, Kernberg believed that early, negative transference developments must be systematically examined and interpreted. Specifically, Kernberg stressed that the therapist must focus on envy and how it prevents the patient from receiving or acknowledging help. When patients receive something positive from their therapist, it often escalates their envy because it generates feelings of inadequacy or inferiority in response to the therapist's capacity for nurturing and understanding. A sample interpretation might sound like this: "To avoid painful feelings of envy, you may need to dismiss my comments as being ridiculous or meaningless."

Although Kernberg is often misconstrued as focusing exclusively on negative transference, he in fact advocated a systematic examination of both positive and negative transference developments (Kernberg 1974b). He warned that therapists who address only the positive aspects of the transference may unconsciously increase their patients' fear of their own envy or rage. A patient who believes that the therapist cannot handle those aspects of the patient may therefore split them off and keep them outside the therapeutic process.

Kernberg also differs significantly from Kohut in important ways regarding the goals of treatment. While Kohut's technique implies that the essence of the cure is not in the cognitive sphere, Kernberg believed that a cognitive understanding via the interpretive process is crucial to therapeutic success. The goal of treatment for Kernberg (1970) included the development of guilt and concern for others, as well as the integration of idealization and trust with rage and contempt (i.e., integrating the "good" aspects of experience with the "bad").

Kernberg viewed persons with a narcissistic personality disorder as among the most difficult patients to treat because much of their effort goes into trying to defeat the therapist. For the treatment and the therapist to be effective, these patients must deal with their intense feelings of envy that someone else has good qualities that they lack. The patient defensively uses devaluation and omnipotent control to keep the therapist at a distance. Kernberg believed that, for the treatment to be viable, these defensive maneuvers must be continually confronted. A patient with significant antisocial features (which are common in narcissistic patients) may simply be untreatable. (The factors that determine the treatability of antisocial patients are discussed in Chapter 16 in some detail.) However, several factors suggest a favorable prognosis (Kernberg 1970): some ability to tolerate depression and mourning, more guilt than paranoid tendencies in the transference, some ability to sublimate primitive drives, relatively good impulse control, and good motivation. Patients who seek therapy or analysis simply for training purposes or because they think it will confer prestige on them in the eyes of others may present a formidable resistance that contributes to a less favorable prognosis.

In the subgroup of patients just mentioned who operate on an overtly borderline level, Kernberg (1984) suggested that a truly supportive psychotherapy is a much more effective treatment than expressive therapy or analysis. This approach should probably be combined with inpatient treatment if the ego weaknesses, such as lack of impulse control, are particularly severe. The indications for supportive therapy in narcissistic personality disorders include: excessive cruelty and sadism, prominent antisocial features, virtually no involvement with other people, intense paranoid reactions to others, and a proneness to chronic rage that is always rationalized as someone else's fault. In these supportive processes, Kernberg (1984) suggested that patients may benefit from "stealing" positive qualities from their therapist. This identification with the therapist may help patients function better, so the process is best left uninterpreted.

Critics of Kernberg's approach argue that it interferes with the natural development of selfobject transferences. Some have even suggested that aggressively confronting the oral aggression of patients may result in their deteriorated functioning (Brandschaft and Stolorow 1984). In this view, the borderline picture of rage, contempt, and devaluation is an artifact of the narcissistic injury induced by the therapist's "critical interventions." Thus the differences in the kinds of patients described by Kernberg and Kohut could be viewed as partially resulting from iatrogenic factors (Adler 1986).

Psychotherapists faced with the formidable task of treating narcissistic patients must avoid the "either/or" approach to the theories of Kernberg and Kohut. Rather than obsessing about which one is "right," therapists may more usefully apply themselves to listening carefully to their patients, observing the transference and countertransference developments, and particularly noting their responses to trial interventions. In this manner therapists will soon reach a tentative conclusion about which theoretical and technical model is the most helpful to the particular patient under consideration. Some patients will simply not tolerate anything but an empathic, experience-near approach based on Kohut's model. Any deviation from that pattern of interventions will be met with prolonged "shut-downs," with the patient refusing to talk and feeling misunderstood, or even by abruptly deciding to quit therapy.

In other cases, the patient may feel understood by interpretations of envy and contempt, and may therefore respond better to Kernberg's technique. Some narcissistic patients do not develop any of the selfobject transferences Kohut described, but instead present the therapist with continual devaluation and rage. In some instances, the therapist must interpret and confront these overt verbal attacks or the patient will find it difficult or impossible to persist in the treatment. Mitchell (1988) has pointed out that it is erroneous to regard Kohut's approach as more empathic than Kernberg's. Both respond empathically to different dimensions of the patient.

Still other patients can benefit from a combination of technical strategies. Although purists would argue that the two theories are incompatible, the patient is not aware of theories. Moreover, the therapist is faced with treating patients, not theories. Many patients require the self psychological approach to technique early in their treatment because it helps build a therapeutic alliance based on a sense that the therapist understands and empathizes with the experience of victimization. After an alliance is established, the therapist may begin to confront patients with their own contributions to their interpersonal difficulties, such as inordinate expectations that others cannot fulfill. Practically speaking, narcissistic pathology can rarely be conceptualized as all the parents' fault or all the patient's fault. More commonly, both parties have contributed to some difficulty, and the comprehensive therapy should address these problems from both angles. Indeed, the majority of analysts and other dynamically oriented clinicians operate from some midpoint between the two extremes (Mitchell 1988).

Finally, we must not assume that the etiology and pathogenesis of narcissistic character pathology will always fit neatly into the theoretical frameworks of Kohut and Kernberg. In sharp contrast to the parent with empathic failures, some parents of narcissistic patients tend to be overly indulgent. They seem to encourage grandiosity through a pattern of excessive mirroring. They shower their children with admiration and approval, making them feel truly special and gifted. When these children grow up, they are repeatedly shattered because others do not respond to them as their parents did. Hence, therapists can benefit from taking a heuristic approach (see Chapter 4) with narcissistic patients; the therapy should be a collaborative effort in which patient and therapist together discover the origins of the patient's difficulties without rigidly forcing the material to fit one theory or another.

Countertransference

Regardless of a therapist's theoretical framework, certain predictable countertransference problems arise in the treatment of narcissistic patients. Some problems are of sufficient magnitude and intensity as to undermine the treatment situation irrevocably. Hence the optimal management of these countertransference patterns cannot be stressed enough.

There is little question that psychotherapy as a career provides an opportunity to gratify wishes to be loved, needed, and idealized (Finnell 1985). The therapist in the throes of an idealizing transference from a narcissistic patient may enjoy basking in the glow of warmth and love to such an extent as to collude with the patient's wish to exclude hatred and anger from the therapy. A frequent development in the treatment of narcissistic patients is that they will initially idealize their current therapist while devaluing all previous treaters. Instead of viewing this process as a defensive maneuver, therapists who long for idealization may simply accept at face value that they have unique gifts that were lacking in their patients' previous therapists.

Narcissistic issues are not the exclusive province of the narcissistic personality disorder. They reside in all patients and in all therapists. Those therapists who cannot acknowledge and accept their own narcissistic needs, and then harness them in the service of delivering effective treatment, may instead disavow and externalize them. These defenses contribute to an erroneous view of the patient as the carrier of all narcissism in the patient-therapist dyad.

Another countertransference problem that regularly arises in the treatment of narcissistic patients is boredom. This usually arises from a feeling that the patient is unaware of or oblivious to the therapist's presence. For prolonged periods, the therapist may have to tolerate a sense of being used as a sounding board by the patient. This pattern is particularly typical of the oblivious narcissistic patient who holds forth as though speaking to an audience, ignoring the therapist as a separate person with separate thoughts and feelings.

> Mr. DD came to therapy after three previously failed attempts. His last treatment had lasted 3 years with a therapist in another city. Mr. DD denigrated that therapeutic experience as "a complete waste of time" and could not even recall his previous therapist's name. (These two signs, an inability to remember a previous therapist's

name and a complete devaluation of the previous therapeutic experience, are often diagnostic clues to narcissistic character pathology.) He said that "doctor what's his name" interrupted him a lot and was not a good listener. Mr. DD talked at great length about his need for a really "special" therapist. He even speculated that there might not be anyone in the city who could really understand him.

As Mr. DD continued to ramble on at some length over many weeks, his therapist began to dread each session. The therapist found his thoughts wandering to his plans for the evening, his financial status, unfinished paperwork, and a variety of other matters with little bearing on Mr. DD and his problems. The therapist also found himself glancing at the clock more often than usual, eagerly awaiting the end of Mr. DD's session. When the therapist intervened, Mr. DD would often ignore his comments and say, "Just let me finish this train of thought first," or "Oh, yes, I'm already aware of that."

After returning from a 3-week vacation, the therapist resumed his sessions with Mr. DD. In the first session, the patient picked right up where he had left off at the end of their last session, as though no time had elapsed. The therapist, exasperated with the sense that he had no importance whatsoever to Mr. DD, said, "You act as though we saw each other yesterday. Didn't the 3-week separation from me have any impact on you?" Mr. DD detected a critical, sarcastic tone in the therapist's voice and replied, "You have the same problem as my last therapist. You're always inserting yourself into this. I'm not paying you to talk about you or your feelings. I'm here to talk about myself."

All of us have a need to be needed, and it is therefore difficult for therapists to tolerate the "satellite existence" (Kernberg 1970) that many narcissistic patients assign them. This feeling of being excluded by the patient may represent a projective identification process (Adler 1986; Finnell 1985) in which the patient excludes the therapist just as he was once excluded by his own parents. In other words, an aspect of the patient is projected into the therapist, who identifies with that self before helping the patient to reintroject it. The containment of this projected aspect of the patient may be a major part of the psychotherapeutic treatment in narcissistic patients. Understanding this pattern may keep the therapist from withdrawing from the patient, from sadistically confronting the patient, or from feeling hurt and abused by the patient.

The hypervigilant variety of narcissistic personality leads the therapist to struggle with countertransference problems of feeling controlled. When the patient reads every movement as an indication of boredom or rejection, the therapist may feel coerced into sitting still and into focusing attention on the patient every moment. Interventions designed to address this interaction may deal productively with this countertransference development. A therapist working from Kernberg's perspective might say, "You seem to have an unrealistic expectation that you can control others and make them behave as extensions of yourself rather than allowing them to respond from within according to their own needs." A self psychological intervention might consist of, "It seems to hurt your feelings when I clear my throat or fidget in my seat because you feel I am not giving you my full attention." Regardless of the pros and cons of these two sample interventions, the main point is that such comments bring a behavioral interaction associated with a countertransference response into a verbal realm, where it can be discussed openly as an issue between therapist and patient.

Finally, the therapist will often have to struggle with countertransference feelings in response to intense devaluation by the patient.

> Ms. EE was a narcissistic patient functioning on an overtly borderline level who had been hospitalized for drug abuse. She demanded barbiturates for insomnia, and became enraged when her hospital doctor refused to prescribe them. Each time the doctor made daily rounds, Ms. EE would recite her doctor's many shortcomings: "You're only a resident, so you don't understand how to relate to patients. When you try to go into practice after your residency, you won't have any patients because you don't know how to relate to people. Instead of listening to my needs, you practice psychiatry out of a book. You don't even know how to dress. You're a complete joke as a physician." The doctor asked, "Why is it that you feel such hatred for me?" Ms. EE responded, "Hatred? You're not worth hating! You're beneath contempt!"

These verbal barrages are all too common with narcissistic patients. When they go on at some length, the doctor feels useless and impotent, as well as hurt and angry. These patients engender strong countertransference hatred that can lead to vengeful comments or ill-advised management decisions as a way to get back at the patient. Although as therapists we can contain a certain amount of abuse, we all have a limit that only we can determine. When that line is crossed, the therapist may need to confront the patient's contempt forcefully by pointing out how the barrage is destroying the patient's chance of getting effective treatment.

Group Psychotherapy

Dynamic group psychotherapy with narcissistic personality disorders is fraught with difficulties if it is the only treatment (Azima 1983; Horner 1975; Wong 1979, 1980; Yalom 1985). Oblivious narcissistic patients may enjoy the idea of having an audience in group psychotherapy, but they may also resent the fact that other people take some of the therapist's time and attention. One such patient quit group therapy because he never got enough "air time." The hypervigilant narcissistic patient may be injured at even the suggestion of group therapy. The referral itself is experienced as a rejection or as an indication that the therapist is not interested in the patient. Most narcissistic patients will see group psychotherapy as a situation in which their specialness and uniqueness will be overlooked. When narcissistic patients do enter group therapy, they often monopolize the group discussions or take on the role of "doctor's assistant," making observations about other people's problems but denying their own (Wong 1979).

Despite the problems inherent in group settings for narcissistic patients, there are clearly some advantages. In groups, narcissistic patients must confront and accept the fact that others have needs and that they themselves cannot expect to be the center of attention at all times. Moreover, narcissistic patients may also benefit from the feedback that others provide about the impact of their character traits on others. Narcissistic patients can have therapeutic effects on others in the group by activating latent feelings of envy and greed in patients with other forms of characterological disturbance (Azima 1983).

Some authors have suggested that combined individual and group psychotherapy may benefit narcissistic patients more than either approach alone (Horwitz 1977; Wong 1979, 1980). Few groups can absorb the narcissistic patient's intense demands for attention, but if an individual process is begun first, the patient may make fewer demands on the group. Wong (1979, 1980) specifically recommended a rather long preparatory period of individual therapy with a technical approach along the lines described by Kohut so that there is a solid therapeutic alliance by the time the patient enters the group. This preparatory period also gives the patient time to explore personal fantasies about group psychotherapy. Wong recommended using the same therapist both for individual and for group psychotherapy. Even with the combination, however, the therapist must actively support the patient if the other group members begin to scapegoat the narcissistic member. The group therapist can help the other patients empathize with the narcissistic patient's need to be recognized and admired.

As discussed in Chapter 5, group psychotherapy can serve to dilute intense negative transferences. This principle is certainly applicable to narcissistic patients, and the other patients in the group are often helpful in pointing out the distortions involved in devaluing or idealizing the therapist. Similarly, the countertransference reactions that are so problematic in the treatment of narcissistic patients can also be diluted in group therapy (Wong 1979). However, it is advisable to have only one narcissistic patient at a time in a heterogeneous group, lest the impact of these patients' demandingness overwhelm other members.

Narcissistic Personality Disorder Over the Course of the Life Cycle

Narcissistic patients who come to treatment as young adults often complain about the quality of their intimate relationships. They may have had repeated infatuations that are short-lived and unsatisfying. After the initial luster of the relationship wears off, idealization of the partner turns either to devaluation or boredom, and they withdraw and seek new partners who can fulfill their needs for admiration, affirmation, unconditional love, and perfect attunement. This pattern of sucking people dry and discarding the empty shells may eventually become tiresome. These patients frequently settle down and marry in their 30s or 40s.

Not surprisingly, characteristic patterns of marital difficulty occur in the marriages of patients with narcissistic personality disorder. They may first seek marital therapy under the guise of sexual problems, depression, or impulsive behavior (Lansky 1982). Beneath the disguised presentation is often a dread of being shamed or humiliated by the marital partner (i.e., a fear of self-fragmentation, in self psychological terms). A narcissistic husband, for example, may blame his wife for deliberately trying to humiliate him rather than acknowledging that he has a problem with being excessively vulnerable, dependent, and extraordinarily needy of selfobject responses, such as mirroring, from his wife. This same husband may eventually reach a state of chronic narcissistic rage, in which he maintains an intractable resentment and bitterness toward his wife for not treating him in the manner to which he feels entitled. Such marriages may be highly refractory to marital therapy because the narcissistic spouse perceives the injury as so damaging that forgiveness is out of the question and nothing the offending spouse can do could possibly redress the grievances.

Regardless of whether or not narcissistic patients choose to marry as they travel through life, they are likely to find the aging process highly distressing. In many cases these patients are physically attractive or interpersonally charming and have achieved a certain degree of success during their young adult years. However, although they can postpone facing the emptiness at their core, they cannot ultimately escape it. Kernberg (1974b) noted:

> If we consider that throughout an ordinary life span most narcissistic gratifications occur in adolescence and early adulthood, and that even though the narcissistic triumphs and gratifications are achieved

throughout adulthood, the individual must eventually face the basic conflicts around aging, chronic illness, physical and mental limitations, and above all, separations, loss, and loneliness—then we must conclude that the eventual confrontation of the grandiose self with the frail, limited and transitory nature of human life is unavoidable. (p. 238)

Narcissistic patients do not age well. Their grandiose fantasies of unending youth and beauty are torn asunder by the vicissitudes of aging. To prove their youth and vigor, they may frantically seek extramarital affairs with partners half their age or take on ill-advised pursuits such as marathon running. Also common are dramatic religious conversions in which the narcissist avoids mourning by a manic flight into the shadow of an idealized object (God).

Much of the pleasure of midlife and old age involves vicarious enjoyment of the success of younger people, such as one's children (Kernberg 1974b). One of the tragedies facing persons who suffer from narcissistic personality disorder is that they are robbed of this source of pleasure because of their envy and despair. These feelings may bring patients to treatment for the first time when they are well into their 40s. Faced with a sense of having missed something and the feeling that their lives are on a faulty course, they may finally be amenable to treatment. They often find themselves lonely, without any supportive relationships, and with a devastating feeling of being unloved. They see themselves confirming the warning of Benjamin Franklin, "He who loves himself will have no rivals."

Narcissistic patients provide enormous challenges for therapists. Kernberg (1974b) argued that the effort is well worthwhile, however, because if even partially successful, it will help attenuate the ravages of the second half of life. If, through treatment, narcissistic patients can achieve some degree of empathy, can partially replace their envy with admiration, and can begin to accept others as separate individuals with their own needs, then they may be able to avoid ending their lives in embittered isolation.

References

Adler G: Psychotherapy of the narcissistic personality disorder patient: two contrasting approaches. Am J Psychiatry 143:430–436, 1986
American Psychiatric Association: Diagnostic and Statistical Manual of Mental Disorders, 3rd Edition, Revised. Washington, DC, American Psychiatric Association, 1987
Azima FJC: Group Psychotherapy With Personality Disorders, in Comprehensive Group Psychotherapy, 2nd Edition. Edited by Kaplan HI, Sadock BJ. Baltimore, Williams & Wilkins, 1983, pp 262–268
Brandschaft B, Stolorow R: The Borderline Concept: Pathological Character or Iatrogenic Myth? In Empathy II. Edited by Lichtenberg

J, Bornstein M, Silver D. Hillsdale, NJ, Analytic Press, 1984, pp 333–357

Broucek FJ: Shame and its relationship to early narcissistic development. In J Psychoanal 63:369–377, 1982

Bursten B: Some narcissistic personality types. Int J Psychoanal 54:287–300, 1973

Cooper AM, Michels R: Book review of Diagnostic and Statistical Manual of Mental Disorders, 3rd Edition, Revised (DSM-III-R by the American Psychiatric Association). Am J Psychiatry 145:1300–1301, 1988

Curtis HC: Clinical perspectives on self psychology. Psychoanalytic Quarterly 54:339–378, 1985

Finnell JS: Narcissistic problems in analysts. Int J Psychoanal 66:433–445, 1985

Gabbard GO: Further contributions to the understanding of stage fright: narcissistic issues. J Am Psychoanal Assoc 31:423–441, 1983

Gabbard GO: Two subtypes of narcissistic personality disorder. Bull Menninger Clin 53:527–532, 1989

Glassman M: Kernberg and Kohut: a test of competing psychoanalytic models of narcissism. J Am Psychoanal Assoc 36:597–625, 1988

Horner AJ: A characterological contraindication for group psychotherapy. J Am Academy of Psychoanal 3:301–305, 1975

Horwitz L: Group psychotherapy of the borderline patient, in Borderline Personality Disorders: The Concept, the Syndrome, the Patient. Edited by Hartocollis P. New York, International Universities Press, 1977, pp 399–422

Kernberg OF: Factors in the psychoanalytic treatment of narcissistic personalities. J Am Psychoanal Assoc 18:51–85, 1970

Kernberg OF: Contrasting viewpoints regarding the nature and psychoanalytic treatment of narcissistic personalities: a preliminary communication. J Am Psychoanal Assoc 22:255–267, 1974a

Kernberg OF: Further contributions to the treatment of narcissistic personalities. Int J Psychoanal 55:215–240, 1974b

Kernberg OF: Severe Personality Disorders: Psychotherapeutic Strategies. New Haven, Yale University Press, 1984

Kohut H: The Analysis of the Self: A Systematic Approach to the Psychoanalytic Treatment of Narcissistic Personality Disorders. New York, International Universities Press, 1971

Kohut H: The Restoration of the Self. New York, International Universities Press, 1977

Kohut H: How Does Analysis Cure? Edited by Goldberg A. Chicago, University of Chicago Press, 1984

Lansky MR: Masks of the narcissistically vulnerable marriage. International Journal of Family Psychiatry 3:439–449, 1982

Lasch C: The Culture of Narcissism: American Life in an Age of Diminishing Expectations. New York, WW Norton, 1979

Maccoby M: The Gamesman: The New Corporate Leaders. New York, Simon & Schuster, 1976

Mahler M, Pine F, Bergman A: The Psychological Birth of the Human Infant: Symbiosis and Individuation. New York, Basic Books, 1975

Meissner WW: Can psychoanalysis find its self? J Am Psychoanal Assoc 34:379-400, 1986

Miller JP: How Kohut actually worked. Progress in Self Psychology 1:13–30, 1985

Mitchell SA: Relational Concepts in Psychoanalysis: An Integration. Cambridge, Harvard University Press, 1988

Modell AH: "The holding environment" and the therapeutic action of psychoanalysis. J Am Psychoanal Assoc 24:285–307, 1976

Ornstein P: A discussion of the paper by Otto F. Kernberg on 'Further contributions to the treatment of narcissistic personalities.' Int J Psychoanal 55:241–247, 1974a

Ornstein PH: On narcissism: beyond the introduction, highlights of Heinz Kohut's contributions to the psychoanalytic treatment of narcissistic personality disorders. Annual of Psychoanalysis 2:127–149, 1974b

Person ES: Manipulativeness in entrepreneurs and psychopaths, in Unmasking the Psychopath: Antisocial Personality and Related Syndromes. Edited by Reid WH, Dorr D, Walker JI, et al. New York, WW Norton, 1986, pp 256–273

Rangell L: The self in psychoanalytic theory. J Am Psychoanal Assoc 30:863-891, 1982

Rinsley DB: The developmental etiology of borderline and narcissistic disorders. Bull Menninger Clin 44:127–134, 1980

Rinsley DB: A comparison of borderline and narcissistic personality disorders. Bull Menninger Clin 48:1–9, 1984

Rinsley DB: Notes on the pathogenesis and nosology of borderline and narcissistic personality disorders. J Am Academy Psychoanal 13:317–328, 1985

Rinsley DB: The adolescent, the family, and the culture of narcissism: a psychosocial commentary. Adolesc Psychiatry 13:7–28, 1986

Rinsley DB: Notes on the developmental pathogenesis of narcissistic personality disorder. Psychiatric Clin North Am 12:695–707, 1989

Rosenfeld H: Impasse and Interpretation: Therapeutic and Anti-Therapeutic Factors in the Psychoanalytic Treatment of Psychotic, Borderline, and Neurotic Patients. Edited by Tuckett D. London, Tavistock Publications, 1987

Rothstein A: The Narcissistic Pursuit of Perfection. New York, International Universities Press, 1984 (Original work published 1980)

Stein MH: Book review of The Restoration of the Self by Heinz Kohut. J Am Psychoanal Assoc 27:665–680, 1979

Stolorow RD: Toward a functional definition of narcissism. Int J Psychoanal 56:179–185, 1975

Wallerstein RS: How does self psychology differ in practice? Int J Psychoanal 66:391–404, 1985

Winnicott DW: Psychiatric disorder in terms of infantile maturational processes, in The Maturational Processes and the Facilitating Environment: Studies in the Theory of Emotional Development. New York, International Universities Press, 1965, pp 230–241

Wong N: Clinical considerations in group treatment of narcissistic disorders. Int J Group Psychother 29:325–345, 1979

Wong N: Combined group and individual treatment of borderline and narcissistic patients: heterogeneous versus homogeneous groups. Int J Group Psychother 30:389–404, 1980

Yalom ID: The Theory and Practice of Group Psychotherapy, 3rd Edition. New York, Basic Books, 1985 (Original work published 1970)

CHAPTER 16

The Antisocial Patient

Antisocial patients are perhaps the most extensively studied of all those with personality disorders, but they are also the patients that clinicians tend to avoid the most. In the therapeutic situation, these patients may lie, cheat, steal, threaten, and otherwise act irresponsibly and deceptively. They have been referred to as "psychopaths," "sociopaths," and "character disorders"—terms that, in psychiatry, have traditionally been equated with being untreatable. Some might even argue that such patients should be regarded as "criminals" and should not be included under the purview of psychiatry. Clinical experience suggests, however, that the antisocial label is applied to a broad spectrum of patients, ranging from the totally untreatable to those who are treatable under certain conditions. The existence of this latter group warrants a detailed understanding of these patients so that those amenable to help can receive the best possible treatment.

In his classic 1941 work, *The Mask of Sanity,* Hervey Cleckley provided the first comprehensive clinical description of these patients (Table 16-1). As his title implies, Cleckley viewed the psychopath as an individual who was not overtly psychotic but whose behavior was so chaotic and so poorly attuned to the demands of reality and society that it indicated a psychosis beneath the surface. While psychopaths seemed to be able to relate superficially to other people, they were completely irresponsible in all their relationships and had no regard for the feelings or concerns of others. Moreover, they seemed utterly incapable of learning from experience. Cleckley believed that psychopaths lacked a fundamental humanness. Their irresponsibility and exploitativeness in relationships caused enormous distress among their family and friends. As a result of this observation, Cleckley saw the education of the psychopath's significant others as one of the major values of his work.

The term *psychopath* fell out of favor during the decades following the appearance of Cleckley's landmark work. *Sociopath* was used for a while, ostensibly as a reflection of the social rather than psychological origins of some of the difficulties faced by these individuals. By the time the American Psychiatric Association's second Diagnostic and Statistical Manual (DSM-II) was published in 1968, the term *antisocial personality* became the preferred nomencla-

Table 16-1. Cleckley's 1941 criteria for psychopathy

1. Superficial charm and good "intelligence"
2. Absence of delusions and other signs of irrational thinking
3. Absence of "nervousness" or psychoneurotic manifestations
4. Unreliability
5. Untruthfulness and insincerity
6. Lack of remorse or shame
7. Inadequately motivated antisocial behavior
8. Poor judgment and failure to learn from experience
9. Pathological egocentricity and incapacity for love
10. General poverty in major affective reactions
11. Specific loss of insight
12. Unresponsiveness in general interpersonal relations
13. Fantastic and uninviting behavior with drink and sometimes without
14. Suicide rarely carried out
15. Sex life impersonal, trivial, and poorly integrated
16. Failure to follow any life plan

ture. With the arrival of DSM-III in 1980, the antisocial personality disorder had been considerably altered from Cleckley's original description. The DSM-III criteria provided more diagnostic detail than those of any other personality disorder, but they narrowed the focus of the disorder to a criminal population likely to be connected with oppressed and disadvantaged lower socioeconomic groups (Halleck 1981; Meloy 1988; Modlin 1983). Detailed studies of prison populations indicate that only 40–50 percent of incarcerated criminals have an antisocial personality (Guze 1976; Hare 1983).

Another problem with the DSM-III criteria was that they were so atheoretical that they provided little more than behavioral descriptions of activities commonly found in criminals. Cleckley's description more closely approximated a true personality disorder in the sense that there were psychodynamic underpinnings to such qualities as incapacity for love, loss of insight, lack of remorse or shame, and failure to learn from experience (Meloy 1988; Modlin 1983). The authors of DSM-III-R (American Psychiatric Association 1987) attempted to respond to these criticisms by adding "lacks remorse" to the criteria (see Table 16-2).

In the last few years, the term *psychopath* has made a comeback in the clinical and research literature (Meloy 1988; Person 1986; Reid et al. 1986). This usage has grown in popularity with an awareness that psychopathy implies particular psychodynamic and even biological features that are not captured in the DSM-III-R criteria of antisocial personality disorder. Meloy (1988) employs the term to describe persons with a total absence of empathy and a sadomasochistic interactional style based on power rather than emotional attachment. Person (1986) views psychopathy as "an impulse disorder in which the short-term relief of anxiety is more important than any long-term consequence" (p. 266). This return to Cleckley's term is useful clinically because a person can be a psychopath without having an antisocial personality disorder by DSM-III-R criteria. Conversely, a person can meet the DSM-III-R criteria for antisocial personality disorder but not be a psychopath. As Cleckley was fond of pointing out, physicians, attorneys, politicians, and others in respected or powerful positions may be psychopathic.

One final problem with the DSM-III-R criteria is that they are not particularly useful in determining treatability. With antisocial patients, the clinician must determine first and foremost whether a particular patient is treatable under the circumstances. This dilemma can be conceptualized by viewing the antisocial patient as a subcategory of narcissistic personality disorder (Kernberg 1984; Meloy 1988; Reid 1985). Indeed, there is a narcissistic continuum of antisocial pathology ranging from the most primitive psychopath in its purest form to narcissistic personality disorder with ego-syntonic antisocial features to narcissistic patients who are simply dishonest in the transference (Kernberg 1984).

Clinicians will encounter many patients with antisocial features. The dynamic psychiatrist should approach each patient with this narcissistic continuum in mind. Using the dynamic understanding (discussed later in this chapter) related to narcissistic and antisocial pathology, clinicians can make a dynamically informed decision about whether a patient is treatable and what conditions warrant a treatment effort. In this chapter the term *psychopath* refers only to patients at the lower end of Kernberg's (1984) continuum (although he uses "antisocial personality" to describe such patients), the subgroup that fits the clinical and dynamic descriptions of Meloy (1988) and Person (1986). "Antisocial patients" will be used generically to describe patients along the continuum who show varying degrees of antisocial behavior. In this sense, psychopath is viewed as a dynamic construct, while the DSM-III-R category of antisocial personality disorder is purely descriptive.

Epidemiology

A considerable body of knowledge has been accumulated regarding the epidemiology of antisocial personality disorder (Cadoret 1986), which has a 2–3 percent lifetime prevalence in the United States population. Persons with this disorder are more commonly found in impoverished central city areas, and many of them drop out of

Table 16-2. DSM-III-R criteria for antisocial personality disorder

A. Current age at least 18.
B. Evidence of conduct disorder with onset before age 15, as indicated by a history of three or more of the following:
   (1) was often truant
   (2) ran away from home overnight at least twice while living in parental or parental surrogate home (or once without returning)
   (3) often initiated physical fights
   (4) used a weapon in more than one fight
   (5) forced someone into sexual activity with him or her
   (6) was physically cruel to animals
   (7) was physically cruel to other people
   (8) deliberately destroyed others' property (other than by fire-setting)
   (9) deliberately engaged in fire-setting
   (10) often lied (other than to avoid physical or sexual abuse)
   (11) has stolen without confrontation of a victim on more than one occasion (including forgery)
   (12) has stolen with confrontation of a victim (e.g., mugging, purse-snatching, extortion, armed robbery)
C. A pattern of irresponsible and antisocial behavior since the age of 5, as indicated by at least four of the following:
   (1) is unable to sustain consistent work behavior, as indicated by any of the following (including similar behavior in academic settings if the person is a student):
     (a) significant unemployment for six months or more within five years when expected to work and work was available
     (b) repeated absences from work unexplained by illness in self or family
     (c) abandonment of several jobs without realistic plans for others
   (2) fails to conform to social norms with respect to lawful behavior, as indicated by repeatedly performing antisocial acts that are grounds for arrest (whether arrested or not) (e.g., destroying property, harassing others, stealing, pursuing an illegal occupation)
   (3) is irritable and aggressive, as indicated by repeated physical fights or assaults (not required by one's job or to defend someone or oneself), including spouse- or child-beating
   (4) repeatedly fails to honor financial obligations, as indicated by defaulting on debts or failing to provide child support or support for other dependents on a regular basis
   (5) fails to plan ahead, or is impulsive, as indicated by one or both of the following:
     (a) traveling from place to place without a prearranged job or clear goal for the period of travel or a clear idea about when the travel will terminate
     (b) lack of a fixed address for a month or more
   (6) has no regard for the truth, as indicated by repeated lying, use of aliases, or "conning" others for personal profit or pleasure
   (7) is reckless regarding his or her own or others' personal safety, as indicated by driving while intoxicated, or recurrent speeding

Table 16-2. *(continued)*

    (8) if a parent or guardian, lacks ability to function as a responsible
        parent, as indicated by one or more of the following:
        (a) malnutrition of child
        (b) child's illness resulting from lack of minimal hygiene
        (c) failure to obtain medical care for a seriously ill child
        (d) child's dependence on neighbors or nonresident relatives for
            food or shelter
        (e) failure to arrange for a caretaker for young child when
            parent is away from home
        (f) repeated squandering, on personal items, of money required
            for household necessities
    (9) has never sustained a totally monogamous relationship for more
        than one year
  (10) lacks remorse (feels justified in having hurt, mistreated, or stolen
        from another)
D. Occurrence of antisocial behavior not exclusively during the course
    of schizophrenia or manic episodes.

Note. Reprinted from DSM-III-R, pp. 344–346, with permission from the American
Psychiatric Association.

high school before graduation. There is a downward drift in the lives
of antisocial individuals (Person 1986), who tend to make and lose
money cyclically until they "burn out" in middle age, often at the
price of severe alcoholism and debilitation (Halleck 1981).

    There is a striking correlation between antisocial character
pathology and substance abuse (Cadoret 1986; Halleck 1981; Meloy
1988; Modlin 1983; Reid 1985; Vaillant 1983). The current thinking
on the interrelationship of the two is that they often coexist but that
each has a separate etiology (Cadoret 1986; Reid 1985; Vaillant
1983). It is also well established, of course, that criminal activity is
intimately tied to substance abuse (Holden 1986). Fifty-two to 65
percent of felons have also been found to be drug abusers.

    Patients with antisocial problems are generally thought to be
male, and indeed the male-to-female ratio among antisocial personality disorders varies from 4:1 to 7.8:1 (Cadoret 1986). Familial links
between psychopathy and somatization disorder (hysteria) have
been extensively documented (Cadoret 1978; Cloninger et al. 1984;
Cloninger and Guze 1975; Woerner and Guze 1968). A recently
proposed explanation for this correlation is that gender influences
whether individuals with hysterical or histrionic personality tendencies will develop either antisocial personality or somatization disorder (Lilienfeld et al. 1986).

    Psychopathy can and does occur in female patients, despite its
much more common occurrence among males. Clinicians may
overlook the diagnosis in females because of sex role stereotypes. A

seductive and manipulative woman who exhibits considerable anti-social activity is much more likely to be labeled hysterical, histrionic, or borderline. One 19-year-old hospitalized female patient had been involved in extensive antisocial behavior, including the murder of a man she had said was attempting to rape her, as well as stealing, lying, and undermining the treatment of other patients. At one point during her hospitalization, she convinced two male patients to take a crowbar to her window to help her escape. After flying across country with them (using her parents' credit cards), she abandoned them without money in an airport. Her treatment reached a turning point when she started a fire in her room that threatened the safety of everyone on her hospital unit. Because this patient was attractive, seductive, and not without interpersonal charm, her treaters kept giving her the benefit of the doubt. Some even viewed her behavior as reflecting "depression" rather than antisocial pathology. Yet she met both the DSM-III-R criteria for antisocial personality disorder and the psychodynamic criteria for psychopathy.

This tendency to misdiagnose antisocial women may be changing (Reid 1985), however, as women gain increasing social freedom. As more women modify their life-styles in the direction of tradition-ally male patterns, more of them may be diagnosed with antisocial personality disorder.

Dynamic Understanding

A comprehensive understanding of the antisocial personality disor-der must begin with recognition that biological factors clearly con-tribute to the etiology and pathogenesis of the disorder. Studies of twins offer convincing evidence that genetic factors influence the development of psychopathy (Cadoret 1986). The concordance for criminality, for example, is two to three times higher for monozy-gotic twins than it is for dizygotic twins (Christiansen 1977; Wilson and Herrnstein 1985). One study of psychopaths reported that 91 percent were neuropsychologically impaired (Yeudall 1977). Stud-ies have also linked aggression to hormonal and neurochemical factors (Meloy 1988). Finally, antisocial individuals have been found to be autonomically hyporeactive, possibly because of their inability to learn from experience (Meloy 1988). A lesser degree of auto-nomic arousal in the face of adverse experience may be related to the dynamic inference that psychopaths have less anticipatory anx-iety to deter them from ill-advised actions.

Certain antisocial patients also apparently become violent during neurologically triggered episodes of dyscontrol. However, this subgroup of patients far more commonly uses such physical complaints as an *excuse* for violence (i.e., a disavowal of any personal responsibility for causing harm to others) (Meloy 1988). Similarly, criminals will often use psychiatric constructs, such as dissociation or multiple personality, to avoid prosecution. A celebrated example of this deception was Kenneth Bianchi's attempt to convince authorities that he was suffering from multiple personality disorder when arrested in connection with the "Hillside Strangler" murders. Nearly two-thirds of all murderers claim that they are amnestic for the crime (Bradford and Smith 1979).

These biological factors may in turn contribute to early problems in the infant-mother relationship. Antisocial patients frequently have a history of childhood neglect or abuse by parental figures. Constitutional factors may make these infants particularly difficult to soothe and comfort and may interfere with the normal attachment process (Meloy 1988). Regardless of whether the responsibility belongs with the infant, the mother, or both, psychopaths clearly have not attained the developmental level of object constancy (Mahler et al. 1975). As a result they lack a soothing maternal introject (see Chapter 2). Like patients with narcissistic personality disorder, they form a pathological grandiose self. This structure differs, however, from that of the narcissistic patient in one important way. Kernberg (1975) described the narcissistic personality's grandiose self as a fusion of the real self, the ideal self, and the ideal internal object. In the psychopath, on the other hand, the "ideal object" is an *aggressive* introject, often referred to as the "stranger selfobject" (Grotstein 1982; Meloy 1988). Unlike the selfobjects of Kohut's self psychology (see Chapter 2), this version reflects an experience of the parent as a stranger who cannot be trusted and who harbors malevolence toward the infant. This threatening internalized figure may derive from real experiences of parental cruelty and neglect.

Lack of basic trust, combined with the absence of loving experiences with a maternal figure, has grave implications for the psychopath's further development. The maturational process apparently reaches a stalemate before the completion of separation-individuation and the development of object constancy. At the same time, the infant's emotional attachment to the mother is derailed because the mother is experienced as a stranger or predator. In the child's subsequent development, two separate processes coexist (Meloy 1988). One is characterized by a profound detachment from all relationships and from affective experience, while the other is a more object-related path characterized by sadistic attempts to bond with others through the exercise of power and destructiveness.

Another implication of the child's early relationship with the mother is that the subsequent withdrawal from relatedness precludes a normal passage into the depressive position and the oedipal phase of development. The psychopathic patient never becomes aware of other people as separate individuals with feelings of their own. Hence these patients do not develop a capacity for depressive anxieties or for guilt stemming from concern that their actions can hurt others. A corollary of this fact is that psychopaths are incapable of true depression. When psychopaths refer to depression, they may actually be describing a state of rageful resentment at the world for not conforming to their wishes, a reaction accompanied by feelings of emptiness and boredom (Yochelson and Samenow 1977). Suicide attempts among these patients thus tend to grow out of narcissistic rage rather than out of genuine hopelessness and a wish to die, as in affectively disordered patients (Meloy 1988). The presence of an Axis I major depressive episode precludes the diagnosis of true psychopathy. However, a number of patients with antisocial behavior and even some meeting the DSM-III-R criteria of antisocial personality disorder will have a concomitant Axis I diagnosis of major depression (Gabbard and Coyne 1987; Woody et al. 1985).

The serious impairment of internalization in the psychopath obviously leads to a massive failure of superego development—the classical hallmark, in a dynamic sense, of the psychopath. The absence of any moral sense in these individuals is one of the chilling qualities that make them seem lacking in basic humanness. Their only value system of any consequence is the exercise of aggressive power, and their only trace of superego development may be the sadistic superego precursors (or stranger selfobjects) manifested by their sadistic and cruel behavior (Kernberg 1984).

Higher-level patients, who do not fit the category of the pure psychopath, may exhibit superego lacunae (Johnson 1949). These individuals, because of their relatively more favorable constitutional factors and environmental experiences with parenting, have some semblance of a conscience with circumscribed areas where the superego does not seem to operate. Some of these individuals have been subtly or not-so-subtly encouraged in their antisocial behavior by one or both parents.

> Allen was a 10-year-old boy who was admitted to the hospital by his parents. During the admission interview with the psychiatrist and social worker, his mother and father described a long history of aggressive behavior. Allen had repeatedly fought at school, engaged in minor acts of vandalism on neighbors' property, and refused to obey his parents. Allen's father described the incident that finally precipitated his son's admission to the hospital: "This old guy was driving by our house, and Allen was out in the yard with his bow and arrow. Even though the guy was driving 35 miles an hour, Allen was able to shoot an arrow through the car's windshield and hit the guy in the eye. You have to admit that it was a pretty good shot." As a smile flickered across Allen's father's lips, a confused look appeared on Allen's face.

White-collar criminals often fit this category of superego lacunae. Their narcissistic personality structure has allowed them to succeed, but certain defects in their conscience eventually become manifested in antisocial behaviors that are detected by others. It is important in this context to distinguish between antisocial *behavior* and true antisocial personality. Behavior of an antisocial nature may arise from peer pressure, from neurotic conflict, or from psychotic thinking. In these cases it may bear no relation to antisocial personality disorder.

Another aspect of superego pathology that typifies the true psychopath more than the higher-level narcissistic variants is a complete lack of effort to morally justify or rationalize the antisocial behavior (Meloy 1988). When confronted with their antisocial behavior, psychopaths are likely to respond with self-righteousness, declaring that the victims of their antisocial acts deserved what they got. Psychopaths may also choose to lie and to avoid any responsibility for their behavior.

Mr. FF was a 23-year-old man who had been involuntarily committed to long-term hospitalization by the court. Shortly after admission, he was seen by a consultant, and the following dialogue took place:

Consultant:	What brings you to the hospital?
Patient:	The court sent me.
Consultant:	How come?
Patient:	I was in a car accident, and my best friend was accidentally killed.
Consultant:	How did it happen?
Patient:	I was driving down the street, minding my own business, when the guy in front of me slams on his brakes. I plow into his rear end, and the gun in my glove compartment goes off and accidentally shoots my friend through the head.
Consultant:	Why did you have a gun in your glove compartment?
Patient:	You gotta have a gun in the neighborhood I come from. I gotta protect myself. There's all kinds of drug dealers around.
Consultant:	Why did the court commit you to a hospital as the result of an accident?
Patient:	Good question.
Consultant:	Do you have any emotional problems?
Patient:	No, I'm a pretty happy-go-lucky guy.
Consultant:	Have you had any other problems with the law?
Patient:	The only other thing that happened wasn't my fault either. These buddies of mine ripped off a dollar changing machine from a laundromat and left it on my porch as a gag. The police thought I did it and arrested me.

Mr. FF's disavowal of responsibility shows his absence of concern about his "best friend" and his complete inability to acknowledge any of his own problems that might have contributed to his situation. This vignette underscores the difficulty therapists may have engaging antisocial patients in treatment because they externalize all problems.

Psychopathy is best understood as a primitive variant of the narcissistic personality disorder (see Chapter 15) described by Kernberg (1984; Meloy 1988; Reid 1985), with the same underlying borderline personality organization that relies on primitive defenses and highly pathological internal object relations (Kernberg 1975). There are five main differences between the psychopath and the nonpsychopathic narcissistic personality disorder (see Table 16-3).

Both the narcissist and the psychopathic variant are plagued with boredom and emptiness because their envy precludes meaningful relationships with others. The psychopath simply manages these affects more aggressively than does the narcissistic personality. Both manipulate others with charm, but the charm of the narcissistic patient is based more on stabilization of self-esteem in contrast to the psychopath, whose primary motivation for manipulation is symbolic destruction, humiliation, and domination of the other person (Person 1986). Although the psychopath's object-seeking may appear hedonistic, it is best understood as satisfying the aggressive need to dominate.

One form of splitting is particularly prominent in antisocial patients. The discontinuity in their self-representations often takes the form of disavowal of past behavior. A female antisocial patient, for example, who was asked about antisocial behavior on admission, denied having any problems. When she was confronted with having written bad checks that had resulted in her arrest, her response was, "That was over a month ago. What's that got to do with anything

Table 16-3. Features that distinguish the psychopath from other forms of narcissistic personality disorder

1. All interactions with others are characterized by aggression and power rather than attachment.
2. The only evidence of superego development is the presence of sadistic superego precursors that are manifested by sadistic and cruel behavior toward others.
3. The internalized "ideal object" is a highly aggressive introject (the stranger selfobject) based on an abusive or neglectful parental figure.
4. No interest is shown in rationalizing or morally justifying one's behavior.
5. There is no adherence to any value system other than the exploitative, aggressive exercise of power.

Note. Based on Kernberg (1984) and Meloy (1988).

now?" Thus the same bland denial of contradictory self-representations common to borderline patients is also operative in antisocial patients.

Psychodynamically differentiating the treatable narcissistic patient from the pure psychopath may be difficult in many clinical situations because antisocial patients tend to deceive clinicians. In the next section, we will examine more objective criteria for determining treatability.

Hospital Treatment

There is a broad consensus that patients with serious antisocial behavior are unlikely to benefit from a treatment approach characterized exclusively by outpatient psychotherapy (Frosch 1983; Gabbard and Coyne 1987; Person 1986; Reid 1985). Some form of institutional or residential setting is necessary for even modest improvement. If psychotherapy is employed as a treatment, it must begin while the antisocial patient is contained by the structure of a round-the-clock milieu. These action-oriented individuals will never get in touch with their affective states as long as they have the outlet of behavior to discharge their impulses. It is only when they are immobilized by an inpatient setting that the treatment staff will begin to see them display emotions such as anxiety and emptiness (Frosch 1983; Person 1986).

The decision to hospitalize an antisocial patient in a general psychiatry unit containing patients with a variety of diagnoses usually leads to regret. The psychopath's disruptive behavior may grossly interfere with the treatment of other patients and may bring all therapeutic programs in the milieu to a grinding halt. These patients will steal from, sexually exploit, and assault other patients; they also lie to and ridicule staff members, smuggle drugs and alcohol into the unit, ridicule the treatment philosophy, and corrupt staff members into dishonest and unethical behavior. Some will systematically destroy any therapeutic alliance that other patients have developed with the treatment staff.

> Mr. GG was a 46-year-old clergyman forced into hospital treatment by his superiors in the church because his behavior was creating chaos in his congregation. He had seduced a number of women connected with his church and had delighted in "undermining their faith" by challenging the basic tenets of their beliefs. Similar patterns of behavior and object relations occurred in the hospital. Mr. GG was silent in most group meetings, but he insidiously "poisoned" the milieu by devaluing staff members in private one-to-one meetings with other patients and by systematically eroding other patients' faith that treatment could be helpful. He viewed all his relationships with

female patients and female treaters as sexualized conquests, and even when his sexual acting out was blocked by the structure of the hospital unit, Mr. GG would find other ways to dominate and humiliate women. He often joked with other patients about the relative sexual merits of various female nurses and doctors on the unit, and he devalued the expertise of all staff members regardless of gender. His treatment ended when he planned and executed an elopement with a female inpatient. For several months after Mr. GG's departure, however, his impact was still felt on the unit because of the patients' pervasive doubt about the value of treatment—a doubt that he had fueled by his comments and actions.

More sophisticated and intelligent psychopaths may present a different problem in the hospital milieu. Because they are aware that hospitalization is far more comfortable than prison, they may deceive the treatment staff into thinking that they are benefiting greatly from treatment. Such patients may be highly skilled charmers who convince the staff that they should be discharged sooner than initially expected. The behavioral changes of antisocial patients that occur during hospitalization, however, do not usually continue beyond discharge (Frosch 1983). These patients often just go through the motions of treatment without being touched by it. When they revert to their antisocial behavior after discharge, the hospital staff may feel outraged because they have been conned.

To avoid wasting an enormous investment of time, money, and energy, hospital clinicians must determine which antisocial patients warrant a trial of psychiatric hospitalization. There is a broad consensus that true psychopaths do not belong on general psychiatry units because they are unable to benefit from such treatment, perhaps because they tend to transform the experience into an exploitative situation of the proverbial "fox in the chicken coop." Specialized units, such as those in prison settings (Kiger 1967; Sturup 1968), nonmedical community residential programs (Reid and Solomon 1981), and wilderness programs (Reid 1985) have had somewhat better success with psychopathic patients and are generally viewed as the only hope for those in this diagnostic category.

In specialized institutional settings, such as the Patuxent Institution in Maryland or the Herstedvester Institution in Denmark, the treatment of the psychopath is enhanced by the homogeneous composition of the milieu. These programs rely heavily on group confrontation by peers. Other psychopaths are familiar with the "con artist" techniques of their cohorts; when these are consistently confronted, their effectiveness is neutralized. These programs also employ tight structure with clear and rigidly enforced rules. The consequences for rule-breaking of any kind are implemented swiftly without any allowance for bargaining or rationalizations on the part of the patients (Reid 1985; Yochelson and Samenow 1977).

Once these institutions have established control over the lives of the patients and have blocked their usual channels for discharging unpleasant affects through action, these patients may begin to come to terms with their anxiety and aggression. The staff's predictable and consistent responses to all breaks in structure frustrate the usual efforts to get around "the system." These programs depend on court-mandated treatment, however, because the patients may wish to leave the institution as soon as untoward feelings creep into awareness.

A small subsample of patients with antisocial features, usually those with borderline or narcissistic personality disorders, may benefit from voluntary hospitalization in a general psychiatry unit (Gabbard and Coyne 1987). However, differentiating these patients from the pure psychopath may be difficult because of the intense countertransference reactions evoked by antisocial patients. Mental health professionals, by the very nature of their career choice, are inclined to be charitable and kindly toward those they treat. They are prone to give patients the benefit of the doubt and to see them as somehow treatable no matter how resistant they may appear. This tendency may lead treaters to downplay the extent of ruthlessness in psychopathic patients and to assume that antisocial behavior is really a "cry for help." Hospital staff members in particular often have a deep-seated need to see themselves as capable of treating the untreatable patient. They may take extraordinary steps to connect with a patient who has no interest in meaningful human relationships. In reaching out to such patients, they may collude with the tendency of these patients to minimize the extent of their antisocial behavior and superego pathology. One aspect of this countertransference denial is that clinicians may underdiagnose psychopaths and thus view them as more treatable than they actually are. For example, in one study only half the patients meeting DSM-III-R criteria for antisocial personality disorder were given that diagnosis (Gabbard and Coyne 1987).

Underdiagnosis may result in viewing the patient as simply narcissistic rather than psychopathic, as immature—with a character structure that is "not yet crystallized," or as primarily a substance abuser. In fact, substance abuse may be an excuse used by psychopaths themselves. In some cases, treatment staff collude with this excuse by arguing vehemently that a patient's crimes occurred only under the influence of drugs and alcohol so the patient should not be viewed as antisocial. These professionals will often argue that treating the patient's substance abuse will eliminate the problematic antisocial behavior. This point of view fails to consider the extensive overlap between psychopathy and drug abuse, which was described earlier in this chapter. Moreover, some studies have demonstrated that drug abuse in no way improves a psychopath's prospects for

Table 16-4. Predictors of positive and negative treatment
response on a general psychiatric unit

Negative response
  1. History of felony arrest
  2. History of repeated lying, aliases, conning
  3. Unresolved legal situation at admission
  4. History of felony conviction
  5. Hospitalization forced as an alternative to incarceration
  6. History of violence toward others
  7. Diagnosis on Axis I of organic brain impairment
Positive response
  1. Presence of anxiety
  2. Axis I diagnosis of depression
  3. Axis I psychotic diagnosis other than depression or organic
     brain syndrome

Note. Based on Gabbard and Coyne (1987).

psychological change (Gabbard and Coyne 1987; Woody et al.
1985).

Because of countertransference contamination in distinguishing between the treatable antisocial patient and the pure psychopath, objective criteria are essential to such determinations. "Gut feelings" about particular patients are notoriously unreliable. The data from one study of hospitalized patients with antisocial features found that there are three predictors of a reasonably positive treatment outcome for these patients in a general psychiatry unit (Gabbard and Coyne 1987) (Table 16-4).

As explained earlier in this chapter, the presence of an Axis I diagnosis of a major depressive episode effectively rules out (by definition) the presence of true psychopathy. Patients who meet the Axis I criteria for depression have some superego development and some capacity, however minimal, for remorse. Similarly, the presence of anxiety represents some concern about one's behavior and its consequences. Finally, the presence of an Axis I psychotic diagnosis, such as mania, suggests that pharmacological treatment may improve the prognosis. It is certainly well known that individuals in the midst of a manic episode often exhibit antisocial behavior. Pharmacological treatment has not been particularly effective for the true psychopath (Halleck 1981).

The same study delineated several predictors of negative treatment response for the same population (see Table 16-4). When there is no other way to keep psychopathic patients involved in treatment, they may benefit from involuntary hospitalization in a specialized penal setting. Psychopaths who are forced to seek hospital treatment as an alternative to prison, however, will simply exploit the opportunity to con the staff of the unit who are predisposed anyway to see such patients as "sick" or "disturbed" rather than as criminals in need of punishment. Under these conditions, the patients will either disrupt the unit or merely go through the motions of treatment. Many patients will use the hospital to "hide out" from an unresolved legal situation that requires a court appearance. A serious history of violence bodes poorly for treatment because, when these patients become frustrated, they may resort to violence, either against staff members or other patients. Likewise, a serious organic brain impairment may interfere with a patient's ability to understand and benefit from the constructive feedback provided in a hospital milieu, which in turn may increase frustration.

Antisocial patients rarely have all the positive predictors and rarely lack any of the negative predictors in Table 16-4. Although there is no ideal antisocial patient, each additional positive predictor improves a patient's suitability for hospital treatment, and each negative predictor worsens the patient's amenability to hospital treatment (Gabbard and Coyne 1987).

Even with a relatively favorable profile, antisocial patients present a host of difficulties in a typical psychiatric milieu. Only long-term hospital treatment has a chance of producing any lasting change in these patients. They naturally attempt to continue their pattern of impulsively translating their feelings into actions. The cornerstone of treatment must therefore be a tightly controlled structure. From day one, treaters must anticipate and address likely forms of acting out in the hospital. Certain expectations must be spelled out at admission. For example, the patient must be told that substance abuse, violence, theft, and sexual relationships with other patients will not be tolerated. If the patient is a drug abuser, all mail must be opened in front of staff members to help prevent the smuggling in of drugs. Patients must be clearly told that they will be accompanied by staff whenever they leave the unit and that they will remain at that level of responsibility for a considerable time. Phone calls and access to cash and credit cards also must be restricted. The patient should be made aware that any breaks in structure will result in clear-cut consequences, such as room restriction. Treatment must be viewed initially as being conducted on a trial basis only—as a period of evaluation (usually of several weeks)—to determine the patient's suitability for treatment. All these conditions may be written out as a "contract" at the time of admission, so that the patient will have a copy for reference.

Staff members must scrupulously monitor their countertransference reactions, both as individuals and in the group context. Three common staff reactions are disbelief, collusion, and condemnation (Symington 1980). Disbelief may surface as denial that the patient is really "that bad." Rationalizing antisocial behavior, as due to such problems as drug abuse or adolescent rebellion, may cause staff members to deny the presence of psychopathic features and instead view the patient as depressed or misunderstood.

Collusion is one of the most problematic forms of counter-transference. A common development in the hospital treatment of antisocial patients is for the patient to corrupt one or more staff members. In the belief that they are helping the patient, the staff members involved in such countertransference acting out may commit illegal acts or otherwise behave unethically. Staff members have been known to lie on behalf of such patients; they also have falsified records, been seduced into sexual relationships, and helped these patients to elope from the hospital. These countertransfer-ence developments can be understood as part of the projective identification process whereby a corrupt aspect of the patient's self enters the treater and transforms that individual's behavior. Staff members who are involved in such countertransference acting out often report that "I was not acting like myself."

Another way to conceptualize these countertransference col-lusions is that they are the result of what Meloy (1988) referred to as *malignant pseudo-identification*. In this process, "the psychopath consciously imitates or unconsciously simulates a certain behavior to foster the victim's identification with this individual, thus increas-ing the victim's vulnerability to exploitation" (p. 139). Through simulated tearfulness, remorse, or sadness, antisocial patients ma-nipulate clinicians into empathizing with them. If only one clinician sees this simulated self-presentation of the patient, it can lead to splitting among the hospital staff. The staff member involved in the malignant pseudo-identification will adamantly defend the patient against the "attacks" of other staff members. Meloy points out that these simulated affects in the patient can often be identified by sadistic countertransference feelings in the face of the patient's outpouring of sadness and by the patient's apparently rapid recom-pensation, leaving observers with the impression that they have witnessed a performance.

Condemnation is a third common countertransference reac-tion. It is often manifested in expressions by hospital staff that a patient is totally untreatable, and that no effort should be made to establish a treatment relationship. Such a decision can be made by rationally assessing objective factors, but it is more often a knee-jerk reaction to hearing some history of antisocial activity. This auto-matic reaction may be countertransference in the narrow sense, because it is based on the treater's past experience with similar individuals. Condemnation that stems from intensive work with the patient may be understood as a projective identification with the aggressive introject of the patient.

Other common countertransference reactions in the treatment of antisocial patients include feelings of helplessness and impotence in the face of a treatment-resistant patient, wishes to destroy the patient that grow out of anger, and feelings of invalidity and loss of identity (Strasberger 1986). The staff may also fear an assault by these patients, who are often threatening and menacing. (Certain psychopathic patients evoke an intense fear of predation in treaters merely by looking at them [Meloy 1988].) Fear of assault may lead staff members to avoid implementing the firm structure that the patient so desperately needs. To avoid arousing the patient's anger or violence, staff members may rationalize their loose structure and indulgence of the patient. For example, although a muscular young man in a long-term hospital unit had beaten up other patients on several occasions, he was allowed to freely wander the grounds. His treatment team justified this loose structure by saying that they were not going to be provoked into responding punitively to the patient as his parents had.

A major aspect of the hospital treatment of antisocial patients must be the continual focus on their faulty thought processes (Yochelson and Samenow 1976). When they pose as the victim because of being held accountable for their behavior, they must be confronted with how they are responsible for what happens to them. Staff members must also perform as auxiliary egos in terms of judgment. The staff must point out over and over that these patients fail to anticipate the consequences of their behavior.

The antisocial patient tends to move directly from impulse to action. The hospital staff must therefore help these patients insert *thought between* impulse and action. In other words, each time an antisocial patient has an impulse, the staff must encourage the patient to think about what may result from the action. In milieu treatment, patients must also learn that impulses and actions grow out of feelings. Often the language of emotions is so foreign to the patients that they cannot identify their internal states.

All these strategies focus on the "here and now" in the milieu, because exploring the childhood origins of such problems is often useless with antisocial patients. Any attempt by the antisocial patient to corrupt staff members must also be confronted *as it occurs*. If an intervention is not made immediately after the acting-out behavior, then the patient may dismiss it or forget it.

A case example of a treatable antisocial patient will illustrate many of the principles described here.

Mr. HH was a single 24-year-old who came to a long-term hospital unit after being released from prison where he had served time for selling cocaine. The hospitalization was not a condition of parole, and Mr. HH was seeking admission voluntarily. He said that he needed to change his life-style so that he would stop abusing drugs and destroying any chance he had to become successful. In addition to a history of selling and abusing cocaine, Mr. HH also had a history of extensive antisocial behavior, including lying, cheating, stealing, and operating as a building contractor without a license. His object relations were characterized by exploitative and manipulative patterns. Despite this ominous-sounding history, Mr. HH experienced genuine anxiety about his destructive behavior and was motivated to change it. Moreover, he was not under pressure to seek hospitalization, so he was viewed as having a reasonable chance to improve. Diagnostically, he was best described as having a narcissistic personality with antisocial features.

The cornerstone of Mr. HH's treatment plan was a contractual agreement between him and the treatment team. This contract stipulated that Mr. HH would have to adhere to a specific structure in order to be adequately treated. This structure included staff accompaniment to all activities and appointments outside the unit during the first 4 months of hospitalization, telephone calls monitored by staff members, a $25-per-week allowance and no access to credit cards, no visits from friends, attendance at all treatment activities and meetings, no violent behavior, no sexual behavior with other patients, no substance abuse, and no negotiation of this structure during the first 4 months of treatment. By frustrating the various outlets for impulses, the staff forced the patient to deal with his anxiety and internal emptiness rather than to discharge it through acting-out behavior.

The patient found this structure enormously frustrating and restricting, but he seemed to realize that it was necessary. Mr. HH was repeatedly confronted by staff members about his tendency to externalize problems that occurred in relationships on the unit. He was told that he was not a passive victim under the influence of others, but rather, that he was an active contributor to the problems that occurred with other people on the unit. He was a handsome and charming man, who behaved seductively toward a number of female patients but then complained that he could not possibly please them all.

Mr. HH also devalued the treatment structure, openly saying that it was ridiculous and that he did not require such restrictions. He aroused considerable sympathy from other patients by portraying himself as a victim of an extremely harsh and sadistic treatment team. The clinicians working to deal with this manipulation conducted a good deal of group work on the unit. In the group meetings, Mr. HH was confronted with his efforts to appear as a victim instead of as a manipulative patient whose history warranted such tight structure. Since he would not mention his antisocial behavior in the treatment meetings, the staff often had to remind him, and the other patients, of the reasons for Mr. HH's hospitalization. He had developed an artificial split between his "bad self," which he had left outside the hospital, and his "good self," which was in the hospital. He repeatedly minimized his antisocial past as being "past history." The treatment staff, on the other hand, confronted him with the reality that *he* had committed those antisocial acts and that he still had the potential for such behavior. Thus Mr. HH's splitting maneuvers were challenged, and his "good self" and "bad self" were brought together.

Early in the treatment, Mr. HH broke the established structure on several occasions by using the phone to call friends who might supply him with cocaine. Whenever this occurred, the staff immediately implemented further restrictions, such as unit confinement, without discussion or negotiation. Mr. HH also had to open all his mail in front of a staff member, who checked to be sure that no drugs or contraband were being mailed to him.

On one occasion Mr. HH was able to manipulate a female mental health technician (who found him charming and attractive) into loaning him a dollar to buy a Coke. After buying the Coke, he did not return any change to her. While the mental health technician dealt with her countertransference acting out in supervision, Mr. HH was confronted about his actions in a group treatment meeting. He went on at great length about how "totally ridiculous" it was to focus on such a small amount of money. He said that he had fully intended to return the change, but that he had simply forgotten. The treatment team confronted his minimization and denial and pointed out that his behavior outside the hospital was being repeated, only on a smaller scale.

Over several months, Mr. HH became increasingly psychologically minded. He was referred for twice-weekly psychotherapy after he began to show an ability to reflect on the staff's confrontations rather than to respond defensively and automatically. A turning point occurred when a female patient in his "harem" attempted suicide because she could not stand the way he was leading her on while simultaneously sharing his attention with several other women. Only then did Mr. HH begin to realize that his exploitative relationships with women could be highly destructive. He also eventually realized that he lacked empathy for others and was simply using women to gratify his own needs. By the time he left the hospital after 18 months of treatment, he had begun to piece together how internal anxiety states led him to drug abuse and other impulsive actions as a way to "treat" his anxiety. Specifically, he realized that he was extremely concerned about being rejected or abandoned by women, so he maintained several relationships at a time to reduce his vulnerability. He called this manipulation his "spare tire" strategy.

After discharge, Mr. HH continued psychotherapy and joined Narcotics Anonymous as well. In his final meeting with his hospital psychiatrist, Mr. HH noted that his inpatient experience was the first time that he had ever really felt understood. In his own words, "You guys knew what a con artist I was." At 4-year follow-up, Mr. HH had remained abstinent from cocaine and other drugs of abuse and was working full-time in a business-related field. He had become quite active in the stock market, where he was able to sublimate his thrill-seeking and risk-taking tendencies in a legal and socially acceptable manner.

Mr. HH is unusual among hospitalized antisocial patients. Many will leave treatment when the frustration becomes too great to bear. A small subgroup, however, can benefit from long-term hospitalization. As with borderline patients, milieu treatment combined with psychotherapy provides these patients with an opportunity to internalize new patterns of object relatedness. One reason for Mr. HH's improvement was the "softening" or modification of his aggressive self- and object-representations. Clearly, the enormous expense of such intensive treatment must not be squandered on patients who will misuse the treatment or who will not benefit from it.

Individual Psychotherapy

Outpatient individual psychotherapy of the severely antisocial patient is doomed to failure. Affects will be discharged through action because there is no contained environment in which to control such channeling. In addition, the patient's lies and deceptions are so pervasive that the therapist will have no idea what is really going on in the patient's life. In an institutional or hospital setting, there is some reason for guarded optimism about psychotherapy with a select subgroup of antisocial patients such as Mr. HH. As with hospital treatment, the clinician's task is to determine which patients are worth the time, energy, and money required by a long-term therapy process with an uncertain outcome. The pure psychopath, in the dynamic sense, will not respond to psychotherapy, and so it should not be attempted (Kernberg 1984; Meloy 1988; Woody et al. 1985). Further along the continuum, the patient who has a narcissistic personality disorder with severe antisocial features is somewhat more amenable to psychotherapy. These patients may subtly reveal dependency in the transference, their antisocial behavior may have an enraged quality about it, and their internal "ideal object" may be somewhat less aggressive than that of the pure psychopath (Kernberg 1984; Meloy 1988). Meloy (1988) has suggested that the superego pathology of these patients may be more related to environmental factors than is the biogenic etiology of the psychopath. They may attempt to rationalize or justify their behavior, thus reflecting some rudimentary value system. Their treatability will be essentially determined by their ability to form some semblance of an emotional attachment to others and to exercise some rudimentary superego functions.

Projective psychological testing may be extraordinarily helpful in assessing the antisocial patient's superego development and object relations. The Rorschach has been used, for example, to quantitatively evaluate the severity of the antisocial pathology (Exner and Weiner 1986). Although patients may successfully deceive clinicians during an interview by simulating guilt or concern for others, they have much more difficulty with the ambiguous stimuli of an inkblot, where there are no obviously "correct" answers.

The presence of bona fide depression appears to be a sign of amenability to psychotherapy just as it is a positive predictor of hospital treatment response. In a study of patients with antisocial personality disorder who were opiate addicts, the presence of depression appeared to indicate suitability for psychotherapy even if there continued to be behavioral manifestations of psychopathy (Woody et al. 1985). The antisocial patients in the study who were not depressed fared poorly in psychotherapy. In addition, the absence of relatedness to others was the most negative predictor of psychotherapy response.

Clinicians who evaluate antisocial patients must feel comfortable making a recommendation for no treatment. Such a decision may be a perfectly rational determination based on the patient's strengths and weaknesses and the danger that the patient might pose to those attempting to treat him. This manner of evaluating treatability differs greatly from the knee-jerk countertransference response described earlier. Meloy (1988), using his extensive experience in the psychotherapy of psychopaths, has identified five clinical features that absolutely contraindicate any attempt in psychotherapy (see Table 16-5). Sadistic cruelty toward others, total absence of remorse, and lack of emotional attachment are three key features that differentiate the psychopath from the more treatable narcissistic patient. The chilling countertransference feelings that lead therapists to fear for their personal safety can paralyze them and preclude any constructive efforts at treatment. Finally, the paradoxical contraindications of both high and low intelligence reflect the extremely bright patient's adeptness at thwarting the process and the dull patient's cognitive inability to grasp the therapist's interventions.

Table 16-5. Clinical features that contraindicate psychotherapy of any kind

1. A history of sadistic, violent behavior toward others that resulted in serious injury or death
2. A total absence of remorse or rationalization for such behavior
3. Intelligence that is either in the very superior or mildly mentally retarded range
4. A historical incapacity to develop emotional attachments to others
5. An intense countertransference fear of predation on the part of experienced clinicians even without clear precipitating behavior on the part of the patient

Note. Based on Meloy (1988).

Therapists who attempt psychotherapy with severely antisocial patients must be able to quickly confront their patients or they will be deceived again and again. For, while the therapist's goal is an unflinching search for truth, the patient's goal is deception. Therapists must also learn to accept that they will be conned despite all their diligent efforts to avoid it. The therapeutic alliance is either completely absent or glimpsed only in brief, intermittent flashes of collaboration.

Deceiving or conning others is a way of life for antisocial patients. They experience a powerful sense of delight, or even exhilaration, whenever they "put something over" on their therapist (Bursten 1972; Meloy 1988). Unconscious envy of the therapist's positive qualities often leads to this repetitive cycle of deception. The exhilarating feeling of triumph at a successful con is laced with contempt, which serves as a defense against envy. The patient's avoidance of a meaningful relationship with the therapist also wards off feelings of envy, but leaves the patient feeling empty.

If therapists can accept the fact that these patients will practice deception, they can proceed with psychotherapy based on the recommendations of those therapists who have had extensive experience with this population (Adler and Shapiro 1969; Frosch 1983; Kernberg 1984; Lion 1978; Meloy 1988; Person 1986; Reid 1985; Strasberger 1986; Vaillant 1975). These recommendations can be distilled into six basic principles of technique.

1. *The therapist must be stable, persistent, and thoroughly incorruptible.* More than with any other patient group, the therapist must be absolutely scrupulous about maintaining normal procedures in therapy (Person 1986). Deviating from the structure and usual context of the hours is inadvisable. These patients will do whatever they can to corrupt the therapist into unethical or dishonest conduct. David Mamet's recent movie, *House of Games* (1987), portrays the perils of attempting to help the antisocial patient by departing from the role of therapist and becoming overinvolved in the patient's life.
2. *The therapist must repeatedly confront the patient's denial and minimization of antisocial behavior.* Pervasive denial even infiltrates the antisocial patient's choice of words. If the patient says, "I ripped off this guy," the therapist needs to clarify, "So, you are a thief." If the patient says, "I offed this dude," the therapist may confront the patient by responding, "So, you are a murderer then." This technique of repeated confrontation enables the therapist to help these patients become aware of their tendency to externalize all responsibility, and they can therefore begin to acknowledge and accept responsibility for their antisocial behavior.

3. *The therapist must help the patient connect actions with internal states.*
   Just as with antisocial patients undergoing hospital treatment,
   those in individual psychotherapy require education in this regard.
4. *Confrontations of here-and-now behavior are more effective than interpre-*
   tations of unconscious material from the past. In particular, the
   patient's denigration of the therapist and contemptuous devaluation of the process must be repeatedly challenged.
5. *Countertransference must be rigorously monitored to avoid acting out by*
   the therapist. Any collusion must also be carefully avoided, despite
   the tendency to "take the path of least resistance."
6. *The therapist must avoid having excessive expectations for improvement.*
   Antisocial patients will detect this *furor therapeuticus* and will take
   great delight in thwarting their therapist's wishes to change them.
   Therapists whose self-esteem depends on the improvement of
   their patients should not treat antisocial patients.

Progress is painstakingly slow with antisocial patients in psychotherapy. At some level, these patients experience therapy as a
threat to the grandiose self. They will fight their therapist every step
of the way to avoid giving up their cherished grandiosity. Therapists
must therefore be cognizant of this resistance and must realize that
the patient's internal cohesiveness depends on a grandiose self-concept (Reid 1985). For long periods in the therapy process, the
therapist may feel paralyzed by the patient's overt or covert threats
(Kernberg 1984). This intimidation may deskill therapists and effectively stalemate their efforts. To avoid becoming victimized by their
patients, therapists must be constantly attuned to these attempts at
control.

One final comment about neutrality is in order. Therapists
treating antisocial patients cannot reasonably expect to maintain a
neutral position regarding the patient's antisocial activities. Attempting to do so would be tantamount to a silent endorsement of
or collusion with the patient's actions. More to the point, the
therapist's moral outrage will be evident in a myriad of nonverbal
communications and vocal intonations, so the patient will view any
effort at neutrality as hypocritical. When therapists are shocked at a
patient's antisocial behavior, they should simply say so (Gedo 1984).
Empathy, in accord with the self psychological approach, is both
misguided and collusive in such instances.

Even when therapists are capable of navigating the various
obstacles of resistance presented by the antisocial patient, their
attempts to be effective can still backfire. Competent therapists who
are able to avoid being destroyed by the patient are the ones most
likely to evoke intense envy, which may surface as hatred toward the
loving or idealized object (i.e., the therapist), eventually leading to

an intractable negative therapeutic reaction. Despite these pitfalls, however, many experienced clinicians believe that psychotherapeutic efforts with these patients pay off frequently enough to warrant such heroic treatment.

References

Adler G, Shapiro LN: Psychotherapy with prisoners. Curr Psychiatr Ther 9:99–105, 1969

American Psychiatric Association: Diagnostic and Statistical Manual of Mental Disorders, 2nd Edition. Washington, DC, American Psychiatric Association, 1968

American Psychiatric Association: Diagnostic and Statistical Manual of Mental Disorders, 3rd Edition. Washington, DC, American Psychiatric Association, 1980

American Psychiatric Association: Diagnostic and Statistical Manual of Mental Disorders, 3rd Edition, Revised. Washington, DC, American Psychiatric Association, 1987

Bradford JMW, Smith SM: Amnesia and homicide: the Padola case and a study of thirty cases. Bull Am Acad Psychiatry Law 7:219–231, 1979

Bursten B: The manipulative personality. Arch Gen Psychiatry 26:318–321, 1972

Cadoret RJ: Psychopathology in the adopted-away offspring of biologic parents with antisocial behavior. Arch Gen Psychiatry 35:176–184, 1978

Cadoret RJ: Epidemiology of antisocial personality, in Unmasking the Psychopath: Antisocial Personality and Related Syndromes. Edited by Reid WH, Dorr D, Walker JI, et al. New York, WW Norton, 1986, pp 28–44

Christiansen KO: A preliminary study of criminality among twins, in Biosocial Bases of Criminal Behavior. Edited by Mednick SA, Christiansen KO. New York, Gardner Press, 1977, pp 89–108

Cleckley HM: The Mask of Sanity: An Attempt to Clarify Some Issues About the So-Called Psychopathic Personality, 5th Edition. St. Louis, CV Mosby, 1976

Cloninger CR, Guze SB: Hysteria and parental psychiatric illness. Psychol Med 5:27–31, 1975

Cloninger CR, Sigvardsson S, von Knorring A-L, et al: An adoption study of somatoform disorders, II: identification of two discrete somatoform disorders. Arch Gen Psychiatry 41:863–871, 1984

Exner JE, Jr, Weiner IB: The Rorschach: A Comprehensive System, Vol I: Basic Foundations, 2nd Edition. New York, John Wiley, 1986

Frosch JP: The treatment of antisocial and borderline personality disorders. Hosp Community Psychiatry 34:243–248, 1983

Gabbard GO, Coyne L: Predictors of response of antisocial patients to hospital treatment. Hosp Community Psychiatry 38:118–1185, 1987

Gedo JE: Psychoanalysis and Its Discontents. New York, Guilford Press, 1984

Grotstein JS: Newer perspectives in object relations theory. Contemporary Psychoanalysis 18:43–91, 1982

Guze SB: Criminality and Psychiatric Disorders. New York, Oxford University Press, 1976

Halleck SL: Sociopathy: ethical aspects of diagnosis and treatment. Curr Psychiatr Ther 20:167–176, 1981

Hare RD: Diagnosis of antisocial personality disorder in two prison populations. Am J Psychiatry 140:887–890, 1983

Holden C: Growing focus on criminal careers. Science 233:1377–1378, 1986

Johnson AM: Sanctions for superego lacunae of adolescents, in Searchlights on Delinquency: New Psychoanalytic Studies. Edited by Eissler KR. New York, International Universities Press, 1949, pp 225–245

Kernberg OF: Borderline Conditions and Pathological Narcissism. New York, Jason Aronson, 1975

Kernberg OF: Severe Personality Disorders: Psychotherapeutic Disorders. New Haven, Yale University Press, 1984

Kiger RS: Treating the psychopathic patient in a therapeutic community. Hosp Community Psychiatry 18:191–196, 1967

Lilienfeld SO, VanValkenburg C, Larntz K, et al: The relationship of histrionic personality disorder to antisocial personality and somatization disorders. Am J Psychiatry 143:718–722, 1986

Lion JR: Outpatient treatment of psychopaths, in The Psychopath: A Comprehensive Study of Antisocial Disorders and Behaviors. Edited by Reid WH. New York, Brunner/Mazel, 1978, pp 286–300

Mahler MS, Pine F, Bergman A: The Psychological Birth of the Human Infant: Symbiosis and Individuation. New York, Basic Books, 1975

Meloy JR: The Psychopathic Mind: Origins, Dynamics, and Treatment. Northvale, NJ, Jason Aronson, 1988

Modlin HC: The antisocial personality. Bull Menninger Clin 47:129–144, 1983

Person E: Manipulativeness in entrepreneurs and psychopaths, in Unmasking the Psychopath: Antisocial Personality and Related Syndromes. Edited by Reid WH, Dorr D, Walker J, et al. New York, WW Norton, 1986, pp 256–273

Reid WH: The antisocial personality: a review. Hosp Community Psychiatry 36:831–837, 1985

Reid WH, Solomon G: Community-based offender programs, in The Treatment of Antisocial Syndromes. Edited by Reid WH. New York, Van Nostrand Reinhold, 1981, pp 76–94

Reid WH, Dorr D, Walker J, et al (eds): Unmasking the Psychopath: Antisocial Personality and Related Syndromes. New York, WW Norton, 1986

Strasberger LH: The treatment of antisocial syndromes: the therapist's feelings, in Unmasking the Psychopath: Antisocial Personality and Related Syndromes. Edited by Reid WH, Dorr D, Walker J, et al. New York, WW Norton, 1986, pp 191–207

Sturup GK: Treating the Untreatable: Chronic Criminals at Herstedvester. Baltimore, Johns Hopkins University Press, 1968

Symington N: The response aroused by the psychopath. Int Rev Psychoanal 7:291–298, 1980

Vaillant GE: Sociopathy as a human process: a viewpoint. Arch Gen Psychiatry 32:178–183, 1975

Vaillant G: Natural history of male alcoholism, V: is alcoholism the cart or the horse to sociopathy? Br J Addict 78:317–326, 1983

Wilson JQ, Herrnstein RJ: Crime and Human Nature. New York, Simon & Schuster, 1985

Woerner PI, Guze SB: A family and marital study of hysteria. Br J Psychiatry 114:161–168, 1968

Woody GE, McLellan AT, Luborsky L, et al: Sociopathy and psychotherapy outcome. Arch Gen Psychiatry 42:1081–1086, 1985

Yeudall LT: Neuropsychological assessment of forensic disorders. Canada's Mental Health 25(2):7–15, 1977

Yochelson S, Samenow SE: The Criminal Personality, Vol I: A Profile for Change. New York, Jason Aronson, 1976

Yochelson S, Samenow SE: The Criminal Personality, Vol II: The Treatment Process. New York, Jason Aronson, 1977

CHAPTER 17

Hysterical and Histrionic Personality Disorders

In the transition from DSM-II (American Psychiatric Association 1968) to DSM-III (American Psychiatric Association 1980), hysterical personality disorder disappeared from the official diagnostic nomenclature of American psychiatry. This change eliminated a diagnostic entity with a time-honored clinical tradition paralleled by few other psychiatric syndromes. DSM-III replaced it with histrionic personality disorder which, the manual suggests, is synonymous with hysterical personality disorder. In fact, the diagnostic criteria for DSM-III histrionic personality disorder described a much more primitive, much more impulsive, and much less stable variant that sounded remarkably like borderline personality disorder. Indeed, in one study 74 percent of a sample of patients with borderline personality disorder also fulfilled DSM-III criteria for histrionic personality disorder (Pope et al. 1983).

Because of widespread criticism that the DSM-III entity of histrionic personality disorder overlapped too much with borderline personality disorder, the criteria were modified in DSM-III-R (American Psychiatric Association 1987) (Widiger et al. 1988). The criteria of angry outbursts and tantrums, as well as manipulative suicidal behavior, were deleted because they suggested borderline features. To make the characteristics of the diagnosis sound more like the classic hysterical personality disorder, the diagnostic criteria were emended to include "inappropriately sexually seductive in appearance or behavior" (p. 349) (see Table 17-1).

Despite these modifications, however, the diagnostic criteria for histrionic personality fail to capture the well-integrated and higher-functioning hysterical personality disorder well known by dynamic clinicians for decades (Cooper and Michels 1988). Since both the higher-level hysterical personality disorder and the more primitive histrionic personality disorder are encountered in clinical practice, both will be considered in this chapter despite the omission of the former from DSM-III-R.

Table 17-1.   DSM-III-R diagnostic criteria for histrionic
                  personality disorder

A pervasive pattern of excessive emotionality and attention-seeking,
beginning by early adulthood and present in a variety of contexts, as
indicated by at least *four* of the following:
  (1) constantly seeks or demands reassurance, approval, or praise
  (2) is inappropriately sexually seductive in appearance or behavior
  (3) is overly concerned with physical attractiveness
  (4) expresses emotion with inappropriate exaggeration, e.g.,
       embraces casual acquaintances with excessive ardor,
       uncontrollable sobbing on minor sentimental occasions, has
       temper tantrums
  (5) is uncomfortable in situations in which he or she is not the center
       of attention
  (6) displays rapidly shifting and shallow expression of emotions
  (7) is self-centered, actions being directed toward obtaining
       immediate satisfaction; has no tolerance for the frustration of
       delayed gratification
  (8) has a style of speech that is excessively impressionistic and lacking
       in detail, e.g., when asked to describe mother, can be no more
       specific than, "She was a beautiful person."

Note.   Reprinted from DSM-III-R, p. 349, with permission from the American Psychiatric Association.

Hysterical Versus Histrionic

The staunchly atheoretical nature of the personality disorder criteria in DSM-III-R is particularly problematic when considering patients with hysterical or histrionic tendencies. To determine the appropriate treatment for this diverse group of patients, a careful psychodynamic assessment is far more crucial than a descriptive cataloging of overt behaviors. One primary source of confusion in the related literature has been a tendency to rely on behavioral characteristics instead of dynamic understanding.

A further source of confusion is that the term *hysterical* has been used not only to describe a personality disorder but also to refer to a disease largely of women, characterized by frequent surgeries and multiple somatic complaints, and to characterize various conversion symptoms, such as paralysis or blindness, that have no organic basis. The former condition, known as Briquet's hysteria or Briquet's syndrome, is currently subsumed by somatization disorder in DSM-III-R. Conversion symptoms may now be found in Axis I under conversion disorder, alternatively labeled *hysterical neurosis, conversion type*. Hysterical conversion symptomatology is what opened the gates of the unconscious to Freud and led to the development of psychoanalysis. Freud understood conversion symptoms as symbolic physical symptoms that represented displaced and repressed instinctual wishes. However, there is a broad consensus in modern psychiatry that hysterical conversion symptoms and hysterical personality disorder are not related either clinically or dynamically (Chodoff 1974). Although conversion symptoms can occur in patients with hysterical personality disorder, they also can occur across a wide variety of other character diagnoses.

During the first half of the century, the intrapsychic conflicts associated with the hysterical personality were thought to derive from genital-oedipal developmental issues. Part of the legacy of Freud's work with hysterical conversion symptoms was the more generalized view that repressed sexuality was of paramount importance in both character neuroses and neurotic symptoms. Clinically unsuccessful psychoanalytic efforts to treat these patients led some to question Freud's formulation. Beginning with Marmor's classic 1953 article, the psychiatric literature has strongly identified pregenital (particularly oral) issues as central to the pathogenesis of hysterical personality disorder (Chodoff 1974).

The literature of the last three decades has seen a convergence of opinion regarding the existence of both the "healthy" and the "sick" hysterical patient (Baumbacher and Amini 1980-81; Blacker and Tupin 1977; Chodoff 1974; Easser and Lesser 1965; Kernberg 1975; Lazare 1971; Sugarman 1979; Wallerstein 1980-81; Zetzel 1968). The healthy hysterical patients are referred to by a variety of names, including "good," "phallic," and "true." Even more labels have been applied to those in the latter group—"oral hysterics," "so-called good hysterics," "hysteroids," and "infantile personalities." For reasons of clarity, in this chapter we will refer to the healthier group as *hysterical personality disorders* and the more disturbed group as *histrionic personality disorders*.

Defining the exact interrelationship between the hysterical and histrionic personalities is a controversial process. While some have argued that the two are simply gradations along a continuum (Blacker and Tupin 1977; Lazare 1971; Wallerstein 1980-81; Zetzel 1968), others viewed the two groups as so different as to constitute sharply distinct entities (Baumbacher and Amini 1980-81; Sugarman 1979). What appears to link hysterical persons and histrionic persons is an overlap in overt behavioral characteristics such as labile and shallow emotionality, attention-seeking, disturbed sexual functioning, dependency and helplessness, and self-dramatization. These qualities have come to be associated with the use of "hysterical" by laypersons to mean dramatic overreaction. The paradox is that these characteristics are far more typical of histrionic patients than of hysterical patients. As Wallerstein (1980-81) noted: "Those who behaviorally look more hysterical in the sense of the dramatic or flamboyant hysterical character type are the very ones who look less hysterical in the sense of the dynamics of the 'good' or 'true' hysteric" (p. 540). Zetzel (1968) similarly observed that the "so-called good hysterics" who appear floridly hysterical are often mistaken for analyzable, high-level hysterical patients although they are actually primitively organized and unanalyzable—what we refer to here as *histrionic personalities*.

The literature distinguishing the two groups can be summarized by listing the characteristics that differentiate hysterical personality disorder from the histrionic personality disorder (Easser and Lesser 1965; Kernberg 1975; Lazare 1971; Sugarman 1979; Zetzel 1968) (see Table 17-2). The histrionic personality is more florid than the hysteric in virtually every way. All the DSM-III-R criteria symptoms are more exaggerated in the histrionic person. Greater lability of affect, more impulsivity, and a more overt seduc-

Table 17-2. Differentiation of hysterical personality disorder from histrionic personality disorder

Hysterical Personality Disorder	Histrionic Personality Disorder
1. Restrained and circumscribed emotionality.	1. Florid and generalized emotionality.
2. Sexualized exhibitionism and need to be loved.	2. Greedy exhibitionism with a demanding, oral quality that is "cold" and less engaging.
3. Good impulse control.	3. Generalized impulsivity.
4. Subtly appealing seductiveness.	4. Crude, inappropriate, and distancing seductiveness.
5. Ambition and competitiveness.	5. Aimlessness and helplessness.
6. Mature triangular object relations.	6. Primitive, dyadic object relations, characterized by clinging, masochism, and paranoia.
7. Separations from love objects can be tolerated.	7. Overwhelming separation anxiety occurs when abandoned by love objects.
8. Strict superego and some obsessional defenses.	8. Lax superego and a predominance of primitive defenses, such as splitting and idealization.
9. Sexualized transference wishes develop gradually and are viewed as unrealistic.	9. Intense sexualized transference wishes develop rapidly and are viewed as realistic expectations.

tiveness are all hallmarks. The sexuality of these patients is often so direct and unmodulated that it may actually "turn off" members of the opposite sex. Their demanding, exhibitionistic need to be the center of attention may also fail to engage others because of its ruthless nature. In this regard, these patients clearly have much in common with persons who have narcissistic personality disorder.

By contrast, persons who have true hysterical personality disorder may be much more subtly dramatic and exhibitionistic, and their sexuality may be expressed more coyly and engagingly. In addition, Wallerstein (1980-81) has suggested that a sizable group of high-level hysterics are not dramatic or flamboyant at all. He described these patients as "constricted wall flowers, shy and even tongue-tied in interpersonal encounter, at extremes mousy and totally inhibited in demeanor and interaction" (p. 540). He persuasively pointed out that a focus on overt behavior rather than underlying dynamics can result in a misdiagnosis.

Patients with hysterical personality disorder are often reasonably successful in work and demonstrate ambition as well as constructive competitiveness. This active mastery can be juxtaposed with the aimless, helpless, dependent quality that keeps histrionic patients from succeeding except in the sense of passively manipulating others to meet their needs. Whereas the true hysterical patient has attained mature whole-object relations characterized by triangular oedipal themes and has been able to form significant relationships with both parents, the histrionic patient is fixated at a more primitive dyadic level of object relations often characterized by clinging, masochism, and paranoia.

Hysterical patients can tolerate separation from their love objects even though they may identify those relationships as their main area of difficulty. Histrionic patients, on the other hand, are often overwhelmed with separation anxiety when apart from their love objects. The strict superego and other obsessional defenses of the hysterical patient contrast with the histrionic patient's typically lax superego and predominantly more primitive defenses, such as splitting and idealization.

When hysterical patients enter psychotherapy or psychoanalysis, sexualized transference wishes develop gradually over a considerable time and are generally viewed as unrealistic by the patients themselves. Histrionic patients, on the other hand, develop intense erotic transference wishes almost immediately, and often view these wishes as realistic expectations. When the wishes are frustrated, the patient may become furious with the therapist for not being more gratifying. Zetzel (1968) has pointed out that the hysterical patient's capacity to differentiate the therapeutic alliance from transference feelings is intimately linked to the ability to separate internal from

external reality, an ego function that is compromised in the histrionic patient.

The distinguishing features of the histrionic personality disorder highlight its close relationship with the borderline personality
disorder. Kernberg (1975), for example, explicitly conceptualized
the infantile personality as having an underlying borderline personality organization. These patients do not defend against genital
sexuality so much as against passive and primitive orality (Lazare
1971).

Patients with hysterical personality disorder, on the other
hand, usually present with problems that revolve around either
genital sexuality per se or around difficulties with the sexual objects
in their lives. Although the hysterical female has classically been
described as "frigid" or anorgasmic, she may also be promiscuous or
fully orgasmic but basically dissatisfied with her sexual relationships.
She may be unable to make a romantic or sexual commitment to a
man who is appropriate for her, instead falling hopelessly in love
with an unavailable man. Another recurrent problem for the female
hysterical patient is that men often misinterpret her actions as sexual
advances, and she is continually surprised at this misunderstand-
ing—a fact that reflects the *unconscious* nature of her seductiveness.

Gender and Diagnosis

The more flamboyant descriptive characteristics of the hysterical—
and particularly the histrionic—personality disorder paint a picture
that is often described as a caricature of femininity (Chodoff and
Lyons 1958). These diagnoses are so commonly applied to women
that some clinicians would regard the term *male hysteric* as an oxy-
moron. Throughout the history of psychiatry, the hysterical personality has been associated with the female gender. This tendency to
think of the diagnosis only in relation to women probably relates
more to cultural sex role stereotypes than to psychodynamics.
Halleck (1967) has pointed out that deprived males in our society
tend to deny their own needs and attack those they believe have
rejected them. Women in our society, however, are not expected to
deny their dependency needs and have "little opportunity to express
aggression directly" (p. 753). Female children "are more likely to
adapt to deprivation by seeking to bind people to...(them) through
relationships in which...(the women assume) a highly dependent
role" (p. 753). Others (Hollender 1971; Lerner 1974) have noted
that the hysterical personality characteristics reflect cultural expectations of how women are supposed to adapt in American society.
Another glaring contributor to the overwhelming tendency to view
hysterical personality as a female disease is the fact that, with few

exceptions, the literature on the disorder has been written entirely by men (Chodoff and Lyons 1958; Luisada et al. 1974).

Despite the predominant association between hysterical personality and femininity, hysterical personality disorder has been extensively documented in males (Blacker and Tupin 1977; Cleghorn 1969; Kolb 1968; Halleck 1967; Luisada et al. 1974; MacKinnon and Michels 1971; Malmquist 1971). The descriptions of male hysterical patients fall into two broad subtypes: the hypermasculine and the passive, effeminate. Those in the hypermasculine subtype are directly analogous to the classical female hysteric in that they are caricatures of masculinity. They may be Don Juans who act seductively toward all women and may even engage in antisocial behavior. The latter subtype of passive, effeminate males may be "foppish" (MacKinnon and Michels 1971), flamboyant homosexuals or passive, impotent heterosexuals who are fearful of women. The same distinction between the high-level hysterical person and the lower-level histrionic person can be made in male patients, based largely on the same criteria used to distinguish the two groups in females.

In a study of 27 male patients with hysterical personality disorder, Luisada et al. (1974) found that the vast majority were heterosexual, but that all had some form of disturbed sexual relationships. Antisocial behavior, such as lying and unreliability, were common problems in the group, as were alcohol and drug abuse. These investigators identified both effeminate and hypermasculine subtypes, with unstable relationships typical of both. Many of these patients would probably receive a diagnosis of narcissistic personality disorder, some with antisocial features, but as a group they tended to have much more warmth toward and empathy for others than the true narcissist.

Despite the overt differences in the behavior of the passive, effeminate subtype and the hypermasculine subtype, the underlying dynamics in the male hysterical personality disorder are remarkably similar. These dynamics and their contribution to the behavioral facade of the male hysterical patient will be discussed later in this chapter.

Cognitive Style and Defense Mechanisms

One aspect of intrapsychic functioning that links the hysterical and the histrionic personality disorders is cognitive style. Shapiro (1965) has identified the cognitive style typical of these personality disorders as generally "global, relatively diffuse, and lacking in sharpness, particularly in sharp detail. In a word, it is *impressionistic*" (p. 111). When a therapist asks a patient with this cognitive style, "How was your weekend?" the response is likely to be along the lines of "just great" or "really awful," without any supportive detail. The same order of response is likely to apply to significant figures in the patient's life. When one hysterical patient was asked to describe her father, she responded, "He's just super!" Similarly, when patients with this form of cognitive style approach a task, such as psychological testing, they are inclined to avoid concentrating on facts and to instead respond with a hunch. The therapist may encounter considerable frustration, for example, in getting historical facts about a patient's family background.

This global, impressionistic cognitive style is complementary to two of the chief defense mechanisms of the hysterical personality: repression and denial (Horowitz 1977a). Repression is facilitated by this cognitive style (Shapiro 1965) because of the patient's sketchy original retention of facts and the patient's impressionistic and poorly focused subsequent recall of facts. Because of the distractible deployment of attention, aspects of reality are disavowed as well, in keeping with the defense mechanism of denial. In the early literature on hysteria, the patient's attitude was often described as *la belle indifference,* referring to the female patient's apparent lack of concern about her conversion symptoms. Although this phrase is rarely used in modern psychiatry, patients with hysterical personality disorder do manifest a blasé attitude about certain aspects of reality that they appear to scotomize. The hysterical cognitive style may account for this failure to integrate or recognize implications, consequences, and details of experience.

This same attitude of indifference occurs in patients with histrionic personality disorder after they have displayed intense emotions during an outburst. Like the borderline patient, the histrionic patient may react with bland denial to the contradiction between the self-representation associated with the outburst and the self-representation associated with calm, subdued functioning *after* the outburst. Kernberg (1975) has suggested that hysterical patients use repression as a predominant defense, while infantile patients (histrionic patients for purposes of this discussion) use splitting instead of repression as their major defense. Recent research (Perry and Cooper 1986), suggests, however, that repression and splitting are not necessarily at opposite ends of the same continuum. Indeed, the two defenses commonly coexist in hysterical and histrionic patients. For example, histrionic patients who use splitting will often report pervasive amnesia (indicative of repression) regarding early childhood experiences. Nevertheless, Kernberg's distinction is useful in the sense that repression is probably *more prominent* than splitting in most hysterical persons and vice versa in histrionic persons.

Dissociative states, like conversion symptoms, have often been classified as hysterical phenomena, even though they are found in patients with a variety of diagnoses. The most extreme manifestation of dissociation is multiple personality disorder, which involves both splitting—in the sense that different self-representations are maintained as separate—and repression—in the sense that the primary personality usually has no memory of the alternates. The reactions of histrionic patients to their emotional outbursts resemble dissociation and multiple personality disorder, albeit in attenuated form. These patients often have poor recall of their actions, which they say seemed to be like those of "someone else."

One histrionic patient who also suffered from dissociative symptoms discovered cuts on her left breast but could not explain how they got there. Shortly after this discovery, her husband found her in the bathroom at 3 A.M.; she was in a dissociated state and was cutting her left breast lightly with a razor blade. Hypnotized for diagnostic purposes, the patient said, "I must suffer as my mother suffered." Her mother had just undergone surgery for breast cancer. This patient also illustrates the defense mechanism of identification, another common hysterical defense (MacKinnon and Michels 1971).

One final defense mechanism that may be found in both hysterical and histrionic patients is emotionality itself. Becoming intensely, yet superficially and shallowly, emotional may defend against deeper, more heartfelt affects that the patient wishes to avoid (MacKinnon and Michels 1971). Knee-jerk emotionality in concert with the global, impressionistic cognitive style serves to keep the histrionic patient from being in touch with any genuine affective states or attitudes toward self and others.

Horowitz (1977a) has incorporated the hysterical defensive patterns and cognitive style into an operational definition of hysterical personality based on long-range, medium-range, and short-range patterns. The short-range patterns involve the hysterical patient's information-processing style. These patterns last only minutes or seconds, and include global deployment of attention and incomplete communications lacking in detail. The medium-range patterns, occurring over hours or days, are referred to as "traits." These include behaving in a childlike manner, suggestibility, fluid transitions from one mood or emotion to another, sex appeal, and attention-seeking behavior. Finally, the longer-range patterns, covering months to years, focus on interpersonal relationships. Typical stereotyped patterns for all three frames are victim-aggressor or child-parent interactions, and rescue or rape themes.

Psychodynamic Understanding

Because a variety of overt behaviors in both genders are subsumed by the categories of hysterical and histrionic personality disorders, a careful psychodynamic assessment is crucial to the informed assignment of the appropriate type of psychotherapy. Female patients with hysterical or histrionic personality styles tend to encounter difficulties at two of the classical psychosexual stages of development: they experience relative maternal deprivation during the oral stage, and they have difficulty resolving the oedipal situation and emerging with a clear sexual identity (Blacker and Tupin 1977). Although both hysterical and histrionic patients have some difficulty with oral and phallic-oedipal issues, the histrionic patient obviously encounters greater difficulty at the earlier stage while the hysteric is fixated primarily at the later stage.

In the case of the histrionic female patient, the lack of maternal nurturance leads her to turn to her father for the gratification of dependency needs (Blacker and Tupin 1977; Hollender 1971; MacKinnon and Michels 1971). She soon learns that flirtatiousness and dramatic exhibitionistic displays of emotion are required to gain her father's attention. As she matures, she learns that she must repress her genital sexuality to remain "daddy's little girl." When the little girl grows up, the primitive neediness characteristic of all her sexual relations may be termed the *breast-penis equation*. She often engages in promiscuous sexual behavior that is ultimately unsatisfying since the male penis only serves as a substitute for the maternal breast she unconsciously longs for.

The female with hysterical personality disorder has negotiated the oral stage of development with a reasonable degree of success. She, too, is disappointed with her mother, but the disappointment occurs at a more advanced stage of development. In the phallic stage of development directly preceding the full-blown oedipal situation, the little girl must come to terms with the fact that she cannot physically possess her mother as her father can. The narcissistic injury ensuing from this awareness of genital difference normally leads the little girl to transfer her libidinal phallic strivings from her mother to her father during the oedipal phase of development.

Some hysterical patients who have been unable to shift from mother to father maintain an unconscious phallic attachment to their mother (Baumbacher and Amini 1980-81). By maintaining this attachment, they ward off the narcissistic injury connected with their feelings of inadequacy. They also may displace their phallic strivings from the genitals to the entire body. The hyperfemininity that results is sometimes referred to as the *body phallus*, in the sense that the patient "adorns her body...makes herself and her presence intrusive, creates a stir wherever she goes, and in her childishness or naiveté...may be very aggressive" (Baumbacher and Amini 1980-81, p. 515). The patient thus defends against her anger and disappointment in her mother by a positive, even idealized attachment to her mother.

The end result of this developmental constellation is that the overtly heterosexual hysterical woman continues to have her mother as a (homosexual) unconscious love object. She lacks any real investment in male relationships, however, because no man can compete with her unconscious attachment to her mother. These patients have relatively good ego functioning, but their unconscious self-representations are inadequate because they lack a coherent sexual identity due to an inability to shift their attachment to their mother into a more oedipal attachment to their father.

Other hysterical patients are able to shift from their mother to their father but then cannot let go of the father. As little girls, these women often idealized their father, perhaps as the only man worth having. This intense attachment led to rivalrous feelings toward the mother and active wishes to replace her. In the course of therapy or analysis, many hysterical patients recover previously repressed fantasies of this nature. If they perceive that their brothers are granted special status with their fathers by virtue of their male gender, they also may develop deep resentment and may become highly competitive with men.

The common finding of anorgasmia in hysterical patients may be partly related to an unconscious wish to achieve power over men through the sexual act (MacKinnon and Michels 1971). Alternatively, all sexuality may be tinged with incestuous meanings because of the oedipal attachment to the father. These women also may choose inappropriate partners as a further defense against giving up oedipal longings. These dynamics are often covert, however, and often only become clear after a careful evaluation. While some hysterical patients may have overt, conscious attachments to their father, others will have repressed this dimension of development. Their conscious experience of their father may be tinged with anger as a defense against their underlying longing. Similarly, they may be unaware of their rivalrous feelings toward their mother, whom they consciously love. Evidence of hysterical dynamics in the female patient may come instead from persistent patterns of triangular relationships, such as falling in love with married men, or from slowly emerging developments in the transference, such as intense rivalry with other female patients. Whether the dynamics are repressed may depend on the father's response to his daughter's oedipal longings. If he views such feelings as unacceptable, he will convey this attitude to his daughter, who will then feel that she must repress them.

The developmental dynamics outlined for the female patient may be similarly applied to the male. The histrionic male patient will have experienced maternal deprivation and will have looked to his father for nurturance. If the father is absent or emotionally unavailable, the boy child is faced with two alternatives: he may model himself after his mother and develop a passive, effeminate identity, or (in the absence of a true masculine role model) he may mimic various cultural stereotypes of hypermasculinity to take flight from any anxiety about effeminacy and to counteract his regressive pull to be like his mother (Blacker and Tupin 1977).

The male patient with hysterical personality disorder resembles his female counterpart in that he enters the phallic stage intensely attached to his mother. He also experiences feelings of genital inadequacy when comparing himself to his father or other adult males. The narcissistic injury associated with greater genital awareness prevents him — just as it does some females — from entering the competitive arena of the Oedipus complex. He remains attached to his mother and may become passive and effeminate by identification (Baumbacher and Amini 1980-81). He does not become homosexual, but his heterosexual relationships are largely related to efforts to reassure himself about his underlying genital inadequacy. He is always disappointed with women, since none of them can measure up to his mother. Some men with this hysterical configuration will choose a celibate life-style, such as the priest-hood, to unconsciously maintain unswerving loyalty to their mother. Other boys will deal with their perceived genital inadequacy by indulging in hypermasculine activity, such as body-building and the compulsive seduction of women. Thus they can reassure themselves that they are "real men" with nothing to feel inferior about.

No discussion of female hysteria would be complete without reference to incest and childhood seduction. Freud originally believed that many of his hysterical patients had been seduced by their fathers because he so often heard such reports from his patients. He later became convinced that many of these reports were fantasies stemming from oedipal wishes. We now know that many little girls are indeed victims of actual incestuous sexuality with their fathers, stepfathers, or other male relatives. Amidst the furor over whether Freud's view was correct, many clinicians have adopted an either/or position. Either little girls are actually seduced, or they merely fantasize seduction. This dichotomy is further complicated by the fact that many women who have been victimized by incest nevertheless have powerful fantasies about and yearnings for the perpetrator of the incest. Even women who have never been violated by their father may still have powerful conscious or unconscious sexual wishes for him. Finally, there is considerable middle ground where erotized interactions occur that do *not* result in overt incest, but that *do* encourage fantasies.

In terms of the developmental pathogenesis of histrionic and hysterical personality disorder, a history of actual incest is much more likely to be found in the histrionic patient. These patients may go through their adult life repeating the original trauma by seeking out men who are forbidden in one way or another, such as therapists, married men, or bosses. They may be unconsciously attempting to actively master a passively experienced trauma by being the one to initiate it rather than the one to passively submit.

The higher-level hysterical patient is much less likely to have a history of overt incest but may have had what she perceived as a special relationship with her father. Hysterical patients frequently have a father who was unhappy with his wife and turned to the patient for fulfillment and gratification not possible in the marriage. The patient may receive an implicit message that she must remain loyal to her father forever to rescue him from an unhappy marriage. Fathers in this situation may give subtle or even overt signs of disapproval whenever their daughters show interest in other men. In this scenario, the hysterical patient will find herself surrounded with dynamics similar to incest, only in attenuated form. Hysterical patients with these dynamics and family constellations may find themselves unable to give up their dependency on their father and get on with their lives.

Individual Psychotherapy

Patients with hysterical personality disorder generally respond well to expressive individual psychotherapy or to psychoanalysis. The discussion here will focus on those patients, since therapeutic strategies appropriate to the lower-level histrionic patient are similar to those employed in the treatment of the borderline personality disorder (Allen 1977) discussed earlier (see Chapter 14). Where appropriate, modifications of technique required for the treatment of histrionic personality disorders will be discussed.

Although some patients with hysterical personality disorder will present with a discrete symptom, such as sexual dysfunction, more commonly they enter psychotherapy because of a general dissatisfaction with their relationship patterns. The precipitating event may be the breakup of a marriage or a love relationship. They also may experience vague feelings of depression or anxiety related to disappointment with their current partner (MacKinnon and Michels 1971). Unlike many patients with the personality disorders in Clusters A and B of DSM-III-R, the patient with hysterical personality disorder readily becomes attached to the therapist and quickly develops a therapeutic alliance in which the therapist is perceived as helpful. The psychotherapy process will generally go well if the therapist adheres to several general principles.

Principles of Technique

A rule of thumb in expressive work is to address resistance before attempting to interpret the underlying content. In the case of the hysterical patient, this axiom dictates that the patient's cognitive style must be dealt with first, since it is so intimately bound up with the patient's defensive configuration. Hysterical patients often begin psychotherapy with an unconscious expectation that the therapist should be able to understand them intuitively, nonverbally, and globally without details of their intrapsychic world (Allen 1977). Therapists confronting this expectation must matter-of-factly let their patients know that the only way they can develop understanding is if the patients provide a detailed account of their internal experience. Hence the initial approach must be geared to eliciting as much detail as possible from the patient (Allen 1977; Horowitz 1977b; MacKinnon and Michels 1971).

As soon as the therapist has established the need for detail, the patient is likely to struggle with compliance. Hysterical patients are not accustomed to thinking in such terms, and the therapist can expect responses along the lines of "I don't know." At this point in the process, therapists can gently encourage the patients with comments such as, "Let's not accept 'I don't know' and see what comes to mind as you reflect on it." Over and over again, the therapist must help the patient learn how to *reflect* instead of simply reporting an impressionistic feeling. Therapists may thus call the patient's attention to the vagueness of perception and interpret defensive reasons for not wanting to fully recognize certain thoughts or feelings (Horowitz 1977b).

The internal experience of the hysterical patient is often that of a leaf in the wind buffeted by powerful feeling states. There may be a complete repression of the ideas that connect one feeling with another. In urging the hysterical patient to reflect and to attend in detail to internal and external reality, the therapist helps the patient retrieve the ideational connections between feelings. As Allen (1977) has noted, part of this process involves teaching the hysterical person to feel more in-depth and more genuinely. Superficial and shallow feelings defend against more disturbing and more deeply experienced affects. As the patient's tolerance for these deeper feeling states increases, there is a concomitant increase in the patient's ability to attend to details (Horowitz 1977b).

When hysterical patients identify their feelings, attitudes, and ideational states, they develop a greater sense of self-as-agent in active interaction with the environment rather than self-as-passive-victim of the environment (Horowitz 1977b). Hysterical patients often experience vivid visual images and fantasies, but they will not translate these into words unless the therapist assists in this process.

Thus, therapists help their patients identify what they want and feel. The patient also learns that having certain thoughts or feelings is not dangerous.

When threatening thoughts and feelings emerge, hysterical patients frequently express a wish to know all about the therapist's life. They are highly suggestible, and if therapists share a lot about their own life and beliefs, their patients will rapidly adopt similar qualities so as to please their therapists and to thereby avoid the arduous task of getting in touch with their own feelings and beliefs. A cardinal rule in the treatment of hysterical patients is to frustrate rather than to gratify their wish for personal information about the therapist. Gratifying these demands leads to their becoming endless (Allen 1977). The wish to know about the therapist may be interpreted as a defensive maneuver to avoid anxiety about self-disclosure (Allen 1977). Therapists should similarly avoid giving advice to their hysterical patients, who need to learn that they have considerable resources within themselves with which to approach their problems.

Patients in long-term therapy will find that the process of modifying their cognitive style leads to a modification of object relatedness as well. As these patients begin to attend in more detail to self and others in interpersonal contexts, they develop new patterns of perceiving relationships (Horowitz 1977b). Instead of always seeing themselves as the victim of others, patients begin to understand that they play an active role in perpetuating certain patterns of relating to others. They develop a capacity to compare the actual facts of an interpersonal situation to the internal patterns often superimposed on external situations. Ultimately, the self-representation of the passive child so typical of the hysterical patient is replaced by a more mature representation involving activity and sexuality. This transition may take years, however, because patients frequently experience the loss of the hysterical cognitive style as a threat to a basic sense of identity.

In the psychotherapy of the hysterical personality disorder, therapeutic work within the transference is the main vehicle for change. The problems that the patient encounters in relationships outside the therapy will be reproduced within the transference. Although psychotherapy can be effective and gratifying with hysterical patients, the mishandling of transference, particularly erotic transference, is probably the most frequent cause of therapeutic failure.

Management of Erotic Transference

Despite the pervasiveness of the phenomenon of erotic transference, not only in hysterical patients but also in others, many therapists do not receive adequate training in the effective and therapeutic management of transference feelings. One female psychiatric resident who was struggling with a male patient's sexual feelings toward her took the problem to her psychotherapy supervisor, an analyst. He responded by scratching his head and replying, "I don't know what you girls do about this problem." Historically, a subtle (or not-so-subtle) sexism has pervaded psychotherapy training programs. Because the vast majority of erotic transference reports in the literature, from Freud to the present, have been of female patients who have fallen in love with their male therapists or analysts, male supervisors have sometimes inadvertently promoted among their male supervisees a casual, denigrating attitude toward female patients who develop an erotic transference. One male resident, who was beginning psychotherapy training, told his male supervisor that he was uncertain about how to approach his first psychotherapy patient. His supervisor informed him, "It's really very simple. Do you know how to seduce a woman?" The supervisor went on to draw an analogy between "hooking" the patient in a psychotherapy process and seducing a woman. This unprofessional attitude typifies an unfortunate historical trend to "enjoy" the erotic transference rather than to analyze and understand it.

Since the term is used loosely to describe a number of different transference developments, a clear definition of the phenomenon is relevant to a discussion of its management. Person (1985) provided a succinct definition that applies to psychotherapy as well as to psychoanalysis:

> The term *erotic transference* is used interchangeably with the term *transference love*. It refers to some mixture of tender, erotic, and sexual feelings that a patient experiences in reference to his or her analyst and, as such, forms part of a positive transference. Sexual transference components alone represent a truncated erotic transference, one that has not been fully developed or is not fully experienced. (p. 161)

In hysterical patients, the erotic transference usually develops gradually and with considerable shame and embarrassment. Sexual longings for the therapist are often experienced as ego-dystonic, and the patient knows that the fulfillment of these wishes would be inappropriate.

Histrionic and borderline patients may develop a subtype of erotic transference that Blum (1973) has termed the *erotized transference*. In contrast to ordinary transference love, the patient in the throes of an erotized transference makes a tenacious and ego-syntonic demand for sexual gratification. Because of ego impairments in these patients, their internal and external reality are blurred, and they view their expectation of sexual consummation with their therapist as reasonable and desirable. Their seeming obliviousness to the crossing of symbolically incestuous boundaries may stem from a childhood history of being victimized in actual sexual seductions by parents or parental figures (Blum 1973; Kumin 1985-86).

The spectrum of transferences ranging from the erotic to the erotized is aptly described by Person (1985) as "both gold mine and minefield" (p. 163). These transferences can set the scene for devastating countertransference acting out. Therapist-patient sex has severely stigmatized the mental health professions, has ruined the careers of a number of psychotherapists, and has caused severe psychological damage to the patients who are its victims (Gabbard 1989; Pope and Bouhoutsos 1986). Surveys reveal that as many as 10 percent of all male therapists have engaged in such behavior (Gabbard 1989), so it cannot be dismissed as an occasional aberration of only the seriously disturbed therapist. Many of these unfortunate therapists appear to be seeking a cure for themselves as well as to be making a desperate attempt to cure their patients (Twemlow and Gabbard 1989).

The "gold mine" aspect of erotic transferences is that they provide the therapist an in vivo recapitulation of a past relationship in the present situation of the transference relationship. Such patients show their therapists what contributions they bring to similar relationships outside the therapeutic situation. Thus a patient's problems with love and sexuality can be examined and understood as they develop in a safe relationship where that patient will not be exploited or abused. To mine the gold in the experience without being destroyed by the minefield requires therapists to adhere to four principles of technique (see Table 17-3). Although there are definite gender differences in the expression of erotic transference, we will first discuss the handling of erotic transference in general and then examine the specific gender-determined aspects of the phenomenon.

Examination of countertransference feelings. The therapist's countertransference reactions to erotic transference feelings in the patient may represent countertransference narrowly as a reactivation of a relationship in the therapist's past, broadly as an identification with a projected aspect of the patient, or as a mixture

Table 17-3. Therapeutic management of erotic transference

1. Examination of countertransference feelings
2. Nonexploitative acceptance of erotic transference as important therapeutic material to be understood
3. Assessment of the multiple meanings of the transference in its function as a resistance to a deepening of the therapeutic process
4. Interpretation of connections between transference and both current and past relationships

of both (Kumin 1985-1986; Sandler 1976). The patient may well represent a forbidden but sexually arousing object from the therapist's past, but the therapist's desire for the patient may also be linked to the actual incestuous desire of a parental figure from the patient's oedipal phase of development. So the first step in monitoring countertransference, in keeping with the practice of dynamic psychiatry, is for therapists to assess the relative weight of their own contributions versus those of the patient. Therapists who attempt to manage erotic transference in intensive psychotherapy without a personal treatment experience, however, will be at a serious disadvantage.

Several common countertransference patterns relate to erotic transference. The first, common in male residents treating attractive female patients, is to see erotic transference where none exists. Male therapists may respond to their own sexual arousal by projectively disavowing it and instead seeing it in their patients, whom they label as "seductive." In these circumstances, the resident who is pressed for details about why the patient is seductive or why she is sexually interested in him, is often at a loss to present convincing evidence. Because of anxieties about his own sexual feelings, he has avoided them much as the hysterical patient attempts to avoid her sexual feelings. Although this avoidance may simply reflect beginner's anxiety about having sexual feelings in psychotherapy, it may also be a repetition of the patient's father's response to his own sexual arousal to his daughter (Gorkin 1985). If beginning therapists ignore these feelings, they unconsciously act them out by making phallic, "penetrating" interpretations too often and too soon, another common pitfall of the new therapist.

A second countertransference reaction is cold aloofness in response to the patient's confessions of erotic longings for the therapist (MacKinnon and Michels 1971). To control any sexual countertransference reactions to the patient's feelings the therapist may become more silent, less empathic, and more distant. This "straitjacketing" of all emotions helps to rigidly maintain control of sexual impulses that seem threatening.

A third common countertransference reaction is anxiety stemming from the fear that sexual feelings, either in the patient or therapist, will get out of control. This anxiety may lead the therapist to divert the conversation from the patient's expressions of love or sexual arousal, or to interpret such feelings prematurely as "resistance," a digression from the therapeutic task. When a male therapist inappropriately tells his female patient that he will not allow the therapy to be sidetracked by her feelings for him, he forces her to stick to the problems outside therapy that brought her to treatment. Such an anxious attempt to eliminate erotic transference feelings may give patients the message that sexual feelings are unacceptable and possibly disgusting, a view that often mirrors feelings of these patients. The therapist's own underlying disgust relates to the covert message in intense erotic transference that therapy is useless—that only sex or "love" can cure (Gorkin 1985).

In the fourth countertransference pattern, which may be more insidious than the others, therapists may encourage and foster erotic feelings for their personal gratification. These therapists, who listen with voyeuristic delight to the details of their patient's sexual fantasies, may have been drawn to the profession because they long to be idealized and loved. Underneath this wish, they may gain sadistic pleasure by arousing their patients' futile sexual wishes. This pattern can often be traced to the therapist's childhood interactions where they felt they were aroused by the opposite-sex parent only to be frustrated. By practicing psychotherapy, these individuals may be trying to reverse that childhood situation. Thus therapists must be aware of their own desires in the therapeutic relationship. As Kumin (1985-86) noted, "Both the analyst's capacity and incapacity to interpret accurately the patient's wishes in the transference requires an appreciation of not only what and whom the patient desires but also what and whom the analyst desires" (p. 13). Kumin has also suggested that the desires of the therapist for the patient may present a more formidable resistance than do the patient's desires for the therapist. Numerous psychotherapy processes have become stalemated in the throes of intense erotic transference because the therapist has been too busy basking in the glow of sexual feelings.

Nonexploitative acceptance of erotic transference as important therapeutic material to be understood. After the therapist has carefully monitored countertransference feelings, the next step is to convey to the patient that sexual or loving feelings are acceptable aspects of the therapeutic experience. The therapist may make an educational comment such as, "In psychotherapy you are likely to experience a broad range of feelings—hate, love, envy, sexual arousal, fear, anger, and joy—all of which must be dealt with as acceptable topics for discussion and as carriers of important information for the therapy." While it is true that erotic transference may serve as resistance to the emergence of other material in the therapy, it is a technical error to immediately interpret such feelings as resistance. To understand what is being repeated from the past, the erotic transference must be allowed to develop fully.

Freud (1914) first used the term *acting out* to describe a patient's tendency to repeat in action something from the past rather than to remember and verbalize it. Patients can be told that the feelings developing in the therapy will provide important information about feelings that develop in their other relationships, both past and present. If a patient insists on having the therapist gratify the transference wishes, the therapist can point out that not gratifying the wishes can lead to a better understanding of what happens in other relationships. The therapist should keep in mind that erotic transference may be intensely unpleasant for the patient (just as it may be for the therapist), not only because of the frustration it brings, but also because it may be embarrassing. The therapist may wish to communicate an empathic understanding of the patient's shame: "I know it is difficult and painful for you to have these feelings without being able to gratify them, but if we can explore them together we may be able to help you understand more fully the problems that brought you here."

Assessment of the multiple meanings of the transference in its function as a resistance. Erotic transference is a resistance in the sense that something is being repeated rather than remembered and verbalized. Resistance should not be equated, however, with "something bad that must be removed immediately," as it often is by beginning therapists. As just noted, erotic transference is also an important communication that should be understood. Like all other mental phenomena, erotic transference is determined by the principle of multiple function. It should not be taken simply at face value, but rather should be explored via the patient's associations, dreams, and memories for all its multiple meanings, some of which may be unconscious. For example, a male patient's erotic transference to a female therapist may represent passive homosexual longings even though the therapist is of the opposite sex (Torras de Beà 1987). Because erotic transference must also be understood in terms of its function at a particular moment in therapy, the therapist must assess what preceded its development and what follows its flourishing.

One male patient began his therapy session with his male therapist by saying that he had been helped enormously in the previous session by the therapist's explanation. After commenting on how much the therapist's interpretation had helped him at work, the patient began to contradict what he had just said by maintaining that his relationships were deteriorating. As he continued to talk, he revealed that he had been having sexual fantasies about the therapist and that he believed the therapist could only help him by ejaculating semen into his rectum to make him more masculine. The therapist pointed out that the patient was devaluing the help of the insights that he had received in the previous session by holding onto a magical belief that a sexual liaison was the only way to be helped. The patient acknowledged that he needed to devalue the therapist's help because he felt so inferior to the therapist, who he said was "on Mt. Olympus." The therapist then explained that the patient's envy had increased as he was helped, so he had sexualized the transference to devalue the help. (If the therapist's insights were not particularly effective or useful, there was much less to envy.) In response, the patient said that his liberating feelings of having been helped had alternated with

feelings of humiliation because he had to acknowledge that the
therapist knew something the patient did not know, which made him
feel vulnerable.

In this instance, the patient's erotic transference was a way to defend
against his envy of the therapist's competence by devaluing it.
Sexualization in the transference may be a way to defend against
other feelings as well.

> A male patient was seeing his female therapist for the last time prior
> to her departure at the end of her residency training program. He
> told her that he had seen a movie the night before in which a female
> psychiatrist had kissed one of her male patients. He observed that
> the patient had seemed to benefit from the therapist's affection, and
> he asked his therapist if she might do the same with him. After an
> initially anxious reaction to the request, the therapist asked if the
> unexpected request might be related to the termination of the
> therapy. The patient responded that he would rather not think about
> that subject. The therapist then pointed out to the patient that his
> wish to sexualize their relationship might be a defense against facing
> the grief associated with termination.

Sexualizing the end of a relationship is a common phenomenon (in therapy and in life in general). It serves to avoid the
mourning process connected with loss of an important figure. In
this vignette, the patient's wish to become physically involved with
his therapist was also a way to deny the definitive nature of termination: A kiss might lead to a *beginning*, rather than an ending.

Therapists who view transference love as a natural and understandable response to their enormous sexual appeal are overlooking
the darker side of erotic transference. One of the many stories told
about Dr. Karl Menninger illustrates this dilemma:

> A somewhat depressed and hysterical 40-year-old woman was hospi-
> talized at the Menninger Clinic for over a year with essentially no
> change in her condition. She had developed an intense and intrac-
> table erotic transference toward her male psychotherapist. Dr. Men-
> ninger was asked to consult on the case because of the therapeutic
> stalemate that had been reached. Throughout much of the interview,
> the patient repeatedly commented on her great love for her thera-
> pist. After listening to her protestations of love for several minutes,
> Dr. Menninger reportedly said, "You know, if you really loved him,
> you would get better for him."

Dr. Menninger was addressing the hostility that often lies just
beneath the surface of a patient's transference love. Indeed, erotic
transferences frequently mask considerable aggression and sadism,
even to the extent that an erotic transference might be considered

a form of negative transference (Kumin 1985-1986). Exploration of transference wishes for a sexual relationship regularly reveal wishes to hurt, embarrass, or destroy the therapist. A patient's demands for sexual boundary-crossing may be so tormenting, especially in instances of the erotized variant typical of histrionic and borderline patients, that the therapist dreads each session. The therapist may feel used and transformed into a need-gratifying object whose only function is to fulfill the patient's inappropriate demands (Frayn and Silberfeld 1986).

> Ms. II was a 24-year-old homosexual histrionic patient functioning at a borderline level of ego organization who had a history of sexual abuse by male relatives. She formed an intense erotized transference to her female therapist almost immediately. She flirted with her provocatively in the sessions by touching the therapist's foot lightly with her own foot and asking, "Does this make you nervous?" Ms. II steadfastly maintained that her therapist could only get to know her if she slept with her. She also demanded to know her therapist's sexual orientation. Although the therapist frustrated the patient's wish to destroy their professional relationship by transforming it into a sexual one, the patient continued her efforts at seduction.
>
> The patient would regularly bring in explicit sexual fantasies about her therapist:
>
> > I am caressing your body—your back, your hips, your thighs. I gently and quickly stroke my hand across your pussy. You moan softly and tighten your grip across my back. I kiss you and whisper softly in your ear that I'm going to make love to you. I softly massage your breasts and kiss them. I kiss your stomach and move down toward your pussy. I kiss the inside of your thighs while stroking your clitoris with my tongue. I continue to kiss, suck, and caress you with my tongue. You moan with pleasure as you have an orgasm. I kiss your thighs again and lightly squeeze your breasts and run my fingers down your sides to your hips. I begin to lick at your clitoris again and stick my tongue inside you. I then lick and suck on your clitoris while I gently ease one, then two of my fingers into you. You have a long, multiple, satisfying orgasm which ends with you stroking my hair and me lightly kissing your pussy.
>
> Needless to say, the patient's expression of such fantasies made the therapist feel uncomfortable and anxious, as well as controlled. If she interrupted the fantasies, she felt that she was revealing her discomfort and disapproval of the patient's transference feelings. If she remained silent, she felt that she was colluding in an exhibitionist-voyeur pairing.
>
> The patient finally revealed some of the underlying aggressive feelings that were masquerading as erotized transference. She commented to the therapist, "You know I'm aware of still wanting to piss you off. Probably force you into rejecting me. Make you hate me. Am

> I succeeding? I really want you to like me. But since I know that's out of the question, I'll just drive you away. It's the shits, isn't it? You see, I see our relationship in two ways: either we fuck, or I make you hate my guts."

To a large extent, Ms. II had induced a paralysis in the therapist, who felt cruel and sadistic by frustrating the patient's wishes. A consultation helped the therapist understand that she was being controlled by a projective identification process so that the normal, professional limits of psychotherapy seemed ruthless and unreasonable. In other words, a cold depriving object from the patient's past had been projected into the therapist, who unconsciously identified with this projected material. Moreover, her own anger at the patient for her relentless control of the therapy also contributed to her feeling that any intervention would appear cold and ruthless. As the psychotherapy continued, it became clearer that the overt sexual wish was only the tip of an iceberg.

> During one session, Ms. II reported a dream in which she was in a high-tech office. There was a machine that could translate the patient's thoughts, so that she did not have to tell them to her therapist. In the patient's associations to the dream, she acknowledged that her longings for the therapist were not truly sexual, but rather a wish for her therapist to really know her intimately. The therapist eventually helped Ms. II to see that her wish for sex was really a wish for merger—a wish that her therapist would know her thoughts without her having to voice them.

This regressive longing to return to the mother-infant symbiotic state is often a powerful component of erotic or erotized transferences in the female patient-female therapist dyad. The sexualized wish may be preferable to the more threatening wish for merger.

Interpretation of connections between transference and both current and past relationships. A correct interpretation of the erotic transference will often reduce the desire and the resistance inherent in transference love (Kumin 1985-86). To avoid premature interpretation, the therapist may need to silently formulate the interpretation to help with countertransference desires even before delivering the interpretation to the patient. The timing of transference interpretations is a matter of judgment, but a rule of thumb is to not interpret the transference until it becomes a resistance. Another guideline is to avoid interpreting it until the underlying linkages to past relationships and to current extratransference relationships are near conscious awareness. The therapist can use the model of the triangle of insight described in Chapter 4 to construct connections between the transference feelings and past relationships, as well as between the transference and current extratransference relationships. By pointing out that transference love is a repetition of something from the past, and by asking the patient if the situation is reminiscent of past situations, the therapist can lay the groundwork for interpretive interventions. An actual transcript of a psychotherapy session may illustrate some of the technical approaches to interpreting erotic transference.

> Ms. JJ was a 26-year-old married patient with a diagnosis of hysterical personality disorder. She was seen twice weekly by a male therapist in expressive-supportive psychotherapy with a predominantly expressive emphasis. She began psychotherapy with complaints of anorgasmia, headaches, constant marital difficulties, fear of "standing on her own two feet," feelings of being unloved and unwanted, and a generalized concern that she was too dependent. Midway through the second year of treatment, the following interchange occurred in one session:

Patient:	My husband and I haven't been getting along. We don't see each other much, and when we do, we argue. I wanted to make you a buddy again today, but when I walked in, something changed. I don't know what to say today. I'd like to get real mad at you, but I don't know why. Probably because I need attention and my husband's not giving me any. When I don't have anything to say, it's usually because I have feelings for you—I had butterflies just now when I said that. There are two kinds of feelings I get in here—one is when I feel that you're like my dad and I want you to cradle me and give me the pat on the back. The other is when I want you to hold me real tight...(patient stops)
Therapist:	You had a feeling just now that stopped you in mid-sentence. What was it?
Patient:	I don't want to say it. It's ridiculous. (with great hesitation) I can't just come in here...and look at you...and think, "I want to make love with you." I can't feel that way. That's not me.
Therapist:	To think that you could have sexual feelings is so unacceptable to you that you cannot own the feelings as yours.
Patient:	I'm just not like that. Not even with my husband. My subconscious wants to hang on to you and hold you tightly, but my conscious mind wants to pretend I don't have the feelings. I'd rather go back to just having the feeling that you were like my dad and I need a pat on the back.
Therapist:	It's particularly unacceptable for you to have sexual feelings for someone that you also view as a dad. I

	wonder if the same thing happened as a little girl in your relationship with your father.
Patient:	I was always very special to my dad. When he walked me down the aisle and gave me away at the wedding, he told me that I was always his favorite of his three daughters. I shouldn't be talking like this. I have to go out and get in the car with my husband and spend the evening with him, but my thoughts are going to be about you.
Therapist:	It sounds like there is a similarity between your attachment to me and your attachment to your dad in that both make it difficult for you to invest emotionally in your husband.

In this vignette, the therapist draws a connection between the patient's erotic transference and her feelings for her father. Sexual feelings are forbidden in both relationships because she sees them as incompatible with her otherwise paternal view of the therapist and her father. After linking the transference feelings to the patient's past relationship with her father, the therapist connects these longings to her difficulty with her husband, a current extratransference relationship.

These four principles of technique may be helpful to the psychotherapist who is treating a patient struggling with erotic transference feelings. However, adherence to these principles requires rational, level-headed thinking. As poets have long known, passion clouds judgment. When therapists begin to observe that they are being swept away by erotic feelings toward a patient, they would be wise to seek out consultation or supervision from a respected colleague.

Gender Differences in Erotic Transference

The overwhelming majority of case reports in the literature involving erotic or erotized transferences are of female patients with male therapists. Lester (1985) has pointed out that the absence of reports involving male patients and female therapists may reflect the general rarity of transference love in those dyads. She has speculated that the male patient's anxiety about the female analyst as a powerful preoedipal phallic mother, who makes "penetrating" interpretations, can overshadow and greatly inhibit his expression of sexual feelings toward the analyst as an oedipal mother. Lester also noted that the regressive passivity in analytic therapy goes against the grain of the traditional active male sexual role.

Lester's experience has not been corroborated by all female therapists. Gornick (1986) has viewed Lester's scenario of the phallic mother as only applicable to some male patients working with female therapists. Other male patients, she has asserted, find it much more unacceptable to be passive and dependent vis-à-vis a female than to express direct sexual feelings. The shame of being dependent may lead certain male patients to defend against such feelings by "turning the tables" and using sexual feelings in the transference to restore a sense of male dominance.

Although male patients apparently experience a spectrum of erotic transference manifestations with female therapists, these do not seem to be as intense, as prolonged, and as fully developed as the erotic transference that female patients in general experience. Person (1985) has related this variance to the differences in moral development between men and women (Gilligan 1982). While women are raised to define themselves more through affiliation and relationships, men are socialized to value autonomy over related-ness. As a result, men may feel that their masculinity is threatened by dependency, whereas women do not feel an analogous threat to their femininity. Person (1985) has also suggested that erotic trans-ference in women is more often a longing for love, while in men the feelings are more often specifically sexual.

Another distinction between male and female erotic transfer-ences is that female patients more often use it as a resistance, while male patients display a resistance to the awareness of any erotic transference (Person 1985). Male patients will frequently displace erotic feelings for their therapist onto a woman outside the therapy, because acknowledging such longings for the therapist might threaten their sense of autonomy.

Group Psychotherapy

Clinicians have often noted that patients who are good candidates for dynamic individual psychotherapy are also good candidates for dynamic group psychotherapy. Such is the case with hysterical patients, who often become "stars" in their groups. They are highly valued by other group members for their ability to express feelings directly and for their care and concern about others in the group. The hysterical patient's cognitive style and its associated defenses of repression and denial can be dealt with quite effectively in group psychotherapy. Other patients in the group will help hysterical patients see how they tend to distort their view of self and others by omitting details from interactional situations. For example, when one female hysterical patient described how she was misunderstood as being seductive when she was simply being friendly with a man at work, male patients in the group pointed out that she might be overlooking what she had said (or how she had said it) in the interaction. Furthermore, they pointed out how this patient behaved similarly in the group itself and how she seemed oblivious to the flirtatious signals she gave men in the group as well.

Hysterical patients generally form a positive maternal transference to the group as a whole. They seize group therapy as an opportunity to receive some of the maternal nurturance that they believe they missed during childhood. They are therefore well motivated to attend group therapy and to encourage others to view it as a valuable resource. Histrionic patients, however, can be more problematic in groups, because they will often "upstage" other patients by demanding to be the center of attention through florid displays of emotionality. Such patients can be effectively treated in group psychotherapy only if they are also in individual psychotherapy, much as with group psychotherapy of borderline patients (see Chapter 14).

References

Allen DW: Basic treatment issues, in Hysterical Personality. Edited by Horowitz MJ. New York, Jason Aronson, 1977, pp 283–328

American Psychiatric Association: Diagnostic and Statistical Manual of Mental Disorders, 2nd Edition. Washington, DC, American Psychiatric Association, 1968

American Psychiatric Association: Diagnostic and Statistical Manual of Mental Disorders, 3rd Edition. Washington, DC, American Psychiatric Association, 1980

American Psychiatric Association: Diagnostic and Statistical Manual of Mental Disorders, 3rd Edition, Revised. Washington, DC, American Psychiatric Association, 1987

Baumbacher G, Amini F: The hysterical personality disorder: a proposed clarification of a diagnostic dilemma. International Journal of Psychoanalytic Psychotherapy 8:501–532, 1980-81

Blacker KH, Tupin JP: Hysteria and hysterical structures: developmental and social theories, in Hysterical Personality. Edited by Horowitz MJ. New York, Jason Aronson, 1977, pp 95–141

Blum HP: The concept of erotized transference. J Am Psychoanal Assoc 21:61–76, 1973

Chodoff P: The diagnosis of hysteria: an overview. Am J Psychiatry 131:1073–1078, 1974

Chodoff P, Lyons H: Hysteria, the hysterical personality and "hysterical" conversion. Am J Psychiatry 114:734–740, 1958

Cleghorn RA: Hysteria—multiple manifestations of semantic confusion. Canadian Psychiatry Association Journal 14:539–551, 1969

Cooper A, Michels R: Book review of Diagnostic and Statistical Manual of Mental Disorders, Third Edition, Revised (DSM-III-R). Am J Psychiatry 145:1300–1301, 1988

Easser BR, Lesser SR: Hysterical personality: a re-evaluation. Psychoanal Q 34:390–405, 1965

Frayn DH, Silberfeld M: Erotic transferences. Can J Psychiatry 31:323–327, 1986

Freud S: Remembering, repeating and working-through (further recommendations on the technique of psycho-analysis II) (1914), in The Standard Edition of the Complete Psychological Works of Sigmund Freud, Vol 12. Translated and edited by Strachey J. London, Hogarth Press, 1958, pp 145–156

Gabbard GO (ed): Sexual Exploitation in Professional Relationships. Washington, DC, American Psychiatric Press, 1989

Gilligan C: In a Different Voice: Psychological Theory and Women's Development. Cambridge, MA, Harvard University Press, 1982

Gorkin M: Varieties of sexualized countertransference. Psychoanal Rev 72:421–440, 1985

Gornick LK: Developing a new narrative: the woman therapist and the male patient. Psychoanalytic Psychology 3:299–325, 1986

Halleck SL: Hysterical personality traits: psychological, social, and iatrogenic determinants. Arch Gen Psychiatry 16:750–757, 1967

Hollender M: Hysterical personality. Comment on Contemporary Psychiatry 1:17–24, 1971

Horowitz MJ: The core characteristics of hysterical personality (introduction), in Hysterical Personality. Edited by Horowitz MJ. New York, Jason Aronson, 1977a, pp 3–6

Horowitz MJ: Structure and the processes of change, in Hysterical Personality. Edited by Horowitz MJ. New York, Jason Aronson, 1977b, pp 329–399

Kernberg OF: Borderline Conditions and Pathological Narcissism. New York, Jason Aronson, 1975

Kolb LC: Noyes' Modern Clinical Psychiatry, 7th Edition. Philadelphia, WB Saunders, 1968

Kumin I: Erotic horror: desire and resistance in the psychoanalytic situation. International Journal of Psychoanalytic Psychotherapy 11:3–20, 1985-86

Lazare A: The hysterical character in psychoanalytic theory: evolution and confusion. Arch Gen Psychiatry 25:131–137, 1971

Lerner HE: The hysterical personality: a "woman's disease." Compr Psychiatry 15:157–164, 1974

Lester EP: The female analyst and the erotized transference. Int J Psychoanal 66:283–293, 1985

Luisada PV, Peele R, Pitard EA: The hysterical personality in men. Am J Psychiatry 131:518–521, 1974

Malmquist C: Hysteria in childhood. Postgraduate Medicine 50:112–117, 1971

Marmor J: Orality in the hysterical personality. J Am Psychoanal Assoc 1:656–671, 1953

MacKinnon R, Michels R: The Psychiatric Interview in Clinical Practice. Philadelphia, WB Saunders, 1971

Perry J, Cooper S: A preliminary report on defenses and conflicts associated with borderline personality disorder. J Am Psychoanal Assoc 34:863–893, 1986

Person ES: The erotic transference in women and in men: differences and consequences. J Am Acad Psychoanal 13:159–180, 1985

Pope HG Jr, Jonas JM, Hudson JI, et al: The validity of DSM-III border-
    line personality disorder: a phenomenologic, family history, treat-
    ment response, and long-term follow-up study. Arch Gen
    Psychiatry 40:23–30, 1983
Pope KS, Bouhoutsos JC: Sexual intimacy between therapists and pa-
    tients. New York, Praeger, 1986
Sandler J: Countertransference and role-responsiveness. International
    Review of Psychoanalysis 3:43–47, 1976
Shapiro D: Neurotic Styles. New York, Basic Books, 1965
Sugarman A: The infantile personality: orality in the hysteric revisited.
    Int J Psychoanal 60:501–513, 1979
Torras de Beà E: A contribution to the papers on transference by Eva
    Lester and Marianne Goldberger and Dorothy Evans. Int J Psy-
    choanal 68:63–67, 1987
Twemlow SW, Gabbard GO: The lovesick therapist, in Sexual Exploita-
    tion in Professional Relationships. Edited by Gabbard GO. Wash-
    ington, DC, American Psychiatric Press, 1989, pp 71–87
Wallerstein RS: Diagnosis revisited (and revisited): the case of hysteria
    and the hysterical personality. International Journal of Psycho-
    analysis and Psychotherapy 8:533–547, 1980-81
Widiger TA, Frances A, Spitzer RL, et al: The DSM-III-R personality
    disorders: an overview. Am J Psychiatry 145:786–795, 1988
Zetzel ER: The so called good hysteric. Int J Psychoanal 49:256–260,
    1968

CHAPTER 18

Cluster C Personality Disorders: Obsessive-Compulsive, Avoidant, Dependent, and Passive-Aggressive

The four personality disorders classified in Cluster C of DSM-III-R (American Psychiatric Association 1987)—obsessive-compulsive, avoidant, dependent, and passive-aggressive—are grouped together because persons suffering from these disorders supposedly have anxiety or fear in common as a prominent characteristic. A long clinical-psychoanalytic tradition is associated with the obsessive-compulsive personality disorder, but no similar traditions exist for the other three characterological entities of Cluster C. The fact that all four personality disorders are considered here in one chapter reflects the paucity of contributions to the psychodynamic literature regarding avoidant, dependent, and passive-aggressive personality disorders.

Obsessive-Compulsive Personality Disorder

The distinction between obsessive-compulsive disorder (or neurosis) and obsessive-compulsive personality disorder is based on the difference between symptoms and enduring character traits. As described in Chapter 9, the patient suffering from obsessive-compulsive disorder is plagued with recurring thoughts of an unpleasant nature and is driven to perform ritualistic behaviors. These symptomatic manifestations are ego-*dystonic* in that the patient recognizes them as problems and ordinarily wishes to be rid of them. In contrast, the traits that constitute the DSM-III-R diagnosis of obsessive-compulsive personality disorder (see Table 18-1) are lifelong patterns of behavior that are ego-*syntonic*. These traits seldom cause distress to the patients themselves and may even be regarded as highly adaptive. Indeed, studies of physicians, for example, suggest that certain obsessive-compulsive characteristics contribute significantly to success as a physician (Gabbard 1985; Krakowski 1982; Vaillant et al. 1972). The unswerving devotion to work typical of the obsessive-compulsive person also leads to high achievement in professions other than medicine where attention to detail is essential. However, success in the work sphere often comes at a high price to

Table 18-1. DSM-III-R criteria for obsessive-compulsive
personality disorder

A pervasive pattern of perfectionism and inflexibility, beginning by early
adulthood and present in a variety of contexts, as indicated by at least
five of the following:
  (1) perfectionism that interferes with task completion, e.g., inability to
      complete a project because own overly strict standards are not met
  (2) preoccupation with details, rules, lists, order, organization, or
      schedules to the extent that the major point of the activity is lost
  (3) unreasonable insistence that others submit to exactly his or her
      way of doing things, or unreasonable reluctance to allow others to
      do things because of the conviction that they will not do them
      correctly
  (4) excessive devotion to work and productivity to the exclusion of
      leisure activities and friendships (not accounted for by obvious
      economic necessity)
  (5) indecisiveness: decision making is either avoided, postponed, or
      protracted, e.g., the person cannot get assignments done on time
      because of ruminating about priorities (do not include if
      indecisiveness is due to excessive need for advice or reassurance
      from others)
  (6) overconscientiousness, scrupulousness, and inflexibility about
      matters of morality, ethics, or values (not accounted for by cultural
      or religious identification)
  (7) restricted expression of affection
  (8) lack of generosity in giving time, money, or gifts when no personal
      gain is likely to result
  (9) inability to discard worn-out or worthless objects even when they
      have no sentimental value

Note. Reprinted from DSM-III-R, p. 356, with permission from the American Psychiatric Association.

these people. Their significant others often find them difficult to
live with and frequently instigate their coming to psychiatric attention.

Although the distinctions between obsessive-compulsive disorder and obsessive-compulsive personality disorder in DSM-III-R are
clear and useful, there is some controversy over the extent of the
overlap between these two diagnostic entities. Psychodynamic clinicians, noting the similarities in the psychodynamic basis of both
disorders, have observed that many individuals with obsessive-compulsive neurotic symptoms also have an underlying obsessive-compulsive character structure (Nemiah 1980). Symptoms of an obsessive-compulsive nature have also been reported as transitory
occurrences during the psychoanalytic treatment of patients with
obsessive-compulsive personality disorder (Munich 1986). How-

ever, nondynamic empirical studies indicate that a wide range of personality disorders may occur in patients with obsessive-compulsive disorder. In one study, less than half the patients with obsessive-compulsive disorder satisfied the criteria for obsessive-compulsive personality disorder (Rasmussen and Tsuang 1986). Another investigation of 23 patients with obsessive-compulsive disorder found that only one subject also suffered from obsessive-compulsive personality disorder (Joffe et al. 1988). In fact, the most common characterological diagnosis in this sample was a mixed personality disorder with avoidant, dependent, and passive-aggressive features.

Psychodynamic Understanding

Early psychoanalytic contributions (Abraham 1921; Freud 1908; Jones 1948; Menninger 1943) connected certain character traits, particularly obstinacy, parsimony, and orderliness, with the anal phase of psychosexual development. Patients with these personality features were viewed as having regressed from the castration anxiety associated with the oedipal phase of development to the relative safety of the anal period. Driven by a punitive superego, they presumably employed characteristic defensive operations of the ego, including isolation of affect, intellectualization, reaction formation, undoing, and displacement (see Chapter 2). Their obsessive orderliness, for example, was conceptualized as a reaction formation against an underlying wish to engage in anal messiness and its derivatives. The considerable difficulty that the obsessive-compulsive personality has expressing aggression was related to early power struggles with maternal figures around toilet training. The stubbornness of the obsessive individual could also be viewed as an outgrowth of those same struggles.

More recent contributions (Gabbard 1985; Gabbard and Menninger 1988; Horowitz 1988; Salzman 1968, 1980, 1983; Shapiro 1965) have gone beyond the vicissitudes of the anal phase to focus on interpersonal elements, self-esteem, management of anger and dependency, cognitive style, and the problems of balancing work and emotional relationships. Individuals with obsessive-compulsive personality disorder suffer from a good deal of self-doubt. Their experience as children was that they were not sufficiently valued or loved by their parents. In some cases, this perception may relate to actual coldness or distance in parental figures, while in others the children may simply have required more reassurance and affection than the ordinary child to feel a sense of parental approval. Psychodynamic treatment of these patients reveals strong unfulfilled dependent yearnings and a reservoir of rage directed at the parents for not being more emotionally available. Since obsessive-compulsive patients find both anger and dependency consciously unacceptable, they defend against those feelings with defenses such as reaction formation and isolation of affect. In a counterdependent effort to deny any dependency on anyone, many obsessive-compulsive persons go to great lengths to demonstrate their independence and their "rugged individualism." Similarly, they strive for complete control over all anger, and they may even appear deferential and obsequious to avoid any impression of harboring angry feelings.

Intimate relationships pose a significant problem to the obsessive-compulsive patient. Intimacy raises the possibility of being overwhelmed by powerful wishes to be taken care of, with the concomitant potential for frustration of those wishes, resulting in feelings of hatred and resentment, and a desire for revenge. The feelings inherent to intimate relationships are threatening because they have the potential for becoming "out of control," one of the fundamental fears of the obsessive-compulsive person. Significant others frequently complain that their obsessive-compulsive loved one is too controlling. Stalemates and impasses often occur in such relationships because obsessive-compulsive persons refuse to acknowledge that anyone else might have a better way to do things. This need to control others often stems from a fundamental concern that sources of nurturance in the environment are highly tenuous and may disappear at any moment. Somewhere in every obsessive-compulsive person is a child who feels unloved. The low self-esteem connected with this childhood sense of not being valued often leads to an assumption that others would prefer not to put up with obsessive-compulsive persons. The high level of aggression and the intense destructive wishes lurking in the unconscious of the obsessive-compulsive person may also contribute to this fear of losing others. These patients often fear that their destructiveness will drive others away or that it will lead to counteraggression, a projection of their own rage.

Obsessive-compulsive persons are also characterized by a quest for perfection. They seem to harbor a secret belief that if they can only reach a transcendent stage of flawlessness, then they will finally receive the parental approval and esteem they missed as children. These children often grow up with the conviction that they simply did not try hard enough, and as adults, they chronically feel that they are "not doing enough." The parent who seems always unsatisfied is internalized as a harsh superego that expects more and more from the patient. Many obsessive-compulsive individuals become workaholics because they are unconsciously driven by this conviction that love and approval can be obtained only through heroic efforts to achieve extraordinary heights in their chosen profession. The irony in this striving for perfection, however, is that obsessive-compulsive persons rarely seem satisfied with any of their achievements. They appear driven more by a wish to gain relief from their tormenting superego than by a genuine wish for pleasure.

These dynamic underpinnings lead to a characteristic cognitive style (Horowitz 1988; Shapiro 1965). Whereas hysterical and histrionic patients tend to overvalue affective states at the expense of careful thought, the reverse is true for obsessive-compulsive persons. Not unlike Mr. Spock of *Star Trek* fame, obsessive-compulsive individuals seek to be thoroughly rational and logical in every endeavor. They dread any situation of uncontrolled emotion, and their mechanistic tendency to be totally without affect may drive those around them to distraction. Moreover, their thinking is only logical within certain narrow parameters. Their thought patterns can be characterized as rigid and dogmatic (Shapiro 1965). Dynamically, these qualities can be understood as compensatory for the underlying self-doubt and ambivalence that plague the obsessive-compulsive person.

In contrast to the cognitive style of the hysterical patient, that of the obsessive-compulsive individual involves careful attention to detail but an almost complete lack of spontaneity or flexibility, with impressionistic hunches being automatically dismissed as "illogical." Obsessive-compulsive persons expend extraordinary energy to maintain their rigid cognitive and attentional styles, so that absolutely nothing they do is without effort. Taking vacations, or even relaxing, generally hold no allure whatsoever for the true obsessive-compulsive person. In one survey of 100 self-professed obsessive-compulsive physicians (Krakowski 1982), only 11 percent took vacations exclusively for the sake of a vacation and only 10 percent regularly took time away from work to relax.

Although many of these individuals are high achievers, some find that their character style impairs their ability to succeed at work. Obsessive-compulsive persons may ruminate endlessly about small decisions, exasperating those around them. They often get bogged down in details and lose track of the main purpose of the task at hand. Their indecision may be dynamically related to deep feelings of self-doubt. They may feel that the risk of making a mistake is so great as to preclude a definite decision one way or another. Similarly, their concern that the final outcome of a project may be less than perfect may contribute to their indecisiveness. Many obsessive-compulsive persons are extraordinarily articulate verbally but encounter major psychological obstacles in their writing because of this concern that the end result will not be flawless.

The "driven" quality inherent in the actions of the obsessive-compulsive person has been well described by Shapiro (1965) as having "the appearance of being pressed or motivated by something beyond the interest of the acting person. He does not seem that enthusiastic. His genuine interest in the activity, in other words, does not seem to account for the intensity with which he pursues it" (p. 33). These patients are always driven by their own internal overseer who issues commands about what they "should" or "ought to" do. Dynamically speaking, they have little autonomy from their own superego injunctions. They behave the way they do because they must, regardless of how their behavior impinges on others.

The hypertrophied superego of the obsessive-compulsive patient is relentless in its demands for perfection. When those demands are not satisfied over a long time, depression may set in. This dynamic link between the obsessive-compulsive character and depression has been observed by clinicians for many years. The obsessive-compulsive person may be at particularly high risk for depression in middle age, when the idealistic dreams of youth are shattered by the reality of time running out with advancing age. These patients may become suicidal at this point in their life cycle and may require hospitalization, despite a long history of functioning reasonably well in a work situation.

Psychotherapeutic Considerations

In contrast to the refractory nature of the obsessive-compulsive disorder, obsessive-compulsive *personality* disorder is often greatly improved by psychoanalysis or individual psychotherapy with an expressive emphasis (Gunderson 1988; Horowitz 1988; Munich 1986; Salzman 1980). Dynamic group psychotherapy may also be effective for patients with obsessive-compulsive personality disorder. Whether individual or group psychotherapy is chosen, similar therapeutic problems arise, requiring similar approaches.

In considering the resistances commonly encountered in the psychotherapy of obsessive-compulsive patients, one must first empathize with the implications that dynamic psychotherapy has for such patients. The very idea of the unconscious threatens their sense of control. Psychodynamic theory teaches that we are unconsciously controlled and consciously confused. Hence, the typical obsessive-compulsive patient is going to resent the basic premise of dynamic therapy. To deal with the feeling of being threatened, the obsessive-compulsive person may discount all the therapist's insights as "nothing new." Obsessive-compulsive patients may at first be reluctant to admit that the therapist is saying anything that they are not already aware of (Salzman 1980). Resistance can be understood as a patient's typical defensive operations as manifested in the psychotherapeutic process. Isolation of affect, then, may present itself as a lack of awareness of any feelings toward the therapist, particularly dependency or anger. The patient may talk at great length about factual information from both past and present situations, with no apparent emotional reaction to these events. When the therapist returns from a lengthy vacation, the obsessive-compulsive patient is likely to be reluctant to admit any emotional reaction to the separation. If reaction formation is a prominent defense, the patient will probably respond with: "Oh, no, I wasn't bothered by it. I just hope that you had a wonderful time and feel refreshed."

Obsessive-compulsive persons also respond to the threat of intense affect by obsessional rambling that serves as a smoke screen to mask their real feelings. More precisely, it may serve as an anesthetizing cloud that puts others to sleep. As the patient wanders farther and farther afield from the original point, the therapist may lose track of the thread that links the patient's associations and may begin to "tune out" the patient. Because these persons may experience thoughts as having as much power as actions, the patient may feel the need to undo what has already been said, as follows:

> During the weekend visit with my parents, I became somewhat irritated with my father. Well, I wouldn't really say that I was irritated, in the sense that I truly felt any anger toward him. It's just that he sat and watched TV and seemed to have no interest in speaking to me. At one point, I had the thought of turning the TV off and confronting him, but of course I didn't really do that. I would never actually be that rude to anyone.

The rambling speech pattern typical of the obsessive-compulsive patient in psychotherapy is the frequent canceling of thoughts or wishes that have just been verbalized. In addition, an overinclusiveness of thinking leads the patient to bring in peripheral events that take the content of the rambling progressively farther from the main theme of the session.

Many obsessive-compulsive patients will attempt to become the "perfect patient." They may attempt to produce exactly what they think the therapist wants to hear, with the unconscious fantasy that they will finally get the love and esteem they feel they missed as children. Since they are certain that any expression of anger will result in disapproval, they may consciously experience no anger while unconsciously expressing it by completely monopolizing the session. One obsessive-compulsive patient talked nonstop for 50 minutes, only to cease exactly on time, without ever letting the therapist get a word in edgewise. In this manner, the patient was able to express his anger without having to acknowledge any angry feelings.

Other obsessive-compulsive patients will manifest their resistance by re-creating in the transference relationship with the therapist their power struggle with their mother.

> Mr. KK was an obsessive-compulsive printer who came to psychoanalytic therapy twice a week. He initially presented as a rather submis-

sive and passive "good boy," who was completely unable to express any anger within the therapy sessions. However, he developed a pattern of not speaking for approximately half the 50-minute session and of not paying his bill. Although he denied any anger toward the therapist when this behavior was brought out in the open, he developed a pattern of ventilating his anger with an exit line. One day, after failing to voice anger about the therapist "staring" at him during the session, he strode to the door and said, "I guess you didn't catch my cold," referring to a previously expressed concern that he might give his therapist his cold. On another occasion, after he was confronted about his failure to pay his bill, he exited with the following comment: "Don't freeze to death!" Shortly thereafter, another session ended with, "Don't slip on the ice!"

One of Mr. KK's most remarkable exit lines occurred after a session where he was largely silent except for an occasional comment on the failure to pay his bill. The therapist connected his failure to produce payment for the bill with his failure to produce verbal material for the sessions. After a prolonged silence, Mr. KK was informed that the time was up. As he went to the door, he turned to the therapist and said, "I almost bought you a book at a sale yesterday. It was by a physician and was entitled *Thirty Years of Rectal Practice.*" Then he rapidly left the room and slammed the door. During the next session, his therapist brought up this comment about his seemingly benevolent wish to buy him a gift. Mr. KK was able to explore his feeling that the therapist's attempt to extract money and words was comparable to an intrusive finger in his anus attempting to extract feces.

In the transference, Mr. KK had re-created a highly ambivalent relationship with his mother, which involved issues of withholding and control. He experienced his therapist as a mother who was demanding that he produce his feces (words and money) when and where she ordered him to. To defy what he felt as a sadistic and unreasonable command, he withheld his productions until the last moment, then let them go under his own control. In so doing, he attempted to make active what was passively experienced, ventilating his sadistic aggression in angry comments. However, as these examples illustrate, his characterological defense of reaction formation got the best of him in each exit line. Seeing through the reaction formation, the exit lines can be heard as follows: "Don't slip on the ice!" would be, "I hope you slip on the ice." "Don't freeze to death!" would mean, "I wish you would freeze to death." Even Mr. KK's attempt to equate his therapist with a sadistic and intrusive mother who was forcibly extracting his bodily contents had to be cloaked in the thought of buying him a gift. Despite the reaction formation, the anger in these exit lines still came through to the therapist. Because of Mr. KK's omnipotent concerns about the devastating power of his anger, he had to exit immediately after any hostile expression. He feared that his therapist would be so profoundly affected by these comments that he would retaliate in a massive and destructive fashion. Hence Mr. KK could only express his anger as he left the office, out of danger from retaliation (Gabbard 1982).

Therapeutic approaches to address these characteristic resistances of obsessive-compulsive patients begin with careful attention to countertransference. The therapist may feel a strong pull to disengage from the rambling, mechanistic presentation of factual material. Therapists may begin to isolate affect just as the patient does rather than to experience the irritation and anger as an important part of the process that needs to be interpreted to the patient. For example, when the therapist begins to feel bored and distanced by the material, a useful comment might be, "Is it possible that you are presenting all this factual material as a way of keeping emotionally distant from me?" Another countertransference pitfall is for the therapist to scotomize certain aspects of the patient's psychopathology because of the therapist's own obsessive-compulsive tendencies. To get through medical school and psychiatric residency training, obsessive-compulsive traits are highly adaptive (Gabbard 1985), so therapists may be prone to overlook how those traits might negatively affect a patient's relationships. To acknowledge that impact may make therapists feel uncomfortable because the patient's situation may resonate with similar tendencies in the therapist's own personal relationships.

One effective strategy in the psychotherapeutic treatment of patients with obsessive-compulsive character structure is to cut through the smoke screen of words to go directly after feelings. The therapy process will frequently get bogged down in the patient's search for facts to avoid feelings, as in the following example:

> Mr. LL was a 29-year-old graduate student who sought psychotherapy with the chief complaint of not being able to complete his dissertation. His therapist was a psychiatric resident slightly younger than him. In the first few sessions, the patient struggled with his concern about the therapist's age by attempting to establish certain facts.

Mr. LL:	You look like you're probably not old enough to be a fully trained psychiatrist. I would guess you're approximately the same age as me. Is that correct?
Therapist:	Yes. I'm approximately the same age as you.
Mr. LL:	I assume, of course, that you've had considerable training in psychotherapy. Isn't that correct?
Therapist:	Yes, I have.
Mr. LL:	How long is a psychiatric residency anyway?
Therapist:	Four years.
Mr. LL:	And what year are you in?
Therapist:	I'm in my third year.
Mr. LL:	I guess you probably have a supervisor, though, don't you?

At this point, the resident became aware that this question-and-answer approach was bypassing the patient's feelings. Instead of merely answering all the patient's factual questions, the therapist chose to address the process itself.

Therapist: Mr. LL, it seems to me that this attempt to establish the facts of my training is a way of not addressing the feelings you're having about seeing a therapist who is approximately your own age and who is in training. I wonder if there isn't some anger and possibly even a bit of humiliation about having been assigned to a resident.

This vignette illustrates how the therapist should aggressively address the patient's feelings even when the patient is denying their existence. Obsessive-compulsive patients will also flee from transference feelings by retreating into long discourses about historically distant events. The therapist may have to bring the patient back to the here and now in the transference and may have to attempt to establish what is going on in the present situation that caused the patient to seek refuge in the past (Salzman 1980, 1983). By keeping certain overarching themes and goals of the treatment in mind, often those with which the patient originally came to treatment, the therapist *can* maintain anchoring points for the process (Salzman 1980, 1983). When the patient endlessly ruminates about seemingly irrelevant minutiae, the therapist may have to interrupt the ruminations and bring the patient back to the central theme or issue that began the session. Group psychotherapy is often highly effective in dealing with this problem, because the patient may accept such feedback from peers without the same power struggle that accompanies feedback from the therapist.

An overall goal in the psychotherapeutic treatment of the obsessive-compulsive patient is superego modification. In the simplest terms, this means that these patients must accept their humanness. They must accept that their wish to transcend feelings of anger, hatred, lust, dependency, and so forth is doomed to failure. Feelings must finally be embraced as part of the human condition. They must be integrated as part of the person's self-experience rather than suppressed, denied, repressed, or disavowed as belonging to someone else. To accomplish this goal of making the superego a more benign structure, reassurance is rarely useful. Comments such as, "You're not really as bad as you think you are," or "You're much too hard on yourself," will sound hollow to the patient.

Superego changes are more likely to occur through detailed interpretation of the patient's conflicts around dependency, aggression, and sexuality, and by the therapist's stable neutrality over time. By remaining nonjudgmental and equidistant from the superego, the ego, and the id, the therapist helps the patient discover that perceptions of the therapist are distorted according to templates forged by past relationships. The patient will repeatedly try to view the therapist as critical and judgmental, but the therapist can facilitate recognition that the patient is attributing his or her own critical, judgmental attitude to the therapist.

As these patients begin to understand that others are not nearly as critical as they themselves are, their self-esteem may correspondingly increase. They realize that others have accepted them all along much more than they had imagined. As they experience their therapist's acceptance of them for who they are, they also gain an increasing self-acceptance. As they learn that their conflicts over aggression and dependency stem from childhood situations, they gain greater mastery over these feelings and accept them as part of being human. The therapist *can* use periodic confrontations about the unrealistic expectations these patients so frequently harbor about themselves. One patient, for example, berated himself in a psychotherapy session over his feelings of rivalry with his older brother at a Christmas family gathering. The therapist commented, "You seem to believe that you should be able to transcend all feelings of competition with your brother and that you're a failure if you don't."

As in the psychotherapy of most patients, resistances are interpreted before underlying content. Defenses against anger, such as reaction formation, may have to be addressed for some time before the patient can see the defensive pattern clearly enough to relate it to underlying anger. For example, the therapist might have to deliver an interpretation such as the following: "Each time I announce a vacation, I notice that you say, 'No problem!' I wonder if that response covers up some other feelings that are more unacceptable." When obsessive-compulsive patients can finally experience and express undisguised anger toward the therapist, they eventually learn that it is not nearly as destructive as they had thought. The therapist is a consistent, durable figure who is there week after week, clearly unscathed by expressions of anger. Similarly, these patients discover that they themselves are not transformed by their anger into monsters much like David Banner's metamorphosis into the Incredible Hulk.

To the obsessive-compulsive patient, sexual feelings are frequently just as unacceptable as anger or dependency. Again, the transference will reenact the childhood situation in which the patient sees the therapist as a parent who disapproves of sexuality. By maintaining a position of concerned neutrality, the therapist allows the patient to eventually see that such prohibitions are *internal,* not external. The threat (of castration or loss of love) attributed to the therapist can be understood, then, as an illusory one emanating from within the patient.

Avoidant Personality Disorder

This controversial disorder was designed to characterize a group of socially withdrawn individuals distinct from schizoid patients. As discussed in Chapter 13, the avoidant patient, unlike the schizoid patient, longs for close interpersonal relationships but is also afraid of them. These individuals avoid relationships and social situations because they fear the humiliation connected with failure and the pain connected with rejection. Their desire for relationships may not be readily apparent because of their shy, self-effacing self-presentation.

The distinction between avoidant and schizoid personality disorders has been criticized on several grounds: for having no "clinical, empirical, or even widely accepted theoretical rationale" (Gunderson 1983, p. 23), for impoverishing the historical concept of schizoid personality disorder by obscuring some of its key features (Livesley et al. 1985; Livesley and West 1986), and for not adequately differentiating the two groups of patients (Reich and Noyes 1986). In a study of 82 psychiatric outpatients, Reich and Noyes (1986) found that a large percentage of those with schizoid personality disorder also met the diagnostic criteria for avoidant personality disorder. Their data suggested that schizoid personality might actually be a variant of avoidant personality disorder.

The data on diagnostic overlap, however, are contradictory. Two studies (Kass et al. 1985; Trull et al. 1987) found that avoidant and schizoid diagnoses had a very low correlation, but that *dependent* personality disorder had considerable overlap with avoidant personality disorder. Trull et al. (1987) argued that in actual practice the diagnosis of schizoid personality disorder is rare, so that the overlap of avoidant and schizoid disorders has little clinical significance. They suggested that much more concern should be directed at the overlap between avoidant and dependent personality disorders.

In response to these criticisms, the DSM-III-R criteria for avoidant personality disorder (see Table 18-2) were modified from the DSM-III (American Psychiatric Association 1980) version. Nonspecific criteria, such as "low self-esteem" and "desire for affection and acceptance" were deleted because they apply to many other personality disorders. Also, new features, including an exaggeration of the risks in everyday life and an inordinate fear of being embarrassed, were added to bring the entity more in line with the psychoanalytic concept of the phobic character (Widiger et al. 1988). The DSM-III-R definition was also expanded to encompass avoidance of

Table 18-2. DSM-III-R criteria for avoidant personality disorder

A pervasive pattern of social discomfort, fear of negative evaluation, and timidity, beginning by early adulthood and present in a variety of contexts, as indicated by at least *four* of the following:

 (1) is easily hurt by criticism or disapproval
 (2) has no close friends or confidants (or only one) other than first-degree relatives
 (3) is unwilling to get involved with people unless certain of being liked
 (4) avoids social or occupational activities that involve significant interpersonal contact, e.g., refuses a promotion that will increase social demands
 (5) is reticent in social situations because of a fear of saying something inappropriate or foolish, or of being unable to answer a question
 (6) fears being embarrassed by blushing, crying, or showing signs of anxiety in front of other people
 (7) exaggerates the potential difficulties, physical dangers, or risks involved in doing something ordinary but outside his or her usual routine, e.g., may cancel social plans because she anticipates being exhausted by the effort of getting there

Note. Reprinted from DSM-III-R, pp. 352–353, with permission from the American Psychiatric Association

situations as well as interpersonal relationships. Although this revision of the diagnostic category is still somewhat problematic, it provides clear gains from a psychodynamic perspective. The new definition is more closely linked to the psychoanalytic tradition of the phobic personality described by Fenichel (1945). Moreover, this improvement further defines the avoidant personality disorder as a *neurotic* character rather than a more primitive one. A number of authors (Akhtar 1986; Kernberg 1975; Meissner 1988) view the schizoid personality disorder as part of the borderline spectrum because identity diffusion and splitting are prominent features. In contrast, the avoidant personality disorder may be neurotic in the sense that identity diffusion is not present, and repression and other high-level defense mechanisms are much more prominent than splitting. Akhtar (1986) noted: "Avoidant personality is an ego-syntonic characterological counterpart of the phobic neurosis, just as obsessional personality is an ego-syntonic characterological counterpart of obsessional neurosis" (p. 1061).

The modification of the DSM-III-R criteria in the direction of phobic character, however, presents some difficulty in overlap with social phobia. The DSM-III-R differentiates them by defining social phobias as focused around a specific situation that must be avoided while the avoidance is more generalized in the avoidant personality disorder. However, the manual also suggests that the two diagnoses may coexist. One study of relatively small sample size (Turner et al. 1986) compared 10 people with social phobias with 8 patients suffering from avoidant personality disorder. Avoidant patients were found to be less socially skilled, more interpersonally hypersensitive, more pervasively avoidant of social situations, more subjectively distressed, and more likely to have symptoms such as anxiety, depression, and compulsive rituals. More research is required to substantiate these differences.

The criteria for avoidant personality disorder are frequently present in clinical populations. However, the disorder is rarely the primary or sole diagnosis in clinical practice (Gunderson 1988). It is most commonly a supplementary diagnosis to another personality disorder, or is used in conjunction with an Axis I diagnosis. The centrality of shame in the avoidant patient provides a psychodynamic link with certain types of narcissistic patients (particularly the phenomenologically hypervigilant type and some of those described by Kohut). Both narcissistic and avoidant patients may be prone to shame, but the former are also often characterized by a sense of entitlement and a quiet grandiosity.

Psychodynamic Understanding

People can be shy and avoidant for a variety of reasons. They may have a constitutional predisposition to avoid stressful situations based on inborn temperament that is secondarily elaborated into their entire personality style (Gunderson 1988). Some research data suggest that the trait of shyness is of genetic-constitutional origin but that it requires a specific environmental experience to develop into a full-blown trait (Kagan et al. 1988). Shyness or avoidance defends against embarrassment, humiliation, rejection, and failure. As with any other form of anxiety, the psychodynamic meaning of the anxiety must be explored to understand fully its origins with each individual patient. However, the psychotherapeutic and psychoanalytic treatment of individuals with these concerns often uncovers shame as a central affective experience.

Shame and the exposure of the self are intimately connected. What avoidant patients generally fear is any situation in which they must reveal aspects of themselves that leave them vulnerable. While guilt involves concerns about punishment for having violated some internal rule, shame relates more to an assessment of the self as somehow inadequate, as not measuring up to an internal standard. In this sense, guilt is more closely related to the superego in the structural model, while shame is more closely connected to the ego ideal (see Chapter 2).

Individuals with avoidant personality disorder may feel that social situations must be avoided because they allow their inadequacies to be displayed for all to see. They may feel ashamed about many different aspects of the self, including the perception of oneself as weak, as unable to compete, as physically or mentally defective, as messy and disgusting, as unable to control bodily functions, and as exhibitionistic (Wurmser 1981).

Shame is etymologically derived from the verb "to hide" (Nathanson 1987), and the avoidant patient often withdraws from interpersonal relationships and situations of exposure out of a wish to "hide out" from the highly unpleasant affect of shame. Shame cannot be reductionistically linked with one developmental moment in the life of the child, but seems instead to evolve from many different developmental experiences at various ages (Nathanson 1987). Apparently present from very early in life, shame certainly is evident at the onset of stranger anxiety around 8 months of age (Broucek 1982). It is also connected with feelings that arise from bladder and bowel accidents and from an internalization of the parental reprimands often associated with those accidents. The 2-year-old child who is exhilarated by romping in the buff may also develop shame when a stern parent stops such activity by insisting that the child get dressed (Gabbard 1983). All these developmental experiences may be reactivated in the avoidant patient upon exposure to a group of people or an individual who matters a great deal to the patient.

Psychotherapeutic Approaches

Both individual and group psychotherapy of an expressive-supportive nature can be highly effective with patients suffering from avoidant personality disorder. Supportive elements involve an empathic appreciation of the embarrassment and humiliation associated with exposure, coupled with a firm encouragement to nevertheless expose oneself to the feared situations. The expressive elements of the psychotherapy involve exploring the underlying causes of shame and their linkage to past developmental experiences. The expressive aspect of therapy is greatly enhanced if the patient is willing to risk confronting the feared situations. More of the anxieties and fantasies will be activated in the actual situation of exposure than in the defensive posture of withdrawal. This fact can be explained to these patients in an educational intervention to help them see the value of actively seeking out the feared situations.

Initial exploratory efforts may be frustrating because avoidant patients will not be entirely sure what it is that they fear. Avoidant patients often resort to psychiatric clichés, such as "rejection." The therapist must seek out more detail of actual situations to help the patient move beyond such vague explanations for avoidance. The therapist may ask, "What was your actual fantasy of what your coworkers might think of you when you sat in the lunch room with them yesterday?" Similarly, specific fantasies can be explored in the context of the transference. Avoidant patients usually have a good deal of anxiety about the exposure inherent in psychotherapy. When a patient blushes about something that has been verbalized, the therapist might ask, "Can you share with me what's embarrassing you right now? Is there some reaction that you imagine I'm having to what you just said?" By pursuing the details of specific situations, the patient will develop a greater awareness of the cognitive correlates of the shame affect.

Ms. MM was a 24-year-old nursing student who came to psychotherapy because she felt dissatisfied with her life, had difficulty establishing heterosexual relationships, and experienced anxiety in social situations. She described chronic problems with feeling timid and shy around men. Since she was exceptionally attractive, she was frequently asked out, but her anxiety about each date would escalate to the point where she had to drink alcohol to relax. She told her therapist that she felt at risk for developing a dependence on alcohol, because she was only able to "open up" to men when she was under the influence. Ms. MM also noted the same experience of anxiety when she found herself "loosening up" with other people, such as peers in nursing school.

She had tried group psychotherapy for several months, but found herself tongue-tied and self-conscious in the group. She would rarely speak for fear of "saying the wrong thing." When she began missing group psychotherapy sessions, she rationalized her absence by saying that it did not matter since she was not participating anyway. Ms. MM decided to seek individual psychotherapy because she thought it would be easier to open up to one person instead of eight.

In her third session in psychotherapy, she began to fall silent frequently. The therapist was patient during these silences, but after a few more sessions, he noted that her silences seemed to occur when she was about to experience strong feelings. She acknowledged that she was terribly afraid of losing control when she became emotional. The therapist asked Ms. MM if she were concerned about his response to her expression of emotion. Ms. MM said that she felt certain he would criticize her and "shame" her for "acting like a baby."

At this point the therapist asked Ms. MM if this fear was based on any similar past experiences. She launched into an extensive description of how her father had treated her as a child. She said that he was "a big man who couldn't take criticism but could deal it out." Each time she brought home a report card, he would yell at her, demanding, "Why didn't you get an A?" She also remembered spilling her milk at the supper table and being severely reprimanded by her father, who railed at her, "Why can't you be more like your sister?" With considerable embarrassment, she said her father had never made her feel comfortable about being female. He teased her on the day of her first period by telling her she now had an excuse for being "bad" once a month. She recalled being extraordinarily mortified and crying in her room for hours. When she came home one day full of excitement because she had been selected as a cheerleader, her father called her "conceited and spoiled." She held a strong conviction that she would never be able to measure up to her father's expectations.

At one point in the therapy, Ms. MM was talking about her difficulty in attending parties or other social situations. Again the therapist asked about past situations that might be related to this fear. Ms. MM remembered that when she had been a little girl, her mother would dress her up and take her over to a friend's house, and everyone would always comment on how "cute" she was. She remembered her sense of embarrassment at these compliments, as though she had been "showing off." As the therapist helped her explore that feeling further, she realized that to some extent she had enjoyed the exposure because she had received such positive feedback in contrast to the constant criticism from her father. The therapist encouraged her to attend some of the social functions to which she was invited to see what other associations came to mind during an anxiety attack.

When Ms. MM began socializing more without first becoming inebriated, she realized that she feared enjoying herself. If she enjoyed the compliments of the men who hovered around her at a social gathering, then she was convinced that she was "conceited and spoiled," just as her father had used to say. This conviction made her feel that she was a "bad girl."

The case of Ms. MM illustrates that success in interpersonal situations often may be feared every bit as much as failure. The thrill of an exhibitionistic display may automatically trigger earlier parental reprimands about "showing off." Many individuals with avoidant personality disorder fear that they will become intoxicated with themselves when they are in the spotlight. This dynamic is central to the experience of stage fright (Gabbard 1979, 1983). Coexisting with Ms. MM's fear of enjoying her moment at center stage was another fear that she would fall short of the high expectations she had set for herself. These expectations were internalized by living with a father who had excessively high expectations. In the therapy, she was eventually able to acknowledge her intense anger at her father for repeatedly shaming her and making her feel so conflicted about her sexuality and her femaleness. Miller (1985) has noted a consistent connection between the inhibition of anger and the shame experience. Ms. MM could never freely express her anger at her father, and she felt ashamed of even having such feelings.

Dependent Personality Disorder

Dependency, like rejection, has become something of a psychiatric cliché. Everyone is dependent to some degree, and most patients in a clinical setting will have some conflict over their feelings of dependency. Particularly in American culture, where a powerful myth centers on rugged individualism and independence, the word "dependency" is often used pejoratively. Yet self psychologists would argue that true independence is neither possible nor desirable (see Chapter 2). We are all in need of various selfobject functions, such as approval, empathy, validation, and admiration, to sustain us and to regulate our self-esteem.

The DSM-III-R category of dependent personality disorder is meant to capture a dependency so extreme as to be pathological. These individuals are unable to make decisions for themselves, are unusually submissive, are always in need of reassurance, and cannot function well without someone else to take care of them. Dependent personality disorder was not listed in DSM-II (American Psychiatric Association 1968) and was only added to DSM-III because some contributors were convinced that a "passive-dependent" type of personality disorder was needed as a counterpart to the "active-dependent" type characterized by the criteria for histrionic personality disorder (Gunderson 1983). Although the category is somewhat related to the traditional "oral character" identified in psychoanalytic writings, there are no empirical data to support the active-dependent and passive-dependent distinction.

The DSM-III version of dependent personality disorder was criticized for being too vague—it had only three diagnostic criteria—and for being too gender biased in its examples, which suggested that women were more likely to suffer from the disorder (Widiger et al. 1988). The revised category expands the criteria to nine items (see Table 18-3) and, to some extent, corrects the gender bias by changing the examples. Although the diagnosis may actually be applied more frequently to women (Gunderson 1988), this fact may be related to entrenched sexual stereotypes in our culture, which allow women to be more dependent than men.

Dependent personality disorder, like avoidant personality disorder, is rarely used as a principal or single diagnosis. It is often associated with dysthymic disorder, with depression, and with anxiety. It is also commonly diagnosed in conjunction with other personality disorders, such as borderline, histrionic, and avoidant. The key item that differentiates avoidant and dependent personality disorders is social withdrawal, but an individual can be diagnosed as avoidant without being socially withdrawn since only four criteria are necessary for the diagnosis. Trull et al. (1987) pointed out the following problem in distinguishing the two:

> The avoidant and dependent disorders are distinguished by the difficulty of the person with dependent disorder in separation and the difficulty of the person with avoidant disorder in initiation, but it is conceivable that a person would have difficulty in both initiating and separating from a relationship. A lonely person who intensely

desires involvements is likely to be very fearful of losing a relationship once it has been established. (p. 770)

Psychodynamic Understanding

Many patients with dependent personality have grown up in households where the parents have communicated in one way or another that independence is fraught with danger. Overinvolved and over-intrusive mothers are common to this group of patients. Like many histrionic and borderline patients, dependent patients have a history of being subtly rewarded for maintaining loyalty to their parents, who subtly reject them in the face of any move toward separation and independence.

Despite this similarity to patients with borderline personality disorder, the patient with dependent personality does not react to separation exactly like the borderline individual does. Both may dread abandonment, both may cling to the significant other, and both may feel lost in the absence of the significant other. Borderline patients commonly react to separation with a sense of panic, leading to impulsive self-destructive behavior. Such dramatic reactions in those with dependent personality disorder are uncommon. The dependent patient is much more likely to simply sit and cry. This difference might be related to greater object constancy in the

Table 18-3. DSM-III-R criteria for dependent personality disorder

A pervasive pattern of dependent and submissive behavior, beginning by early adulthood and present in a variety of contexts, as indicated by at least *five* of the following:
  (1) is unable to make everyday decisions without an excessive amount of advice or reassurance from others
  (2) allows others to make most of his or her important decisions, e.g., where to live, what job to take
  (3) agrees with people even when he or she believes they are wrong, because of fear of being rejected
  (4) has difficulty initiating projects or doing things on his or her own
  (5) volunteers to do things that are unpleasant or demeaning in order to get other people to like him or her
  (6) feels uncomfortable or helpless when alone, or goes to great lengths to avoid being alone
  (7) feels devastated or helpless when close relationships end
  (8) is frequently preoccupied with fears of being abandoned
  (9) is easily hurt by criticism or disapproval

Note. Reprinted from DSM-III-R, p. 354, with permission from the American Psychiatric Association.

developmental histories of those with dependent personality disorder. An alternative hypothesis would be that dependent patients lack the genetic-constitutional predisposition to flamboyant self-destructive behavior characteristic of borderline patients.

Although early psychoanalytic writers believed that problems with dependency were connected with disturbances during the oral phase of psychosexual development, this view is not widely held today (Gunderson 1988). Such a formulation has the same problem as other phase-specific explanations for psychopathology. A pervasive pattern of parental reinforcement for dependency throughout all phases of development is more likely to be operative in the backgrounds of patients with dependent personality disorder.

A submissive stance toward others may have a myriad of meanings. Just as the avoidant patient shuns exposure as a result of multiply determined unconscious factors, the dependent patient seeks caretaking because of anxieties that lie beneath the surface. The clinician should ask each individual, "What is it about independence or separation that is frightening?" Dependent clinging often masks aggression. It may be viewed as a compromise formation in the sense that it defends against hostility that is also concomitantly expressed. As many mental health professionals know from first-hand experience, the person who is the object of the dependent patient's clinging may experience the patient's demands as hostile and tormenting.

Dependent behavior may also be a way to avoid the reactivation of past traumatic experiences. The therapist should explore with the patient any memories of past separations and their impact.

Mr. NN was a 29-year-old, married postal clerk. He had a long-standing dysthymic disorder and chronically complained of insomnia, lack of energy, difficulty making decisions, and anxiety. Nevertheless, he managed to show up at his job conscientiously, even though he found it difficult to take any initiative when it was expected of him. Prior to his psychiatric hospitalization for suicidal thoughts and wishes, Mr. NN had broken down in tears in front of his supervisor when he was told he was not doing his job properly.

During the admission interview, Mr. NN expressed extreme concern about being away from his wife during the hospitalization, even though he realized that his suicidal wishes were dangerous enough to necessitate inpatient treatment. Mrs. NN explained that her husband had never liked to be away from her. He relied on her to make all decisions in the home, and he could not function very well without her. Almost immediately after being admitted, Mr. NN latched onto a female patient approximately his age and looked to her for guidance in the same way he had related to his wife. He ate all his meals with her and spent all his leisure time with her when he was not involved in treatment activities. He made no sexual overtures toward this other patient, but simply reported that he felt safe in her company.

Mr. NN's history revealed a lifelong pattern of anxious dependency. He had always experienced considerable anxiety at the prospect of doing something alone or upon initiating any plan of action without consulting others. He had school phobia when he started elementary school, and his mother reported that he had cried until she would take him home. Similarly, at the age of 10, he had been sent to visit his uncle overnight and had cried so hard that his mother had had to return to the uncle's house and bring him home. When he graduated from high school, all his friends in his peer group enlisted in the service, so he followed suit. Upon discharge from the service, they went to work for the post office, so he applied along with them. Any independent action on his part seemed to reactivate the painful anxiety associated with early separations. He behaved as though convinced that he would be abandoned for any autonomous behavior.

The origins of Mr. NN's dependency and separation anxiety became clearer when his mother began to call him in the hospital. She complained about his decision to enter the hospital: "How can you justify being away from us like this? Your condition can't be that bad. What if we need you to do something and you're not available?" The patient explained that even as an adult, he had responded to his mother's call to come over to her house each week to do various menial jobs. He went on to say that his parents were virtually non-communicative and that his mother had relied on him for conversation. Mr. NN had grown up in a household where his mother had conveyed a powerful message—namely, that she needed him as a stand-in for her emotionally estranged husband. Independence was thus regarded as an aggressive and disloyal act that would lead to the loss of his mother's love.

Psychotherapeutic Considerations

The psychotherapy of patients with dependent personality disorder presents an immediate therapeutic dilemma—for these patients to overcome their problems with dependency, they must first develop dependency on their therapist. This dilemma often becomes elaborated into a specific form of resistance in which the patient sees dependency on the therapist as an end in itself rather than as a means to an end. After a period in therapy, these patients may forget the nature of the complaint that brought them to treatment, and their only purpose becomes the maintenance of their attachment to the therapist. Dreading termination, they may repeatedly remind their therapist of how awful they feel to assure continuation of the treatment. If the therapist comments on any improvement whatsoever, the patient may paradoxically worsen since the thought of improvement is equated with termination.

One rule of thumb in treating dependent patients is to remember that what they say they want is probably not what they need. They will attempt to get their therapist to tell them what to do, to allow them to continue their dependency, and to collude in the avoidance of making decisions or asserting their own wishes. The therapist must feel comfortable in frustrating these wishes and instead promoting independent thinking and action in the patient. The therapist must convey that the anxiety produced by this frustration is tolerable and also productive in that it may lead to associations about the origins of the dependency and the fears associated with it.

Time-limited dynamic psychotherapy has been successful with a number of these patients (Gunderson 1988). Knowing from the beginning of the psychotherapy that the patient-therapist relationship will end after 12, 16, or 20 sessions forces these patients to confront their deepest anxieties about loss and independence. Moreover, this approach also helps patients address powerful fantasies involving the never-ending availability of nurturing figures. When long-term, open-ended therapy reaches something of a stalemate, a modification of the time-limited technique can be utilized by setting a deadline for termination. Anxieties that may have lain dormant will be brought rapidly to the surface when the end of therapy is in sight.

A subgroup of dependent patients are simply unable or unwilling to make use of the framework of brief psychotherapy. The prospect of losing the therapist after "just getting started" creates too much anxiety. Because of lesser amounts of ego strength or greater degrees of separation anxiety, these patients need to develop a positive dependent transference to a therapist over a long time. Nevertheless, considerable therapeutic gains are possible with this supportive strategy, as documented by Wallerstein's (1986) research (discussed in Chapter 4). Some patients change as part of a "transference trade" (Wallerstein, p. 690) with the therapist. They are willing to make certain alterations in their lives in return for the therapist's approval. Others may become "lifers" who can maintain change as long as they know that the therapist will always be there for them. These patients may do well even when the therapist tapers down the sessions to one every few months, provided there is no threat of termination.

Patients with dependent personality disorder commonly create countertransference problems related to dependency conflicts in their treaters. Physicians in general, and psychiatrists in particular, may feel conflicted about their own dependency (Gabbard 1985; Gabbard and Menninger 1988; Vaillant et al. 1972). Psychotherapists must be wary of countertransference contempt or disdain toward the dependent patient. The longings of the patient may resonate with the unconscious longings of the therapist, and an empathic attunement with such dependency wishes may be acutely uncomfortable. Therapists who repudiate their patient's longings may be repudiating their own longings as well.

Passive-Aggressive Personality Disorder

Of all the DSM-III-R personality disorders, passive-aggressive personality is possibly the most problematic. Its inclusion in Cluster C is puzzling since many passive-aggressive individuals are remarkably free of anxiety or fear. In many respects, the diagnostic criteria describe more of a trait or a specific kind of behavior than a true personality disorder (see Table 18-4). Clinicians rarely use this diagnosis because passive-aggressive behavior occurs in a wide variety of personality disorders, and clinicians are much more likely to diagnose another personality disorder and to simply refer to passive-aggressive traits or behavior as part of the clinical picture. The diagnosis is designed to capture a certain style of passive resistance that occurs in response to demands made on the patient. A passive-aggressive individual may go through the motions of obeying a command but will subtly undermine the task or take a great deal of

Table 18-4. DSM-III-R criteria for passive-aggressive personality disorder

A pervasive pattern of passive resistance to demands for adequate social and occupational performance, beginning by early adulthood and present in a variety of contexts, as indicated by at least *five* of the following:
  (1) procrastinates, i.e., puts off things that need to be done so that deadlines are not met
  (2) becomes sulky, irritable, or argumentative when asked to do something he or she does not want to do
  (3) seems to work deliberately slowly or to do a bad job on tasks that he or she really does not want to do
  (4) protests, without justification, that others make unreasonable demands on him or her
  (5) avoids obligations by claiming to have "forgotten"
  (6) believes that he or she is doing a much better job than others think he or she is doing
  (7) resents useful suggestions from others concerning how he or she could be more productive
  (8) obstructs the efforts of others by failing to do his or her share of the work
  (9) unreasonably criticizes or scorns people in positions of authority

Note. Reprinted from DSM-III-R, pp. 357–358, with permission from the American Psychiatric Association.

time to do it. Passive-aggressive people infuriate others around them because of this style of relating, even though they themselves rarely show overt anger. In other words, this behavior is a passive way to handle anger since the overt expression of hostility is too threatening.

The responses of the anesthetist in the following dialogue between a surgeon and a nurse anesthetist during an operation illustrate the passive-aggressive style:

> Surgeon: How's the patient doing?
> Anesthetist: (pause) What?
> Surgeon: I said, how is the patient doing?
> Anesthetist: (pause) Oh, fine.
> Surgeon: (somewhat irritated) I'm asking you how his blood pressure is!
> Anesthetist: Oh! Looks okay to me.
> Surgeon: (more irritated) What are the numbers?
> Anesthetist: Systolic or diastolic?
> Surgeon: (quite angry now) Both numbers!
> Anesthetist: (pause) Let's see. 95/65.
> Surgeon: (sarcastically) Thank you! I hope I didn't put you to too much trouble!

As this example indicates, passive-aggressive behavior usually occurs in the context of a hierarchical structure in which authority is resented. In fact, this diagnosis was present in DSM (American Psychiatric Association 1952) and DSM-II largely as a result of experiences in the military (Millon 1981). In preparing the first edition of DSM-III, serious consideration was given to excluding the diagnosis since it sometimes seems to represent the situational reaction of someone who is powerless in the face of a domineering authority figure (Widiger et al. 1988). The diagnosis should not be applied unless passive-aggressive behavior is present in many different situations, including those where there is not a clear authoritarian structure. Like other Cluster C personality disorders, passive-aggressive personality disorder has no clinical tradition, and factor analytic studies have failed to verify it as a discrete entity (Gunderson 1988).

Psychodynamic Understanding

Because of the controversy surrounding this diagnosis, it is easier to speak of the dynamics of passive-aggressive *behavior* rather than to attempt a thorough-going explanation of an entire character style. The psychoanalytic literature is sparse on the subject of the etiology and pathogenesis of passive-aggressive behavior. Gunderson (1988) suggested that power struggles during the anal phase of development may be contributory factors as well as exercises of exaggerated parental authority.

The object relations theory model of projective identification as both an intrapsychic defense and an interpersonal mode of relatedness also has considerable explanatory value. For the passive-aggressive patient, a self-representation associated with anger is highly unacceptable. Therefore, the patient projectively disavows this aspect of the self and coerces others into identifying with the projection by covertly noncompliant behavior. This process operates at an unconscious level, so that these patients often feel that they are completely free of anger and that others unjustly pick on them. For example, an interview with the nurse anesthetist in the previous vignette might reveal that the nurse believed that he had simply misunderstood the surgeon's request and had been unfairly blasted by the surgeon's anger. Passive-aggressive behavior is usually ego-syntonic.

Psychotherapeutic Considerations

Since the passive-aggressive style of relatedness is unconscious and rarely a source of distress for the patient, it is an unlikely target as a goal of therapy by the patient. Difficulties in getting along with others, or even "problems with anger," may be among the presenting complaints, but it is rare for passive-aggressive patients to identify their behavior itself as a reason for therapy.

Passive-aggressive behavior usually becomes evident in one of two ways. Either the patient describes a characteristic pattern of provoking anger in others, or the therapist begins to experience uncharacteristic anger in session after session, despite the fact that the patient is not expressing any overt rage. The diagnosis of passive-aggressive behavior may be regarded as a countertransference diagnosis.

After a psychotherapist has made this diagnosis, the countertransference feelings can be used to constructively say to the patient, "I get the feeling that you're trying to make me angry with you. Do you have any thoughts about why you would want to do that?" This inquiry will usually meet with vehement denial because these patients view themselves as completely without anger. The therapist can then proceed to identify specific aspects of the patient's behavior that evoke anger in others. When the patient can accept these observations, connections can be made with behavior in other relationships in the patient's current life and in the patient's childhood. The patient and therapist can then collaborate in a search for reasons that the patient must repudiate all anger.

Group psychotherapy may be particularly helpful in getting these patients to the point where they can accept their projective disavowal of aggression. When several people are confronting the patient with the same pattern in different situations, the patient is hard pressed to dismiss it as the unique problem of one person, as one might do in individual psychotherapy.

Other Personality Disorders

Having completed our survey of the DSM-III-R personality disorders, it is worth noting that patients generally do not present themselves as "pure cultures" of any one personality disorder. DSM-III-R has created an extra category of personality disorder to acknowledge this fact. A great many personality disorders are "mixed" in the sense that elements of several different personality disorders are blended into a unique constellation of defenses and interpersonal relatedness. The uniqueness of each individual is a source of continued delight and challenge for the dynamic psychiatrist. In Chapter 1 we noted that the dynamic psychiatrist is more interested in how patients differ from one another than in how they are similar. Nowhere in psychiatry is this axiom more relevant than in the treatment of personality disorders.

References

Abraham K: Contributions to the theory of the anal character (1921), in Selected Papers of Karl Abraham, M.D. London, Hogarth Press, 1942, pp 370–392

Akhtar S: Differentiating schizoid and avoidant personality disorders (letter to editor). Am J Psychiatry 143:1061–1062, 1986

American Psychiatric Association: Diagnostic and Statistical Manual of Mental Disorders. Washington, DC, American Psychiatric Association, 1952

American Psychiatric Association: Diagnostic and Statistical Manual of Mental Disorders, 2nd Edition. Washington, DC, American Psychiatric Association, 1968

American Psychiatric Association: Diagnostic and Statistical Manual of Mental Disorders, 3rd Edition. Washington, DC, American Psychiatric Association, 1980

American Psychiatric Association: Diagnostic and Statistical Manual of Mental Disorders, 3rd Edition, Revised. Washington, DC, American Psychiatric Association, 1987

Broucek FJ: Shame and its relationship to early narcissistic developments. Int J Psychoanal 63:369–378, 1982

Fenichel O: The Psychoanalytic Theory of the Neurosis. New York, Norton, 1945

Freud S: Character and anal erotism (1908), in The Standard Edition of the Complete Psychological Works of Sigmund Freud, Vol 9.

Translated and edited by Strachey J. London, Hogarth Press, 1959, pp 167–175

Gabbard GO: Stage fright. Int J Psychoanal 60:383–392, 1979

Gabbard GO: The exit line: heightened transference-countertransference manifestations at the end of the hour. J Am Psychoanal Assoc 30:579–598, 1982

Gabbard GO: Further contributions to the understanding of stage fright: narcissistic issues. J Am Psychoanal Assoc 31:423–441, 1983

Gabbard GO: The role of compulsiveness in the normal physician. JAMA 254:2926–2929, 1985

Gabbard GO, Menninger RW: The psychology of the physician, in Medical Marriages. Edited by Gabbard GO, Menninger RW. Washington, DC, American Psychiatric Press, 1988, pp 23–38

Gunderson JG: DSM-III diagnoses of personality disorders, in Current Perspectives on Personality Disorders. Edited by Frosch JP. Washington, DC, American Psychiatric Press, 1983, pp 20–39

Gunderson JG: Personality disorders, in The New Harvard Guide to Psychiatry. Edited by Nicholi AM Jr. Cambridge, MA, Belknap Press of Harvard University Press, 1988, pp 337–357

Horowitz MJ: Introduction to Psychodynamics: A New Synthesis. New York, Basic Books, 1988

Joffe RT, Swinson RP, Regan JJ: Personality features of obsessive-compulsive disorder. Am J Psychiatry 145:1127–1129, 1988

Jones E: Anal-erotic character traits, in Papers on Psycho-Analysis, 5th Edition. Baltimore, Williams & Wilkins, 1948, pp 413–437

Kagan J, Reznick JS, Snidman N: Biological bases of childhood shyness. Science 240:167–171, 1988

Kass F, Skodol AE, Charles E, et al: Scaled ratings of DSM-III personality disorders. Am J Psychiatry 142:627–630, 1985

Kernberg OF: Borderline Conditions and Pathological Narcissism. New York, Jason Aronson, 1975

Krakowski AJ: Stress and the practice of medicine, II: stressors, stresses, and strains. Psychother Psychosom 38:11–23, 1982

Livesley WJ, West M: The DSM-III distinction between schizoid and avoidant personality disorders. Can J Psychiatry 31:59–62, 1986

Livesley WJ, West M, Tanney A: Historical comment on DSM-III schizoid and avoidant personality disorders. Am J Psychiatry 142:1344–1347, 1985

Meissner WW: Treatment of Patients in the Borderline Spectrum. Northvale, NJ, Jason Aronson, 1988

Menninger WC: Characterologic and symptomatic expressions related to the anal phase of psychosexual development. Psychoanal Q 12:161–193, 1943

Miller S: The Shame Experience. Hillsdale, NJ, Analytic Press, 1985

Millon T: Disorders of Personality: DSM-III, Axis-II. New York, John Wiley & Sons, 1981

Munich RL: Transitory symptom formation in the analysis of an obsessional character. Psychoanal Stud Child 41:515–535, 1986

Nathanson DL: A timetable for shame, in The Many Faces of Shame. Edited by Nathanson DL. New York, Guilford Press, 1987, pp 1–63

Nemiah JC: Obsessive-compulsive disorder (obsessive-compulsive neurosis), in Comprehensive Textbook of Psychiatry/III, Vol 2, 3rd Edition. Edited by Kaplan HI, Freedman AM, Sadock BJ. Baltimore, Williams & Wilkins, 1980, pp 1504–1517

Rasmussen SA, Tsuang MT: Clinical characteristics and family history in DSM-III obsessive-compulsive disorder. Am J Psychiatry 143:317–322, 1986

Reich J, Noyes R, Jr: Differentiating schizoid and avoidant personality disorders (letter to editor). Am J Psychiatry 143:1062, 1986

Salzman L: The Obsessive Personality: Origins, Dynamics, and Therapy. New York, Science House, 1968

Salzman L: Treatment of the Obsessive Personality. New York, Jason Aronson, 1980

Salzman L: Psychoanalytic therapy of the obsessional patient. Curr Psychiatr Ther 22:53–59, 1983

Shapiro D: Neurotic Styles. New York, Basic Books, 1965

Trull TJ, Widiger TA, Frances A: Covariation of criteria sets for avoidant, schizoid, and dependent personality disorders. Am J Psychiatry 144:767–771, 1987

Turner SM, Beidel DC, Dancu CV, et al: Psychopathology of social phobia and comparison to avoidant personality disorder. J Abnorm Psychol 95:389–394, 1986

Vaillant GE, Sobowale NC, McArthur C: Some psychologic vulnerabilities of physicians. N Engl J Med 287:372–375, 1972

Wallerstein RS: Forty-two Lives in Treatment: A Study of Psychoanalysis and Psychotherapy. New York, Guilford Press, 1986

Widiger TA, Frances A, Spitzer RL, et al: The DSM-III-R personality disorders: an overview. Am J Psychiatry 145:786–795, 1988

Wurmser L: The Mask of Shame. Baltimore, Johns Hopkins University Press, 1981

Index